Lecture Notes in Computer Science 1682

Edited by G. Goos, J. Hartmanis and J. van Leeuwen

T0216450

Springer

Berlin
Heidelberg
New York
Barcelona
Hong Kong
London
Milan
Paris
Singapore
Tokyo

Mads Nielsen   Peter Johansen
Ole Fogh Olsen   Joachim Weickert (Eds.)

Scale-Space Theories in Computer Vision

Second International Conference, Scale-Space'99
Corfu, Greece, September 26-27, 1999
Proceedings

Springer

Series Editors

Gerhard Goos, Karlsruhe University, Germany
Juris Hartmanis, Cornell University, NY, USA
Jan van Leeuwen, Utrecht University, The Netherlands

Volume Editors

Mads Nielsen
The IT University in Copenhagen
Glentevej 67, DK-2400 Copenhagen NV, Denmark
E-mail: malte@itu.dk

Peter Johansen
Ole Fogh Olsen
University of Copenhagen, Department of Computer Science
Universitetsparken 1, DK-2100 Copenhagen OE, Denmark
E-mail: peterjo/fogh@diku.dk

Joachim Weickert
University of Mannheim, Department of Mathematics and Computer Science
D-68131 Mannheim, Germany
E-mail: Joachim.Weickert@ti.uni-mannheim.de

Cataloging-in-Publication data applied for

Die Deutsche Bibliothek - CIP-Einheitsaufnahme

Scale space theories in computer vision : proceedings / Second International
Conference, Scale Space '99, Corfu, Greece, September 26 - 27, 1999. Mads
Nielsen ... (ed.). - Berlin ; Heidelberg ; New York ; Barcelona ; Hong Kong ;
London ; Milan ; Paris ; Singapore ; Tokyo : Springer, 1999
(Lecture notes in computer science ; Vol. 1682)
ISBN 3-540-66498-X

CR Subject Classification (1998): I.4, I.3.5, I.5

ISSN 0302-9743
ISBN 3-540-66498-X Springer-Verlag Berlin Heidelberg New York

© Springer-Verlag Berlin Heidelberg 1999
Printed in Germany

Typesetting: Camera-ready by author
SPIN: 10704355   06/3142 – 5 4 3 2 1 0   Printed on acid-free paper

Preface

The scale-space conference series dates back to the NSF/ESPRIT transatlantic collaboration on "geometry-driven diffusion"(1993-1996). This collaboration led to a series of very successful workshops followed by a PhD summer school on Gaussian Scale-Space Theory in Copenhagen, in spring 1996. After this, Bart ter Haar Romeny arranged the First International Conference on Scale-Space Theory in Computer Vision (Utrecht, July 2-4, 1997). Indeed the title was appropriate since this was the *first* scale-space conference in a series of so far two conferences. We feel very confident that the series will be much longer. We hope that the scheduling next to ICCV '99 will attract more delegates furthering the integration of scale-space theories into computer vision.

Since the first scale-space conference we have had an increase of more than 50% in the number of contributions. Of 66 high-quality submissions, we could, due to the time limitation of the conference, only select 24 papers for oral presentations. They form Part I of this volume. Many papers were of such high quality, that they would otherwise have qualified for oral presentation. It was decided to include 12 of the remaining papers in full length in the proceedings, creating the category of "Long Posters". They form Part 2 of this volume. Finally, 18 papers were accepted for poster presentations, constituting Part 3. Invited talks were given by Prof. Rüdiger von der Heydt, Department of Neuroscience, Johns Hopkins University School of Medicine and Prof. David L. Donoho, Statistics Department, Stanford University.

We would like to thank everyone who contributed to the success of this 2nd conference on scale-space theories in computer vision; first of all the many authors for their excellent and timely contributions, the referees that in a very short period reviewed the many papers (each paper was reviewed by 3 referees), members of the conference board, program board, and program committee, Ole F. Olsen and Erik B. Dam for their administration and the work of collecting the papers for this volume, ICCV and John Tsotsos for the very flexible hosting of the conference, and, last but not least, all who otherwise participated in making the conference successful.

July 1999   Mads Nielsen

Organization

General Board

Mads Nielsen (Information Technology University, Copenhagen)
Olivier Faugeras (INRIA, Sophia-Antipolis)
Pietro Perona (Caltech, Pasadena)
Bart ter Haar Romeny (Utrecht University)
Guillermo Sapiro (Minnesota University, Minneapolis)

Program Board Committee

Mads Nielsen (Information Technology University, Copenhagen)
Joachim Weickert (Mannheim University)
Peter Johansen (DIKU University Copenhagen)
Ole Fogh Olsen (DIKU University Copenhagen)

Program Committee

Luis Alvarez, Las Palmas University
Rein van den Boomgaard, Amsterdam University
Alfred Bruckstein, Technion, Haifa
Vicent Caselles, Illes Balears University, Palma de Mallorca
Tony Chan, UCLA, Los Angeles
James Damon, North Carolina University
Rachid Deriche, INRIA, Sophia Antipolis
Luc Florack, Utrecth University
Lewis Griffin, Aston University, Birmingham
Frederic Guichard, CEREMADE
Ben Kimia, Brown University, Providence
Ron Kimmel, Technion, Haifa
Jan Koenderink, Utrecth University
Tony Lindeberg, KTH, Stockholm
Ravikanth Malladi, Lawrence Berkeley National Lab, Berkeley
Farzin Mokhtarian, Surrey University
Wiro Niessen, Utrecth University
Eric Pauwels, K.U.Leuven, Heverlee
Steve Pizer, North Carolina University, Chapel Hill
Joachim Rieger, Martin Luther University, Halle–Wittenberg
Christoph Schnörr, Mannheim University

Jayant Shah, Northeastern University, Boston
Jon Sporring, ICS-Forth, Heraklion
Luc Van Gool, K.U.Leuven, Heverlee

Invited Lectures

Rüdiger von der Heydt (Johns Hopkins University School of Medicine, Baltimore)
David L. Donoho (Stanford University, Stanford)

Sponsoring Institutions

Danish National Research Council of Natural Science through the project "Computation of Natural Shape"

Table of Contents

Oral Presentations

Long Posters

Short Posters

Blur and Disorder

Jan J. Koenderink and Andrea J. van Doorn

Department of Physics and Astronomy,
PO Box 80 000, 3508TA Utrecht,
The Netherlands

Abstract. Blurring is not the only way to selectively remove fine spatial detail from an image. An alternative is to scramble pixels locally over areas defined by the desired blur circle. We refer to such scrambled images as "locally disorderly". Such images have many potentially interesting applications. In this contribution we discuss a formal framework for such locally disorderly images. It boils down to a number of intricately intertwined scale spaces, one of which is the ordinary linear scale space for the image. The formalism is constructed on the basis of an operational definition of local histograms of arbitrary bin width and arbitrary support.

1   Introduction

Standing in front of a tree you may believe that you clearly see the leaves. You also see "foliage" (which is a kind of texture), the general shape of the treetop, and so forth[3, 10]. You will be hard put to keep a given leaf in mind (say) and retrieve it the next day, or even a minute later. You fail any idea of the total number of leaves. If you glance away and we would remove a few leaves you would hardly notice. Indeed, it seems likely that you wouldn't notice quite serious changes in the foliage at all: One branch tends to look much like any other. This is what John Ruskin[13, 14] called "mystery". Yet you *would* notice when the treetop were replaced with a balloon of the same shape and identical average color. The foliage texture is important (it makes the foliage look like what it is) even though the actual spatial structure is largely ineffective in human vision.

Something quite similar occurs with images. Given an image we may scramble its pixels or replace all pixels with the average taken over all pixels. Both operations clearly destroy all spatial information. Yet the scrambled picture contains more information than the blurred one. When the blurring or scrambling is done locally at many places in a large image, one obtains something like a blurred photograph in one case, like a "painterly rendering" in the other case. Although the painterly rendering does not reveal more spatial detail than the blurred one, it tells you more about the rendered scene. We call such images "locally disorderly". We became interested because human vision is locally disordered in the peripheral visual field. In pathological cases it may even dominate focal vision[4, 6]. For instance, in cases of (always unilateral) "scrambled vision" the visual field is useless for reading newspapers (even the headlines) say. Yet such patients can discriminate even the highest spatial frequencies from a uniform field: In that respect the scrambled eye is at par with the good one. There is nothing wrong with the optics of such eyes, nor with the sampling. The patients simply don't know where the pixels are, it is a *mental* deficiency, not an optical or neurophysiological disorder.

Apart from the natural urge to understand such locally disorderly images formally, they may have many applications in computer graphics (why compute all leaves on a tree when a painter can do without?), image compression (why encode what the human observer doesn't notice?), and so forth. However, our interest is mainly fundamental.

2 Local histograms

For an image showing an extensive scene the histogram of the full image makes little sense because it is a hodge–podge of mutually unrelated entities. Far more informative are histograms of selected regions of interest that show certain uniform regions (where the precise concept of "uniformity" may vary). Such a region may be part of a treetop for instance. A pixel histogram still might show quite different structure according to the size of the leaf images with respect to the pixel size. In order to understand the structure of the histogram one has to specify both the region of interest and the spatial resolution. Finally, the result will depend upon the resolution in the intensity domain: The histogram for a binary image, an eight bit or a thirty two bit image will all look different. We will refer to this as the bin width. Thus one needs at least the following parameters to specify a local histogram: The location and size of the region of interest (the support), the spatial resolution, and the bin width (that is the resolution in the intensity domain). We will regard the histogram as a function of position, thus one obtains a histogram valued image.

In order to construct histogram valued images one has to measure how much "stuff" should go in a certain bin for a certain region of interest, at a certain resolution. The spatial distribution of this "stuff" is what makes up the histogram valued image for a certain region size, resolution, bin width and intensity value. For each intensity value (keeping the other parameters constant) one has such a stuff distribution image.

Here is how one might construct a stuff distribution image: First one constructs the image at the specified level of resolution. Formally[7, 9, 1] this can be written as a convolution (here "⊗" denotes the convolution operator)

$$I(\mathbf{r}; \sigma) = S(\mathbf{r}) \otimes G_0(\mathbf{r}; \sigma) \tag{1}$$

of the "scene" ($S(\mathbf{r})$; at infinite resolution!) with a Gaussian kernel

$$G_0(\mathbf{r}; \sigma) = \frac{e^{-\frac{\mathbf{r} \cdot \mathbf{r}}{2\sigma^2}}}{2\pi\sigma^2}, \tag{2}$$

where σ denotes the resolution. Of course this is to be understood as merely formal: In reality one *observes* the image, the scene is implicit it cannot be observed other than via images. It is like the horizon that can never be reached.

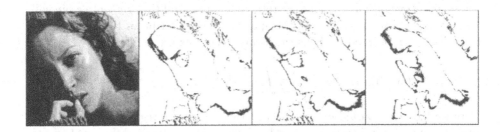

Fig. 1. *An image and three distributions of "histogram stuff". The bin width is 8, fiducial levels are 107, 127 and 147 (intensity ranges from 0 to 255). Notice the shift of the isophote with level. In this respect the soft isophotes behave exactly like regular isophotes (figure 3).*

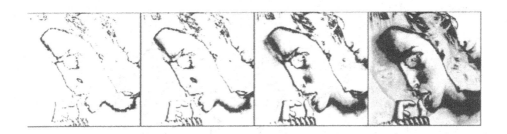

Fig. 2. *Four distributions of "histogram stuff". The image is shown in figure 1 on the left. Fiducial level is 127, bin widths are 8, 16, 32 and 64. Notice that though the location of the soft isophote is constant, its width increases as the bin width is increased. The soft isophotes can be quite broad "ribbons", in fact there is no limit, they may fill the whole image.*

Next one applies the following nonlinear transformation to the intensity of each pixel:

$$F(i; i_0, \beta) = e^{-\frac{(i-i_0)^2}{2\beta^2}}, \tag{3}$$

here i_0 denotes the fiducial intensity value and β denotes the bin width. Notice that the resulting image has pixel values in the range zero to one. These values can be regarded as the value of the membership function of a given pixel to the specified bin. Finally one blurs the result, taking the size of the region of interest as internal scale. The kernel to be used is

$$A(\mathbf{r};\mathbf{r_0},\alpha) = e^{-\frac{(\mathbf{r}-\mathbf{r_0})\cdot(\mathbf{r}-\mathbf{r_0})}{2\alpha^2}}. \tag{4}$$

The function A is the "aperture function" which defines the (soft) region of interest. It is not normalized, thus the total amount of stuff that gets into a bin will be proportional with the area of the aperture. This distributes the membership over the region of interest. Thus the local histograms are defined as

$$H(i;\mathbf{r_0},\sigma,\beta,\alpha) = \frac{1}{2\pi\alpha^2}\int_{image} A(\mathbf{r};\mathbf{r_0},\alpha)e^{-\frac{(I(\mathbf{r};\sigma)-i)^2}{2\beta^2}}\,d\mathbf{r} \tag{5}$$

Here we have normalized with respect to the area of the region of interest. The resulting image will have an overall level zero with a certain diffuse ribbon (or curve like) object that may reveal values up to one. This ribbon is intuitively a representation of a "soft isophote". It is in many respects a more useful object than a true "isophote". For instance, in regions where the intensity is roughly constant the "true" isophotes are ill defined and often take on a fractal character. The smallest perturbation may change their nature completely. In such regions the ribbon spreads out and fills the roughly uniform region with a nonzero but low value: The membership is divided over the pixels in the uniform region. For a linear gradient, the steeper the gradient, the narrower the isophote. (See figures 1, 2 and 3.)

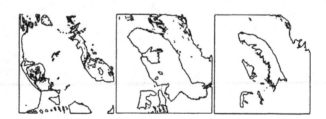

Fig. 3. *Three regular isophotes of the image shown in figure 1 on the left. Notice that the isophotes are not smooth curves but have a fractal character. Compare with the soft isophotes in figure 2.*

Notice that we deal with a number of closely intertwined scale spaces here. First there is the regular scale space of the image at several levels of resolution. Here the extentional parameter is $\mathbf{r}$ and the scale parameter σ. Then there is the scale space of histograms. Here the "extentional" parameter is the intensity i whereas the "resolution" parameter is the bin width. It is indeed (by construction) a neat linear scale space. One may think of it as the histogram at maximum resolution, blurred with a Gaussian kernel at the bin width. Thus each pixel in the image may be thought of as contributing a delta pulse at its intensity, these are then blurred to obtain the histogram: This is formally identical to the Parzen estimator[12] of the histogram. Finally, there is the scale space of stuff images with the size of the region of interest as inner scale. The extentional parameter is r_0 and the scale parameter α.

3 Locally disorderly images

Consider an image and its histogram (in the classical sense, no scale space). When we do arbitrary permutations on the pixels we obtain images that look quite distinct (the spatial structure can differ in arbitrary ways), yet they all have the same histogram. Thus the histogram can be regarded as the image modulo its spatial structure. That it why we refer to such images as "disorderly" in the first place. Histograms are zeroth order summary descriptions of images, the conceptually simplest type of "texture". A histogram valued image is likewise to be considered "locally disorderly". Notice that a disorderly image is not completely lacking in spatial discrimination. For instance, consider an image that consists of vertical stripes at the maximum frequency, say pixels with even horizontal index white, with odd index black. When this image is scrambled it can still be discriminated from a uniform image that is uniformly fifty percent gray. On the other hand, this discrimination fails when we completely blur the image, that is say, replace every pixel value with the average over all pixels. Yet the rudimentary spatial discrimination is not perfect, for instance one cannot discriminate between vertical and horizontal stripes.

Fig. 4. Left: *Original image; Middle: Blurred image; Left: Locally disorderly image. The blur and local disorder destroy roughly the same spatial detail. Notice that the locally disordered image looks "better" than the blurred one and indeed retains more information, for instance the bright pixels of the specularity on the nose.*

Quite apart from spatial discrimination, locally disorderly images retain much information that exists at a scale that is not resolved and would be lost in a totally blurred image[11, 2]. The type of information that is retained often lets you recognize material properties that would be lost by total blurring. Locally disorderly images are very similar to "painterly" renderings. In an impressionist painting there is often no spatial information on the scale of the brush strokes (*touches*). At this scale one has structure that reveals the *facture*, often a signature of the artist. Yet the strokes contribute much to the realistic rendering. The artist doesn't paint leaves when he/she paints a treetop, he/she "does foliage". Although no leaves are ever painted you can often recognize the genus by the way the foliage is handled. Pointillists were quite explicit about such things. For instance, Seurat[5] lists the colors of *touches* that go in a rendering of grass. He never paints leaves of grass, yet the grass is not uniformly green: There are blues (shadow areas), yellows (translucency) and oranges (glints of sunlight). These *touches* appear in a locally disorderly pattern.

Locally disorderly images can be rendered (see figure 4) by using the histograms as densities for a random generator. Every instance will be different, their totality is the locally disorderly image. Although all instances are different, they look the same. Indeed, they are the same on the scale where disorder gives way to order, and on finer scales the histograms are identical. Such renderings are not unlike "dithered" representations[15, 16].

4 Generalizations

In this paper we have considered histograms of pixel values. It is of course an obvious generalization to include local histograms of derivatives or (better) differential invariants. Then one essentially considers local histograms of the local jets up to some order[8], or perhaps the jets modulo some transformation, say a rotation or a left/right symmetry. Such higher order locally disorderly images specify the distribution of textural qualities. Such structures have indeed be used (albeit in an *ad hoc* fashion) to create instances of textures given a single prototypical example. The local disorder is to be considered "zeroth order texture": The local image structure is summarized via the intensity values (zeroth order) alone. Adding gradient information (histograms of the first order "edge detectors") would yield "first order texture", and so forth.

The formal description of such structures appears straightforward and would indeed yield a very attractive and (most likely) useful description of image structure.

5 Disorderly images and segmentation

When the boundary between two uniform regions is blurred the pixels appear to lose their origin. For instance, blurring the boundary between a uniformly red and a uniformly green field yields a ribbon of yellow pixels that appear to belong to neither side. This has been a major incentive for the construction of nonlinear blurring methods: The idea was to blur areas, but not over edges. With locally disorderly images this dilemma is automatically solved in an unexpected way. Although the boundary indeed becomes spatially less and less defined, the individual pixels hold on to their origin. In the example given above no yellow pixels are ever generated. One doesn't know where the red area ends and the green begins because there are red pixels to be found in the green area and *vice versa*. But the pixels themselves don't change their hue. In terms of segmentation the red and green areas may be said to *overlap* in the boundary area.

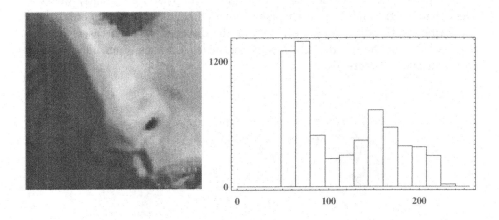

Fig. 5. *The histogram of a patch straddling the bodyshadow edge is bimodal.*

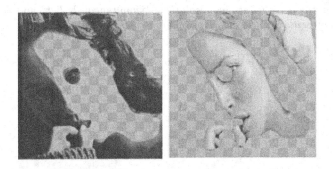

Fig. 6. *Segments belonging to the major modes of the histogram shown in figure 5. These are the illuminated and the shadow side of the face. The segments overlap over the ridge of the nose.*

In figures 5 and 6 we show a segmentation of a face on the basis of major modes in the local histograms. The light and dark halves of the face are segmented. There is some minor overlap on the bridge of the nose. In figure 7 we show a more extreme case: Here the segments belonging to two major modes are extensively overlapping. This example illustrates that the locally disorderly images can be thought of as entertaining multiple intensity levels at any given location in the image[11, 2]. For instance, one may take the major modes in the local histograms as intensity values. When there exists only a single major mode the representation is much like the conventional one (one intensity per pixel). But if there are two or more major modes the advantage of the locally disorderly representation becomes clear. In figure 7 the person apparently wears a dress that is light and dark at the same time! Of course this occurs only when the stripes of the dress have been lost in the disorder. In such cases the difference between the blurred and locally scrambled versions of an image are of course dramatic (figure 8).

Fig. 7. *An example of "transparent segments". On the left the original image. In the middle the segment belonging to the light stripes of the dress, on the right that belonging to the dark stripes. Note that in the latter case the dark hair is included in the segment, in the former case the light interstice between the arm and the leg. In the body part the dress is (at this resolution) "simultaneously light and dark": In the disorderly representation the locations of the stripes are lost.*

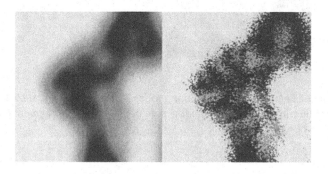

Fig. 8. *Blurred and locally scrambled versions of the striped dress image.*

6 Conclusion

Locally disorderly images admit of a neat formal description in terms of a number of intimately interlocked scale spaces. They can easily be rendered and can thus be used in image compression. They have distinct advantages over blurred images when one is interested in image segmentation. This is often desirable, for instance, one may treat the blue sky as continuous even where it is partly occluded by numerous twigs when seen through a tree top. Thus locally disorderly images may well find applications in image processing and interpretation.

References

1. Florack, L. M. J. 1997. *Image Structure*. Dordrecht: Kluwer.
2. Griffin, L. D. 1997. Scale–imprecision space. *Image and Vision Computing*, 15: 369–398.
3. Helmholtz, H. 1866. Handbuch der physiologischen Optik. Hamburg and Leipzig: Voss.
4. Hess, R. 1982. Developmental sensory impairment: Amblyopia or tarachopia? *Human Neurobiology*, 1: 17–29.
5. Homer, W. I. 1964. *Seurat and the science of painting*. Cambridge, Mass.: The M.I.T. Press.
6. Koenderink, J. J. and van Doorn, A. J. 1978. Invariant features of contrast detection: An explanation in terms of self–similar detector arrays. *Biological Cybernetics*, 30: 157–167.
7. Koenderink, J. J. 1984. The structure of images. *Biological Cybernetics*, 50: 363–370.
8. Koenderink, J. J. and van Doorn, A. J. 1992. Generic neighborhood operators. *IEEE Transactions on Pattern Analysis and Machine Intelligence*, 14: 597–605.
9. Lindeberg, T. 1994. *Scale–space theory in computer vision*. Boston, Mass.: Kluwer.
10. Metzger, W. 1975. Gesetze des Sehens. Frankfurt a.M.: Verlag Waldemar Kramer.
11. Noest, A. J. and Koenderink, J. J. 1990. Visual coherence despite transparency or partial occlusion. *Perception*, 19: 384.
12. Parzen, E. 1962. On estimation of a probability density function and mode. *Annual Mathematical Statistics*, 33: 1065–1076.
13. Ruskin, J. 1900. *Elements of drawing* (first ed. 1857). Sunnyside, Orpington: George Allen.
14. Ruskin, J. 1873. *Modern Painters* (Vol. I). Boston: Dana Estes & Company.
15. Ulichney, R. A. 1987. *Digital halftoning*. Cambridge, Mass.: The M.I.T. Press.
16. Ulichney, R. A. 1988. Dithering with blue noise. *Proc. IEEE*, 76: 56–79.

Applications of Locally Orderless Images

Bram van Ginneken and Bart M. ter Haar Romeny

Image Sciences Institute, Utrecht University, The Netherlands.
E-mail: bram@isi.uu.nl, URL: http://www.isi.uu.nl/

Abstract. In a recent work [1], Koenderink and van Doorn consider a family of three intertwined scale-spaces coined the *locally orderless image* (LOI). The LOI represents the image, observed at inner scale σ, as a local histogram with bin-width β, at each location, with a Gaussian-shaped region of interest of extent α. LOIs form a natural and elegant extension of scale-space theory, show causal consistency and enable the smooth transition between pixels, histograms and isophotes. The aim of this work is to demonstrate the wide applicability and versatility of LOIs. We consider a range of image processing tasks, including variations of adaptive histogram equalization, several methods for noise and scratch removal, texture rendering, classification and segmentation.

1 Introduction

Histograms are ubiquitous in image processing. They embody the notion that for many tasks, it is not the spatial order but the intensity distribution within a region of interest that contains the required information. One can argue that even at a single location the intensity has an uncertainty, and should therefore be described by a probability distribution: physical plausibility requires non-zero imprecision. This led Griffin [2] to propose a *scale-imprecision space* with spatial scale parameter σ and an intensity, or tonal scale β, which can be identified with the familiar *bin-width* of histograms.

Koenderink and Van Doorn [1] extended this concept to *locally orderless images* (LOIs), an image representation with three scale parameters in which there is no local but only a global topology defined. LOIs are *local histograms*, constructed according to scale-space principles, viz. without violating the causality principle. As such, one can apply to LOIs the whole machinery of techniques that has been developed in the context of scale-space research.

In this paper, we aim to demonstrate that LOIs are a versatile and flexible framework for image processing applications. The reader may conceive this article as a broad feasibility study. Due to space limitations, we cannot give thorough evaluations for each application presented. Obviously, local histograms are in common use, and the notion to consider histograms at different scales (soft binning) isn't new either. Yet we believe that the use of a consistent mathematical framework in which all scale parameters are made explicit can aid the design of effective algorithms by reusing existing scale-space concepts. Additional insight may be gained by taking into account the behavior of LOIs over scale.

2 Locally orderless images

We first briefly review locally orderless images [1] by considering the scale parameters involved in the calculation of a histogram:

- the inner scale σ with which the image is observed;
- the outer scale, or extent, or scope α that parameterizes the size of the field of view over which the histogram is calculated;
- the scale at which the histogram is observed, tonal scale, or bin-width β.

The locally orderless images $H(\mathbf{x_0}, i; \sigma, \alpha, \beta)$ are defined as the family of histograms, i.e. a function of the intensity i, with bin-width β of the image observed at scale σ calculated over a field of view centered around $\mathbf{x_0}$ with extent α. The unique way to decrease resolution without creating spurious resolution is by convolution with Gaussian kernels [3] [4]. Therefore Gaussian kernels are used for σ, α and β. We summarize this with a recipe for calculating LOIs:

1. Choose an inner scale σ and blur the image $L(x; \sigma)$ using the diffusion

$$\Delta_{(\mathbf{x})} L(\mathbf{x}; \sigma) = \frac{\partial L(\mathbf{x}; \sigma)}{\partial \frac{\sigma^2}{2}}. \tag{1}$$

2. Choose a number of (equally spaced) bins of intensity levels i and calculate the "soft isophote images", representing the "stuff" in each bin through the Gaussian gray-scale transformation

$$R(\mathbf{x}, i; \sigma, \beta) = \exp(-\frac{(L(\mathbf{x}; \sigma) - i)^2}{2\beta^2}) \tag{2}$$

3. Choose a scope α for a Gaussian aperture, normalized to unit amplitude

$$A(\mathbf{x}; \mathbf{x_0}, \alpha) = \exp \frac{-(\mathbf{x} - \mathbf{x_0})(\mathbf{x} - \mathbf{x_0})}{2\alpha^2} \tag{3}$$

and compute the locally orderless image through convolution

$$H(\mathbf{x_0}, i; \sigma, \alpha, \beta) = \frac{A(\mathbf{x}; \mathbf{x_0}, \alpha)}{2\pi\alpha^2} * R(\mathbf{x}, i; \sigma, \beta). \tag{4}$$

Note that $H(\mathbf{x_0}, i; \sigma, \beta, \alpha)$, is a stack of isophote images, and therefore has a dimensionality 1 higher than that of the input image.

The term *locally orderless* image refers to the fact that we have at each location the probability distribution at our disposal, which is a mere orderless set; the spatial structure within the field of view α centered at $\mathbf{x}$ has been obliterated. This is the key point: instead of a (scalar) intensity, we associate a probability distribution with each spatial location, parameterized by σ, α, β. Since a distribution contains more information then the intensity alone, we may hope to be able to use this information in various image processing tasks.

The LOI contains several conventional concepts. The original image and its scale-space $L(\mathbf{x}; \sigma)$ that can be recovered by integrating $iH(\mathbf{x_0}, i; \sigma, \alpha, \beta)$ over i.

The "conventional" histogram is obtained by letting $\alpha \to \infty$. The construction also includes families of isophote images, which for $\beta > 0$ are named *soft isophote images* by Koenderink. And maybe even more important, by tuning the scale parameters the LOI can fill intermediate stages between the image, its histogram and its isophotes. This can be useful in practice. The framework generalizes trivially to nD images or color images, if a color metric is selected.

3 Median and maximum mode evolution

If we replace the histogram at each location with its mean, we obtain the input image $L(\mathbf{x}; \sigma)$ blurred with a kernel with width α. This holds independently of β, since blurring a histogram does not alter its mean. If, however, we replace the histogram with its median or its maximum mode (intensity with highest probability), we obtain a diffusion with scale parameter α that is reminiscent of some non-linear diffusion schemes . The tonal scale β works as a tuning parameter that determines the amount of non-linearity. For $\beta \to \infty$, the median and the maximum mode are equal to the mean, so the diffusion is linear. Griffin [2] has studied the evolution of the median, and the stable mode (defined as the mode surviving as β increases), which is usually equal to the maximum mode. He always sets $\sigma = \alpha$. This ensures that for $\alpha \to \infty$ the image attains its mean everywhere, as in linear diffusion. With only a few soft isophote level images in the LOI, maximum mode diffusion also performs some sort of quantizing, and one obtains piecewise homogenous patches with user-selectable values. This can be useful, e.g. in coding for data-compression and knowledge driven enhancements.

4 Switching modes in bi-modal histograms

Instead of replacing each pixel with a feature of its local histogram, such as the median or the maximum mode, we can perform more sophisticated processing if we take the structure of the local histograms into account. If this histogram is bi-modal, this indicates the presence of multiple "objects" in the neighborhood of that location. Noest and Koenderink [5] have suggested to deal with partial occlusion in this way.

Fig. 1. Left: Text hidden in a sinusoidal background, dimensions 230×111, intensities in the range $[0, 1]$. Middle: bi-modal locations in an LOI of $\sigma = 0$, $\beta = 0.15$ and $\alpha = 1.5$. Right: bi-modal locations have been replaced with the high mode. Text is removed and the background restored.

Consider locations with bi-modal histograms. We let locations "switch mode", i.e. if they are in the high mode (that is, their original value is on the right of the minimum mode in between the two modes), we replace their value with the low mode (or vice versa, depending on the desired effect). The idea is to replace a bright/dark object with the most likely value that the darker/brighter object that surrounds it has, namely the low/high maximum mode. Note that this a two-step process: the detection of bi-modal locations is a segmentation step, and replacing pixels fills in a value from its surroundings, using statistical information from only those pixels that belong to the object to be filled in.

This scheme allows for a scale-selection procedure. For fixed σ, β, α, there may be locations with more than two modes in their local distribution. This indicates that it is worthwhile to decrease α, focusing on a smaller neighborhood, until just two modes remain. Thus we use a locally adaptive α, ensuring that the replaced pixel value comes from information from locations "as close as possible" to the pixel to be replaced.

We have applied this scheme successfully for the removal of text on a complicated background (Figure 1), the detection of dense objects in chest radiographs, and noise removal. Figure 2 shows how shot noise can be detected and replaced with a probable value, obtained from the local histogram. The restoration is near perfect. Figure 3 shows three consecutive frames from an old movie with severe deteriorations. To avoid to find bi-modal locations due to movement between frames, we considered two LOIs, one in which the frame to be restored was the first and one in which it was the last image. Only locations that were bi-modal in both cases were taken in consideration. Although most artifact are removed, there is ample room for improvements. One can verify from the middle

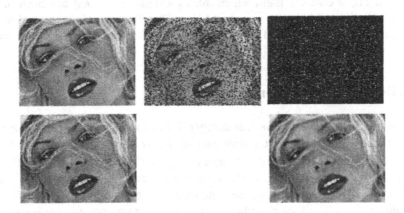

Fig. 2. (top-left) Original image, 249 × 188 pixels, intensities scaled to [0, 1]; (top-middle) Original image with shot noise. This is the input image for the restoration procedure; (top-right) Locations in (top-middle) with bi-modal histograms and pixels in the lowest mode using $\sigma = 0, \beta = 0.04, \alpha = 0.5$. (bottom-left) Restoration using mode-switching for bi-modal locations gives excellent results; (bottom-right) Restoration using using 5x5 median filter. This removes most shot noise, but blurs the image.

Fig. 3. The top row shows three consecutive frames (337×271 pixels, intensities scaled to $[0, 1]$) from a movie with severe local degradations, especially in the first frame shown. LOIs were calculated with $\sigma = 0$, $\beta = 0.1$, and $\alpha = 2.0$. The second row shows the detected artifact locations for each frame. The bottom row shows the restored frames, using histogram mode switching.

column in Fig. 3 that the hand which makes a rapid movement has been partly removed. Distinguishing such movements from deteriorations is in general a very complicated task, that would probably require a detailed analysis of the optic flow between frames.

5 Histogram transformations

Any generic histogram can be transformed into any other histogram by a non-linear, monotonic gray-level transformation. To see this, consider an input histogram $h_1(i)$ and its cumulative histogram $\int_{-\infty}^{i} h_1(i')di' = H_1(i)$ and the desired output histogram $h_2(i)$ and $H_2(i)$. If we replace every i with the i' for which $H_1(i) = H_2(i')$ we have transformed the cumulative histogram H_1 into H_2 and thus also h_1 into h_2. Since cumulative histograms are monotonically increasing, the mapping is monotonically increasing as well.

An example is histogram equalization. When displaying an image with a uniform histogram (within a certain range), all available gray levels or colors will be used in equal amounts and thus "perceptual contrast" is maximal. The idea to use local histograms (that is, selecting a proper α for the LOI) for equalization, to obtain optimal contrast over each region in the image stems from the 1970s

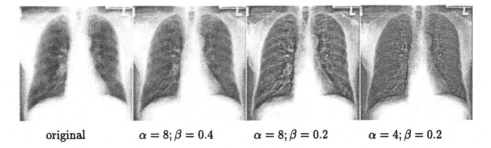

original $\alpha = 8; \beta = 0.4$ $\alpha = 8; \beta = 0.2$ $\alpha = 4; \beta = 0.2$

Fig. 4. A normal PA chest radiograph of 512 by 512 pixels with intensities in the range [0,1]. (a) Original image, in which details in lung regions and mediastinum are not well visible due to the large dynamic range of gray levels. (b)-(d) Adaptive histogram equalization (AHE) based on the LOI with $\sigma = 0$ and 3 combinations of α and β.

[6] and is called *adaptive histogram equalization* (AHE). However, it was noted that these operations blow up noise in homogeneous regions. Pizer et al. [7] proposed to *clip* histograms, viz. for each bin with more pixels than a certain threshold, truncate the number of pixels and redistribute these uniformly over all other bins. It can be seen that this ad hoc technique amounts to the same

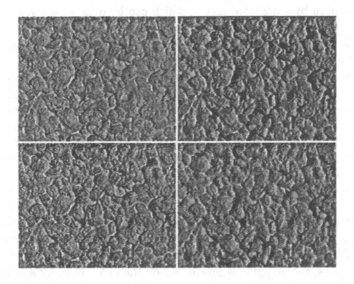

Fig. 5. Top-left is an image (332 by 259 pixels) of rough concrete viewed frontally, illuminated from 22°. Top-right: the same material illuminated from 45°. Bottom-left shows the top-left image with its histogram mapped to the top-right image to approximate the change in texture. Bottom-right shows the result of local histogram transformation, with $\alpha = 2$. The approximation is especially improved in areas that show up white in the images on the left. These areas are often partly shadowed with illumination from 45°, and using a local histogram may correctly "predict" such transitions.

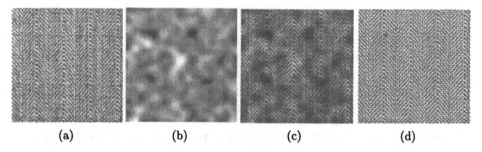

(a)   (b)   (c)   (d)

Fig. 6. (a) A texture from the Brodatz set [11], resolution 256^2, intensities in the range
[0, 1]. (b) Blurred Gaussian noise, scaled to range from [0, 1]. (c) Multiplication of (a)
and (b). (d) Reconstruction of (a) from (c) from the LOI with $\sigma = 0, \beta = 0.1, \alpha = 2$
and computing for each point a mapping to the local histogram at the randomly chosen
location (80,80).

effect as increasing β in the LOI; notably, for $\beta \to \infty$, AHE has no effect. Thus
we see that the two scale parameters α and β determine the size of structures
that are enhanced and the amount of enhancement, respectively. Figure 4 shows
a practical example of such a continuously tuned AHE for a medical modality
(thorax X-ray) with a wide latitude of intensities.

An alternative to histogram equalization is to increase the standard deviation
of the histogram by a constant factor, which can be done by a linear gray level
transformation, or variations on such schemes [8]. Again, the LOI provides us
with an elegant framework in which the scale parameters that determine the
results of such operations are made explicit.

Another application of histogram transformation is to approximate changes
in texture due to different viewing and illumination directions [9]. In general, the
textural appearance of many common real-world materials is a complex function
of the light field and viewing position. In computer graphics it is common practice, however, to simply apply a projective transformation to a texture patch
in order to account for a change in viewing direction and to adjust the mean
brightness using a bi-directional reflection distribution function (BRDF), often
assumed to be simply Lambertian. In [9] it is shown that this gives poor results
for many materials, and that histogram transformations often produce far more
realistic results. A logical next step is to consider *local* histogram transformations. An example is shown in Figure 5, using a texture of rough concrete taken
from the CURET database [10]. Instead of using one mapping function for all
pixel intensities, the mapping is now based on the pixel intensity and the intensities in its surroundings. Physical considerations make clear that this approach
does make sense: bright pixels which have dark pixels due to shadowing in their
neighborhood are more likely to become shadowed for more oblique illumination
than those that are in the center of a bright region.

Finally, histogram transformations can be applied to restore images that have
been corrupted by some noise process, but for which the local histogram properties are known or can be estimated from the corrupted image. Such cases are

encountered frequently in practice. Many image acquisition systems contain artifacts that are hard to correct with calibration schemes. One example in medical image processing is the inhomogeneity of the magnetic field of an MR scanner or of the sensitivity of MR surface coils, leading to low frequency gradients over the image. A generated example is shown in Figure 6 where we multiplied a texture image with Gaussian noise. By randomly choosing a point in the corrupted image and computing the mapping that transforms each local histogram to the local histogram at that particular location we obtain the restored image in Figure 6(d). Apart from it being low frequency, the LOI method does not make any assumption about the noise process and works for multiplicative, additive, and other kinds of noise processes.

6 Texture classification and discrimination

LOIs can be used to set up a framework for texture classification. The histogram is one of the simplest texture descriptions; the spatial structure has been completely disregarded and only the probability distribution remains. This implies that any feature derived from LOIs is rotationally invariant. There are several ways possible to extend LOIs:

Locally orderless derivatives
Instead of using $L(\mathbf{x}; \sigma)$ as input for the calculation of LOIs, we can use $L_n^\theta(\mathbf{x}; \sigma)$, which denotes the nth order spatial derivative of the image at scale σ in the direction θ. These images can be calculated for any θ from a fixed set of basis filters in several ways, for a discussion see [12], [13]. For $n = 0$, these locally orderless derivatives (LODs) reduce to the LOIs. Alternatively, one could choose another family of filters instead of directional derivatives of Gaussians, such as differences of offset Gaussians [14], [15], or Gabor filters [16].

Directional locally orderless images
Another way to introduce orientation sensitivity in LOIs is to use anisotropic Gaussians as local regions of interest. This would extend the construction with an orientation $0 < \theta < \pi$, and an anisotropy factor.

Cooccurrence matrices
Haralick [17],[18] introduced cooccurrence matrices, which are joint probability densities for locations at a prescribed distance and orientation. Texture features can be computed from these matrices. It is straightforward to modify the LOIs into a construction equivalent to cooccurrence matrices. It leads to joint probability functions as a function of location.

Results from psychophysics suggest that if two textures are to be pre-attentive discriminable by human observers, they must have different spatial average $\int \int_{T_1} R(x,y)$ and $\int \int_{T_2} R(x,y)$ of some locally computed neural response R [14]. We use this as a starting point and compute features derived from LODs, averaged over texture patches. Averaging will give identical results for any α if we use linear operations on LODs to compute local features. Thus we include non-linear operations on the local histograms as well. An obvious choice is to use higher-order moments.

Which combinations of scales σ, α, β are interesting to select? First of all, we should have $\sigma < \alpha$, otherwise local histograms are peaked distributions and higher order moments of these distributions are fully predictable. Furthermore, in practice σ and β will often be mutually exclusive. Haralick [18] defined texture as a collection of typical elements, called tonal primitives or textons, put together according to placement rules. As the scope α is much larger than the spatial size of the textons, the local histograms will not change much anymore. Therefore it does not make sense to consider more than one LOI with α much larger than the texton size. Using $\alpha = \infty$ is the obvious choice for this large scope histogram. Secondly, if we vary σ at values below the texton size, we study the spatial structure of the textons. For σ much larger than the texton size, we are investigating the characteristics of the placement rules.

We performed an experiment using texture patches from 16 large texture images from the USC-SIPI database available at `http://sipi.usc.edu`, 11 of which originated from the Brodatz collection [11]. From each texture, 16 nonoverlapping regions were cropped and subsampled to a resolution of 128×128. Intensity values of each patch were normalized to zero mean and unit variance. Figure 7 shows one patch for each texture class.

We classified with the nearest-neigbor rule and the leave-one-out method. A small set of 9 features was already able to classify 255 out of all 256 textures correctly. This set consisted of 3 input images, $L_0(\mathbf{x}; \sigma = 0)$ (used in feature 1-3), $L_1^{0°}(\mathbf{x}; \sigma = 1)$ (used in feature 4-6), and $L_0^{90°}(\mathbf{x}; \sigma = 1)$ (used in feature 7-9) for which we calculated the averaged second moment (viz. the local standard deviation) for $\beta = 0.1$ and $\alpha = 1, 2, \infty$.

To gain more insight into the discriminative power of each of the calculated features separately, we performed the classification for any possible combination of 1, 2 or 3 out of the 9 features. The best and worst results are given in Table 1. It is interesting to see that there is no common feature in the best single set, the best 2 features and the 3 best ones, which indicates that all features contain discriminant power. Since we use only 2nd moments, features are invariant to gray-level inversion. This can be solved by adding higher moments, which was apparently unnecessary for the test set we considered.

Fig. 7. The 16 different textures used in a texture classification experiment.

features set	best single	worst single	best 2	worst 2	best 3	worst 3	full set
features used	7	3	4,9	2,3	1,5,8	3,8,9	all
result	47.6%	12.9%	91.4%	41.0%	99.2%	71.5%	99.6%

Table 1. Classification results for various combinations of features.

7 Texture segmentation based on local histograms

Many "general" (semi-)automatic segmentation schemes are based on the notion that points in spatial proximity with similar intensity values are likely to belong to the same object. Such methods have problems with textured areas, because the intensity values may show wild local variations. A solution is to *locally* compute texture features and replace pixel values with these features, assuming that pixels that belong to the same texture region will now have a similar value. The framework of LOIs is ideally suited to be used for the computation of such local features. One could use LODs, or another extension of LOIs put forward in the previous section. Shi and Malik [15] have applied their normalized cut segmentation scheme to texture segmentation in this way, using local histograms and the correlation between them as a metric.

Here we present an adapted version of a seeded region growing (SRG), that is popular in medical image processing. For $\alpha \to 0$, our adaptation reduces to a scheme very similar to the original SRG. This is directly due to the fact that LOIs *contain* the original image.

SRG segments an image starting from seed regions. A list is maintained of pixels connected to one of the regions, sorted according to some metric. This metric is originally defined as the squared difference between the pxiel intensity and the mean intensity of the region. The pixel at the top of the list is added to the region it is connected to, and the neighbors of the added pixel are added to the list. This procedure is repeated until all pixels are assigned to a region.

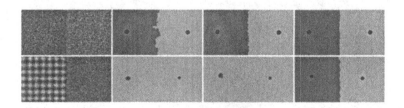

Fig. 8. Top row, from left to right: A 256×128 test image composed of two homogenous regions with intensity 0 and 1 and Gaussian noise with zero mean and unit variance. An LOI with $\sigma = 0$ and $\beta = 0.2$ and $\alpha = 0, 1, 4$, respectively is used for seeded region growing from the two seeds shown in white. Since the mean of the two region is different, regular seeded region growing ($\alpha = 0$) works well. Bottom row: same procedure for a partly textured image; the left half was filled with $\sin(x/3) + \sin(y/3)$, the right half was set to zero, and Gaussian noise with zero mean and $\sigma = 0.5$ was added. Regular seeded region growing now fails, but if α is large enough, the segmentation is correct.

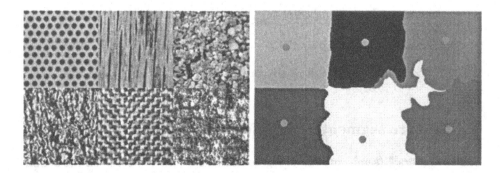

Fig. 9. Left: A test image composed of 6 texture patches of pixel size 128 × 128 each. Intensity values in each patch are normalized to zero mean and unit variance. Right: The result of segmentation with seeded region growing based on a LOI with $\sigma = 0$, $\beta = 0.2$ and $\alpha = 8$. The circles are the seeds.

We propose to compute a metric based on the local histograms of a pixel and a region. We subtract the histograms and take the sum of the absolute values of what is left in the bins. For $\alpha \to 0$ this reduces to a scheme similar to the original scheme, except that one considers for the region the global mode instead of the mean (most likely pixel value instead of the mean pixel value). Figures 8 to 10 illustrate the use of seeded region growing based on local histograms.

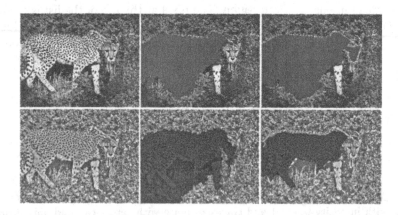

Fig. 10. Top row, left: Wildlife scene with leopard, size 329 × 253 pixels, intensities scaled between [0, 1]; Bottom row, left: A locally ($\sigma = 8$) normalized version of the input image; Middle and right: Segmentation by SRG based upon LOI with $\sigma = 0$, $\beta = 0.05$ and $\alpha = 0, 4$, respectively. Note how well the textured area is segmented in the lower right image.

8 Concluding remarks

In the applications presented, we have used many aspects of LOIs. They are a natural extension of techniques that usually use pixels, e.g. seeded region growing. They extend techniques that use "conventional" histograms with an extra degree of freedom, e.g. histogram transformation techniques. Other applications exploit the behavior of LOIs over scale to obtain non-linear diffusions, for scale selection in noise removal, and to derive texture features. We conclude that LOIs are image representations of great practical value.

Acknowledgments

This work is supported by the IOP Image Processing funded by the Dutch Ministry of Economic Affairs. We thank Peter van Roosmalen for providing the movie sequence.

References

1. J.J. Koenderink and A.J. van Doorn. The structure of locally orderless images. *IJCV*, 31(2/3):159–168, 1999.
2. L.D. Griffin. Scale-imprecision space. *Image and Vision Comp.*, 15:369–398, 1997.
3. J.J. Koenderink. The structure of images. *Biol. Cybern.*, 50:363–370, 1984.
4. J. Weickert, S. Ishikawa, and A. Imiya. On the history of Gaussian scale-space axiomatics. In *Gaussian Scale-Space Theory*, pp. 45–59. Kluwer, Dordrecht, 1997.
5. A.J. Noest and J.J. Koenderink. Visual coherence despite transparency or partial occlusion. *Perception*, 19:384, 1990.
6. R.A. Hummel. Image enhancement by histogram transformation. *Comp. Graph. and Im. Proc.*, 6:184–195, 1977.
7. S. Pizer, E. Amburn, J. Austin, R. Cromartie, A. Geselowitz, T. Greer, B. ter Haar Romeny, J. Zimmerman, and K. Zuiderveld. Adaptive histogram equalization and its variations. *Comp. Vis., Graph. and Im. Proc.*, 39:355–368, 1987.
8. D.C. Chan and W.R. Wu. Image contrast enhancement based on a histogram transformation of local standard deviation. *IEEE TMI*, 17(4):518–531, 1998.
9. B. van Ginneken, J.J. Koenderink, and K.J. Dana. Texture histograms as a function of illumination and viewing direction. *IJCV*, 31(2/3):169–184, 1999.
10. K.J. Dana, B. van Ginneken, S.K. Nayar, and J.J. Koenderink. Reflectance and texture of real-world surfaces. *ACM Trans. on Graphics*, 18(1):1–34, 1999.
11. P. Brodatz. *Textures*. Dover, New York, 1966.
12. W.T. Freeman and E.H. Adelson. The design and use of steerable filters. *IEEE PAMI*, 13(9):891–906, 1991.
13. P. Perona. Deformable kernels for early vision. *IEEE PAMI*, 17(5):488–499, 1995.
14. J. Malik and P. Perona. Preattentive texture discrimination with early vision mechanisms. *JOSA-A*, 7(5):923–932, 1990.
15. J. Shi and J. Malik. Self inducing relational distance and its application to image segmentation. In *ECCV*, 1998.
16. A.C. Bovik, M. Clark, and W.S. Geisler. Multichannel texture analysis using localized spatial filters. *IEEE PAMI*, 12(1):55–73, 1990.
17. R.M. Haralick, K. Shanmugam, and I. Dinstein. Textural features for image classification. *IEEE PAMI*, 3:610–621, 1973.
18. R.M. Haralick. Statistical and structural approaches to texture. *Proc. of the IEEE*, 67(5):786–804, 1979.

Scale Space Technique for Word Segmentation in Handwritten Documents *

R. Manmatha and Nitin Srimal

Computer Science Department,
University of Massachusetts, Amherst MA 01003, USA,
manmatha,nsrimal@cs.umass.edu,
WWW home page: http://ciir.cs.umass.edu

Abstract. Indexing large archives of historical manuscripts, like the papers of George Washington, is required to allow rapid perusal by scholars and researchers who wish to consult the original manuscripts. Presently, such large archives are indexed manually. Since optical character recognition (OCR) works poorly with handwriting, a scheme based on matching word images called word spotting has been suggested previously for indexing such documents. The important steps in this scheme are segmentation of a document page into words and creation of lists containing instances of the same word by word image matching.

We have developed a novel methodology for segmenting handwritten document images by analyzing the extent of "blobs" in a scale space representationof the image. We believe this is the first application of scale space to this problem. The algorithm has been applied to around 30 grey level images randomly picked from different sections of the George Washington corpus of 6,400 handwritten document images. An accuracy of 77 − 96 percent was observed with an average accuracy of around 87 percent. The algorithm works well in the presence of noise, shine through and other artifacts which may arise due aging and degradation of the page over a couple of centuries or through the man made processes of photocopying and scanning.

1   Introduction

There are many single author historical handwritten manuscripts which would be useful to index and search. Examples of these large archives are the papers

---

* This material is based on work supported in part by the National Science Foundation, Library of Congress and Department of Commerce under cooperative agreement number EEC-9209623, in part by the United States Patent and Trademark Office and Defense Advanced Research Projects Agency/ITO under ARPA order number D468, issued by ESC/AXS contract number F19628-95-C-0235, in part by the National Science Foundation under grant number IRI-9619117, in part by NSF Multimedia CDA-9502639 and in part by the Air Force Office of Scientific Research under grant number F49620-99-1-0138. Any opinions, findings and conclusions or recommendations expressed in this material are the authors and do not necessarily reflect those of the sponsors.

of George Washington, Margaret Sanger and W. E. B Dubois. Currently, much of this work is done manually. For example, 50,000 pages of Margaret Sanger's work were recently indexed and placed on a CDROM. A page by page index was created manually. It would be useful to automatically create an index for an historical archive similar to the index at the back of a printed book. To achieve this objective a semi-automatic scheme for indexing such documents have been proposed in [8]. In this scheme known as *Word Spotting* the document page is segmented into words. Lists of words containing multiple instances of the same word are then created by matching word images against each other. A user then provides the ASCII equivalent to a representative word image from each list and the links to the original documents are automatically generated. The earlier work in [8] concentrated on the matching strategies and did not address full page segmentation issues in handwritten documents. In this paper, we propose a new algorithm for word segmentation in document images by considering the scale space behavior of blobs in line images.

Most existing document analysis systems have been developed for machine printed text. There has been little work on word segmentation for handwritten documents. Most of this work has been applied to special kinds of pages - for example, addresses or "clean" pages which have been written specifically for testing the document analysis systems. Historical manuscripts suffer from many problems including noise, shine through and other artifacts due to aging and degradation. No good techniques exist to segment words from such handwritten manuscripts. Further, scale space techniques have not been applied to this problem before. [1] We outline the various steps in the segmentation algorithm below.

The input to the system is a grey level document image. The image is processed to remove horizontal and vertical line segments likely to interfere with later operations. The page is then dissected into lines using projection analysis techniques modified for gray scale image. The projection function is smoothed with a Gaussian filter (low pass filtering) to eliminate false alarms and the positions of the local maxima (i.e. white space between the lines) is detected. Line segmentation, though not essential is useful in breaking up connected ascenders and descenders and also in deriving an automatic scale selection mechanism. The line images are smoothed and then convolved with second order anisotropic Gaussian derivative filters to create a scale space and the *blob* like features which arise from this representation give us the focus of attention regions (i.e. words in the original document image). The problem of automatic scale selection for filtering the document is also addressed. We have come up with an efficient heuristic for scale selection whereby the correct scale for blob extraction is obtained by finding the scale maxima of the blob extent. A connected component analysis of the blob image followed by a reverse mapping of the bounding boxes allows us to

---

[1] It is interesting to note that the first scale space paper by T. Iijima was written in the context of optical character recognition in 1962 (see [12]). However, scale space techniqes are rarely used in document analysis today and as far as we are aware it has not been applied to the problem of character and word segmentation.

extract the words. The box is then extended vertically to include the ascenders and descenders. Our approach to word segmentation is novel as it is the first algorithm which utilizes the inherent scale space behavior of words in grey level document images. This paper gives a brief description of the techniques used. More details may be found in [11].

1.1 Related Work

Character segmentation schemes proposed in the literature have mostly been developed for machine printed characters and work poorly when extended to handwritten text. An excellent survey of the various schemes has been presented in [3]. Very few papers have dealt exclusively with the issue of word segmentation in handwritten documents and most of these have focussed on identifying gaps using geometric distance metrics between connected components. Seni and Cohen [9] evaluate eight different distance measures between pairs of connected component for word segmentation in handwritten text. In [7] the distance between the convex hulls is used. Srihari et all [10] present techniques for line separation and then word segmentation using a neural network. However, existing word segmentation strategies have certain limitations.

1. Almost all the above methods require binary images. Also, they have been tried only on clean white self-written pages and not manuscripts.
2. Most of the techniques have been developed for machine printed characters and not handwritten words. The difficulty faced in word segmentation is in combining discrete characters into words.
3. Most researchers focus only on word recognition algorithms and considered a database of clean images with well segmented words (see for example [1]). Only a few [10] have performed full, handwritten page segmentation. However, we feel that schemes such as [10] are not applicable for page segmentation in manuscript images for the reasons mentioned below.
4. Efficient image binarization is difficult on manuscript images containing noise and shine through.
5. Connected ascenders and descenders have to be separated.
6. Prior character segmentation was required to perform word segmentation and accurate character segmentation in cursive writing is a difficult problem. Also the examples shown are contrived (self written) and do not handle problems in naturally written documents.

2 Word Segmentation

Modeling the human cognitive processes to derive a computational methodology for handwritten word segmentation with performance close to the human visual system is quite complex due to the following characteristics of handwritten text.

1. The handwriting style may be cursive or discrete. In case of discrete handwriting characters have to be combined to form words.

2. Unlike machine printed text, handwritten text is not uniformly spaced.
3. Scale problem. For example, the size of characters in a header is generally larger than the average size of the characters in the body of the document.
4. Ascenders and descenders are frequently connceted and words may be present at different orientations.
5. Noise, artifacts, aging and other degradation of the document. Another problem is the presence of background handwriting or shine through.

We now present a brief background to scale space and how we have applied it to document analysis.

2.1 Scale Space and Document Analysis

Scale space theory deals with the importance of scale in any physical observation i.e. objects and features are relevant only at particular scales. In scale space, starting from an original image, successively smoothed images are generated along the scale dimension. It has been shown by several researchers [4, 6] that the Gaussian uniquely generates the linear scale space of the image when certain conditions are imposed.

We feel that *scale space* also provides an ideal framework for document analysis. We may regard a document to be formed of features at multiple scales. Intuitively, at a finer scale we have characters and at larger scales we have words, phrases, lines and other structures. Hence, we may also say that there exists a scale at which we may derive words from a document image. We would, therefore, like to have an image representation which makes the features at that scale (words in this case) explicit. The linear scale space representation of a continuous signal with arbitrary dimensions consists of building a one parameter family of signals derived from the original one in which the details are progressively removed. Let $f: \Re^2 \to \Re$ represent any given signal. Then, the scale space representation $I: \Re^2 \times \Re_+ \to \Re$ is defined by (see [6]) letting the scale space representation at zero scale be equal to the original signal $I(\cdot; 0) = f$ and for $t > 0$,

$$I(\cdot; t) = G(\cdot; t) \star f, \tag{1}$$

where $t \in \Re_+$ is the scale parameter, and G is the Gaussian kernel which in two dimensions $(x, y \in \Re)$ is written as

$$G(x, y; \sigma) = \frac{1}{2\pi\sigma^2} e^{\frac{-(x^2+y^2)}{(2\sigma^2)}} \tag{2}$$

where $\sigma = \sqrt{2t}$. We now describe the various stages in our algorithm.

2.2 Preprocessing

These handwritten manuscripts have been subjected to degradation such as fading and introduction of artifacts. The images provided to us are scanned versions of the photocopies of the original manuscripts. In the process of photocopying, horizontal and vertical black line segments/margins were introduced. Horizontal lines are also present within the text. The purpose of the preprocessing step is to remove some of these margins and lines so that they will not interfere with the blob analysis stage. Due to lack of space, this step is not described here. More details may be found in [11].

2.3 Line Segmentation

Line segmentation allows the ascenders and descenders of consecutive lines to be separated. In the manuscripts it is observed that the lines consist of a series of horizontal components from left to right. Projection profile techniques have been widely used in line and word segmentation for machine printed documents [5]. In this technique a 1D function of the pixel values is obtained by projecting the binary image onto the horizontal or vertical axis. We use a modified version of the same algorithm extended to gray scale images. Let $f(x, y)$ be the intensity value of a pixel (x, y) in a gray scale image. Then, we define the vertical projection profile as

$$P(y) = \sum_{x=0}^{W} f(x, y) \tag{3}$$

where W is the width of the image. Fig. 1 shows a section of an image in (a) and its projection profile in (b). The distinct local peaks in the profile corresponds to the white space between the lines and distinct local minima corresponds to the text (black ink). Line segmentation, therefore, involves detecting the position of the local maxima. However, the projection profile has a number of false local maxima and minima. The projection function $P(y)$ is therefore, smoothed with a Gaussian (low pass) filter to eliminate false alarms and reduce sensitivity to noise. A smoothed profile is shown in (c). The local maxima is then obtained from the first derivative of the projection function by solving for y such that :

$$P'(y) = P(y) \star G_y = 0 \tag{4}$$

The line segmentation technique is robust to variations in the size of the lines and has been tested on a wide range of handwritten pages. The next step after line segmentation is to create a scale space of the line images for blob analysis.

2.4 Blob Analysis

Now we examine each line image individually to extract the words. A word image is composed of discrete characters, connected characters or a combination of the two. We would like to merge these sub-units into a single meaningful entity which is a word. This may be achieved by forming a blob-like representation of the image. A blob can be regarded as a connected region in space. The traditional way of forming a blob is to use a Laplacian of a Gaussian (LOG) [6], as the LOG is a popular operator and frequently used in blob detection and a variety of multi-scale image analysis tasks [2, 6]. We have used a differential expression similar to

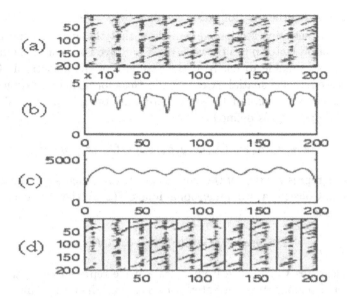

Fig. 1: (a) A section of an image, (b) projection profile, (c) smoothed projection profile (d) line segmented image

a LOG for creating a multi-scale representation for blob detection. However, our differential expression differs in that we combine second order partial Gaussian derivatives along the two orientations at different scales. In the next section we present the motivation for using an anisotropic derivative operator.

Non Uniform Gaussian Filters. In this section some properties which characterize writing are used to formulate an approach to filtering words. In [6] Lindeberg observes that maxima in scale-space occur at a scale proportional to the spatial dimensions of the blob. If we observe a word we may see that the spatial extent of the word is determined by the following :

1. The individual characters determine the height (y dimension) of the word and
2. The length (x dimension) is determined by the number of characters in it.

A word generally contains more than one character and has an aspect ratio greater than one. As the x dimension of the word is larger than the y dimension, the spatial filtering frequency should also be higher in the y dimension as compared to the x dimension. This domain specific knowledge allows us to move from isotropic (same scale in both directions) to anisotropic operators. We choose the x dimension scale to be larger than the y dimension to correspond to the spatial structure of the word. We define the anisotropic Gaussian filter as

$$G(x, y; \sigma_x, \sigma_y) = \frac{1}{2\pi\sigma_x\sigma_y} e^{-(\frac{x^2}{2\sigma_x^2} + \frac{y^2}{2\sigma_y^2})} \tag{5}$$

We may also define the multiplication factor η by $\eta = \frac{\sigma_x}{\sigma_y}$.

In the scale selection section we will show that the average aspect ratio or the multiplication factor η lies between three and five for most of the handwritten documents available to us. Also the response of the anisotropic Gaussian filter (measured as the spatial extent of the *blobs* formed) is maximum in this range. For the above Gaussian, the second order anisotropic Gaussian differential operator $L(x, y; \sigma_x, \sigma_y)$ is defined as

$$L(x, y; \sigma_x, \sigma_y) = G_{xx}(x, y; \sigma_x, \sigma_y) + G_{yy}(x, y; \sigma_x, \sigma_y) \qquad (6)$$

A scale space representation of the line images is constructed by convolving the image with 6. Consider a two dimensional image $f(x, y)$, then the corresponding output image is

$$I(x, y; \sigma_x, \sigma_y) = L(x, y; \sigma_x, \sigma_y) \star f(x, y) \qquad (7)$$

The main features which arise from a scale space representation are blob-like (i.e. connected regions either brighter or darker than the background). The sign of I may then be used to make a classification of the 3-D intensity surface into foreground and background. For example consider the line image in Fig. 2(a). The figures show the blob images $I(x, y; \sigma_x, \sigma_y)$ at increasing scale values. Fig. 2(b) shows that at a lower scale the blob image consists of character blobs. As we increase the scale, character blobs give rise to word blobs (Fig. 2(c) and Fig. 2(d)). This is indicative of the phenomenon of merging in blobs. It is seen that for certain scale values the blobs and hence the words are correctly delineated (Fig. 2(d)). A further increase in the scale value may not necessarily cause word blobs to merge together and other phenomenon such as splitting is also observed. These figures show that there exists a scale at which it is possible to delineate most words. In the next section we present an approach to automatic scale selection for blob extraction.

2.5 Choice of Scale

Scale space analysis does not address the problem of scale selection. The solution to this problem depends on the particular application and requires the use of prior information to guide the scale selection procedure. Some of our work in scale selection draws motivation from Lindeberg's observation [6] that the maximum response in both scale and space is obtained at a scale proportional to the dimension of the object. A document image consists of structures such as characters, words and lines at different scales. However, as compared to other types of images, document images have the unique property that a large variation in scale is not required to extract a particular type of structure. For example, all the words are essentially close together in terms of their scale and can, therefore, be extracted without a large variation in the scale parameter. Hence, there exists a scale where each of the individual word forms a distinct blob. The output (blob) is then maximum at this value of the scale parameter. We will show that

(a) A line image

(b) Blob image at scale $\sigma_y = 1, \sigma_x = 2$

(c) Blob image at scale $\sigma_y = 2, \sigma_x = 4$

(d) Blob image at scale $\sigma_y = 4, \sigma_x = 16$

(e) Blob image at scale $\sigma_y = 6, \sigma_x = 36$

Fig. 2: A line image and the output at different scales

this scale is a function of the vertical dimension of the word if the aspect ratio is fixed.

Now, we highlight, the important differences in Lindeberg's approach to blob analysis and our work. In [6] Lindeberg determines interesting scale levels from the maxima over scale levels of a blob measure. He defines his blob measure to consist of the spatial extent, contrast and lifetime. A scale space blob tree is then constructed to track individual blobs across scales. In our analysis tracking individual blobs across scales is not the relevant issue nor is it computationally advisable because of the presence of a large number of blobs representing characters and words. Also it is impossible to determine whether an extrema corresponds to a character blob or a word blob and as mentioned earlier the variation of the best scale for a word is not large. What is important, however, is that we would like to merge character blobs and yet be able to delimit the word blobs. Therefore, we consider a blob as a connected region in space and measure its spatial extent but do not give it any volumetric significance. Spatial extent as a blob characteristic is computationally available to us and we observe that it shifts with scale giving a maximum as character blobs merge to form word blobs. This is in agreement with the intuitive reasoning that the response of the word at the correct scale of observation should be maximum as every blob has only a range of scales (lifetime) to manifest itself.

Our algorithm requires selecting σ_y and the multiplication factor η for blob extraction. We present an analysis which helped us arrive at a simple scale selection method based on the observation that the maximum of the spatial extent of the blobs corresponds to the best scale for filtering. To measure the variation in spatial extent of the blobs over scale we define ζ_i to represent the extent of a blob i. Then the total extent of the blobs A, for a line is given by $A = \sum_{i=1}^{n} \zeta_i$.

Selecting η. The parameters σ_y and σ_x try to capture the spatial dimensions of a word. An important characteristic of a word is its aspect ratio. A manual analysis of several images was carried out and it was shown that the average aspect ratio of a word in a document image is approximately $3.0 - 5.0$. We had earlier defined the multiplication factor η as $\eta = \sigma_x/\sigma_y$. An analysis of several images reveals that for constant σ_y, the maxima in extent was obtained for η lying in the range between $3 - 5$. A line image and the corresponding plot is shown in Fig. 3. In this Fig. the maximum is obtained in the region between $3.5 - 4$. This analysis along with the observation that the average aspect ratio

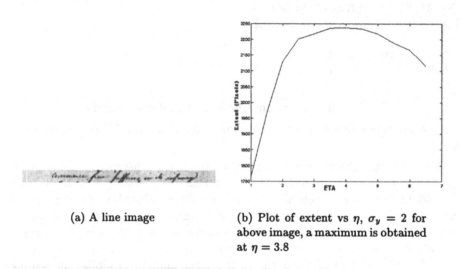

(a) A line image

(b) Plot of extent vs η, $\sigma_y = 2$ for above image, a maximum is obtained at $\eta = 3.8$

Fig. 3: Variation of blob extent vs η with constant σ_y

of the word is between $3 - 5$ allows us to choose a value of η in the range $3 - 5$. Specifically, for further analysis we choose $\eta = 4$.

Selecting σ_y. Fig. 4 shows the line images and corresponding plots of extent versus σ_y for constant η. As seen in the figures the total extent exhibits a peak which depends on σ_y. The figures also show how the peak shifts with the change in the size (height) of the characters. Experimentally it was found that σ_y (y scale) is a function of the height of the words (which is related to the height of the line). An estimate of σ_y is obtained by using the line height i.e.

$$\sigma_y = k \times \text{Line height} \qquad (8)$$

where $0 < k < 1$. The nearby scales are then examined to determine the maximum over scales. For our specific implementation we have used $k = 0.1$ and sampled σ_y at intervals of 0.3. The two values were determined experimentally and worked well over a wide range of images.

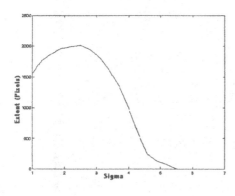

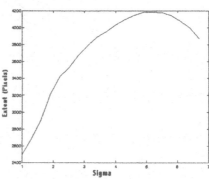

(a) A sample line image with smaller height

(b) A sample line image with larger height

(c) Plot of extent vs σ_y, Maximum is obtained at $\sigma_y = 2.5$

(d) Plot of extent vs σ_y, Maximum is obtained at $\sigma_y = 6.0$

Fig. 4: Variation of blob extent vs σ_y with constant $\eta = 4$.

2.6 Blob Extraction and Post Processing

The blobs are then mapped back to the original image to locate the words. A widely used procedure is to enclose the blob in a bounding box which can be obtained through connected component analysis. In a blob representation of the word, localization is not maintained. Also parts of the words, especially the ascenders and descenders, are lost due to the earlier operations of line segmentation and smoothing (blurring). Therefore, the above bounding box is extended in the vertical direction to include these ascenders and descenders. At this stage an area/ratio filter is used to remove small structures due to noise.

3 Results

The technique was tried on 30 randomly picked images from different sections of the George Washington corpus of 6, 400 images and a few images from the archive of papers of Erasmus Hudson. To reduce the run-time, the images have been smoothed and sub-sampled to a quarter of their original size. The algorithm takes 120 seconds to segment a document page of size 800 x 600 pixels on a PC with a 200 MHz pentium processor running LINUX. A segmentation accuracy ranging from 77 − 96 percent with an average accuracy around 87.6 percent was observed. Fig. 5 shows part of a segmented page image with bounding boxes drawn on the extracted words. The method worked well even on faded, noisy images and Table

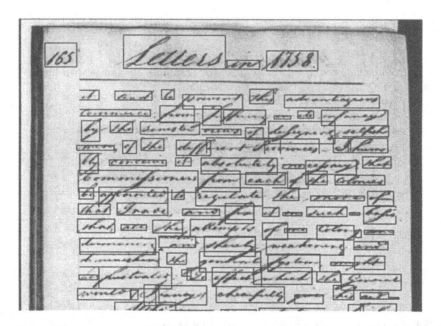

Fig. 5: Segmentation result on part of image 1670165.tif from the George Washington collection

4 shows the results averaged over a set of 30 images. The first column indicates the average no. of distinct words in a page as seen by a human observer. The second column indicates the % of words detected by the algorithm i.e, words with a bounding box around them, this includes words correctly segmented, fragmented and combined together. The next column indicate the % of words fragmented. Word fragmentation occurs if a character or characters in a word have separate bounding boxes or if 50 percent or greater of a character in a word is not detected. Line fragmentation occurs due to the dissection of the image into lines. A word is line fragmented if 50 percent or greater of a character lies outside the top or bottom edges of the bounding box. The sixth column indicates the words which are combined together. These are multiple words in the same bounding box. The last column gives the percentage of correctly segmented words.

4 Conclusion

We have presented a novel technique for word segmentation in handwritten documents. Our algorithm is robust and efficient for the following reasons:

1. We use grey level images and, therefore, image binarization is not required. Image binarization requires careful pre-selection of the threshold and generally results in a loss of information. The threshold parameter has to be selected locally and is very sensitive to noise, fading and other phenomenon.
2. Since the images are heavily smoothed, insignificant *blobs* can easily be eliminated. Therefore, the technique is comparatively unaffected by the presence

of speckles which otherwise would have greatly affected techniques requiring binarization as the first step.

3. One of the major advantages of our approach is that the scheme is largely unaffected by shine through. This is because the algorithm is based on blurring and the information is extracted in the form of blobs.

4. The algorithm makes minimal assumptions about the nature of handwriting and fonts and may be extended to word segmentation in other language documents where words are delineated by spaces. Also, the method does not require prior training.

No. of documents	Average no. of words per image	% words detected	% fragmented words + line	% words combined	% words correctly correctly
30	220	99.12	1.75 + 0.86	8.9	87.6

Table 1. Table of segmentation results

References

1. A.J. Robinson A.W. Senior. An off-line cursive handwriting recognition system. *IEEE transactions on PAMI*, 3:309–321, 1998.

2. D. Blostein and N. Ahuja. A multi-scale region detector. *CVGIP*, 45:22–41, January 1989.

3. R. G. Casey and E. Lecolinet. A survey of methods and strategies in character segmentation. *IEEE Transactions on PAMI*, 18:690–706, July 1996.

4. L. M. J. Florack. *The Syntactic Structure of Scalar Images*. Kluwer Academic Publishers, 1997.

5. J. Ha, R. M. Haralick, and I. T. Phillips. Document page decomposition by the bounding-box projection technique. In *ICDAR*, pages 1119–1122, 1995.

6. T. Lindeberg. *Scale-space theory in computer vision*. Kluwer Academic Publishers, 1994.

7. U. Mahadevan and R. C. Nagabushnam. Gap metrics for word separation in handwritten lines. In *ICDAR*, pages 124–127, 1995.

8. R. Manmatha and W. B. Croft. Word spotting : Indexing handwritten manuscripts. In Mark Maybury, editor, *Intelligent Multi-media Information Retrieval*. AAAI/MIT press, April 1998.

9. G. Seni and E. Cohen. External word segmentation of off-line handwritten text lines. *Pattern Recognition*, 27:41–52, 1994.

10. S. Srihari and G. Kim. Penman : A system for reading unconstrained handwritten page images. In *Symposium on document image understanding technology (SDIUT 97)*, pages 142–153, April 1997.

11. N. Srimal. Indexing handwritten documents, *M.S. Thesis, University of Massachusetts Computer Science Tech Report. 1999*.

12. J. A. Weickert, S. Ishikawa, and A. Imiya. On the history of gaussian scale-space axiomatics. In J. Sporring, M. Nielsen, L. M. J. Florack, and P. Johansen, editors, Gaussian Scale-Space Theory, *pages 45–59. Kluwer Academic Press, 1997.*

Fast Geodesic Active Contours

Roman Goldenberg, Ron Kimmel,
Ehud Rivlin, and Michael Rudzsky

Computer Science Department, Technion—Israel Institute of Technology
Technion City, Haifa 32000, ISRAEL
romang/ron/ehudr/rudzsky@cs.technion.ac.il,
WWW home page: http://www.cs.technion.ac.il/~ron

Abstract. *We use an unconditionally stable numerical scheme to implement a fast version of the geodesic active contour model. The proposed
scheme is useful for object segmentation in images, like tracking moving
objects in a sequence of images. The method is based on the Weickert-
Romeney-Viergever [33] AOS scheme. It is applied at small regions, motivated by Adalsteinsson-Sethian [1] level set narrow band approach, and
uses Sethian's fast marching method [26] for re-initialization. Experimental results demonstrate the power of the new method for tracking in color
movies.*

1 Introduction

An important problem in image analysis is object segmentation. It involves the
isolation of a single object from the rest of the image that may include other
objects and a background. Here, we focus on boundary detection of one or several
objects by a dynamic model known as the 'geodesic active contour' introduced
in [4–7], see also [18, 28].

Geodesic active contours were introduced as a geometric alternative for 'snakes'
[30, 17]. Snakes are deformable models that are based on minimizing an energy
along a curve. The curve, or snake, deforms its shape so as to minimize an
'internal' and 'external' energies along its boundary. The internal part causes
the boundary curve to become smooth, while the external part leads the curve
towards the edges of the object in the image.

In [2, 21], a geometric alternative for the snake model was introduced, in
which an evolving curve was formulated by the Osher-Sethian level set method
[22]. The method works on a fixed grid, usually the image pixels grid, and automatically handles changes in the topology of the evolving contour.

The geodesic active contour model was born latter. It is both a geometric
model as well as energy functional minimization. In [4, 5], it was shown that the
geodesic active contour model is related to the classical snake model. Actually, a
simplified snake model yields the same result as that of a geodesic active contour
model, up to an arbitrary constant that depends on the initial parameterization.
Unknown constants are an undesirable property in most automated models.

Although the geodesic active contour model has many advantages over the
snake, its main drawback is its non-linearity that results in inefficient implementations. For example, explicit Euler schemes for the geodesic active contour

limit the numerical step for stability. In order to overcome these limitations, a multi-resolution approach was used in [32], and coupled with some additional heuristic steps, as in [23], like computationally preferring areas of high energy.

In this paper we introduce a new method that maintains the numerical consistency and makes the geodesic active contour model computationally efficient. The efficiency is achieved by canceling the limitation on the time step in the numerical scheme, by limiting the computations to a narrow band around the the active contour, and by applying an efficient re-initialization technique.

2 From snakes to geodesic active contours

Snakes were introduced in [17, 30] as an active contour model for boundary segmentation. The model is derived by a variational principle from a non-geometric measure. The model starts from an energy functional that includes 'internal' and 'external' terms that are integrated along a curve.

Let the curve $\mathcal{C}(p) = \{x(p), y(p)\}$, where $p \in [0, 1]$ is an arbitrary parameterization. The snake model is defined by the energy functional

$$S[\mathcal{C}] = \int_0^1 \left(|\mathcal{C}_p|^2 + \alpha |\mathcal{C}_{pp}|^2 + 2\beta g(\mathcal{C}) \right) dx dy,$$

where $\mathcal{C}_p \equiv \{\partial_p x(p), \partial_p y(p)\}$, and α and β are positive constants.

The last term represents an external energy, where $g()$ is a positive edge indicator function that depends on the image, it gets small values along the edges and higher values elsewhere. Taking the variational derivative with respect to the curve, $\delta S[\mathcal{C}]/\delta \mathcal{C}$, we obtain the Euler Lagrange equations

$$\mathcal{C}_{pp} - \alpha \mathcal{C}_{pppp} - \beta \nabla g = 0.$$

One may start with a curve that is close to a significant local minimum of $S[\mathcal{C}]$, and use the Euler Lagrange equations as a gradient descent process that leads the curve to its proper position. Formally, we add a time variable t, and write the gradient descent process as $\partial_t \mathcal{C} = \delta S[\mathcal{C}]/\delta \mathcal{C}$, or explicitly

$$\frac{d\mathcal{C}}{dt} = \mathcal{C}_{pp} - \alpha \mathcal{C}_{pppp} - \beta \nabla g.$$

The snake model is a linear model, and thus an efficient and powerful tool for object segmentation and edge integration, especially when there is a rough approximation of the boundary location. There is however an undesirable property that characterizes this model. It depends on the parameterization. The model is not geometric.

Motivated by the theory of curve evolution, Caselles et al. [2] and Malladi et al. [21] introduced a geometric flow that includes an internal and external geometric measures. Given an initial curve $\mathcal{C}_0$, the geometric flow is given by the planar curve evolution equation $\mathcal{C}_t = g(\mathcal{C})(\kappa - v)\mathcal{N}$, where, $\mathcal{N}$ is the normal to the curve, $\kappa \mathcal{N}$ is the curvature vector, v is an arbitrary constant, and $g()$, as before, is an edge indication scalar function. This is a geometric flow, that is, free of the parameterization. Yet, as long as g does not vanish along the boundary, the curve continues its propagation and may skip its desired location. One remedy, proposed in [21], is a control procedure that monitors the propagation and sets g to zero as the curve gets closer to the edge.

The geodesic active contour model was introduced in [4–7], see also [18, 28], as a geometric alternative for the snakes. The model is derived from a geometric functional, where the arbitrary parameter p is replaced with a Euclidean arclength $ds = |C_p|dp$. The functional reads

$$S[C] = \int_0^1 (\alpha + \tilde{g}(C)) |C_p| dp.$$

It may be shown to be equivalent to the arclength parameterized functional

$$S[C] = \int_0^{L(C)} \tilde{g}(C)ds + \alpha L(C),$$

where $L(C)$ is the total Euclidean length of the curve. One may equivalently define $g(x, y) = \tilde{g}(x, y) + \alpha$, in which case

$$S[C] = \int_0^{L(C)} g(C)ds,$$

i.e. minimization of the modulated arclength $g(C)ds$. The Euler Lagrange equations as a gradient descent process is

$$\frac{dC}{dt} = (g(C)\kappa - \langle \nabla g, \mathcal{N} \rangle) \mathcal{N}.$$

Again, internal and external forces are coupled together, yet this time in a way that leads towards a meaningful minimum, which is the minimum of the functional. One may add an additional force that comes from an area minimization term, and known as the balloon force [10]. This way, the contour may be directed to propagate outwards by minimization of the exterior. The functional with the additional area term reads

$$S[C] = \int_0^{L(C)} g(C)ds + \alpha \int_C da,$$

where da is an area element, for example, $\int_C da = \int_0^{L(C)} \mathcal{N} \times Cds$. The Euler Lagrange as steepest descent is

$$\frac{dC}{dt} = (g(C)\kappa - \langle \nabla g, \mathcal{N} \rangle - \alpha) \mathcal{N}.$$

We can use our freedom of parameterization in the gradient descent flow and multiply the right hand side again by an edge indicator, e.g. g. The geodesic active contour model with area as a balloon force modulated by an edge indicator is

$$\frac{dC}{dt} = (g(C)\kappa - \langle \nabla g, \mathcal{N} \rangle - \alpha)\, g(C)\mathcal{N}.$$

The connection between classical snakes, and the geodesic active contour model was established in [5] via Maupertuis' Principle of least action [12]. By Fermat's Principle, the final geodesic active contours are geodesics in an isotropic non-homogeneous medium.

Recent applications of the geodesic active contours include 3D shape from multiple views, also known as shape from stereo [13], segmentation in 3D movies [19], tracking in 2D movies [23], and refinement of efficient segmentation in 3D medical images [20]. The curve propagation equation is just part of the whole model. Subsequently, the geometric evolution is implemented by the Osher-Sethian level set method [22].

2.1 Level set method

The Osher-Sethian [22] level set method considers evolving fronts in an implicit form. It is a numerical method that works on a fixed coordinate system and takes care of topological changes of the evolving interface.

Consider the general geometric planar curve evolution

$$\frac{dC}{dt} = V\mathcal{N},$$

where V is any intrinsic quantity, i.e., V does not depend on a specific choice of parameterization. Now, let $\phi(x, y) : \mathbf{R}^2 \to \mathbf{R}$ be an implicit representation of C, such that $C = \{(x, y) : \phi(x, y) = 0\}$. One example is a distance function from C defined over the coordinate plane, with negative sign in the interior and positive in the exterior of the closed curve.

The evolution for ϕ such that its zero set tracks the evolving contour is given by

$$\frac{d\phi}{dt} = V|\nabla \phi|.$$

This relation is easily proven by applying the chain rule, and using the fact that the normal of any level set, $\phi = constant$, is given by the gradient of ϕ,

$$\frac{d\phi}{dt} = \langle \nabla \phi, C_t \rangle = \langle \nabla \phi, V\mathcal{N} \rangle = V\left\langle \nabla \phi, \frac{\nabla \phi}{|\nabla \phi|} \right\rangle = V|\nabla \phi|.$$

This formulation enable us to implement curve evolution on the x, y fixed coordinate system. It automatically handles topological changes of the evolving curve. The zero level set may split from a single simple connected curve, into two separate curves.

Specifically, the corresponding geodesic active contour model written in its level set formulation is given by

$$\frac{d\phi}{dt} = \operatorname{div}\left(g(x, y)\frac{\nabla \phi}{|\nabla \phi|}\right)|\nabla \phi|.$$

Including an area minimization term that yields a constant velocity, modulated by the edge indication function (by the freedom of parameterization of the gradient descent), we have

$$\frac{d\phi}{dt} = g(x,y)\left(\alpha + \operatorname{div}\left(g(x,y)\frac{\nabla\phi}{|\nabla\phi|}\right)\right)|\nabla\phi|.$$

We have yet to determine a numerical scheme and an appropriate edge indication function g. An explicit Euler scheme with forward time derivative, introduces a numerical limitation on the time step needed for stability. Moreover, the whole domain needs to be updated each step, which is a time consuming operation for a sequential computer. The narrow band approach overcomes the last difficulty by limiting the computations to a narrow strip around the zero set. First suggested by Chopp [9], in the context of the level set method, and later developed in [1], the narrow band idea limits the computation to a tight strip of few grid points around the zero set. The rest of the domain serves only as a sign holder. As the curve evolves, the narrow band changes its shape and serves as a dynamic numerical support around the location of the zero level set.

2.2 The AOS scheme

Additive operator splitting (AOS) schemes were introduced by Weickert et al. [33] as an unconditionally stable numerical scheme for non-linear diffusion in image processing. Let us briefly review its main ingredients and adapt it to our model.

The original AOS model deals with the Perona-Malik [24], non-linear image evolution equation of the form $\partial_t u = \operatorname{div}(g(|\nabla u|)\nabla u)$, given initial condition as the image $u(0) = u_0$. Let us re-write explicitly the right hand side of the evolution equation

$$\operatorname{div}(g(|\nabla u|)\nabla u) = \sum_{l=1}^{m} \partial_{x_l}\left(g(|\nabla u|)\partial_{x_l}u\right),$$

where l is an index running over the m dimensions of the problem, e.g., for a 2D image $m = 2, x_1 = x$, and $x_2 = y$.

As a first step towards discretization consider the operator

$$A_l(u^k) = \partial_{x_l}g(|\nabla u^k|)\partial_{x_l},$$

where the superscript k indicates the iteration number, e.g., $u^0 = u_0$. We can write the explicit scheme

$$u^{k+1} = \left[I + \tau\sum_{l=1}^{m}A_l(u^k)\right]u^k,$$

where, τ is the numerical time step. It requires an upper limit for τ if one desires to establish convergence to a stable steady state. Next, the semi-implicit scheme

$$u^{k+1} = \left[I - \tau\sum_{l=1}^{m}A_l(u^k)\right]^{-1}u^k,$$

is unconditionally stable, yet inverting the large bandwidth matrix is a computationally expensive operation.

Finally, the consistent, first order, semi-implicit, additive operator splitting scheme

$$u^{k+1} = \frac{1}{m} \sum_{l=1}^{m} \left[I - m\tau A_l(u^k) \right]^{-1} u^k,$$

may be applied to efficiently solve the non-linear diffusion.

The AOS semi-implicit scheme in $2D$ is then given by a linear tridiagonal system of equations

$$u^{k+1} = \frac{1}{2} \sum_{l=1}^{2} [I - 2\tau A_l(u^k)]^{-1} u^k,$$

where $A_l(u^k)$ is a matrix corresponding to derivatives along the l-th coordinate axis. It can be efficiently solved for u^{k+1} by Thomas algorithm, see [33].

In our case, the geodesic active contour model is given by

$$\partial_t \phi = \text{div} \left(g(|\nabla u_0|) \frac{\nabla \phi}{|\nabla \phi|} \right) |\nabla \phi|,$$

where u_0 is the image, and ϕ is the implicit representation of the curve. Since our interest is only at the zero level set of ϕ, we can reset ϕ to be a distance function every numerical iteration. One nice property of distance maps is it unit gradient magnitude almost everywhere. Thereby, the short term evolution for the geodesic active contour given by a distance map, with $|\nabla \phi| = 1$, is

$$\partial_t \phi = \text{div} \left(g(|\nabla u_0|) \nabla \phi \right).$$

Note, that now $A_l(\phi^k) = A_l(u_0)$, which means that the matrices $[I - 2\tau A_l(u_0)]^{-1}$ can be computed once for the whole image. Yet, we need to keep the ϕ function as a distance map. This is done through re-initialization by Sethian's fast marching method every iteration.

It is simple to introduce a 'balloon' force to the scheme. The resulting AOS scheme with the 'balloon' then reads

$$\phi^{k+1} = \frac{1}{2} \sum_{l=1}^{2} [I - 2\tau g(u_0) A_l(u_0)]^{-1} (\phi^k + \tau \alpha g(u_0)),$$

where α is the area/balloon coefficient.

In order to reduce the computational cost we use a multi-scale approach [16]. We construct a Gaussian pyramid of the original image. The algorithm is first applied at the lower resolution. Next, the zero set is embedded at a higher resolution and the ϕ distance function is computed. Moreover, the computations are performed only within a limited narrow band around the zero set. The narrow band automatically modifies its shape as we re-initiate the distance map.

2.3 Re-initialization by the fast marching method

In order to maintain sub-grid accuracy, we detect the zero level set curve with sub-pixel accuracy. We apply a linear interpolation in the four pixel cells in which ϕ changes its sign. The grid points with the exact distance to the zero level set are then used to initialize the fast marching method.

Sethian's fast marching method [27, 26], is a computationally optimal numerical method for distance computation on rectangular grids. The method keeps a front of updated points sorted in a heap structure, and constructs a numerical solution iteratively, by fixing the smallest element at the top of the heap and expanding the solution to its neighboring grid points. This method enjoys a computational complexity bound of $O(N \log N)$, where N is the number of grid points in the narrow band. See also [8, 31], where consistent $O(N \log N)$ schemes are used to compute distance maps on rectangular grids.

3 Edge indicator functions for color and movies

Paragios and Deriche [23], introduced a probability based edge indicator function for movies. In this paper we have chosen the geometric philosophy to extract an edge indicator. What is a proper edge indicator for color images? Several generalizations for the gradient magnitude of gray level images were proposed, see e.g. [11, 25, 29]. Here we consider a measure suggested by the Beltrami framework in [29], to construct an edge indicator function.

3.1 Edges in Color

According to the Beltrami framework, a color image is considered as a two dimensional surface in the five dimensional spatial-spectral space. The metric tensor is used to measure distances on the image manifold. The magnitude of this tensor is an area element of the color image surface, which can be considered as a generalization of the gradient magnitude. Formally, the metric tensor of the 2D image given by the 2D surface $\{x, y, R(x,y), G(x,y), B(x,y)\}$ in the $\{x, y, R, G, B\}$ space, is given by

$$(g_{ij}) = \begin{pmatrix} 1 + R_x^2 + G_x^2 + B_x^2 & R_x R_y + G_x G_y + B_x B_y \\ R_x R_y + G_x G_y + B_x B_y & 1 + R_y^2 + G_y^2 + B_y^2 \end{pmatrix},$$

where $R_x \equiv \partial_x R$. The edge indicator function is given by $q = \det(g_{ij})$. It is simple to show that

$$q = 1 + \sum_i |\nabla u^i|^2 + \frac{1}{2} \sum_{i=1}^{3} \sum_{j=1}^{3} (\nabla u^i \times \nabla u^j)^2,$$

where $u^1 = R, u^2 = G, u^3 = B$. Then, the edge indicator function g is given by a decreasing function of q, e.g., $g = q^{-1}$.

3.2   Tracking objects in movies

Let us explore two possibilities to track objects in movies. The first, considers the whole movie volume as a Riemannian space, as done in [7]. In this case the active contour becomes an active surface. The AOS scheme in the spatial-temporal $3D$ hybrid space is

$$\phi^{k+1} = \frac{1}{3} \sum_l [I - 3\tau A_l(u_0)]^{-1} \phi^k,$$

where $A_l(u_0)$ is a matrix corresponding to derivatives along the l-th coordinate axis, where now $l \in [x, y, \mathcal{T}]$.

The edge indicator function is again derived from the Beltrami framework, where for color movies we pull-back the metric

$$(g_{ij}) = \begin{pmatrix} 1 + R_x^2 + G_x^2 + B_x^2 & R_x R_y + G_x G_y + B_x B_y & R_x R_\mathcal{T} + G_x G_\mathcal{T} + B_x B_\mathcal{T} \\ R_x R_y + G_x G_y + B_x B_y & 1 + R_y^2 + G_y^2 + B_y^2 & R_y R_\mathcal{T} + G_y G_\mathcal{T} + B_y B_\mathcal{T} \\ R_x R_\mathcal{T} + G_x G_\mathcal{T} + B_x B_\mathcal{T} & R_y R_\mathcal{T} + G_y G_\mathcal{T} + B_y B_\mathcal{T} & 1 + R_\mathcal{T}^2 + G_\mathcal{T}^2 + B_\mathcal{T}^2 \end{pmatrix}.$$

Which is the metric for a 3D volume in the 6D $\{x, y, \mathcal{T}, R, G, B\}$ spatial-temporal-spectral space. Again, setting $q = \det(g_{ij})$, we have $\sqrt{q}dx dy d\mathcal{T}$ as a volume element of the image. Intuitively, the larger q gets, the smaller spatial-temporal steps one should apply in order to cover the same volume. That is, q integrates the changes with respect to the x, y, and $\mathcal{T}$ coordinates, and can, thereby, be considered as an edge indicator.

A different approach uses the contour location in frame n as an initial condition for the 2D solution in frame $n + 1$, see e.g. [3, 23]. The above edge indicator is still valid in this case. Note, that the aspect ratios between the time, the image space, and the intensity, should be determined according to the application.

The first approach was found to yield accurate results in off line tracking analysis. While the second approach gives up some accuracy, that is achieved by temporal smoothing in the first approach, for efficiency in real time tracking.

4   Experimental Results

As a simple example, the proposed method can be used as a consistent, unconditionally stable, and computationally efficient, numerical approximation for the curvature flow. The curvature flow, also known as curve shortening flow or geometric heat equation, is a well studied equation in the theory of curve evolution. It is proven to bring every simple closed curve into a circular point in finite time [14, 15]. Figure 1 shows an application of the proposed method for a curve evolving by its curvature and vanishes at a point. One can see how the number of iterations needed for the curve to converge to a point decreases as the time step is increased.

We tested several implementations for the curvature flow. Figure 2 shows the CPU time it takes the explicit and implicit schemes to evolve a contour into a circular point. For the explicit scheme we tested both the narrow band and the naive approach in which every grid point is updated every iteration. The tests

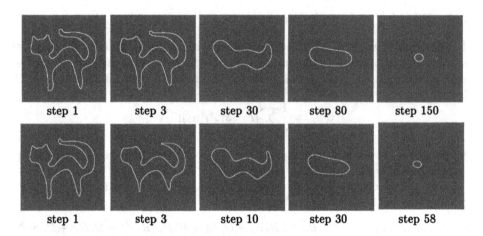

Fig. 1. Curvature flow by the proposed scheme. A non-convex curve vanishes in finite time at a circular point by Grayson's Theorem. The curve evolution is presented for two different time steps. Top: $\tau = 20$; bottom: $\tau = 50$.

were performed on an Ultra SPARC $360MHz$ machine for a 256×256 resolution image.

It should be noted that when the narrow band approach is used, the band width should be increased as the τ grows to ensure that the curve does not escape the band in one iteration.

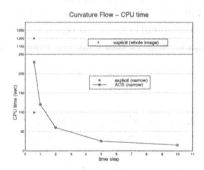

Fig. 2. Curvature flow CPU time for the explicit scheme and the implicit AOS scheme. First, the whole domain is updated, next, the narrow band is used to increase the efficiency, and finally the AOS speeds the whole process. For the explicit scheme the maximal time step that still maintains stability is choosen. For the AOS scheme, CPU times for several time steps are presented.

Figures 3 and 4 show segmentation results for color movies with difficult spatial textures. The tracking is performed at two resolutions. At the lower resolution we search for temporal edges and at the higher resolution we search for strong spatial edges. The contour found in the coarse grid is used as the initial contour at the fine grid.

There are some implementation considerations one should be aware of. For example, if we choose a relatively large time step, the active contour may skip

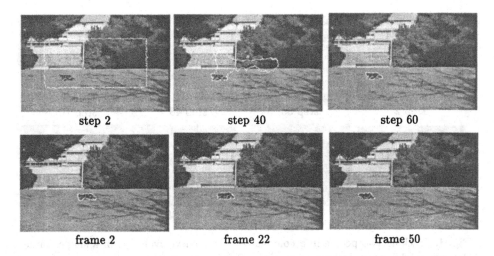

step 2	step 40	step 60
frame 2	frame 22	frame 50

Fig. 3. Tracking a cat in a color movie by the proposed scheme. Top: Segmentation of the cat in a single frame. Bottom: Tracking the walking cat in the 50 frames sequence.

over the boundary. The time step should thus be of similar order as the numerical support of the edges. One way to overcome this limit is to use a coarse to fine scales of boundary smoothing, with an appropriate time step for each scale.

It is possible to compute the inverse matrices of the AOS once for the whole image, or to invert small sub-matrices as new points enter or exit the narrow band. There is obviously a trade-off between the two approaches. For initialization, we have chosen the first approach, since the initial curve starts at the frame of the image and has to travel over most of the image until it captures the moving objects. While for tracking of moving objects in a movie, we use the local approach, since now the curve has only to adjust itself to local changes.

5   Concluding Remarks

It was shown that an integration of advanced numerical techniques yield a computationally efficient algorithm that solves a geometric segmentation model. The numerical algorithm is consistent with the underlying continuous model. The proposed 'fast geodesic active contour' scheme was applied successfully for image segmentation and tracking in movie sequences and color images. It combines the narrow band level set method, with adaptive operator splitting, and the fast marching method.

6   Acknowledgments

We thank Irad Yavne for intriguing conversations and Nikolaos Paragios for useful correspondence.

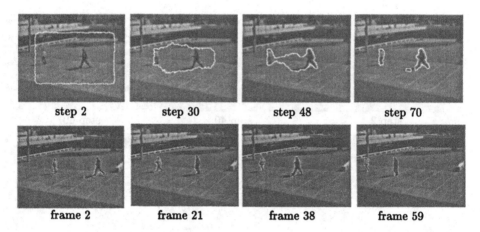

step 2   step 30   step 48   step 70

frame 2   frame 21   frame 38   frame 59

Fig. 4. Tracking two people in a color movie. Top: curve evolution in a single frame. Bottom: tracking two walking people in a 60 frame movie.

References

1. D Adalsteinsson and J A Sethian. A fast level set method for propagating interfaces. *J. of Comp. Phys.*, 118:269–277, 1995.
2. V Caselles, F Catte, T Coll, and F Dibos. A geometric model for active contours. *Numerische Mathematik*, 66:1–31, 1993.
3. V Caselles and B Coll. Snakes in movement. *SIAM J. Numer. Analy.*, 33(6):2445–2456, 1996.
4. V Caselles, R Kimmel, and G Sapiro. Geodesic active contours. In *Proceedings ICCV'95*, pages 694–699, Boston, Massachusetts, June 1995.
5. V Caselles, R Kimmel, and G Sapiro. Geodesic active contours. *IJCV*, 22(1):61–79, 1997.
6. V Caselles, R Kimmel, G Sapiro, and C Sbert. Minimal surfaces: A geometric three dimensional segmentation approach. *Numerische Mathematik*, 77(4):423–425, 1997.
7. V Caselles, R Kimmel, G Sapiro, and C Sbert. Minimal surfaces based object segmentation. *IEEE Trans. on PAMI*, 19:394–398, 1997.
8. C S Chiang, C M Hoffmann, and R E Lync. How to compute offsets without self-intersection. In *Proc. of SPIE*, volume 1620, page 76, 1992.
9. D L Chopp. Computing minimal surfaces via level set curvature flow. *J. of Computational Physics*, 106(1):77–91, May 1993.
10. L D Cohen. On active contour models and balloons. *CVGIP: Image Understanding*, 53(2):211–218, 1991.
11. S Di Zenzo. A note on the gradient of a multi image. *Computer Vision, Graphics, and Image Processing*, 33:116–125, 1986.
12. B A Dubrovin, A T Fomenko, and S P Novikov. *Modern Geometry - Methods and Applications I.* Springer-Verlag, New York, 1984.
13. O Faugeras and R Keriven. Variational principles, surface evolution PFE's, level set methods, and the stereo problem. *IEEE Trans. on Image Processing*, 7(3):336–344, 1998.

14. M Gage and R S Hamilton. The heat equation shrinking convex plane curves. *J. Diff. Geom.*, 23, 1986.
15. M A Grayson. The heat equation shrinks embedded plane curves to round points. *J. Diff. Geom.*, 26, 1987.
16. Bertrand Leroy Isabelle L Herlin and Laurent Cohen. Multi-resolution algorithms for active contour models. In *Proc. 12th Int. Conf. on Analysis and Optimization of Systems (ICAOS'96)*, Paris, France, June 1996.
17. M Kass, A Witkin, and D Terzopoulos. Snakes: Active contour models. *International Journal of Computer Vision*, 1:321–331, 1988.
18. S Kichenassamy, A Kumar, P Olver, A Tannenbaum, and A Yezzi. Gradient flows and geometric active contour models. In *Proceedings ICCV'95*, pages 810–815, Boston, Massachusetts, June 1995.
19. R Malladi, R Kimmel, D Adalsteinsson, V Caselles, G Sapiro, and J A Sethian. A geometric approach to segmentation and analysis of 3d medical images. In *Proceedings of IEEE/SIAM workshop on Biomedical Image Analysis*, San-Francisco, California, June 1996.
20. R Malladi and J A Sethian. An O(N log N) algorithm for shape modeling. *Proceedings of National Academy of Sciences, USA*, 93:9389–9392, 1996.
21. R Malladi, J A Sethian, and B C Vemuri. Shape modeling with front propagation: A level set approach. *IEEE Trans. on PAMI*, 17:158–175, 1995.
22. S J Osher and J A Sethian. Fronts propagating with curvature dependent speed: Algorithms based on Hamilton-Jacobi formulations. *J. of Comp. Phys.*, 79:12–49, 1988.
23. N Paragios and R Deriche. A PDE-based level set approach for detection and tracking of moving objects. In *Proc. of the 6th ICCV*, Bombay, India, 1998.
24. P Perona and J Malik. Scale-space and edge detection using anisotropic diffusion. *IEEE-PAMI*, 12:629–639, 1990.
25. G Sapiro and D L Ringach. Anisotropic diffusion of multivalued images with applications to color filtering. *IEEE Trans. Image Proc.*, 5:1582–1586, 1996.
26. J A Sethian. *Level Set Methods: Evolving Interfaces in Geometry, Fluid Mechanics, Computer Vision and Materials Sciences.* Cambridge Univ. Press, 1996.
27. J A Sethian. A marching level set method for monotonically advancing fronts. *Proc. Nat. Acad. Sci.*, 93(4), 1996.
28. J Shah. A common framework for curve evolution, segmentation and anisotropic diffusion. In *Proceedings IEEE CVPR'96*, pages 136–142, 1996.
29. N Sochen, R Kimmel, and R Malladi. A general framework for low level vision. *IEEE Trans. on Image Processing*, 7(3):310–318, 1998.
30. D Terzopoulos, A Witkin, and M Kass. Constraints on deformable models: Recovering 3D shape and nonrigid motions. *Artificial Intelligence*, 36:91–123, 1988.
31. J N Tsitsiklis. Efficient algorithms for globally optimal trajectories. *IEEE Trans. on Automatic Control*, 40(9):1528–1538, 1995.
32. J Weickert. Fast segmentation methods based on partial differential equations and the watershed transformation. In *Mustererkennung*, pages 93–100, Berlin, 1998. Springer.
33. J Weickert, B M ter Haar Romeny, and M A Viergever. Efficient and reliable scheme for nonlinear diffusion filtering. *IEEE Trans. on Image Processing*, 7(3):398–410, 1998.

Morphing Active Contours

Marcelo Bertalmio[2] and Guillermo Sapiro[1] and Gregory Randall[1]

[1] I.I.E. Facultad de Ingenieria
Universidad de la Republica
Montevideo, Uruguay
[2] Electrical and Computer Engineering
University of Minnesota
Minneapolis, MN 55455
guille@ece.umn.edu

Abstract. A method for deforming curves in a given image to a desired position in a second image is introduced in this paper. The algorithm is based on deforming the first image toward the second one via a partial differential equation, while tracking the deformation of the curves of interest in the first image with an additional, coupled, partial differential equation. The tracking is performed by projecting the velocities of the first equation into the second one. In contrast with previous PDE based approaches, both the images and the curves on the frames/slices of interest are used for tracking. The technique can be applied to object tracking and sequential segmentation. The topology of the deforming curve can change, without any special topology handling procedures added to the scheme. This permits for example the automatic tracking of scenes where, due to occlusions, the topology of the objects of interest changes from frame to frame. In addition, this work introduces the concept of projecting velocities to obtain systems of coupled partial differential equations for image analysis applications. We show examples for object tracking and segmentation of electronic microscopy. We also briefly discuss possible uses of this framework for three dimensional morphing.

Key words: *Partial differential equations, curve evolution, morphing, segmentation, tracking, topology.*

1 Introduction

In a large number of applications, we can use information from one or more images to perform some operation on an additional image. Examples of this are given in Figure 1. On the top row we have two consecutive slices of a 3D image obtained from electronic microscopy. The image on the left has, superimposed, the contour of an object (a slice of a neuron). We can use this information to drive the segmentation of the next slice, the image on the right. On the bottom row we see two consecutive frames of a video sequence. The image on the left shows a marked object that we want to track. Once again, we can use the image on the left to perform the tracking operation in the image on the right. These are the type of problems we address in this paper.

Our approach is based on deforming the contours of interest from the first image toward the desired place in the second one. More specifically, we use a system of coupled Partial Differential Equations (PDE's) to achieve this (coupled PDE's have already been used in the past to address other image processing tasks, see [15, 16] and references therein). The first partial differential equation deforms the first image, or features of it, toward the second one. The additional PDE is driven by the deformation velocity of the first one, and it deforms the curves of interest in the first image toward the desired position in the second one. This last deformation is implemented using the level-sets numerical scheme developed in [11], allowing for changes in the topology of the deforming curve. That is, if the objects of interest split or merge from the first image to the second one, these topology changes are automatically handled by the algorithm. This means that we will be able to track scenes with dynamic occlusions and to segment 3D medical data where the slices contain cuts with different topologies.

2 Basic curve evolution

Let $\mathcal{C}(p, t) : \mathbb{R} \times [0, \tau) \rightarrow \mathbb{R}^2$ be a set of closed planar curves. Assume these curves deform "in time" according to

$$\frac{\partial \mathcal{C}(p, t)}{\partial t} = \beta \mathcal{N}, \tag{1}$$

where β is a given velocity and $\mathcal{N}$ the inner unit normal to $\mathcal{C}(p, t)$. We should note that a tangential velocity can be added to the flow, although it will not affect the geometry of the deformation, just the internal parametrization of the curve $\mathcal{C}$. Therefore, (1) gives the most general form of geometric deformations for planar curves.

Let's now assume that $\mathcal{C}(p, t)$ is the level-set of a given function $u : \mathbb{R}^2 \times [0, \tau) \rightarrow \mathbb{R}$. Then, in order to represent the evolution of $\mathcal{C}$ by that of u, u must satisfy

$$\frac{\partial u}{\partial t} = \beta \parallel \nabla u \parallel, \tag{2}$$

where β is computed at the level-sets of u. This is the formulation introduced by Osher and Sethian [11] to implement curve evolution flows of the type of (1). This implementation has several advantages over a direct discretization of (1). Probably the main advantage is that changes in the topology of $\mathcal{C}(p, t)$ are automatically handled when evolving u, that is, there is no need for any special tracking of the topology of the level-sets; see [11] for details and [6, 7] for theoretical analysis of this flow. The discretization of (2) is performed with an Eulerian approach (fixed coordinate system), as opposed to a Lagrangian approach classically used to discretized (1), where marker particles are used. This gives a numerically stable digital-grid implementation. These reasons have motivated the use of this formulation for a large number of applications, including shape from shading, segmentation, mathematical morphology, stereo, and regularization. Extensions of the level-sets algorithm to higher dimensions are of course straightforward.

3 Morphing active contours

Let $\mathcal{I}_1(x, y, 0) : \mathbb{R}^2 \rightarrow \mathbb{R}$ be the current frame (or slice), where we have already segmented the object of interest. The boundary of this object is given by $\mathcal{C}_{\mathcal{I}_1}(p, 0) : \mathbb{R} \rightarrow \mathbb{R}^2$. Let $\mathcal{I}_2(x, y) : \mathbb{R}^2 \rightarrow \mathbb{R}$ be the image of the next frame, where we have to detect the new position of the object originally given by $\mathcal{C}_{\mathcal{I}_1}(p, 0)$ in $\mathcal{I}_1(x, y, 0)$. Let us define a continuous and Lipschitz function $u(x, y, 0) : \mathbb{R}^2 \rightarrow \mathbb{R}$, such that its zero level-set is the curve $\mathcal{C}_{\mathcal{I}_1}(p, 0)$. This function can be for example the signed distance function from $\mathcal{C}_{\mathcal{I}_1}(p, 0)$. Finally, let's also define $\mathcal{F}_1(x, y, 0) : \mathbb{R}^2 \rightarrow \mathbb{R}$ and $\mathcal{F}_2(x, y) : \mathbb{R}^2 \rightarrow \mathbb{R}$ to be images representing features of $\mathcal{I}_1(x, y, 0)$ and $\mathcal{I}_2(x, y)$ respectively (e.g., $\mathcal{F}_i \equiv \mathcal{I}_i$, or $\mathcal{F}_i$ equals the edge maps of $\mathcal{I}_i$, $i = 1, 2$). With these functions as initial conditions, we define the following system of coupled evolution equations (t stands for the marching variable):

$$\frac{\partial \mathcal{F}_1(x, y, t)}{\partial t} = \beta(x, y, t) \parallel \nabla \mathcal{F}_1(x, y, t) \parallel \qquad (3)$$

$$\frac{\partial u(x, y, t)}{\partial t} = \hat{\beta}(x, y, t) \parallel \nabla u(x, y, t) \parallel$$

where the velocity $\hat{\beta}(x, y, t)$ is given by

$$\hat{\beta}(x, y, t) := \beta(x, y, t) \frac{\nabla \mathcal{F}_1(x, y, t)}{\parallel \nabla \mathcal{F}_1(x, y, t) \parallel} \cdot \frac{\nabla u(x, y, t)}{\parallel \nabla u(x, y, t) \parallel} \qquad (4)$$

The first equation of this system is the *morphing* equation, where $\beta(x, y, t) : \mathbb{R}^2 \times [0, \tau) \rightarrow \mathbb{R}$ is a function measuring the 'discrepancy' between the selected features $\mathcal{F}_1(x, y, t)$ and $\mathcal{F}_2(x, y)$. This equation is morphing $\mathcal{F}_1(x, y, t)$ into $\mathcal{F}_2(x, y, t)$, so that $\beta(x, y, \infty) = 0$.

The second equation of this system is the *tracking* equation. The velocity in the second equation, $\hat{\beta}$, is just the velocity of the first one projected into the normal direction of the level-sets of u. Since tangential velocities do not affect the geometry of the evolution, both the level-sets of $\mathcal{F}_1$ and u are following exactly the same geometric flow. In other words, being $\mathcal{N}_{\mathcal{F}_1}$ and $\mathcal{N}_u$ the inner normals of the level-sets of $\mathcal{F}_1$ and u respectively,[1] these level-sets are moving with velocities $\beta \mathcal{N}_{\mathcal{F}_1}$ and $\hat{\beta} \mathcal{N}_u$ respectively. Since $\hat{\beta} \mathcal{N}_u$ is just the projection of $\beta \mathcal{N}_{\mathcal{F}_1}$ into $\mathcal{N}_u$, both level sets follow the same geometric deformation. In particular, the zero level-set of u is following the deformation of $\mathcal{C}_{\mathcal{I}_1}$, the curves of interest (detected boundaries in $\mathcal{I}_1(x, y, 0)$). It is important to note that since

---

[1] Recall that the normal to the level-sets is parallel to the gradient.

$C_{\mathcal{I}_1}$ is not necessarily a level-set of $\mathcal{I}_1(x, y, 0)$ or $\mathcal{F}_1(x, y, 0)$, u is needed to track the deformation of this curve.

Since the curves of interest in $\mathcal{F}_1$ and the zero level-set of u have the same initial conditions and they move with the same geometric velocity, they will then deform in the same way. Therefore, when the morphing of $\mathcal{F}_1$ into $\mathcal{F}_2$ has been completed, the zero level-set of u should be the curves of interest in the subsequent frame $\mathcal{I}_2(x, y)$.

One could argue that the steady state of (3) is not necessarily given by the condition $\beta = 0$, since it can also be achieved with $\| \nabla \mathcal{F}_1(x, y, t) \| = 0$. This is correct, but it should not affect our tracking since we are assuming that the boundaries to track are not placed over regions where there is no information and then the gradient is flat. Therefore, for a certain band around our boundaries the evolution will only stop when $\beta = 0$, thus allowing for the tracking operation.

4 Examples

For the examples in this paper, we have opted for a very simple selection of the functions in the tracking system, namely

$$\mathcal{F}_i = \mathcal{L}(\mathcal{I}_i), \quad i = 1, 2, \tag{5}$$

and

$$\beta(x, y, t) = \mathcal{F}_2(x, y)) - \mathcal{F}_1(x, y, t), \tag{6}$$

where $\mathcal{L}(\cdot)$ indicates a band around $C_{\mathcal{I}_1}$. That is, for the evolving curve $C_{\mathcal{I}_1}$ we have an evolving band B of width w around it, and $\mathcal{L}(f(x, y, t)) = f(x, y, t)$ if (x, y) is in B, and it is zero otherwise. This particular *morphing* term is a local measure of the difference between $\mathcal{I}_1(t)$ and $\mathcal{I}_2$. It works increasing the grey value of $\mathcal{I}_1(x_0, y_0, t)$ if it is smaller than $\mathcal{I}_2(x_0, y_0)$, and decreasing it otherwise. Therefore, the steady state is obtained when both values are equal $\forall x_0, y_0$ in B, with $\|\nabla \mathcal{I}_1\| \neq 0$. Note that this is a *local* measure, and that no hypothesis concerning the shape of the object to be tracked has been made. Having no model of the boundaries to track, the algorithm becomes very flexible. Being so simple, the main drawback of this particular selection is that it requires an important degree of similarity among the images for the algorithm to track the curves of interest and not to detect spurious objects. If the set of curves $C_{\mathcal{I}_1}$ isolates an almost uniform interior from an almost uniform exterior as in Figure 3, then there is no need for a high similarity among consecutive images. On the other hand, when working with images such as those in Figure 2, if $C_{\mathcal{I}_1}(0)$ is too far away from the expected limit $lim_{t \to \infty} C_{\mathcal{I}_1}(t)$, then the abovementioned errors in the tracking procedure may occur. This *similarity* requirement concerns not only the shapes of the objects depicted in the image but especially their grey levels, since this β function measures grey-level differences. Therefore, histogram equalization is always performed as a pre-processing operation.

We should also note that this particular selection of β involves information of the two present images. Better results are expected if information from additional images in the sequence are taken into account to perform the *morphing* among these two.

The first example of our tracking algorithm is presented in Figure 2. This figure shows nine consecutive slices of neural tissue obtained via electronic microscopy (EM). The goal of the biologist is to obtain a three dimensional reconstruction of this neuron. As we observe from these examples, the EM images are very noisy, and the boundaries of the neuron are not easy to identify or to tell apart from other similar objects. Segmenting the neuron is then a difficult task. Before processing for segmentation, the images are regularized using anisotropic diffusion [1, 2, 14]. Active contours techniques as those in [5, 8–10] will normally fail with this type of images. Since the variation between consecutive slices is not too large, we can use the segmentation obtained for the first slice (segmentation obtained either manually or with the technique described in [17]), to drive the segmentation of the next one, and then automatically proceed to find the segmentation in the following images. In this figure, the top left image shows the manual or semi-automatic segmentation superimposed, while the following ones show the boundaries found by our algorithm.[2] Due to our particular choice of the β function, dissimilarities among the images cause the algorithm to mark as part of the boundary small objects which are too close to our object of interest. These can be removed by simple morphological operations. Cumulative errors might cause the algorithm to lose track of the boundaries after several slices, and re-initialization would be required.

One could argue that we could also use the segmentation of the first frame to initialize the active contours techniques mentioned above for the next frame. We still encounter a number of difficulties with this approach: 1- The deforming curve gets attracted to local minima, and often fails to detect the neuron; 2- Those algorithms normally deform either inwards or outwards (mainly due to the presence of balloon-type forces), while the boundary curve corresponding to the first image is in general neither inside nor outside the object in the second image. To solve this, more elaborated techniques, e.g., [13], have to be used. Therefore, even if the image is not noisy, special techniques need to be developed and implemented to direct different points of the curve toward different directions.

Figure 3 shows an example of object tracking. The top left image has, superimposed, the contours of the objects to track. The following images show the contours found by our algorithm. For sake of space, only one every three frames is shown. Notice how topological changes are handled automatically. A pioneering topology independent algorithm for tracking in video sequences, based on the general geodesic framework introduced in [5, 9] can be found in [12] (an extension to this, with a number of key novel features, was recently reported in [13]). In contrast with our approach, that scheme is based on a unique PDE (no morphing flow), deforming the curve toward a (local) geodesic curve, and it is very sensible to spatial and temporal noisy gradients. We should also not that although the authors of [12] propose a fast technique to implement their flow, this technique

---

[2] A preliminary version of this algorithm has been compared with the segmentation component of [4] and found to produce better results.

is not actually implementing their proposed algorithm. Therefore, to fully implement their scheme, other much slower techniques need to be applied. Due to the similarity between frames, our algorithm converges very fast. Both [12,13] use much more elaborated models to track, and testing on some of the same sequences (e.g., the highway and two-man-walking sequences), we found that a much simpler algorithm as the one here proposed already achieves satisfactory results. The elaborated models in their work might be needed for more difficult scenes than the ones reported in this paper. The CONDENSATION algorithm described in [3] can also achieve, in theory, topology-free tracking, though to the best of our knowledge real examples showing this capability have not been yet reported. In addition, this algorithm requires having a model of the object to track and a model of the possible deformations, even for simple and useful examples as the ones shown in this paper (note that the algorithm here proposed requires no previous or learned information). On the other hand, the outstanding tracking capabilities for cluttered scenes shown with the CONDENSATION scheme can not be obtained with the simple selections for $\mathcal{F}_i$ and β used for the examples in this paper, and more advanced selections must be investigated.

Additional tracking examples are given in the next three figures.

5 Concluding remarks

In this paper we have presented a system of coupled PDE's developed for image segmentation and tracking. We are also investigating the use of this technique for 3D, topology independent, morphing, and Figure 7 shows a toy example to illustrate this. There are a number of additional directions to continue the framework described in this paper, we discuss some of them now.

It is of course of great importance to develop more robust selections of the feature map $\mathcal{F}_i$ and the discrepancy function β. One possible direction is to use recent image metrics based on steerable (wavelets) decompositions. This is the subject of current research.

The use of singular value decomposition and principal components analysis became very popular in computer vision and image processing in the past years. The basic idea is to represent a given event as a linear combination of principal components from learned events. We can see the technique here described as a first step toward the deformation of principal components. That is, we can look at the curve obtained from the current slice as a principal component. We are currently investigating the extension of this technique to the deformation of a number of principal components, thereby representing a given event as a combination of *deformed* learned principal components. The deformations will be obtained as a system of coupled PDE's.

The equations introduced in this paper are basically "short in memory," that is, only the present frame is used to segment the next one. We can incorporate past information to these equations, in the form of optical flow or Kalman filtering (or the techniques in the novel scheme developed in [3]), in order to improve the detection results. Some modeling of the object of interest could be introduced in the *morphing* function β as well. This will be the subject of further study.

We are also studying the extension of previous theoretical results for the system of coupled PDE's presented in this paper. The equations introduced in this paper are one example of systems of coupled PDE's where the velocity in the second equation is obtained by projecting the corresponding velocity in the first flow. It turns out that this technique has applications in other areas like denoising of vector-valued images and surface mapping.

Acknowledgments

Prof. Allen Tannenbaum provided the heart sequence, and Prof. Rachid Deriche and Dr. Nikos Paragios provided the highway and walking sequences. This work was partially supported by a grant from the Office of Naval Research ONR-N00014-97-1-0509, the Office of Naval Research Young Investigator Award, the Presidential Early Career Awards for Scientists and Engineers (PECASE), the National Science Foundation CAREER Award, the National Science Foundation Learning and Intelligent Systems Program (LIS), and by CSIC and CONICYT.

References

1. L. Alvarez, P. L. Lions, and J. M. Morel, "Image selective smoothing and edge detection by nonlinear diffusion," *SIAM J. Numer. Anal.* **29**, pp. 845-866, 1992.
2. M. Black, G. Sapiro, D. Marimont, and D. Heeger, "Robust anisotropic diffusion," *IEEE Trans. Image Processing* **7:3**, pp. 421-432, 1998.
3. A. Blake and M. Isard, *Active Contours*, Springer-Verlag, New York, 1998.
4. I. Carlbom, D. Terzopoulos, and K. Harris, "Computer-assisted registration, segmentation, and 3D reconstruction from images of neuronal tissue sections," *IEEE Transactions on Medical Imaging* **13:2**, pp. 351-362, 1994.
5. V. Caselles, R. Kimmel, and G. Sapiro, "Geodesic active contours," *International Journal of Computer Vision* **22:1**, pp. 61-79, 1997.
6. Y. G. Chen, Y. Giga, and S. Goto, "Uniqueness and existence of viscosity solutions of generalized mean curvature flow equations," *J. Diff. Geom.* **33**, 1991.
7. L. C. Evans and J. Spruck, "Motion of level sets by mean curvature, I," *J. Diff. Geom.* **33**, 1991.
8. M. Kass, A. Witkin, and D. Terzopoulos, "Snakes: Active contour models," *International Journal of Computer Vision* **1**, pp. 321-331, 1988.
9. S. Kichenassamy, A. Kumar, P. Olver, A. Tannenbaum, and A. Yezzi, "Conformal curvature flows: from phase transitions to active vision," *Archive for Rational Mechanics and Analysis* **134**, pp. 275-301, 1996.
10. R. Malladi, J. A. Sethian and B. C. Vemuri, "Shape modeling with front propagation: A level set approach," *IEEE-PAMI* **17**, pp. 158-175, 1995.
11. S. J. Osher and J. A. Sethian, "Fronts propagation with curvature dependent speed: Algorithms based on Hamilton-Jacobi formulations," *Journal of Computational Physics* **79**, pp. 12-49, 1988.
12. N. Paragios and R. Deriche, "A PDE-based level-set approach for detection and tracking of moving objects," *Proc. Int. Conf. Comp. Vision '98*, Bombay, India, January 1998.

13. N. Paragios and R. Deriche, "Geodesic active regions for motion estimation and tracking," *Technical Report - INRIA - Sophia Antipolis* **3631**, March 1999.
14. P. Perona and J. Malik, "Scale-space and edge detection using anisotropic diffusion," *IEEE-PAMI* **12**, pp. 629-639, 1990.
15. B. Romeny, Editor, *Geometry Driven Diffusion in Computer Vision*, Kluwer, The Netherlands, 1994.
16. M. Proesmans, E. Pauwels, and L. van Gool, "Coupled geometry-driven diffusion equations for low-level vision," in [15].
17. L. Vazquez, G. Sapiro, and G. Randall, "Segmenting neurons in electronic microscopy via geometric tracing," *Proc. IEEE ICIP*, Chicago, October 1998.

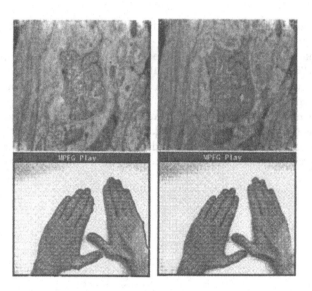

Fig. 1. *Examples of the problems addressed in this paper. See text.*

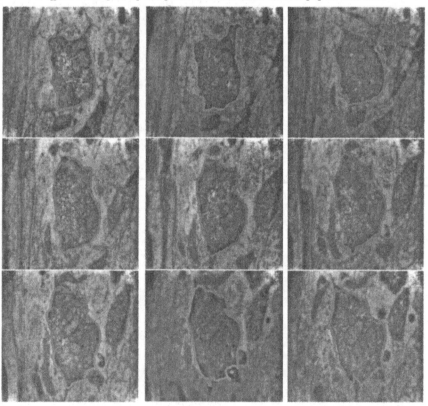

Fig. 2. *Nine consecutive slices of neural tissue. The first image has been segmented manually. The segmentation over the sequence has been performed using the algorithm described in this paper.*

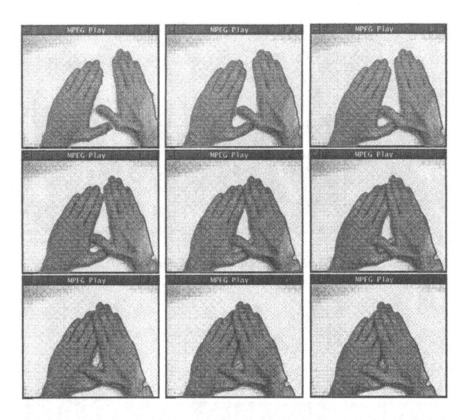

Fig. 3. *Nine frames of a movie. The first image has been segmented manually. The segmentation over the sequence has been performed using the algorithm described in this paper. Notice the automatic handling of topology changes.*

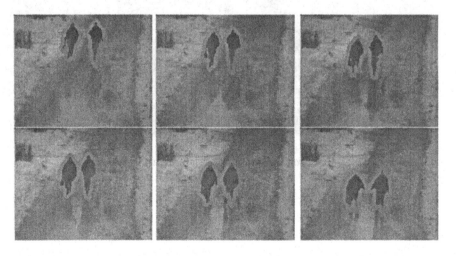

Fig. 4. *Tracking example on the "Walking swedes" movie.*

Fig. 5. *Tracking example on the "Highway" movie.*

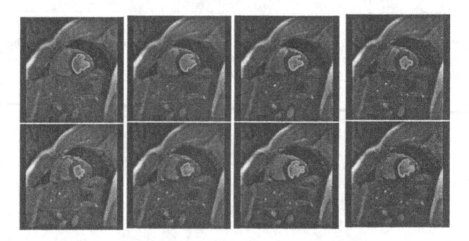

Fig. 6. *Tracking example on the "Heart" movie.*

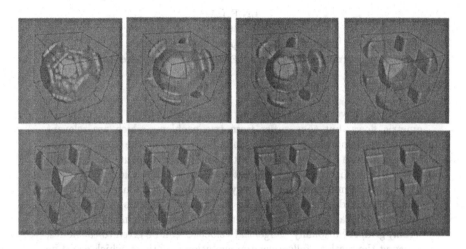

Fig. 7. *Eight steps of 3D morphing, from a given volume (top left) to eight given cubes (bottom right). This toy example uses the algorithm described in the text.*

Unfolding the Cerebral Cortex Using Level Set Methods

Gerardo Hermosillo, Olivier Faugeras and José Gomes

I.N.R.I.A
BP. 93, 2004 Route des Lucioles
06902 Sophia Antipolis Cedex, France
{Gerardo.Hermosillo, Olivier.Faugeras, Jose.Gomes}@inria.fr

Abstract. Level set methods provide a robust way to implement geometric flows, but they suffer from two problems which are relevant when using smoothing flows to unfold the cortex: the lack of point-correspondence between scales and the inability to implement tangential velocities. In this paper, we suggest to solve these problems by driving the nodes of a mesh with an ordinary differential equation. We state that this approach does not suffer from the known problems of Lagrangian methods since all geometrical properties are computed on the fixed (Eulerian) grid. Additionally, tangential velocities can be given to the nodes, allowing the mesh to follow general evolution equations, which could be crucial to achieving the final goal of minimizing local metric distortions. To experiment with this approach, we derive area and volume preserving mean curvature flows and use them to unfold surfaces extracted from MRI data of the human brain.

1 Introduction

Neural activity in high-level tasks of the brain takes place mainly in the cortex, which in humans is a highly folded surface with more than half of its area hidden inside sulci [22, 28, 29]. Regions of neural activity which are close together in three-dimensional space may therefore be far apart when following the shortest path connecting them on the cortical surface. This suggests that a surface representation is better suited than a volumetric one for the task of functional analysis [8, 12, 28].

Once such a representation is available, it may be necessary to "unfold" the surface in order to improve visualization and analysis of the neural activity. Presently, this is done by representing the surface as a triangulated mesh which is forced to move depending on the gradient of a discrete energy measure [8, 28].

This is a geometric Lagrangian formulation which can be exchanged for an Eulerian one, viewing the problem as a front propagation driven by a PDE which is solved on a fixed grid. This so-called "level set formulation" was initially proposed by Osher and Sethian in [23] and has been extensively applied to plane curve evolutions [3, 9, 19, 24] and, to a lesser extent, to the evolution of closed surfaces [4, 6, 14, 18].

Replacing the discrete-energy minimization approach by a surface evolution is interesting since formal results concerning existence, uniqueness, stability and correctness of the evolution may be established using results in the theory of PDE's. When implementing the evolution, the Eulerian approach provides two primary advantages. First, it is more numerically stable since the computations are performed on a fixed grid, unlike the Lagrangian approach, in which heuristic regriding procedures are necessary to avoid numerical explosions [23]. The fixed-grid approach has also been shown to regularize originally ill-posed problems in [17]. The second advantage is the ability to handle topological changes. This is useful even when the topology of the initial and final curve/surface are the same, since this ability may be required at an early stage in the evolution to escape blocking configurations (see for example the discussion on min-max flow in [27]).

On the other hand, at least three questions which are relevant to our goal arise when migrating to a level set approach and here we suggest an answer to the second and third of these questions. The first one is that when unfolding the cortex, topological changes are not desirable. This brings up the problem of finding a surface evolution which is topology-preserving. For planar curves, such an evolution is given by the curvature flow, but unfortunately this is not the case for surfaces. Much research has been devoted to this problem, but it remains an open one [21]. The second question is that of achieving point correspondence between surfaces at different scales. In the level set approach this correspondence is lacking since the surface is only implicitly defined. This gives rise also to the third problem which is that with the level set approach, only flows that do not contain tangential velocities can be implemented. Tangential velocities do not affect the geometry of the surface, but they may be important in our application since they *do* affect extrinsic functions defined on the surface.

Although very closely related, the last two problems are not exactly the same. In [1] the authors propose a solution to the correspondence problem by tracking region boundaries. Their solution however, does not allow tangential terms to be implemented.

We suggest to solve this problems by mapping the function of interest on the nodes of a mesh and subsequently tracking these nodes by means of their corresponding differential equation. The tracking of the mesh solves the correspondence problem and, at the same time, tangential velocities are applicable to the mesh nodes. Although it may seem that this approach brings back the problems of Lagrangian formulations, this is not the case since the mesh is passively driven, all the geometric quantities relevant to the evolution being computed on the fixed (Eulerian) grid. The proposed approach is described in detail in Section 4.

In Section 2, we derive area and volume preserving mean curvature flows, which are the three-dimensional extensions of the Euclidean flows presented in [26]. Although the obtained flows are not Euclidean invariant and may develop topological changes, they allow to evaluate the tracking approach by smoothing the surface without shrinkage and have yielded reasonable results in practice.

Section 5 provides experimental results on their use to unfold the human cortex while tracking the initial triangulated representation. Conclusions and future research directions are discussed in Section 6.

2 Normalized 3D Mean Curvature Flows

In this section we present the evolution equations for mean curvature flows with constant total area or enclosed volume. These are direct three-dimensional extensions of the Euclidean flows described by Sapiro and Tannenbaum [26] for planar curves, and have also been studied in [2, 11, 25]. In the following discussion, bold letters will represent 3D vector quantities, the integral symbol will always denote a closed surface integral over the surface and the scalar and cross product between two vectors $v1$ and $v2$ will be denoted $v1 \cdot v2$ and $v1 \times v2$ respectively. Subscripts will denote partial differentiation with respect to the subscripted parameter.

We consider the family of orientable surfaces in $\mathbb{R}^3$ denoted $\mathbf{S}(u, v, t)$, where u and v parameterize each surface and t parameterizes time (scale), which is obtained by the time evolution of an initial surface $\mathbf{S}_o(u, v) = \mathbf{S}(u, v, 0)$ governed by the following PDE:

$$\mathbf{S}_t = H\mathbf{N} \tag{1}$$

where $H(u, v)$ is the mean curvature and $\mathbf{N}(u, v)$ is the unit inward normal vector. This evolution is known as the mean curvature flow and its properties have been extensively studied in the past [5, 7, 15, 16, 20].

The key idea to obtain a normalized flow is to apply a scaling to the space at each instant during the evolution. The scaling factor will be denoted $\psi(t)$. Let $\tilde{\mathbf{S}}$ be the image of $\mathbf{S}$ under this scaling:

$$\tilde{\mathbf{S}}(t) = \psi(t)\mathbf{S}(t) \tag{2}$$

Initially, $\psi(t) = 1$ and the two surfaces coincide. As time evolves, $\tilde{\mathbf{S}}$ describes another family of surfaces which adopts the same shapes as $\mathbf{S}$, since scaling is a similarity transformation. For the same reason, all the geometric properties of $\mathbf{S}$ can be inferred from those of $\tilde{\mathbf{S}}$. The function $\psi(t)$ can be chosen such that the volume of $\tilde{\mathbf{S}}$ remains constant:

$$\tilde{V} = \psi^3 V = V_0 \tag{3}$$

or such that the total area is preserved:

$$\tilde{A} = \psi^2 A = A_0 \tag{4}$$

By performing a change of temporal variable, from t to $\tau(t)$ such that $\frac{dt}{d\tau} = \psi^{-2}$, and taking into account the relations $H = \psi\tilde{H}$ and $\mathbf{N} = \tilde{\mathbf{N}}$, the evolution of $\tilde{\mathbf{S}}$ may be written as:

$$\tilde{\mathbf{S}}_\tau = \frac{dt}{d\tau}\tilde{\mathbf{S}}_t = \tilde{H}\tilde{\mathbf{N}} + \frac{d\psi}{dt}\psi^{-3}\tilde{\mathbf{S}} \tag{5}$$

The value of the second term of equation (5) will depend on which quantity we wish to preserve. From (4) we obtain the area preserving value,

$$\frac{d\psi}{dt}\psi^{-3} = -\frac{1}{2A_0}\frac{dA}{dt} \tag{6}$$

and from (3) the volume preserving one:

$$\frac{d\psi}{dt}\psi^{-3} = -\frac{\psi}{3V_0}\frac{dV}{dt} \tag{7}$$

We see that in order to achieve constant area or volume, we need to determine the evolutions of these quantities under the flow. For a surface evolving as

$$\mathbf{S}_t = \beta\mathbf{N} \tag{8}$$

the volume variation (see e.g. [2, 11]) is given by the closed integral of the speed:

$$\frac{dV}{dt} = \int \beta \, d\sigma \tag{9}$$

To compute the evolution of the area, we show in the appendix that the evolution of the vector $\mathbf{S}_u \times \mathbf{S}_v$ can be written as

$$(\mathbf{S}_u \times \mathbf{S}_v)_t = |\mathbf{S}_u \times \mathbf{S}_v| \, (2\beta H \mathbf{N} - \nabla\beta) \tag{10}$$

where $\nabla\beta$ is the vector on the tangent plane representing the gradient of the function β. Using the definition of the area element,

$$d\sigma = |\mathbf{S}_u \times \mathbf{S}_v| \, du \, dv \tag{11}$$

the evolution of the area can be obtained from (10):

$$\frac{dA}{dt} = 2 \int \beta H \, d\sigma \tag{12}$$

Interestingly, equation (10) can be used to prove the following proposition.

Proposition *Let $\beta : \mathbf{S} \to \mathbb{R}$ be a differentiable function defined on a closed regular surface $\mathbf{S} \subset \mathbb{R}^3$. Then the following equality holds:*

$$\int \beta \, d\sigma = \frac{1}{3} \int \left(\beta - \mathbf{S} \cdot \nabla\beta + 2 \, \beta H \, (\mathbf{S} \cdot \mathbf{N}) \right) d\sigma$$

Proof The volume enclosed by the surface is given by[1]

$$V = \frac{1}{3} \int \mathbf{S} \cdot \mathbf{N} \, d\sigma \tag{13}$$

---

[1] The divergence theorem relates the volume integral of the divergence of a vector $\mathbf{A}$ to a surface integral over the surface bounding the volume as

$$\int_V \nabla \cdot \mathbf{A} \, dv = \int_S \mathbf{A} \cdot \mathbf{N} \, d\sigma$$

The fact that $\nabla \cdot \mathbf{S} = 3$ implies relation (13).

Using the definition of the normal vector $\mathbf{N} = (\mathbf{S}_u \times \mathbf{S}_v)/|\mathbf{S}_u \times \mathbf{S}_v|$, its evolution can be obtained from (10): $\mathbf{N}_t = -\nabla\beta$. The volume variation is given by the time-derivative of (13):

$$\frac{dV}{dt} = \frac{1}{3} \int \left(\beta - \mathbf{S} \cdot \nabla\beta + 2\,\beta H\,(\mathbf{S} \cdot \mathbf{N}) \right) d\sigma \tag{14}$$

which completes the proof by identifying with (9). $\square$

Taking into account the relations $H = \psi\tilde{H}$ and $d\sigma = \psi^{-2}d\tilde{\sigma}$, the area and volume variations under mean curvature flow may be computed on $\tilde{\mathbf{S}}$, allowing us to write the corresponding area and volume preserving flows by substitution in (5) of (6) and (7) respectively:

$$\tilde{\mathbf{S}}_\tau = \left(\tilde{H} - \frac{\tilde{\mathbf{S}} \cdot \tilde{\mathbf{N}}}{A_0} \int \tilde{H}^2 \, d\tilde{\sigma} \right) \tilde{\mathbf{N}} \tag{15}$$

$$\tilde{\mathbf{S}}_\tau = \left(\tilde{H} - \frac{\tilde{\mathbf{S}} \cdot \tilde{\mathbf{N}}}{3V_0} \int \tilde{H} \, d\tilde{\sigma} \right) \tilde{\mathbf{N}} \tag{16}$$

Note that the flows are geometrically intrinsic to $\tilde{\mathbf{S}}$. Also note that we have taken only the normal component of the second term in the equations since only this term affects the geometry of the surface [26]. It is also interesting to note that, unlike the 2D case, the volume preserving flow is not local.

3 Level Set Formulation

We proceed to describe the computed flows under the level-set approach. A more formal analysis may be found in [13, 23]. The surface is represented in an implicit form, as the zero level-set of a function $u(\mathbf{X}, t)$:

$$S_o(u, v) \equiv \{\mathbf{X} \in \mathbb{R}^3 : u(\mathbf{X}, 0) = 0\} \tag{17}$$

If the surface is evolving according to

$$\frac{\partial \mathbf{S}}{\partial t} = \beta \mathbf{N} \tag{18}$$

then

$$S(u, v, t) = \{\mathbf{X} \in \mathbb{R}^3 : u(\mathbf{X}, t) = 0\} \qquad \forall t \tag{19}$$

provided that the function $u(\mathbf{X}, t) : \mathbb{R}^3 \times \mathbb{R} \to \mathbb{R}$ evolves according to

$$\frac{\partial u}{\partial t} = \beta|\nabla u| \tag{20}$$

Intrinsic geometric properties of the surface have implicit expressions on u. For example the unit inward normal vector and the mean curvature are given by

$$\mathbf{N} = -\frac{\nabla u}{|\nabla u|} \qquad \text{and} \qquad H = \text{div}\frac{\nabla u}{|\nabla u|} \tag{21}$$

Actually the above values give the normal vector and mean curvature of the iso-level of u at $\mathbf{X}$.

Finally, since the evolution equations are not local, the integrals must be approximated by extracting the corresponding integrands with a marching cubes technique.

4 Maintaining point correspondences at different scales

In this section we describe the tracking of the initial mesh of the surface, which contains information that is to be kept during the evolution. Formally, let

$$f(\mathbf{X}) : S \to \mathbb{R} \tag{22}$$

be a function on the surface, sampled at a finite number of points

$$\{\mathbf{X}_i \in S : f(\mathbf{X}_i) = f_i\} \tag{23}$$

Since the surface is evolving as $S_t = \beta \mathbf{N}$, each of the points moves according to the following differential equation:

$$\frac{d\mathbf{X}_i}{dt} = -\beta(\mathbf{X}_i) \, \frac{\nabla u}{|\nabla u|}(\mathbf{X}_i) \qquad \forall i \tag{24}$$

Its trajectory can be followed by updating its position as

$$\mathbf{X}_i(t + \Delta t) \approx \mathbf{X}_i(t) - \beta \Delta t \, \frac{\nabla u}{|\nabla u|}(\mathbf{X}_i) \tag{25}$$

at each step of the PDE. Note that all computations are performed on the function u and therefore no harm is done by the nodes getting too close or too far from each other. Small systematic errors due to the approximation may be corrected at every iteration by projecting the points on the zero level set of u:

$$\mathbf{X}_i(t + \Delta t) \leftarrow \left(\mathbf{X}_i(t + \Delta t) - \frac{u}{|\nabla u|} \frac{\nabla u}{|\nabla u|}(\mathbf{X}_i(t + \Delta t)) \right) \tag{26}$$

This projection can also be used when given tangential velocities to the nodes, in order to force them to stay on the zero level set.

Topological changes may be handled automatically by re-sampling the function on the new triangulation extracted from the level set at each step. This can be done in the following way. Let

$$Y = \{\mathbf{Y}_j \in S : u(\mathbf{Y}_j) = 0\} \tag{27}$$

be the set of nodes of the new mesh, which is extracted from u by a marching cubes technique. The function f can be remapped on Y by assigning to each $\mathbf{Y}_j$ the linear interpolation of f_k, f_l and f_m, where the three nodes $\mathbf{X}_k, \mathbf{X}_l$ and $\mathbf{X}_m$

are such that $\mathbf{Y}_j$ is inside the triangle of the tangent plane defined by the three points:

$$\begin{cases} \mathbf{P}_1 = \mathbf{X}_k - u\nabla u \ / \ |\nabla u|^2 \ (\mathbf{X}_k) \\ \mathbf{P}_2 = \mathbf{X}_l - u\nabla u \ / \ |\nabla u|^2 \ (\mathbf{X}_l) \\ \mathbf{P}_3 = \mathbf{X}_m - u\nabla u \ / \ |\nabla u|^2 \ (\mathbf{X}_m) \end{cases} \qquad (28)$$

To find such a triangle, a search is necessary among the closest triangles to $\mathbf{Y}_j$ and therefore this procedure is computationally expensive. For this reason, and to make more obvious where undesirable topological changes occur, we do not perform this step in the experiments.

5   Results

Here we describe the results obtained by applying the normalized mean curvature flows together with the tracking framework described in the previous section, to unfold surfaces extracted from pre-segmented MRI data of the human brain. The tracked function in the examples is the sign of the mean curvature, light regions indicating concave folds.

Fig. 1 shows a first example starting with a reduced and slightly smoothed version of the cortex. This surface was obtained by applying a scaling flow:

$$\mathbf{S}_t = -(\mathbf{S} \cdot \mathbf{N})\mathbf{N} \qquad (29)$$

to the surface in order to reduce its size, followed by a few steps of Mean Curvature Flow (MCF). The columns correspond to three different views. The first row shows the initial surface. It can be observed that the relative areas of light and dark regions are approximately the same. This qualitative evaluation may already be useful in discarding flows that obviously change this balance. This is the case for the area-preserving flow, whose results are shown in the second row of Fig. 1. It is clear that the dark regions become too wide while the light regions grow too thin. The balance between light and dark regions is not preserved at all. This is undesirable since the goal of the unfolding is to improve visibility in the light regions, i.e. the sulci. The third row is the result obtained with the volume-preserving flow. Here the proportion of dark and light regions is better preserved. The fourth row is the result obtained by applying MCF alone. The proportions are again qualitatively well preserved. Quantitative measures are required to evaluate more precisely these results.

The second example (Fig. 2) shows results with the original cortical surface extracted from the MRI data (i.e. no preprocessing was applied as in the previous example). In this case, only mean curvature flow and its volume-preserving version were tested. The first row shows the initial geometry of the cortex, while the second row presents the geometry as obtained by applying volume-preserving MCF. In the third row, the sign-of-curvature function has been mapped on this same surface. The last row shows the result of applying MCF alone. In this example, the results are very similar with respect to the distribution of the tracked regions.

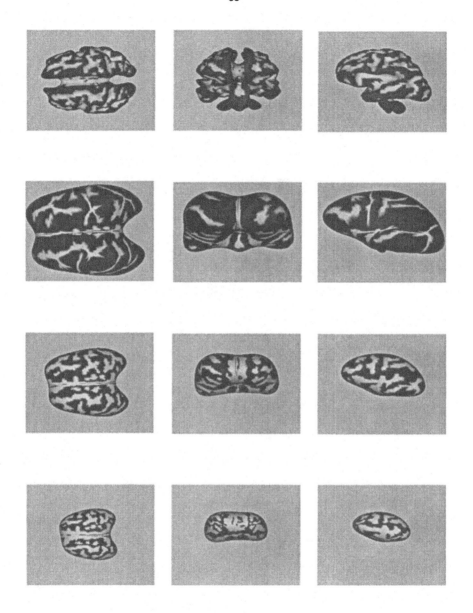

Fig. 1. Results of cortex unfolding using the normalized flows. The columns represent three different views of the corresponding surface. From top to bottom: Original surface, area-preserving MCF, volume-preserving MCF, MCF alone. Note that due to the time normalization, the same number of steps corresponds to different stages of the shape evolution. Scale is the same in all three cases to make the amount of shrinkage evident. The starting surface is a reduced and smoothed version of the actual cortex.

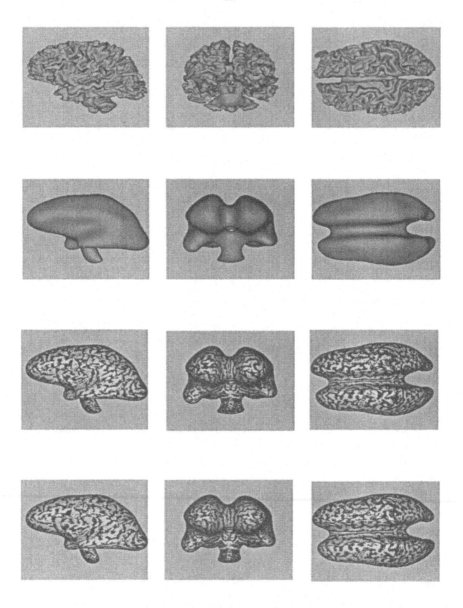

Fig. 2. Unfolding the cortex as segmented from the MRI image. The first two rows show the geometry of the initial and final surfaces, without mapping the sign-of-curvature function. In the third row, the function is mapped using volume-preserving MCF, while the fourth row shows the result of applying MCF alone. In this last row the zoom is larger in order to better visualize the sign-of-curvature function.

6 Conclusion

We have presented normalized mean curvature flows together with a tracking framework that allows to maintain the knowledge of an extrinsic function defined on the surface. These flows were used as first attempts to solve the problem of unfolding the cortex using level set techniques, and have indeed yielded encouraging results. Nevertheless, further research is needed in order to obtain a front propagation model that takes into account the physical constraints of the problem, i.e. minimum variation of geodesic distances and no topological changes. By allowing tangential movements of the tracked nodes, our approach makes general propagation models (i.e. containing normal as well as tangential terms) applicable to those nodes.

Appendix

Here we show how to obtain equation (10), which gives the evolution of $\mathbf{S}_u \times \mathbf{S}_v$. Direct differentiation with respect to time gives:

$$(\mathbf{S}_u \times \mathbf{S}_v)_t = (\beta_u \mathbf{N} + \beta \mathbf{N}_u) \times \mathbf{S}_v + \mathbf{S}_u \times (\beta_v \mathbf{N} + \beta \mathbf{N}_v) \tag{30}$$

$$= \overbrace{\Big(\beta(\mathbf{N}_u \times \mathbf{S}_v + \mathbf{S}_u \times \mathbf{N}_v)\Big)}^{\mathcal{N}} - \overbrace{\Big(\beta_u \mathbf{S}_v \times \mathbf{N} + \beta_v \mathbf{N} \times \mathbf{S}_u\Big)}^{\mathcal{T}} \tag{31}$$

The first term is normal since $\mathbf{N}_u$, $\mathbf{N}_v$, $\mathbf{S}_u$ and $\mathbf{S}_v$ are all four tangential. Moreover, using the fact ([10]) that $\mathbf{N}_u$ and $\mathbf{N}_v$ are decomposed in the tangent plane as:

$$\begin{aligned} \mathbf{N}_u &= a_{11}\mathbf{S}_u + a_{12}\mathbf{S}_v \\ \mathbf{N}_v &= a_{21}\mathbf{S}_u + a_{22}\mathbf{S}_v \end{aligned} \tag{32}$$

with

$$a_{11} + a_{22} = 2H \tag{33}$$

We have

$$\mathcal{N} = |\mathbf{S}_u \times \mathbf{S}_v|\, 2\,\beta H\, \mathbf{N} \tag{34}$$

The second term is obviously tangential and actually gives the gradient of β in the tangent plane. To see this, we will show that its scalar product with an arbitrary vector v of the tangent plane is proportional to the directional derivative of β in the direction of v, which is the definition of a gradient operator. Let v be expressed as

$$v = \alpha_1\, \mathbf{S}_u + \alpha_2\, \mathbf{S}_v \tag{35}$$

We have

$$\mathcal{T} \cdot v = \alpha_1 \beta_u\, \mathbf{S}_u \cdot (\mathbf{S}_v \times \mathbf{N}) + \alpha_2 \beta_v\, \mathbf{S}_v \cdot (\mathbf{N} \times \mathbf{S}_v) \tag{36}$$

but

$$\mathbf{S}_u \cdot (\mathbf{S}_v \times \mathbf{N}) = \mathbf{S}_v \cdot (\mathbf{N} \times \mathbf{S}_v) = |\mathbf{S}_u \times \mathbf{S}_v| \tag{37}$$

so that

$$\frac{1}{|\mathbf{S}_u \times \mathbf{S}_v|} \mathcal{T} \cdot v = \alpha_1 \beta_u + \alpha_2 \beta_v \tag{38}$$

The right-hand side of equation (38) is the directional derivative of β in the direction of v. We therefore may write

$$\mathcal{T} = |\mathbf{S}_u \times \mathbf{S}_v| \, \nabla \beta \tag{39}$$

Combining equations (31), (34) and (39) gives equation (10):

$$(\mathbf{S}_u \times \mathbf{S}_v)_t = |\, \mathbf{S}_u \times \mathbf{S}_v \,| \ (2\beta H \mathbf{N} - \nabla \beta) \tag{40}$$

Acknowledgments

We thank the anonymous reviewers for their constructive comments. G. H. acknowledges the grant given by Conacyt.

References

1. M. Bertalmio, G. Sapiro, and G. Randall. Region tracking on level-sets methods. *IEEE Transactions On Medical Imaging*, to appear.
2. Lia Bronsard and Barbara Stoth. Volume-preserving mean curvature flow as a limit of a nonlocal ginzburg-landau equation. *SIAM Journal on Mathematical Analysis*, 28(4):769–807, July 1997.
3. V. Caselles, R. Kimmel, and G. Sapiro. Geodesic active contours. *The International Journal of Computer Vision*, 22(1):61–79, 1997.
4. V. Caselles, R. Kimmel, G. Sapiro, and C. Sbert. 3d active contours. In M-O. Berger, R. Deriche, I. Herlin, J. Jaffre, and J-M. Morel, editors, *Images, Wavelets and PDEs*, volume 219 of *Lecture Notes in Control and Information Sciences*, pages 43–49. Springer, June 1996.
5. Y.G. Chen, Y. Giga, and S. Goto. Uniqueness and existence of viscosity solutions of generalized mean curvature flow equations. *J. Differential Geometry*, 33:749–786, 1991.
6. David L. Chopp. Computing minimal surfaces via level set curvature flow. *Journal of Computational Physics*, 106:77–91, 1993.
7. D.L. Chopp and J.A. Sethian. Flow under curvature: singularity formation, minimal surfaces, and geodesics. *Experimental Mathematics*, 2(4):235–255, 1993.
8. Anders M. Dale and Martin I. Sereno. Improved localization of cortical activity by combining eeg and meg with mri cortical surface reconstruction: A linear approach. *Journal of Cognitive Neuroscience*, 5(2):162–176, 1993.
9. Rachid Deriche, Stéphane Bouvin, and Olivier. Faugeras. Front propagation and level-set approach for geodesic active stereovision. In *Third Asian Conference On Computer Vision*, Bombay, India, January 1998.
10. M. P. DoCarmo. *Differential Geometry of Curves and Surfaces*. Prentice-Hall, 1976.

11. Joachim Escher and Gieri Simonett. The volume preserving mean curvature flow near spheres. *Proceedings of the american Mathematical Society*, 126(9):2789–2796, September 1998.
12. D. C. Van Essen, H.A. Drury, S.Joshi, and M.I. Miller. Functional and structural mapping of human cerebral cortex: Solutions are in the surfaces. In *Proceedings of the National Academy of Science*, 1998.
13. L.C. Evans and J. Spruck. Motion of level sets by mean curvature: I. *Journal of Differential Geometry*, 33:635–681, 1991.
14. Olivier Faugeras and Renaud Keriven. Variational principles, surface evolution, pde's, level set methods and the stereo problem. *IEEE Trans. on Image Processing*, 7(3):336–344, March 1998.
15. M. Gage and R.S. Hamilton. The heat equation shrinking convex plane curves. *J. of Differential Geometry*, 23:69–96, 1986.
16. M. Grayson. The heat equation shrinks embedded plane curves to round points. *J. of Differential Geometry*, 26:285–314, 1987.
17. Eduard Harabetian and Stanley Osher. Regularization of ill-posed problems via the level set approach. *SIAM J. APPL. MATH*, 58(6):1689–1706, December 1998.
18. L. Lorigo, O. Faugeras, W.E.L. Grimson, R. Keriven, R. Kikinis, and C-F. Westin. Co-dimension 2 geodesic active contours for mra segmentation. In *International Conference on Information Processing in Medical Imaging*, June 1999.
19. R. Malladi, J. A. Sethian, and B.C. Vemuri. Shape modeling with front propagation: A level set approach. *PAMI*, 17(2):158–175, February 1995.
20. R. Malladi and J.A. Sethian. Image processing: Flows under min/max curvature and mean curvature. *Graphical Models and Image Processing*, 58(2):127–141, March 1996.
21. Peter J. Olver, Guillermo Sapiro, and Allen Tannenbaum. Invariant geometric evolutions of surfaces and volumetric smoothing. *SIAM J. APPL. MATH*, 57(1):176–194, February 1997.
22. G. Orban. *Cerebral Cortex*, chapter 9, pages 359–434. Plenum Press, New York, 1997.
23. S. Osher and J. Sethian. Fronts propagating with curvature dependent speed : algorithms based on the Hamilton-Jacobi formulation. *Journal of Computational Physics*, 79:12–49, 1988.
24. N. Paragios and R. Deriche. A PDE-based Level Set Approach for Detection and Tracking of Moving Objects. In *Proceedings of the 6th International Conference on Computer Vision*, Bombay,India, January 1998. IEEE Computer Society Press.
25. A. H. Salden. *Dynamic Scale-Space Paradigms*. PhD thesis, Utrecht University, The Netherlands, 1996.
26. G. Sapiro and A. Tannenbaum. Area and length preserving geometric invariant scale-spaces. *PAMI*, 17(1):67–72, January 1995.
27. J. A. Sethian. *Level Set Methods*. Cambridge University Press, 1996.
28. R. B. H. Tootell, J. D. Mendola, N. K. Hadjikhani, P. J. Leden, A. K. Liu, J. B. Reppas, M. I. Sereno, and A. M. Dale. Functional analysis of v3a and related areas in human visual cortex. *The Journal of Neuroscience*, 17(18):7060–7078, September 1997.
29. K. Zilles, E. Armstrong, A. Schleicher, and H.-J.Kretschmann. *The Human Pattern of Gyrification in the Cerebral Cortex*, pages 173–179. 1988.

Reconciling Distance Functions and Level Sets

José Gomes and Olivier Faugeras

I.N.R.I.A
BP. 93, 2004 Route des Lucioles
06902 Sophia Antipolis Cedex, France

Abstract. This paper is concerned with the simulation of the Partial Differential Equation (PDE) driven evolution of a closed surface by means of an implicit representation. In most applications, the natural choice for the implicit representation is the signed distance function to the closed surface. Osher and Sethian propose to evolve the distance function with a Hamilton-Jacobi equation. Unfortunately the solution to this equation is *not* a distance function. As a consequence, the practical application of the level set method is plagued with such questions as when do we have to "reinitialize" the distance function? How do we "reinitialize" the distance function? Etc... which reveal a disagreement between the theory and its implementation. This paper proposes an alternative to the use of Hamilton-Jacobi equations which eliminates this contradiction: in our method the implicit representation always remains a distance function by construction, and the implementation does not differ from the theory anymore. This is achieved through the introduction of a new equation. Besides its theoretical advantages, the proposed method also has several practical advantages which we demonstrate in two applications: (i) the segmentation of the human cortex surfaces from MRI images using two coupled surfaces [26], (ii) the construction of a hierarchy of Euclidean skeletons of a 3D surface.

1   Introduction and previous work

We consider a family of hypersurfaces $\mathcal{S}(\mathbf{p}, t)$ in $\mathbb{R}^3$, where $\mathbf{p}$ parameterizes the surface and t is the time, that evolve according to the following PDE:

$$\frac{\partial \mathcal{S}}{\partial t} = \beta \mathcal{N} \tag{1}$$

with initial conditions $\mathcal{S}(t = 0) = \mathcal{S}_0$, where $\mathcal{N}$ is the inward unit normal vector of $\mathcal{S}$, β is a velocity function and $\mathcal{S}_0$ is some initial closed surface.

Methods of curves evolution for segmentation, tracking and registration were introduced in computer vision by Kass, Witkin and Terzopoulos [15]. These evolutions were reformulated by Caselles, Kimmel and Sapiro [7] and by Kichenassamy *et al.* [16] in the context of PDE-driven curves and surfaces. There is an extensive literature that addresses the theoretical aspects of these PDE's and offers geometrical interpretations as well as results of uniqueness and existence [13, 14, 9].

Level set methods were first introduced by Osher and Sethian in [21] in the context of fluid mechanics and provide both a nice theoretical framework and efficient practical tools for solving such PDE's. In those methods, the evolution (1) is achieved by means of an implicit representation of the surface $\mathcal{S}$.

The key idea in Osher and Sethian's approach is to introduce a function $u : \mathbb{R}^3 \times \mathbb{R} \to \mathbb{R}$ such that

$$u(\mathcal{S}, t) = 0 \ \forall t \tag{2}$$

By differentiation (and along with $\mathcal{N} = -\frac{\nabla u}{|\nabla u|}$ and (1)), we obtain the Hamilton-Jacobi [1] equation:

$$\frac{\partial u}{\partial t} = \beta |\nabla u| \tag{3}$$

with initial conditions $u(\cdot, 0) = u_0(.)$, where u_0 is some initial function $\mathbb{R}^3 \to \mathbb{R}$ such that $u_0(\mathcal{S}_0) = 0$. It has been proved that for a large class of functions u and u_0, the zero level set at time t of the solution of (3) is the solution at time t of (1).

Regarding the function u_0, it is most often chosen to be the signed distance function to the closed surface $\mathcal{S}_0$. This particular implicit function can be characterized by the two equations:

$$\{x \in \mathbb{R}^3, u_0(x) = 0\} = \mathcal{S}_0 \quad \text{and} \quad |\nabla u_0| = 1$$

Indeed, the magnitude of the gradient of u_0 is equal to the magnitude of the derivative of the distance function from $\mathcal{S}_0$ in the direction normal to $\mathcal{S}_0$, *i.e.*, it is equal to 1.

It is known from [5] that the solution u of (3) *is not* the signed distance function to the solution $\mathcal{S}$ of (1). This causes several problems which are analyzed in the following section.

It is also important to notice that β in (3) is defined in $\mathbb{R}^3$ whereas in (1) it is defined on the surface $\mathcal{S}$. The extension of β from $\mathcal{S}$ to the whole domain $\mathbb{R}^3$ is a crucial point for the analysis and implementation of (3). There are mainly two ways of doing this.

(i) Most of the time this extension is natural. For example, if $\beta = H_{\mathcal{S}}$, the mean curvature of $\mathcal{S}$ in (1), one can choose $\beta = H_u$, the mean curvature of the level set of u passing though x in (3).

(ii) In some cases [24, 20, 2], this extension is not possible. Then one may assign to $\beta(x)$ in (3) the value of $\beta(y)$ in (1) where y is the closest point to x belonging to $\mathcal{S}$. The problem with this extension is that it hides an important dependence of β in (3) with respect to u and we show in section 4 that in this case (3) is *not* a Hamilton-Jacobi equation.

The thrust of this paper is a reformulation of the level set methods introduced by Osher and Sethian in [21] to eliminate some of the problems that are attached to it, e.g. the need to reinitialize periodically the distance function or the need to "invent" a velocity field away from the evolving front or zero level set. The implications of our work are both theoretical and practical.

2 Why Hamilton-Jacobi equation (3) does not preserve distance functions

In this section, we suppose that β is extended as explained in (i). The fact that the solutions to Hamilton-Jacobi equations of the form (3) are not distance functions has been proved formally in [5]. A convincing geometrical interpretation of this fact is now given through two short examples.

---

[1] The difference between a Hamilton-Jacobi equation and a general first order PDE is that the unknown function (here u) does not appear explicitly in the equation.

2.1 First example

Let us consider the problem of segmenting a known object (an ellipse) in an image by minimizing the energy of a curve [8]. Let us force the initial curve to be exactly the solution (the known ellipse) and initialize u_0 to the signed distance function to this ellipse, then evolve u with the Hamilton-Jacobi equation (3).

It is obvious that the zero level set of u (let us call S_0 this ellipse) will not evolve, since it is the solution to (1) and $\beta(x \in S_0) = 0$.
Notice however that replacing 0 by $\epsilon \in \mathbb{R}$ in (2) implies by differentiation the same equation (3), which means that the ϵ level set of u (let us call this S_ϵ curve) also evolves according to $\frac{\partial S}{\partial t} = \beta \mathcal{N}$. In consequence, $\beta(x \in S_\epsilon) \neq 0$ and S_ϵ evolves toward S_0 in order to minimize its energy (cf. fig. (1)).

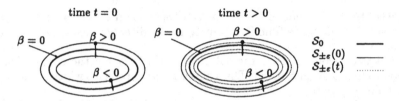

Fig. 1. All the level sets of u (shown as single curves) move towards the ellipse S_0 in order to minimize their own energy with the effect that the distance function is not preserved.

This shows that the shock wave equation (3) requires that all the level sets of u should converge to the ellipse S_0 and therefore that $|\nabla u|$ increases dangerously.

2.2 Second example

A point M with coordinate $x \in \mathbb{R}$ and energy $E(x) = \frac{x^2}{2}$ is moving along the real line in order to minimize its energy. We force the point M to be at $x_0 \neq 0$ at $t = 0$. The level set version of this problem is to define u_0 on the real line as $u_0(x) = x - x_0$ and to evolve u with the Hamilton-Jacobi equation $\frac{\partial u}{\partial t} = x \frac{\partial u}{\partial x}$. The solution is $u(x,t) = e^t x - x_0$. The figure (2) shows u at 3 time instants $(0 = t_0 < t_1 < t_2)$. The zero level set of u is indeed traveling to the origin O but the slope of u is $\frac{\partial u}{\partial x} = e^t$ and increases exponentially in time.

The second example is a rephrasing of what happens in the normal direction to the evolving curve in the first example. It is now obvious why driving all the level sets of u with (3) cannot conserve distance functions and in addition leads to unbounded values of $|\nabla u|$. In practical applications, one is compelled to "reinitialize" the implicit function u to be a distance function which is obviously a contradiction and which shows a gap between the theory and its real application.

In the next section, we convince the reader that maintaining u as a distance function (i.e. such that $|\nabla u| = 1$) during all the time of the evolution is definitely desirable, sometimes crucial.

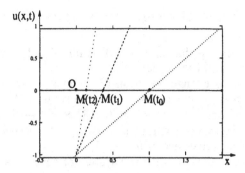

Fig. 2. The point M moves on the horizontal line in order to minimize its energy $E(x) = \frac{x^2}{2}$. The function u, initially of slope 1, becomes more and more vertical.

3   Why we should preserve the distance function

There are at least two reasons for preserving the signed distance function to the evolving surface, a theoretical one and a practical one.

(i) From the theoretical viewpoint, the implicit description of S (seen as a subset of $\mathbb{R}^3$) and its signed distance function u are **equivalent descriptions**. Indeed, given any surface S, its signed distance function is uniquely defined. Conversely, any implicit function u satisfying $|\nabla u| = 1$ is the signed distance function to a surface plus a constant (this last constant is taken equal to 0 on the surface) [4]. Since these descriptions are equivalent, one can transpose immediately properties of the first one into properties of the second one and vice versa. For example, **u has converged if and only if S has converged** (which is not true with Hamilton-Jacobi equation (3) according to the last section).

Moreover, one can deduce interesting intrinsic properties of S by a local knowledge of u. In [3], it is proved that the second fundamental form of S can be computed using the derivatives of the squared distance function. In addition, some applications in medical image analysis such as the segmentation of the cortex using two coupled surfaces [26] assume that the distance between the surfaces is known at any time. As a last example, the computation of the skeleton of a surface requires the detection of the singularities of its distance function [18].

(ii) From the practical viewpoint, the numerical approximation of the derivatives of u by finite differences requires the choice of a spatial step dx. One chooses a small dx if the slope (the gradient) of the function is large and a larger dx if the function has small variations. Since level sets are most often implemented on regular grids, it is more efficient to use the same step $dx = 1$ for each grid point. It is obvious that this approximation is more accurate if the norm of the gradient of u is known which is the case with distance functions since $|\nabla u| = 1$. Keeping $|\nabla u|$ bounded assures that the derivatives of u are always computable without the need to "reinitialize" u.

We now describe a new approach that preserves the signed distance function and therefore meets these two requirements.

4 How to preserve the signed distance function

In this section, we suppose that $u_0 = u(.,0)$ is initialized at $t = 0$ as the signed distance function to the initial surface S_0.

The basic idea is to change equation (3) in such a way that at each time instant u is the signed distance function to the solution S of (1). In order to achieve this goal, we look for a function $B : \mathbb{R}^3 \times \mathbb{R}^+ \to \mathbb{R}$ such that $\frac{\partial u}{\partial t} = B$ and which satisfies the two constrains: (i) $x \to u(x,.)$ is a distance function, (ii) the zero level set of u evolves according to (1).

We express these constrains with the system of equations:

$$\begin{cases} B_{|u=0} = \beta & (4) \\[2mm] \dfrac{\partial u}{\partial t} = B & (5) \\[2mm] |\nabla u| = 1 & (6) \end{cases}$$

where $B_{|u=0}$ denotes the restriction of B to the zero level set of u. By differentiating (5) and (6), we obtain:

$$\nabla\left(\frac{\partial u}{\partial t}\right) = \nabla B \text{ and } \frac{\nabla u}{|\nabla u|} \cdot \frac{\partial \nabla u}{\partial t} = 0 \tag{7}$$

using the Schwartz equality $\frac{\partial \nabla u}{\partial t} = \nabla\left(\frac{\partial u}{\partial t}\right)$, we get:

$$\nabla u \cdot \nabla B = 0 \tag{8}$$

which, together with (4) and (5) determines the function B. Relation (8) states that the function B does not vary along the characteristics of u (the characteristics of u are the integral curves of ∇u). It also means that the characteristics of u and B are orthogonal.

In order to go one step further in the resolution of the system, we must recall an important property [4]: **the characteristics of distance functions are straight lines** (cf. fig. (3)).

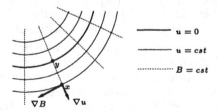

Fig. 3. Characteristic curves of the field ∇u.

This implies that B is constant along straight lines. These lines (or rays) intersect the zero level set of u at a point where B is known according to (4).

Given any point $x \in \mathbb{R}^3$, an equation of the characteristic of u passing through x is $\lambda \to x - \lambda \nabla u$. Since the distance of x to the zero level is $u(x)$ and $|\nabla u(x)| = 1$, the point $y = x - u\nabla u$ is on the zero level set of u. Notice that y is the closest point to x such that $u(y) = 0$. According to the last reasoning, we have $B(x) = B(y) = \beta(x - u\nabla u)$. Therefore, the solution to the initial system is:

$$\frac{\partial u}{\partial t} = \beta(x - u\nabla u) \tag{9}$$

with initial condition $u(.,0) = u_0(.)$. This equation[2] is the main result of the paper. Note that equation (9) is not a Hamilton-Jacobi equation since u appears in the right-hand side and plays a major role. An interpretation of (9) is the following: the zero level set of u is driven by $\frac{\partial u}{\partial t} = \beta$ as proposed by Osher and Sethian. The evolution of this particular surface geometrically defines (by propagation) the evolution of all other level sets.

Remark: *a posteriori*, one guesses that **the integral version** of equation (9) is the equation $u(S + \lambda\mathcal{N}) = \lambda \;\; \forall t, \lambda$. This can be proved by differentiation with respect to t and λ. It states that the surface parallel to S at distance λ from S should be the λ level set of u. This is to be compared to the constrain $u(S, t) = 0 \;\; \forall t$ introduced by Osher and Sethian.

The uniqueness of the closest point y to x such that $u(y) = 0$ is only guaranteed if $\nabla u(x)$ exists. The set of points of $\mathbb{R}^3$ where ∇u is not defined is called the **skeleton** of S (cf. fig. (4)).

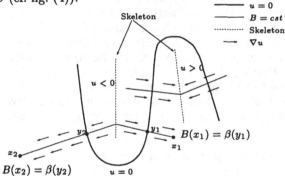

Fig. 4. The skeleton of the zero level set is determined by the points where ∇u is not defined.

Skeletons are very important in computer vision [6, 17, 22]. Since it turns out that they are a byproduct of our new proposed evolution, we describe in the next section an implementation of equation (9) in which special care is taken of the computation of the skeleton.

---

[2] Equation (9) looks simple but is not. Consider for example the case of mean curvature flow: (9) writes $\frac{\partial u}{\partial t}(x, t) = div(\nabla u(x - u(x, t)\nabla u(x, t), t))$, which is not a PDE (Indeed, two different points in $\mathbb{R}^n \times \mathbb{R}^+$ are considered, namely (x, t) and $(x - u\nabla u, t)$). However, notice that $u(x - u\nabla u) = 0$, $\nabla u(x - u\nabla u) = \nabla u(x)$, and according to [3], the second fundamental form at $x - u\nabla u$ can be computed using the derivatives of $u(x, t)$ up to the third order. This shows that for a large class of velocity functions (in particular for mean-curvature flow), (9) is indeed a PDE.

5   Implementation

In this section, we propose a straightforward implementation of the previous theory. u is initialized as the signed distance function to the initial surface. We fix u at a particular instant t and compute the real field $B(x,t) = \beta(x-u\nabla u)$ on a narrow band [10, 19, 1] of S. Once B is known, u can be updated by $u(x,t+dt) = u(x,t) + B(x,t)dt$. The computation of B is done in two steps corresponding respectively to equations (4) and (8). The difficulty is that we work on a discrete grid and this can have dramatic consequences if proper care is not taken of the sampling effects.

In order to deal with those effects, we introduce some notations. Points of $\mathbb{R}^3$ such that none of their coordinates is an integer will be denoted by lower case letters, e.g. x, and called real points. Points of $\mathbb{N}^3$, where N is the set of integers, will be denoted by upper case letters, e.g. X, and called voxels. We can think of x as a point falling in a cube formed by eight voxels. We note $V(x)$ this set of eight voxels.

If f is a function defined on $\mathbb{R}^3$, and x is a real point such that the values of f are known at all voxels of $V(x)$, we note $f_l(x)$ the value of the trilinear interpolation at x. In detail, if $x = (x_1, x_2, x_3) = (n_1 + \epsilon_1, n_2 + \epsilon_2, n_3 + \epsilon_3)$, where $n_i \in \mathbb{N}$ and $0 \le \epsilon_i < 1$, then we have by a simple linear interpolation $f_l(x_1, x_2, x_3) = (1-\epsilon_1)f(n_1, x_2, x_3) + \epsilon_1 f(n_1+1, x_2, x_3)$. By applying recursively this rule to $f(n_1, x_2, x_3)$ and $f(n_1 + 1, x_2, x_3)$, one expresses $f_l(x)$ as a linear combination of the samples of f at the voxels of $V(x)$, the weights being third order polynomials of the coordinates $(\epsilon_1, \epsilon_2, \epsilon_3)$.

Let $A(X)$ be the 26-neighborhood of the voxel X. Since generically the zero level set of u is composed of real points, we need to determine when a voxel X is adjacent to this zero level set. Consider the function C_u defined on the voxels of the grid such that $C_u(X) = 0$ if $u(X) > 0$ and $C_u(X) = 1$ if $u(X) \le 0$. A voxel X is said to be adjacent to the zero level set of u if $\exists Y \in A(X), C_u(Y) \ne C_u(X)$. We call $\mathcal{Z}$ the set of voxels adjacent to the zero level set of u. We are now in position to describe the two steps of our computation.

5.1   First step: computation of β on $\mathcal{Z}$

The first step is the computation of β on $\mathcal{Z}$. These values are stored in a temporary buffer called $B^{\mathcal{Z}}$. There are two ways to do this. If β is defined on $\mathbb{R}^3$, then one can assign $B^{\mathcal{Z}}(X) = \beta(X) \quad \forall X \in \mathcal{Z}$. If β is only defined on the nodes of a mesh describing the zero level set of u, then one can assign $B^{\mathcal{Z}}(X) = \beta(\nu_i) \quad \forall X \in \mathcal{Z}$, where ν_i is the closest node of the mesh to the voxel X. In both cases, the final value of $B(X)$ is *not* the value of $B^{\mathcal{Z}}(X)$, as explained in the second step.

Notice that the definition of $\mathcal{Z}$ ensures that if $u_l(x) = 0$ then $V(x) \subset \mathcal{Z}$ and in consequence $B_l^{\mathcal{Z}}(x)$ can be computed.

5.2   Second step: computation of B on the narrow band

The purpose is to propagate the values of B from $\mathcal{Z}$ to the whole narrow band. This is done by $B(X,t) = B_l^{\mathcal{Z}}(y,t)$ where $u_l(y) = 0$ and y lies on the same characteristic of u than X. Computing directly $y = X - u\nabla u$ is not robust since small errors in ∇u may introduce larger errors (proportional to u) in y. Instead, we follow the characteristic passing through X by unit steps:

$$
\begin{cases}
y_0 = X \\
y_{n+1} = y_n - \begin{cases} \text{if} & u_l(y_n) < 0 & \text{then} & max(u_l(y_n), sign(u_l(y_n))) \nabla_l u(y_n) \\ \text{if} & u_l(y_n) > 0 & \text{then} & min(u_l(y_n), sign(u_l(y_n))) \nabla_l u(y_n) \end{cases} & \text{until} \\
u_l(y_n) = 0
\end{cases}
$$

This marching is done for each voxel in the narrow band, even those of $\mathcal{Z}$. The computation of the march direction $\nabla_l u(y_n)$ requires the evaluation of ∇u at voxels of the grid. The choice of the numerical scheme for $\nabla u(X)$ is crucial since it may introduce unrecoverable errors if X lies on the skeleton of $\mathcal{S}$. Our choice is based on the schemes used in the resolution of Hamilton-Jacobi equations where shocks occur [25, 23]. These schemes use switch functions which turn on or off whenever a shock is detected. We explicit here our choice. Let $D_x^+ u = u(i+1, j, k) - u(i, j, k)$ and $D_x^- u = u(i, j, k) - u(i-1, j, k)$, with similar expressions for D_y and D_z. We form the eight estimators $D^i, i = 1, \dots, 8$ of ∇u, namely $D^1 u = \left(D_x^+ u, D_y^+ u, D_z^+ u\right)$, $D^2 u = \left(D_x^+ u, D_y^+ u, D_z^- u\right)$, $\cdots$, $D^8 u = \left(D_x^- u, D_y^- u, D_z^- u\right)$.

In our current implementation we use $\nabla u(X) = \text{ArgMax}_i(|D^i u(X)|)$. Indeed, apart from points on the skeleton of $\mathcal{S}$ where ∇u is undefined, $|\nabla u(X)|$ which should be equal to 1 since u is a distance function is found to be in practice less than or equal to 1 depending on which of the operators D^i we use. Hence the direction of maximum slope at X is the direction of the closest point to X of the zero level set of u. The fact that the skeleton can be detected by comparing the vectors $D^1 u, D^2 u, \dots, D^8 u$ is discussed in section 6.2.

6 Applications

We now describe two applications where our new method is shown to work significantly better than previous ones.

6.1 Cortex segmentation using coupled surfaces

We have implemented the segmentation of the cortical gray matter (a volumetric layer of variable thickness ($\approx$ 3mm)) from MRI volumetric data using two coupled surfaces proposed in [26] by Zeng et al. The idea put forward in [26] is to evolve simultaneously two surfaces with equations of the form (1). An inner surface $\mathcal{S}_{in}$ captures the boundary between the white and the gray matter and an outer surface $\mathcal{S}_{out}$ captures the exterior boundary of the gray matter. The segmented cortical gray matter is the volume between these two surfaces. The velocities of the two surfaces are:

$$\beta_{in} = f(I - I_{in}) + C(u_{out} + \epsilon) \tag{10}$$
$$\beta_{out} = f(I - I_{out}) + C(u_{in} - \epsilon) \tag{11}$$

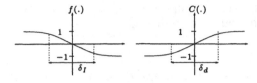

Fig. 5.

where I is the local gray intensity of the MRI image, I_{in} and I_{out} are two thresholds (I_{in} for the white matter and I_{out} for the gray matter), ϵ is the desired thickness and C and f have the shape of figure (5).

Let us interpret equation (10). The first term $f(I - I_{in})$ forces the gray level values to be close to I_{in} on S_{in}: it is the data attachment velocity term. The second term $C(u_{out} + \epsilon)$ models the interaction between S_{out} and S_{in}: it is the coupling term. According to the shape of C, see figure (5), if locally the two surfaces are at a distance $\epsilon = 3mm$, then the coupling term has no effect ($C = 0$) and S_{in} evolves in order to satisfy its data attachment term. If the local distance between S_{in} and S_{out} is too small ($< \epsilon$) then $C > 0$ and S_{in} slows down in order to get further from S_{out}. If the local distance between S_{in} and S_{out} is too large ($> \epsilon$) then $C < 0$ and S_{in} speeds up in order to move closer to S_{out}. A similar interpretation can be done for (11).

If these evolutions are implemented with the Hamilton-Jacobi equation (3), then the following occurs: the magnitudes of the gradients of u_{out} and u_{in} increase with time ($| \nabla u_{out} | > 1$ and $| \nabla u_{in} | > 1$). As a consequence, the estimation of the distance between S_{in} and S_{out} which is taken as $u_{in}(x)$ for x on S_{out} and $u_{out}(x)$ for x on S_{in}, is overestimated. Since the coupling term is negative in (10) and positive in (11), both S_{out} and S_{in} evolve in order to become closer and closer from each other (until the inevitable reinitialization of the distance functions is performed). In other words, with the standard implementation of the level sets, the incorrect evaluation of the distance functions prevents the coupling term to act correctly and, consequently, also prevents the data attachment terms to play their roles.

On the other hand, if these evolutions are implemented with our new PDE, then a much better interaction between the two terms is achieved since the data attachment term can fully play its role as soon as the distance between the two surfaces is correct (cf. fig.(6)).

These results are demonstrated in the figure (6) which we now comment. Each row corresponds to a different 32×32 sub-slice of an MRI image. The first column shows the original data and some regions of interest (concavities) are labeled A, B and C. The second column shows a simple thresholding at I_{in} and I_{out}. The third column shows the cross-sections of S_{in} and S_{out} through the slices if the coupling terms are not taken into account. This is why these curves have the same shape as in the second column. One observes that the segmented gray matter has not the wanted regular thickness. In the fourth column, the coupling terms are taken into account and the evolutions (10) and (11) are implemented with Hamilton-Jacobi equation (3). One observes (in particular at the concavities indicated in the first column) that the distance constraint is well satisfied but the data attachment term was neglected. This is due to the fact that with (3) the distance between the two surfaces is overevaluated. In the fifth column, this same evolution is implemented with the new PDE introduced in this paper (9). One can observe a much better result at concavities. This is due to the fact that the coupling terms stop having any effect as soon as the distance between

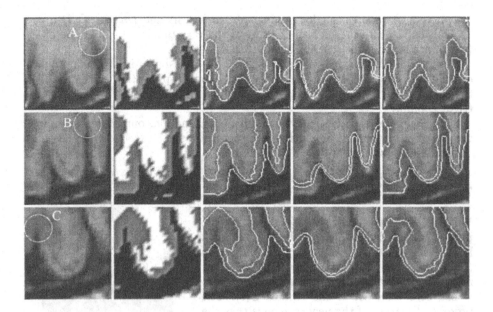

Fig. 6. Results of the segmentation of the gray matter using different algorithms, see text.

the surfaces is correct allowing the data term to drive correctly the surfaces according to the gray level values.

6.2 Extraction of the skeleton of an evolving surface

Skeletons are widely used in computer vision to describe global properties of objects. This representation is useful in tasks such as object recognition and registration because of its compactness [6, 17, 22].

One of the advantages of our new level set technique is that it provides, almost for free, at each time instant a description of the skeleton of the evolving surface or zero level set.

We show an example of this on one of the results of the segmentation described in the previous section. We take the outside surface of the cortex and simplify it using mean-curvature flow, i.e. the evolution $\frac{\partial S}{\partial t} = H\mathcal{N}$ where H is the mean curvature. This evolution is shown in the first column of figure 7. Since the distance function u to the zero level set is preserved at every step, it is quite simple to extract from it the skeleton by using the fact that it is the set of points where ∇u is not defined [6]. This is shown in the right column of figure 7. Each surface is rescaled in order to occupy the whole image.

The skeletons are computed using the distance function to the evolving surface as follows. We look for the voxels where the eight estimators $D^i u$ of ∇u defined in section 5 differ a lot and threshold the simple criterion:

$$\sum_i \left(\frac{D^i u}{|D^i u|}, \frac{\overline{Du}}{|\overline{Du}|} \right)^2$$

where $(.,.)$ denotes the dot product of two vectors and $\overline{Du} = \frac{1}{8}\sum_i D^i u$.

This can be interpreted as a measure of the variations of the direction of ∇u (which are large in the neighborhood of the skeleton).

The results for the left column of figure (7) are shown in the right column of the same figure where we clearly see how the simplification of the shape of the cortex (left column) goes together with the the simplification of its skeleton (right column).

Note that because it preserves the distance function, our framework allows the use of more sophisticated criteria for determining the skeleton [18] based on this distance function.

7 Conclusion

We have proposed a new scheme for solving the problem of evolving through the technique of level sets a surface $S(t)$ satisfying a PDE such as (1). This scheme introduces a new PDE, (9),that must be satisfied by the auxiliary function $u(t)$ whose zero level set is the surface $S(t)$. The prominent feature of the new scheme is that the solution to this PDE is the distance function to $S(t)$ at each time instant t. Our approach has many theoretical and practical advantages that were discussed and demonstrated on two applications. Since the distance function to the evolving surface is in most applications the preferred function, we believe that the PDE that was presented here is an interesting alternative to Hamilton-Jacobi equations which do not preserve this function.

References

1. D. Adalsteinsson and J. A. Sethian. A Fast Level Set Method for Propagating Interfaces. *Journal of Computational Physics*, 118(2):269–277, 1995.
2. D. Adalsteinsson and J. A. Sethian. The fast construction of extension velocities in level set methods. *Journal of Computational Physics*, 1(148):2–22, 1999.
3. L. Ambrosio and C. Mantegazza. Curvature and distance function from a manifold. *J. Geom. Anal.*, 1996. To appear.
4. V. I. Arnold. *Geometrical Methods in the Theory of Ordinary Differential Equations*. Springer-Verlag New York Inc., 1983.
5. G. Barles, H.M. Soner, and P.E. Souganidis. Front propagation and phase field theory. *SIAM J. Control and Optimization*, 31(2):439–469, March 1993.

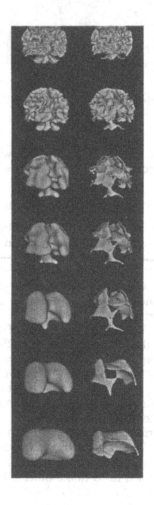

Fig. 7.

6. Harry Blum and Roger N. Nagel. Shape description using weighted symmetric axis features. *Pattern Recog.*, 10:167–180, 1978.
7. V. Caselles, R. Kimmel, and G. Sapiro. Geodesic active contours. In *Proceedings of the 5th International Conference on Computer Vision*, pages 694–699, Boston, MA, June 1995. IEEE Computer Society Press.
8. V. Caselles, R. Kimmel, and G. Sapiro. Geodesic active contours. *The International Journal of Computer Vision*, 22(1):61–79, 1997.
9. Y.G. Chen, Y. Giga, and S. Goto. Uniqueness and existence of viscosity solutions of generalized mean curvature flow equations. *J. Differential Geometry*, 33:749–786, 1991.
10. David L. Chopp. Computing minimal surfaces via level set curvature flow. *Journal of Computational Physics*, 106:77–91, 1993.
11. Frédéric Devernay. *Vision stéréoscopique et propriétés différentielles des surfaces.* PhD thesis, École Polytechnique, February 97.
12. O. Faugeras and R. Keriven. Level set methods and the stereo problem. In Bart ter Haar Romeny, Luc Florack, Jan Koenderink, and Max Viergever, editors, *Proc. of First International Conference on Scale-Space Theory in Computer Vision*, volume 1252 of *Lecture Notes in Computer Science*, pages 272–283. Springer, 1997.
13. M. Gage and R.S. Hamilton. The heat equation shrinking convex plane curves. *J. of Differential Geometry*, 23:69–96, 1986.
14. M. Grayson. The heat equation shrinks embedded plane curves to round points. *J. of Differential Geometry*, 26:285–314, 1987.
15. M. Kass, A. Witkin, and D. Terzopoulos. SNAKES: Active contour models. *The International Journal of Computer Vision*, 1:321–332, January 1988.
16. S. Kichenassamy, A. Kumar, P. Olver, A. Tannenbaum, and A. Yezzi. Gradient flows and geometric active contour models. In *Proceedings of the 5th International Conference on Computer Vision*, Boston, MA, June 1995. IEEE Computer Society Press.
17. B. Kimia, A. R. Tannenbaum, and S. W. Zucker. Shapes, schoks and deformations i: The components of two-dimensional shape and the reaction-diffusion space. *ijcv*, 15:189–224, 1995.
18. G. Malandain and S. Fernández-Vidal. Euclidean skeletons. *Image and Vision Computing*, 16:317–327, 1998.
19. R. Malladi, J. A. Sethian, and B.C. Vemuri. Evolutionary fronts for topology-independent shape modeling and recovery. In J-O. Eklundh, editor, *Proceedings of the 3rd European Conference on Computer Vision*, volume 800 of *Lecture Notes in Computer Science*, Stockholm, Sweden, May 1994. Springer-Verlag.
20. R. Malladi, J. A. Sethian, and B.C. Vemuri. Shape modeling with front propagation: A level set approach. *PAMI*, 17(2):158–175, February 1995.
21. S. Osher and J. Sethian. Fronts propagating with curvature dependent speed : algorithms based on the Hamilton-Jacobi formulation. *Journal of Computational Physics*, 79:12–49, 1988.
22. Jean Serra. *Image Analysis and Mathematical Morphology.* Academic Press, London, 1982.
23. J. A. Sethian. *Level Set Methods.* Cambridge University Press, 1996.
24. J.A. Sethian and J. Strain. Crystal growth and dendritic solidification. *Journal of Computational Physics*, 98:231–253, 1992.
25. C. W. Shu and S. Osher. Efficient implementation of essentially non-oscillatory shock-capturing schemes, ii. *Journal of Computational Physics*, 83:32–78, 1989.
26. X. Zeng, L. H. Staib, R. T. Schultz, and J. S. Duncan. Volumetric layer segmentation using coupled surfaces propagation. In *Proceedings of the International Conference on Computer Vision and Pattern Recognition*, Santa Barbara, 1998.

Computation of Ridges via Pullback Metrics from Scale Space

Michael Kerckhove *

University of Richmond, Richmond VA 23173, USA,
mkerckho@richmond.edu

Abstract. Properties of points in images are often measured using convolution integrals with each convolution kernel associated to a particular scale and perhaps to other parameters, such as an orientation, as well. Assigning to each point the parameter values that yield the maximum value of the convolution integral gives a map from points in the image to the space of parameters by which the given property is measured. The range of this map is the optimal parameter surface. In this paper, we argue that ridge points for the measured quantity are best computed via the pullback metric from the optimal parameter surface. A relatively simple kernel used to measure the property of medialness is explored in detail. For this example, we discuss connectivity of the optimal parameter surface and the possibility of more than one critical scale for medialness at a given point. We demonstrate that medial loci computed as ridges of medialness are in general agreement with the Blum medial axis.

1 Introduction

In the article "Scale in Perspective," [1], Koenderink illustrates the importance of scale in measuring how cloudlike a point in the atmosphere is. The property of "cloudlikeness" is discussed in terms of the density of condensed water vapor, and Koenderink, citing Mason [2], eventually settles on what amounts to the following definition: the cloudlikeness at a point in the atmosphere is the average density of condensed water vapor in a ball of volume 1 m^3 centered at the point. The size of the ball used in this measurement is crucial, and Koenderink reminds us that all physical measures of density should be thought of as part of a one-parameter family of density measures, with the level of resolution of the measuring instrument as the parameter.

Thresholding the value of cloudlikeness (at 0.4 gm^{-3}) gives a way to determine the boundary of a particular cloud; but there are other ways that the scalar field of cloudlikeness measures might be used. For example, a more detailed understanding of the cloud might be obtained by examining height ridges [3], generalized maxima of condensed water vapor density, within the cloud. To finish with this introductory example, consider whether we can be truly confident that the single scale represented by balls of volume 1 m^3 is exactly correct

---

* This work supported by NSF Grant BIR-951-0228

in all situations. A more prudent strategy would be to measure the cloudlikeness at a point over a range of scales, say from balls of size 0.5 m^3 to balls of size 2 m^3. We could then agree to define the cloudlikeness at a point to be the maximum, over the agreed upon range of scales, of these measured densities. This gives another bit of information; not only do we have the cloudlikeness at a point, but the scale at which the maximum density occurs, and perhaps this extra bit will reveal a deeper level of structure within the cloud.

In their papers on "Zoom-invariant Figural Shape", [5][6], Pizer and Morse, et. al., employ the principles outlined above to define and measure a property they call "medialness" at a point within an image. For an object with clearly defined boundary in a 2-dimensional image, the medial axis transform, first described by Blum [7], is the locus of centers of disks that are maximally inscribed in the object, together with the radii of those disks. This information provides a simple description of the size, shape, and location of the object, and is complete in the sense that the original object can be reconstructed exactly from its medial axis transform. In the presence of image disturbances, the exact nature of the reconstruction can be a liability rather than a feature, since the disturbances are also reconstructed from the transform. To overcome this liability, Pizer and his colleagues [5] take a multiscale approach to the extraction of medial loci directly from image intensities (with no pre-processing segmentation of image into objects required). The idea is to measure the medialness of points via a convolution integral whose kernel involves both a scale and an orientation; then to extract ridges from these measurements. In [6] they provide strong experimental evidence that these ridges of medialness are insensitive to small scale image disturbances. They use the term "cores" for such ridges. Having achieved the objective of overcoming small disturbances, they go on to describe applications of cores to problems of segmentation, registration, object recognition, and shape analysis [8], [5]. Indeed, by placing a disk with radius proportional to the optimal scale at each point, a useful Blum-like description of the boundary at the scale of the core (BASOC) is produced.

In this paper we propose that the extraction of height ridges for properties like medialness is best performed using a pullback metric from the parameter space. There are two advantages to using a pullback metric. First, ridges are computed directly in the image instead of being computed in the higher-dimensional product space formed from the image and the measurement parameters. Second, the calculation of ridges is metric dependent and the pullback metric assigns the proper distance between points of the image, based on the optimal parameters for the measurement in question. An outline of the contents of the paper follows. In section 2, we review definitions of medialness at a point in an image and of the optimal scale surface for medialness. In section 3, we describe the mathematics of pullback metrics and make subsequent computations of gradients, hessians, and convexity ridges. In section 4 we apply the pullback metric from the optimal scale surface to the problem of extracting medial loci, illustrating results for rectangles. In principle, any image property measured pointwise at various scales (and with various auxiliary parameters) is amenable to this treatment.

The optimal scale surface for the measurement inherits a metric from the metric on the parameter space; this metric may be pulled back to the original image and provides what we believe to be the correct metric in which to compute ridges for the measured quantity. The approach presented here supplements the recent work of Furst [9] in which a marching cubes like algorithm for tracking ridges is developed.

2 Medialness and the Optimal Scale Surface

We adopt the following definition of medialness at a point in a 2-dimensional image from the paper of Pizer, Eberly, Morse, and Fritsch [5]. In that paper several different medialness kernels are proposed; the kernel below is sufficient for our purposes although other kernels may produce medial loci more closely associated to Blum's medial axis.

Definition 1. *Let x be a point in $\mathbb{R}^2$, let u be a unit vector in $\mathbb{R}^2$ and let σ be a positive scalar. Let $G_\sigma(x) = \sigma^{-2} exp(-|x|^2/2\sigma^2)$ be the standard 2D gaussian with scale σ, denote the matrix of second partials of G_σ at x by $hess(G_\sigma)|_x$, and set $K(x,\sigma,u) = -\sigma^2 u^t.hess(G_\sigma)|_x.u$. Let $I(x)$ be a 2D image intensity, i.e., a bounded nonnegative function on $\mathbb{R}^2$ having compact support.*

Then, the parameter-dependent medialness at the point x, relative to the intensity function I, measured at scale σ and with orientation u is

$$m(I,x,\sigma,u) = \int_{\mathbb{R}^2} I(z)K(z-x,\sigma,u)\,dz.$$

The medialness at the point x, denoted $M(x)$, is the maximum, over scales σ and orientations u, of $m(I,x,\sigma,u)$. The values of σ and u at which the maximum value of $m(I,x,\sigma,u)$ occurs are the optimal parameters.

Lemma 1. *The optimal orientation at a point x is completely determined by the optimal scale.*

Proof. The medialness function $m(I,x,\sigma,u)$ may be re-written in the form $u^t A u$, where A is a symmetric matrix whose entries are integrals with values depending on scale. From this form, we see that the optimal orientation at a given scale is the eigendirection for A corresponding to its largest eigenvalue.

For a given image, denote the support set for the intensity function by Ω. We may "zoom" the image by a constant factor of $\lambda > 0$ by defining a new intensity function $I_\lambda(z) = I(z/\lambda)$. Clearly the support set for the new intensity is the set $\lambda\Omega$. We record the fundamental property of medialness, "zoom-invariance," in the following proposition.

Proposition 1. *The parameter-dependent medialness function is invariant to zoom, meaning that for any positive real number λ,*

$$m(I_\lambda,\lambda x,\lambda\sigma,u) = m(I,x,\sigma,u).$$

Proof. The proof that

$$\int_{\lambda\Omega} I_\lambda(w)K(w - \lambda x, \lambda\sigma, u)\, dw = \int_\Omega I(z)K(z - x, \sigma, u)\, dz.$$

is accomplished by means of the change of variables formula for multiple integrals. This property accounts for the factor of σ^2 in the definition of the medialness kernel.

The graph of the medialness kernel K is centered over the point at which the measurement is made, has the shape of a Gaussian in the direction orthogonal to u, and has the shape of a Gaussian second derivative in the direction of u. This shape makes this kernel particularly effective for locating medial axes of objects having parallel sides and uniform interior intensity: orienting the kernel so that u is perpendicular to the parallel sides will maximize the value of medialness. It is interesting to note that for rectangular objects with aspect ratio less than $1/5$, the scale that maximizes medialness at the center of the rectangle is equal to half the distance between the parallel sides. The other simple plane figure is the disk of radius R: here symmetry dictates that the parameter-dependent medialness measure at the center of the disk is independent of u and the optimal scale is $R/\sqrt{2}$.

By the term scale space, we mean the Cartesian product $\mathbb{R}^2 \times \mathbb{R}^+ = S$ consisting of points x in the image plane and scales σ at which medialness measurements are made. Associating to each point its optimal scale for medialness gives a map σ_o from the image plane into scale space given by $x \mapsto (x, \sigma_o(x))$.

Definition 2. *The set of points in scale space of the form $(x, \sigma_o(x))$ is the optimal scale surface for medialness.*

The nature of the map σ_o is not completely understood: in [5] it is claimed that σ_o is continuous; in [3], the optimal scale surface is redefined in terms of the smallest scale at which a local maximum for medialness occurs and further assumptions of continuity and differentiability are made; while in [9] reference is made to the possibility of folds in the optimal scale surface and the need to use more general coordinate charts. As we shall illustrate in section 4, the optimal scale surface need not be connected. Nevertheless, we shall continue our development by assuming that there are open sets bounded by Jordan curves in the image plane such that the restriction of σ_o to any one of these open sets is twice differentiable. In what follows we shall restrict attention to a single such open set, continuing to refer to the graph of σ_o over that open set as the optimal scale surface.

Under the assumption of differentiability, we proceed to define the tangent map.

Definition 3. *The tangent map σ_{o*} maps vectors in the image plane to vectors in scale space. Let v be a vector in the image plane at the point x. Then the vector $\sigma_{o*}(v)$ is the vector based at the point $\sigma(x)$ that is defined by taking any parametrized curve $c(t)$ in the image plane whose initial position is x and whose initial velocity is v and setting $\sigma_{o*}(v)$ to be the initial velocity of the curve $\sigma(c(t))$.*

The vector $\sigma_{o*}(v)$ is well-defined independent of the curve $c(t)$ by which it is computed. Moreover, the map σ_{o*} is a linear map between the (linear) tangent spaces at x and at $\sigma(x)$. The important vectors at a point (x, y) in the image plane are the coordinate vectors $\partial_x = (1, 0)$ and $\partial_y = (0, 1)$. Using the same notation to denote the coordinate vector fields in scale space, we see that the set of vectors $\{\partial_x, \partial_y, \partial_\sigma\}$ forms a basis for the vectors in scale space. In terms of these coordinate bases, we have the familiar formulas

$$\sigma_{o*}(\partial_x) = (1, 0, \sigma_{ox}) \text{ and } \sigma_{o*}(\partial_y) = (0, 1, \sigma_{oy}).$$

3 The Scale Space Metric, the Induced Metric, the Pullback Metric; Differential Operators and Ridges

Our notation for the coordinate vector fields in the image plane, $\{\partial_x, \partial_y\}$, belies the fact that we consider these vector fields primarily via their action on functions: applying ∂_x to the function f yields the partial derivative f_x, a new function on the image plane. One may extend this action on functions to an action on vector fields and tensors of higher order by defining covariant differentiation. In the presence of a metric, Lemma 2 below indicates that a unique preferred notion of covariant differentiation (via the Levi-Civita connection). The development of a suitable metric on the image plane for the extraction of medial loci will take some time; we emphasize that the role of the metric is to define the differential operators by which ridges of medialness are to be computed. Standard references for the ideas and coordinate free notation of differential geometry presented in this section include [10] and [11].

A Riemannian metric on a differentiable manifold is is a means for computing dot products of tangent vectors. This amounts to the assignment of a nondegenerate, symmetric bilinear form h on each tangent plane of the manifold. Once such a metric is assigned, arclengths, and subsequently distances between points, may be computed by integrating lengths of velocity vectors along differentiable curves. By the term scale space, we mean the product manifold $R^2 \times [\sigma_0, sigma_1]$, where, for a particular 2-dimensional image, the inner scale σ_0 is the smallest scale consistent with the image production process and where the outer scale σ_1 is the largest scale consistent with the image size, [5],[12]. We make the following choice for a metric on scale space.

Definition 4. *Let v and w be vectors in scale space at the point (x, y, σ) and let $[v]$ and $[w]$ be the coordinate vectors of v and w relative to the basis $\{\partial_x, \partial_y, \partial_\sigma\}$. Then $h|_{(x,y,\sigma)}(v, w) = [v]^t[h][w]$, where $[h]$ is the matrix*

$$[h] = \begin{pmatrix} \frac{1}{\sigma^2} & 0 & 0 \\ 0 & \frac{1}{\sigma^2} & 0 \\ 0 & 0 & \frac{1}{\sigma^2} \end{pmatrix}.$$

This metric is often expressed less formally by writing

$$ds^2 = \frac{dx^2 + dy^2 + d\sigma^2}{\sigma^2}.$$

The resulting geometry is hyperbolic, having constant sectional curvature -1. The rationale for this choice of metric is as follows: if the spatial distance between points p and q in R^2 is L when measured at scale σ, then the distance between those points when measured at scale $\frac{\sigma}{2}$ is $2L$. Similarly, reported scale differences exhibit the same dependence on the scales at which they are measured. This gives $ds^2 = \frac{dx^2 + dy^2 + d\sigma^2}{\rho^2 \sigma^2}$. and for convenience we may assume that the conversion factor ρ between the units of spatial distance and the units of scale difference is 1.

The metric h induces a metric h_o on the optimal scale surface, simply by restricting h to the tangent planes to that surface. Re-expressing the restriction in terms of the coordinate basis for the tangent plane to the optimal scale surface at the point $\sigma_o(x, y)$ given by $\{\sigma_{o*}(\partial_x), \sigma_{o*}(\partial_y)\}$ yields the 2-by-2 matrix

$$[h_o] = \begin{pmatrix} \frac{1 + \sigma_{ox}^2}{\sigma_o^2} & \frac{\sigma_{ox}\sigma_{oy}}{\sigma_o^2} \\ \frac{\sigma_{ox}\sigma_{oy}}{\sigma_o^2} & \frac{1 + \sigma_{ox}^2}{\sigma_o^2} \end{pmatrix} = [\sigma_o^* h_o] = [g]. \tag{1}$$

To explain the notation on the right hand side of (1), we may consider the induced metric h_o as a metric on the original image plane, the so-called pullback metric, denoted by $g = \sigma_o^*(h)$ and defined for vectors v and w in the plane of the original image by $g(v, w) = h_o(\sigma_{o*}(v), \sigma_{o*}(w))$. In particular, we have that the matrix $[g]$ relative to the coordinate basis $\{\partial_x, \partial_y\}$ is identical to the matrix for $[h_o]$ as indicated in (1). It is this metric g, expressed by the matrix $[g]$ in (1), that we will use to study the medialness function M.

Our next task is to define the gradient and hessian of M relative to our metric g. We rely on covariant differentiation (which gives a way to differentiate tensor fields) in order to accomplish this task. That the task can be accomplished in only one way once a metric is prescribed is a consequence of the following lemma [11] (in the statement of the lemma g is used to denote an arbitrary metric).

Lemma 2 (Fundamental Lemma of Riemannian Geometry). *On a differentiable manifold N with metric g there is a unique way to define covariant differentiation that is compatible with both the manifold structure of N and with the metric g in the sense that the covariant derivative of g satisfies $Dg = 0$.*

As indicated in the beginning paragraph of this section, covariant differentiation of functions along vector fields amounts to directional derivatives. For a vector field v and a function f, we write $D_v f$ to indicate this derivative. In terms of the coordinate vector fields $\{\partial_x, \partial_y\}$, we may write $v = v_1 \partial_x + v_2 \partial_y$, and the expression for the directional derivative becomes $D_v f = v_1 f_x + v_2 f_y$. The gradient grad f of the function f is defined by means of the metric g by setting grad f to be the unique vector field satisfying $D_v f = g(\text{grad } f, v)$ for every vector field v.

Next we consider the covariant derivative of a vector field w along the vector field v. Denoted by $D_v w$, this new vector field may again be computed in terms of the metric via the Koszul formula for $g(D_v w, u)$. In this formula, given below, u is an arbitrary vector field and terms of the form $[v, w]$ involve the Lie bracket of of two vector fields (the Lie bracket is a non-metric derivative of one vector field along another; compatibility of D with the manifold structure of N means precisely that $[v, w] = D_v w - D_w v$).

$$2g(D_v w, u) = D_v g(w, u) + D_w g(u, v) - D_u g(v, w)$$
$$-g(v, [w, u]) + g(w, [u, v]) + g(u, [v, w]).$$

We shall have little use for Lie brackets below, as we will revert to expressing the tensors of interest to us in terms of coordinate vector fields and the Lie bracket of coordinate vector fields is zero. We note in passing that the Koszul formula, when applied to coordinate vector fields, yields expressions for the classical Christoffel symbols.

The metric-dependent hessian (a symmetric tensor of type $(2, 0)$), defined for any twice differentiable function f, may now be written concisely as

$$\operatorname{hess}_f(v, w) = g(D_v \operatorname{grad} f, w).$$

When N has dimension 2, we may choose a basis for the tangent space at each point and compute a 2-by-2 matrix $[\operatorname{hess}_f]$. The trace of this matrix is a new function on N, the metric-dependent Laplacian of f. Note further that the matrix $[\operatorname{hess}_f]$ is symmetric and hence diagonalizable over the reals. This leads directly to the consideration of convexity ridges for f.

Definition 5. *Let f be a twice differentiable function on a 2-dimensional manifold N with metric g. On the open subset of N where the eigenvalues $\lambda_+ > \lambda_-$ of hess_f are distinct, with corresponding eigenvectors e^+ and e^-, the maximum convexity ridge for f is the set of points where $\lambda_- < 0$ and where $g(\operatorname{grad} f, e^-) = 0$.*

As mentioned in the introduction, convexity ridges [3], [4] are generalized maxima for f; at each ridge point, f has a local maximum in the direction of e^- which is transverse to the ridge. It is also worth noting that the current ridge-tracking algorithms of [5] and [9] involve computing the hessian of the medialness function m in 3-dimensional scale space, then considering the restriction of the hessian of m to a 2-dimensional subspace in scale space. The restriction of the 3D hessian to the optimal scale surface in scale space is not the same as the hessian obtained by first restricting the function m to obtain M on the optimal scale surface then computing in the metric intrinsic to the surface; the restricted 3D hessian involves a second term resulting from the (generally nonzero) curvature of the optimal scale surface in scale space.

With these generalities as foundation, we return to the image plane furnished with its metric g, the pullback of the restriction of the hyperbolic scale space metric to the optimal scale surface. The matrix for this metric, in terms of the coordinate vector fields $\{\partial_x, \partial_y\}$, is given by formula (1). The medialness function $M = M(x, y)$ is a function on the image plane, and relative to the basis of coordinate vector fields we have

$$[\text{hess}_M] = \begin{pmatrix} M_{xx} - g(D_{\partial_x}\partial_x, \text{grad}\,M) & M_{xy} - g(D_{\partial_y}\partial_x, \text{grad}\,M) \\ M_{yx} - g(D_{\partial_x}\partial_y, \text{grad}\,M) & M_{yy} - g(D_{\partial_y}\partial_y, \text{grad}\,M) \end{pmatrix}. \tag{2}$$

The maximum convexity ridge for M relative to the metric g constitutes the medial locus for the image. To compute the matrix $[\text{hess}_M]$ in practice requires knowledge of the second partial derivatives of M and, because the Koszul formula for covariant derivatives of coordinate vector fields involves derivatives of the metric g, knowledge of the second partial derivatives of the function σ_o. We emphasize that no higher order derivatives are required and that by using the pullback metric, ridges of dimension 1 are computed directly in the 2-dimensional image plane rather than being computed in, then projected from a higher dimensional parameter space.

4 Medial Loci for Rectangles

In this section, we compute medial loci for binary images of rectangles, using the eigenvalues and eigenvectors of $[\text{hess}_M]$. Computations are performed using a grid of 1600 equally spaced points on the square $[-1, 1] \times [-1, 1]$. At each point in the grid, approximate values of the optimal scale function σ_o and of the medialness function M are computed by sampling scales σ with $0.05 \le \sigma \le 1$. These values are then used to generate two-variable quadratic Taylor polynomials for σ_o and M centered at each point in the grid using a least squares fit to the sampled data. Coefficients of these Taylor expansions are then used as approximate values for the derivatives of σ_o and M in the formula for $[\text{hess}_M]$. Determination of eigenvalues, eigenvectors, and ridges points follows.

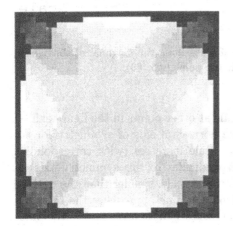 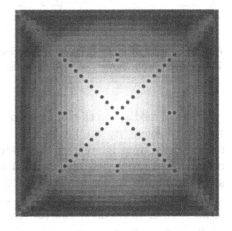

Fig. 1. The optimal scale surface and the medial locus for a square.

In Figure 1, we show the optimal scale surface and medial locus for a square as determined by our algorithm. The original intensity function is 1 at each point in the square. The plot at left shows optimal scales for medialness at each point in the square, with lighter shading indicating larger scale. Approximately 1400 of the 1600 grid points have optimal scales larger than 0.75 with a maximum of 0.90, while the remaining points, those nearest the edges and corners of the square, have optimal scales smaller than 0.45, the optimal scale being 0.05 at points along the square's boundary. At right, the maximum convexity ridge for the medialness function M, computed using the pullback metric, is shown. The ridge is overlaid on a plot of medialness values, again with lighter shading indicating a higher value. Points on the ridges shown here lie within the set of points where $\sigma_o \geq 0.75$ and satisfy $|g(\text{grad}\, M, e^-)| < 0.01$. Near the midpoints of the edges of the square, it can be seen that extremely small scales increase medialness values.

In Figure 2, we consider the function $m(I, (x, x), \sigma, (-1, 1)/\sqrt{2})$ at the points $(.625, .625)$, $(.65, .65)$, $(.675, .675)$. Note the two local maxima for medialness at $(.65, .65)$. From the information in this figure we may conclude that the optimal scale surface for the square is either disconnected or has a fold. The global picture of Figure 1 allows us to see that it is not possible to go from $(0.65, 0.65, smaller\ critical\ scale)$ to $(0.65, 0.65, larger\ critical\ scale)$ along a path that remains on the optimal scale surface; the option of a fold is not possible and we conclude that the optimal scale surface is disconnected.

m

scale

Fig. 2. Graphs of medialness as a function of scale along the diagonal of the square. The center graph shows two critical scales at the point $(.65, .65)$.

Plots of medialness as a function of scale at other points in the figure exhibit similar behavior. As one moves along the horizontal axis of symmetry for the square away from its center, the optimal scale increases (with corresponding optimal orientation occurring with u perpendicular to this symmetry axis) as shown in Figure 1. Meanwhile, a second critical scale, smaller than the optimal scale, develops (starting at about $x = 0.60$). As one approaches the midpoint of an edge of the square, the two critical scales persist until finally the value of medialness at the smaller critical scale becomes maximal and the optimal orientation of the medialness kernel rotates through 90 degrees.

In Figure 3, the extracted medial loci for rectangles with aspect ratios 0.85 and 0.70 are illustrated. Solid lines indicate the Blum medial axis for each rectangle. As in Figure 2, the medial loci are overlaid upon plots of values for the medialness function M and ridges are computed over an open subset wherein σ_o is large and the optimal scale surface is connected. Our computations indicate that convexity ridges for medialness computed from pullback metrics branch in much the same way as does the Blum medial axis. Our failure to detect branches of the medial axis for smaller aspect ratios is due to the nature of the kernel employed for these computations, a kernel that over-emphasizes long parallel sides in object boundaries and under-emphasizes corners.

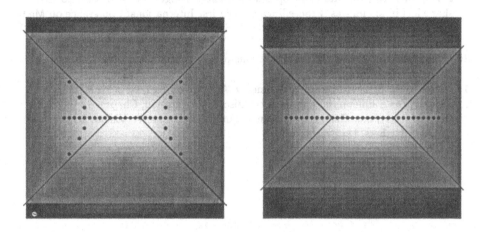

Fig. 3. The medial axes and ridges of medialness for rectangles having aspect ratio 0.85 and 0.70.

5 Acknowledgements

The author gratefully acknowledges Stephen Pizer and his research group for introducing him to medialness measurements and is pleased to acknowledge the work of undergraduate student James Tripp on this project.

References

1. Koenderink, J.: Scale in perspective. In Gaussian Scale Space Theory, J. Sporring, M. Nielsen, L. Florack, P. Johansen, eds., Kluwer Academic Press, Dordrecht, 1997.
2. Mason, B. J.: Clouds, Rain, and Rainmaking. Cambridge Univ Press, London, 1962.
3. Eberly, D.: Ridges in Image & Data Analysis. Kluwer Academic Press, Dordrecht, 1996.
4. Furst, J., Keller, R., Miller, J.,Pizer, S.: Image loci are ridges in geometric spaces. Scale-Space Theory in Computer Vision: Proceedings of First International Conference, Scale-Space '97, LNCS **1252** (1997) 176-187.

5. Pizer, S., Eberly, D., Morse, B., Fritsch, D.: Zoom-invariant figural shape: the mathematics of cores. Computer Vision and Image Understanding **69** (1998) 55–71.
6. Morse, B., Pizer, S., Puff, D., Gu, C.: Zoom-invariant vision of figural shape: effects on cores of image disturbances. Computer Vision and Image Understanding **69** (1998) 72–86.
7. Blum, H.: Biological shape and visual science (part I). J. Theoret. Biol. **38** (1973) 205–287.
8. Pizer, S., Burbeck, C., Coggins, J., Fritsch, D., Morse, B.: Object shape before boundary shape: scale-space medial axes. Journal of Mathematical Imaging and Vision **4** (1994) 303–313.
9. Furst, J., Pizer, S.: Marching optimal-parameter ridges: an algorithm to extract shape loci in 3D images. Proceedings of the First International Conference on Medical Image Computing and Computer-Assisted Intervention - MICCAI'98 (1998) 780–787.
10. Kobayashi, S., Nomizu, K.: Foundations of Differential Geometry, Volumes I and II. Wiley, New York, 1963.
11. O'Neill, B.: Semi-Riemannian Geometry. Academic Press, New York, 1983.
12. Eberly, D.: A differential approach to anisotropic diffusion, Chapter 14 in B.M. ter Haar Romeny, ed., Geometry-Driven Diffusion in Computer Vision, Kluwer Academic Publishers, Dordrecht, 1994.

The Maximal Scale Ridge

Incorporating scale into the ridge definition

Jason Miller[1], Jacob Furst[2]

[1] Truman State University
Division of Mathematics and Computer Science
Kirksville, Missouri, USA
millerj@truman.edu
[2] DePaul University
School of Computer Science, Telecommunications,
and Information Systems
Chicago, Illinois, USA
jfurst@cti.depaul.edu

Abstract. The maximal convexity ridge is not well suited for the analysis of medial functions or, it can be argued, for the analysis of any function that is created via convolution with a kernel based on the Gaussian. In its place one should use the maximal scale ridge, which takes scale's distinguished role into account. We present the local geometric structure of the maximal scale ridge of smooth and Gaussian blurred functions, a result that complements recent work on scale selection. We also discuss the subdimensional maxima property as it relates to the maximal scale ridge, and we prove that a generalized maximal parameter ridge has the subdimensional maxima property as well.

1 Introduction

One of the central tasks in the field of computer vision is the analysis of greyscale images with a view toward extracting geometric loci that are intrinsic to the scene. Such analysis includes, for example, edge detection [1], skeleton extraction (*e.g.*, via cores [5]), and ridge extraction [11] [4]. In [7], we, along with Pizer and Keller, take the position that one can think of the geometric loci in an image as the height ridges of some function. This function is derived from an image's pixel intensity function by means of convolution with kernels that may involve, in addition to the image's spatial variables, orientation and scale parameters. In [7] we also reported preliminary results [10] [13] on the local generic structure of maximal convexity ridges of pixel intensity functions [2] on $\mathbb{R}^3$, and their related relative critical sets. Though those results appeared unrelated to the material that preceeded them insofar as the maximal convexity ridge can not distinguish scale or orientation from any other function variable, those results are important to computer vision. They provide the standard against which the success of (maximal convexity) ridge extraction methods can be judged. It is in this same spirit that we present structure results for the maximal scale ridge, a ridge that takes scale's distinguished role into account [4], [5]. We report its generic local geometric structure for both the case of smooth functions and functions derived from a pixel intensity function $I : \mathbb{R}^2 \to \mathbb{R}$ via convolution with a particular medial kernel. We conclude the paper with a discussion of the subdimensional maxima property as it relates to ridge definitions that involve multiple parameters.

Recall that the (one dimensional) maximal convexity ridge of a C^2-function f defined on an open subset $U \subset \mathbb{R}^3$ is defined as follows. Let $\lambda_1(x) < \lambda_2(x) < \lambda_3(x)$ be the eigenvalues of the 3×3 Hessian matrix $H(f)(x)$, and let $v_1(x)$ and $v_2(x)$ be unit eigenvectors associated to the first two eigenvalues. The point $x \in U$ lies on the ridge if and only if $\nabla f \cdot v_i = 0$ for $i = 1, 2$ and $\lambda_2 < 0$ at x. These conditions are not enough to guarantee that $f(x)$ is a locally maximum value of f, but they are enough to guarantee that $f(x)$ is locally a maximum value of $f|W$, the restriction of f to the plane $W(x) = \text{span}(v_1(x), v_2(x))$ [7], [13], [3]. As discussed in [7], this geometric property characterizes what it means for x to be an abstract ridge point of f. We will follow Kalitzin [9] and call this the *subdimensional maximum* property.

As was noted in [7], the height ridge as defined in [7] need not have the subdimensional maxima property. Therefore, when we use this definition as a basis for the creation of a specialized ridge definition we must be careful to verify that the newly defined ridge has the subdimensional property. We will do so for the maximal scale ridge and, at the end of the paper, we show that under certain conditions multiparameter ridges have the subdimensional maxima property.

To motivate interest in a ridge definition that treats scale as a distinguished parameter, consider how one uses ridge theory to identify the shape skeleton of objects in a greyscale image. Let $I : \mathbb{R}^2 \to \mathbb{R}$ represent the pixel intensity function of a greyscale image, and let $K(\mathbf{x}, \sigma) = -\sigma^2 \Delta G(\mathbf{x}, \sigma)$ where $G(\mathbf{x}, \sigma)$ is the standard Gaussian kernel with standard deviation σ, which we call scale. The convolution $I * K$ is a C^∞ function called a medial function because the value $I * K(\mathbf{x}, \sigma)$ reflects how well the point $\mathbf{x}$ is in the center of a figure of width σ in the original image.

By means of example, see that in Fig. 1 we chose a point $\mathbf{x}$ in the center of a vertical bar. Of the three circles centered at $\mathbf{x}$, the middle circle seems to be the largest circle centered at $\mathbf{x}$ that sits within the bar. Its radius determines a scale σ_0 at which medialness at $\mathbf{x}$ will be locally maximal. Once we know the scale value at which medialness at $\mathbf{x}$ is locally maximal, we can analyze the spatial directions to determine the skeleton's tangent and normal directions at $\mathbf{x}$. In this example, the scale parameter and the spatial variables play vitally distinct roles. This compels us to develop a ridge definition in which the scale and spatial components are treated separately. More generally, insofar as scale-space based analysis uses filters built on the Gaussian, and scale parameterizes the blurring away of detail, any geometric image analysis in scale space ought to treat spatial and scale variables differently. In what follows, we define a variant of the maximal

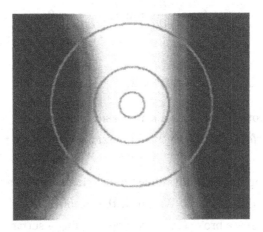

Fig. 1. The three circles represent scales at which medialness is measured. Medialness is highest at the scale represented by the middle circle because, of the three concentric circles, it fits most snugly *into* the bar.

convexity ridge called the *maximal scale ridge* that does just that. This ridge will be defined for a function of three variables, two spatial and one scale. The definition is closely related to the criteria Lindeberg uses for his method of automatic scale selection [11]. (This ridge definition can be used in any setting involving two spatial variables and one distinguished parameter. Moreover, it can be easily adapted to contexts where one is interested in minimal parameters values. For these reasons, one might choose to call the ridge under discussion the *optimal parameter ridge*.) We will observe that (1) the the maximal scale ridge is defined in terms of a maximal convexity ridge, and (2) this relationship does *not* imply that the two varieties of ridge have the same local generic structure. We shall observe that the ridge-valley-connector curves of these two are remarkably different. Reasons for the difference are explained by classical catastrophe theory. Finally, we shall prove that this new definition indeed gives us a ridge; every point in the locus is a subdimensional maxima in a well defined sense.

2   The Definition

Let $f(\mathbf{x}, \sigma)$ be a smooth differentiable function on U an open subset of $\mathbb{R}^2 \times \mathbb{R}_{++}$ scale space. The demand that ridge points $(\mathbf{x}, \sigma)$ be local maxima in scale gives the following necessary condition

$$\text{at } (\mathbf{x}, \sigma), \frac{\partial f}{\partial \sigma} = 0 \text{ and } \frac{\partial^2 f}{\partial \sigma^2} < 0. \tag{1}$$

Because the set

$$X = \{(\mathbf{x}, \sigma) \in \mathbb{R}^2 \times \mathbb{R}_{++} \mid \frac{\partial f}{\partial \sigma}(\mathbf{x}, \sigma) = 0\}. \tag{2}$$

is generically smooth, (1) defines a smooth surface $X_M \subset \mathbb{R}^2 \times \mathbb{R}_{++}$ called the *maximal scale surface*. Consequently, all maximal scale ridge points must lie in the surface X_M.

One of the computational advantages of defining a critical scale surface is the dimensional reduction it offers. We break the problem of defining a ridge in a three dimensional space broken into two steps: finding a surface in $\mathbb{R}^2 \times \mathbb{R}_{++}$ and then finding a ridge on the surface. The two problems together are simpler than the original problem. We know of three approaches that exploit this reduction in dimension to calculate ridges on X_M.

1. Calculate height ridges of $f|X_M$
2. Calculate height ridges using approximate derivatives calculated by selectively ignoring the change in scale on X_M
3. Calculate height ridges of f on coordinate patches mapping $\mathbb{R}^2 \times \{0\} \subset \mathbb{R}^2 \times \mathbb{R}_{++}$ to X_M

Eberly demonstrates how height ridges of $f|X_M$ can be computed using the intrinsic geometry of X_M [4]; however, even for the case of a surface in $\mathbb{R}^3$, this approach is computationally expensive and has never been implemented. Kalitzin [9] implements (2) using a maximal orientation surface (rather than a maximal scale surface) and reports good results for a single test case. This approach, however, disregards effects the geometry of X_M has on the derivative calculations. Fritsch uses approach (3) because it is both computationally tractable and it incorporates the geometry of X_M into the computation. The rest of this paper is devoted to examining the mathematics of (3) and what it tells us about the local geometric structure of the maximal convexity ridge.

Eberly described a mathematical approach one could use to extract the maximal scale ridges from an image. He showed that that maximal scale ridge can be computed using a parameterization of X_M from the spatial subspace $\mathbb{R}^2 \times \{0\}$ [4]. To be more precise, he used a coordinate patch $\phi : \mathbb{R}^2 \to X_M$ to define $g(\mathbf{x}) = f \circ \phi(\mathbf{x})$ and he claimed that $R \subset \mathbb{R}^2$ is the ridge set of $g(\mathbf{x}) = f|X_M$. Consequently, $\phi(R) \subset X_M$ is the maximal scale ridge of f. Fritsch used Eberly's mathematics to find the cores[1] of figures in portal images [5] and he did so with notable success, but some of what he saw bothered him. His extraction method relied on a ridge tracking algorithm, which works best when the ridge is a set of long unbroken curve segments. Given the figures in his images, he expected the cores to be exactly that. Contrary to his expectations, the maximal scale cores he extracted had a tendency to end abruptly (at points he certainly expected a shape skeleton to pass through smoothly). Moreover, after searching the vicinity of the core's endpoint he would find the endpoint of another core. If one ignored the gap between the core segments, this new core segment essentially picked up where the previous segment left off. Fritsch knew of the structure classification for maximal convexity ridges and cores in $\mathbb{R}^2$ and $\mathbb{R}^3$ [3],[13], and found nothing in that context that could explain this consistent aberrant structure. Going

---

[1] In general, cores are ridges of functions created by filtering greyscale images for medialness. Fritsch's cores were maximal scale ridges of medialness. See [5].

back to [4] one sees that Eberly does not address the issue of the existence of the parameterizations he needs to establish his theory. This observation led us to an explanation of the "gap" phenomena Fritsch observed.

At each point $(\mathbf{x}, \sigma)$ on the maximal scale ridge, ∇f is necessarily orthogonal to a subspace of the tangent space $T_{(\mathbf{x}, \sigma)} X_M$ on which f has a local maxima at $(\mathbf{x}, \sigma)$. Eberly showed that this subspace can be identified using a local parameterization $\phi : U \to \mathbb{R}^2 \times \mathbb{R}_{++}$ where U is an open subset of the spatial subspace $\mathbb{R}^2 \times \{0\}$. But such a parameterization is not guaranteed to exist.

Points at which such a local parameterization exists are characterized as those points at which the projection $\pi : X \to \mathbb{R}^2$ is a submersion. An elementary result from Thom's catastrophe theory implies that the surface X contains a subset of codimesion 1 on which π fails to be a submersion. This curve on X_M is called the fold curve, and the maximal scale ridge abruptly ends when the two intersect. (See Figure 2.) We must note three things at this point. First, at points away from the fold, Eberly's results hold and the maximal scale ridge in $\mathbb{R}^2 \times \mathbb{R}_{++}$ is diffeomorphic to the maximal convexity ridge in $\mathbb{R}^2$ (see Theorem 5, properties 1-3).

Theorem 1 (Eberly). *Suppose at $(\mathbf{x}, \sigma) \in X$ there is a local para-metrization $\phi : U \to \mathbb{R}^2 \times \mathbb{R}_{++}$ of X with $\mathbf{x} \in U \subset \mathbb{R}^2$. The point $(\mathbf{x}, \sigma)$ is a maximal scale ridge point of f if and only if the point x is a maximal convexity ridge point of $f \circ \phi : U \to \mathbb{R}_{++}$.*

Second, the fold is characterized as the set of point $(\mathbf{x}, \sigma)$ at which $\frac{\partial^2 f}{\partial \sigma^2}$ vanishes [12]. This is exactly the boundary of X_M, on which the maximal scale ridge is undefined. Third, although Damon showed how maximal convexity ridges when viewed as relative critical sets can be continued as connector curves, this fold singularity means we cannot call on these results to continue the maximal scale ridge.

Note 2. It is a straightforward exercise to verify that those points $(\mathbf{x}, \sigma)$ that are maximal scale ridge points according to Theorem 1 are subdimensional maxima with respect to the plane $\text{span}(\frac{\partial}{\partial \sigma}, d\phi(\mathbf{v}))$, Where $\mathbf{v}$ is an vector for the most negative eigenvector of $H(f \circ \phi)$. In the last section of the paper we will establish the subdimensional maxima property for an analogously defined multiparameter ridge.

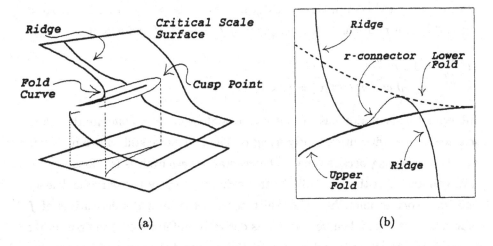

(a)   (b)

Fig. 2. Notice the geometry at the fold curve of the critical scale surface pictured in the Fig.2a. If there were a maximal scale ridge on X, it can be expected to intersect the fold curve and come to an end. This is the behavior Fritsch observed which tracking the ridge. Fig 2b. shows how the ridge can be continued using a connector curve (see Definition 6) which may lead to a nearby ridge segment. This illustrates why Fritsch saw small gaps in his maximal scale ridges.

To explain the phenomena Fritsch observed, and to show how the ridge can be continued as a connector curve, the first author used mathematical machinery Eberly employed to prove Theorem 1 and techniques used to establish properties of relative critical sets in [13].

One of Eberly's innovations in the proof of Theorem 1 was his use of a 3×3 generalized eigensystem.

Definition 3. *The generalized eigensystem of 3×3 matrices M and N consists of vectors $\mathbf{v} \in \mathbb{R}^3 \setminus \{0\}$ and scalars $\gamma \in \mathbb{R}$ that satisfy the matrix equation $M\mathbf{v} = \gamma N\mathbf{v}$.*

Eberly used $M = H(f)$ and $N = P$, the matrix representation of π. Let $\gamma_1 \leq \gamma_2$ be the two generalized eigenvalues of $H(f)$ [13] and let $\mathbf{v}_1$ and $\mathbf{v}_2$ be corresponding unit generalized eigenvectors. With this data we can give an alternate definition for the maximal scale ridge.

Definition 4 (Maximal Scale Ridge). *Let* $U \subset \mathbb{R}^2 \times \mathbb{R}_{++}$ *be open. A point* $(\mathbf{x}, \sigma) \in U$ *is a maximal scale ridge point of* $f : U \to \mathbb{R}$ *if and only if at* $(\mathbf{x}, \sigma)$,

1. $\dfrac{\partial f}{\partial \sigma} = 0$ *and* $\dfrac{\partial^2 f}{\partial \sigma^2} < 0$, *and*
2. $\nabla f \cdot \mathbf{v}_1 = 0$ *and* $\mathbf{v}_1^t H(f) \mathbf{v}_1 = \gamma_1 < 0$.

Adopting this definition has the advantage of allowing us to compute the maximal scale ridge without explicitly using ϕ. The fold curve still causes problems in this new setting because one of the generalized eigenvalues is unbounded in a neighborhood of the fold [13]. At this point we employ Catastrophe Theory and its theory of unfoldings [12] which tells us the form the derivatives of f may take near the fold curve. Using this derivative information, the first author determined the asymptotic behavior of the unbounded generalized eigenvalue and used that to define preridge maps [3] and relative critical surfaces that allowed us to complete Eberly's geometric description of the maximal scale ridge in $\mathbb{R}^2 \times \mathbb{R}_{++}$ [13].

By using the generalized eigensystem and techniques used to establish the generic structure of relative critical sets , the first author proved that the generic structure of the maximal scale ridge in $\mathbb{R}^2 \times \mathbb{R}_{++}$ differs from that of the maximal convexity ridge in $\mathbb{R}^2$ only insofar as the maximal scale ridge comes to an end at the singularities of $\pi | X$.

3   The Properties

By using elements of Eberly's proof of Theorem 1, methods used in the analysis of relative critical sets, and Catastrophe Theory, we proved the following structure theorem for the maximal scale ridge of smooth functions on $U \subset \mathbb{R}^2 \times \mathbb{R}_{++}$ [13].

Theorem 5. *For* $U \subset \mathbb{R}^3$, *there is a residual set of* $f \in C^\infty(U)$ *whose maximal scale ridges have the following properties:*

1. *The ridge is a finite collection of smooth, embedded one dimensional submanifolds which may have boundary. In particular, they neither cross nor branch.*
2. *The ridge passes smoothly through critical points of* f, *but such critical points are Morse critical points of* f *with Hessian having distinct, nonzero eigenvalues.*

3. Components of the ridge have a boundary point where $\gamma_1 = 0$ or $\gamma_1 = \gamma_2$.

4. In addition, components of the ridge can have a boundary point at fold singularities of $\pi|X$.

If $C \subset U$ is compact, the set of $f \in C^\infty(U)$ that exhibit these properties on C is open and dense.

Properties (1) through (3) are analogous to those of the maximal scale ridge in $\mathbb{R}^2$, and property (4) is caused by the fold curve. It should be noted that these results continue to hold for maximal scale ridges of medial functions on $\mathbb{R}^2 \times \mathbb{R}_{++}$ generated as the convolution of a greyscale pixel intensity function $I : \mathbb{R}^2 \to \mathbb{R}$ with the medial kernel $-\sigma^2 \Delta G(\mathbf{x}, \sigma)$ [13].

Furthermore, the techniques used to Theorem 5 lead to a natural definition of relative critical sets in $\mathbb{R}^2 \times \mathbb{R}_{++}$ that distinguish the role of scale. In particular, we obtain a ridge-valley-connector set that facilitates the use of ridge tracking methods for extracting cores from two dimensional greyscale images.

Definition 6. *Let $(\mathbf{x}, \sigma) \in X$ and let $\gamma_1 \le \gamma_2$ be the generalized eigenvalues of $H(f)$, and $\mathbf{v}_1$ and $\mathbf{v}_2$ their generalized eigenvectors. Then $(\mathbf{x}, \sigma)$ is a*

1. r-connector point of f if at $(\mathbf{x}, \sigma)$ $\nabla f \cdot \mathbf{v}_1 = 0$ and $\gamma_1 > 0$
2. valley point of f if, at $(\mathbf{x}, \sigma)$, $\nabla f \cdot \mathbf{v}_2 = 0$, $\frac{\partial^2 f}{\partial \sigma^2} > 0$ and $\gamma_2 > 0$,
3. v-connector point of f if at $(\mathbf{x}, \sigma)$ $\nabla f \cdot \mathbf{v}_2 = 0$ and $\gamma_2 < 0$,

Notice that when the maximal scale ridge hits the fold curve it is continued by a r-connector curve (see Fig. 2). This curve can be followed (possibly through some transitions to other connector curves) to an intersection with another fold curve at which point the curve becomes a maximal scale ridge curve again.

4 Generalized Optimal Parameter Ridges

The previous sections of this paper have dealt with the maximal scale surface in great detail. However, there are instances in which we may want to deal with other parameters. Kalitzin has already experimented with optimal orientation, as did Canny in his definition of edges. We motivated distinguishing scale in the case of medialness measurements and, more generally, Gaussian derivative measurements. However, Gaussian filters of two or more dimensions may have more than one scale component. Further, the second author [6] has described medialness measurements that use both scale and orientation. In all cases described, the distinguished role of orientation and scale leads naturally to optimal parameter ridges. To define optimal parameter ridges in arbitrary spaces, let $\mathbb{R}^n$ be a Euclidean space (typically the domain of a greyscale image) and let $\mathbb{R}^p$ be the domain of the parameters.

Let $V \subset \mathbb{R}^n \times \mathbb{R}^p$ be open and let $f : V \to \mathbb{R}$ be smooth. Define X_M to be the set of $(\mathbf{x}, \sigma) \in V$ where

$$\frac{\partial f}{\partial \sigma_i} = 0 \text{ and } \left(\frac{\partial^2 f}{\partial \sigma_i \partial \sigma_j} \right)_{1 \leq i,j \leq p} \text{ is negative definite}$$

By the Generalized Maximal Rank theorem ([8], Theorem 4.4) and results in [13] X_M is generically (with respect to the space of all smooth functions on V) a smooth manifold called the *maximal parameter* manifold.

Definition 7. *Suppose at* $(\mathbf{x}, \sigma)$ *there is a local parameterization* $\phi : U \to \mathbb{R}^n \times \mathbb{R}^p$ *of* X_M *with* $U \subset \mathbb{R}^n \times \{0\}$. *The point* $(\mathbf{x}, \sigma)$ *is a maximal parameter ridge point of* f *if and only if the point* $\mathbf{x}$ *is a maximal convexity ridge point of* $f \circ \phi$.

A special case of this definition is the maximal scale ridge, which enjoys the subdimensional maxima property. It is not clear, however, that the maximal parameter ridge has this property. Moreover, there are instances (see [7]) where maximal parameter values determine geometrically important spatial subspaces that are not necessarily eigenspaces of the Hessian of $f \circ \phi$. When this is the case, the ridge that is natural in that context is not compatible with Definition 7. However we choose to define this new class of ridge, the definition must imply that the ridge has the subdimensional maxima property. What follows is a definition that allows for such distinguished spatial subspaces and a proof that the ridges so definition do in fact enjoy the subdimensional maxima property.

Let $U' \subset \mathbb{R}^n$ be open, $U = U' \times \mathbb{R}^p$, and $f : U \to \mathbb{R}$ be smooth. Define X_M the maximal parameter manifold as above. Let $(\mathbf{x}, \sigma) \in X_M$ at which a local parameterization ϕ of X_M from U' exists. Finally, our idea for ridge definition must specify a subspace $W(\mathbf{x}) \subset \mathbb{R}^n$ (e.g.,in the case of the maximal scale ridge $W(\mathbf{x})$ was a one dimensional eigenspace of $H(f \circ \phi)$).

Definition 8. *The point* $(\mathbf{x}, \sigma)$ *is a generalized maximal parameter ridge point of* f *with respect to* $W(\mathbf{x})$ *if and only if* $f \circ \phi$ *is has the subdimensional maxima property on* $W(x)$.

For $(\mathbf{x}, \sigma)$ to be a true ridge point, f must have the subdimensional maxima property on $W(\mathbf{x}) \times \mathbb{R}^p$. It is not immediately clear from Definition 8 that this is the case. We conclude this paper with its proof.

Theorem 9. *Every point on the generalized maximal parameter ridge of f as defined above is a subdimensional maxima of f with respect to the subspace $W(\mathbf{x}) \times \mathbb{R}^p$.*

Proof. Let $H(f|(W \times \mathbb{R}^p))$ be defined as follows:

$$\begin{pmatrix} H_{\mathbf{w}} & D \\ D & H_{\mathbf{p}} \end{pmatrix} = \begin{pmatrix} \left(\dfrac{\partial^2 f}{\partial w_i \partial w_j}\right) & \left(\dfrac{\partial^2 f}{\partial w_i \partial p_j}\right) \\ \left(\dfrac{\partial^2 f}{\partial p_i \partial w_j}\right) & \left(\dfrac{\partial^2 f}{\partial p_i \partial p_j}\right) \end{pmatrix} \tag{3}$$

Because $\nabla(f|\mathbb{R}^p)$ vanishes on X_M, and because $\nabla((f \circ \phi)|W)$ is defined to vanish on optimal parameter ridge points, $\nabla(f|(W \times \mathbb{R}^p))$ also vanishes on optimal parameter ridge points.

Let w be defined as $\alpha u + \beta v$, $u \in W$ and $v \in \mathbb{R}^p$. Then

$$w^t H(f|(W \times \mathbb{R}^n))w = \alpha u^t H_w \alpha u + \alpha u^t D\beta v + \beta v^t D\alpha u + \beta v^t H_p \beta v$$

And because $H((f \circ \phi)|W)$ is negative definite,

$$w^t H(f|(W \times \mathbb{R}^n))w < \alpha u^t (H_w - H((f \circ \phi)|W))\alpha u + \\ \alpha u^t D\beta v + \beta v^t D\alpha u + \beta v^t H_p \beta v$$

The definition of $H((f \circ \phi)|W)$ allows the following substitution:

$$w^t H(f|(W \times \mathbb{R}^n))w < \alpha u^t D H_p D\alpha u + \\ \alpha u^t D\beta v + \beta v^t D\alpha u + \beta v^t H_p \beta v$$

Finally, the introduction of $H_p^{-1} H_p$ and an algebraic rearrangement of terms yields

$$w^t H(f|(W \times \mathbb{R}^n))w < (\alpha u^t D + \beta v^t H_p)^t H_p^{-1}(\alpha u^t D + \beta v^t H_p)$$

and, since H_p^{-1} is negative definite everywhere on X_M, $H(f|(W \times \mathbb{R}^p))$ is also negative definite. Therefore, $f|(W \times \mathbb{R}^n)$ is locally maximal at $(\mathbf{x}, \sigma)$. This completes the proof.

References

1. J Canny. A computational approach to edge detection. *IEEE PAMI*, 8(6):679–698, 1987.

2. J. Damon. Singularities with scale threshold and discrete functions exhibiting generic properties. In *Proc. Int. Workshop on Real and Complex Singularities*, 1996.

3. J. Damon. Generic structure of two dimensional images under Gaussian blurring. *SIAM J. Appl. Math.*, 59(1):97–138, 1998.

4. D. Eberly. *Ridges in Image and Data Analysis*, volume 7 of *Series Comp. Imaging and Vision*. Kluwer, 1996.

5. Fritsch, D., Eberly, D., Pizer, S., and McAuliffe, M. Stimulated cores and their application in medical imaging. Preprint, 1998.

6. Jacob Furst. *Height Ridges of Oriented Medialness*. PhD thesis, Univ. of North Carolina, 1999.

7. Furst, J., Keller, R., Miller, J., and Pizer, S. Image loci are ridges in geometric spaces. In *Scale Space Theory in Computer Vision: Proceedings of the First International Conference on, Scale Space '97*, number 1252 in Springer Lecture Notes in Comp. Sci., pages 176–187, 1997.

8. Golubitsky, M. and Guillemin, V. *Stable Mappings and Their Singularities*. Number 14 in GTM. Springer-Verlag, 1973.

9. Kalitzin, S., Staal, J., ter Haar Romeny, B., and Viergever, M. Frame-relative critical point sets in image analysis. Image Sciences Institute, Utrecht University.

10. R. Keller. *Generic Transitions of Relative Critical Sets in Parametrized Families with Applications to Image Analysis*. PhD thesis, Univ, of North Carolina, 1998.

11. Tony Lindeberg. Edge detection and ridge detection with automatic scale selection. *Int. J. of Computer Vision*, 30(2):117–156, 1998.

12. J. Martinet. *Singularities of Smooth Functions and Maps*. Number 58 in London Math. Soc. Lec. Notes. Cambridge Univ. Press, 1982.

13. J Miller. *Relative Critical Sets in $\mathbb{R}^n$ and Applications to Image Analysis*. PhD thesis, University of North Carolina, 1998.

Detection of Critical Structures in Scale Space

Joes Staal, Stiliyan Kalitzin, Bart ter Haar Romeny, and Max Viergever

Image Sciences Institute
University Hospital Utrecht, E01.334
Heidelberglaan 100
3584 CX Utrecht
The Netherlands
{joes,stiliyan,bart,max}@isi.uu.nl

Abstract. In this paper we investigate scale space based structural grouping in images. Our strategy is to detect (relative) critical point sets in scale space, which we consider as an extended image representation. In this way the multi-scale behavior of the original image structures is taken into account and automatic scale space grouping and scale selection is possible. We review a constructive and efficient topologically based method to detect the (relative) critical points. The method is presented for arbitrary dimensions. Relative critical point sets in a Hessian vector frame provide us with a generalization of height ridges. Automatic scale selection is accomplished by a proper reparameterization of the scale axis. As the relative critical sets are in general connected submanifolds, it provides a robust method for perceptual grouping with only local measurements.

Key words: deep structure, feature detection, scale selection, perceptual grouping.

1   Introduction

The goal in this paper is to perform scale space based structural grouping in images. We accomplish this by detection of the maximal response in scale space of the desired image structures. Our strategy is to detect (relative) critical point sets in scale space. Rather than to investigate the evolution of the critical sets of the original D-dimensional image across scale, we consider the scale space as an extended image representation and detect the critical sets in this $D + 1$-dimensional image. In this way the multi-scale behavior of the original image structures is taken into account and automatic scale space grouping and scale selection is possible.

Critical points and relative critical point sets play an essential role in uncommitted image analysis as described in [11–13]. These topological structures are studied in the context of multi-scale image analysis in [6, 15, 16]. They form a topological "back-bone" on which the image structures are mounted.

We introduce a non-perturbative method for detecting critical and relative critical points. The method is based on computing a surface integral of a functional of the gradient vector on the border of a closed neighborhood around every image point [8,9]. This integral evaluates to zero for regular image points and to an integer number for critical points. The value and sign of this number discriminates between the different critical points.

The main advantage of our method for localizing critical points lies in its explicit and constructive nature. To illustrate this, note that in finding the zero crossings of a real function, the only sensible task would be to find the intervals where the function changes sign. The size of these intervals is the precision with which we are searching for the zero crossings. Our topological construction is in many aspects analogous to this generic example. The size of the neighborhood (the closed surface) around the test image point is the spatial precision with which we want to localize the critical point. Therefore our method is a natural generalization of interval mathematics to higher dimensional signals.

Another advantage of the method is its non-perturbative nature. To compute the integrals, we do not need to know the values of the gradient or higher order derivatives *in* the point, but only *around* the given image location as opposed to [2,3,5,6,13,16].

In the paper we first give a review on the detection of critical points and relative critical point sets as introduced by [10]. The method is based on the computation of homotopy class numbers. We show that detecting relative critical point sets in a Hessian frame provides us with a generalization of height ridges. We turn to the detection of critical point sets in scale space in Sect. 3. Because the properties of Gaussian scale spaces prohibit automatic scale selection, we deform the scale space with a form factor. We apply the method in Sect. 4 for the grouping and detection of elongated structures at a scale of maximum response in some synthetical examples and in a medical fundus reflection image of the eye. In the last section we discuss some practical and conceptual issues concerning our approach.

2 Critical Points and Relative Critical Points

Critical points are those points in an image at which the gradient vanishes, i.e. extrema and (generalized) saddle points. We define a relative critical point as a critical point in a subdimensional neighborhood around an image pixel. The neighborhood can be defined in intrinsically or extrinsically subdimensional vector frames. In this section we show how to detect critical points in arbitrary dimensions. The detection of the relative critical points is then straightforward, because they are critical points themselves in a subdimensional vector frame.

For the detection of the critical points we use the topological homotopy class numbers as introduced by [7,10]. This number reflects the behavior of the image gradient vector in a close neighborhood of an image point. For regular points it equals zero, whereas for critical points it has an integer value. In the simplest, one-dimensional, case it is defined as half the difference of the sign of the signal's derivative taken from the right side and the left side of the point. For regular points the topological number equals zero, for local maxima -1 and for local minima $+1$.

Extension to higher dimensions can be done (borrowing from homotopy theory) by computing an $D-1$-dimensional form on a $D-1$-dimensional hypersurface [10]. We will only give the main outline without elaborating on the theory of homotopy classes, see [14] for a detailed discussion on homotopy classes. For the introduction of homotopy class numbers in image analysis we refer to [10].

2.1 Review on Critical Point Detection

The main construction lies in the definition of a topological quantity ν which describes the behavior of the image gradient vector around a point P of the image. Suppose V_P is a D-dimensional neighborhood around P which does not contain any critical points except possibly P and let ∂V_P be the $D-1$-dimensional closed oriented hypersurface which is the boundary of V_P. Because there are no critical points at the boundary of V_P, we can define the normalized gradient vector field of the image L at ∂V_P

$$\xi_i = \frac{L_i}{\sqrt{L_j L_j}} \qquad i = 1, \ldots, D \tag{1}$$

$$L_i = \partial_i L \ .$$

Throughout the paper a sum over all repeated indices is assumed. Now we give the operational definition of the topological quantity ν. The quantity ν is a surface integral of a $D-1$ form over ∂V_P. The form Φ is defined as, see [10],

$$\Phi = \xi_{i_1} \, d\xi_{i_2} \wedge \cdots \wedge d\xi_{i_D} \, \varepsilon^{i_1 \cdots i_D} \ , \tag{2}$$

where $\varepsilon^{i_1 \cdots i_D}$ is the Levi-Civita tensor of order D

$$\varepsilon^{i_1 \cdots i_k \cdots i_l \cdots i_D} = \begin{cases} -\varepsilon^{i_1 \cdots i_l \cdots i_k \cdots i_D} & \text{for any } l \neq k \\ 0 & \text{for } l = k \end{cases}, \tag{3}$$

$$\varepsilon^{12 \cdots D} = 1 \ . \tag{4}$$

The topological integer number ν is now given as the natural integral of the form Φ over ∂V_P

$$\nu = \frac{1}{A_D} \oint_{Q \in \partial V_P} \Phi(Q) \ . \tag{5}$$

The factor A_D is the area of a D-dimensional hypersphere of radius 1. The form (2) has the important property that it is a closed form [10], i.e. the total differential vanishes

$$d\Phi = 0 \ . \tag{6}$$

This property is essential for the applications of the topological quantity (5). If W is a region where the image has no singularities, then the form Φ is defined for the entire region and we can apply the generalized Stokes theorem [1,4]

$$\oint_{\partial W} \Phi = \int_W d\Phi = 0 \ , \tag{7}$$

because of (6). This has the important implication that the number ν of (5) is zero at those points where L is regular. Furthermore, ν is invariant under smooth deformations of the oriented hypersurface ∂W as long as no singularities are crossing the boundary. This property justifies the term "topological" assigned to ν, since it depends on the properties of the image at the point P and not on the surface ∂W around P. The number ν depends only on the number and type of singularities surrounded by ∂W. Therefore (5) defines the topological number ν for the image point P, as long as the singularities are isolated. The last is always true for generic images [10]. We can compute (5) for every location in the image, obtaining an integer scalar density field $\nu(x_1, \ldots, x_D)$ that represents the distribution of the critical points of the image L.

2.2 Detecting Critical Points in 1, 2 and 3 Dimensions

As we discussed above, in the one-dimensional case the number ν reduces to

$$\nu(x) = \frac{1}{2}\left(\xi_x(b) - \xi_x(a)\right) = \frac{1}{2}\left(\mathrm{sign}(L_x)_b - \mathrm{sign}(L_x)_a\right), \quad \text{for } a < x < b, \quad (8)$$

showing that ν is -1 for maxima, $+1$ for minima and 0 for regular points.

In two dimensions, the form Φ becomes

$$\Phi = \xi_x d\xi_y - \xi_y d\xi_x, \tag{9}$$

which is just the angle between the normalized gradients in two neighboring points. Equation (5) becomes a closed contour integral which integrates this angle and we find the winding number associated with this contour. Therefore, $\nu(x, y)$ equals $+1$ in maxima and minima, -1 in non-degenerate saddle points, and 0 in regular points. For degenerate saddle points, or so-called monkey saddles, ν is $-n+1$ where n is the number of ridges or valleys converging to the point.

In three dimensions the form becomes

$$\Phi = \xi_i d\xi_j \wedge d\xi_k \varepsilon^{ijk} = \xi_i \partial_l \xi_j \partial_m \xi_k dx^l \wedge dx^m \varepsilon^{ijk}, \tag{10}$$

where we used $d\xi_i = \partial_j \xi_i dx^j$. In the appendix we give the form in Cartesian coordinates for a surface at which z is constant. It is possible to give a geometrical interpretation in three dimensions as in one and two dimensions. The form in (10) is the solid angle determined by normalized gradients in three neighboring points. Integrating this solid angle over a closed surface around an image points defines the number ν. It is 1 for minima and one type of saddle points, -1 for maxima and another type of saddle points and 0 for regular points. The discussion on the saddle points is deferred to Sect. 2.4.

2.3 Detecting Relative Critical Points

For detecting relative critical points we project the image gradient vector to a local subdimensional vector frame. Let $h_\alpha^i(x)$ be a local subdimensional vector frame of dimension $D_{CP} \leq D$. Roman indices run from 1 to D, Greek indices from 1 to D_{CP}. The gradient in this frame is the projection of L_i to it

$$L_\alpha(x) = h_\alpha^i(x)L_i(x), \quad i = 1,\ldots,D \quad \alpha = 1,\ldots,D_{CP} . \tag{11}$$

For the detection of the relative critical points we use (5) and (2) but with the projected — normalized — gradient vector ξ_α, D_{CP} replacing D and Greek indices replacing Roman ones.

One can show that relative critical points, detected in a frame of subdimension D_{CP}, belong to a set which is locally isomorphic to a linear space of dimension $C_{CP} = D - D_{CP}$. A proof can be found in [8,9]. Note that C_{CP} is the codimension of the dimension in which the relative critical point is detected.

If, e.g. in three dimensions, $D_{CP} = 1$ the local vector frame is of dimension 1 and detection of the critical points reduces to (8), taking half the difference of sign of the gradient in the direction of h_1^i. The critical points form a manifold of dimension 2, i.e. a surface. For $D_{CP} = 2$, we compute the winding number (9) in the plane spanned by h_1^i and h_2^i. These winding numbers form manifolds of dimension 1, which are strings. For $D_{CP} = 3$ we obtain (10), i.e. (5) in a full D-dimensional neighborhood of the test point. In this case the manifold reduces to a point.

2.4 Detecting Relative Critical Sets in a Hessian Frame

So far we have made no choice for the vector frame in which to detect the relative critical sets. In this section we take frames formed by eigenvectors $h^i(x)$ of the local Hessian field $H_{ij}(x) = \partial_i\partial_j L(x)$. The eigenvectors of the Hessian are aligned with the principal directions in the image and the eigenvalues λ_i measure the local curvature[1]. From now on we assume that the eigenvectors are labeled in decreasing order of the magnitude of the curvature, i.e. $|\lambda_1| > \cdots > |\lambda_D|$. We take as subdimensional frames the first D_{CP} eigenvectors of the Hessian field. With this choice we can interpret the relative critical sets as a generalization of height ridges. In fact, if there are m_+ positive and m_- negative eigenvalues, we define a topological ridge set $R^{m_+,m_-}(L)$ of codimension $C_{CP} = m_+ + m_-$ as a relative critical set associated with the first D_{CP} eigenvectors corresponding to the largest absolute eigenvalues of the Hessian field. We exclude the points at which the Hessian is degenerate. The obtained ridge set contains only those points at which there are exactly m_+ positive and m_- negative eigenvalues. Note that there is a close relationship between our ridge set definition and the one by Damon [2]. In [2] the eigenvalues are ordered by their signed value and the sets $R^{m_+,0}$ and R^{0,m_-} coincide for both definitions. For mixed signatures the two definitions will delineate different topological sets.

The number and signs of the eigenvalues put a natural label on the ridge sets. If all D_{CP} eigenvalues are negative we obtain a height ridge whereas for all eigenvalues positive we get a valley. In the general case where both $m_+ \neq 0$

---

[1] These curvatures are to be distinguished from the isophote curvature.

and $m_- \neq 0$ we can speak of "saddle" ridges. The definition extends to the case $D_{\mathrm{CP}} = D$ when the ridge is of dimension zero. If all D eigenvalues are negative we are dealing with a maximum and if they are all positive with a minimum. For mixed numbers of signs we get saddle points of different signature.

In the three-dimensional case, as discussed at the end of Sect. 2.2, we have four different critical points, which using (10) and (5) can only be divided in two groups. With the use of the ridge sets R^{m_+,m_-} we can differentiate between all four signatures. This shows clearly that the choice of the Hessian field allows in the form of the ridge sets R^{m_+,m_-} for a richer description of the relative critical sets than (5) does. In Table 1 we give an overview of all relative critical sets which can be detected in three dimensions using the Hessian frame.

The topological ridge sets have a few other properties we like to discuss. First, as a direct consequence of their definition we can infer the following inclusion relation

$$R^{m_+,m_-} \subset R^{m'_+,m'_-} \quad \text{for any } m_+ \geq m'_+ \text{ and } m_- \geq m'_- . \tag{12}$$

This relation shows that ridge sets can contain lower dimensional ridges as subsets. For example, a maximum can be included in a positive string or a positive surface. In Sect. 4 this property will show to be important in the detection of elongated structures at a scale of maximum response while establishing a link to the finest scale simultaneously.

As a second property, we like to remark that one can prove that topological ridge sets are locally orthogonal to the Hessian vector frame $h^i_\alpha(x)$, see [8].

Table 1. Classification of the relative critical sets that can be detected in three dimensions using a Hessian frame. The value of $m_+ + m_-$ determines the codimension of the detected set. The cases in which $m_+ + m_- > D$ are marked with a '$-$'. There are two types of saddle points which can be found.

m_- \ m_+	0	1	2	3
0	regular	negative surface	negative string	minimum
1	positive surface	saddle string	saddle point (1)	$-$
2	positive string	saddle point (2)	$-$	$-$
3	maximum	$-$	$-$	$-$

3 Relative Critical Sets in Scale Space

In Sect. 2 we have shown how to detect relative critical sets for images of arbitrary dimensions. Our aim here is to detect objects and structures in scale space at a scale of maximum response. In this section we will focus on the detection of relative critical sets in linear Gaussian scale spaces of two-dimensional images. Note that, like [16], we look for the critical sets in scale space and not for the evolution across scale of the critical sets of the image itself [13]. Therefore we will regard the scale space of a two-dimensional image $L(x, y)$ as a three-dimensional entity, i.e. an image which depends on the three coordinates (x, y, σ)

$$L(x, y, \sigma) = \frac{1}{2\pi\sigma^2} \iint L(x', y') \exp\left(-\frac{(x-x')^2 + (y-y')^2}{2\sigma^2}\right) dx' dy' \ . \quad (13)$$

In doing so, we must take into account that in its present form (13) Gaussian scale space is not suited for the grouping of image structures by detecting critical sets. For the detection of an elongated structure at its scale of maximum response, e.g., the strings of Table 1 seem the obvious choice. However, the sets that can be found are restricted by the properties of the Gaussian filters. For example, it is well known that there are no local extrema in scale space. Indeed, if $L_x = L_y = 0$ and if H_{xx} and H_{yy} are of the same sign, which is required for an extremum, we always have for non-umbilic points that $\partial_\sigma L = \sigma(H_{xx} + H_{yy}) \neq 0$.

Extremal points can still be detected in scale space if we modify the Gaussian kernels by multiplying them with a monotonically increasing form factor $\phi(\sigma)$ to obtain a deformed scale space of the image

$$L(x, \sigma) \rightarrow \phi(\sigma) L(x, \sigma) = \tilde{L}(x, \sigma) \ . \quad (14)$$

The factor ϕ carries the essential information of the desired model structures we want to localize in the scale space. Note that the locations of the critical points ($L_i = 0$, $i \in \{x, y\}$) and therefore the locations of the catastrophes do not change. For appropriate choices of the form factor ϕ it will be possible to make $\tilde{L}_\sigma$ equal to zero and to find extrema in the deformed image.

As an example, let us take in a D-dimensional image a C_{CP}-dimensional Gaussian ridge which is aligned with the first $D_{\mathrm{CP}} = D - C_{\mathrm{CP}}$ coordinate axes

$$L(x, 0) = \left(\sqrt{2\pi\sigma_0^2}\right)^{-D_{\mathrm{CP}}} \exp\left(-\frac{x_\alpha x^\alpha}{2\sigma_0^2}\right) \quad \alpha = 1, \ldots, D_{\mathrm{CP}} \ . \quad (15)$$

The scale space representation of (15) reads,

$$L(x, \sigma) = \left(\sqrt{2\pi(\sigma^2 + \sigma_0^2)}\right)^{-D_{\mathrm{CP}}} \exp\left(-\frac{x_\alpha x^\alpha}{2(\sigma^2 + \sigma_0^2)}\right) \ . \quad (16)$$

If we take the form factor $\phi(\sigma) = \sigma^\gamma$, similar to [13], the derivatives $\tilde{L}_{x_\alpha}$ and $\tilde{L}_\sigma$ are zero for

$$x_\alpha = 0 \quad \text{and} \quad \sigma = \sqrt{\frac{\gamma}{D_{\mathrm{CP}} - \gamma}} \sigma_0 \ , \quad (17)$$

which defines a C_{CP}-dimensional surface in scale space. Note that D refers here to the image dimensions. The scale space has a dimension of $D + 1$. Equation (17) shows that only for γ in the range $0 < \gamma < D_{\mathrm{CP}}$ an extremum in the scale direction can be generated. For $\gamma \downarrow 0$ the extremum in the scale direction goes to zero whereas for $\gamma \uparrow D_{\mathrm{CP}}$ the extremum moves to infinity.

In general, the valid range for $\gamma > 0$ will be determined by the profile of the ridge and a choice of γ which is close to zero seems reasonable.

4 Examples

In this section we give several examples of the constructions made in the previous sections. Our main focus is on detection of elongated structures at a scale of maximum response with respect to a form factor ϕ. But we first show the difference between the non-deformed (13) and a deformed (14) scale space of an anisotropic Gaussian, $L(x,y) = (2\pi\sigma_x\sigma_y)^{-1}\exp(-(x/\sqrt{2}\sigma_x)^2 - (y/\sqrt{2}\sigma_y)^2)$, which we regard as a two-dimensional elongated, ridge like, structure. For both scale spaces we detect all detectable sets. Figure 1 shows in the left frame the image, with $\sigma_x = 2.0$ and $\sigma_y = 30.0$ pixels, in the middle frame the detected sets of the non-deformed scale space and in the right frame the detected sets of the deformed scale space. At the bottom of the boxes we have shown the left frame again. The light grey surface in the middle and left frame is the ridge set $R^{0,1}$, i.e. $m_+ = 0$ and $m_- = 1$. The dark grey string in the middle frame is the ridge set $R^{0,2}$ and represents the scale evolution of the maximum of the anisotropic Gaussian. The string is a subset of the surface which is in correspondence with (12). In the right frame we have detected more $R^{0,2}$ strings and a maximum that is depicted in white. Some straightforward calculation shows that the maximum is found at

$$\sigma = \sqrt{\frac{(\gamma-1)(\sigma_x^2+\sigma_y^2) + \sqrt{(\gamma-1)^2(\sigma_x^2-\sigma_y^2)^2 + 4\sigma_x^2\sigma_y^2}}{2(2-\gamma)}}. \tag{18}$$

The γ value used was 0.5. The scale at which the maximum is found is $\sigma = 1.98$, which is in agreement with (18).

The inclusion relation (12) between the relative critical point sets can be used to establish a link from the detected scale space structure at its optimal scale and the location of this structure at the original scale. In the example above the connection is provided by the vertical string in the right frame of Fig. 1.

For the examples in the rest of this paper we consider only deformed scale spaces.

The horizontal string of the right frame of Fig. 1 can be used to detect elongated structures in an image at their scale of maximum response with respect to the form factor $\phi(\sigma)$. We can optimize the intrinsically defined Hessian vector frame to reduce the response of the vertical strings, which represent the evolution of extrema in scale space. Since the elongated structures are one-dimensional structures in the original image and we want them to be detected at a scale of maximum response in scale space, we define the vector frame as follows: one vector is always pointing in the direction of increasing scale whereas the other is the eigenvector belonging to the largest curvature of the two-dimensional Hessian $H_{ij} = L_{ij}(x,y,\sigma)$, $\{i,j\} \in \{x,y\}$. We can use the signs of the eigenvalues to discriminate between saddle strings, maxima strings and minima strings if we take the value of the second derivative in the scale direction as the eigenvalue belonging to the vector $(0,0,1)$.

In the next example we apply the above defined vector frame for the detection of two perpendicular Gaussian ridges with scales $\sigma_1 = 2.0$ and $\sigma_2 = 5.0$

respectively. Figure 2 depicts in the left frame the image and in the right frame the strings with respect to the modified Hessian frame. We will refer to these strings as scale space strings. The γ value used here is 0.5 and the maximum responses are found at $\sigma = 2.0$ and $\sigma = 5.0$ in correspondence with (17). The strings are broken in the middle, which is due to interference of the two ridges. In this region there is no well defined ridge, except at scale $\sigma = 3.8$ where we find a string of small length.

Now we consider the image in the top left frame of Fig. 3, which consists of a sequence of identical horizontal bars equally spaced along the vertical axis. In the top right frame we show the strings and observe that the bars give maximal response at two distinct scales. At the fine scales the bars are detected as elongated structures separately, but at larger scales they have grouped together to one elongated structure in the perpendicular direction. The objects group themselves to different structures at different scales. In the bottom left frame the ridges change their orientation in a continuous way. We included a magnification of the ridges in the bottom right frame. In accordance with (12) we see that the strings always lie on a higher dimensional ridge (vertical surface) which provides the connection to the original scale.

As a final example we detect the vessel structure of a retina in a two-dimensional fundus reflection image from a scanning laser ophthalmoscope, see the left frame of Fig. 4. In this example we used the form factor $\phi(\sigma) = (\sigma/(\sigma + \sigma_0))^\gamma$. The positive strings are depicted in the right frame.

All these examples lead us to the observation that the deformed scale spaces can serve as a grouping mechanism.

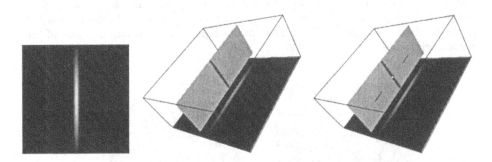

Fig. 1. Example 1: The left frame shows an image of an anisotropic Gaussian blob with $\sigma_x = 2.0$ and $\sigma_y = 30.0$ pixels. Middle and right frames show the detected ridge sets for a non-deformed and a deformed scale space respectively. The scale runs from 1.0 pixel from the bottom of the box to 4.0 pixels at the top. Light grey corresponds to the sets $R^{0,1}$, dark grey to $R^{0,2}$ and white to $R^{0,3}$.

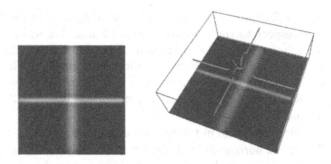

Fig. 2. Example 2: Scale space strings of two Gaussian ridges.

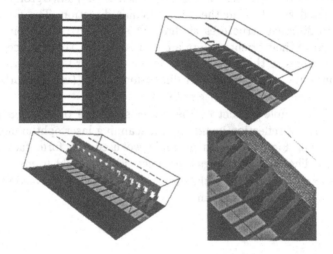

Fig. 3. Example 3: Scale space grouping of bars. The top left frame shows the original image. In the top right frame the scale space strings are depicted. In the bottom left frame we show the ridge sets $R^{0,1}$. The bottom right frame is a magnification of the bottom left frame. We used $\gamma = 0.25$.

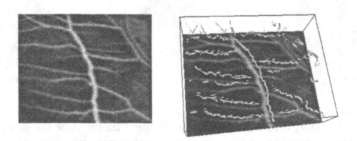

Fig. 4. Example 4: In the left frame a fundus reflection image of the eye is depicted. The interlacing artefacts are due to the method of the acquisition. The right frame shows the detected scale space strings. We used $\phi(\sigma) = (\sigma/(\sigma + \sigma_0))^\gamma$, $\sigma_0 = 1$, $\gamma = 0.5$. Scale runs exponentially from 1.0 pixel to 4.0 pixels in 32 steps.

5 Discussion

In the present paper we reviewed a constructive definition of relative critical sets in images of any number of spatial dimensions. The definition is very flexible because it associates critical sets to an arbitrarily chosen local vector frame field. Depending on the visual task, different model structures can be identified with the relative critical sets. As a consequence our construction can be purely intrinsic (defined only by the image structures), or it can involve externally specified frames. We demonstrated that the intrinsic Hessian frame leads to the detection of ridge sets. As an externally specified frame we defined a modified Hessian frame for the detection of elongated structures at their scale of maximum response with respect to a multiplication form factor. This factor together with a selected vector frame contains the model information we want to incorporate in our detection strategy.

The relative critical sets are in general connected sub-manifolds. Therefore, our technique provides indeed a method for perceptual grouping achieved with only local measurements. In a sense such a technique can be viewed as a particular generalization of the threshold techniques where the connected entities are the level surfaces (or lines in 2D).

All examples showed the grouping properties of the system of ridges for optimal scale selection of multi-scale connected objects. The method also provides a linkage from the scale space structure down to the original image space. We observe that scale space performs a grouping mechanism in itself. We refer to those applications as to topological deep structure analysis.

A   Appendix

Here we give an expression in Cartesian coordinates for the form (2) in three dimensions. As shown in (10), in three dimensions (2) reads

$$\Phi = \xi_i \partial_l \xi_j \partial_m \xi_k dx^l \wedge dx^m \varepsilon^{ijk} \ . \tag{19}$$

Performing the contraction on l and m gives

$$\begin{aligned}
\Phi = \varepsilon^{ijk}\xi_i((\partial_x\xi_j\partial_y\xi_k - \partial_y\xi_j\partial_x\xi_k)dx \wedge dy \\
+ \ (\partial_y\xi_j\partial_z\xi_k - \partial_z\xi_j\partial_y\xi_k)dy \wedge dz \\
+ \ (\partial_z\xi_j\partial_x\xi_k - \partial_x\xi_j\partial_z\xi_k)dz \wedge dx) \ .
\end{aligned} \tag{20}$$

On a surface z is constant (20) reduces to

$$\Phi = \varepsilon^{ijk}\xi_i(\partial_x\xi_j\partial_y\xi_k - \partial_y\xi_j\partial_x\xi_k)dx \wedge dy \ . \tag{21}$$

Performing the contraction on i, j and k gives

$$\begin{aligned}
\Phi = 2(\xi_x(\partial_x\xi_y\partial_y\xi_z - \partial_y\xi_y\partial_x\xi_z) \\
+ \ \xi_y(\partial_x\xi_z\partial_y\xi_x - \partial_y\xi_z\partial_x\xi_x) \\
+ \ \xi_z(\partial_x\xi_x\partial_y\xi_y - \partial_y\xi_x\partial_x\xi_y))dx \wedge dy \ .
\end{aligned} \tag{22}$$

Similar relations hold for the other surfaces.

Acknowledgments

This work is carried out in the framework of the NWO research project STW/4496.

References

1. W. M. Boothby. *An introduction to differential geometry and Riemannian geometry*. Academic Press, New York, San Francisco, London, 1975.
2. J. Damon. Generic structure of two-dimensional images under Gaussian blurring. *SIAM Journal on Applied Mathematics*, 59(1):97–138, 1998.
3. D. Eberly, R. Gardner, B. Morse, S. Pizer, and C. Scharlach. Ridges for image analysis. *Journal of Mathematical Imaging and Vision*, 4(4):351–371, 1994.
4. T. Eguchi, P. Gilkey, and J. Hanson. Gravitation, gauge theories and differential geometry. *Physics Reports*, 66(2):213–393, 1980.
5. L. Griffin. Critical point events in affine scale space, in *Gaussian Scale Space Theory*, J. Sporring and M. Nielsen and L. Florack and P. Johansen, eds., pages 165–180. Kluwer Academic Publishers, Dordrecht, 1997.
6. P. Johansen. On the classification of toppoints in scale space. *Journal of Mathematical Imaging and Vision*, 4(1):57–68, 1994.
7. S. N. Kalitzin. Topological numbers and singularities in scalar images, in *Gaussian scale space theory*, J. Sporring and M. Nielsen and L. Florack and P. Johansen, eds., pages 181–189. Kluwer Academic Publishers, Dordrecht, Boston, London, 1997.
8. S. N. Kalitzin, J. J. Staal, B. M. ter Haar Romeny, and M. A. Viergever. Computational topology in multi-scale image analysis. Submitted to IEEE Transactions on Pattern Analysis and Machine Intelligence.
9. S. N. Kalitzin, J. J. Staal, B. M. ter Haar Romeny, and M. A. Viergever. Frame-relative critical point sets in image analysis. Accepted for the 8th International Conference on Computer Analysis of Images and Patterns, Ljubljana, Slovenia, September 1–3, 1999.
10. S. N. Kalitzin, B. M. ter Haar Romeny, A. H. Salden, P. F. M. Nacken, and M. A. Viergever. Topological numbers and singularities in scalar images: scale space evolution properties. *Journal of Mathematical Imaging and Vision*, 9(3):253–269, 1998.
11. J. J. Koenderink. The structure of images. *Biological Cybernetics*, 50:363–370, 1984.
12. T. Lindeberg. Scale space behavior of local extrema and blobs. *Journal of Mathematical Imaging and Vision*, 1(1):65–99, 1992.
13. T. Lindeberg. Edge detection and ridge detection with automatic scale selection. *Int. Journal of Computer Vision*, 30(2):117–154, 1998.
14. M. Nakahara. *Geometry, topology and physics*. Adam Hilger, Bristol, New York, 1989.
15. O. F. Olsen. Multi-scale watershed segmentation, in *Gaussian Scale Space Theory*, J. Sporring and M. Nielsen and L. Florack and P. Johansen, eds., pages 191–200. Kluwer Academic Publishers, Dordrecht, 1997.
16. S. M. Pizer, D. Eberly, D. S. Fritsch, and B. S. Morse. Zoom-invariant vision of figural shape: the mathematics of cores. *Computer Vision and Image Understanding*, 69(1):55–71, 1998.

Qualitative Multi-scale Feature Hierarchies for Object Tracking

Lars Bretzner and Tony Lindeberg

Computational Vision and Active Perception Laboratory (CVAP)
Dept. of Numerical Analysis and Computing Science
KTH, S-100 44 Stockholm, Sweden

Abstract. This paper shows how the performance of feature trackers can be improved by building a view-based object representation consisting of qualitative relations between image structures at different scales. The idea is to track all image features individually, and to use the qualitative feature relations for resolving ambiguous matches and for introducing feature hypotheses whenever image features are mismatched or lost. Compared to more traditional work on view-based object tracking, this methodology has the ability to handle semi-rigid objects and partial occlusions. Compared to trackers based on three-dimensional object models, this approach is much simpler and of a more generic nature. A hands-on example is presented showing how an integrated application system can be constructed from conceptually very simple operations.

1 Introduction

To maintain a stable representation of a dynamic world, it is necessary to relate image data from different time moments. When analysing image sequences frame by frame, as is commonly done in computer vision applications, it is therefore useful to include an explicit tracking mechanisms into the vision system.

When constructing such a tracking mechanism, there is a large freedom in design, concerning how much a priori information should be included into and be used by the tracker. If the goal is to track a single object of known shape, then it may be natural to build a three-dimensional object model, and to relate computed views of this internal model to the image data that occur. An alternative approach is store a large number of actual views in a database, and subsequently match these to the image sequence.

Depending on what type of object representation we choose, we can expect different trade-offs between the complexity of constructing the object representation and the complexity in matching the object representation to image data. In particular, different design strategies will imply different amounts of additional work when the database is extended with new objects.

The subject of this article is to advocate the use of *qualitative* multi-scale object models in this context, as opposed to more detailed models. The idea is to represent only dominant image features of the object, and relations between those that are reasonably stable under view variations. In this way, a new object model can be constructed with only minor additional work, and it will be demonstrated that such a weaker approach to object representation is powerful enough to give a significant improvement in the robustness of feature trackers. Specifically, we will show how an integrated non-trivial application to human-computer interaction can be constructed in a straightforward and conceptually very simple way, by combination with a set of elementary scale-space operations.

2 Choice of Image Representation for Feature Tracking

The framework we consider is one in which image features are detected at multiple scales. Each feature is associated with a region in space as well as a range of scales, and relations between features at different scales impose hierarchical links across scales. Specifically, we assume that the image features are detected with a mechanism for automatic scale selection. In earlier work (Bretzner & Lindeberg 1998a), we have demonstrated how such a scale selection mechanism is essential to obtain a robust behaviour of the feature tracker if the image features undergo large size variations in the image domain.

The rationale for using a hierarchical multi-scale image representation for feature tracking originates from the well-known fact that real-world objects consist of different types of structures at different scales. An internal object representation should reflect this fact. One aspect of this, which we shall make particular use of, is that certain hierarchical relations over scales tend to remain reasonably stable when the viewing conditions are varied. Thus, even if some features are lost during tracking (e.g. due to occlusions, illumination variations, or spurious errors by the feature detector or the feature matching algorithm), it is rather likely that a sufficient number of image features remain to support the tracking of the other features. Thereby, the feature tracker will have higher robustness with respect to occlusions, viewing variations and spurious errors in the lower-level modules. As we shall see, the qualitative nature of these feature relations will also make it possible to handle semi-rigid objects within the same framework.

In this way, the approach we will propose is closely related to the notion of object representation. Compared to the more traditional problem of object recognition, however, the requirements are different, since the primary goal is to maintain a stable image representation over time, and we do not need to support indexing and recognition functionalities into large databases. For these reasons, a qualitative image representation can be sufficient in many cases, and offer a higher flexibility by being more generic than detailed object models.

Related works. This topic of this paper touches on both the subjects of feature tracking and object representation. The literature on tracking is large and impossible to review here. Hence, we focus on the most closely related works.

Image representations involving linking across scales have been presented by several authors. (Crowley & Parker 1984, Crowley & Sanderson 1987) detected peaks and ridges in a pyramid representation. In retrospect, a main reason why stability problems were encountered is that the pyramids involved a rather coarse sampling in the scale direction. (Koenderink 1984) defined links across scales using iso-intensity paths in scale-space, and this idea was made operational for medical image segmentation by (Lifshitz & Pizer 1990) and (Vincken et al. 1997). (Lindeberg 1993) constructed a scale-space primal sketch, in which a morphological support region was associated with each extremum point and paths of critical points over scales were computed delimited by bifurcations. (Olsen 1997) applied a similar approach to watershed minima in the gradient magnitude. (Griffin et al. 1992) developed a closely related approach based on maximum gradient paths, however, at a single scale. In the scale-space primal sketch, scale selection was performed, by maximizing measures of blob strength over scales, and significance was measured by the volumes that image structures occupy in scale-space, involving the stability over scales as a major component. A generalization of this scale selection idea to more general classes of image structures was presented in (Lindeberg 1994, Lindeberg 1998b, Lindeberg 1998a), by detecting scale-space maxima, *i.e.* points in scale-space at which normalized differential measures of feature strength assume local maxima with respect to scale. (Pizer et al. 1994) and his co-workers have proposed closely related descriptors, focusing on multiscale ridge representations for medical image analysis. Psychophysical results by (Burbeck & Pizer 1995) support the belief that such hierarchical multi-scale representations are relevant for object representation.

With respect to the problem of object recognition, (Shokoufandeh et al. 1998) detect extrema in a wavelet transform in a way closely related to the detection of scale-space maxima, and define a graph structure from these image features. This graph structure is then matched to corresponding descriptors for other objects, based on topological and geometric similarity. In relation to the large number of works on model based tracking, there are similar aims between our approach and the following works: (Koller et al. 1993) used car models to support the tracking of vehicles in long sequences with occlusions and illumination variations. (Smith & Brady 1995) defined clusters of coherently moving corner features as to support the tracking of cars in a qualitative manner. (Black & Jepson 1998b) constructed a view-based object representation using an eigenimage approach to compactly represent and support the tracking of an object seen from a large number of different views. The recently developed condensation algorithm (Isard & Blake 1998, Black & Jepson 1998a) is of particular interest, by explicitly constructing statistical distributions to capture relations between image features. Concerning the specific application to qualitative hand tracking that will be addressed in this paper, more detailed hand models have been presented by (Kuch & Huang 1995, Heap & Hogg 1996, Yasumuro et al. 1999). Related graphlike representations for hand tracking and face tracking have been presented by (Triesch & von der Malsburg 1996, Mauerer & von der Malsburg 1996).

3 Image Features and Qualitative Feature Relations

We are interested in representing objects which can give rise to a rich variety of image features of different types and at different scales. Generically, these image features can be (i) zero-dimensional (junctions), (ii) one-dimensional (edges and ridges), or (iii) two-dimensional (blobs), and we assume that each image feature is associated with a region in space as well as a range of scales.

3.1 Computation of Image Features

When computing a hierarchical view-based object representation, one may at first desire to compute a detailed representation of the multi-scale image structure, as done by the scale-space primal sketch or some of the closely related representations reviewed in section 2. Since we are interested in processing temporal image data, however, and the construction of such a representation from image data requires a rather large amount of computations, we shall here follow a computationally more efficient approach.

We focus on image features expressed in terms of *scale-space maxima*, *i.e.* points in scale-space at which differential geometric entities assume local maxima with respect to space and scale. Formally, such points are defined by

$$(\nabla \left(\mathcal{D}_{norm} L(x; \ s) \right) = 0) \quad \wedge \quad (\partial_s \left(\mathcal{D}_{norm} L(x; \ s) \right) = 0) \tag{1}$$

where $L(\cdot; \ s)$ denotes the scale-space representation of the image f constructed by convolution with a Gaussian kernel $g(\cdot; s)$ with scale parameter (variance) s and $\mathcal{D}_{norm}$ is a differential invariant normalized by the replacement of all spatial derivatives ∂_{x_i} by γ-normalized derivatives $\partial_{\xi_i} = s^{\gamma/2} \partial_{x_i}$.

Two examples of such differential descriptors, which we shall make particular use of here, include the normalized Laplacian (with $\gamma = 1$) for blob detection

$$\nabla^2_{norm} L = s \left(L_{xx} + L_{yy} \right) \tag{2}$$

and the square difference between the eigenvalues L_{pp} and L_{qq} of the Hessian matrix (with $\gamma = 3/4$) for ridge detection

$$\mathcal{A}L_{\gamma-norm} = s^{2\gamma} |L_{pp} - L_{qq}|^2 = s^{2\gamma} \left((L_{xx} - L_{yy})^2 + 4L_{xy}^2 \right) \tag{3}$$

see (Lindeberg 1998*b*, Lindeberg 1998*a*) for a more general description. A computationally very attractive property of this construction is that the scale-space maxima can be computed by architecturally very simple and computationally highly efficient operations involving: (i) scale-space smoothing, (ii) pointwise computation of differential invariants, and (iii) detection of local maxima.

Furthermore, to simplify the geometric analysis of image features, we shall reduce the spatial representation of image descriptors to ellipses, by evaluating a second moment matrix

$$\mu = \int_{\eta \in \mathbb{R}^2} \begin{pmatrix} L_x^2 & L_x L_y \\ L_x L_y & L_y^2 \end{pmatrix} g(\eta; s_{int}) \, d\eta \tag{4}$$

at integration scale s_{int} proportional to the detection scale of the scale-space maximum (equation (1)). Thereby, each image feature will we represented by a point $(x; \ s)$ in scale-space and a covariance matrix Σ describing the shape, graphically illustrated by an ellipse. For one-dimensional features, the corresponding ellipses will be highly elongated, while for zero-dimensional and two-dimensional features, the ellipse descriptors of the second moment matrices will be rather circular. Attributes derived from the covariance matrix include its anisotropy derived from the ratio $\lambda_{max}/\lambda_{min}$ between its eigenvalues, and its orientation defined as the orientation of its main eigenvector.

Figure 3 shows an example of such image descriptors computed from a grey-level image, after ranking on a significance measure defined as the magnitude of the response of the differential operator at the scale-space maximum. A trivial but nevertheless very useful effect of this ranking is that it substantially reduces the number of image features for further processing, thus improving the computational efficiency. In a more detailed representation of the multi-scale deep structure of a real-world image, it will often be the case that a large number of the image features and their hierarchical relations correspond to image structures that will be regarded as insignificant by later processing stages.

3.2 Qualitative Feature Relations

Between the abovementioned features, various types of relations can be defined in the image plane. Here, we consider the following types of qualitative relations:

Spatial coincidence (inclusion): We say that a region A at position x_A and scale s_A is in spatial coincidence relation to a region B at position x_B and at a (coarser) scale $s_B > s_A$ if

$$(x_A - x_B)^T \Sigma_B^{-1} (x_A - x_B) \in [D_1, D_2] \qquad (5)$$

where D_1 and D_2 are distance thresholds. By using a Mahalanobis distance measure, we introduce a directional preference which is highly useful for expressing spatial relations between elongated image features. While the special case $D_1 = 0$ corresponds to an inclusion relation, there are also cases where one may want to explicitly represent distant features, using $D_1 > 0$

Stability of scale relations: For two image feature at times t_k and $t_{k'}$, we assume that the ratio between their scales should be approximately the same. This is motivated by the requirement of scale invariance under zooming

$$\frac{s_A(t_k)}{s_B(t_k)} \approx \frac{s_A(t_{k'})}{s_B(t_{k'})}. \qquad (6)$$

To accept small variations due to changes in view direction and spurious variations from the scale selection mechanism of the feature tracker, we measure relative distances in the scale direction and implement the "$\approx$" operation by $q \approx q' \iff |\log \frac{q}{q'}| < \log T$, where $T > 1$ is a threshold in the scale direction.

Directional relation (bearing): For a feature A related to a one-dimensional feature B, the angle is measured between the main eigenvector of Σ_B and the vector $x_A - x_B$ from the center x_B of B to the center x_A of A.

Trivially, these relations are invariant to translations and rotations in the image plane. The scale invariance of these relations follows from corresponding scale invariance properties of image descriptors computed from scale-space maxima — if the size of an image structure is scaled by a factor c in the image domain, then the corresponding scale levels are transformed by a factor c^2.

3.3 Qualitative Multi-Scale Feature Hierarchy

Let us now consider a specific example with images of a hand. From our knowledge that a hand consists of five fingers, we construct a model consisting of: (i) the palm, (ii) the five fingers, (iii) a finger tip for each finger, (see figure 1).

Each finger is in a spatial coincidence relation to the palm, as well as a directional relation. Moreover, each fingertip is in a spatial relationship to its finger, and satisfies a directional relation to this feature. In a similar manner, each finger is in a scale stability relation with respect to the palm, and each fingertip is in a corresponding scale stability relation relative to its finger.

Such a representation will be referred to as a *qualitative multi-scale feature hierarchy*. Figure 2 shows the relations this representation is built from, using UML notation. An attractive property of this view-based object representation is that it only focuses on qualitative object features. There is no assumption of rigidity, only that the qualitative shape is preserved.

The idea behind this construction is of course that the palm and the fingertips should give rise to blob responses (equation (2)) and that the fingers give rise to ridge responses (equation (3)). Figure 3 shows an example of how this model can be initialized and matched to image data with associated image descriptors.

To exclude responses from the background, we have here required that all image features should correspond to bright blobs or bright ridges. Alternatively, one could define spatial inclusion relations with respect to other segmentation cues relative to the background, *e.g.* chromaticity or depth.

Here, we have constructed the graph with feature relations manually, using qualitative knowledge about the shape of the object and its primitives. In a more general setting, however, one can also consider the learning of stable feature relations in an actual setting, based on a (possibly richer) vocabulary of qualitative feature relations. The list of feature relations in section 3.2 should by no means be regarded as exhaustive. Additional feature relations can be introduced whenever motivated by their effectiveness in specific applications. For example, in several cases it is natural to introduce a richer set of inter-feature relations between the primitives that are the ancestors of a coarser scale features.

4 Feature Tracking with Hierarchical Support

One idea that we are going to make explicit use of in this paper is to let features at different scales support each other during feature tracking. If fine-scale features are lost, then the coarse scale features combined with the other fine-scale features should provide sufficient information so as to generate hypotheses for recapturing

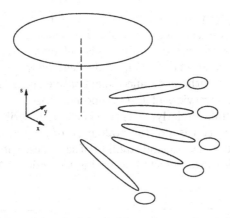

Fig. 1. A qualitative multi-scale feature hierarchy constructed for a hand model.

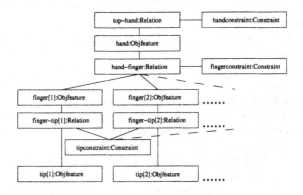

Fig. 2. Instance diagram for the feature hierarchy of a hand (figure 1).

20 strongest blobs and ridges   *Initialized hand model*   *All hand features captured*

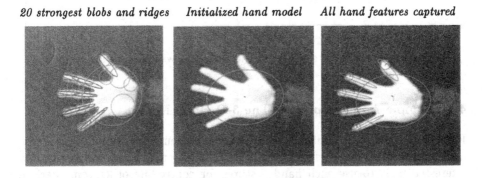

Fig. 3. Illustration of the initialization stage of the object tracker. Once the coarse-scale feature is found (here the palm of the hand), the qualitative feature hierarchy guides the top-down search for the remaining features of the representation. (The left image shows the 20 most significant blob responses (in red) and ridge responses (in blue).)

the lost feature. Similarly, if a coarse scale feature is lost, *e.g.* due to occlusion or a too large three-dimensional rotation, then the fine-scale features should support the model based tracking. While this behaviour can be easily achieved with a three-dimensional object model, we are here interested in generic feature trackers which operate without detailed quantitative geometric information.

Figure 4 gives an overview of the composed object tracking scheme. The feature tracking module underlying this scheme is described in (Bretzner & Lindeberg 1998*a*), and consists of the evaluation of a multi-cue similarity measure involving patch correlation, and stability of scale descriptors and significance measures for image features detected according to section 3.1.

Scheme for object tracking using qualitative feature hierarchies:

Initialization:
    Find and match top-level feature using initial position and top-level parent-children constraints.

Tracking:
    For each frame:
        For each feature in the hierarchy (top-down):
            Track image features (see separate description)
            If a feature is lost (or not found)
                If parent matched
                    Find feature using parent position and parent-feature relation constraints
                else if child(ren) matched
                    Find feature using child(ren) position and feature-children relation constraints.
        Parse feature hierarchy, verify relations and reject mismatches.

Fig. 4. Overview of the scheme for object tracking with hierarchical support.

4.1 Sample Application I — The 3-D Hand Mouse

From the trajectories of image features, we can compute the motion of the hand, assuming that the hand is kept rigid. An application that we are particularly interested in is to use such hand gestures for controlling other computerized equipment. Examples of applications include (i) interaction with visualization systems and virtual environments, (ii) control of mechanical systems and (iii) immaterial remote control functionality for consumer electronics (Lindeberg & Bretzner 1998). The mathematical foundation for this "3-D hand mouse" was presented in (Bretzner & Lindeberg 1998*b*). Our previous experimental work, however, was done with image sequences where an individual feature tracker with

Steady-state model   *One feature disappears*   *Feature recaptured*

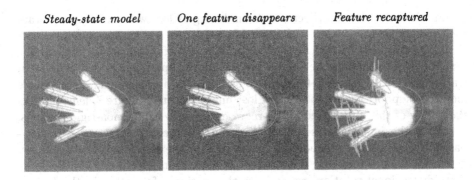

Fig. 5. The proposed qualitative representation makes it possible to maintain tracking even if parts of the object are occluded. Later in the sequence, the occluded part (in this case the finger), can be captured again using the feature hierarchy. (Here, all image features are illustrated by red, while the feature trajectories are green.)

Steady-state model   *Fine scale features occluded*   *All features captured*

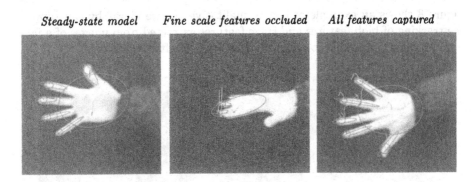

Fig. 6. Illustration of how the qualitative feature hierarchy makes it possible to maintain object tracking under view variations. The images show how most finger features are lost due to occlusion when the hand turns, and how the qualitative feature hierarchy guides the search to find these features again.

The behaviour of the qualitative feature hierarchy tracker under semi-rigid motion

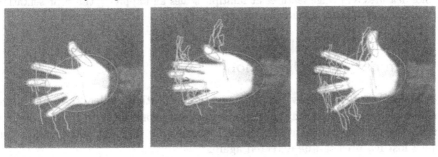

Fig. 7. Due to the qualitative nature of the feature relations, the proposed framework allows objects to be tracked under semi-rigid motion.

automatic scale selection (Bretzner & Lindeberg 1998a) was sufficient to obtain the extended feature trajectories needed for structure and motion computations.

The qualitative feature hierarchy provides a useful tool for extending this functionality, by making the system less sensitive to spurious errors of individual feature tracking. Figures 5–6 show two examples of how the qualitative feature hierarchy support the recapturing of lost image features. Figure 7 demonstrates the ability of this view-based image representation to handle non-rigid motions.

While the image representation underlying these computations is a view-based representation, it should be remarked that the step is not far to a three-dimensional object model. If the hand is kept rigid over a sufficiently large three-dimensional rotation, we can use the motion information in the feature trajectories of the fingers and the finger tips for computing the structure and the motion of the object (see (Bretzner & Lindeberg 1998b) for details).

4.2 Sample Application II — View-Based Face Model

Figure 8 shows an example of how a qualitative feature hierarchy can support the tracking of blob features and ridge features extracted from images of a face. Again a main purpose is to recapture lost features after occlusions.

| *Steady-state model* | *Occlusion by rotation* | *Features recaptured* |

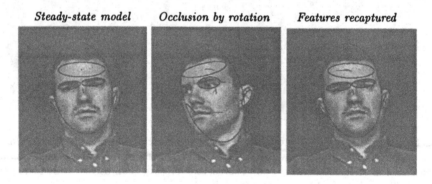

Fig. 8. Results of building a qualitative feature hierarchy for a face model consisting of blob features and ridge features at multiple scales and applying this representation to the tracking of facial features over time.

5 Summary and Discussion

We have presented a view-based image representation, called the qualitative multi-scale feature hierarchy, and shown how this representation can be used for improving the performance of a feature tracker, by defining search regions in which lost features can be detected again.

Besides making explicit use of the hierarchical relations that are induced by different features in a multi-scale representation, the philosophy behind this approach is to build an internal representation that supports the processing of those image descriptors we can expect to extract from image data. This knowledge is represented in a qualitative manner, without need for constructing geometrically detailed object models.

In relation to other graph-like object representations, the discriminative power of the qualitative feature hierarchy may of course be lower than for geometrically more accurate three-dimensional object models or more detailed view-based representations involving quantitative information. Therefore the qualitative feature hierarchies may be less suitable for object recognition, but still enough for pre-segmentation of complex scenes, or as a complement to filling in missing information given partial information from other modules (here the individual feature trackers). Notably, the application of this concept does not suffer from similar complexity problems as approaches involving explicit graph matching.

It should be pointed out that we do not claim that the proposed framework should be regarded as excluding more traditional object representations, such as three-dimensional object models or view-based representations. Rather different types of representations could be used in a complementary manner, exploiting their respective advantages. For example, in certain applications it is natural to complement the qualitative feature hierarchy with a view-based representation at the feature level, in order to enable more reliable verification of the image features. Moreover, regarding our application to the 3-D hand mouse, it is worth pointing out that the qualitative feature hierarchy is used as a major tool in a system for computing three-dimensional structure and motion, thus at the end deriving a quantitative three-dimensional object model from image data.

The main advantages of the proposed approach are that it is very simple to implement in practice, and that it allows us to handle semi-rigid objects, occlusions, as well as variations in view direction and illumination conditions. Specifically, with respect to the topic of scale-space theory, we have demonstrated how an integrated computer vision application with non-trivial functionally can be constructed essentially just from the following components: (i) basic scale-space operations (see section 3.1), (ii) a straightforward graph representation, and (iii) a generic framework for multi-view geometry (described elsewhere).

References

Black, M. J. & Jepson (1998a), A probabilistic framework for matching temporal trajectories: Condensation-based recognition of gestures and expressions, in H. Burkhardt & B. Neumann, eds, 'ECCV'98', Vol. 1406 of Lecture Notes in Computer Science, Springer Verlag, Berlin, Freiburg, Germany, 909–924.

Black, M. J. & Jepson, A. (1998b), 'Eigentracking: Robust matching and tracking of articulated objects using a view-based representation', IJCV 26(1), 63–84.

Bretzner, L. & Lindeberg, T. (1998a), 'Feature tracking with automatic selection of spatial scales', Computer Vision and Image Understanding 71(3), 385–392.

Bretzner, L. & Lindeberg, T. (1998b), Use your hand as a 3-D mouse or relative orientation from extended sequences of sparse point and line correspondances using the affine trifocal tensor, in H. Burkhardt & B. Neumann, eds, 'ECCV'98', Vol. 1406 of Lecture Notes in Computer Science, Springer Verlag, Berlin, 141–157.

Burbeck, C. A. & Pizer, S. M. (1995), 'Object representation by cores: Identifying and representing primitive spatial regions', *Vis. Res.* **35**(13), 1917–1930.

Crowley, J. L. & Parker, A. C. (1984), 'A representation for shape based on peaks and ridges in the Difference of Low-Pass Transform', *IEEE-PAMI* **6**(2), 156–170.

Crowley, J. L. & Sanderson, A. C. (1987), 'Multiple resolution representation and probabilistic matching of 2-D gray-scale shape', *IEEE-PAMI* **9**(1), 113–121.

Griffin, L. D., Colchester, A. C. F. & Robinson, G. P. (1992), 'Scale and segmentation of images using maximum gradient paths', *IVC* **10**(6), 389–402.

Heap, T. & Hogg, D. (1996), Towards 3D hand tracking using a deformable model, *in* 'Int. Conf. Automatic Face and Gesture Recognition', Killington, Vermont, 140–145.

Isard, M. & Blake, A. (1998), A mixed-state condensation tracker with automatic model switching, *in* '6th ICCV', Bombay, India, 107–112.

Koenderink, J. J. (1984), 'The structure of images', *Biol. Cyb.* **50**, 363–370.

Koller, D., Daniilidis, K. & Nagel, H. (1993), 'Model-based object tracking in monocular image sequences of road traffic scenes', *IJCV* 257–281.

Kuch, J. J. & Huang, T. S. (1995), Vision based hand modelling and tracking for virtual teleconferencing and telecollaboration, *in* '5th ICCV', Cambridge, MA, 666–671.

Lifshitz, L. & Pizer, S. (1990), 'A multiresolution hierarchical approach to image segmentation based on intensity extrema', *IEEE-PAMI* **12**(6), 529–541.

Lindeberg, T. (1993), 'Detecting salient blob-like image structures and their scales with a scale-space primal sketch: A method for focus-of-attention', *IJCV* **11**(3), 283–318.

Lindeberg, T. (1994), *Scale-Space Theory in Computer Vision*, Kluwer, Netherlands.

Lindeberg, T. (1998*a*), 'Edge detection and ridge detection with automatic scale selection', *IJCV* **30**(2), 117–154.

Lindeberg, T. (1998*b*), 'Feature detection with automatic scale selection', *IJCV* **30**(2), 77–116.

Lindeberg, T. & Bretzner, L. (1998), Förfarande och anordning för överföring av information genom rörelsedetektering, samt användning av anordningen. Patent pending.

Mauerer, T. & von der Malsburg, C. (1996), Tracking and learning graphs and pose on images of faces, *in* 'Int. Conf. Automatic Face and Gesture Recognition', Killington, Vermont, 176–181.

Olsen, O. F. (1997), Multi-scale watershed segmentation, *in* J. Sporring, M. Nielsen, L. Florack & P. Johansen, eds, 'Gaussian Scale-Space Theory: Proc. PhD School on Scale-Space Theory', Kluwer, Copenhagen, Denmark, 191–200.

Pizer, S. M., Burbeck, C. A., Coggins, J. M., Fritsch, D. S. & Morse, B. S. (1994), 'Object shape before boundary shape: Scale-space medial axis', *J. Math. Im. Vis.* **4**, 303–313.

Shokoufandeh, A., Marsic, I. & Dickinson, S. J. (1998), View-based object matching, *in* '6th ICCV', Bombay, India, 588–595.

Smith, S. M. & Brady, J. M. (1995), 'Asset-2: Real-time motion segmentation and shape tracking', *IEEE-PAMI* **17**(8), 814–820.

Triesch, J. & von der Malsburg, C. (1996), Robust classification of hand postures against complex background, *in* 'Int. Conf. Automatic Face and Gesture Recognition', Killington, Vermont, 170–175.

Vincken, K., Koster, A. & Viergever, M. (1997), 'Probabilistic multiscale image segmentation', *IEEE-PAMI* **19**(2), 109–120.

Yasumuro, Y., Chen, Q. & Chihara, K. (1999), 'Three-dimensional modelling of the human hand with motion constraints', *IVC* **17**(2), 149–156.

Riemannian Drums, Anisotropic Curve Evolution and Segmentation

Jayant Shah[1]

Mathematics Department, Northeastern University,

Boston, MA 02115. email: shah@neu.edu

Abstract. The method of curve evolution is a popular method for recovering shape boundaries. However isotropic metrics have always been used to induce the flow of the curve and potential steady states tend to be difficult to determine numerically, especially in noisy or low-contrast situations. Initial curves shrink past the steady state and soon vanish. In this paper, anisotropic metrics are considered which remedy the situation by taking the orientation of the feature gradient into account. The problem of shape recovery or segmentation is formulated as the problem of finding minimum cuts of a Riemannian manifold. Approximate methods, namely anisotropic geodesic flows and solution of an eigenvalue problem are discussed.

1 Introduction

In recent years, there has been extensive development of methods for shape recovery by curve evolution. These methods are gaining in popularity due to their potential for very fast implementation. A parametric form of it was developed by Katz, Witkin and Terzoupolous [6]. A geometrically intrinsic formulation of active contours was introduced by Caselles, Catte, Coll and Dibos in [2] and developed over the years by several authors [3,7,8,14]. A formulation based on curve evolution introduced by Sethian [13] is also in use where the flow velocity consists of a constant component and a component proportional to the curvature (see for example, [18]). The evolving curve in this case is stopped near the shape boundary or at least slowed by means of a stopping term. From a geometric perspective, the image domain may be viewed as a Riemannian manifold endowed with a metric defined by the image features. An initial curve flows towards a geodesic with normal velocity proportional to its geodesic curvature. Several techniques for fast implemetation of geodesic flows have been developed. The speed of the method is due to two essential factors. First, noise suppression and edge detection are done in a hierarchical fashion: the image is smoothed first and then the geodesic flow is calculated. This is in contrast to the flows defined by segmentation functionals in which noise suppression and edge detection are done simultaneously. The second reason for the speed-up is that the object boundaries are found by tracking one closed curve at a time and thus the computational effort can be focused on a small neighborhood of the evolving curve.

Throughout the development of this approach, the metric used has always been an isotropic metric. In this paper, fully general anisotropic metrics are considered. One reason for developing such a generalization is that in noisy or low contrast situations,

---

[1]This work was partially supported by PHS Grant 2-R01–NS34189–04 from NINDS, NCI and NIMH, and NSF Grant DMS-9531293.

the steady states for the isotropic flows are not robust and one has to resort to devices such as a stopping term. For instance, when the image gradient is large everywhere due to noise, curves with the same Euclidean length will have their Riemannian length approximately equal if the metric is isotropic, indicating reduced sensitivity of the method. In practice, the curves tend to continuously shrink and vanish. A way to improve this situation is to take into account the orientation of the gradient by considering anisotropic metrics. Another reason to consider anisotropic metrics comes from the impressive results obtained by Shi and Malik [17] who formulate the problem of shape recovery in natural scenes as a problem of finding the minimum cut in a weighted graph. An ingredient essential for their method to work is the implied anisotropic metric. Finally, use of anisotropic metrics is implied in boundary detection by means of segmentation functionals. This connection is briefly reviewed in Section 2. However its implementation is computationally expensive and it is worthwhile to formulate anisotripic curve evolution directly.

2 Segmentation Functionals and Curve Evolution

Consider the segmentation functional [11]

$$(1) \qquad E(u,C) = \int\int_{D\backslash C} \|\nabla u\|^2 dx_1 dx_2 + \mu^2 \int\int_{D} |u - I|^2 dx_1 dx_2 + \nu|C|$$

where D is the image domain, I is the image intensity, C is the segmenting curve, $|C|$ its length and u is a piecewise smooth approximation of I. Let $e = \mu^2(u - I)^2 + \|\nabla u\|^2$ denote the energy density. Then with u fixed, the gradient flow for C is given by the equation

$$(2) \qquad \frac{\partial C}{\partial t} = \left[(e^+ - e^-) - \nu\kappa \right] N$$

where C now denotes the position vector of the segmenting curve, superscripts $+, -$ denote the values on the two sides of C, N is the normal to C pointing towards the side of C marked $+$ and κ denotes the curvature. To see anisotropicity, look at the limiting case as $\mu \to \infty$. Then C minimizes the limiting functional

$$(3) \qquad E_\infty(C) = \int_C \left[\frac{\mu\nu}{2} - \left(\frac{\partial I}{\partial n} \right)^2 \right] ds$$

The metric is an anisotropic (non-Riemannian) Finsler metric. It is singular and non-definite, exhibiting space-like and time-like behaviors [11]. Existence of space-like geodesics is an open question.

At the other extreme, as $\mu \to 0$ the behavior is governed by the isotropic Euclidean metric. The curve minimizes

$$(4) \qquad E_0(C) = \sum_i \int_{D_i} (I - \bar{I}_i)^2 + \frac{\nu}{\mu^2}|C|$$

where D_i's are the segments of D and $\bar{I}_i$ is the average value of I in D_i. The curve evolution is given by the equation

$$(5) \qquad \frac{\partial C}{\partial t} = \left[(\bar{I}^+ - \bar{I}^-)(\bar{I}^+ + \bar{I}^- - 2I) - \frac{\nu}{\mu^2}\kappa \right]$$

The equation is similar to the one used in [18] where the first term is replaced by a constant. The advantage of using the segmentation functional is that it avoids the problem of choosing this constant.

Another segmentation functional that leads to isotropic curve evolution is formulated using L^1–norms [15]:

$$(6) \qquad E(u, C) = \int\!\!\int_{D \backslash C} \|\nabla u\| dx_1 dx_2 + \frac{\nu}{\mu} \int\!\!\int_D |u - I| dx_1 dx_2 + \int_C \frac{J_u}{1 + \mu J_u} ds$$

where J_u is the jump in u across C, that is, $J_u = |u^+ - u^-|$. In order to implement the functional by gradient descent, curve C is replaced by a continuous function v, the edge-strength function:

$$(7) \qquad E_\rho(u, v) = \int\!\!\int_D \{\mu(1 - v)^2 \|\nabla u\| + \nu|u - I| + \frac{\rho}{2}\|\nabla v\|^2 + \frac{v^2}{2\rho}\} dx_1 dx_2$$

The gradient descent equations for u and v are:

$$(8) \qquad \begin{aligned} \frac{\partial u}{\partial t} &= \left[(1 - v)^2 \, curv(u) - 2(1 - v)\nabla v \cdot \frac{\nabla u}{\|\nabla u\|} - \frac{\nu}{\mu}\frac{(u - I)}{|u - I|} \right] \|\nabla u\| \\ \frac{\partial v}{\partial t} &= \nabla^2 v - \frac{v}{\rho^2} + \frac{2\mu}{\rho}(1 - v)\|\nabla u\| \end{aligned}$$

where $curv(u)$ is the curvature of the level curves of u:

$$(9) \qquad curv(u) = \frac{u_{x_2}^2 u_{x_1 x_1} - 2u_{x_1} u_{x_2} u_{x_1 x_2} + u_{x_1}^2 u_{x_2 x_2}}{\|\nabla u\|^3}$$

The term in the brackets in the first equation prescribes the three components of the velocity with which the level curves of u move. The first term is the usual Euclidean curvature term except for the factor of $(1 - v)^2$, the second term is the advection induced by the edge-strength function v and the last term prescribes the constant component of the velocity. The sign is automatically chosen such that this component of velocity pushes the level curve towards the corresponding level curve of I. The implied metric is isotropic.

3 Anisotropic Geodesic Flows

It is helpful to start with a slightly more general framework to derive the equation of anisotropic geodesic flow. Let M denote the image domain D when it is endowed with a Riemannian metric, $g = \{g_{ij}\}$. Let C be a curve dividing M into two disjoint submanifolds, M_1 and M_2. Following Cheeger [4], define

$$(10) \qquad h(C) = \frac{L(C)}{\min_i A(M_i)}$$

where $L(C)$ is the length of C and $A(M_i)$ is the area of M_i, both being measured with respect to the metric on M. Then the problem of shape recovery may be viewed as the problem of finding the minimum cut of M by minimizing $h(C)$. (Note the dependence of the minimum cut on the size and shape of the image domain due to the term in the denominator.) The gradient flow obtained by calculating the first variation of $h(C)$ is given by the equation

$$(11) \qquad \frac{\partial C}{\partial t} = [-\kappa_g \pm h(C)]N_g$$

where κ_g is now the *geodesic* curvature and N_g is the normal defined by the metric; plus sign is to be used if the area bounded by the curve is smaller than its complement, minus otherwise. In the isotropic case with the metric equal to a scalar function θ times the identity metric, the relation between the geodesic curvature κ_g and the Euclidean curvature κ is given by the equation

$$(12) \qquad \kappa_g = \frac{1}{\theta}\left[\kappa + \frac{\nabla\theta \cdot N}{\theta}\right]$$

Thus the geodesic curvature includes the advection term. The term $h(C)$ is the component of the velocity which is constant along the curve and varies in magnitude as the curve moves. To implement the flow, the initial curve is embedded as a level curve of a function u and the evolution equation for u is derived such that its level curves move with velocity proportional to their geodesic curvature augmented by the component β, constant along each level curve. If only the motion of the original curve C is of interest, we may assume that all the level curves have the same constant component β equal to $h(C)$, updated continuously as C evolves. However, if motion of all the level curves is of interest, then the value of h for each level curve must be calculated, making the implementation considerably more difficult. In this paper, purely anisotropic geodesic flow is studied by setting $\beta = 0$.

The functional for u may be derived using the coarea formula, taking care to define all the quantities involved in terms of the metric g. Let $g^{-1} = \{g^{ij}\}$ be the metric dual to g given by the inverse of the matrix $\{g_{ij}\}$. Let

$$(13) \qquad <X,Y>_A = \sum_{i,j} X_i A_{ij} Y_j$$

be the binary form defined by a given matrix A and let

$$(14) \qquad \|X\|_A = \sqrt{< X, X \underset{A}{>}}$$

Then the functional for u may be obtained by the coarea formula and has the form

$$(15) \qquad \int_M \left[\|\nabla u\|_{g^{-1}} + \beta u \right] = \int_D \left[\|\nabla u\|_{g^{-1}} + \beta u \right] \sqrt{det(g)}$$

where β is assumed to constant. Here, ∇u is the Euclidean gradient vector $\{u_{x_i}\}$. (In fact, $g^{-1}\nabla u$ is the gradient vector $\nabla_g u$ defined by the metric g and $\|\nabla_g u\|_g = \|\nabla u\|_{g^{-1}}$.) The evolution equation for u has the form

$$(16) \qquad \frac{\partial u}{\partial t} = div_g \left(\frac{g^{-1}\nabla u}{\|\nabla u\|_{g^{-1}}} \right) - \beta$$

where

$$(17) \qquad div_g(X) = \sum_i \frac{1}{\sqrt{det(g)}} \partial_i \left(X_i \sqrt{det(g)} \right)$$

is the divergence operator defined with respect to g. The equations (16) and (17) are valid in arbitrary dimension. The first term in Equation (16) is the mean geodesic curvature of the level hypersurfaces of u.

In dimension 2, the evolution equation (16) for u assumes a fairly simple form and is not much more difficult to implement than in the isotropic case. In dimension 2, after multiplying the right hand side of Equation (16) by a positive function, we get

$$(18) \qquad \frac{\partial u}{\partial t} = curv(u)\|\nabla u\| + \frac{\gamma\|\nabla u\|_K^2 - \frac{1}{2}\|\nabla u\|_Q^2 - \beta\|\nabla u\|_K^3 \sqrt{det(K)}}{\|\nabla u\|^2 det(K)}$$

where as before, $curv(u)$ is the Euclidean curvature of the level curves of u, ∇u is the Euclidean gradient of u, $\|\nabla u\|$ is its Euclidean norm, and

$$(19) \qquad \begin{aligned} K &= det(g)g^{-1} \\ \gamma &= \sum_{i,j} \partial_i K_{ij} \partial_j u \\ Q_{ij} &=< \nabla u, \nabla K_{ij} \underset{K}{>} \end{aligned}$$

Comparison with the corresponding equation for the isotropic flow shows that anisotropy does not affect the second order curvature term, but the advection term is more finely tuned. To have the effect of anisotropy on the second order term in dimension 2, more general Finsler metrics must be considered [1].

4 Approximation: Riemannian Drums

As in the isotropic case, Equation (18) is hyperbolic in the direction normal to the level curves so that its solution is capable of developing shocks. A shock-capturing numerical method [12] must be used to implement the equation. An alternative is to convert the minimum-cut problem into an eigenvalue problem as suggested by the Cheeger inequality

$$(20) \qquad \lambda \geq \frac{1}{4}\left(\min_C h(C)\right)^2$$

where λ is the second smallest eigenvalue of the Laplace–Beltrami operator. Therefore, instead of minimizing $h(C)$, consider minimizing the Rayleigh quotient

$$(21) \qquad \frac{\int_D \|\nabla u\|_{g^{-1}}^2 \sqrt{det(g)}}{\int_D u^2 \sqrt{det(g)}}$$

which is equivalent to solving the eigenvalue problem

$$(22) \qquad \Delta_g u + \lambda u = 0, \text{ Neumann boundary conditions}$$

where

$$(23) \qquad \Delta_g u = \frac{1}{\sqrt{det(g)}} \sum_{i,j} \partial_i \left(g^{ij}\sqrt{det(g)}\partial_j u\right)$$

is the Laplace–Beltrami operator. When g is the Euclidean metric, the operator reduces to the ordinary Laplacian and the eigenvalue problem describes the modes of vibration of an elastic membrane. When discretized, the eigenvalue problem takes the form

$$(24) \qquad Hu = \lambda M u$$

where u is now a vector, H is the "stiffness" matrix and M is the mass matrix. An important point to note is that Equation (22) does not involve β, its approximate value is determined automatically by the Cheeger inequality. Another important point to note is that for the approximation to work, an anisotropic metric is essential. In dimension 2, if the metric is isotropic, the numerator in the Rayleigh quotient is independent of g and since we expect g to deviate substantially from the Euclidean metric only near the shape boundary, the denominator is insensitive to g as well. As a result, the eigenvalue problem reduces to essentially the Euclidean case.

The eigenvalue problem (22) is an analytic version of the formulation proposed by Shi and Malik in the framework of graph theory, motivated by the principles of gestalt psychology. They regard the image as a weighted graph by viewing the pixels as vertices and assigning weights to the edges in proportion to the proximity of the corresponding vertices and similarity between the feature values at these vertices. The minimum cut of the graph is defined in some normalized way. There is a standard way to define the Laplacian of a graph from its adjacency matrix [9,10] and approximate the minimum cut problem as the problem of determining the eigenvector corresponding to the second smallest eigenvalue of this Laplacian. Since this eigenvalue is zero if the graph is disconnected, it is called the algebraic connectivity of the graph. For a more detailed comparison between the graph-theoretic formulation and the formulation presented here, see [16]. Note that here too, anisotropicity is essential. Isotropicity would mean that all the edges have the same weight and hence the graph cannot carry any information about the image.

The eigenvalue problem may be approximately solved by one of the special methods for large sparse matrices such as the Lanczos method [5]. Care must be taken to ensure that the matrix H is symmetric so that the Lanczos method is applicable. One of the ways to ensure this is to derive Equation (24) by discretizing the Rayleigh quotient (21) instead of Equation (22). Details of the Lanczos method may be found in [16]. The method is an efficient procedure to find the vector which minimizes the Rayleigh quotient over the vector space $\mathcal{K}_m = \{u_0, M^{-1}Hu_0, (M^{-1}H)^2u_0, \cdots, (M^{-1}H)^mu_0\}$. Here, u_0 is a user-supplied initial vector and m is chosen so that satisfactory numerical convergence is obtained. In principle, the only requirement for the method to work is that the initial vector must have a component along the true eigenvector. However, the greater the number of higher eigenvectors significantly present in u_0, the larger the value of m needed for the method to converge to the second eigenvector. Moreover, as m increases, it becomes harder and harder to orthogonalize the vector space $\mathcal{K}_m$ as required by the Lanczos method. Therefore, the choice of the initial vector is a non-trivial problem.

5. Anisotropic Metrics

In dimension 2, the obvious starting point for intensity images is the matrix

$$(25) \qquad \nabla I^\sigma \otimes \nabla I^\sigma = \begin{bmatrix} \partial_1 I^\sigma \partial_1 I^\sigma & \partial_1 I^\sigma \partial_2 I^\sigma \\ \partial_1 I^\sigma \partial_2 I^\sigma & \partial_2 I^\sigma \partial_2 I^\sigma \end{bmatrix}$$

where I^σ denotes the smoothing of the image by a Gaussian filter. There are two problems with the metric defined in this way. First of all, the metric is degenerate since the determinant is zero. This may be remedied by adding a small multiple of the identity matrix to the above matrix. (Shi and Malik solve this problem by exponentiating the metric.) The second objection is that the length of each level curve of I^σ is just a constant multiple of its Euclidean length. Since we expect the object boundaries to coincide more or less with the level curves, evolving curves will shrink and vanish. A solution to this problem is to divide the augmented matrix by its determinant. The final result is the metric given by the matrix

$$(26) \qquad \begin{bmatrix} \dfrac{1+\alpha\partial_1 I^\sigma \partial_1 I^\sigma}{1+\alpha\|\nabla I^\sigma\|^2} & \dfrac{\alpha\partial_1 I^\sigma \partial_2 I^\sigma}{1+\alpha\|\nabla I^\sigma\|^2} \\ \dfrac{\alpha\partial_1 I^\sigma \partial_2 I^\sigma}{1+\alpha\|\nabla I^\sigma\|^2} & \dfrac{1+\alpha\partial_2 I^\sigma \partial_2 I^\sigma}{1+\alpha\|\nabla I^\sigma\|^2} \end{bmatrix}$$

where α is a constant. Finally, just as in the isotropic case [14], the metric may be raised to some power p. The effect of p is to sharpen the maxima and the minima of the smaller eigenvalue of the metric over the image domain, resulting in sharper edges and corners. In the gradient direction, the infinitestimal length is the Euclidean arclength ds, independent of the gradient. Along the level curves of I^σ, the infinitestimal length is $ds/(1 + \alpha\|\nabla I^\sigma\|^2)^{p/2}$. Thus the metric provides a generalization compatible with the isotropic case as it is usually formulated [14]. Its generalization to vector valued images, for instance to the case where we have a set of transforms $\{I^{(k)}\}$ of the image by a bank of filters, is straightforward. In matrix (26), simply replace $\partial_i I^\sigma \partial_j I^\sigma$ by $\Sigma_k \alpha^{(k)} \partial_i I^{(k)} \partial_j I^{(k)}$. Generalizaton to arbitrary dimension n is obtained by letting the indices i, j run from 1 to n and normalizing the metric by dividing it by the $(n-1)^{th}$ root of its determinant. Of course, determining the weights $\{\alpha^{(k)}\}$ is a difficult problem.

6. Experiments

In the first experiment, different methods considered here are compared from the point of view of smoothing intensity images. In the second experiment, in addition to smoothing an MR image, anisotropic flow is applied to smoothing of the zero-crossings of the Laplacian of the image presmoothed by a Gaussian.

In these experiments, the constant β was set equal to zero and α was chosen so that the smallest value achieved by the smaller eigenvalue of the matrices $\{g_{ij}\}$ over the image domain was equal to a small constant c, less than 1. The closer the value of c is to 1, the closer the metric is to the Euclidean metric. (The Euclidean geodesic flow is a purely curvature-driven flow without advection. The image is eventually smoothed out to uniform intensity.) In the case of the eigenvalue problem, the closer the value of c is to 1, the more the behavior is like a Euclidean drum and the second eigenvector is dominated by the fundamental mode of Euclidean vibration.

In order to clearly bring out the differences among the different methods, the first experiment is that of a synthetic image with greatly exaggerated noise. The image is shown in Figure 1a (top-left) and was created by adding noise to a white ellipse on a black background. The top-right frame shows a horizontal and a vertical cross-section through the middle of the image. The metric was calculated from the the the filtered image I^σ obtained by filtering the original image by a Gaussian with standard deviation equal to $\sqrt{2}$. I^σ was also used as the initial vector for the geodesic flow as well as for the Lanczos iteration. (Uniformly sampled random noise was also tried as initial u for solving the eigenvalue problem, but the convergence was unacceptably slow.) .

Under the isotropic flow, with $\theta = 1/(1 + \alpha\|\nabla I^\sigma\|^2)^2$ in Equation (12), all the significant level curves shrank and vanished in a few thousand iterations. The bottom frames of Figure 1a show the results of anisotropic geodesic flow. The numerically steady state shown in the figure remained stable even after a few hundred thousand iterations. Sharpening of the edges can be clearly seen in the graph of the cross-sections.

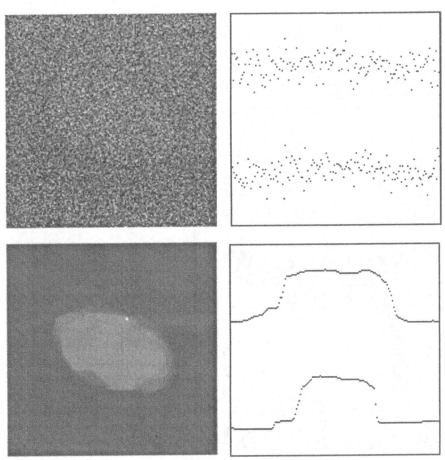

Fig. 1a. Top Right: A synthetic image . Top Left: Horizontal and
vertical sections through the middle. Bottom Right: Smoothing
by anisotropic geodesic flow. Bottom Left: The two sections.

The solution to the eigenvalue problem is shown in the top-row of Figure 1b. The
figure shows that the method is not as effective as the method of geodesic flow for
denoising or deblurring. In fact, the solution is very close to the initial vector I^σ.

The best results were obtained using Equations (8) corresponding to the segmentation functional (6) as shown in the bottom row of Figure 1b. The advantage of the
segmentation functional over the curve evolution formulation is that denoising and
edge detection are done simultaneously. The formulation makes it possible for the
smoothed intensity u and the edge-strength function v to interact and reinforce each
other. In the example shown, u is in fact almost piecewise constant.

Figures 2a and 2b portray the results for an MR image. This is a more difficult
image to deal with since the intensity gradient and the curvature vary widely along
the object boundaries, resulting in varying degrees of smoothing. This is especially
true of the thin protrusions and indentations. The top row in Figure 2a shows the
original image togetherwith graphs of two horizontal cross-sections. The top graph is

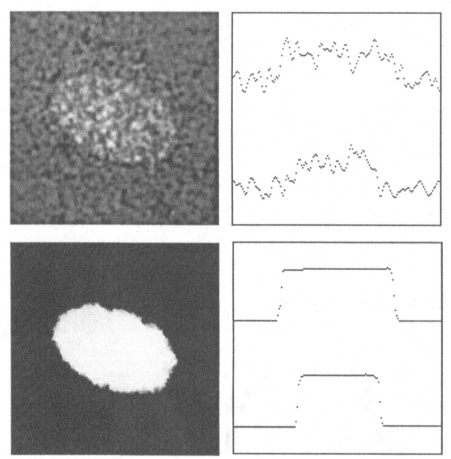

Fig. 1b. Top Right: Result of solving the eigenvalue problem. Top Left: The two sections. Bottom Right: Result by L1 functional. Bottom Left: The two sections.

a section near the top of the image while the bottom graph is through the two ventricles in the middle. The bottom row shows the effect of smoothing under anisotropic flow using the original image as the initial u as well as for calculating the metric. Figure 2b shows the results of smoothing the zero-crossings of $\nabla^2 I^\sigma$. The case $\sigma = 1/2$ is shown in the top row, the left frame being the initial zero-crossings. The case $\sigma = 3/\sqrt{2}$ is shown in the bottom row. The anisotropic metric was computed from the original (unsmoothed) image. Stability of the significant boundaries is indicated by the close similarity between the curves in the two figures.

References

(1) G. Bellettini and M. Paolini: "Anisotropic Motion by Mean Curvature in the Context of Finsler Geometry", Tech. Report, Universita Degli Studi di Milano, (1994).
(2) V. Caselles, F. Catte, T. Coll and F. Dibos: "A Geometric Model for Active Contours", Numerische Mathematik 66, (1993).
(3) V. Caselles, R. Kimmel and G. Sapiro: "Geodesic Active Contours", Fifth International Conference on Computer Vision, (1995).

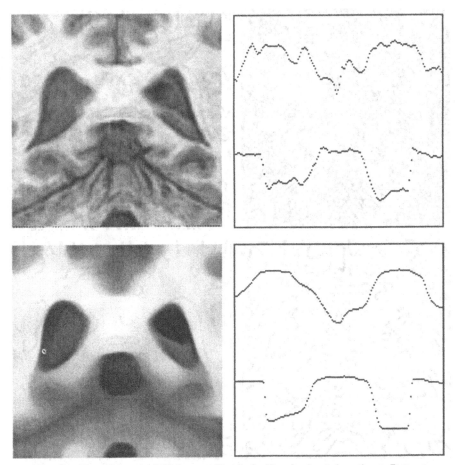

Fig. 2a. Top Right: An MR image. Top Left: Two horizontal sections. Bottom Right: Smoothing by anisotropic geodesic flow. Bottom Left: The two sections.

(4) J. Cheeger: "A Lower Bound for the Smallest Eigenvalue of the Laplacian", in *Problems in Analysis*, Ed: R.C. Gunning, Princeton University Press, (1970).

(5) Golub and Van Loan: *Matrix Computation*, John Hopkins University Press, (1989).

(6) M. Kass, A. Witkin and D. Terzopoulos: "Snakes: Active Contour Models", International J. of Computer Vision, v.1, (1988).

(7) S. Kichenassamy, A. Kumar, P. Olver, A. Tannenbaum and A. Yezzi: "Gradient Flows and Geometric Active Contour Models", Fifth International Conference on Computer Vision, (1995).

(8) R. Malladi, J.A. Sethian and B.C. Vemuri: "Shape Modeling with Front Propagation: A Level Set Approach", IEEE-PAMI 17, (1995).

(9) R. Merris: "Laplacian Matrices of Graphs: A Survey", Linear Algebra and its Applications 197,198, (1994).

(10) B. Mohar: "Laplace Eigenvalues of Graphs — A Survey", Discrete Math. 109, (1992).

(11) D. Mumford and J. Shah: "Optimal Approximations by Piecewise Smooth Functions and Associated Variational Problems", Comm. on Pure and Appl. Math, v.XLII, n.5, pp.577–684, (July, 1989).

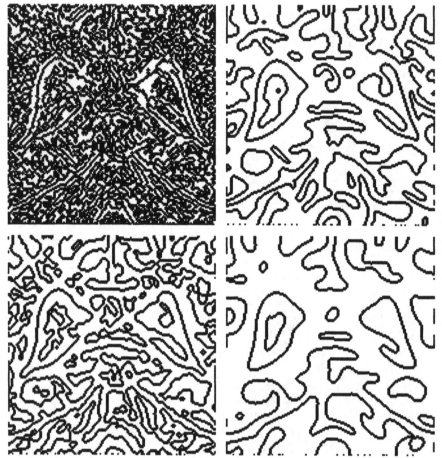

Fig. 2b. Top Right: Zero–crossings of $\nabla^2 I^\sigma, \sigma = 1/2$. Top Left: Smoothing of
the zero-crossings by anisotropic flow. Bottom Right: Zero–crossings of
$\nabla^2 I^\sigma, \sigma = 3/\sqrt{2}$. Bottom Left: Smoothing of the zero-crossings by anisotropic flow.

(12) S. Osher and J. Sethian: "Fronts Propagating with Curvature Dependent Speed: Algorithms based on the Hamilton-Jacobi Formulation", J. Comp. Physics, 79, (1988).

(13) J. Sethian: "Numerical Algorithms for Propagating Interfaces", J. of Diff. Geom. v.31, (1990).

(14) J. Shah: "Shape Recovery from Noisy Images by Curve Evolution", IASTED International Conference on Signal and Image Processing, (1995).

(15) J. Shah: "A Common Framework for Curve Evolution, Segmentation and Anisotropic Diffusion", IEEE Conference on Computer Vision and Pattern Re:cogntion, June, 1996.

(16) J. Shah: "Segmentation as a Riemannian Drum problem", IEEE International Conference on Image Processing, October, 1998.

(17) J. Shi and J. Malik: "Normalized Cuts and Image Segmentation", IEEE Conf. on Computer Vision and Pattern Recognition, (1997).

(18) H. Tek and B.B. Kimia: "Image Segmentation by Reaction-Diffusion Bubbles", Fifth International Conference on Computer Vision, (1995).

An Active Contour Model without Edges

Tony Chan and Luminita Vese

Department of Mathematics, University of California, Los Angeles,
520 Portola Plaza, Los Angeles, CA 90095-1555
chan,lvese@math.ucla.edu
WWW home page: http://www.math.ucla.edu

Abstract. In this paper, we propose a new model for active contours to detect objects in a given image, based on techniques of curve evolution, Mumford-Shah functional for segmentation and level sets. Our model can detect objects whose boundaries are not necessarily defined by gradient. The model is a combination between more classical active contour models using mean curvature motion techniques, and the Mumford-Shah model for segmentation. We minimize an energy which can be seen as a particular case of the so-called minimal partition problem. In the level set formulation, the problem becomes a "mean-curvature flow"-like evolving the active contour, which will stop on the desired boundary. However, the stopping term does not depend on the gradient of the image, as in the classical active contour models, but is instead related to a particular segmentation of the image. Finally, we will present various experimental results and in particular some examples for which the classical snakes methods based on the gradient are not applicable.

1 Introduction

The basic idea in active contour models or snakes is to evolve a curve, subject to constraints from a given image u_0, in order to detect objects in that image. For instance, starting with a curve around the object to be detected, the curve moves toward its interior normal under some constraints from the image, and has to stop on the boundary of the object.

Let Ω be a bounded and open subset of $I\!\!R^2$, with $\partial\Omega$ its boundary. Let u_0 be a given image, as a bounded function defined on $\overline{\Omega}$ and with real values. Usually, $\overline{\Omega}$ is a rectangle in the plane and u_0 takes values between 0 and 255. Denote by $C(s):[0,1]\to I\!\!R^2$ a piecewise C^1 parameterized curve.

In all the classical snakes and active contour models (see for instance [7], [3], [9], [4]), an edge detector is used to stop the evolving curve on the boundaries of the desired object. Usually, this is a positive and regular edge-function $g(|\nabla u_0|)$, decreasing such that $\lim_{t\to\infty} g(t) = 0$. For instance,

$$g(|\nabla u_0|) = \frac{1}{1+|\nabla G_\sigma * u_0|^2},$$

where $G_\sigma * u_0$ is the convolution of the image u_0 with the Gaussian $G_\sigma(x,y) = \sigma^{-1/2}\exp(-|x^2+y^2|/4\sigma)$ (a smoother version of u_0). The function $g(|\nabla u_0|)$ will be strictly positive in homogeneous regions, and near zero on the edges. The evolving curve moves by a variant of the mean curvature motion [14] with the edge-function $g(|\nabla u_0|)$ as an extra factor in the velocity.

All these classical snakes or active contour models rely on this edge-function g, depending on the gradient $|\nabla u_0|$ of the image, to stop the curve evolution. Therefore, these models can detect only objects with edges defined by gradient. Also, in practice, the discrete gradients are bounded and then the stopping function g is never zero on the edges, and the curve may pass through the boundary. On the other hand, if the image u_0 is noisy, then the isotropic smoothing Gaussian has to be strong, which will smooth the edges too. In this paper, we propose a different active contour model, without a stopping edge-function, i.e. a model which is not based on the gradient of the image u_0 for the stopping process. The stopping term is based on Mumford-Shah segmentation techniques [13]. In this way, we obtain a model which can detect contours both with or without gradient, for instance objects with very smooth boundaries or even with discontinuous boundaries. For a discussion on different types of contours, we refer the reader to [6].

The outline of the paper is as follows. In the next section we introduce our model as an energy minimization and discuss the relationship with the Mumford-Shah functional for segmentation. In Section 3, we formulate the model in terms of level set functions, compute the associated Euler-Lagrange equations, and discuss the algorithm. We end the paper validating our model by numerical results. We show in particular how we can detect contours without gradient or cognitive contours [6], for which the classical models are not applicable, and also how we can automatically detect interior contours.

Before describing our proposed model, we would like to refer the reader to the works [10] and [11] for shape recovery using level sets and edge-function, and to more recent and related works by [19], [17], and [8].

Finally, we would also like to mention [21] and [12] on shape reconstruction from unorganized points, and to the recent works [15] and [16], where a probability based geodesic active region model combined with classical gradient based active contour techniques is proposed.

2   Description of the model

Let C be the evolving curve. We denote by c_1 and c_2 two constants, representing the averages of u_0 "inside" and "outside" the curve C.

Our model is the minimization of an energy based-segmentation. Let us first explain the basic idea of the model in a simple case. Assume that the image u_0 is formed by two regions of approximatively piecewise-constant intensities, of distinct values u_0^i and u_0^o. Assume further that the object to be detected is represented by the region with the value u_0^i and let denote his boundary by C. Then we have $u_0 \approx u_0^i$ inside the object (inside C) and $u_0 \approx u_0^o$ outside the object (outside C). Now let us consider the following "fitting energy", formed by two terms:

$$F_1(C) + F_2(C) = \int_{inside(C)} |u_0 - c_1|^2 dx dy + \int_{outside(C)} |u_0 - c_2|^2 dx dy,$$

where C is any other variable curve. We say that the boundary of the object $\mathcal{C}$ is the minimizer of the fitting energy:

$$\inf_C \left\{ F_1(C) + F_2(C) \right\} \approx 0 \approx F_1(\mathcal{C}) + F_2(\mathcal{C}).$$

This can be seen easily. For instance, if the curve C is outside the object, then $F_1(C) > 0$ and $F_2(C) \approx 0$. If the curve C is inside the object, then $F_1(C) \approx 0$ but $F_2(C) > 0$. Finally, the fitting energy will be minimized if the $C = \mathcal{C}$, i.e. if the curve C is on the boundary of the object. These remarks are illustrated in Fig. 1.

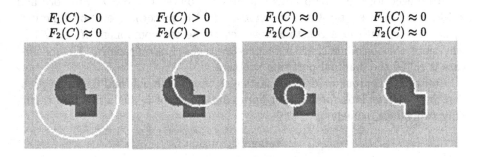

Fig. 1. Consider all possible cases in the position of the curve. The "fitting energy" is minimized only for the case when the curve is on the boundary of the object.

Therefore, in our active contour model we will minimize this fitting energy and we can add some regularizing terms, like the length of C and/or the area inside C. We introduce the energy $F(C, c_1, c_2)$ by:

$$F(C, c_1, c_2) = \mu \cdot \text{length}(C) + \nu \cdot \text{area}(inside C)$$
$$+ \lambda_1 \int_{inside(C)} |u_0 - c_1|^2 dx dy + \lambda_2 \int_{outside(C)} |u_0 - c_2|^2 dx dy,$$

where c_1 and c_2 are constant unknowns, and $\mu > 0$, $\nu \geq 0$, $\lambda_1, \lambda_2 > 0$ are fixed parameters.

In almost all our computations, we take $\nu = 0$ and $\lambda_1 = \lambda_2$. Of-course that one of these parameters can be "eliminated", by fixing it to be 1. In almost all our computations, we take $\nu = 0$ and $\lambda_1 = \lambda_2$. The area term in the energy can be used for instance when we may need to force the curve to move only inside.

In order to balance the terms and their dimensions in the energy, if d is the unit distance in the Ω-plane, then μ has to be measured in units of $(size\ of\ u_0)^2 \cdot d$, and ν has to be measured in units of $(size\ of\ u_0)^2$.

Finally, we consider the minimization problem:

$$\inf_{C, c_1, c_2} F(C, c_1, c_2). \tag{1}$$

2.1 Relation with the Mumford-Shah functional for segmentation

The Mumford-Shah functional for segmentation is [13]:

$$F^{MS}(u, C) = \int_{\Omega \backslash C} (\alpha |\nabla u|^2 + \beta |u - u_0|^2) dx dy + \text{length}(C), \tag{2}$$

where α, β are positive parameters. The solution image u obtained by minimizing this functional is formed by smooth regions R_i and with sharp boundaries, denoted here by C.

A reduced form of this problem, as it was pointed out by D. Mumford and J. Shah in [13], is simply the restriction of F^{MS} to piecewise constant functions u, i.e. $u = c_i$ with c_i a constant, on each connected component R_i of $\Omega \backslash C$. Therefore, the constants c_i are in fact the averages of u_0 on each R_i. The reduced case is called the minimal partition problem.

Our active contour model is a particular case of the minimal partition problem, in which we look for the best approximation u of u_0, as a function taking only two values, namely:

$$u = \begin{cases} \text{average}(u_0) \text{ inside } C \\ \text{average}(u_0) \text{ outside } C, \end{cases}$$

and with one edge C, represented by the snake or the active contour.

This particular case of the minimal partition problem can be formulated and solved using the level set method [14]. This is presented in the next section.

2.2 The level set formulation of the model

In the level set method [14], an evolving curve C is represented by the zero level set of a Lipschitz continuous function $\phi : \Omega \to \mathbb{R}$. So, $C = \{(x, y) \in \Omega : \phi(x, y) = 0\}$, and we choose ϕ to be positive inside C and negative outside C. For the level set formulation of our variational active contour model we essentially follow [20]. Therefore, we replace the unknown variable C by the unknown variable ϕ and the new energy, still denoted by $F(\phi, c_1, c_2)$, becomes:

$$F(\phi, c_1, c_2) = \mu \cdot \text{length}\{\phi = 0\} + \nu \cdot \text{area}\{\phi \geq 0\}$$
$$+ \lambda_1 \int_{\phi \geq 0} |u_0 - c_1|^2 dx dy + \lambda_2 \int_{\phi < 0} |u_0 - c_2|^2 dx dy.$$

Using the Heaviside function H defined by

$$H(x) = \begin{cases} 1, \text{ if } x \geq 0 \\ 0, \text{ if } x < 0 \end{cases}$$

and the one-dimensional Dirac measure δ concentrated at 0 and defined by

$$\delta(x) = \frac{d}{dx} H(x) \text{ (in the sense of distributions)},$$

we express the terms in the energy F in the following way:

$$\begin{cases} \text{length}\{\phi = 0\} = \int_\Omega |\nabla H(\phi)| = \int_\Omega \delta(\phi)|\nabla\phi|, \\ \text{area}\{\phi \geq 0\} = \int_\Omega H(\phi) dx dy, \end{cases}$$

and

$$\begin{cases} \int_{\phi \geq 0} |u_0 - c_1|^2 dx dy = \int_\Omega |u_0 - c_1|^2 H(\phi) dx dy \\ \int_{\phi < 0} |u_0 - c_2|^2 dx dy = \int_\Omega |u_0 - c_2|^2 (1 - H(\phi)) dx dy. \end{cases}$$

Then the energy $F(\phi, c_1, c_2)$ can be written as:

$$F(\phi, c_1, c_2) = \mu \int_\Omega \delta(\phi)|\nabla\phi| + \nu \int_\Omega H(\phi) dx dy$$
$$+ \lambda_1 \int_\Omega |u_0 - c_1|^2 H(\phi) dx dy + \lambda_2 \int_\Omega |u_0 - c_2|^2 (1 - H(\phi)) dx dy.$$

Keeping ϕ fixed and minimizing the energy $F(\phi, c_1, c_2)$ with respect to the constants c_1 and c_2, it is easy to express these constants function of ϕ by:

$$c_1(\phi) = \frac{\int_\Omega u_0 H(\phi) dx dy}{\int_\Omega H(\phi(x,y)) dx dy} \qquad \text{(the average of } u_0 \text{ in } \{\phi \geq 0\}), \qquad (3)$$

$$c_2(\phi) = \frac{\int_\Omega u_0 (1 - H(\phi)) dx dy}{\int_\Omega (1 - H(\phi(x,y))) dx dy} \qquad \text{(the average of } u_0 \text{ in } \{\phi < 0\}). \qquad (4)$$

Keeping c_1 and c_2 fixed, and formally minimizing the energy with respect to ϕ, we obtain the Euler-Lagrange equation for ϕ (parameterizing the descent direction by an artificial time):

$$\begin{cases} \frac{\partial\phi}{\partial t} = \delta(\phi)\left[\mu\text{div}\left(\frac{\nabla\phi}{|\nabla\phi|}\right) - \nu - \lambda_1(u_0 - c_1)^2 + \lambda_2(u_0 - c_2)^2\right] \text{ in } \Omega, \\ \frac{\delta(\phi)}{|\nabla\phi|} \frac{\partial\phi}{\partial n} = 0 \text{ on } \partial\Omega. \end{cases}$$

In practice, we have to consider slightly regularized versions of the functions H and δ, denoted here by H_ε and δ_ε, such that $\delta_\varepsilon(x) = H'_\varepsilon(x)$.

A first possible regularization by C^2 and respectively C^1 functions, as proposed for instance in [20], is:

$$H_{1,\varepsilon}(x) = \begin{cases} 1 \text{ if } x > \varepsilon \\ 0 \text{ if } x < -\varepsilon \\ \frac{1}{2}\left[1 + \frac{x}{\varepsilon} + \frac{1}{\pi}\sin\left(\frac{\pi x}{\varepsilon}\right)\right] \text{ if } |x| \leq \varepsilon \end{cases}$$

and

$$\delta_{1,\varepsilon}(x) = H'_{1,\varepsilon}(x) = \begin{cases} 0 \text{ if } |x| > \varepsilon \\ \frac{1}{2\varepsilon}\left[1 + \cos\left(\frac{\pi x}{\varepsilon}\right)\right], \text{ if } |x| \leq \varepsilon. \end{cases}$$

In our calculations, we use instead the following C^∞ regularized versions of H and δ, defined by:

$$H_{2,\varepsilon}(x) = \frac{1}{2}(1 + \frac{2}{\pi}\arctan(\frac{x}{\varepsilon})), \ \delta_{2,\varepsilon}(x) = H'_{2,\varepsilon}(x) = \frac{1}{\pi} \cdot \frac{\varepsilon}{\varepsilon^2 + x^2}.$$

As $\varepsilon \to 0$, both approximations converge to H and δ. The first approximations $H_{1,\varepsilon}$ and $\delta_{1,\varepsilon}$ are C^2 and respectively C^1 functions, with $\delta_{1,\varepsilon}$ with small compact support, arround the zero-level set. The second approximations $H_{2,\varepsilon}$ and $\delta_{2,\varepsilon}$ are both C^∞ functions, with $\delta_{2,\varepsilon}$ different of zero everywhere.

We want to formally explain here why we need to introduce the second approximations, instead of the first approximations, which have been used in previous papers (for instance in [20]). Because our energy is non-convex (allowing therefore many local minima), and because $\delta_{1,\varepsilon}$ has a very small compact support, the interval $[-\varepsilon, \varepsilon]$, the iterative algorithm may depend on the initial curve, and will not necessarily compute a global minimizer. In some of our tests using the first approximation, we obtained only a local minimizer of the energy. Using the second approximations, the algorithm has the tendency to compute a global minimizer. One of the reasons is that, the Euler-Lagrange equation acts only locally, on a few level curves arround $\phi = 0$ using the first approximation, while by the second approximation, the equation acts on all level curves, of course stronger on the zero level curve, but not only locally. In this way, in practice, we can obtain a global minimizer, independently of the position of the initial curve. Moreover, interior contours are automatically detected. We could also extend the motion to all level sets of ϕ replacing $\delta(\phi)$ in the equation by $|\nabla\phi|$ (this method is for instance used in [20]).

To discretize the equation in ϕ, we use a finite differences implicit scheme (we refer the reader to [1], for details).

We also need at each step to reinitialize ϕ to be the signed distance function to its zero-level curve. This procedure is standard (see [18] and [20]), and prevences the level set function to become too flat, or it can be seen as a L^∞ stability for ϕ and a rescaling.

This reinitialization procedure is made by the following evolution equation [18]:

$$\begin{cases} \psi_\tau = sign(\phi(t))(1 - |\nabla\psi|) \\ \psi(0,\cdot) = \phi(t,\cdot), \end{cases} \quad (5)$$

where $\phi(t,\cdot)$ is our solution ϕ at time t. Then the new $\phi(t,\cdot)$ will be ψ, such that ψ is obtained at the steady state of (5).

3 Experimental results

We present here numerical results using our model. For the examples in Figures 2-5, we show the image and the evolving contour (top), together with the piecewise-constant approximations given by the averages c_1 and c_2 (bottom). In all cases, we start with a single initial closed curve. We choose the level set function ϕ to be positive "inside" the initial curve, and negative "outside" the initial curve, but in our model this choice is not important. We could consider the opposite signs, and the curve would still be attracted by the object. Also, the position of the initial curve is not important.

In Fig. 2 we show how our model can detect contours without gradient or cognitive contours (see [6]) and an interior contour automatically, starting with only one initial curve. This is obtained using our second approximations for H and δ. In Fig. 3 we consider a very noisy image. Again the interior contour of the torus is automatically detected.

In Fig. 4 we validate our model on a very different problem: to detect features in spatial point processes in the presence of substantial cluster. One example is the detection of minefields using reconnaissance aircraft images that identify many objects that are not mines. These problems are for instance solved using statistical methods (see for instance [5] and [2]). By this application, we show again that our model can be used to detect objects or features with contours without gradient. This is not possible using classical snakes or active contours based on the gradient.

We end the paper with results on two real images (Fig. 5 and 6.), illustrating all the properties of our model: detecting smooth boundaries, scaling role of the length term in the size of the detected objects, and automatic change of topology.

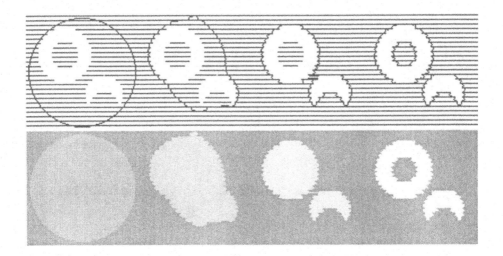

Fig. 2. Detection of different objects in a synthetic image, with various convexities and with an interior contour, which is automatically detected. Here we illustrate the fact that our model can detect edges without gradient. Top: u_0 and the contour. Bottom: the piece-wise constant approximation of u_0.

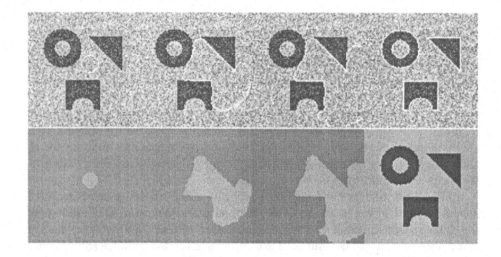

Fig. 3. Results for a very noisy image, with the initial curve not surrounding the objects. Top: u_0 and the contour. Bottom: the piece-wise constant approximation of u_0.

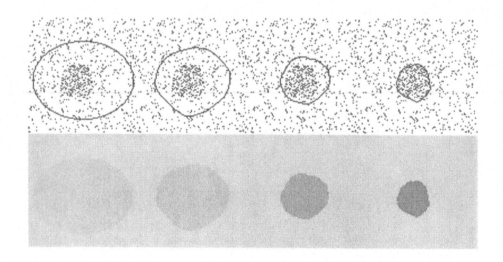

Fig. 4. Detection of a simulated minefield, with contour without gradient.

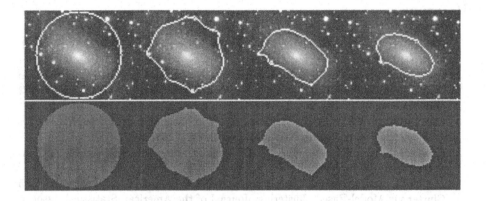

Fig. 5. Detection of a galaxy with very smooth boundaries.

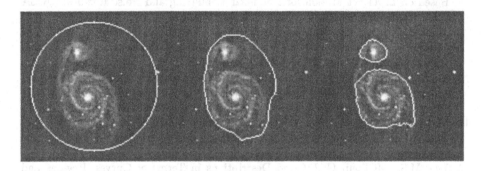

Fig. 6. Detection of the contours of a galaxy.

4 Concluding remarks

In this paper we proposed an active contour model based on Mumford-Shah segmentation techniques and level set methods. Our model is not based on an edge-function, like in the classical active contour models, to stop the evolving curve on the desired boundary. We do not need to smooth the initial image, even if it is very noisy and in this way, the locations of boundaries are very well detected. Also, we can detect objects whose boundaries are not necessarily defined by gradient or with very smooth boundaries. The model automatically detects interior contours, starting with only one initial curve. The initial curve does not necessarily start around the objects to be detected. Finally, we validated our model by various numerical results.

References

1. Aubert, G., Vese, L.: A variational method in image recovery. SIAM J. Num. Anal. **34/5** (1997) 1948-1979.
2. Byers, S., Raftery, A.: Nearest-Neighbor Clutter Removal for Estimating Features in Spatial Point Processes. Journal of the American Statistical Association **93/442** (1998) 577-584.
3. Caselles, V., Catté, F., Coll, T., Dibos, F.: A geometric model for active contours in image processing. Numerische Mathematik **66** (1993) 1-31.
4. Caselles, V., Kimmel, R., Sapiro, G.: On geodesic active contours. Journal of Computer Vision **22(1)** (1997) 61-79.
5. Dasgupta, A., Raftery, A.: Detecting Features in Spatial Point Processes With Clutter via Model-Based Clustering. Journal of the American Statistical Association **98/441** (1998) 294-302.
6. Kanizsa, G.: La Grammaire du Voir. Essais sur la perception. Diderot Editeur, Arts et Sciences (1997).
7. Kass, M., Witkin, A., Terzopoulos, D.: Snakes: Active contour models. International Journal of Computer Vision **1** (1988) 321-331.
8. Marquina, A., Osher, S.: Explicit Algorithms for a New Time Dependent Model Based on Level Set Motion for Nonlinear Deblurring and Noise Removal. UCLA CAM Report **99-55** (1999).
9. Malladi, R., Sethian, J.A., and Vemuri, B.C.: A Topology Independent Shape Modeling Scheme. Proc. SPIE Conf. on Geometric Methods in Computer Vision II, San Diego, **2031** (1993), 246-258.
10. Malladi, R., Sethian, J.A., and Vemuri, B.C.: Evolutionary Fronts for Topology-Independent Shape Modeling and Recovery. Proceedings of the Third European Conference on Computer Vision, LNCS **800** (1994), Stockholm, Sweden, 3-13.
11. Malladi, R., Sethian, J.A., Vemuri, B.C.: Shape Modeling with Front Propagation: A Level Set Approach. IEEE Transactions on Pattern Analysis and Machine Intelligence, **17**, No. 2 (1995), 158-175.
12. Lee, M.S., Medioni, G: Inferred Descriptions in Terms of Curves, Regions and Junctions from Sparse, Noisy Binary Data. Proceedings of the IEEE International Symposium on Computer Vision, Coral Gable, Florida (1995), 73-78.
13. Mumford, D., Shah, J.: Optimal approximation by piecewise smooth functions and associated variational problems. Comm. Pure Appl. Math. **42** (1989) 577-685.
14. Osher, S., Sethian, J. A.: Fronts Propagating with Curvature-Dependent Speed: Algorithms Based on Hamilton-Jacobi Formulation. Journal of Computational Physics **79** (1988) 12-49.
15. Paragios, N., and Deriche, R.: Geodesic Active Regions for Texture Segmentation. INRIA Research Report **3440** (1998).
16. Paragios, N., and Deriche, R.: Geodesic Active Regions for Motion Estimation and Tracking. INRIA Research Report 3631 (1999).
17. Siddiqi, K., Lauzière, Y. B., Tannenbaum, A., and Zucker, S. W.: Area and Length Minimizing Flows for Shape Segmentation. IEEE Transactions on Image Processing (Special Issue) **7/3** (1998) 433-443.
18. Sussman, M., Smereka, P., Osher, S.: A Level Set Approach for Computing Solutions to Incompressible Two-Phase Flow. UCLA CAM Report **93-18** (1993).
19. Xu, C., Prince, J. L.: Snakes, Shapes and Gradient Vector Flow. IEEE Transactions on Image Processing (Special Issue) **7/3** (1998) 359-369.

20. Zhao, H. K., Chan, T., Merriman, B., Osher, S.: A Variational Level Set Approach to Multiphase Motion. Journal of Computational Physics **127** (1996) 179-195.
21. Zhao, H.-K., Osher, S., Merriman, B. and Kang, M.: Implicit, Nonparametric Shape Reconstruction from Unorganized Points Using A Variational Level Set Method. UCLA CAM Report **98-7** (1998) (revised February 1999).

A Compact and Multiscale Image Model Based on Level Sets

Jacques Froment

PRISME, UFR de Math. et Info., Univ. Paris 5 R.Descartes,
45 rue des Saints-Pères, 75270 Paris cedex 06, France
and
CMLA, Ecole Normale Supérieure de Cachan,
61 avenue du Président Wilson, 94235 Cachan cedex, France

Abstract. Multiscale segmentation respectful of the visual perception is an important issue of Computer Vision. We present an image model derived from the level sets representation which offers most of the properties sought to a good segmentation : the borders are located at the perceptual edges; they are invariant by affine map and by contrast change; they are sorted according to their perceptual significance using a scale parameter. At last, a compact version of this model has been developed to be used in a progressive, and artifact-free, image compression scheme.

1 Introduction

One of the basic problem of image analysis is to define a mathematical representation that offers suitable properties upon which subsequent computer vision algorithms would operate.

The edge detection theory of Hildreth and Marr [19] [26] was one of the first attempts to solve this problem using a multiscale analysis. The *raw primal sketch* of D.Marr is based on the detection of the intensity changes in the image, by recording the zero-crossing location of the image filtered by the Laplacian of the Gaussian at a given scale. The edges are then defined as discontinuity lines, and the scale parameter allows to discriminate the important *atoms*. This approach has been successfully developed in the past, since it meets almost all the requirements of a "good primal sketch" (see e.g. [10] for an optimal edge detector). These last years have seen interesting reformalizations of this multiscale edges representation, in a wavelet [18] and in a variational [21] framework.

However, this approach still suffers of some drawbacks that do not make it always suitable for some processes : the representation is not invariant under contrast changes. This means that the edge locations of an image on which a contrast change has been applied differ from the original edge locations. It is well known since M.Wertheimer [25] that the visual perception of edges does not depend of the light level. Therefore, edges should not be computed using a discrete derivative. This deviation is a major inconvenience for pattern recognition processes, but it does not really apply to compression problem. This last domain is concerned by the completeness of the representation. Although the classical linear multiscale edges representation is mathematically not complete, algorithms which allow to reconstruct an image close to the original have been described [14] [18]. But when the representation is altered by a compression process, visual artifacts (e.g. Gibbs phenomena) appear on the reconstructed image.

More recently, it has been proved in [2] that, under fairly conditions (including invariance under change of contrast, under change of scale and under affine map), there exists only one regular multiscale analysis, the so-called AMSS (for Affine Morphological Scale Space). An image is decomposed into this scale-space using a parabolic evolution equation, for which viscosity solutions [9] exist. Because of the morphological invariance, the evolution of the image along the scales is equivalent to the evolution of its level curves, which are defined as the border of the level sets. A level set is a set of pixels with gray levels below (or above) a given threshold.

The representation of an image by its level sets has been proposed by the Mathematical Morphology school [22] as a geometrical decomposition which offers the contrast invariance. This representation can be viewed as another raw primal sketch, for which all good properties are met but the compactness. Recently, such a decomposition based on the connected components of the level lines has been described [20], together with a fast algorithm. This representation is well adapted to number of image analysis problems (as pattern matching) but it still suffers of a relatively large amount of data. Using AMSS, a simplification of the image can be performed to reduce the amount of data. However, the structure of the image is then considerably weakened and the filtered image does not sound natural.

In this paper, we introduce another model based on the level sets that can be coded using a very small amount of data. We propose in Section 2 a new definition of morphological edges, based on the selection of the most perceptive level sets. We use the conjecture expressed in [6] about the atoms of the visual perception, made by pieces of level lines joining junctions. The regions formed by these level sets compose a segmentation at a given scale. Section 3 describes our image model : using an elliptic PDE [7], the image is approximated by smooth and non-oscillating functions on each regions given by the segmentation. This defines a sketch image which carries the most important structures, up to the scale of the less perceptive edges. According to the quantity of pixel's values retained in the border's regions, the image model may be used as a compact image representation. A straightforward application of this compact model is the design of a compression scheme that respects the human visual system. We illustrate this capacity in Section 4.

2 Morphological edges and multiscale segmentation

This section addresses the problem of computing a multiscale and morphological segmentation $\mathcal{P} = \{P_i/i = 1, \ldots, n\}$ such that the borders of the most important structures match the borders of the regions P_i. A classical answer would be to try to extract the edges, in the sense of the discontinuity lines in the image. However, the use of classical edge detectors is not consistent with the morphological approach, as it is well explained in [6], essentially because such edges are not contrast invariant. In this paper, V.Caselles, B.Coll and J.M.Morel argue that the atoms of the perception, that is, the basic elements on which further representations may be built, are not edges but "pieces of level lines joining junctions".

Let us first recall what level lines are. Let Ω be an open bounded subset of $\mathbb{R}^2$. The total variation of an image $u : \Omega \to \mathbb{R}$ can be simply defined, if $u \in C^1(\Omega)$, as

$$\text{TV}(u) = \int_\Omega |\nabla u(x)| \, dx. \tag{1}$$

If the gradient of u, ∇u, does not exist or is not continuous but if $u \in L^1(\Omega)$, (1) is generalized into

$$\text{TV}(u) = \sup_\phi \{ \int_\Omega u(x)(\text{div}\phi)(x) \, dx \, / \, \phi \in C_c^1(\Omega, \mathbb{R}^2) \text{ and } |\phi| \leq 1 \}. \tag{2}$$

We say that u is of bounded variation ($u \in \text{BV}(\Omega)$) if $\text{TV}(u) < +\infty$. A set $P \subset \Omega$ has finite perimeter if $\text{per}(P) = \text{TV}(\mathbb{1}_P) < +\infty$. In that case $\partial^* P$, the essential boundary of P, is an union of a countable set of Jordan curves [8].

Let L_λ be the lower level set λ and M_μ the upper level set μ of u:

$$L_\lambda = \{x \in \Omega / u(x) \leq \lambda\}, M_\mu = \{x \in \Omega / u(x) \geq \mu\}. \tag{3}$$

We shall call level set any lower or upper level set. The family $(L_\lambda)_\lambda$ or $(M_\mu)_\mu$ is a complete representation, since one can reconstruct the image by

$$u(x) = \inf_\lambda \{x \in L_\lambda\} = \sup_\mu \{x \in M_\mu\}. \tag{4}$$

If u is BV, then all level sets are of finite perimeter and their essential boundaries constitute the level lines of u. If we map the level lines of an image for a given set of levels $\{\lambda_1 < \lambda_2 \ldots < \lambda_n = +\infty\}$, we get a segmentation of the image with sets of type $\{x \in \Omega / \lambda_{i-1} < u(x) < \lambda_i\}$, also called topographic map [6] (see first line of Figure 3). More generally, one can consider a segmentation achieved using only some connected components of lower levet sets $(L_\lambda)_\lambda$ and upper level sets $(M_\mu)_\mu$. Notice that pieces of some (but not all) level lines are located at the perceptive edges and that conversely, all perceptive edges correspond to pieces of some level lines. A topographic map has also interesting invariance properties : the map commutes with any affine transformation performed on the image (translation, rotation, and zoom) and it does not change when the contrast of the image is modified (the so-called morphological property). Thus, a topographic map achieves a morphological segmentation with suitable properties to build an image model based on perceptual edges. The question is now : how should we select the level sets so that the level lines match as well as possible the visual perception of edges ?

We shall emphasize that the physical generation process of an image implies some events (as occlusions and transparencies) which cause singularities on the topographic map : level lines joining some other level lines with a shape (more or less) like a T in case of an occlusion. The T-junction singularity is one of the most significant principles of the visual reconstruction, which allows a geometrical constitution of the visual objects. It is in the heart of the Gestaltist's theory, and in particular of the Kanizsa's work [15] [16]. Each time a T-junction is detected, our perception reconstructs the occlusion of an object by another one, and the border of the occluded object is mentally extended behind the horizontal bar of the T. In the left drawing of Figure 1, the observer reconstructs black disks from quarters of disks only. This phenomenological description, originally formulated by G.Kanizsa in the case of drawings, can be easily adapted to digital images using level lines [1]. The main difference lies in the fact that on drawings, T-junctions occur where the line of the pen meets a previous line only, that is, at places where an object begins to come in front of another. On digital images of natural world, the objects are never uniformly shined, and therefore even unvaried colored surfaces present lot of level lines. At the borders of an object, these level lines meet the level lines of the background and generate multiple T-junctions : occlusions occur along all the borders. The shapes of the objects is then essentially characterised by the T-junctions on them, and by the pieces of the level lines joining these junctions. In this way, one may give a morphological definition of edges : we call *morphological edge* a piece of level line joining any number of T-junctions. The more a morphological edge contains T-junctions, the more it is perceptually significant : the number of T-junctions contained in a morphological edge behaves as an inverse scale parameter.

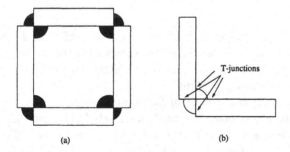

(a)   (b)

Fig. 1. The visual power of T-junctions. The human visual system reconstructs the black objects of the drawing (a) as disks partially covered by boxes. This reconstruction is due to the T-junctions, which are abvious on the topographic map (b). One of the Kanizsa's principle says that the border of the occluded object has to be extended so that to preserve its curvature.

To detect the significant T-junctions on natural images, we use an algorithm adapted from [6] which ensures the existence of three connected components with non-negligible size, one belonging to the occulting object, one belonging to the occulted object and one part of the background. The geometry of every recorded T-junction is characterized by only two of these three connected components. For our image model, we consider the one wich is a lower level set L_λ and the one which is an upper level set M_μ (see Figure 2). In this way, morphological edges are composed by borders of connected components denoted L_λ^k and M_μ^k. Notice that in the discrete case $\Omega \subset \mathbb{Z}^2$, the border of a region lies in the shifted grid $(\mathbb{Z} + 1/2)^2$. If we note ∂P the internal border of a region P (which lies in the $\mathbb{Z}^2$ grid), at every T-junction $x \in (\mathbb{Z}+1/2)^2$ can be associated the neighbor pixels $x_\lambda^k \in \partial L_\lambda^k$ and $y_\mu^k \in \partial M_\mu^k$.

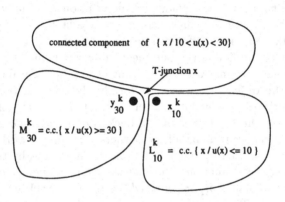

Fig. 2. The T-junction detection algorithm ensures the existence of three significant connected components, one being part of a lower level set L_λ and one being part of an upper level set M_μ (in this example, $\lambda = 10$ and $\mu = 30$). The T-junction point x does not belong to the pixel's grid, but the points x_λ^k and y_μ^k do.

Since each morphological edge belongs to a border of a set L_λ^k or M_μ^k, the issue is to choice, from all possible connected components of the level sets family $(L_\lambda)_\lambda$ and $(M_\mu)_\mu$, the ones that contain the greatest numbers of T-junctions :

Multiscale segmentation algorithm -

Parameter : $s \in [0,1]$ is the scale of the segmentation.

Step 1 : decompose the image u into its level sets $(L_\lambda)_\lambda$ and $(M_\mu)_\mu$.

Step 2 : compute the sequences of T-junctions $T_L = (x_\lambda^k)_{\lambda,k}$, $T_M = (y_\mu^k)_{\mu,k}$ and the associated connected components L_λ^k and M_μ^k. Let N be the number of T-junctions : $N = |T_L| = |T_M|$.

Step 3 : sort the sequences L_λ^k and M_μ^k in the order given by the number of T-junctions : L_λ^k is before $L_{\lambda'}^{k'}$ if $|T_L \cap \partial L_\lambda^k| > |T_L \cap \partial L_{\lambda'}^{k'}|$ and M_μ^k is before $M_{\mu'}^{k'}$ if $|T_M \cap \partial M_\mu^k| > |T_M \cap \partial M_{\mu'}^{k'}|$.

Step 4 : the multiscale segmentation $\mathcal{P}$ is made by the first $N(1-s)$ connected components of the sequences L_λ^k and M_μ^k.

When this algorithm ends, the topographic map defined by the level sets in $\mathcal{P}$ is a morphological segmentation of u so that each ∂P_i is made by pieces of morphological edges : $\mathcal{P} = \{P_i\}_i = \{L_\lambda^k\}_{k,\lambda} \cup \{M_\mu^k\}_{k,\mu}$. The resolution of the segmentation that is, the visual significance of the less perceptive edge, is given by the scale parameter s : when s tends to 0 almost all level sets are mapped (even those which are not perceptually significant), and when s tends to 1 only level sets with borders matching the most important perceptual edges are considered. Example of a segmentation at two different scales is shown Figure 3, at the first column of the second and third lines.

Remark

- The scale is not directly related to the size of the regions. Although level sets of big size are likely to contain more T-junctions than level sets of smaller size, the level lines corresponding to a border of a small object may be recorded at a coarse scale, while the level lines corresponding to the gradation of the light inside a large surface may not.
- The algorithm works for natural images (i.e. photographs of the real world) only. For synthetic images, one would like to replace the T-junction criterion by something related to the contrast of the level lines. With natural images, we should not use the contrast, since the segmentation would not be morphological.

3   Compact and multiscale image model

The compact image model is based on the multiscale segmentation and on pixel's values needed to reconstruct an approximation of the original image.

We use a piecewise-smooth and non-oscillating approximation v_s of the image u in each region defined by the multiscale segmentation. In this way, we remove the upper part of the total variation of u. In [13], we show how the total variation can be related to perceptual microtextures : microtextures correspond to fast oscillating parts at every scales, and therefore are associated to high variations. On the other hand, edges surrounding flat regions generate little variations. The coarea formula [11] allows to link the total variation of u with the total length of its level lines :

$$TV(u) = \int_{\mathbb{R}} \operatorname{per}(L_\lambda) \, d\lambda. \tag{5}$$

Therefore, our morphological approach leads us to split the information between edges and microtextures. More precisely, the compact image model tends to remove the microtextures when the scale s increases, whereas borders of the main structures are kept. For this reason, the approximation v_s is a sketch of u at the scale s of the segmentation. One may also want to conserve the microtexture and to code them apart. This can be done by computing the error image $w_{1-s} = u - v_s$ and by removing some residual sketch information in w_{1-s}. This problem is developed in [13] and will not be addressed here.

Our model contains two types of data : geometrical data record pixel locations on the grid, and numerical data are related to the gray level values at these locations. The numerical data are used to compute the sketch v_s on u defined on each region P_i of the segmentation. The multiscale segmentation algorithm ensures that no important edge can be located inside P_i : this explains why the image may be well approximated by a piecewise-smooth function v_s. In addition, the approximating function is chosen non-oscillating so that it catches the sketch and not the textures. How should be chosen the data to allow a good approximation ? Since the border of P_i is made by morphological edges, the knowledge of u in the internal and external side of each edge is the basic information. In order to get a compact model, we propose to retain only two samples of u for each level line (one for the internal side and one for the external). Since the external side corresponds to the internal side of the adjacent level line (remember that both lower and upper level sets are recorded), it is actually enough to retain one value per level line.

A pixel x of ∂P_i may be associated to several morphological edges (it may belong to different level sets). In that case, $v_s(x)$ is set to be the closest value to $u(x)$. This operation corresponds to chose the smallest level set, and it is implemented by means of an "inf" (lower level sets) or a "sup" (upper level sets) on all level lines containing x. In the internal side of a level line ∂P_i, we have to chose how to represent a sequence of gray level values by only one. The values may be chosen to lower the variation of v_s between two neighbouring regions of a T-junction. This not only helps to get a non-oscillating function, but also prevents the appearance of visual artefacts near the edges by keeping a low contrast. In that case, the value is the "sup" of the gray levels (lower level sets) or the "inf" (upper level sets). Another possibility is to try to preserve the average gray level of the border by computing the median or the mean value.

These remarks lead the following algorithm which computes the values $\phi_i(x)$ of v_s on each ∂P_i :

Algorithm to get samples of the approximating function -

Step 1 : Compute v_s on internal boundary associated to lower level sets, as follows. $\forall P_i \in \mathcal{P}, \forall x \in \partial P_i$, if $\exists k, \lambda / x \in \partial L_\lambda^k$, and if $\phi_i(x)$ has not been already defined, define

$$\phi_i(x) = \inf_{\lambda,k/x \in \partial L_\lambda^k} \sup_{y \in \partial L_\lambda^k} u(y). \tag{6}$$

Step 2 : Compute v_s on internal borders associated to upper level sets, as follows. $\forall P_i \in \mathcal{P}, \forall x \in \partial P_i$, if $\exists k, \mu / x \in \partial M_\mu^k$, and if $\phi_i(x)$ has not been already defined, define

$$\phi_i(x) = \sup_{\mu,k/x \in \partial M_\mu^k} \inf_{y \in \partial M_\mu^k} u(y). \tag{7}$$

To summarize our discussion, the compact image model contains the following data :

- the segmentation map $(\partial P_i)_i$;
- the sequence of samples $(\phi_i(x))_{i; x \in \partial P_i}$.

Example of such data is shown Figure 3, at the second column of the second and third lines.

The issue of computing an approximating function v_s from the samples $(\phi_i(x))_{i; x \in \partial P_i}$ belongs to the class of interpolation problems. Different approaches using image interpolation techniques have been described in the literature (see for example [17],[4],[12]), some of them including the same motives than ours of catching the image sketch in a compact way. Recently, a morphological interpolation technique for image coding has been proposed by J.Casas in [5]. In our knowledge, our work is the first one to use a segmentation map not based on a classical (and non morphological) edge detector, but on a selection of the level sets that carry the atoms of the perception.

We shall retain the work of V.Caselles, B.Coll and J.M.Morel in [7], where they extend the Casas' morphological interpolation technique, and where they prove that any interpolation operator (satisfying fairly conditions, such as morphological, invariance and regularity properties) comes down to let evolve the interpolating function r_i on each P_i with the following equation :

$$\begin{cases} \dfrac{\partial w}{\partial t} = D^2 w \left(\dfrac{Dw}{|Dw|}, \dfrac{Dw}{|Dw|} \right) & \forall t > 0, \ \forall x \in P_i; \\ w(0, x) = w_0(x) & \forall x \in P_i; \\ w(t, x) = w_0(x) = \phi_i(x) & \forall t > 0, \ \forall x \in \partial P_i. \end{cases} \tag{8}$$

We have written by Dw the gradient of w along the spatial coordinates, and by $D^2 w$ the Hessian of w, that is, the matrix of the second derivatives of w.

Under some reasonable conditions [3], there exists a unique continuous viscosity solution $w(t, x)$ of (8) such that $w(t, .)$ is a Lipshitz function for all $t > 0$ on each P_i, with uniformly bounded Lipschitz norm. When $t \to +\infty$, $w(t, .) \to r_i$ with $r_{i|\partial P_i} = \phi_i$. The function r_i is an absolutely minimizing Lipschitz interpolant of ϕ_i inside P_i, or AMLE for short. The evolution equation (8) can be solved using an implicit Euler scheme, so that to transform the evolution problem to a sequence of non linear elliptic problems, which leads in a discrete case to an implicit difference scheme. The sketch v_s is defined by $v_s = r_i$ on each region P_i of the multiscale segmentation $\mathcal{P}$.

Figures 3 and 4 give examples of a sketch image at different scales.

4   Application to image compression

In order to show how the multiscale image model is compact, the geometrical and numerical data have been error-free compressed using adapted coding techniques. We do not claim that our compression scheme gives better results than well established compression standards, further developments are needed before we could present a fair comparison. We just wish to mention the main advantage of a model based on level sets : the segmentation is not only invariant by affine map and by contrast change, but it permits to code very precisely the perceptual edges. On the contrary, compression schemes based on a space-frequency or on a linear scale-space representation cannot respect the perceptual edges when the compression ratio is to high : blocking artifact called Gibbs phenomena appears in the neighborhood of the edges, due to the quantization of the Fourier coefficients which have a bad decay at discontinuities. The same phenomena occurs with wavelet coefficients, although their space-localization reduces the artifacts.

Fig. 3. This plate illustrates the multiscale image model. First line, from left to right: Original Lenna 256×256 image; a topographic map which gives the borders of the lower level sets L_λ for $\lambda = 8n, n = 0, \ldots, 32$; reconstruction using the lower level sets of the previous image only. Second line, from left to right: segmentation at scale $s = 0.65$; samples $\phi_i(x)$ used to compute the sketch; sketch at scale $s = 0.65$. Third line, from left to right: segmentation at scale $s = 0.90$; samples $\phi_i(x)$ used to compute the sketch; sketch at scale $s = 0.90$.

Figure 5 illustrates this problem. We have compressed the "House" (a simple image with strong edges) at a high compression ratio of 38. Both JPEG [24] (the standard for Fourier-based compression) and the Shapiro's EZW [23] (Embedded Zerotrees Wavelet, one of the best wavelet-based compression scheme) algorithms give very poor results. Our compact image model allows to code the "House" at the same compression ratio without distortion of the edges. Of course, only the most important structures are preserved. To keep some texture, we propose

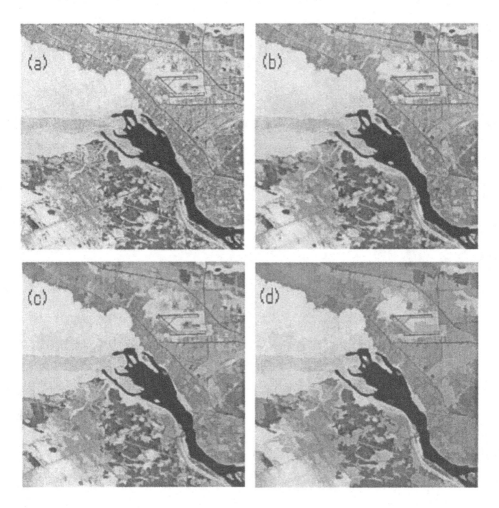

Fig. 4. Multiscale analysis of a view from a satellite. (a): original 256×256 image. (b): sketch at scale $s = 0.90$. (c): sketch at scale $s = 0.96$. (d): sketch at scale $s = 0.99$. Only 1% of all lower level sets and 1% of all upper level sets are used to reconstruct this image.

in [13] to compute the error image and to compress it using a linear scale-space representation : since the error image does not have to code edges, we do not introduce blocking artifact.

5 Conclusion

The level sets decomposition is a well-known tool to get an invariant and morphological image representation. But it is perceived as a redundant structure generating an huge quantity of data. In this paper, we propose a method to select the most representative level sets. From these level sets, a sketch image

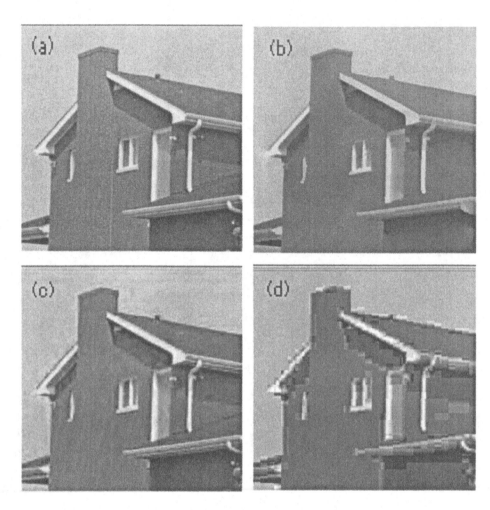

Fig. 5.

Comparison with linear scale-space and space-frequency compression schemes. (a): original "House" image. Size 256 × 256, 8 bpp (bit per pixel). (b): Compact image model of (a) at a scale that leads a bit rate of 0.21 bpp. This bit rate corresponds to a compression ratio of 38. (c): Image (a) compressed at the same ratio using a biorthonormal wavelet scheme (EZW). (d): Image (a) compressed at the same ratio using a windowed Fourier scheme (JPEG).

can be reconstructed. It contains the borders of the most important structure, up to a scale parameter. This requires a new definition of edges, as level lines containing a great number of topological singularities (the T-junctions). This approach allows to build a non-linear scale-space image model respectful of the human visual system, and with a compactness that makes it suitable to perform image compression at low bit rate.

References

1. J.P. D'Alès, J. Froment and J.M. Morel, "Reconstruction visuelle et généricité", *Sec. Euro. Work. on Image Proc. and Mean Curv. Motion*, Spain, p. 1-21, 1995.
2. L. Alvarez, F. Guichard, P.L. Lions and J.M. Morel, "Axioms and fundamental equations of image processing", *Arch. Rational Mechanics and Anal.*, vol. 16, no. 9, p 200-257, 1993.
3. F. Cao, "Absolutely minimizing Lipschitz extension with discontinuous boundary data", *C.R. Acad. Sci. Paris*, t.327, Série I, p. 563-568, 1998.
4. S. Carlsson, "Sketch based coding of grey level images", *Signal Processing North-Holland*, vol. 15 no. 1, July 1988, p. 57-83.
5. J.R. Casas, "Morphological Interpolation for Image Coding", 12th Int. Conf. on Analysis and Optimization of Systems. Images, Wavelets and PDEs. MO.Berger, R.Deriche, I.Herlin, J.Jaffré, JM.Morel (Eds), Springer, Paris, June 1996.
6. V. Caselles, B. Coll and J.M. Morel, "A Kanizsa programme", *Progress in Nonlinear Differential Equs. and their Applications*, vol. 25, p 35-55, 1996.
7. V. Caselles, J.M. Morel and C. Sbert, "An Axiomatic Approach to Image Interpolation", *IEEE Trans. on Image Processing*, vol. 7, no. 3, 1998, p. 376-386.
8. V. Caselles, B. Coll and J.M. Morel, "The Connected Components of Sets of Finite Perimeter in the Plane", Preprint, 1998.
9. M.G. Crandall, H. Ishii, P.L. Lions, "User's Guide to Viscosity Solution of Second Order P.D.E.", vol. 27, *Bull. Amer. Math. Soc*, 1992, p. 1-67.
10. R. Deriche, "Using Canny's criteria to derive a recursively implemented optimal edge detector", *Int. J. of Comp. Vision*, p. 167-187, 1987.
11. L.C. Evans and R.F. Gariepy, "Measure theory and fine properties of functions", *Studies in Advanced Mathematics*, CRC Press Inc., 1992.
12. J. Froment and S. Mallat, "Second Generation Compact Image Coding with Wavelets", *Wavelets - A Tutorial in Theory and Applications*, C.K. Chui (ed.), Academic Press, 1992, p 655-678.
13. J. Froment, "A Functional Analysis Model for Natural Images Permitting Structured Compression", *TR 9833*, ENS Cachan, 1998.
14. R. Hummel and R. Moniot, "Reconstruction from zero-crossings in scale-space", *IEEE Trans. on Acoustic, Speech and Signal Processing*, vol. 37, no. 12, 1989.
15. G. Kanisza, "Grammatica del Vedere", Il Mulino, Bologna, 1980.
16. G. Kanisza, "Vedere e pensare", Il Mulino, Bologna, 1991.
17. M. Kunt, M. Bénard, R. Leonardi, "Recent Results in High-Compression Image Coding" *IEEE Trans. on Circuits and Systems*, nov. 1987, p. 1306-1336.
18. S. Mallat and S. Zhong, "Characterization of signals from multiscale edges" *IEEE Trans. on Pattern Recog. and Machine Intel.*, vol. 14, no. 7, 1992, p. 710-732.
19. D. Marr, *"Vision"*, W.H.Freeman and Co., 1982.
20. P. Monasse and F. Guichard, "Fast computation of a contrast-invariant image representation", *TR 9815*, CMLA, ENS Cachan, France, 1998.
21. J.M. Morel and S. Solimini, *"Variational methods in image processing"*, Birkhäuser, 1994.
22. J. Serra, *"Image analysis and mathematical morphology"*, Academic Press, 1982.
23. J. Shapiro, "Embedded Image Coding Using Zerotrees of Wavelet Coefficients", *IEEE Trans. on Signal Processing*, vol. 41, no. 12, p 3445-3462, 1993.
24. G.K. Wallace, "JPEG", *Comm. of the ACM*, vol. 34, no. 4, p. 31-44, 1991.
25. M. Wertheimer, "Untersuchungen zur Lehre der Gestalt", Psychologische Forschung, IV, p. 301-350, 1923.
26. A.P. Witkin, "Scale-space filtering", *Proc. of IJCAI*, Karlsruhe, p. 1019-1021, 1983.

Morphological Scale Space and Mathematical Morphology

Frédéric CAO

Centre de Mathmatiques et leurs Applications
Ecole Normale Suprieure de Cachan
61 Avenue du Prsident Wilson
94235 CACHAN Cedex FRANCE
cao@cmla.ens-cachan.fr

Abstract. It is well known that a conveniently rescaled iterated convolution of a linear positive kernel converges to a Gaussian. Therefore, all iterative linear smoothing methods of a signal or an image boils down to the application to the signal of the Heat Equation. In this survey, we explain how a similar analysis can be performed for image iterative smoothing by contrast invariant monotone operators. In particular, we prove that all iterated affine and contrast invariant monotone operators are equivalent to the unique affine invariant curvature motion. We also prove that under very broad conditions, weighted median filters are equivalent to the Mean Curvature Motion Equation.

Introduction

The goal of this paper is to precise rigorously the link between the morphological Scale Space Theory and the Mathematical Morphology Theory. The equations we will consider are the affine morphological scale space of Alvarez, Guichard, Lions and Morel [1] and the Motion by Mean Curvature (see for example [12], [9]) . The reason why these equations are so relevant is that they are invariant with respect to some large classes of geometric transformations and contrast change. We will introduce approximation schemes which shall have a theoretical interest in the affine invariant case, and both theoretical and practical interest for the Mean Curvature Motion. The plan is the following: in the first section, we recall some of the main results of Mathematical Morphology and particularly the characterization of operator commuting with continuous nondecreasing functions (contrast change). In section 2, we prove that, under very smooth assumptions, any rescaled affine and contrast invariant operator is asymptotically equivalent to the only affine and contrast invariant differential operator. This consistency results will provide the convergence result is section 3, in which we prove that if the scale is adequately chosen, then the iterated operator converges to the affine and contrast invariant nonlinear semi-group. Section 4 will be devoted to the proof of the convergence of an algorithm previously introduced by Bence,Merriman and Osher in [5]. The results we prove are a generalization of the results proved by Guichard and Morel in [14] and Catt in [7] for the affine case, and generalize or revisit the results in [5], [8], [10], [11], [15].

1 Mathematical Morphology

1.1 Basic Results

It is well known that in image analysis, one of the most basic tasks is to smooth an image $u_0(x)$ for noise removal and shape simplification. Such a smoothing should preserve as much as possible the essential features of an image. This requirement is most easily formalized in terms of invariance. Two invariance requirements are basic in this context : given a smoothing operator T, it should commute with contrast changes, that is, increasing functions. Indeed, for physical and technological reasons, most digital images are known up to a contrast change. The second obvious requirement is geometric invariance : since the position of the camera is in general arbitrary or unknown, the operator T should commute with translations, rotations, and, when possible, with affine and even projective transforms of the image plane. The School of Mathematical Morphology [18] [21] was one of the first to rigorously study and characterize operators acting on sets. We shall see that this theory is intimately linked with contrast invariant operators acting on images. As an image in known up to a contrast change, it is better suited to consider the equivalence classes of functions that can be obtained from one another *via* a contrast change. An obvious consequence of this, is that an image is completely determined by the geometry of its level sets: if $u : \mathbb{R}^N \to \mathbb{R}$ is a grey level image and $\lambda \in \mathbb{R}$, we call level set of u at the value λ the subset of $\mathbb{R}^N$ $\chi_\lambda(u) = \{x \in \mathbb{R}^N, u(x) \geq \lambda\}$. It is obvious that two elements of the same equivalent class will have the same level sets. We also note that the family $\chi_\lambda(u)$ satisfies the following properties :

$$\lambda \leq \mu \Rightarrow \chi_\mu(u) \subset \chi_\lambda(u), \tag{1}$$

$$\chi_\lambda(u) = \bigcap_{\mu < \lambda} \chi_\mu(u). \tag{2}$$

Conversely, we can prove that if $(X_\lambda)_{\lambda \in \mathbb{R}}$ is any family of subsets satisfying equations (1) and (2), then it determines an equivalence class of images. More precisely, if we set $u(x) = \sup\{\lambda \text{ s.t. } x \in X_\lambda\}$, we see that the level sets of u are the X_λ's. It is true (though not trivial) that any function with the same level sets is obtained from u by applying a contrast change. For this reason, the first object of Mathematical Morphology was to study operators acting on sets respecting the usual ordering given by inclusion. Since no point is *a priori* a privileged reference, translation invariant operators are particularly interesting and we shall always make this assumption.

Definition 1. *Let* $\mathbb{T}$ *be an operator acting on a subsets of* $\mathbb{R}^N$. *We say that* $\mathbb{T}$ *is morphological if it is nondecreasing for the inclusion ordering and commutes with translations.*

Matheron proved the following

Theorem 1 (Matheron1). *If* $\mathbb{T}$ *is a morphological operator acting on sets, then there is a family* $\mathbb{B}$ *of subsets of* $\mathbb{R}^N$ *called structuring elements, such that*

$$\forall X \subset \mathbb{R}^N, \quad \mathbb{T}X = \bigcup_{B \in \mathbb{B}} \bigcap_{y \in B} (X - y).$$

The family $\mathbb{B}$ *is not unique but we can take* $\mathbb{B} = \{X \subset \mathbb{R}^N, 0 \in \mathbb{T}X\}$.

We saw that the knowledge of families of sets satisfying equations (1) and (2) is the same as the knowledge of a function up to a contrast change. We would like to transpose Definition 1 and Theorem 1 to functions. We are led to

Definition 2. *Let* $\mathcal{F}$ *be a set of functions on* $\mathbb{R}^N$ *containing continuous functions and characteristics functions of level sets of elements of* $\mathcal{F}$. *We say that* $T : \mathcal{F} \longrightarrow \mathcal{F}$ *is morphological if and only if* T *is monotone (that is* $u \leq v$ *in* $\mathbb{R}^N$ *implies* $Tu \leq Tv$ *in* $\mathbb{R}^N$*), commutes with translations and continuous nondecreasing functions (contrast changes).*

Matheron then proved the expected result

Theorem 2 (Matheron2). *Let* T *be an operator defined on a set of functions* $\mathcal{F}$ *as in Definition 2. Then* T *is morphological if and only if there exists a family* $\mathbb{B}$ *of subsets of* $\mathbb{R}^N$ *called structuring elements, such that*

$$Tu(\mathbf{x}) = \sup_{B \in \mathbb{B}} \inf_{\mathbf{y} \in \mathbb{B}} u(\mathbf{x} + \mathbf{y}). \tag{3}$$

In the same way there exists an other family $\mathbb{B}'$ *such that*

$$Tu(\mathbf{x}) = \inf_{B \in \mathbb{B}'} \sup_{\mathbf{y} \in \mathbb{B}} u(\mathbf{x} + \mathbf{y}). \tag{4}$$

1.2 Scale Space and Mathematical Morphology

In a completely different setting, the concept of Scale Space was introduced in [16] [17] [22]. To fix notations, it consists in a family of operators $(T_t)_{t \geq 0}$ over real valued functions (grey level images) in $\mathbb{R}^N$ ($N \geq 2$). Let $u_t = T_t u_0$: it corresponds to smoothed versions of the image depending upon a scale parameter t. A complete axiomatization was presented in [1] [2] and all scale spaces were classified with respect to their geometrical invariance properties. It is then proved that u_t is solution of a second order parabolic PDE. Among the relevant PDEs, we find the Mean Curvature Motion (MCM)

$$\frac{\partial u}{\partial t} = \Delta u - \frac{(D^2 u Du, Du)}{|Du|^2}. \tag{5}$$

Another important result is that there exists a single Affine Morphological Scale Space ($AMSS$), *i.e.* commuting with nondecreasing functions, invariant by translation, grey level shift and affine mapping of $\mathbb{R}^N$. Moreover, this scale space is not projective invariant. Thus, in the frame of scale space theory, projective invariance and contrast invariance are incompatible. The affine and contrast invariant PDE in $\mathbb{R}^N$ is

$$\frac{\partial u}{\partial t}(\mathbf{x}, t) = |Du| t^{\frac{1}{N+1}} \left(\prod_{i=1}^{N-1} \lambda_i \right)^{\frac{1}{N+1}} H(\lambda_1, \cdots, \lambda_{N-1}), \qquad (6)$$

where λ_i is the ith principal curvature of the level surface of $u(\cdot, t)$ at $\mathbf{x}$ and H is equal to 1 if and only if the λ_i are all strictly positive, to -1 if they are strictly negative and 0 otherwise. The principal curvatures of u are the eigenvalues of the second derivative $D^2 u$ restricted to the hyperplane orthogonal to Du, divided by $|Du|$. Of course, these curvatures are only defined when the gradient is different from 0. Note that from Matheron Theorem, if the considered scale space is morphological the operator T_t can be written in an "*inf-sup*" form with a family of structuring elements $\mathbb{B}_t$ depending on the scale t. When t tends to 0, the operator $T_t - Id$ is approximately the infinitesimal generator of the nonlinear semigroup of the equation. The basic idea, is to retrieve the solution of the PDE by constructing an operator that is tangent to the infinitesimal generator. In [8], Catt, Dibos and Koepfler already established a link between both point of views (Matheron's Mathematical Morphology and geometrical PDEs) by proving that if the family of structuring elements $\mathbb{B}$ is an isotropic family of segments centered at the origin with equal length, then adequately rescaled iterated Matheron filters converge to the viscosity solution of the Mean Curvature Equation. A more general result was presented in [20], where structuring elements were exhibited to approximate equations of the type

$$\frac{\partial u}{\partial t} = |Du| (\text{curv } u)^\gamma$$

in the plane, for all $\gamma \geq 0$.

2 Approximation scheme for the Affine Scale Space

In this section, we prove (under some basic assumptions that are not restrictive at all) that if we adequately scale any Matheron morphological affine invariant operators, then the iterated associated operators converge to the semi-group of the affine invariant, geometrical evolution PDE of the classification established in [1]. Let us precise that we say that an operator is affine invariant if it commutes with affine transformation with determinant equal to 1. In [13], it is proved that it must be covariant with respect to any affine transformation, but a scale factor simply depending on the determinant of the transformation must be introduced. We recall that our schemes in the affine invariant case cannot be used to numerically approximate the Affine Scale Space. This has been tested but the results were not much satisfying, since because for numerical reasons, affine invariance is only approximated. In the case of *inf-sup* schemes, this approximation is very poor if the family of structuring elements is the family of ellipses with area 1. On the contrary, a very fast morphological and affine invariant algorithm is presented by Moisan in [19] to compute the solution of the *AMSS* Equation in the two-dimensional case. By Matheron Theorem, this scheme can also be reformulated in terms of *inf-sup*, but the family is less simple. The extension of Guichard and Morel's result to any dimension is interesting because three-dimensional images and even movies of three dimensional images are already available in the medical domain. These last ones can be considered as four-dimensional images, whereas two-dimensional movies can also be seen as three-dimensional images. From Matheron's Theorem 1, we can also assume that T is affine invariant if and only if the family $\mathbb{B}$ is also affine invariant. Let $\mathbb{B}$ be a family of structuring elements. Let us introduce a scale parameter s and consider the family of structuring elements $\mathbb{B}_s$ obtained from $\mathbb{B}$ by a simple dilation: $\mathbb{B}_s = s^{1/N}\mathbb{B}$ (N being the space dimension). The real s is thus a scale parameter linked to the size of the structuring elements. Let us now introduce the operator

$$IS_s u(\mathbf{x}) = \inf_{B \in \mathbb{B}_s} \sup_{\mathbf{y} \in B} u(\mathbf{x} + \mathbf{y}) \tag{7}$$

and the dual operator

$$SI_s u(\mathbf{x}) = \sup_{B \in \mathbb{B}_s} \inf_{\mathbf{y} \in B} u(\mathbf{x} + \mathbf{y}). \tag{8}$$

Proposition 1. *Let $\mathbb{B}$ an affine invariant closed (with respect to the Hausdorff distance) family of structuring elements which are closed, convex, symmetric with respect to 0, with measure 1 and let $u : \mathbb{R}^N \to \mathbb{R}$ be a C^3 function. Then, there exists a positive constant $c_{\mathbb{B}}$ only depending on $\mathbb{B}$ such that*

$$\lim_{s \to 0} \frac{IS_s u(\mathbf{x}) - u(\mathbf{x})}{s^{\frac{2}{N+1}}} = c_{\mathbb{B}}|p|(\lambda_1^+ \cdots \lambda_{N-1}^+)^{\frac{1}{N+1}} \tag{9}$$

where $p = |Du(\mathbf{x})|$ and $\lambda_1, \ldots, \lambda_{N-1}$ are the principal curvatures of the level surface going through $\mathbf{x}$ (in the formula above, the "+" exponent is the positive part of a number, that is to say $\lambda^+ = \max(\lambda, 0)$).
We have a similar result by replacing IS_s by SI_s (obtained by swapping inf and sup) and the λ_i^+ by λ_i^-.

We shall also need consistency results on the alternate operator $SI_s IS_s$. To this end, we prove that except at critical points, consistency is uniform. We then establish the link between consistency and convergence. Let $h = s^{2/(N+1)}$ and $T_h = SI_s IS_s$.

Theorem 3. *Let $u_0 \in BUC(\mathbb{R}^N)$ (bounded and uniformly continuous). The approximate solutions u_h defined by*

$$\forall n \in \mathbb{N}, \forall t \in [(n-1)h, nh[, \qquad u_h(\mathbf{x}, t) = T_h^n u_0(\mathbf{x}) \tag{10}$$

converge towards the unique solution in $BUC(\mathbb{R}^N)$ of

$$\frac{\partial u}{\partial t} = c_{\mathbb{B}}|Du|\left(\prod_{i=1}^{N-1}\lambda_i\right)^{\frac{1}{N+1}}H(\lambda_1,\cdots,\lambda_{N-1}). \qquad (11)$$

with initial data u_0. Here $H(\lambda_1,\cdots,\lambda_{N-1}) = -1$ if the λ_i are all negative, 1 if they are all positive and 0 otherwise. Convergence is uniform on every compact set of $\mathbb{R}^N \times \mathbb{R}_+$.

We sever the proof of consistency in a serie of lemmas. We do not enter into details since the proofs are a bit long a technical. A complete version is given in [6]. To simplify the notations, we denote by $IS_s(px + ax^2 + \sum_{i=1}^{N-1} b_iy_i^2 + \sum_{i=1}^{N-1} c_ixy_i)$, the value of the operator IS_s applied to the polynomial function and taken at the origin. Let $s = r^{N+2}$.

Lemma 1. *Set*

$$c_{\mathbb{B}} = IS_1(x + y_1^2 + \cdots + y_{N-1}^2).$$

If the structuring elements are closed, convex, symmetric with respect to the origin and with measure 1, then $c_{\mathbb{B}} > 0$.

Lemma 2. *Assume that $p > 0$. If $b_1,\ldots,b_{N-1} > 0$ then*

$$IS_s(px + b_1y_1^2 + \cdots + b_{N-1}y_{N-1}^2) = c_{\mathbb{B}}ps^{\frac{2}{N+1}}(\lambda_1\cdots\lambda_{N-1})^{\frac{1}{N+1}} \qquad (12)$$

where $\lambda_i = 2b_i/p$ is the ith principal curvature. If one of the b_i is nonpositive, then

$$IS_s(px + b_1y_1^2 + \cdots + b_{N-1}y_{N-1}^2) = o(s^{2/N+1}) \qquad (13)$$

Moreover, in both cases, the Inf-Sup is attained for structuring element included in a ball with radius which is $o(r)$.

Lemma 3. *There exists a function $G(p,(b_i),(c_i))$ bounded on every compact subset of $\mathbb{R}_*^+ \times \mathbb{R}^{N-1} \times \mathbb{R}^{N-1}$ such that*

$$IS_s(px + ax^2 + \sum_{i=1}^{N-1} b_iy_i^2 + \sum_{i=1}^{N-1} c_ixy_i) = c_{\mathbb{B}}p^{\frac{2}{N+1}}s^{\frac{2}{N+1}}\left(\prod_{i=1}^{N-1} b_i^+\right)^{\frac{1}{N+1}}$$
$$+G(p,(b_i),(c_i))s^{\frac{1}{2(N+2)}+\frac{2}{N+1}}.$$

All these lemmas are based on estimates of the size in any directions on structuring elements attaining values near the infimum in the IS_s operator. The proof of these lemmas, though not very complicated and using only basic mathematical tools, are heavy and can be find in [6]. Theorem 1 is a simple consequence of this bench of lemmas, since it suffices to use translation and rotation invariance to write Taylor expansion of any regular function in the form used in Lemma 3. We did insist in Lemma 2 on the fact that the structuring elements attaining the right value of the *inf-sup* operator were included in a ball with radius $r = s^{1/N+2}$.

This technical detail is in fact crucial since it allows to assert that IS_s is basically a local operator (which it is *a priori* not, since the family of structuring element is not bounded). More precisely, we can bound IS_s from below and from above by two operators that are really local. Define

$$I_s u(\mathbf{x}) = \inf_{B \in \mathbb{B}} \sup_{\mathbf{y} \in B \cap B(0,r)} u(\mathbf{x} + \mathbf{y}), \qquad (14)$$

and

$$S_s u(\mathbf{x}) = \inf_{\substack{B \in \mathbb{B} \\ B \subset B(0,r)}} \sup_{\mathbf{y} \in B} u(\mathbf{x} + \mathbf{y}). \qquad (15)$$

Then, it is clear that $I_s u \leq IS_s u \leq S_s u$ (for I_s we take the supremum on smaller sets, and for S_s, we take the infimum on a subfamily of structuring elements). Now, the fact that, in Lemma 2 above, the structuring elements for quadratic forms are included in the ball $B(0,r)$ implies that I_s, S_s and IS_s are nearly equal since by only taking points in $B(0,r)$, no information vanished. By construction, $I_s u(0)$ and $S_s u(0)$ are local (they only depend on values of u in the ball $B(0,r)$. Thus, to compute $IS_s u(0)$ for a C^3 function, we can only consider the values of u in $B(0,r)$ by using Taylor expansion. The rest in this expansion is $O(r^3)$ and the definition of r is precisely chosen to make this rest negligible in front of the asymptotic term we give in Lemmas 2 and 3. In addition, we can prove that this argument also implies that the error term appearing in the consistency results is uniformly bounded in a ball with fixed radius near a point where the gradient and the curvature are not zero. A consequence is that consistency is uniform near those points. Uniform consistency in a sufficient condition to prove convergence. Another consequence is that we also get consistency results for the alternate operator $SI_s IS_s$.

Proposition 2. *Let $\mathbb{B}$ a family of structuring elements invariant by $SL(\mathbb{R}^N)$ with elements that are closed, convex symmetric with respect to the origin and with Lebesgue measure equal to 1. There exists $c_{\mathbb{B}} > 0$ such that for any C^3 function u, such that $Du(\mathbf{x}) \neq 0$*

$$\lim_{s \to 0} \frac{SI_s IS_s u(\mathbf{x}) - u(\mathbf{x})}{s^{\frac{2}{N+1}}} = c_{\mathbb{B}} |Du(\mathbf{x})| (\lambda_1 \cdots \lambda_{N-1})^{\frac{1}{N+1}} H(\lambda_1, \ldots, \lambda_{N-1}) \quad (16)$$

where the (λ_i) are the principal curvatures of the level surface passing through $\mathbf{x}$, $H = 1$ if all the curvatures are positive, $H = -1$ if they are negative and $H = 0$ elsewhere.

The gain here is that this operator is consistent with the true generator of the Affine Morphological Scale Space (contrary to the IS_s operator, see Proposition 1). The convergence of the scheme is then nearly guaranteed. Nevertheless, we saw that problems may occur at points where the gradient is equal to zero. To rigorously prove convergence, we first need the following lemma that allows to control the growth of T_h at critical points.

Lemma 4. *Let $a(\mathbf{x}) = |\mathbf{x}|^2$. Then,*

$$\lim_{(\mathbf{x},h)\to(0,0)} \frac{T_h a(\mathbf{x}) - a(\mathbf{x})}{h} = 0 \tag{17}$$

The main point here is that the limit is taken for $\mathbf{x} \to 0$ and $h \to 0$ independently. The T_h operator can either be IS_h, SI_h or SI_hIS_h.

A direct consequence of this lemma is the following.

Lemma 5. *Let u be a C^3 bounded function such that $Du(\mathbf{x}) = 0$. Let $\mathbf{x}_h$ tending to $\mathbf{x}$ as h tends to 0. Then*

$$\lim_{h\to 0} \frac{T_h u(\mathbf{x}_h) - u(\mathbf{x}_h)}{h} = 0.$$

In [4], Barles and Souganidis proved the convergence of any monotone, stable and consistent scheme. Proposition 2 and Lemma 5 are sufficient conditions to satisfy the hypotheses they gave. This directly ensures Theorem 3.

3   Mean Curvature Motion and Median Filters

This last section is devoted to a new proof that all properly rescaled and iterated *weighted median filters*, a class of isotropic morphological operators widely used in image processing, converge to Mean Curvature Motion. This result has already been proved by Ishii (see [15]), generalizing the proof by Barles and Georgelin ([3]) and Evans ([11]) and answering a conjecture of Bence, Merriman and Osher ([5], but the tools we use here are different and perhaps better adapted to the mathematical morphology theory. Precisely, let k a continuous radial probability density that decreases fast enough at infinity (this will be precised below) and define $\mathbb{B} = \{B \subset \mathbb{R}^N, \text{meas}_k B \geq \frac{1}{2}\}$. Let also define the weighted median filter associated with the density k by

$$\text{med}_k u(\mathbf{x}) = \inf_{B \in \mathbb{B}} \sup_{\mathbf{y} \in B} u(\mathbf{x} + \mathbf{y}).$$

Scale k in k_h by $k_h(\mathbf{x}) = h^{-N}k(h^{-1}\mathbf{x})$, let $T_h = \text{med}_{k_h}$. We prove the following

Theorem 4. *Define*

$$u_h(\mathbf{x}, t) = T_h^n u_0(\mathbf{x}) \text{ if } nh^2 \leq t < (n+1)h^2.$$

Then (up to a linear rescaling of time), u_h converge uniformly on every compact set towards the solution of the Mean Curvature Motion defined by

$$\frac{\partial u}{\partial t} - \left(\Delta u - \frac{(D^2uDu, Du)}{|Du|^2}\right) = 0$$

and with initial condition $u_0 \in BUC(\mathbb{R}^N)$.

The result has been proved by Guichard and Morel in [14] if k is compactly supported. In this case, the median filter is really local and standard approximation arguments give the result. The other references above give a convergence result without this assumption. In this paper, we show that the formalism used by Guichard and Morel can also be adapted to this more general situation. Except in [15], the main part of the proof of the convergence relies on consistency arguments. We also adopt this technique as in the affine invariance case. As soon as k is not compactly supported, this is not clear that the median filter only depends on the local features of the image. In [3] [5] [11], k is a normalized Gaussian. As the decay is very fast in this case, we can expect that the associated median filter is local. Here we shall give weaker conditions of decay and prove the same result. The lack of space prevents us from giving the detailed proofs that the reader may find in [6].

As k is radial we can a define a function f by $f(|\mathbf{x}|) = k(\mathbf{x})$. Assume that f is continuous, and that it is decreasing outside a bounded interval. The speed of decay is given by the condition

$$\int t^{\gamma+N-1} f(t)\,dt < +\infty$$

where γ is any number such that $\gamma > 3$. Set also

$$c(k) = \frac{1}{2}(N-1)\frac{\displaystyle\int_0^\infty t^N f(t)\,dt}{\displaystyle\int_0^\infty t^{N-2} f(t)\,dt}.$$

We introduce another scale parameter $r = h^\alpha$ where $\frac{2}{3} < \alpha < 1$ is determined in the analysis. We now define two local operators I_h^r and S_h^r

$$I_h^r u(\mathbf{x}) = \inf_{B \in \mathbb{B}_h} \sup_{\mathbf{y} \in B \cap D(0,r)} u(\mathbf{x}+\mathbf{y}) \tag{18}$$

and

$$S_h^r u(\mathbf{x}) = \inf_{\substack{B \in \mathbb{B}_h \\ B \subset D(0,r)}} \sup_{\mathbf{y} \in B} u(\mathbf{x}+\mathbf{y}). \tag{19}$$

They obviously satisfy $I_h^r \le T_h \le S_h^r$. It suffices to prove that I_h^r and S_h^r are consistent with the same differential operator to obtain the same results for T_h. It is even sufficient to prove some inequalities in this case. Precisely, we prove

Lemma 6. *Let $p > 0$.*

$$I_h^r\left(px + ax^2 + \sum_{i=1}^{N-1} b_i y_i^2 + \sum_{i=1}^{N-1} c_i x y_i\right) \ge c(k)\kappa h^2 + o(h^2) \tag{20}$$

where κ is the mean curvature at the origin.

Lemma 7.

$$S_h^\tau(px + ax^2 + \sum_{i=1}^{N-1} b_i y_i^2 + \sum_{i=1}^{N-1} c_i xy_i) \le c(k)\kappa h^2 + o(h^2). \tag{21}$$

These lemmas provide consistency for C^3 functions since it suffices to use translation invariance and rotation invariance (which is true since k is radial) and apply the results to the Taylor expansion of the function to analyze. We also get an error term of the form $o(h^2)$ which is uniform around a point where the gradient is not equal to zero. Gathering both previous lemmas, we get

Proposition 3. *Let u be a C^3 function. Assume that $Du(\mathbf{x}) \neq 0$. Then*

$$\frac{T_h u(\mathbf{x}) - u(\mathbf{x})}{h^2} = c(k)\kappa + o(1),$$

the term $o(1)$ being uniform in a neighborhood of $\mathbf{x}$.

Near critical points, we have to describe more precisely the behaviour of T_h.

Lemma 8. *Let φ a C^3 function. Let $\mathbf{x}_0 \in \mathbb{R}^N$ such that*

$$\begin{cases} D\varphi(\mathbf{x}_0) = 0 \\ D^2\varphi(\mathbf{x}_0) = 0. \end{cases}$$

and let $\mathbf{x}_h \to \mathbf{x}_0$ when $h \to 0$. Then

$$\lim_{h\to 0} \frac{T_h \varphi(\mathbf{x}_h) - \varphi(\mathbf{x}_h)}{h^2} = 0.$$

To conclude, we apply the convergence results in [4] to prove Theorem 4.

Acknowledgments. The author would like to thank Jean-Michel Morel and Vicent Caselles for informing him of this subject and all the conversations they had.

References

1. L. Alvarez, F. Guichard, P.L. Lions, and J.M. Morel. Axiomatisation et nouveaux oprateurs de la morphologie mathmatique. *Compte rendu de l'Acadmie des Sciences de Paris*, 1(315):265–268, 1992.
2. L. Alvarez, F. Guichard, P.L. Lions, and J.M. Morel. Axioms and fundamental equations of image processing. *Arch. for Rat. Mech.*, 123(3):199–257, 1993.
3. G. Barles and C. Georgelin. A simple proof of convergence for an approximation scheme for computing motion by mean curvature. *SIAM J.Numer.Anal.*, 32(2):484–500, 1995.
4. G. Barles and P.M. Souganidis. Convergence of approximation schemes for fully nonlinear second order equations. *Asymptotic Analysis*, 4:271–283, 1991.
5. J. Bence, B. Merriman, and S. Osher. Diffusion motion generated by mean curvature. CAM Report 92-18. Dept of Mathematics. University of California Los Angeles, April 1992.

6. F. Cao. Partial differential equations and mathematical morphology. *Journal de Mathmatiques Pures et Appliques*, 77(9):909–941, 1998.

7. F. Catt. Convergence of iterated affine and morphological filters by nonlinear semi-groups theory. *Proceedings of ICAOS-96 INRIA-CEREMADE*, June 1996.

8. F. Catt, F. Dibos, and G. Koepfler. A morphological scheme for mean curvature motion and application to anisotropic diffusion and motion of level sets. *SIAM Jour. of Numer. Anal.*, 32(6):1895–1909, Dec 1995.

9. Y.G. Chen, Y. Giga, and S. Goto. Uniqueness and existence of viscosity solutions of generalized mean curvature flow equations. *J. Diff. Geometry*, 33:749–786, 1991.

10. M.G. Crandall and P.L. Lions. Convergent difference schemes for nonlinear parabolic equations and mean curvature motion. *Numerische Mathematik*, 75:17–41, 1996.

11. L.C. Evans. Convergence of an algorithm for mean curvature motion. *Indiana Univ. Math. Journal*, 42:533–557, 1993.

12. L.C. Evans and J. Spruck. Motion of level sets by mean curvature. I. *J. of Differential Geometry*, 33:635–681, 1991.

13. F. Guichard. *Axiomatisation des analyses multichelles d'images et de films*. PhD thesis, Universit Paris Dauphine, 1993.

14. F. Guichard and J.M. Morel. *Partial Differential Equations and Image Iterative Filtering*. Tutorial of ICIP95, Washington D.C., 1995.

15. H. Ishii. A Generalization of the Bence, Merriman and Osher Algorithm for Motion By Mean Curvature. In GAKUTO, editor, *Curvature flows and related topics*, volume 5, pages 111–127. Levico, 1994.

16. J.J. Koenderink. The structure of images. *Biol. Cybern.*, 50:363–370, 1984.

17. D. Marr. *Vision*. N.York, W.H. and Co, 1982.

18. G. Matheron. *Random Sets and Integral Geometry*. John Wiley N.Y., 1975.

19. L. Moisan. Affine plane curve evolution: a fully consistent scheme. Technical Report 9628, Cahiers du Ceremade, 1996.

20. D. Pasquignon. Approximation of viscosity solutions by morphological filters. Preprint, 1997.

21. J. Serra. *Image Analysis and Mathematical Morphology*. Academic Press, 1982.

22. A.P. Witkin. Scale space filtering. In *Proc. of IJCAI, Karlsruhe*, pages 1019–1021, 1983.

Scale-Space from a Level Lines Tree

Pascal Monasse[1] and Frédéric Guichard[2]

[1] CMLA, ENS Cachan
61, av du Président Wilson
94235 Cachan Cedex, France
monasse@cmla.ens-cachan.fr
[2] Inrets/Dart
2, av du Général Malleret-Joinville
F-94114 Arcueil Cedex, France
fguichar@ceremade.dauphine.fr
http://www.ceremade.dauphine.fr/~fguichar

Abstract. We decompose images into "shapes", based on connected components of level sets, which can be put in a tree structure. This tree contains the purely geometric information present in the image, separated from the contrast information. This structure allows to suppress easily some shapes without affecting the others, which yields a peculiar kind of scale-space, where the information present at each scale is already present in the original image.

1 Introduction

Depending on the problem at hand, different representations of images must be used. For deblurring, restoration and denoising purposes, representations based on Fourier transform are well adapted because they rely on the generation process of the image (Shannon theory for the sampling step) and frequency models of degradations, for example concerning additive noise. Achieving a localization of the frequencies, wavelets decompositions [1, 2] are known to be very efficient for compression of images. These representations are said to be additive in the sense that they decompose the image on a given a priori basis of elementary images and it is represented as the weighted sum of the basis images, the weights being the coefficients of the decomposition. From the image analysis point of view, these representations are not necessarily as well adapted because wavelets are not translation invariant, the Fourier transform is not local and both yield quantized scales of observation.

Scale-space and edge detection theories represent the images by "significant edges", the image being smoothed (linearly or not [3, 4]) and then convolved with an edge detector filter. This was first proposed by Marr [5] and then generalized by [6], whereas many developments where proposed for edge detection [7].

Extraction of "edges" was shown to be generally the output of a variational formulation [8, 9]. The image is approximated by a function from a class for which the definition of edge becomes clear. The balance between the precision of the approximation and its complexity (which can be measured for example by the length of the edges) yields a multi-scale representation of the image. Despite its generality, this approach suffers from the absence of an universal model.

Scale-space representations based on edges are however incomplete (they do not allow to reconstruct the image) and the images at different scales are redundant [10, 11, 2].

Furthermore most of them do not take into account the fact that contrast may strongly change without affecting much our perception of images, a problem underlined and considered as central by the mathematical morphology school[12, 13]. It proposes a parameter free, complete and contrast insensitive representation of an image by its level sets. A recent variant [14] proposed to take as basic elements the boundaries of the level sets (called level lines), a representation named the "topographic map".

Our work [15] decomposes the image into connected components of level lines structured in a tree representing their geometrical inclusion.

This tree allows to compute easily the effect of a multi-scale operator introduced in section 3 which is special because it proceeds by eliminating some level lines while keeping the others without smoothing them. The advantage is that important structures of the image are not damaged throughout the scale-space derived from this operator.

The pyramidal decomposition of the image given by the tree can also be seen as a region growing decomposition (see [9] and references therein), where two regions corresponding to interiors of nested level lines are merged when the smaller enclosed region is too small. But here, no edge is moved and no spurious edge is created. The operator proceeds by removing level lines, and the contrast between two adjacent regions cannot increase, so no new gray level is introduced.

The paper is organized as follow: Section 2 is devoted to the decomposition of images by connected components of their level sets into an inclusion tree-like structure. Section 3 describes the natural multi-scale operator to simplify this tree, which yields a "scale-space" representation of the image. At last, in section 4 some experiments are shown.

2 Level Sets and Connected Components

2.1 Contrast Insensitive Representations

Here an image u is defined as a function from a rectangle $\Omega = [O, W] \times [0, H]$ to $\mathbb{R}$ being constant on each "pixel" $(j, j+1) \times (i, i+1)$. The value attributed to each edgel $\{i\} \times (j, j+1)$ and $(i, i+1) \times \{j\}$ is the max of the values at the two adjacent pixels and at each point $\{i\} \times \{j\}$, the max value of u at the 4 adjacent pixels. It is convenient to extend the image on the plane $\mathbb{R}^2$ by setting $u = u_0$ outside Ω where u_0 is an arbitrary fixed real value. This gives a continuously defined representation of a discrete array of pixels. Notice that with these conventions, u is upper semi-continuous.

Given an image u, upper (noted $\mathcal{X}_\lambda$) and lower ($\mathcal{X}^\mu$) level sets are defined as

$$\mathcal{X}_\lambda = \{x \in \mathbb{R}^2,\ u(x) \geq \lambda\} \qquad \mathcal{X}^\mu = \{x \in \mathbb{R}^2,\ u(x) < \mu\}. \tag{1}$$

u can be rebuilt from the data of any of the families of upper and lower level sets [12, 16, 17]:

$$u(x) = \sup \{\lambda\ /\ x \in \mathcal{X}_\lambda\} = \inf \{\mu\ /\ x \in \mathcal{X}^\mu\}. \tag{2}$$

The interest of these representations is their insensitivity to contrast change, that is to say $g(u)$ and u have the same families of level sets whenever g is a real strictly increasing function, representing a global contrast change.

A fundamental property of the level sets is their monotonicity:

$$\forall \lambda \leq \mu,\ \mathcal{X}_\lambda \supset \mathcal{X}_\mu,\ \mathcal{X}^\lambda \subset \mathcal{X}^\mu. \tag{3}$$

As in [14], to alleviate the global aspect of these basic elements, only connected components (cc)[1] will be used (which are invariant to a local contrast change):

$$\mathcal{X}_\lambda = \bigcup_{i=1}^{i=N_\lambda} cc_i(\mathcal{X}_\lambda) \qquad \mathcal{X}^\mu = \bigcup_{i=1}^{i=N^\mu} cc_i(\mathcal{X}^\mu)$$

Relation (3) translates to cc's into:

$$\forall \lambda < \lambda',\ i \in [1, N_{\lambda'}],\ \exists! j \in [1, N_\lambda]\ \text{s.t.}\ cc_i(\mathcal{X}_{\lambda'}) \subset cc_j(\mathcal{X}_\lambda) \tag{4}$$

Indeed, $cc_i(\mathcal{X}_{\lambda'}) \subset \mathcal{X}_{\lambda'} \subset \mathcal{X}_\lambda$ and since it is connected, it is included in some cc_j of $\mathcal{X}_\lambda$, with j unique. Equation (4) yields a tree structure for the cc's of upper level sets (the same can be said of the cc's of lower level sets).

Actually, suppose the image takes its values in the discrete set $\{0, \dots, U\}$ (typically, $U = 255$) and consider the graph where the nodes represent all cc's of all level sets $\mathcal{X}_0, \dots, \mathcal{X}_U$. Let us write N_λ^i the node corresponding to $cc_i(\mathcal{X}_\lambda)$. Since a cc of upper level set may be extracted from several upper level sets (when it is sufficiently contrasted w.r.t. its neighborhood), suppose to avoid redundancy that only the one with greatest λ is kept. Then put a link between N_λ^i and $N_{\lambda-1}^j$ whenever $cc_i(\mathcal{X}_\lambda) \subset cc_j(\mathcal{X}_{\lambda-1})$. This graph is in fact a tree $\mathcal{T}_u$, of root N_0^1 corresponding to $cc_1(\mathcal{X}_0) = \mathbb{R}^2$. Equation (4) ensures that the graph is connected and without circuit, which are the two properties defining a tree. For each pixel P,

$$\bigcap_{\lambda, i\ \text{s.t.}\ P \in cc_i(\mathcal{X}_\lambda)} cc_i(\mathcal{X}_\lambda)$$

is not empty (since $P \in cc_0^1$) and is an intersection of non disjoint cc's of upper level sets, so that by (4), it is itself a cc of upper level set; call its associated

---

[1] Notice that with the conventions above, connectedness corresponds to 8-connectedness for upper level sets and 4-connectedness for lower level sets in the discretely defined image.

node $N_u(P)$ and let $\mathrm{Gray}(N_u(P))$ the corresponding gray level λ from which it is extracted. Then we get

$$
\begin{aligned}
u(P) &= \max\{\lambda : P \in \mathcal{X}_\lambda\} \\
&= \max\{\lambda : \exists i \in [1, N_\lambda] \text{ s.t. } P \in cc_i(\mathcal{X}_\lambda)\} \\
&= \mathrm{Gray}(N_u(P))
\end{aligned}
\tag{5}
$$

In other words, reconstructing the image from the tree is made by attributing to each pixel the gray level value of the smallest cc of upper level set that contains it. Thus the data of u is equivalent to the data of $\mathcal{T}_u$ and of $N_u(P)$ for all pixels P. Notice that nothing obliges us to store the values $\mathrm{Gray}(N)$ when N is a node of $\mathcal{T}_u$. If we do not want to store them, but still have a reconstruction formula as (5), we attribute to each node N a gray level which is strictly decreasing when we follow up the (unique) path from N to the root in $\mathcal{T}_u$ (e.g. the depth of the node in $\mathcal{T}_u$). Then we can easily verify that the image reconstructed from it is u modulo a local contrast change. Reciprocally, if v is u modulo a local contrast change, the trees of u and v are the same.

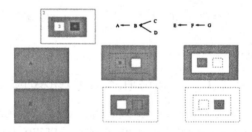

Fig. 1. Up: originqal image and associated trees $\mathcal{T}_u$ (left) and $\mathcal{T}_l$ (right)(arrows are directed from child to parent). Middle: cc's of upper level sets. Down: cc's of lower level sets.

All the above results can be stated with the appropriate changes for lower level sets to construct another tree $\mathcal{T}_l$, and for each pixel P the node associated to the smallest containing cc of upper level set, $N_l(P)$. An example of such a decomposition is given in fig. 1. This is what is done by [18].

2.2 The Inclusion Tree

Each one of the trees $\mathcal{T}_u$ and $\mathcal{T}_l$ satisfy our requirements stated in the introduction, nevertheless they make an a priori choice of the "objects" in the image: $\mathcal{T}_u$ is adapted to clear objects on a darker background. We would like to deal simultaneously with clear objects and with dark objects. It is not satisfactory to keep both trees, because they are redundant, each one individually being sufficient to represent the image. Thus, we have to eliminate some cc from the trees. Two hypotheses will guide us:

1. The "interesting objects" in u stretch over a finite portion of the plane.
2. The "interesting objects" have no holes.

Our "interesting objects" will be cc's of upper or lower level sets. The first hypothesis tells us to eliminate non bounded cc of level sets, the second one allows us to build a new tree from the remaining nodes.

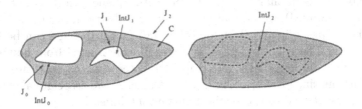

Fig. 2. C is a cc of a level set. Three level lines compose its border. The exterior level line is J_2. Int $J_2 = C \cup$ Int $J_0 \cup$ Int J_1 is shown at the right.

Each bounded cc of level set C has a topological border that is composed of one or several sets of connected edgels, called *level lines*. A level line separates the plane in two disjoint connected parts[2], its interior (which is the bounded part) and its exterior (the unbounded one) [27]. C is comprised in the interior of one of the level lines composing its frontier, called its exterior border, and in the exterior of all others, called its interior borders (see fig. 2). The interiors of its interior borders constitute its holes. The hypothesis 2 leads us to consider not C but C union its holes, which we call a **"shape"** $S(C)$. The border of $S(C)$ is now only the exterior border of C. Therefore, we are led to consider the interiors of level lines.

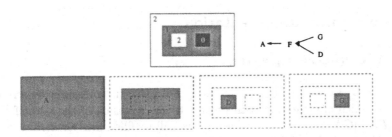

Fig. 3. The inclusion tree $\mathcal{T}$ corresponding to a simple image. Notice that D is a hole in F. Compare with the upper and lower trees $\mathcal{T}_u$ and $\mathcal{T}_l$ given in fig. 1

---

[2] The connectedness considered here does not correspond to the topological connectedness in the continuous plane $\mathbb{R}^2$, but to the discrete notions of connectedness (4- and 8-connectedness). More precisely, if C comes from an upper level set, the part of the plane containing C is taken in 8-connectedness and the other part in 4-connectedness, whereas it is the contrary if C is extracted from a lower level set.

A property similar to (4) can be proved for shapes, namely that if two shapes are not disjoint, one of them is included in the other. This relies on the fact that level lines do not cross: a level line cannot meet altogether the interior and the exterior of another level line. The proof of this is not trivial, and involves hypotheses on the function (semi-continuity is a sufficient condition), see [21]. Our definition of image ensures such sufficient conditions.

The following operations are done for constructing the inclusion tree: Associate a node to each shape. Consider the entire plane (which is not a shape, because not bounded), as the root node. Put a link between two nodes whenever one of the shapes is included in the other and no third shape can be inserted between both. The resulting graph is a tree $\mathcal{T}$, constructed from bounded cc's of both upper and lower level sets [15]. The "interesting objects" are now represented in one single tree (see fig. 3). For a pixel P, we associate also the node $N(P)$ in $\mathcal{T}$ associated to the smallest shape containing P.

A reconstruction formula similar to (5) holds: $u(P) = \text{Gray}(N(P))$.

2.3 Summary

We consider functions made of closed upper level sets whose topological boundaries are a finite number of "level lines". Such class of functions contains discrete images (pixel-wise defined), or functions having a minimal regularity.

- We call shape the interior of a level line.
- Level lines are closed curves that do not cross.
- Thus two shapes are either disjoint, so that they are contained in a third shape, or nested, in which case one is a descendent of the other. This yields a tree structure for the set of shapes, where the relation child-parent means the topological inclusion.

3 Scale-Space Representation

3.1 A Multi-Scale Operator

For a set B, we denote by $|B|$ its area, i.e. Lebesgue measure, or any other measure which is increasing with respect to the inclusion of the sets (if $B \subset C$ then $|B| \leq |C|$). For a connected set B, we call its filled interior $\phi(B)$ the union of B and its holes and its filled area the area of its filled interior. In other words, $\phi(B)$ is the smallest simply connected set containing B. Let $\mathcal{B}_t$ be the family of closed connected sets B whose filled interior contains the origin $\mathbf{O}$, $|\phi(B)| \geq t$ and such that if $\mathbf{O}$ is in a hole H of B, then $|\phi(H)| < t$.

Let us introduce our multi-scale operator:

$$T_t u(\mathbf{x}) = \sup_{B \in \mathcal{B}_t} \inf_{\mathbf{y} \in \mathbf{x} + B} u(\mathbf{y}). \tag{6}$$

The operator T_t applied to the image u is equivalent to removing all the shapes of area strictly less than t from the inclusion tree of u and constructing back the image. This yields another formulation of the operator T:[3]

$$T_t'u(\mathbf{x}) = \inf_{B \in \mathcal{B}_t} \sup_{\mathbf{y} \in \mathbf{x}+B} u(\mathbf{y}). \tag{7}$$

This operator is at the same time a morphological opening and closing [13]! It is close to a filter proposed independently by several authors [22, 18, 23, 24] but in their case the applied filter was equivalent to remove only nodes from the tree of cc's of superior level sets or from the tree of inferior level sets, so that they get two different operators which do not commute (the opening and the closing version). The operator presented here is the grain filter studied in [19].

3.2 Properties

Let us consider the properties of this multi-scale operator. Some of the properties suppose that the image is at least continuous, which is impossible with the continuously defined versions of discretely defined images we considered (except for trivial cases). Nevertheless, whereas the notion of the inclusion tree is not clear in such a case, the operator T_t can be defined as in equation (6).

[**Causality**] The scale-space is causal, meaning that each scale can be deduced from any anterior scale by a transition operator.

$$\forall s, t, \ s \leq t, \ \exists T_{t,s} \text{ so that } T_t = T_{t,s} \circ T_s \tag{8}$$

The transition operator is the operator itself: $T_{t,s} = T_t$.

[**Monotonicity**] This scale-space is monotonous:

$$u \leq v \Rightarrow \forall t, T_t u \leq T_t v \tag{9}$$

[**Contrast covariance**] If g is a contrast change (an increasing real valued function), then

$$\forall t \ \ g \circ T_t = T_t \circ g \tag{10}$$

[**Negative covariance**] Some other interesting feature of the operator is its negative covariance, that is that it commutes with taking a negative of the image:[4]

$$\forall t \ \ T_t(-u) = -T_t u \tag{11}$$

Notice that this is not the case with the operator defined in [18], where regional maxima and regional minima do not play symmetrical roles.

---

[3] $T = T'$ if one switches the connectedness for upper and lower level sets. We conjecture that they are also equal when acting on continuous functions.

[4] However, $-u$ is lower semi-continuous, so that appropriate changes of connectedness must be applied: lower (resp. upper) level sets of $-u$ must be considered in 8- (resp. 4-) connectedness.

[**Local extrema conservation**] A local regional extremum in the image u remains either a local regional extremum at scale t, or is included in a bigger local regional extremum or disappears. In other words, regional extrema can grow, but they are never split during the scale-space and the operator proceeds by growing local regional extrema. Moreover, at scale t each regional extremum of $T_t u$ contains a regional extremum of u. This implies that the number of regional extrema is a decreasing function of the scale. Notice that this property is not true with the linear scale-space (convolution by a gaussian) in two dimensions.

[**Idempotent**] The operator has the property to be idempotent.

$$\forall t, \; T_t \circ T_t = T_t \tag{12}$$

[**No asymptotic evolution**] If u is C^2, there is no asymptotic evolution of the image. We have the two behaviors:

$$\forall \mathbf{x}, \nabla u(\mathbf{x}) \neq 0 \Rightarrow \exists t > 0 \text{ so that } \forall h \leq t, (T_h u - u)(\mathbf{x}) = 0 \tag{13}$$

$$\forall \mathbf{x}, \text{ if } \exists r > 0 \text{ so that } \forall \mathbf{y} \in B(\mathbf{x}, r), \nabla u(\mathbf{y}) = 0 \text{ then} \\ \exists t > 0 \text{ so that } \forall h \leq t, (T_h u - u)(\mathbf{x}) = 0 \tag{14}$$

[**Conservation of T-junctions**] Since the level lines at $T_t u$ are level lines of u, the T-junctions involving sufficient areas in u remain the same without alteration. Notice that this is not the case with all other usual scale-spaces: it is clearly false for the linear scale-space, for the median filter (mean curvature motion), but also for the affine invariant morphological scale-space, as shown in [25].

[**Conservation of some regularity**] If u is Lipschitz, so is $T_t u$ with an inferior or equal Lipschitz norm. Indeed,

$$\forall \mathbf{x}, \mathbf{z}, u(\mathbf{z}) - k|\mathbf{x}| \leq u(\mathbf{z} - \mathbf{x}) \leq u(\mathbf{z}) + k|\mathbf{x}|$$

so that

$$\forall \mathbf{x}, \mathbf{y}, \inf_{\mathbf{z} \in \mathbf{y} + B} u(\mathbf{z}) - k|\mathbf{x}| \leq \inf_{\mathbf{z} \in \mathbf{y} + B} u(\mathbf{z} - \mathbf{x}) \leq \inf_{\mathbf{z} \in \mathbf{y} + B} u(\mathbf{z}) + k|\mathbf{x}|$$

$$\forall \mathbf{x}, \mathbf{y}, \sup_{B \in B_t} \inf_{\mathbf{z} \in \mathbf{y} + B} u(\mathbf{z}) - k|\mathbf{x}| \leq \sup_{B \in B_t} \inf_{\mathbf{z} \in \mathbf{y} + B} u(\mathbf{z} - \mathbf{x}| \leq \sup_{B \in B_t} \inf_{\mathbf{z} \in \mathbf{y} + B} u(\mathbf{z}) + k|\mathbf{x}|,$$

meaning

$$T_t u(\mathbf{y}) - k|x| \leq \inf_{\mathbf{z} \in \mathbf{y} + B} u(\mathbf{z} - \mathbf{x}) = \inf_{\mathbf{z} \in \mathbf{x} + \mathbf{y} + B} u(\mathbf{z}) = T_t u(\mathbf{x} + \mathbf{y}) \leq T_t u(\mathbf{y}) + k|x|.$$

A similar demonstration shows that an *uniformly* continuous u remains uniformly continuous throughout the scale-space. We conjecture that if u is continuous, so is $T_t u$ for all t (a demonstration for the case of area opening and closing is shown in [26], we think our operator would behave similarly). Nevertheless, we cannot say more about regularization: it is not true that if u is C^1 so would be $T_t u$. This scale-space is peculiar because it does not allow to estimate more reliably the results of differential operators!

[**Affine covariance**] The operator commutes with all affine transforms of determinant 1:

$$\forall t, \forall A \in AG(\mathbb{R}^2), T_t(u \circ A) = (T_{t/|\det A|}u) \circ A \qquad (15)$$

Notice that equations (8), (9), (10) and (15) are properties that our scale-space shares only with the affine morphological scale-space. Nevertheless, the latter has an infinitesimal evolution law, whereas the former has not.

Remark: the geometrical covariance of the operator is linked to the geometrical invariance of the measure, here the area under any affine transformation of determinant 1. With a different measure invariant under another group of transformations preserving the connectedness (so probably continuous transformations would be welcome) and non decreasing with respect to inclusion, our operator would commute with these transformations.

4 Experiments

Fig. 4 illustrates the fact that this scale-space is different from the one deduced by iterating area opening and closing (see [18]) with increasing area.

Different scales of the scale-space based on the inclusion tree are shown in fig. 5. Another example showing also the level lines is shown in fig. 6. Notice how the important structures of the image (in particular T-junctions) are preserved.

The inclusion tree can also be used to remove impulsional noise: supposing that speckle noise creates only small shapes, we represent the image at a sufficiently large scale (see fig. 7). This suppresses most of noise, without attempting to restore the image, so a subsequent treatment should follow [19].

Other uses of the inclusion tree are proposed in [15].

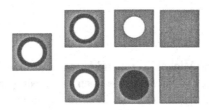

Fig. 4. Left: an image. Up: Successive removals of the cc's of upper, then lower level sets with increasing area threshold. The black ring disappears before the white circle. Down: The image across the scales of the inclusion tree: the circles disappear according to their interior size.

Fig. 5. Up-left: original image 650 × 429, Up-right: image at scale 50 (all shapes of area less than 50 pixels are removed), Down: image at scale 500, and 5000.

5 Summary and Conclusions

The inclusion tree is a complete and non-redundant representation of image, insensitive to local changes of contrast. The basic elements are the interiors of connected components of level lines, called "shapes". The structure of tree represents the geometrical inclusion, allowing to easily manipulate it, like removing some shapes, which is the fundamental operation. This yields a scale-space representation of the image which, on the contrary to most other scale-space representations, does not smooth the image, but rather selects the information to keep at each scale. As a consequence, its application field will be different from the classical scale-space.

These shapes, appearing as natural geometrical contrast insensitive information, can also be used for various image analysis tasks, like image simplification, image comparison and registration [15, 20].

Acknowledgments

The authors thank Jean-Michel Morel and Vicent Caselles for fruitful discussions about the subject. Part of this work has been done using the MegaWave2 image processing environment (http://www.ceremade.dauphine.fr), Cognitech, Inc. image processing facilities (http://www.cognitech.com), and Inrets facilities.

References

1. Meyer, Y.: Wavelets: Algorithms and Applications, SIAM, Philadelphia (1993)
2. Mallat, S.: A Wavelet Tour of Signal Processing, Academic Press (1998)

Fig. 6. Up-left: original image 508 × 500, Up-right: image at scale 150, Down: the level lines of the original image (left) and of the image at scale 150 (right). All the level lines displayed in right are present and identical to level lines of the original image (left).

3. Alvarez, L., Guichard, F., Lions, P.L., Morel, J.M.: Axioms and Fundamental Equations of Image Processing, Arch. Rational Mech. and Anal., **16**, 9 (1993) 200–257
4. Ed. Romeny, B.M. ter Haar: Geometry-Driven Diffusion in Computer Vision, Kluwer Academic Publishers (1994)
5. Marr, D.: Vision, Freeman and Co. (1982)
6. Hummel, R.A.: Representations Based on Zero-Crossing in Scale-Space, Proc. of CVPR. IEEE (1986) 204–209
7. Canny, J.: A Computational Approach to Edge Detection, IEEE Trans. on PAMI, **8**, 6 (1986) 679–698
8. Nitzberg, M., Mumford, D.: The 2.1 Sketch, Proc. of ICCV, Osaka, Japan (1990)
9. Morel, J.M., Solimini, S.: Variational Methods in Image Processing, Birkhäuser (1994)
10. Koenderink, J.J.: The Structure of Images, Biological Cybernetics, **50** (1984) 363–370
11. Witkin, A.P.: Scale-Space Filtering, Proc. of IJCAI, Karlsruhe (1983) 1019–1022
12. Matheron, G.: Random Sets and Integral Geometry, John Wiley, N.Y. (1975)
13. Serra, J.: Image Analysis and Mathematical Morphology, Academic Press (1982)
14. Caselles, V., Coll, B., Morel, J.M.: Topographic Maps, preprint CMLA (1997)
15. Monasse, P., Guichard, F.: Fast Computation of a Contrast-Invariant Image Representation, Preprint CMLA 9815, available from http://www.cmla.ens-cachan.fr/index.html (1998)

Fig. 7. Left: an image (size 240 × 255) where 50% of the pixels are changed to an arbitrary value. Right: this image at scale 30 pixels.

16. Guichard, F., Morel, J.M.: Partial Differential Equations and Image Iterative Filtering, Tutorial ICIP, Washington D.C. (1995)
17. Guichard, F., Morel, J.M.: Partial Differential Equations and Image Iterative Filtering, State of the Art in Numerical Analysis (1996)
18. Vincent, L.: Grayscale Area Openings and Closings, Their Efficient Implementation and Applications, Proc. of 1st Workshop on Math. Morphology and its Appl. to Signal Proc., J. Serra and Ph. Salembrier, Eds. (1993) 22–27
19. Masnou, S., Morel, J.M.: Image Restoration Involving Connectedness, Proc. of the 6th Int. Workshop on Digital I.P. and Comp. Graphics, SPIE **3346**, Vienna, Austria (1998)
20. Monasse, P.: Contrast Invariant Image Registration, Proc. of ICASSP, Vol. 6, (1999) 3221–3224
21. Monasse, P.: An Inclusion Tree Describing the Topological Structure of an Image, in preparation
22. Cheng, F., Venetsanopoulos, A.N.: An Adaptive Morphological Filter for Image Processing, IEEE Trans. on PAMI, Vol. 1, 4 (1992) 533–539
23. Andrew Bangham, J., Ling, P.D., Harvey, R.: Scale-Space from Nonlinear Filters, IEEE Trans. on PAMI, Vol. 18, 5 (1996) 520–528
24. Andrew Bangham, J., Ling, P.D., Harvey, R., Aldridge, R.V.: Morphological Scale-Space Preserving Transforms in Many Dimensions, Journal of Electronic Imaging, Vol. 5, 3 (1996) 283–299
25. Caselles, V., Coll, B., Morel, J.M.: Is Scale-Space Possible?, Proc. of the 1st Workshop on Scale-Space Theories in Computer Vision, Utrecht, the Netherlands (1997)
26. Guichard, F., Morel, J.M.: Image Iterative Filtering, Lecture Notes of Institut Henri Poincaré (1998)
27. Kong, T.Y., Rosenfeld, A.: Digital Topology: Introduction and Survey, CVGIP, Vol. 48, 3 (1989) 357–393

Morphological Scale-Space Representation with Levelings

Fernand Meyer[1] and Petros Maragos[2]

[1] Centre de Morphologie Mathématique, Ecole des Mines de Paris,
35, Rue Saint Honoré, 77305 Fontainebleau, France. Email: meyer@cmm.ensmp.fr
[2] National Technical University of Athens, Dept. of Electrical & Computer
Engineering, Zografou 15773, Athens, Greece. Email: maragos@cs.ntua.gr

Abstract. A morphological scale-space representation is presented based on a morphological strong filter, the levelings. The scale-properties are analysed and illustrated. From one scale to the next, details vanish, but the contours of the remaining objects are preserved sharp and perfectly localised. This paper is followed by a companion paper on pde formulations of levelings.

1 Introduction

In many circumstances, the objects of interest which have to be measured, segmented or recognised in an image belong to a scale, and all remaining objects, to be discarded, to another scale. In some cases, however, such a threshold in the scales is not possible, and the information of interest is present at several scales: it has to be extracted from various scales. For such situations, multiscale approaches have been developed, where a series of coarser and coarser representations of the same image are derived. The recognition of the objects or segmentation will use the complete set of representations at various scales and not only the initial image.

A multiscale representation will be completely specified, if one has defined the transformations from a finer scale to a coarser scale. In order to reduce the freedom of choice, some properties of these transformations may be specified. Invariance properties are the most general:

- spatial invariance = invariance by translation
- isotropy = invariance by rotation
- invariance under a change of illumination: the transformation should commute with an increasing anamorphosis of the luminance

One may add some requirements on the effect of the transformation itself:

- The transformation should really be a simplification of the image. As such it will not be reversible: some information has to be lost from one scale to the next.

- A particular form of simplification is expressed by the maximum principle: at any scale change, the maximal luminance at the coarser scale is always lower than the maximum intensity at the finer scale, the minimum always larger. [1]
- Causality: coarser scales can only be caused by what happened at finer scales [2]
- It should not create new structures at coarser scales ; the most frequent requirement is that it should not create new regional extrema.[3][4]

Furthermore, if the goal is image segmentation, one may require that the contours remain sharp and not displaced. Finally, one has to care for the relations between the various scales. Many scale-space representations in the literature verify a semi-group property: if g_λ is the representation at scale λ of image g, then the representation at scale μ of g_λ should be the same as the representation at scale $\lambda + \mu$ of $g : g_{\lambda+\mu} = (g_\lambda)_\mu$. We will present another structure by introducing an order relation among scales.

Since one rarely adds images, there is no particular reason, except mathematical tractability, to ask for linear transforms. If one however choses linearity, then various groups of the constraints listed above lead to the same solution: linear scale space theory. The evolution of images with the scale follows the physics of luminance diffusion: the decrease of luminance with scale is equal to the divergence of the luminance gradient [2]. The discrete operator for changing scale is a convolution by a Gaussian kernel. Its major utility is to regularize the images, permitting to compute derivatives: the spatial derivatives of the Gaussian are solutions of the diffusion equation too, and together with the zeroth order Gaussian, they form a complete family of differential operators. Besides this advantage, linear scale space cumulates the disadvantages. After convolution with a Gaussian kernerl, the images are uniformly blurred, also the regions of particular interest like the edges. Furthermore, the localisation of the structures of interest becomes extremely imprecise ; if an object is found at one scale, one has to refine its contours along all finer scales. At very large scales, the objects are not recognisable at all, for excess of blurring, but also due to the apparition of spurious extrema in 2 dimensins. Various solutions have been proposed to reduce this problem. Perona and Malik were the first to propose a diffusion inhibited by high gradient values[5]. Weickert introduced a tensor dependent diffusion [6]. Such approaches reduce the problems but do not eliminate them completely: spurious extrema may still appear.

Other non linear scale-spaces consider the evolution of curves and surfaces as a function of their geometry. Among them we find the morphological approaches producing dilations of increasing size for representing the successive scales [7]. These approaches have also the disadvantage to displace the boundaries. The first morphological scale-space approaches have been the granulometries associated to a family of openings or of closings ; openings operate only on the peaks and the closings only on the valleys [8],[9]. They obey a semi-group relation: $g_{\max(\lambda,\mu)} = (g_\lambda)_\mu$. Using morphological openings also displaces the contours, however openings and closings do not create spurious extrema. If one desires to preserve the contours, one uses openings and closings by reconstruction. If one desires a symmetric treatment of peaks and valleys, one uses alternate sequential filters, which are extremely costly in terms of computation, specially if one uses openings and closings by reconstruction [10][11].

In this paper we present a new and extremely general non linear scale-space representation with many extremely interesting features. The most interesting of them is the preservation of contours. Furthermore, no spurious extrema appear. As a matter of fact, the transformation from one scale to the next, called leveling, respects all the criteria listed abovve, except that it is not linear. From one scale to the next, the structures of the image progressively vanish, becoming flat or "quasi-flat" zone ; however, as long they are visible, they keep exactly the same localisation as in the initial image. Levelings have been introduced by F.Meyer. They have been studied by G.Matheron [12], F.Meyer [13], [14], and J.Serra [15].

In the first section, we present a characterisation and the scale-space properties of the simplest levelings. In a second section we show how to transform any function g into a leveling of a function f. We also present extensions of levelings. The analysis of the algorithm for constructing levelings leads to a PDE formulation, presented in a second paper.In a last section we illustrate the result.

2   Multiscale representation of images through levelings

2.1   Flat and quasi-flat zones

We are working here on grey-tone functions defined on a digital grid. We call $N_G(p)$ the set of neighbors of a pixel p. The maximal (resp. minimal) value of a function g within $N_G(p)$ represents the elementary dilation δg (resp; erosion εg) of the function f at pixel p.

A path P of cardinal n between two pixels p and q on the grid G is an n-tuple of pixels $(p_1, p_2, ..., p_n)$ such that $p_1 = p$ and $p_n = q$, and for all i, (p_i, p_{i+1}) are neighbors.

We will see that simple levelings are a subclass of connected operators [16], that means they extend flat zones and do not create new contours. More general levelings will extend quasi-flat zones, defined as follows.

Definition 1. *Two pixels x, y belong to the same R-flat-zone of a function f if and only if there exists a n-tuple of pixels $(p_1, p_2, ..., p_n)$ such that $p_1 = x$ and $p_n = y$, and for all i, (p_i, p_{i+1}) are neighbours and verify the symmetrical relation: $f_{p_i} \ R \ f_{p_i+1}$.*

The simplest symmetrical relation R is equality: $f_{p_i} = f_{p_i+1}$ for which the quasi-flat zones are flat. As an example of a more complex relation R, let us define for two neighbouring pixels p and q, $f_p \approx f_q$ by $|f_p - f_q| \leq \lambda$. This relation is symmetrical and defines quasi-flat-zones with a maximal slope equal to λ.

2.2 Characterisation of levelings

We will define a non linear scale-space representation of images based on level-ings. An image g will be a representation of an image f at a coarser scale, if g is a leveling of f, characterised by the following definition.

Definition 2. *An image g is a a leveling of the image f iff $\forall (p,q)$ neighbors:*
$$g_p > g_q \quad \Rightarrow \quad f_p \geq g_p \text{ and } g_q \geq f_q$$

Remark 1. If the function g is constant, no couple of neighboring pixels (p,q) may be found for which $g_p > g_q$. Hence the implication $\{g_p > g_q \Rightarrow f_p \geq g_p\}$ is always true, showing that a flat function is a leveling of any other function.

The relation $\{g \text{ is a leveling of } f\}$ will be written $g \prec f$. The characterisation using neighboring points, defining the levelings is illustrated by fig.1b. In [14] we have shown that adopting a different order relation, giving a new meaning to $g_p > g_q$ leads to larger classes of levelings.

2.3 Properties of levelings

Algebraic properties If two functions g_1 and g_2 both are levelings of the same function f then $g_1 \vee g_2$ and $g_1 \wedge g_2$ are both levelings of f. This property permits to associate new levelings to family of levelings. In particular if (g_i) is a family of levelings of f, the morphological centre $(f \vee \bigwedge g_i) \wedge \bigvee g_i$ of this family also is a leveling of f.

Invariance properties In the introduction, we have listed a number of de-sirable properties of transformations on which to build a scale-space. They are obviously satisfied by levelings:

- Invariance by spatial translation
- isotropy: invariance by rotation
- invariance to a change of illumination: g being a leveling of f, if g and f are submitted to a same increasing anamorphosis, then the transformed function g' will still be a leveling of the transformed function f'.

Relation between 2 scales Levelings really will construct a scale-space, when a true simplification of the image occurs between two scales. Let us now charac-terize the type of simplifications implied by levelings.

In this section we always suppose that g is a leveling of f. As shown by the definition, if there is a transition for the function g between two neighboring pixels $g_p > g_q$, then there exists an even greater transition between f_p and f_q, as $f_p \geq g_p > g_q \geq f_q$. In other words to any contour of the function g corresponds a stronger contour of the function f at the very same location, and the localisation of this contour is exactly the same. This bracketing of each transition of the function g by a transition of the function f also shows that the "causality principle" is verified: coarser scales can only be caused by what happened at finer scale.

Furthermore, if we exclude the case where g is a completely flat function, then the "maximum principle" also is satisfied: at any scale change, the maximal luminance at the coarser scale is always lower than the maximum intensity at the finer scale, the minimum is always larger.

Let us now analyse what happens on the zones where the leveling g departs from the function f. Let us consider two neighboring points (p, q) for which $f_p > g_p$ and $f_q > g_q$. For such a couple of pixels, the second half of the definition: $f_p \geq g_p$ and $g_q \geq f_q$ is wrong, showing that the first half must also be wrong: $g_p \leq g_q$. By reason of symmetry we also have $g_p \geq g_q$, and hence $g_p = g_q$. This means that if g is a leveling of f, the connected components of the anti-extensivity zones $\{f > g\}$ are necessarily flat. By duality, the same holds for the extensivity zones $\{f < g\}$.

The last criterion "no new extrema at larger scales" also is satisfied as shown by the following section.

Life and death of the regional minima and maxima Levelings are a particular case of monotone planings:

Definition 3. *An image g is a a monotone planing of the image f iff $\forall (p, q)$ neighbors:*

$$g_p > g_q \quad \Rightarrow \quad f_p > f_q$$

Theorem 1. *A monotone planing does not create regional minima or maxima. In other words, if g is a monotone planing of f, and if g has a regional minimum (resp. maximum) X, then f possesses a regional minimum (resp. maximum) $Z \subset X$.*

Hint of the proof: If X is a regional minimum of g all its neighbors have a higher altitude. To these increasing transitions correspond increasing transitions of f. It is then easy to show that the lowest pixel for f within X belongs to a regional minimum Z for f included in X.

Relations between multiple scales: preorder relation We have now to consider the relations between multiple scales. Until now, we have presented how levelings simplify images. For speaking about scales, we need some structure among scales. This structure is a lattice structure. To be a leveling is in fact an order relation as shown by the following two lemmas.

Lemma: The relation $\{g$ is a leveling of $f\}$ is symmetric and transitive: it is a preorder relations.

Lemma: The family of levelings, from which we exclude the trivial constant functions, verify the anti-symmetry relation: if f is a non constant function and a leveling of g, and simultaneously g is a leveling of f, then $f = g$.

Being an anti-symmetric preorder relation, the relation $\{g$ is a leveling of $f\}$ is an order relation, except for functions which are constant everywhere. With the help of this order relation, we are now able to construct a multiscale representation of an image in the form of a series of levelings $(g_0 = f, g_1, ...g_n)$ where g_k is a leveling of g_{k-1} and as a consequence of the transitivity, g_k also is a leveling of each function g_l for $l < k$.

3 Construction of the levelings

3.1 A criterion characterizing levelings

It will be fruitful to consider the levelings as the intersection of two larger classes: the lower levelings and the upper levelings, defined as follows.

Definition 4. *A function g is a lower-leveling of a function f if and only if for any couple of neighbouring pixels (p, q): $g_p > g_q \Rightarrow g_q \geq f_q$*

Definition 5. *A function g is an upper-leveling of a function f if and only if for any couple of neighbouring pixels (p, q): $g_p > g_q \Rightarrow g_p \leq f_p$*

The name "upper-leveling" comes from the fact that all connected components where $g > f$ are flat: for any couple of neighbouring pixels (p, q):
$$\begin{vmatrix} g_q > f_q \\ g_p > f_p \end{vmatrix} \Rightarrow g_p = g_q.$$
Similarly if g is a lower leveling of f, then all connected components where $g < f$ are flat.

Obviously, a function g is a leveling of a function f if and only if it is both an upper and a lower leveling of the function f. Let us now propose an equivalent formulation for the lower levelings:

Criterion: A function g is a lower-leveling of a function f if and only if for each pixel q with a neighbour p verifying $g_p > g_q$ the relation $g_q \geq f_q$ is satisfied.

But the pixels with this property are those for which the dilation δ will increase the value: $g_q < \delta_q g$. This leads to a new criterion

Criterion: A function g is a lower-leveling of a function f if and only if: $g_q < \delta_q g \Rightarrow g_q \geq f_q$

Recalling that the logical meaning of $[A \Rightarrow B]$ is $[not A$ or $B]$ we may interpret $[g_q < \delta_q g \Rightarrow g_q \geq f_q]$ as $[g_q \geq \delta_q g$ or $g_q \geq f_q]$ or in a equivalent manner $[g_q \geq f_q \wedge \delta_q g]$. This gives the following criterion

Criterion: A function g is a lower-leveling of a function f if and only if: $g \geq f \wedge \delta g$

In a similar way we derive a criterion for upper levelings:

Criterion Up: A function g is an upper-leveling of a function f if and only if: $g \leq f \vee \varepsilon g$

Putting everything together yields a criterion for levelings

Criterion A function g is a leveling of a function f if and only if: $f \wedge \delta g \leq g \leq f \vee \varepsilon g$ (see [12]).

3.2 Openings and closings by reconstruction

We recall that a function g is an opening (resp. closing) by reconstruction of a function f iff $g = f \wedge \delta g$ (resp. $g = f \vee \varepsilon g$). As it verifies the criterion Low (resp. Up), such a function g is then a lower (resp. upper) leveling of f. The reciprocal is also true. Hence:

Proposition 1. *g is an opening (resp. closing) by reconstruction of a function f if and only if g is a lower (resp. upper) leveling of f verifying $g \leq f$ (resp. $g \geq f$).*

Using this characterisation, we may particularize the initial definition of lower levelings in the case where $f \geq g$:

Proposition 2. *g is an opening by reconstruction of a function f if and only if $g \leq f$ and for any couple of neighbouring pixels (p, q): $g_p > g_q \Rightarrow g_q = f_q$.*

Proposition 3. *g is a closing by reconstruction of a function f if and only if $g \geq f$ and for any couple of neighbouring pixels (p, q): $g_p > g_q \Rightarrow g_p = f_p$.*

Remark 2. If g is a (lower) leveling of f then $g \wedge f$ is a lower leveling of f verifying $g \wedge f \leq f$, i.e. an opening by reconstruction. Similarly if g is an upper leveling of f then $g \vee f$ is a closing by reconstruction.

3.3 An algorithm for constructing levelings

We finally adopt the following general criterion of levelings
Criterion: A function g is a leveling of a function f if and only if: $f \wedge \alpha g \leq g \leq f \vee \beta g$, where α is an extensive operator $\alpha g \geq g$ and β an anti-extensive operator $\beta g \leq g$

With the help of this criterion, we may turn each function g into the leveling of a function f. We will call the function f reference function and the function g marker function. Given two functions g and f, we want to transform g into a leveling of f. If g is not a leveling of f, then the criterion $[f \wedge \alpha g \leq g \leq f \vee \beta g]$ is false for at least a pixel p. The criterion is not verified in two cases:

- $g_p < f_p \wedge \alpha_p g$. Hence the smallest modification of g_p for which the criterion becomes true is $g'_p = f_p \wedge \alpha_p g$. We remark that $g_p \leq g'_p \leq f_p$
- $g_p > f_p \vee \beta_p g$. Hence the smallest modification of g_p for which the criterion becomes true is $g'_p = f_p \vee \beta_p g$. We remark that $g_p \geq g'_p \geq f_p$

We remark that for $\{g_p = f_p\}$ the criterion is always satisfied. Hence another formulation of the algorithm:

- lev^-: On $\{g < f\}$ do $g = f \wedge \alpha g$.
- lev^+: On $\{g > f\}$ do $g = f \vee \beta g$

It is easy to check that this algorithm amounts to replace everywhere g by the new value $g = (f \wedge \alpha g) \vee \beta g = (f \vee \beta g) \wedge \alpha g$

We repeat the algorithm until the criterion is satisfied everywhere. We are sure that the algorithm will converge, since the modifications of g are pointwise monotonous: the successive values of g get closer and closer to f until convergence.

In order to optimize the speed of the algorithm, we use a unique parallel step of the algorithm $g = (f \wedge \alpha g) \vee \beta g$ After this first step both algorithms $[lev^-]$ and $[lev^+]$ have no effect on each other and may be used in any order. In particular one may use them as sequential algorithms in which the new value of any pixel is used for computing the values of their neighboring pixels. This may be done during alternating raster scans, a direct scan from top to bottom and left to right being followed by an inverse scan from bottom to top and right to left. Or hierarchical queues may be used, allowing to process the pixels in decreasing order on $\{g < f\}$ and on increasing order on $\{g > f\}$.

Let us illustrate in fig.1a how a a marker function h is transformed until it becomes a function g which is a leveling of f. This leveling uses for α the dilation δ and for β the erosion ε. On $\{h < f\}$, the leveling increases h as little as possible until a flat zone is created or the function g hits the function f: hence on $\{g < f\}$, the function g is flat. On $\{h > f\}$, the leveling decreases h as little as possible until a flat zone is created or the function g hits the function f: hence on $\{g > f\}$, the function g also is flat. For more general levelings, quasi-flat zones are created.

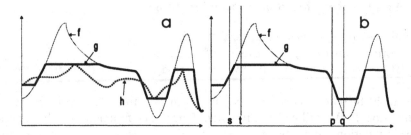

Fig. 1. a) f = reference function ; h = marker function ; g = associated leveling ; b) characterisation of levelings on the transition zones.

If g is not modified, while applying this complete algorithm to a couple of functions (f, g), then g is a leveling of f. If on the other hand g is modified, one repeats the same algorithm until convergence as explained above.

3.4   Robustness of levelings

In this section, we will see that levelings are particularly robust: they are strong morphological filters. We recall that an operator ϕ is called morphological filter if it is:

- increasing: $g > h \Rightarrow \phi g > \phi h$. This implies that $\phi(h \wedge k) < \phi h \wedge \phi k$ and $\phi(h \vee k) > \phi h \vee \phi k$
- idempotent: $\phi\phi = \phi$. This means that the operator is stable: it is sufficient to apply it once in order to get the result (for instance, the median filter, which is not a morphological filter is not stable, it may oscillate when iterated)

It is strong, if furthermore $\phi(Id \vee \phi) = \phi(Id \wedge \phi) = \phi$, where Id represents the identity operator. This property defines that functions within a given range will yield the same result, for any function h verifying $f \wedge \phi f < h < f \vee \phi f$, we have $\phi f = \phi h$.

In our case, we define an operator $\nu_g(f)$ which constructs the leveling of the marker g with reference function f. For a fixed function g and varying f, this operator is a strong morphological filter. If we call $\nu_g^-(f)$ the opening by reconstruction and $\nu_g^+(f))$ the closing by reconstruction of f based on the marker g it can be shown that : $\nu_g(f) = \nu_g^-(\nu_g^+(f)) = \nu_g^+(\nu_g^-(f))$, an opening followed by a closing and simultaneously a closing followed by an opening, a sufficient condition for a leveling to be a strong morphological filter. We use this property for showing that yet another scale space dimension exists, based on levelings. We use here a family of leveling operators, based on a family (α_i) of extensive dilations and the family of adjunct erosions (β_i), verifying for $i > j : \alpha_i < \alpha_j$ and $\beta_i > \beta_j$. We call Λ_i the leveling built with α_i and β_i. Then using the same marker g and the same reference function f, we obtain a family of increasing levelings: for $i > j$ the leveling $\Lambda_i(f; g)$ is a leveling of $\Lambda_j(f; g)$.

4   Illustration

Levelings depend upon several parameters. First of all the type of leveling has to be chosen, this depends upon the choice of the operators α and β. Fig.2 presents three different levelings, applied to the same reference and marker image. The operators α and β used for producing them are, from the left to the right, the following:1) $\alpha = \delta$; $\beta = \varepsilon$; 2) $\alpha = Id \vee (\delta - 1)$; $\beta = Id \wedge (\varepsilon + 1)$; 3) $\alpha = Id \vee \gamma \delta$; $\beta = Id \wedge \varphi \varepsilon$, where γ and φ are respectively an opening and a closing. In Fig.3 a flat leveling based on δ and ε is applied to the same reference image (in the centre of the figure), using different markers produced by an alternate sequential filter applied to the reference image : "marker 1" using disks as structuring elements, and "marker 2" using line segments.

The last series of illustrations presents how levelings may be used in order to derive a multiscale representation of an image. We use as markers alternate sequential filters with disks: m_0 = original image ; $m_i = \varphi_i \gamma_i m_{i-1}$. The levelings are produced in the following manner: l_0 is the original image and l_i is the leveling obtained if one takes as reference the image l_{i-1} and as marker the image m_i. The resulting levelings inherit in this case the semi-group property of the markers [17]. The illustrations are disposed as follows:

m_1 *original* l_1

m_3 *original* l_3

m_5 *original* l_5

Fig. 2. Three different levelings, applied to the same reference and marker image.

5 Conclusion

A morphological scale space representation has been presented, with all desirable features of a scale space. It has been applied with success in order to reduce the bitstream of an MPEG-4 encoder, when the simplified sequence replaces the original sequence. In this case, a sliding temporal window is processed and treated as a 3D volume, with 2 spatial dimensions and one temporal dimension: 3D markers and 3D levelings are then used. Another important application is the simplification of the images prior to segmentation. Since the levelings enlarge flat zones, these flat zones may be used as seeds for a segmentation algorithm.

References

1. R.A. Hummel and B.C. Gidas. Zero crossings and the heat equation. Technical report, New York Univ., Courant Institute of Math. Sciences, Computer Science Division, 1984.
2. J.J Koenderink. The structure of images. *Biol. Cybern.*, 50:363–370, 1984.
3. T. Lindeberg. On scale selection for differential operators. In B. Braathen K. Heia, K.A. Hogdra, editor, *Proc. 8th Scandinavian Conf. Image Analysis*, Trmso, Norway, 1993. Norwegian Society for Image Processing and Pattern Recognition.
4. M. Baudin J. Babaud, A.P. Witkin and R.O. Duda. Uniqueness of the gaussian kernel for scale-space filtering. *IEEE Trans. Pattern Analysis and Machine Intelligence*, 8(1):26–33, 1986.
5. P. Perona and J. Malik. Scale space and edge detection using anisotropic diffusion. *IEEE Trans. Pattern Anal. Machine Intell.*, pages 629–639, July 1989.

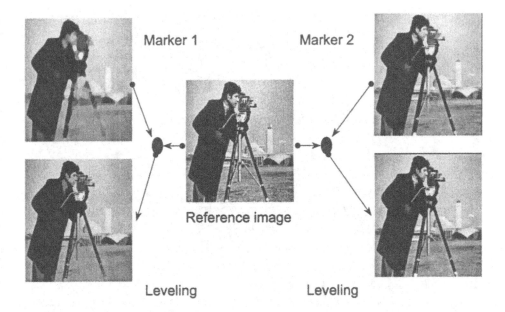

Marker 1   Marker 2

Reference image

Leveling   Leveling

Fig. 3. A same leveling applied to the same reference image with distinct marker images

6. J. Weickert. *Theoretical Foundations of Anisotropic Diffusion in Image Processing*, volume 11 of *Computing Supplement*, pages 221–246. Springer, 1996.
7. P.T. Jackway and M. Deriche. Scale-space properties of multiscale morphological dilation-erosion. *IEEE Trans. Pattern Analysis and Machine Intelligence*, 18(1):38–51, 1996.
8. G. Matheron. *Random Sets and Integral Geometry*. New York: Wiley, 1975.
9. P. Maragos. Pattern spectrum and multiscale shape representation. *IEEE Trans. Pattern Analysis and Machine Intelligence*, 11:701–716, 1989.
10. J. Serra. *Mathematical Morphology: Vol. II*, chapter Alternating Sequential Filters. London: Academic Press, 1988.
11. L. Vincent. Morphological grayscale reconstruction in image analysis: Applications and efficient algorithms. *IEEE Trans. in Image Procesing*, 1993.
12. G. Matheron. Les nivellements. Technical report, Centre de Morphologie Mathématique, 1997.
13. F. Meyer. From connected operators to levelings. In H. Heijmans and J. Roerdink, editors, *Mathematical Morphology and its Applications to Image and Signal Processing*, pages 191–199. Kluwer, 1998.
14. F. Meyer. The levelings. In H. Heijmans and J. Roerdink, editors, *Mathematical Morphology and Its Applications to Image Processing*, pages 199–207. Kluwer, 1998.
15. J. Serra. Quelques propriétés des nivellements. Technical Report 30/98/MM, CMM, 1998.
16. P. Salembier and J. Serra. Flat zone filtering, connected operators and filters by reconstruction. *IEEE Trans. Image Processing*, 4:1153–1160, Aug. 1995.
17. J. Serra. Set connectons and discrete filtering. In M. Couprie G. Bertrand and L. Perroton, editors, *Discrete Geometry for Computer Imagery*, Lecture Notes in Computer Science 1568, pages 191–207. Springer, 1999.

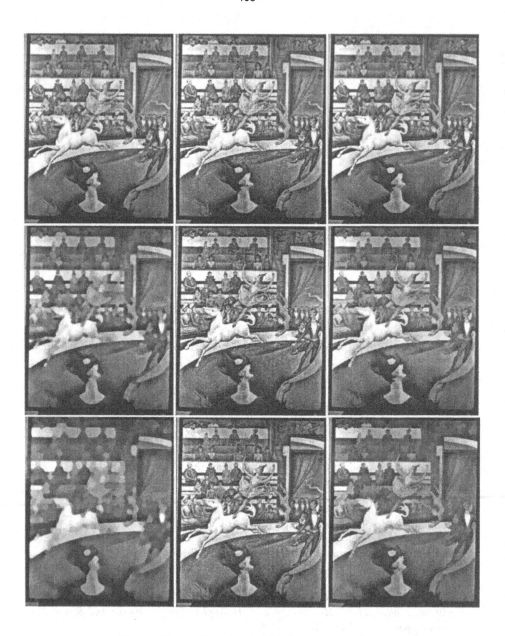

Fig. 4. Illustration of a multiscale representation

Numerical Solution Schemes
for Continuous-Scale Morphology

Rein van den Boomgaard

University of Amsterdam, The Netherlands,
rein@wins.uva.nl

Abstract. The partial differential equations describing the propagation
of (wave) fronts in space are closely connected with the morphological
erosion and dilation. Strangely enough this connection has not been explored in the derivation of numerical schemes to solve the differential
equations. In this paper the *morphological facet model* is introduced in
which an analytical function is locally fitted to the data. This function is
then dilated analytically with an infinitesimal small structuring element.
These *sub-pixel dilations* form the core of the numerical solution schemes
presented in this paper. One of the simpler morphological facet models
leads to a numerical scheme that is identical with a well known classical
upwind finite difference scheme. Experiments show that the morphological facet model provides stable numerical solution schemes for these
partial differential equations.

1   Introduction

The partial differential equations describing the propagation of fronts in space
are known to be closely connected with the morphological erosion and dilation.
These morphological partial differential equations (henceforth abbreviated as
PDE's) known from the work of Alvarez [1], Maragos[2], Matiolli [3] and van
den Boomgaard [4], have gained considerable interest in the past as canonical descriptions of evolutionary shape deformation (see Osher and Sethian [5],
Sapiro [6] and Kimia [7]). Strangely enough the realization that these PDE's are
solved with morphological operations has not been explored in the development
of numerical schemes to solve these differential equations. This paper is a more
detailed paper building on a previous paper [8] in which we have shortly introduced the *morphological facet model* as a tool to construct numerical schemes to
solve these PDE's. This paper deals with the subject in more detail.

In the morphological facet model an analytical function is locally fitted to the
data. This function is then dilated analytically with an infinitesimal small structuring element. These *sub-pixel dilations* form the core of the numerical solution
schemes. One of the simpler morphological facet models leads to a numerical
scheme that is identical with a well known classical upwind finite difference
scheme.

Consider the parameterized shape contour $C(p, t)$ as function of the path
parameter p and "time" parameter t. The generic evolution of shape as a function

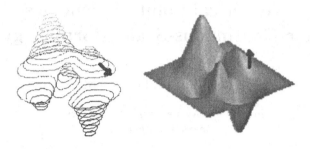

Fig. 1. Contour versus function evolution.

of time is given by:

$$\frac{\partial C}{\partial t} = \Gamma(\kappa)N$$

where Γ is a function of the curvature κ and N is the inwards pointing normal to the curve. The choice of $\Gamma = -1$ is equivalent with the dilation of the shape with a disk of radius t. A pure local description of the dilation (as in the above PDE) leads to self-intersecting curves. Dorst and van den Boomgaard [9] used this local geometrical description as their definition of the *tangential dilation*. The classical morphological dilation corresponds with the entropy solution of the PDE (i.e. the solution without self-intersections).

A robust way of obtaining entropy solutions is to embed the curve as a level set in a function and solve the associated PDE that describes the evolution of the function in time. Let F be a function of space (parameter x) and time (parameter t) and let some level set of F at time $t = 0$ correspond with the original curve C. It can be easily shown that the evolution of the function F such that the level set behaves in time as if the 'curve PDE' is solved, is given by:

$$\frac{\partial F}{\partial t} = -\Gamma(\kappa)\,\|\nabla F\|\,.$$

Note that the embedding of the curve is chosen in such a way that the shape is characterized with high function values. In that case the gradient vector is indeed the inwards pointing normal. For $\Gamma = -1$ we recognize the PDE that is solved by dilating the initial condition (the function F at time $t = 0$) with a flat disk shaped structuring element of radius t. For arbitrary, but positive, Γ, the PDE can be interpreted as geometry controlled dilation. It should be noted that such a spatially variant dilations is completely within the scope of the morphological (complete lattice) framework (see Heijmans [10]).

When a 2D curve is embedded in a 2D function a remarkable thing happens. The geometry of the curve is not measured in the spatial domain alone, but the smoothness of the embedding function is used to measure the geometry of the curve through its function derivatives. Whereas in the curve representation the points on the curve are moved to a new position in the same (horizontal) plane, in the embedding function the points are moved in vertical direction (i.e. the function value is changed). This is only allowed in case the required smoothness of the embedding function (which is a mathematical construct) is guaranteed through out the evolution process.

In this contribution we will not look at the numerous applications of these types of morphological PDE's in the computer vision context. Instead we will concentrate on numerical schemes to find solutions. In the mathematical literature, the derivation of robust and stable numerical schemes is complex and relies on the analysis of the conservation law properties of the PDE.

In [4] it was shown that the morphological dilation, out of all possible solutions (note that these type of PDE's do not have a unique solution), selects the entropy solution (which is unique). With this observation in mind, this paper introduces the *morphological facet model* as an elegant method to derive robust and stable numerical schemes to solve these PDE's. To allow for small time steps in the solution, corresponding with small radii of the dilation disk, the morphological facet model facilitates *sub-pixel dilations*. In section 2 a short introduction to morphological PDE's is given. In section 3.1 two classical numerical schemes for solving these PDE's are given for reference and comparison. In section 3.2 the morphological facet model is introduced. One of the morphological facet models leads to a numerical scheme that is equivalent to a classical scheme. In section 3.3. some numerical experiments are presented.

2 Morphological PDE's

In this section a short introduction to the morphological PDE's is given, a more detailed description can be found in [4]. Consider the one-parameter family of images F obtained by dilating a function f with structuring function g^t for varying t:

$$F(x,t) = (f \oplus g^t)(x)$$

with g a concave function and g^t the umbral scaling of g defined as $g^t(x) = tg(x/t)$. In umbral scaling not only the spatial dimensions are scaled with a factor t but also the grey value dimension is scaled. Essentially the graph of the function, interpreted as a geometrical object, is scaled.

In this section it will be shown what happens if we change the scale from t to $t + dt$. Because umbral scaling of any concave function forms a semi group under dilation (i.e. $g^\lambda \oplus g^\mu = g^{\lambda+\mu}$) we can write:

$$F(x,t+dt) = (f \oplus g^{t+dt})(x)$$
$$= ((f \oplus g^t) \oplus g^{dt})(x)$$
$$= (F(\cdot,t) \oplus g^{dt})(x)$$

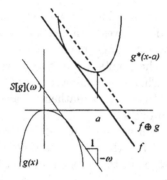

Fig. 2. Dilating a planar function. The vertical shift when dilating a planar function is given by the slope transform of the structuring function.

As we are interested in the case that dt is infinitesimal small, meaning that g^{dt} becomes very sharply pointed and indeed looks like the morphological pulse, we may approximate the function $F(\cdot, t)$ locally around the point x, with its tangent line.

Planar functions are the eigenfunctions of mathematical morphology. Dilating (eroding) a planar function with any structuring function g results in a planar function with the same slope, it is only shifted in space. The vertical shift is equal to the intercept with the function axis (this is illustrated in figure 2) of the tangent plane in the point on the structuring function where the slope equals the slope of the plane to be dilated. This geometrical construction (for all tangent planes to the function g) gives the Legendre transform of the (concave) function g. The generalization of the Legendre transform to arbitrary functions is called the slope transform[9].

The dilation of a planar function $e_\omega(x) = \omega \cdot x + c$ is therefore equal to $e_\omega \oplus g = e_\omega + S[g](\omega)$, where $S[g]$ is the slope transform of g. In the case of the tangent plane to the function F in the point x, we obtain:

$$F(x, t + dt) = F(x, t) + S[g^{dt}](\nabla F(x, t))$$

(note that $\nabla F(x, t)$ is the 'slope' of the tangent plane). In [9] it is proven that umbral scaling in the spatial domain amounts to grey value scaling (i.e. multiplication with a constant) in the slope domain. Thus we have:

$$F(x, t + dt) = F(x, t) + dt S[g](\nabla F(x, t)).$$

Rearranging terms and in the limit $dt \to 0$:

$$\frac{\partial F}{\partial t}(x, t) = S[g](\nabla F(x, t)).$$

This analysis shows that the family of images generated by dilation with the umbral scaling of a concave structuring function is causal in the scale-parameter.

I.e. the change in grey value going from scale t to scale $t + dt$ is determined by the (first order) differential structure of the image at scale t.

In summary, the entropy solution of the PDE $\partial F/\partial t = G(\nabla F)$ with initial condition $F(x, 0) = f(x)$ is given by the dilation $F(x, t) = (f \oplus g^t)(x)$, where G is the slope transform of g.

As an example consider the PDE $\frac{\partial F}{\partial t} = \|\nabla F\|$. The inverse slope transform of $G(\omega) = \|\omega\|$ is the 'indicator' function μ_B:

$$\mu_B(x) = \begin{cases} 0 & : \|x\| \leq 1 \\ -\infty & : \text{elsewhere} \end{cases}.$$

Note that the slope transform *can* be applied to non-differentiable functions like μ_B (for details see [9]). The PDE $\partial F/\partial t = \|\nabla F\|$ is thus solved with a dilation of f using a disk shaped flat structuring element of radius t. This PDE is often encountered not only in morphological image processing where the disk shaped structuring element has radius greater than the pixel size, but also in non-linear curvature controlled deformation of shape boundaries. Here the radius of dilation is controlled by the curvature of the boundary. The dilation to get from $F(\cdot, t)$ to $F(\cdot, t+dt)$ uses a disk with infinitely small radius controlled by the local (position dependent) geometry. This observation already hints at numerical schemes to solve the PDE: dilations with disk smaller than the pixel distance (sub-pixel morphological operators). Another example of the use of sub-pixel dilations is in its use in geometrical measurements where the difference of a shape and a dilated version is proportional to certain geometrical properties of the shape[11].

As a second example, consider the PDE $\frac{\partial F}{\partial t} = \|\nabla F\|^2$, with initial condition $F(x, 0) = f(x)$. The inverse slope transform of $G(\omega) = \|\omega\|^2$ is the quadratic structuring function $g(x) = -\|x\|^2/4$, i.e. the PDE is solved with dilations using a quadratic structuring element of scale t. This PDE is the morphological equivalent of the linear diffusion equation [4].

3 Numerical solutions

In this section we look at numerical schemes to solve the PDE

$$\frac{\partial F}{\partial t} = \|\nabla F\| \tag{1}$$

with initial condition $F(x, 0) = f(x)$. Only forward Euler schemes will be considered. Let $F_{i,j,r} = F(i\Delta x, j\Delta y, r\Delta t)$, then the forward Euler numerical difference scheme is given by:

$$F_{i,j,r+1} = F_{i,j,r} + \Delta t \sqrt{\left(D_{i,j,r}^x F\right)^2 + \left(D_{i,j,r}^y F\right)^2}$$

where $D_{i,j,r}^x F$ is the finite difference approximation to $F_x(i\Delta x, j\Delta y, r\Delta t)$. The choice of these finite difference operators proves to be the crucial step. Simple central differences like

$$D_{i,j,r}^x F = \frac{\left(F_{i+1,j,r}^r - F_{i-1,j,r}^r\right)}{2\Delta x} \tag{2}$$

do *not* work. Even in case very small time steps Δt are used, stability is not guaranteed.

3.1 Upwind finite difference schemes

Based on the analysis of the PDE (especially the fact that it expresses a conservation law and the fact that we are looking for an entropy solution) several *upwind finite difference schemes* are presented in the literature. The simplest one is given by Osher and Sethian[5]:

$$F_{i,j,r+1} = F_{i,j,r} + \Delta t \sqrt{\left(D_{i,j,r}^{-x}F\right)^2 + \left(D_{i,j,r}^{+x}F\right)^2 + \left(D_{i,j,r}^{-y}F\right)^2 + \left(D_{i,j,r}^{+y}F\right)^2} \quad (3)$$

where:

$$D_{i,j,r}^{-x}F = \frac{F_{i-1,j,r} - F_{i,j,r}}{\Delta x} \vee 0, \qquad D_{i,j,r}^{+x}F = \frac{F_{i+1,j,r} - F_{i,j,r}}{\Delta x} \vee 0.$$

Here we use the morphological convention to denote the supremum (maximum) operator with $\vee$. Equivalent expressions are used for the directed differences in y-direction. A second finite difference scheme to solve the same PDE is due to Rouy and Tourin (as cited in [12]):

$$F_{i,j,r+1} = F_{i,j,r} + \Delta t \sqrt{\left(D_{i,j,r}^{-x}F \vee D_{i,j,r}^{+x}F\right)^2 + \left(D_{i,j,r}^{-y}F \vee D_{i,j,r}^{+y}F\right)^2}. \quad (4)$$

It is not within the scope of this paper to give the derivation of these upwind difference schemes. Instead in the following section it will be shown that the upwind schemes are in complete accordance with the schemes that implement the sub-pixel morphological operations.

3.2 The Morphological Facet Model

From a morphological point of view it is not surprising that the classical finite difference schemes needed to solve 'morphological PDE's' contain max and min functions. In this section it will be shown that finite difference schemes that are identical to the schemes cited in the previous section, can be easily derived starting from the fact that the PDE is actually solved by a morphological dilation[1].

In the previous section it was already stated that the operation to derive $F(x, t+\Delta t)$ given $F(x, t)$ is to dilate the function $F(\cdot, t)$ with a disk of radius t. In this section we consider the dilation of a function with a disk shaped structuring element of radius $t < 1$. For these small values of the radius a sampled version of the disk is of no use as only the origin is a grid point. To be able to dilate the sampled function we therefore propose the *morphological facet model*:

---

[1] The use of a morphological dilation to solve these type of differential equations is certainly not new. Burgers [13] himself presented a geometrical construction to solve 'his' PDE, which would nowadays be immediately recognized as a morphological dilation (using a parabolic structuring function).

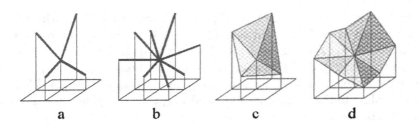

Fig. 3. Morphological facet models. a: 4-beam, b: 8-beam, c: 4-plane and d: 8-plane.

- approximate the discrete data in a small neighborhood with a function, then
- dilate this function analytically and, finally,
- sample the dilated function to give the final result.

We use the term morphological facet model because of its resemblance to the facet model which is used to approximate the derivatives of a sampled function (see Haralick[14]). Any facet model is characterized by:

- the analytical function that is fitted to the data, and
- the size and shape of the neighborhood from which the data is considered in the fitting.

The function used in the local approximation of the function data has to be chosen in such a way that the desired operation (calculating the derivatives in the classical facet model and dilation in the morphological facet model respectively) can be calculated analytically. Whereas in the classical (linear) facet model the function needs to be differentiable (its sole purpose is to calculate the derivatives), in the morphological facet model a crucial requirement is that the local range of function values is preserved. If this would not be the case then the dilation of the approximated function could result in function values that cannot be "explained" by function values in the sampled data. This is exactly the main problem when 'solving' the morphological PDE's with a simple linear finite difference scheme that is based on a facet model that does not obey the range requirement. Differentiability of the function is not a primary concern; dilations tend to result in non differentiable functions anyway. Even continuity of the function is not of primary concern in the morphological facet model.

The first morphological facet model considered is a degenerated facet model. Instead of fitting a surface to the data points , just the "beams" between the central data point and the neighboring points are considered. Two beam models are distinguished. The 4-beam model considers only the beams to the 4-connected neighbors. The 8-beam model also considers the beams to the 8 connected neighbors. Both beam models are illustrated in figure 3. In dilating the facet model, we are only interested in the dilation value in the central pixel. Evidently the final dilation result is the maximum of the dilations of the individual beams. Consider the first beam connecting the central grid point with value $F_{i,j,r}$ with the first neighbor with value $F_{i+1,j,r}$. In case $F_{i+1,j,r} \leq F_{i,j,r}$ the dilation result in the central pixel is $F_{i,j,r}$, i.e. the disk hits the beam in its highest point (the origin). In case the other end of the beam is the highest point (i.e. $F_{i+1,j,r} > F_{i,j,r}$) the dilation value equals $F_{i+1,j,r+dr} = F_{i,j,r} + \Delta t(F_{i+1,j,r} - F_{i,j,r})$. The selection according to the ordering of $F_{i,j,r}$ and $F_{i+1,j,r}$ can elegantly be casted in a maximum operator:

$$F_{i+1,j,r+dr} = F_{i,j,r} + \Delta t \left(0 \vee (F_{i+1,j,r} - F_{i,j,r})\right).$$

An equivalent analysis can be done for all 4-connected neighbors, leading to the following morphological finite dilation scheme:

$$F_{i+1,j,r+dr} = F_{i,j,r} + \Delta t \bigvee_{(k,\ell) \in N_4} (F_{i+k,j+\ell,r} - F_{i,j,r}). \tag{5}$$

The beam model is easily extended to take all 8 neighbors into consideration. For the diagonal neighbors a distance correction is needed then. This leads to:

$$F_{i+1,j,r+dr} = F_{i,j,r} + \Delta t \bigvee_{(k,\ell) \in N_8} w(k,\ell)\, (F_{i+k,j+\ell,r} - F_{i,j,r}), \tag{6}$$

where $w(k,\ell) = 1/\sqrt{2}$ for the diagonal neighbors and 1 for the other points in the 8-connected neighborhood. Note that it is essential that in the above maximum also the central pixel itself (i.e. $(k,\ell) = (0,0)$) is considered as it provides the necessary positivity of the dilation offset.

More complex morphological facet models are obtained when interpolating planar surfaces are used as shown in figure 3 c and d. The 4 plane model interpolates the data points with 4 planar function patches, each of them defined in one of the four octants. Dilation of the facet model is then equivalent with the maximum of the 4 dilations of the individual triangular facets. In section 2 it was indicated that dilating a plane with a disk is equal to the addition of the gradient norm. Because in the planar facet model only a small triangular patch of the plane is dilated, we have to make sure that the 'point-of-contact' is indeed within that patch. Let $p_{i,j}^1$ be the planar function in the first quadrant:

$$p_{i,j}^1(x,y) = \begin{cases} (F_{i+1,j,r} - F_{i,j,r})\,x + (F_{i,j+1,r} - F_{i,j,r})\,y & : x \geq 0, y \geq 0, x+y \leq 1 \\ -\infty & : \text{elsewhere} \end{cases}.$$

The dilation result of this patch with a disk of radius t, in the central point is given by:

$$F_{i,j,r} + \Delta t \begin{cases} \sqrt{(F_{i+1,j,r} - F_{i,j,r})^2 + (F_{i,j+1,r} - F_{i,j,r})^2} & : * \\ 0 \vee (F_{i+1,j,r} - F_{i,j,r}) \vee (F_{i,j+1,r} - F_{i,j,r}) & : \text{elsewhere} \end{cases},$$

where $*$ indicates the condition that $F_{i+1,j,r} - F_{i,j,r} \geq 0$ and $F_{i,j+1,r} - F_{i,j,r} \geq 0$. Thus, in case that the point-of-contact is within the first quadrant, the dilation adds the gradient norm to the function value. When the gradient vector points outside the first quadrant, the disk will hit the triangular planar patch at one of the two 'beams'. The above expression can be simplified to:

$$F_{i,j,r+1} = F_{i,j,r} + \Delta t(\sqrt{\left(F_{i+1,j,r} - F_{i,j,r} \bigvee 0\right)^2 + \left(F_{i,j+1,r} - F_{i,j,r} \bigvee 0\right)^2}.$$

The dilation of the entire 4-plane facet model is equal to the maximum of the 4 individual dilations:

$$F_{i,j,r+1} = F_{i,j,r} + \Delta t($$
$$\sqrt{\left(F_{i+1,j,r} - F_{i,j,r} \bigvee 0\right)^2 + \left(F_{i,j+1,r} - F_{i,j,r} \bigvee 0\right)^2} \vee$$
$$\sqrt{\left(F_{i,j+1,r} - F_{i,j,r} \bigvee 0\right)^2 + \left(F_{i-1,j,r} - F_{i,j,r} \bigvee 0\right)^2} \vee$$
$$\sqrt{\left(F_{i-1,j,r} - F_{i,j,r} \bigvee 0\right)^2 + \left(F_{i,j-1,r} - F_{i,j,r} \bigvee 0\right)^2} \vee$$
$$\sqrt{\left(F_{i,j-1,r} - F_{i,j,r} \bigvee 0\right)^2 + \left(F_{i+1,j,r} - F_{i,j,r} \bigvee 0\right)^2}).$$

Careful analysis[2] of the above equation reveals that it is equivalent with the Rouy and Tourin scheme (equation 4):

$$F_{i,j,r+1} = F_{i,j,r} + \Delta t \left((0 \vee F_{i+1,j,r} - F_{i,j,r} \vee F_{i-1,j,r} - F_{i,j,r})^2 + \right.$$
$$\left. (0 \vee F_{i,j+1,r} - F_{i,j,r} \vee F_{i,j-1,r} - F_{i,j,r})^2\right)^{\frac{1}{2}}.$$

The extension of the 4-plane model to the 8-plane model is straightforward.. In this case the 8 planar patches are defined within an octant, making the check to see whether the point-of-contact is within the region of definition more complex.

3.3 Numerical Experiments

The experiments presented in this section are meant to illustrate the concepts developed in previous sections. The morphological numerical schemes are compared with the classical Rouy and Tourin scheme. More detailed experiments concerning stability and accuracy are the subject of future research.

In figure 4 the experiment is shown in which a pulse (in a 64×64 image) is the initial condition to the PDE given in equation (1). As explained in the previous section, the Rouy and Tourin (abbreviated as the R&T) upwind scheme is equivalent to the morphological 4-plane facet model. From the figures it is clear that the morphological beam models suffer from severe anisotropy and therefore are of little practical use.

---

[2] To prove the equivalence remember that $\sqrt{a} \vee \sqrt{b} = \sqrt{a \vee b}$, and that $(a+b) \vee (a+c) = a + (b \vee c)$ for positive a, b and c. Using these equalities the proof is completely straightforward.

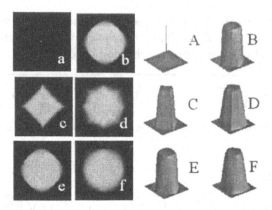

Fig. 4. Sub-pixel dilation of a pulse. In a(A) the original 64 × 64 initial condition of the PDE is shown. The PDE is solved with 5 numerical schemes. In b(B) the R&T scheme is depicted. In c(C) the 4-beam facet model, in d(D) the 8-beam model, in e(E) the 4-plane model and in f(F) the 8-plane model.

Comparison of the morphological 4-plane and 8-plane models, learns that whereas the 8-plane model is the most isotropic solution, it is so at the cost of being more dissipative (i.e. more 'smoothing' is introduced). An advantage of the 8-plane model is that the scale step Δt can be chosen significantly larger than for the 4-plane model. For the 8-plane model we have $\Delta t/\Delta x < \cos \pi/8 \approx 0.92$ compared with $\Delta t/\Delta x < \cos \pi/4 \approx 0.71$ for the 4-plane model. These bounds follow from the observation that stability requires that the disk really hits one of the planes as defined in the small considered neighbourhood (and not the analytical continuation). The 8-plane model therefore can be used with larger time steps, leading to more efficient solutions schemes as fewer iterations are needed.

Figure 5 depicts the second experiment in the same layout, only the initial condition was changed. This time a smooth function (the function 'peaks' from matlab: a weighted addition of several Gaussian functions) is used as initial condition. Again we observe that the morphological beam models perform poorly, whereas any differences between the 4-plane and 8-plane model are hardly noticeable.

Figure 6 finally shows the experiment where noise has been added to the smooth function that has been used in the previous experiment. This experiment shows that smoothness of the functions is not of any influence to the stability of the numerical solution schemes.

4   Conclusions

In this paper we have introduced the morphological facet model as a method to implement sub-pixel morphological dilations (and of course also erosions) and

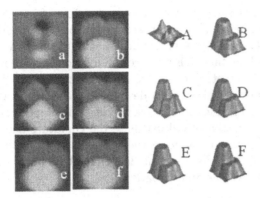

Fig. 5. Sub-pixel dilation of a continuous and smooth function. In a(A) the original 64 × 64 initial condition of the PDE is shown. The PDE is solved with 5 numerical schemes. In b(B) the R&T scheme is depicted. In c(C) the 4-beam facet model, in d(D) the 8-beam model, in e(E) the 4-plane model and in f(F) the 8-plane model.

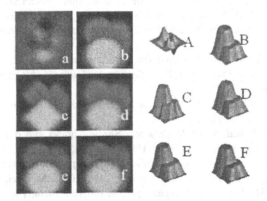

Fig. 6. Sub-pixel dilation of a function with a substantial amount of noise added. In a(A) the original 64 × 64 initial condition of the PDE is shown. The PDE is solved with 5 numerical schemes. In b(B) the R&T scheme is depicted. In c(C) the 4-beam facet model, in d(D) the 8-beam model, in e(E) the 4-plane model and in f(F) the 8-plane model.

thus to provide a stable numerical scheme to solve the class of morphological PDE's. The morphological numerical scheme based on 4-plane facet model proves to be equivalent with the classical upwind numerical scheme of Rouy and Tourin.

Future research will look at the PDE's where the dilation/erosion is locally controlled by the observed geometry of the shape (i.e. its curvature). The simplest way to use the morphological schemes described in this paper is to use a classical facet model (e.g. bicubic) to observe the local differential geometry (or use Gaussian (fuzzy) derivatives) and calculate the curvature and then to use a morphological facet model to perform the sub-pixel erosion/dilation. A more unified approach is to look for facet models that allow both analytical morphological operations as well as differentiation.

References

1. L. Alvarez, F. Guichard, P.L. Lions, and J.M. Morel. Axioms and fundamental equations of image processing. *Archives for rational mechanics*, 123(3):199–257, 1993.
2. P. Maragos. Max-min difference equations and recursive morphological systems. In J. Serra and P. Salembier, editors, *Mathematical Morphology and its Applications to Signal Processing*, pages 128–133. Kluwer academic publishers, 1993.
3. J. Mattioli. Differential equations of morphological operators. In J. Serra and P. Salembier, editors, *Mathematical Morphology and its Applications to Signal Processing*, pages 162–167, Amsterdam, 1993. Kluwer academic publishers.
4. R. v.d. Boomgaard and A.W.M. Smeulders. The morphological structure of images, the differential equations of morphological scale-space. *IEEE transactions PAMI*, 16(11):1101–1113, 1994.
5. S. Osher and J.A. Sethian. Fronts propagating with curvature dependent speed: algorithms based on hamilton-jacobi formulations. *Journal of Computational Physics*, 79:12–49, 1988.
6. G. Sapiro and A. Tannenbaum. Affine invariant scale-space. *International journal of computer vision*, 11:25–44, 1994.
7. B.B. Kimia, A. Tannenbaum, and S.W. Zucker. Shape, shocks and deformations, i. *International journal of computer vision*, 15(3):189–224, 1994.
8. R. v.d.Boomgaard. Numerical solutions of morphological partial differential equations, based on the morphological facet model. In H.J.A.M. Heijmans and J. Roerdink, editors, *Mathematical Morphology and its Applications to Image and Signal Processing*, pages 175 – 182, 1998.
9. L. Dorst and R. v.d. Boomgaard. The slope transform and morphological signal processing. *Signal Processing*, 38:79–98, 1994.
10. H.J.A.M. Heijmans. *Morphological Image Operators*. Academic Press, 1994.
11. L. van Vliet. *Grey-scale measurements in multidimensional digitized images*. PhD thesis, Delft University of Technology, 1993.
12. J.A. Sethian. A fast marching level set method for monotonically advancing fronts. *Proc. Nat. Acad. Sci.*, 93(4):1591–1595, 1996.
13. J.M. Burgers. *The non-linear diffusion equation: asymptotic solutions and statistical problems*. D. Reidel Publishers, 1974.
14. R. Haralick and L. Shapiro. *Computer and robot vision*. Addison and Wesley, 1992.

Scale-Space Properties of Regularization Methods

Esther Radmoser[1], Otmar Scherzer[1], and Joachim Weickert[2]

[1]Industrial Mathematics Institute, University of Linz,
Altenberger Str. 69, A-4040 Linz, Austria
E-Mail: {radmoser, scherzer}@indmath.uni-linz.ac.at
Web Page: http://imagewww.indmath.uni-linz.ac.at

[2]Computer Vision, Graphics and Pattern Recognition Group,
Department of Mathematics and Computer Science,
University of Mannheim, D-68131 Mannheim, Germany
E-Mail: Joachim.Weickert@ti.uni-mannheim.de
Web Page: http://www.ti.uni-mannheim/~bmg/weickert

Abstract. We show that regularization methods can be regarded as scale-spaces where the regularization parameter serves as scale. In analogy to nonlinear diffusion filtering we establish continuity with respect to scale, causality in terms of a maximum–minimum principle, simplification properties by means of Lyapunov functionals and convergence to a constant steady-state. We identify nonlinear regularization with a single implicit time step of a diffusion process. This implies that iterated regularization with small regularization parameters is a numerical realization of a diffusion filter. Numerical experiments in two and three space dimensions illustrate the scale-space behaviour of regularization methods.

1 Introduction

There has often been a fruitful interaction between linear scale-space techniques and regularization methods. Torre and Poggio [28] emphasized that differentiation is ill-posed in the sense of Hadamard, and applying suitable regularization strategies approximates linear diffusion filtering or – equivalently – Gaussian convolution. Much of the linear scale-space literature is based on the regularization properties of convolutions with Gaussians. In particular, differential geometric image analysis is performed by replacing derivatives by Gaussian-smoothed derivatives; see e.g. [8, 14, 25] and the references therein. In a very nice work, Nielsen et al. [15] derived linear diffusion filtering axiomatically from Tikhonov regularization, where the stabilizer consists of a sum of squared derivatives up to infinite order.

Nonlinear diffusion filtering can be regarded both as a restoration method and a scale-space technique [10, 19, 29]. When considering the restoration properties, natural relations between *biased* diffusion and regularization theory exist via the Euler equation for the regularization functional. This Euler equation can be regarded as the steady-state of a suitable nonlinear diffusion process with a bias term [5, 18, 24]. A popular specific energy functional arises from unconstrained total variation denoising [1, 3, 4]. Constrained total variation also leads to a nonlinear diffusion process with a bias term using a time-dependent Lagrange multiplier [21].

When regarding nonlinear diffusion as a scale-space method we have to ensure that *architectural, invariance* and *simplification properties* exist [2]. A typical architectural property is continuity with respect to the scale parameter, a characteristic invariance property is the average grey level invariance, and simplification qualities can be stated in terms of a maximum–minimum principle, Lyapunov functionals and convergence to a constant steady-state [29].

Strong and Chan [27] proposed to regard the regularization parameter of total variation denoising as a scale parameter. However, a corresponding scale-space interpretation of regularization methods, which is in analogy to results for nonlinear diffusion scale-spaces, has been missing so far. This topic will be discussed in the present paper. We show that there exists a scale-space theory for regularization methods which resembles very much the one for nonlinear diffusion filtering. Following [12, 22, 27] we interpret the regularization parameter as a diffusion time by considering regularization as time-discrete diffusion filtering with a single implicit time step. Consequently, iteration of regularization with small regularization parameters can be regarded as an approximation to diffusion filtering.

Our paper is organized as follows: In Section 2 we survey scale-space properties of diffusion filtering. In Sections 3 and 4 an analogous theory for noniterated and iterated regularization techniques is established. Due to the lack of space we can survey only the main results. Proofs and full details can be found in technical reports [23, 20]. In Section 5 we present some experiments with 2D MR images and 3D ultrasound data, and compare the restoration properties of noniterated and iterated regularization.

2 Diffusion Filtering

In this section we review essential scale-space properties of nonlinear diffusion filtering. The presented results can also be extended to a broader class of methods including regularized filters with nonmonotone flux functions and anisotropic filters with a diffusion tensor. More details and proofs can be found in [29].

We consider a *diffusion process* of the form

$$
\begin{cases}
\partial_t u(x,t) = \nabla \cdot \left(g(|\nabla u|^2) \nabla u \right)(x,t) & \text{on } \Omega \times [0, \infty[\\
\partial_n u(x,t) = 0 & \text{on } \Gamma \times [0, \infty[\\
u(x,0) = f(x) & \text{on } \Omega.
\end{cases} \tag{1}
$$

The image domain $\Omega \subseteq \mathbb{R}^d$ is assumed to be bounded with piecewise Lipschitzian boundary Γ with unit normal vector n, and $f \in L^\infty(\Omega)$ is a degraded original image with $a := \operatorname{ess\,inf}_\Omega f$ and $b := \operatorname{ess\,sup}_\Omega f$.

The diffusivity g satisfies the following properties:

1. $g \in C^\infty([0, \infty))$
2. The flux $g(s^2)s$ is monotonically increasing in s.
3. $g(s) > 0$ for all $s \geq 0$.

Under these assumptions there exists a unique solution $u(x,t)$ of (1), such that $\|u(.,t)\|_{L^2(\Omega)}$ is continuous for $t \geq 0$. This continuity property is necessary for relating structures over scales and for retrieving the original image for $t \to 0$. It is one of the fundamental architectural ingredients of scale-space theory. Furthermore, it is possible to show that $u(x,t) \in C^\infty(\bar{\Omega} \times (0, \infty))$.

Moreover, the average grey level is conserved:

$$\frac{1}{|\Omega|} \int_\Omega u(x,t)dx = Mf \quad \text{for all } t > 0,$$

with

$$Mf := \frac{1}{|\Omega|} \int_\Omega f(x)\,dx .$$

A constant average grey level is essential for scale-space segmentation algorithms such as the hyperstack [16]. It is also a desirable quality in medical imaging where grey values measure physical quantities of the depicted object, for instance proton densities in MR images.

The unique solution of (1) fulfills the extremum principle

$$a \leq u(x,t) \leq b \text{ on } \Omega \times (0, T]. \tag{2}$$

The extremum principle is an equivalent formulation of Koenderink's causality requirement [11]. Together with the continuity it ensures that level sets can be traced back in scale.

Another important simplification property can be expressed in terms of Lyapunov functionals. For all $r \in C^2[a, b]$ with $r'' \geq 0$ on $[a, b]$, the function

$$V(t) := \phi(u(t)) := \int_\Omega r(u(x,t))\,dx \tag{3}$$

is a Lyapunov functional since it satisfies

1. $\phi(u(t)) \geq \phi(Mf)$ for all $t \geq 0$
2. (a) $V \in C[0, \infty) \cap C^1(0, \infty)$
   (b) $V'(t) \leq 0$ for all $t > 0$.

Lyapunov functionals show that diffusion filters create simplifying transformations: the special choices $r(s) := |s|^p$, $r(s) := (s - Mf)^{2n}$ and $r(s) = s\ln(s)$, respectively, imply that all L^p norms with $p \geq 2$ are decreasing, all even central moments are decreasing, and the entropy $S[u(t)] := -\int_\Omega u(x,t)\ln u(x,t)\,dx$, a measure of uncertainty and missing information, is increasing with respect to t. Lyapunov functionals have been used for scale-selection and texture analysis [26], for the synchronisation of different diffusion scale-spaces [16], and for the automatic determination of stopping times [31]. Moreover, they allow to prove that the filtered image converges to a constant image as t tends to ∞: $\lim_{t \to \infty} \|u(t) - Mf\|_{L^p(\Omega)} = 0$ for $p \in [1, \infty)$. For $d = 1$ we have even uniform convergence.

3 Regularization

An interesting relation between nonlinear diffusion filtering and regularization methods becomes evident when considering an implicit time discretization [12, 22, 27]. The first step of an implicit scheme with step-size h in t–direction reads as follows.

$$\begin{cases} \frac{u(x,h)-u(x,0)}{h} = \nabla \cdot \left(g(|\nabla u|^2)\nabla u \right)(x,h) \\ \partial_n u(x,h) = 0 \\ u(x,0) = f(x) \ . \end{cases} \qquad (4)$$

In the following we assume the existence of a differentiable function $\hat{g}$ on $[0,\infty)$ which satisfies $\hat{g}' = g$. Then the minimizer of the functional

$$T(u) := \|u - f\|^2_{L^2(\Omega)} + h \int_\Omega \hat{g}(|\nabla u|^2)\, dx \qquad (5)$$

satisfies (4). This can be seen by calculating the formal Gateaux derivative of T in direction v, i.e.

$$(T'(u), v) = \lim_{t\to 0^+} \frac{T(u+tv) - T(u)}{t} = \int_\Omega 2(u-f)v\, dx + h \int_\Omega 2g(|\nabla u|^2)\nabla u \nabla v\, dx.$$

Since a minimizer of (5) satisfies $(T'(u), v) = 0$ for all v, we can conclude that the minimizer satisfies the differential equation (4). If the functional T is convex, then a minimizer of T is uniquely characterized by the solution of equation (4).

$T(u)$ is a typical regularization functional consisting of the approximation functional $\|u-f\|^2_{L^2(\Omega)}$ and the stabilizing functional $\int_\Omega \hat{g}(|\nabla u|^2)\, dx$. The weight h is called *regularization parameter*. An extensive discussion of regularization methods can be found in [7].

Now we present a scale-space theory for a broad class of regularization methods. For proofs and full details we refer to [23]. Let $\hat{g}$ satisfy:

1. $\hat{g}(.)$ is continuous for any compact $K \subseteq [0, \infty)$.
2. $\hat{g}(0) = \min \{\hat{g}(x) : x \in [0, \infty)\} \geq 0$.
3. $\hat{g}(|.|^2)$ is convex from $\mathbb{R}^d$ to $\mathbb{R}$.
4. There exists a constant $c > 0$ such that $\hat{g}(s) \geq cs$.
5. $\hat{g}$ is monotone in $[0, \infty)$.

These assumptions guarantee existence and uniqueness of a minimizer u_h for the regularization functional (5) in the Sobolev space $H^1(\Omega)$.

They are satisfied for the following regularization techniques:

1. Tikhonov regularization:

$$\hat{g}(|s|^2) = |s|^2 \ .$$

2. The modified total variation regularization of Ito and Kunisch [13]:

$$\hat{g}(|s|^2) = \sqrt{|s|^2} + \alpha|s|^2, \text{ with } \alpha > 0.$$

3. The modified total variation regularization of Nashed and Scherzer [17]:

$$\hat{g}(|s|^2) = \sqrt{|s|^2 + \beta^2} + \alpha|s|^2.$$

4. The regularization of Geman and Yang [9] and Chambolle and Lions [3]:

$$\hat{g}(|s|^2) = \begin{cases} \frac{1}{2\varepsilon}|s|^2 & |s| \leq \varepsilon \\ |s| - \frac{\varepsilon}{2} & \varepsilon \leq |s| \leq \frac{1}{\varepsilon} \\ \frac{\varepsilon}{2}|s|^2 + \frac{1}{2}\left(\frac{1}{\varepsilon} - \varepsilon\right) & |s| > \frac{1}{\varepsilon}. \end{cases}$$

5. Schnörr's [24] convex nonquadratic regularization:

$$\hat{g}(|s|^2) = \begin{cases} \lambda_h^2|s|^2 & |s| \leq c_p \\ \lambda_l^2|s|^2 + (\lambda_h^2 - \lambda_l^2)c_p(2|s| - c_p) & |s| > c_p. \end{cases}$$

The assumption 4. on $\hat{g}$ is violated for the total variation regularization in its original formulation by Rudin et al. [21]. In this case our mathematical framework cannot guarantee existence of a minimizer of (5) in $H^1(\Omega)$, and in turn we have no existence theory for the partial differential equation (4). However, this does not mean that it is impossible to establish similar results by using other mathematical tools in the proofs.

The functional $\|u_h\|_{L^2(\Omega)}$ can also be shown to be continuous in $h \geq 0$. Regarding spatial smoothness, the solution belongs to $H^2(\Omega)$. This result is weaker than for the diffusion case.

In analogy to diffusion filtering, the average grey level invariance

$$\int_\Omega u_h \, dx = \int_\Omega f \, dx \quad \text{for all } h \geq 0$$

and the extremum principle

$$a \leq u_h \leq b \quad \text{for all } h \geq 0$$

can be established.

Moreover, Lyapunov functionals for regularization methods can be constructed in a similar way. For all $r \in C^2[a, b]$ with $r'' \geq 0$, the function

$$V(h) := \phi(u_h) := \int_\Omega r(u_h(x)) \, dx \tag{6}$$

is a Lyapunov functional:

1. $\phi(u_h) \geq \phi(Mf)$ for all $h \geq 0$.

2. (a) $V \in C[0, \infty)$,

   (b) $DV(h) := \int_\Omega r'(u_h)(u_h - u_0) \leq 0$, for all $h \geq 0$.

   (c) $V(h) - V(0) \leq 0$ for all $h \geq 0$.

Here, a difference between Lyapunov functionals for diffusion processes and regularization methods becomes evident. For Lyapunov functionals in diffusion processes we have $V'(t) \leq 0$, and in regularization processes we have $DV(h) \leq 0$. $DV(h)$ is obtained from $V'(t)$ by making a time discrete ansatz at time 0. We note that this is exactly the way we compared diffusion filtering and regularization techniques. It is therefore natural that the role of the time derivative in diffusion filtering is replaced by the time discrete approximation around 0.

Again, these Lyapunov functionals allow to prove convergence of the filtered images to a constant image as $h \to \infty$. For $d = 3$, however, the convergence result is slightly weaker than in the diffusion case.

$d = 1$: $\;u_h$ converges uniformly to Mf for $h \to \infty$

$d = 2$: $\;\lim\limits_{h \to \infty} \|u_h - Mf\|_{L^p(\Omega)} = 0$ for any $1 \leq p < \infty$

$d = 3$: $\;\lim\limits_{h \to \infty} \|u_h - Mf\|_{L^p(\Omega)} = 0$ for any $1 \leq p \leq 6$

4 Iterated Regularization

Regularization can be applied iteratively where the regularized solution of the previous step serves as initial image for the next iteration. For small regularization parameters, iterated regularization becomes therefore a good approximation to a nonlinear diffusion filter.

Let us consider an iterative regularization process with positive regularization parameters h_k, $k = 1, ..., \infty$, such that the corresponding "diffusion time" $t_n := \sum_{k=1}^n h_k$ tends to ∞ for $n \to \infty$. The n-th iteration reads as follows:

$$\begin{cases} \dfrac{u(x, t) - u(x, t_{n-1})}{t - t_{n-1}} = \nabla \cdot \left(g(|\nabla u|^2)\nabla u\right)(x, t) & t \in (t_{n-1}, t_n], \; x \in \Omega \\[2mm] \partial_n u(x, t) = 0 & x \in \Gamma \\[2mm] u(x, 0) = f(x) & x \in \Omega \end{cases} \quad (7)$$

where now $t - t_{n-1}$ serves as the regularization parameter in the interval $(t_{n-1}, t_n]$.

It is now possible to prove a similar scale-space theory as for noniterated regularization [20]. The main results are given below.

Under the same assumptions as for the noniterated case there exists a unique minimizer $u(\cdot, t)$. Moreover, the functional $\|u(\cdot, t)\|_{L^2(\Omega)}$ is continuous for $t \geq 0$. However, the spatial smoothness becomes better in each iteration step: after n iterations the solution $u(., t)$ is in the Sobolev space $H^{2n}(\Omega)$ for fixed $t \in (t_{n-1}, t_n]$ (provided the diffusivity g is sufficiently smooth). This suggests that, if one uses the regularized solution for calculating derivatives of order $2n$, one should perform at least n iterations.

As for noniterated regularization, the average grey level invariance and the extremum principle hold.

Even at the risk of boring the reader we introduce for the sake of completeness Lyapunov functionals for iterated regularization: for all $r \in C^2[a, b]$ with $r'' \geq 0$, the function

$$V(t) := \phi(u(.,t)) := \int_{\Omega} r(u(x,t)) \, dx \qquad (8)$$

is a Lyapunov functional:

1. $\phi(u(.,t)) \geq \phi(Mf)$ for all $t \geq 0$.

2. (a) $V \in C[0, \infty)$,

   (b) $DV(t) := \int_{\Omega} r'\left(u(x,t)\right)\left(u(x,t) - u(x,t_{n-1})\right) dx \leq 0$,
   for all $t \in (t_{n-1}, t_n]$,

   (c) $V(t) - V(t_{n-1}) \leq 0$ for all $t \in (t_{n-1}, t_n]$.

In contrast to noniterated regularization, Lyapunov functionals for iterated regularization methods are based on the time discrete ansatz at $t = t_n$. Nevertheless, the convergence results from Section 3 carry over literally.

5 Experiments

The numerical experiments are performed using the software package DIFFPACK from the University of Oslo / Numerical Objects [6]. We have implemented the diffusion equation with $\hat{g}(|\nabla u|^2) = \sqrt{|\nabla u|^2 + \beta^2} + \alpha|\nabla u|^2$ which is a modified total variation regularization. For this diffusion filtering our theoretical results are applicable. The term $\alpha|\nabla u|^2$ is only of theoretical interest; in numerical realizations, the discretized version of the gradient is bounded, and there is no visible difference between using very small values of α (in which the theoretical results are applicable) and $\alpha = 0$ (where our theoretical results do not hold).

Our experiments were carried out for different sequences of time-steps and various smoothing parameters β. The influence of the parameter settings is as follows.

The impact of β on the numerical reconstruction is hardly viewable in the range from $\beta = 10^{-2}$ to 10^{-4}. Even the convergence rate is, although slower for smaller β, hardly affected.

For small values of regularization parameters h (up to approximately 5.0), there is no visible difference between iterated and noniterated regularization. The effect can only be seen for larger values of h. This is illustrated in Figure 2. It shows the result of noniterated and iterated regularization applied to the 2D MR image from Figure 1(a). The results are depicted at times $t = 10, 30$, and 100, respectively. For noniterated regularization this is achieved in one step, and for iterated regularization the regularization parameter $h = 1$ was chosen and 10, 30, or 100 iterations were performed. We observe that differences between the two methods are very small. They only become evident when subtracting one image from the other. This also indicates that even the semigroup property of regularization methods is well approximated in practice. It should be noted that the semigroup property is an ideal continuous concept which can only be approximated in time-discrete algorithms for partial differential equations.

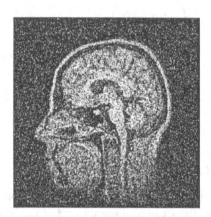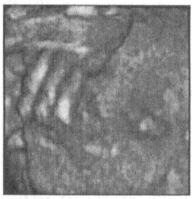

Fig. 1. Test images. (a) **Left:** MR image with additive Gaussian noise ($SNR = 1$). (b) **Right:** Rendering of a three-dimensional ultrasound data set of a human fetus.

As can be seen from the previous sections, the scale-space framework for noniterated and iterated regularization methods carries over to higher space dimensions. In the next figure we present results from a three-dimensional ultrasound data set of a fetus with $80 \times 80 \times 80$ voxels. Also in this case the differences between noniterated and iterated regularization are very small and iterated regularization appears to give slightly smoother results. This is in complete accordance with the theory derived in the previous sections.

6 Conclusions

Traditionally, scale-space techniques have been linked to parabolic or hyperbolic partial differential equations [2]. The novelty of our paper consists of establishing a parameter dependent elliptic boundary value problem (noniterated regularization) and a sequence of elliptic problems (iterated regularization) as scale-space techniques. They satisfy the same scale-space properties as nonlinear diffusion filtering. The key ingredient for understanding this relation is the interpretation of regularization methods as time-implicit approximations to diffusion processes. In this sense, the scale-space theory of regularization methods is also a novel semi-discrete theory to diffusion filtering. This time-discrete framework completes the theory of diffusion scale-spaces where up to now only results for the continuous, the space-discrete and the fully discrete setting have been formulated [29].

The synthesis of regularization techniques and diffusion methods may lead to a deeper understanding of both fields, and it is likely that many more results can be transferred from one of these areas to the other. It would e.g. be interesting to study how results for optimal parameter selection in regularization methods can be used for diffusion filtering. It is also promising to analyse and juxtapose efficient numerical techniques developed in both frameworks. First steps in this direction are reported in [30].

Acknowledgements

The work of E.R. and O.S. is supported by the Austrian Fonds zur Förderung der wissenschaftlichen Forschung, SFB 1310, and J.W. received financial support from the EU-TMR project VIRGO. The authors thank Firma Kretztechnik AG, Austria, for the allowance to publish the ultrasound data in Figure 3.

References

1. ACAR, R.; VOGEL, C.R.: *Analysis of bounded variation penalty methods for ill-posed problems*, Inverse Problems, 10, 1217–1229, 1994
2. ALVAREZ, L.; GUICHARD, F.; LIONS, P.L.; MOREL, J.M., *Axioms and fundamental equations of image processing*, Arch. Rat. Mech. Anal., 16, 200–257, 1993
3. CHAMBOLLE, A.; LIONS P.-L.: *Image recovery via total variation minimization and related problems*, Numer. Math., 76, 167 – 188, 1995
4. CHAN, T.F.; GOLUB, G.H.; MULET, P.: *A nonlinear primal–dual method for total-variation based image restoration*, in Berger, M.O.; Deriche, R.; Herlin, I.; Jaffré, J.; Morel, J.M. (Eds.): ICAOS '96: Images, wavelets and PDEs, Lecture Notes in Control and Information Sciences, 219, Springer, London, 241–252, 1996
5. CHARBONNIER, P.; BLANC–FÉRAUD, L.; AUBERT, G.; BARLAUD, M.: *Two deterministic half-quadratic regularization algorithms for computed imaging*, Proc. IEEE Int. Conf. Image Processing (Austin, Nov. 13–16, 1994), Vol. 2, 168–172, 1994
6. DÆHLEN, M.; TVEITO, A.: *Numerical Methods and Software Tools in Industrial Mathematics*, Birkhäuser, Boston, 1997
7. ENGL, H.W.; HANKE, M.; NEUBAUER, A.: *Regularization of Inverse Problems*, Kluwer, Dordrecht, 1996
8. FLORACK, L.: *Image Structure*, Kluwer, Dordrecht, 1997
9. GEMAN, D.; YANG, C.: *Nonlinear image recovery with half-quadratic regularization*, IEEE Transactions on Image Processing, 4, 932-945, 1995
10. TER HAAR ROMENY, B.M. (ED.): *Geometry-Driven Diffusion in Computer Vision*, Kluwer, Dordrecht, 1994
11. HUMMEL, R.A.: *Representations based on zero crossings in scale space*, Proc. IEEE Comp. Soc. Conf. Computer Vision and Pattern Recognition (Miami Beach, June 22 - 26, 1986), 204 – 209, 1986.
12. MOREL, J.F.; SOLIMINI S.: *Variational Methods in Image Segmentation*; Birkhäuser, Boston, 1995
13. ITO, K.; KUNISCH, K.: *An active set strategy for image restoration based on the augmented Lagrangian formulation*, Preprint No. 410/1994, Fachbereich Mathematik (3), Technische Universität Berlin, Straße des 17. Juni 136, 10623 Berlin, Germany, 1994, submitted to SIAM J. Optimization

14. LINDEBERG, T.: *Scale-Space Theory in Computer Vision*, Kluwer, Boston, 1994

15. NIELSEN, M.; FLORACK, L.; DERICHE, R.: *Regularization, scale-space and edge detection filters*, J. Math. Imag. Vision, 7, 291–307, 1997

16. NIESSEN, W.J., VINCKEN, K.L., WEICKERT, J., VIERGEVER, M.A.: *Nonlinear multiscale representations for image segmentation*, Computer Vision and Image Understanding, 66, 233–245, 1997

17. NASHED, M.Z.; SCHERZER O.: *Least squares and bounded variation regularization with nondifferentiable functionals*, Numer. Funct. Anal. and Optimiz., 19, 873–901, 1998

18. NORDSTRÖM, N.: *Biased anisotropic diffusion – a unified regularization and diffusion approach to edge detection*, Image and Vision Computing, 8, 318–327, 1990

19. PERONA, P.; MALIK, J.: *Scale space and edge detection using anisotropic diffusion*, IEEE Trans. Pattern Anal. Mach. Intell., 12, 629–639, 1990

20. RADMOSER, E.; SCHERZER, O.; WEICKERT, J.: *Lyapunov functionals for nonstationary regularization*, in preparation, 1999.

21. RUDIN, L.I.; OSHER, S.; FATEMI, E.: *Nonlinear total variation based noise removal algorithms*, Physica D, 60, 259–268, 1992

22. SCHERZER, O.: *Stable evaluation of differential operators and linear and nonlinear multi-scale filtering*, Electronic Journal of Differential Equations (http://ejde.math.unt.edu), No. 15, 1–12, 1997

23. SCHERZER, O.; WEICKERT, J.: *Relations between regularization and diffusion filtering*, J. Math. Imag. Vision, to appear.

24. SCHNÖRR, C.: *Unique reconstruction of piecewise smooth images by minimizing strictly convex non-quadratic functionals*, J. Math. Imag. Vision, 4, 189–198, 1994

25. SPORRING, J.; NIELSEN, M.; FLORACK, L.; JOHANSEN, P. (EDS.): *Gaussian Scale-Space Theory*, Kluwer, Dordrecht, 1997

26. SPORRING, J.; WEICKERT, J.: *Information measures in scale-spaces*, IEEE Trans. Information Theory, 45, 1051–1058, 1999

27. STRONG, D.M.; CHAN, T.F.: *Relation of regularization parameter and scale in total variation based image denoising*, CAM Report 96-7, Dept. of Mathematics, Univ. of California, Los Angeles, CA 90024, U.S.A., 1996

28. TORRE, V.; POGGIO, T.A.: *On edge detection*, IEEE Trans. Pattern Anal. Mach. Intell., 8, 148–163, 1986

29. WEICKERT, J.: *Anisotropic Diffusion in Image Processing*, Teubner, Stuttgart, 1998

30. WEICKERT, J.; HEERS, J.; SCHNÖRR, C.; ZUIDERVELD, K.J.; SCHERZER, O.; STIEHL, H.S.: *Fast parallel algorithms for a broad class of nonlinear variational diffusion approaches*, Report 5/99, Computer Science Series, Dept. of Mathematics and Computer Science, University of Mannheim, 68131 Mannheim, Germany, 1999, submitted.

31. WEICKERT, J.; ZUIDERVELD, K.J.; TER HAAR ROMENY, B.M.; NIESSEN, W.J.: *Parallel implementations of AOS schemes: A fast way of nonlinear diffusion filtering*, Proc. 1997 IEEE International Conference on Image Processing (Santa Barbara, Oct. 26–29, 1997), Vol. 3, 396–399, 1997.

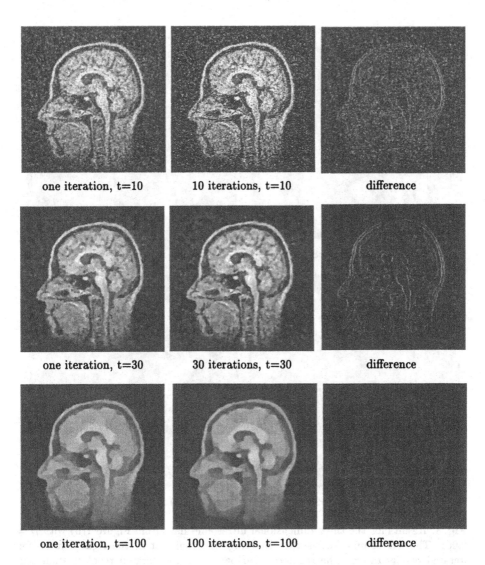

one iteration, t=10   10 iterations, t=10   difference

one iteration, t=30   30 iterations, t=30   difference

one iteration, t=100   100 iterations, t=100   difference

Fig. 2. Results for the MR image from Figure 1(a) with noniterated and iterated regularization ($\beta = 0.001$). The left column shows the results for noniterated, the middle column for iterated regularization. The images in the right column depict the modulus of the differences between the results for the iterated and noniterated method.

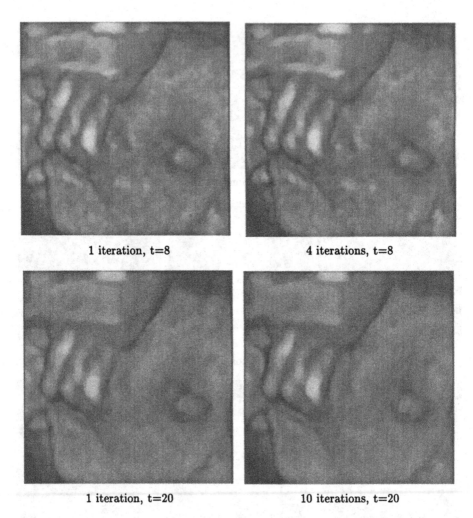

Fig. 3. Results for the three-dimensional ultrasound data from Figure 1(b) with $\beta = 0.001$. The left column shows the renderings for noniterated, the right column for iterated regularization. The regularization parameter for iterated regularization was $h = 2$.

An Adaptive Finite Element Method for Large Scale Image Processing

T. Preußer and M. Rumpf

Institut für Angewandte Mathematik, Universität Bonn,
Wegelerstr. 6, 53115 Bonn, Germany
tpreuss,rumpf@iam.uni-bonn.de

Abstract. Nonlinear diffusion methods have proved to be powerful methods in the processing of 2D and 3D images. They allow a denoising and smoothing of image intensities while retaining and enhancing edges. On the other hand, compression is an important topic in image processing as well. Here a method is presented which combines the two aspects in an efficient way. It is based on a semi–implicit Finite Element implementation of nonlinear diffusion. Error indicators guide a successive coarsening process. This leads to locally coarse grids in areas of resulting smooth image intensity, while enhanced edges are still resolved on fine grid levels. Special emphasis has been put on algorithmical aspects such as storage requirements and efficiency. Furthermore, a new nonlinear anisotropic diffusion method for vector field visualization is presented.

1 Introduction

Nonlinear diffusion methods in image processing have been known for a long time. In 1987 Perona and Malik [17] introduced a continuous diffusion model which allows the denoising of images together with the enhancing of edges. The diffusion driven evolution is started on an initial image intensity. In general, it is either noisy because of unavoidable measurement errors, or it carries partially hidden patterns which have to be intensified and outlined [9, 23]. Such an image smoothing and feature restoration process can be understood as a successive coarsening while certain structures are retained on a fine scale – an approach which is closely related to the major techniques in image compression.
Finite Element methods are widespread to discretize and appropriately implement the diffusion based models. Their general convergence properties were studied for instance by Kačur and Mikula [13]. Furthermore, Schnörr applied Finite Elements in a variational approach to image processing [19]. In various areas of scientific computing adaptive Finite Element methods [6, 4] have been incorporated to substantially reduce the required degrees of freedom while conserving the approximation quality of the numerical solution. Thereby locally defined reliable error estimators or some error indicators steer the local grid refinement, respectively coarsening [22, 5]. The image intensities resulting from the nonlinear parabolic evolution are obviously well-suited to be resolved on adaptive grids. As time evolves, a successive coarsening in areas of smooth image intensity is

near at hand. For instance in case of an d–dimensional image, where the image intensity is constant on piecewise smoothly bounded regions, we obtain the same image quality on a $O(N^{d-1} \log(N))$ complex adaptive grid as on a $O(N^d)$ regular grid. The cost of the numerical algorithm, the storage requirements, and the transmission time on computer networks scale with this complexity in terms of actual degrees of freedom.

These efficiency perspectives have first been studied by Bänsch and Mikula [3], who presented an adaptive Finite Element method. This method is based on simplicial grids generated by bisection and then again successively coarsened in the diffusion process. The major shortcoming of their approach is the enormous memory requirement for the data structures describing the adaptive grid and the sparse matrices used in the linear solver in each implicit time. Therefore, large 3D images – as they are widespread in medical images – are difficult to manage on moderately sized workstations.

Here we present an adaptive multilevel Finite Element method which avoids these shortcomings and comes along with minimal storage requirements. The specific ingredients of our method are:

- adaptive quad– and octrees, with accompanying piecewise bilinear, respectively trilinear Finite Element spaces are procedurally handled only,
- error indicators on grid nodes and a suitable threshold value implicitly describe the adaptive grid (no explicit adaptive grid structure is required),
- invoking a certain saturation condition for the nodal indicators, we ensure robustness and one level transitions only on the resulting adaptive grid,
- the adaptive Finite Element space is defined as an implicitly constrained discrete space on the full grid,
- the grid is completely handled procedurally,
- and instead of dealing with explicitly stored sparse matrices, the hierarchically preconditioned linear solver in each timestep uses "on–the–fly" matrix multiplication based on efficient grid traversals.

Let us mention that this approach benefits from general and efficient multilevel data post processing methodology [16, 18] and is related to the multilevel methods discussed in [1, 24].

Finally, as a – to our knowledge – new area of application we will present a scale space method in vector field visualization. Flow visualization is an important task in scientific visualization. Simply drawing vector plots at nodes of some overlayed regular grid in general produces visual clutter. The central goal is to come up with inituitive methods with more comprehensible results. They should provide an overall as well as detailed view on the flow patterns. Several techniques generating such textures based on discrete models have been presented [8, 15, 20, 21]. We ask for a continuous model which leads to stretched streamline type patterns, which are aligned to the vector field. Furthermore, the possibility to successively coarsen this pattern is obviously a desirable property. For the generation of such field aligned flow patterns we apply anisotropic nonlinear diffusion. A matrix valued diffusion coefficient controls the anisotropy as in

Weickart's method [25] to restore and enhance lower dimensional structures in images.

2 FE-Discretization of Nonlinear Diffusion

Let us look at the modified Perona-Malik [17] model proposed by Catté, Lions, Morel, and Coll [9]. Without any restriction we consider the domain $\Omega := [0,1]^d$, $d = 2, 3$ and ask for solution of the following nonlinear parabolic, boundary and initial value problem: Find $\rho : \mathbb{R}^+ \times \Omega \to \mathbb{R}^m$ such that

$$\frac{\partial}{\partial t}\rho - \text{div}\,(A(\nabla\rho_\epsilon)\nabla\rho) = f(\rho), \quad \text{in } \mathbb{R}^+ \times \Omega,$$
$$\rho(0,\cdot) = \rho_0 \quad , \quad \text{on } \Omega,$$
$$\frac{\partial}{\partial \nu}\rho = 0 \quad , \quad \text{on } \mathbb{R}^+ \times \partial\Omega.$$

where in the basic model $A = g$ for a non negative monotone decreasing function $g : \mathbb{R}_0^+ \to \mathbb{R}+$ satisfying $\lim_{s\to\infty} g(s) = 0$, e. g. $g(s) = (1 + s^2)^{-1}$, and ρ_ϵ is a mollification of ρ with some smoothing kernel. We interpret the solution ρ for increasing $t \in \mathbb{R}^+$ to be a successively filtered version of ρ_0. With respect to the shape of g, the diffusion is of regularized backward type [14] in regions of high image gradients, while noisy regions of ρ_0 will be smoothed by dominant diffusion.

We solve this problem numerically by applying a bilinear, respectively trilinear conforming Finite Element discretization on an adaptive quadrilateral, respectively hexahedral grid. In time a semi-implicit second order Euler scheme is used. As it has become standard the scheme is semi-implicit with respect to the evaluation of the nonlinear diffusion coefficient g and the right hand side. The computation of the mollified intensity ρ_ϵ is based on a single short timestep of the corresponding heat equation (linear diffusion) with given data ρ [13]. In the ith timestep we have to solve the linear system $(M + \tau L(\rho_\epsilon))\bar{\rho}^i = M\bar{\rho}^{i-1} + F$, where $\bar{\rho}^i$ is the corresponding solution vector consisting of the nodal values, τ the current timestep, M is the lumped mass matrix, $L(\rho_\epsilon)$ the weighted stiffness matrix and F the vector representation of the right hand side. The growth of F in the application is moderate compared to chemical reaction diffusion equations. Therefore we have not recognized any instabilities with this source term. The stiffness matrix and the right hand side are computed by applying the midpoint quadrature rule.

The above linear system as well as the linear system resulting from the mollification by the heat equation kernel is solved by a preconditioned conjugate gradient method. We use the Bramble–Pasciak–Xu preconditioning [7], thus making appropriate use of the given grid hierarchy.

As already mentioned above, a peculiarity of our scheme is that no matrices are stored explicitly. Instead, the multiplication of the mass, respectively the stiffness matrix with a coefficient vector consisting of nodal values is done procedurally. Therefore, in each step the hierarchical and adaptive grid is traversed and element wise local contributions are evaluated and successively assembled on the resulting coefficient vector. Thus we avoid storing the matrices explicitly.

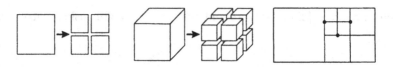

Fig. 1. On the left element types in two and three dimensions and their refinements are shown and on the right a grid configuration with hanging nodes is depicted.

Otherwise we would have been unable to manage typical 3D applications with more than 10 million nodes. Furthermore, this procedural access carries strong provisions for code optimization with respect to a cache optimal numbering of the nodes.

3 Grid Adaptivity and Error Indicators

In this section we will discuss an adaptive approach to the problem of nonlinear diffusion. We will especially focus on the choice and the handling of error indicator values on the grid nodes which steer the adaptive algorithm. It will be outlined that *saturation* plays an essential role in the robustness and implementability of the proposed algorithm. In fact, solely referring to saturated error indicator information and not to some explicit grid hierarchy enables us to define and handle appropriate adaptive meshes for the nonlinear diffusion algorithm. Let us assume the dimension of our image to be $(2^{l_{\max}} + 1)$ in each direction for some $l_{\max} \in \mathbb{N}$. The degrees of freedom are interpretated as nodal values of a regular grid with $2^{l_{\max}d}$ elements for $d = 2, 3$. Above this fine grid level we define a quadtree, respectively octree hierarchy of elements with $l_{\max} + 1$ grid levels. In each local refinement step an element E is subdivided into a set $\mathcal{C}(E)$ of 2^d child elements (cf. Fig. 1). Vice versa we denote by $\mathcal{P}(E)$ the ancestor of an element E. In each refinement step new grid nodes x appear. They are expressed by weighted sums over their parent nodes $x_{\mathcal{P}} \in \mathcal{P}(x)$ from the set of coarser grid level nodes: $x = \sum_{x_{\mathcal{P}} \in \mathcal{P}(x)} \omega(x, x_{\mathcal{P}}) x_{\mathcal{P}}$. The weights $\omega(x, x_{\mathcal{P}}) \in \{\frac{1}{2}, \frac{1}{4}, \frac{1}{8}\}$ depend on the type of the new node, which might be the center of a 1D edge, a 2D face, or a 3D hexahedron. Let us denote by $\mathcal{N}_{\mathcal{C}}(E)$ the set of new nodes on an element E.

We suppose the grid to be adaptive. I. e. depending on data the recursive refinement is stopped locally on elements of different grid levels. Thereby a sequence of nested successively refined grids $\{\mathcal{M}^l\}_{0 \le l \le l_{\max}}$ is generated. On this sequence we define discrete function spaces $\{\mathcal{V}^l\}_{0 \le l \le l_{\max}}$ consisting of continuous piecewise bilinear, respectively trilinear functions, which are ordered by set inclusion: $\mathcal{V}^0 \subset \mathcal{V}^1 \subset \cdots \subset \mathcal{V}^l \subset \mathcal{V}^{l+1} \subset \cdots \subset \mathcal{V}^{l_{\max}}$. Let $\{\phi_i^l\}_i$ denote the basis of $\mathcal{V}^l$ consisting of hat-functions, i.e. if $\{x_1, \ldots, x_N\}$ denotes the set of non constrained vertices of $\mathcal{M}^l$, we have $\phi_i^l(x^j) = \delta_{ij}$, $j = 1, \ldots, N$. Thereby a vertex is called *constrained*, or a *hanging node*, if it is not generated by refinement on every adjacent element (cf. Fig. 1). On adaptive quadtrees, respectively octrees such hanging nodes are unavoidable. The handling of the corresponding nodal values is crucial for the efficiency of the resulting adaptive numerical algorithm. We choose an efficient implicit processing which will be described below.

Usually, for timedependent problems a grid modification consisting of the refinement and coarsening of elements is necessary at certain time steps. In our setting we start on the initial fine grid $\mathcal{M}^{l_{max}}$ and it suffices to coarsen elements, since there is in general no spatial movement of the image edges and complete information of the image is coded on the initial grid. This coarsening is obtained by prescribing a data dependent, boolean valued stopping criterion $S(E)$ on elements, which implies local stopping in a recursive depth first traversal of the hierarchical grid. It turned out to be suitable to let this element stopping criterion depend on a corresponding criterion $S(x)$ on the nodes, respectively basis functions, i. e. we define $S(E):=\bigwedge_{x\in\mathcal{N}_C(E)} S(x)$. $S(\cdot)$ distinguishes which degrees of freedom are actually important, respectively which nodal values can be generated by interpolation of some coarse grid function. If $\eta(x)$ is some error indicator on the nodes x and ϵ is a prescribed threshold value, we obtain such an interpolation criterion by $S(x):=(\eta(x) \leq \epsilon)$. Given an image intensity $\rho \in \mathcal{V}^{l_{max}}$ an intuitive choice for an error indicator is $\eta(x):=|\nabla\rho(x)|$, because the gradient of an image ρ acts like an edge indicator. Hence in regions with nearly constant intensity the grid will be coarsened substantially, whereas in the vicinity of high gradients, indicating preservable edges, the grid size is kept fine.

The stopping criterion on elements is motivated by the fact that in the next refinement step only interpolated nodal values would appear. To ensure every descendent nodal value on such an element – also those on finer grid levels – to be interpolated we require the following natural saturation condition on the error indicator

(Saturation Condition) *An error indicator value $\eta(x)$ for $x \in \mathcal{N}(E)$ is always greater than every error indicator $\eta(x_C)$ for $x_C \in \mathcal{N}_C(E)$.*

In general the saturation condition is not fulfilled, but we can modify the error indicator in a preprocessing step. Typically, this turns out to be necessary only on coarse grid levels. A simple update algorithm for an error indicator η and thereby the corresponding projection criterion S is the following bottom-up traversal of the grid hierarchy, starting on the second finest level and ending on the macro grid.

```
for l= l_max-1 to 0 step -1 do
    for each element E of M^l do
        η* := max_{x∈N_C^{i+1}(E)} η(x);
        for all x ∈ N(E) do if(η(x) < η*) η(x) = η*;
```

Let us emphasize that a depth first traversal of the hierarchy in the adjustment procedure would not be sufficient. This saturation process "transports" fine grid error information up to coarse grid level and prevents us from overlooking important fine grid details [16]. Furthermore, the saturation condition comes along with another desirable property. The corresponding element stopping criterion implies only one level grid transitions at element faces of the actual adaptive grid (cf. Fig. 1). Thus, the possible hanging node configurations confine to the

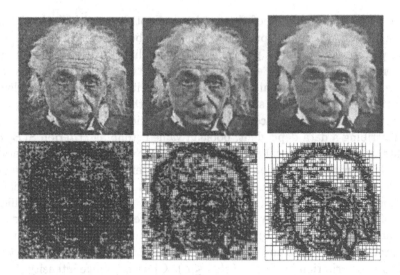

Fig. 2. From left to right several timesteps of the selective image smoothing on adaptive grids are shown.

basic one level cases. I. e. any open face and any edge of an element E contains at most one hanging node (cf. [11] for a general treatment of hanging nodes). Finally, this has straightforward implications on the assurance of continuity of discrete Finite Element functions and the corresponding matrix assembly in the implementation of our nonlinear diffusion algorithm. In general on regular grids the continuity is guaranteed by identifying each local degree of freedom (dof) with the global dof in the assembly of the global stiffness matrices and the right hand side of the corresponding discrete linear problem. However, hanging nodes of the adaptive grid do not represent dofs, due to their dependence upon other dofs. Therefore, when assembling the global stiffness matrices, we have to distribute the contribution of the hanging nodes onto the constraining dofs. This is nothing else but procedurally respecting the appropriate interpolation conditions. For future use let us introduce the following notation:

- NDEP(i) = Number of constraints of the node with local index i of an element. We define NDEP(i):=1 if the node is not constrained.
- CCOEF(i,j) = List of constrained coefficients. In our case we always have CCOEF(i,j) = 1/NDEP(i) for $j = 1, \ldots,$ NDEP(i).
- CDOFM(i,j) = List of global dofs that constrain the node i, $j = 1, \ldots,$ NDEP(i). For non-hanging nodes CDOFM($i,1$) coincides with the global dof of node i.

The CCOEF–values are identical to the weights in the above node generation rule. Figure 2 shows the application of the resulting adaptive algorithm to selectively smoothen some noisy image. In Figure 3 and 4 we have applied the algorithm to a 3D data set [12]. Figure 5 shows results obtained by the application of nonlinear diffusion to image segmentation. The approach is based on a continuous multilevel analogue of the watershed algorithm.

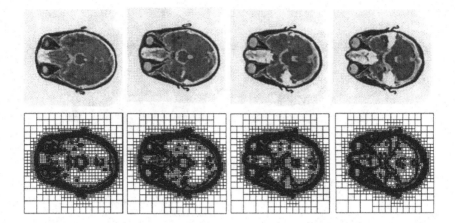

Fig. 3. Nonlinear diffusion has been applied to a 3d medical data set. Several slices through the adaptive grid are depicted showing the corresponding image intensity as well as the intersection lines with element faces.

4 Procedural Grid Handling and Matrix Multiplication

As already mentioned in Section 2 the hierarchical grid is handled solely procedurally and necessary matrix multiplications in the linear system solver are performed on–the–fly traversing the adaptive grid recursively. Let us describe this now in more detail.

Traversing the grid, information that is needed to identify an element E will be generated recursively. If this recursive traversal routine reaches a leaf element of the adaptive grid, i. e. an element for which $S(E)$ is true, a callback-method will perform some action on that element. For instance it calculates the local right hand side. An element E is identified by the index vector of its lower left corner, its grid level and its refinement-type. Every other information like the element's size, the mapping of local dofs to global dofs, and the constrained dofs will be stored in lookup tables as already mentioned in Section 3. In 2D the hierarchical traversal can be formulated in pseudo code as follows:

```
sub traverse(i, j, lev, refType, callback, params)
    if (lev ≠ l_max) and ¬S(element) do
        offset = 2^(l_max-lev-1);
        traverse(i, j, lev+1, 0, callback, params);
        traverse(i + offset, j, lev+1, 1, callback, params);
        traverse(i + offset, j + offset, lev+1, 2, callback, params);
        traverse(i, j + offset, lev+1, callback, params);
    else callback(i, j, lev, refType, params);
```

We can also formulate the "on-the-fly" matrix-vector multiplication using this callback traversal. Multiplying a given vector u with the matrix $M + \tau L(\rho_\epsilon)$ and assembling the result in a vector w requires the following local callback procedure:

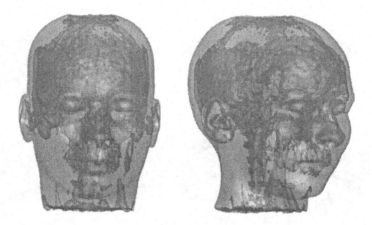

Fig. 4. A transparent isosurface visualization of the brain data set, smoothed by non-linear diffusion (cf. Fig. 3).

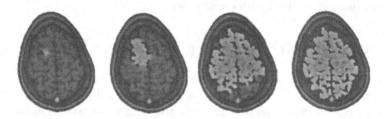

Fig. 5. Brain segmentation on slices of a MRT-image by nonlinear diffusion. Consecutive timesteps of the corresponding evolution are depicted.

```
sub matrixProduct(i, j, lev, refType, (u,w))
    for each pair l,k of local dofs
        for lc=0 to NDEP(l), kc=0 to NDEP(k)
            w(CDOFM(kc)) += localMatrix(CDOFM(lc), CDOFM(kc)) *
                            CCOEFF(lc) * CCOEFF(kc) * u(CDOFM(lc));
```

Similarily the adaptive BPX preconditioning can be implemented.

5 Application to Flow Visualization

As already sketched in the introduction we will now apply nonlinear anisotropic diffusion to vector field visualization. Thereby we consider diffusive smoothing along streamlines and edge enhancing in the orthogonal directions. Applying this to some initial random noise image we generate a scale of successively coarser patterns which represent the flow field.

For a given smooth vector field $v : \Omega \rightarrow \mathbb{R}^n$ we define a family of continuous orthogonal mappings $B(v) : \mathbb{R}^n \rightarrow SO(n)$ such that $B(v)v = e_0$,

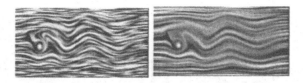

Fig. 6. A single timestep is depicted from the nonlinear diffusion method applied to the vector field describing the flow around an obstacle at a fixed time. A discrete white noise is considered as initial data. We run the evolution on the left for a small and on the right for a large constant diffusion coefficient α.

Fig. 7. Several timesteps are depicted from the nonlinear anisotropic evolution applied to a convective flow field in a 2D box.

where $\{e_i\}_{i=0,\cdots,n-1}$ is the standard base in $\mathbb{R}^n$. We consider a diffusion matrix $A = A(v, \nabla \rho_\epsilon)$ and define

$$A(v, d) = B(v)^T \begin{pmatrix} \alpha(\|v\|) & 0 \\ 0 & g(d) \end{pmatrix} B(v)$$

where $\alpha : \mathbb{R}^+ \to \mathbb{R}^+$ controls the linear diffusion in vector field direction, i. e. along streamlines, and the above introduced edge enhancing diffusion coefficient $g(\cdot)$ acts in the orthogonal directions. We may either choose a linear function α or in case of a velocity field, which spatially varies over several orders of magnitude, we select a monotone function α with $\alpha(0) > 0$ and $\lim_{s \to \infty} \alpha(s) = \alpha_{\max}$.

Different to the problems studied by Weickart in [25] in our case no canonical initial data is given. To avoid aliasing artifacts we thus choose some random noise ρ_0 of an appropriate frequency range. This can for instance be generated running a linear isotropic diffusion simulation on a discrete white noise for a short time. During the evolution the random pattern will grow upstream and downstream, whereas the edges tangential to these patterns are successively enhanced. Still there is some diffusion perpendicular to the field which supplies us for evolving time with a scale of progressively coarser representation of the flow field. Running the evolution for vanishing right hand side f the image contrast will unfortunately decrease successively. Thus the asymptotic limit would turn out to be an averaged grey value. Therefore, we select an appropriate contrast

Fig. 8. Convective patterns in a 2D flow field are displayed and emphasized by the method of anisotropic nonlinear diffusion. The images show the velocity field of the flow at different timesteps. Thereby the resulting alignment is with respect to streamlines of this timedependent flow.

enhancing right hand side $f : [0,1] \to \mathbb{R}^+$ with $f(0) = f(1) = 0$, $f > 0$ on $(0.5, 1)$, and $f < 0$ on $(0, 0.5)$ (cf. reaction diffusion problems in image analysis studied in [2, 10]). Finally we end up with the method of nonlinear anisotropic diffusion to visualize complex vector fields.

We expect an almost everywhere convergence to $\rho(\infty, \cdot) \in \{0, 1\}$ due to the choice of the contrast enhancing function $f(\cdot)$. The set of asymptotic limits significantly influences the richness of the developing pattern. One way to enrich this set significantly is to consider a vector valued $\rho : \Omega \to [0,1]^2$ for some $m \geq 1$ and a corresponding system of parabolic equations. Now, the nonlinear diffusion coefficient $g(\cdot)$ is assumed to depend on the norm $\|\nabla\rho\|$ of the Jacobian of the vector valued density $\nabla\rho$ and as right hand we define $f(\rho) = h(\|\rho\|)\rho$. Here $h(s) = \tilde{f}(s)/s$ for $s \neq 0$, where $\tilde{f}$ is the old right hand side from the scalar case, and $h(0) = 0$. Finally the random initial density is assumed to have values in $B_1(0) \cap [0,1]^2$. Obviously the contrast enhancement leads to asymptotic values which are either 0 or lie on the sphere sector $S^1 \cap [0,1]^2$ in $\mathbb{R}^2$. This method is capable to nicely depict the global structure of flow fields, including saddle points, vortices, and stagnation points on the boundary. This is indicated by Figure 7 and 8. Here the anisotropic diffusion method is applied to an incompressible Bénard convection problem in a rectangular box with heating from below and cooling from above. The formation of convection rolls leads to an exchange of temperature.

The anisotropic nonlinear diffusion problem has already been formulated in Section 2 for arbitrary space dimension. Differing from 2D in 3D we have somehow to break up the volume and open up the view to inner regions. Here a further benefit of the vector valued diffusion comes into play. The asymptotic limits - which differ from 0 - are in mean equally distributed on $S^1 \cap [0,1]^2$. Hence, we reduce the informational content and focus on a ball shaped neighbourhood $B_\delta(\omega)$ of a certain point $\omega \in S^1 \cap [0,1]^2$ (cf. Fig. 9).

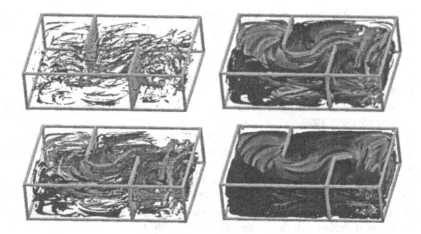

Fig. 9. The incompressible flow in a water basin with two interior walls and an inlet (on the left) and an outlet (on the right) is visualized by anisotropic nonlinear diffusion. Isosurfaces show the preimage of $\partial B_\delta(\omega)$ (for different values of δ) under the vector valued mapping ρ for some point ω on S^1. Color is indicating the velocity.

6 Conclusions

We have discussed an adaptive Finite Element method for the discretization of nonlinear diffusion methods in large scale image processing. Especially, we have introduced a new method to process adaptive grids and corresponding mass- and stiffness matrices procedurally with out storing any matrix or any graph structure for the hierarchical tree of elements. Thus the method enables the handling of large images (257^3 dofs and more) on moderately sized workstations. Furthermore a new method for 2D and 3D flow visualization has been presented.

Acknowledgement
The authors would like to acknowledge Karol Mikula and Jarke van Wijk for inspiring discussions and many useful comments on image processing and flow visualization. Furthermore, they thank Eberhard Bänsch from Bremen University for providing the incompressible flow data sets.

References

1. S. T. Acton. Multigrid anisotropic diffusion. *IEEE Trans. Image Proc.*, 7:280–291, 1998.
2. L. Alvarez and J. Esclarin. Image quantization using reaction-diffusion equations. *SIAM J. Appl. Math.*, 57:153–175, 1997.
3. E. Bänsch and K. Mikula. A coarsening finite element strategy in image selective smoothing. *Computing and Visualization in Science*, 1:53–63, 1997.
4. P. Bastian, K. Birken, K. Johannsen, S. Lang, N. Neuss, H. Rentz-Reichert, and C. Wieners. Ug - a flexible software toolbox for solving partial differential equations. *Comput. Visual. Sci.*, 1:27–40, 1997.

5. R. Becker and R. Rannacher. A feed-back approach to error control in finite element methods: Basic analysis and examples. *East-West J. Numer. Math.*, 4:237–264, 1996.

6. Bornemann, F. and Erdmann, B. and Kornhuber, R. Adaptive multilevel methods in three space dimensions. *Int. J. Numer. Methods Eng.*, 36, No.18:3187–3203, 1993.

7. J. Bramble, J. Pasciak, and J. Xu. Parallel multilevel preconditioners. *Math. of Comp.*, 55:1–22, 1990.

8. B. Cabral and L. Leedom. Imaging vector fields using line integral convolution. In J. T. Kajiya, editor, *Computer Graphics (SIGGRAPH '93 Proceedings)*, volume 27, pages 263–272, Aug. 1993.

9. F. Catté, P. L. Lions, J. M. Morel, and T. Coll. Image selective smoothing and edge detection by nonlinear diffusion. *SIAM J. Numer. Anal.*, 29:182–193, 1992.

10. G.-H. Cottet and L. Germain. Image processing through reaction combined with nonlinear diffusion. *Math. Comp.*, 61:659–673, 1993.

11. L. Demkowicz, K. Gerdes, C. Schwab, A. Bajer, and T. Walsh. HP90: A general and flexible fortran 90 *hp* – FE code. Technical Report 97-17, Seminar für Angewandte Mathematik, ETH Zürich, 1997.

12. T. Gerstner and M. Rumpf. Multiresolutional parallel isosurface extraction based on tetrahedral bisection. In *Proceedings of the Volume Visualization '99 workshop*, 1999.

13. J. Kačur and K. Mikula. Solution of nonlinear diffusion appearing in image smoothing ansd edge detection. *Appl. Numer. Math.*, 17 (1):47–59, 1995.

14. Kawohl, B. and Kutev, N. Maximum and comparison principle for one-dimensional anisotropic diffusion. *Math. Ann.*, 311 (1):107–123, 1998.

15. N. Max and B. Becker. Flow visualization using moving textures. In *Proceedings of the ICASE/LaRC Symposium on Time Varying Data, NASA Conference Publication 3321*, pages 77–87, 1996.

16. M. Ohlberger and M. Rumpf. Adaptive projection operators in multiresolutional scientific visualization. *IEEE Transactions on Visualization and Computer Graphics*, 4 (4), 1998.

17. P. Perona and J. Malik. Scale space and edge detection using anisotropic diffusion. In *IEEE Computer Society Workshop on Computer Vision*, 1987.

18. M. Rumpf. Recent numerical methods – a challenge for efficient visualization. *IEEE Transactions on Visualization and Computer Graphics*, 15:43–58, 1999.

19. C. Schnörr. A study of a convex variational approach for image segmentation and feature extraction. *J. Math. Imaging and Vision*, 8:271–292, 1998.

20. H.-W. Shen and D. L. Kao. Uflic: A line integral convolution algorithm for visualizing unsteady flows. In *Proceedings Visualization '97*, pages 317–322, 1997.

21. J. J. van Wijk. Spot noise-texture synthesis for data visualization. In T. W. Sederberg, editor, *Computer Graphics (SIGGRAPH '91 Proceedings)*, volume 25, pages 309–318, July 1991.

22. R. Verfürth. A posteriori error estimation and adaptive mesh-refinement techniques. *J. Comput. Appl. Math.*, 50:67–83, 1994.

23. J. Weickart. *Anisotropic diffusion in image processing*. Teubner, 1998.

24. J. Weickert, B. M. ter Haar Romeny, and Viergever. Efficient and reliable schemes for nonlinear diffusion. *IEEE Trans. Image Proc.*, 7:398–410, 1998.

25. Weickert, J. Foundations and applications of nonlinear anisotropic diffusion filtering. *Z. Angew. Math. Mech.*, 76:283–286, 1996.

A Scale-Space Approach to Nonlocal Optical Flow Calculations

Luis Alvarez[1], Joachim Weickert[2], and Javier Sánchez[1]

[1] Departamento de Informática y Sistemas,
Universidad de Las Palmas, Campus de Tafira,
SP-35017 Las Palmas, Spain.
E-Mail: {lalvarez,jsanchez}@dis.ulpgc.es
WWW: http://serdis.dis.ulpgc.es/~{lalvarez,jsanchez}

[2] Computer Vision, Graphics, and Pattern Recognition Group,
Department of Mathematics and Computer Science,
University of Mannheim, D-68131 Mannheim, Germany.
E-Mail: Joachim.Weickert@ti.uni-mannheim.de
WWW: http://www.ti.uni-mannheim.de/~bmg/weickert

Abstract. This paper presents an interpretation of a classic optical flow method by Nagel and Enkelmann as a tensor-driven anisotropic diffusion approach in digital image analysis. We introduce an improvement into the model formulation, and we establish well-posedness results for the resulting system of parabolic partial differential equations. Our method avoids linearizations in the optical flow constraint, and it can recover displacement fields which are far beyond the typical one-pixel limits that are characteristic for many differential methods for optical flow recovery. A robust numerical scheme is presented in detail. We avoid convergence to irrelevant local minima by embedding our method into a linear scale-space framework and using a focusing strategy from coarse to fine scales. The high accuracy of the proposed method is demonstrated by means of a synthetic and a real-world image sequence.

1 Introduction

Optical flow computation consists of finding the apparent motion of objects in a sequence of images. It is a key problem in artificial vision and much research has been devoted to this field; for a survey see e.g. [23].

In the present paper we shall consider two images $I_1(x,y)$ and $I_2(x,y)$ (defined on $\mathbb{R}^2$ to simplify the discussion) which represent two consecutive views in a sequence of images. Under the assumption that corresponding pixels have equal grey values, the determination of the optical flow from I_1 to I_2 comes down to finding a function $h(x,y) = (u(x,y), v(x,y))$ such that

$$I_1(x,y) = I_2(x + u(x,y), y + v(x,y)), \qquad \forall (x,y) \in \mathbb{R}^2. \tag{1}$$

To compute $h(x,y)$ the preceding equality is usually linearized yielding the so-called *optical flow constraint*

$$I_1(\overline{x}) - I_2(\overline{x}) \approx \langle \nabla I_2(\overline{x}), h(\overline{x}) \rangle \qquad \forall \overline{x} \in \mathbb{R}^2,$$

where $\overline{x} := (x, y)$. The linearized optical flow constraint assumes that the object displacements $h(\overline{x})$ are small or that the image is slowly varying in space. In other cases, this linearization is no longer valid.

Frequently, instead of equation (1), researchers use the alternative equality

$$I_1(x - u(x, y), y - v(x, y)) = I_2(x, y), \qquad \forall(x, y) \in \mathbb{R}^2. \tag{2}$$

In this case the displacement $h(x, y)$ is centered in the image $I_2(x, y)$.

The determination of optical flow is a classic ill-posed problem in computer vision [7], and it requires to be supplemented with additional regularizing assumptions. The regularization by Horn and Schunck [16] assumes that the optical flow field is smooth. However, since many natural image sequences are better described in terms of piecewise smooth flow fields separated by discontinuities, much research has been done to modify the Horn and Schunck approach in order to permit such discontinuous flow fields; see e.g. [8, 10, 11, 21, 24, 25, 27, 32] and the references therein.

An important improvement in this direction has been achieved by Nagel and Enkelmann [24] in 1986. They consider the following minimization problem:

$$E_{NE}(h) = \int_{\mathbb{R}^2} \left(I_1(x - u(x, y), y - v(x, y)) - I_2(x, y) \right)^2 dx \tag{3}$$
$$+ C \int_{\mathbb{R}^2} trace \left((\nabla h)^T D (\nabla I_1) (\nabla h) \right) dx$$

where C is a positive constant and $D(\nabla I_1)$ is a regularized projection matrix in the direction perpendicular of ∇I_1:

$$D(\nabla I_1) = \frac{1}{|\nabla I_1|^2 + 2\lambda^2} \left\{ \begin{pmatrix} \frac{\partial I_1}{\partial y} \\ -\frac{\partial I_1}{\partial x} \end{pmatrix} \begin{pmatrix} \frac{\partial I_1}{\partial y} \\ -\frac{\partial I_1}{\partial x} \end{pmatrix}^T + \lambda^2 Id \right\}.$$

In this formulation, Id denotes the identity matrix. The advantage of this method is that it inhibits blurring of the flow across boundaries of I_1 where $|\nabla I_1| >> \lambda$. This model, however, uses an optical flow constraint which is centered in I_2, while the projection matrix D in the smoothness term depends on I_1. This inconsistency may lead to erroneous results for large displacement fields. In order to avoid this problem, we consider a modified energy functional where both the optical flow constraint and the smoothness constraint are related to I_1:

$$E(h) = \int_{\mathbb{R}^2} \left(I_1(x, y) - I_2(x + u(x, y), y + v(x, y)) \right)^2 dx \tag{4}$$
$$+ C \int_{\mathbb{R}^2} trace \left((\nabla h)^T D (\nabla I_1) (\nabla h) \right) dx.$$

The associated Euler-Lagrange equations are given by the PDE system

$$C \operatorname{div} \left(D\left(\nabla I_1 \right) \nabla u \right) + \left(I_1(\overline{x}) - I_2(\overline{x} + h(\overline{x})) \right) \frac{\partial I_2}{\partial x} (\overline{x} + h(\overline{x})) = 0, \qquad (5)$$

$$C \operatorname{div} \left(D\left(\nabla I_1 \right) \nabla v \right) + \left(I_1(\overline{x}) - I_2(\overline{x} + h(\overline{x})) \right) \frac{\partial I_2}{\partial y} (\overline{x} + h(\overline{x})) = 0. \qquad (6)$$

In this paper, we are interested in solutions of the equations (5)-(6) in the case of *large* displacement fields and images that are not necessarily slowly varying in space. Therefore, we do not introduce any linearization in the above system. We obtain the solutions by calculating the asymptotic state $(t \to \infty)$ of the parabolic system

$$\frac{\partial u}{\partial t} = C \operatorname{div} \left(D\left(\nabla I_1 \right) \nabla u \right) + \left(I_1(\overline{x}) - I_2(\overline{x} + h(\overline{x})) \right) \frac{\partial I_2}{\partial x} (\overline{x} + h(\overline{x})), \qquad (7)$$

$$\frac{\partial v}{\partial t} = C \operatorname{div} \left(D\left(\nabla I_1 \right) \nabla v \right) + \left(I_1(\overline{x}) - I_2(\overline{x} + h(\overline{x})) \right) \frac{\partial I_2}{\partial y} (\overline{x} + h(\overline{x})). \qquad (8)$$

Interestingly, this coupled system of diffusion–reaction equations reveals a diffusion tensor which resembles the one used for edge-enhancing anisotropic diffusion filtering. Indeed, $D(\nabla I_1)$ has the eigenvectors $v_1 := \nabla I_1$ and $v_2 := \nabla I_1^\perp$. The corresponding eigenvalues are given by

$$\lambda_1(|\nabla I_1|) = \frac{\lambda^2}{|\nabla I_1|^2 + 2\lambda^2}, \qquad (9)$$

$$\lambda_2(|\nabla I_1|) = \frac{|\nabla I_1|^2 + \lambda^2}{|\nabla I_1|^2 + 2\lambda^2}. \qquad (10)$$

We observe, that $\lambda_1 + \lambda_2 = 1$ holds independently of ∇I_1. In the interior of objects we have $|\nabla I_1| \to 0$, and therefore $\lambda_1 \to 1/2$ and $\lambda_2 \to 1/2$. At ideal edges where $|\nabla I_1| \to \infty$, we obtain $\lambda_1 \to 0$ and $\lambda_2 \to 1$. Thus, we have isotropic behaviour within regions, and at image boundaries the process smoothes anisotropically along the edge. This behaviour is very similar to edge-enhancing anisotropic diffusion filtering [30], and it is also close in spirit to the modified mean-curvature motion considered in [3]. In this sense, one may regard the Nagel–Enkelmann method as an early predecessor of modern PDE techniques for image restoration. For a detailed treatment of anisotropic diffusion filtering we refer to [31], and an axiomatic classification of mean-curvature motion and related morphological PDEs for image analysis is presented in [2].

Without any linearization, the optical flow constraint may cause a nonconvex energy functional (4). In this case we cannot expect the uniqueness of solutions of the elliptic system (5)-(6), and the asymptotic state of the above parabolic system depends on the initial data for the flow u and v. In order to encourage convergence to the physically correct solution in case of large displacement flow, we will design a linear scale-space focusing procedure for the optical flow constraint. Using a scale-space approach enables us also to perform a finer and more reliable scale focusing as it would be the case for related pyramid [4] or multigrid approaches [12].

The paper is organized as follows: In Section 2 we sketch existence and uniqueness results for the nonlinear parabolic system (7)-(8). In Section 3 we apply a linear scale-space focusing which enables us to achieve convergence to realistic solutions for large displacement vectors. Section 4 describes a numerical discretization of the parabolic system (7)-(8) based on an explicit finite difference scheme. In Section 5 we present experimental results on a synthetic and a real-world image sequence. Finally, in Section 6 we conclude with a summary.

Related work. Proesmans *et al.* [25] studied a related approach that also dispenses with a linearization of the optical flow constraint in order to allow for larger displacements. Their method, however, requires six coupled partial differential equations and its nonlinear diffusion process uses a scalar-valued diffusivity instead of a diffusion tensor. Their discontinuity-preserving smoothing is flow-driven while ours is image-driven. Another PDE technique that is similar in vein to the work of Proesmans *et al.* is a stereo method due to Shah [28]. With respect to embeddings into a linear scale-space framework our method can be related to the optical flow approach of Florack *et al.* [14]. Their method differs from ours in that it is purely linear, applies scale selection mechanisms and does not use discontinuity-preserving nonlinear smoothness terms. Our focusing strategy for avoiding to end up in irrelevant local minima also resembles the *graduated non-convexity (GNC) algorithms* of Blake and Zisserman [9].

2 Existence and Uniqueness of the Parabolic System

Next we investigate the parabolic system of nonlinear partial differential equations (7)-(8). In [1], the authors develop a theoretical framework to study the existence and uniqueness of solutions of a similar parabolic system, but with a different regularization term. The main techniques used in [1] can be applied in order to obtain the existence and uniqueness of the solutions of the system (7)-(8). This leads to the following result.

Theorem 1. *Let $I_2 \in C^2(\mathbb{R}^2)$ and $I_1 \in C^1(\mathbb{R}^2)$. Then the parabolic system (7)-(8) has a unique generalized solution $h(.,t) \in C\left([0,\infty); L^2(\mathbb{R}^2) \times L^2(\mathbb{R}^2)\right)$ for all initial flows $h_0 \in L^2(\mathbb{R}^2) \times L^2(\mathbb{R}^2)$.*

3 A Linear Scale-Space Approach to Recover Large Displacements

In general, the Euler-Lagrange equations (5)-(6) will have multiple solutions. As a consequence, the asymptotic state of the parabolic system (7)-(8), which we use for approximating the optical flow, will depend on the initial data. Typically, the convergence is the better, the closer the initial data is to the asymptotic state. When we expect small displacements in the scene, the natural choice is to take

$u \equiv v \equiv 0$ as initialization of the flow. For large displacement fields, however, this may not work, and we need better initial data. To this end, we embed our method into a linear scale-space framework [17, 33]. Considering the problem at a coarse scale avoids that the algorithm gets trapped in physically irrelevant local minima. The coarse-scale solution serves then as initial data for solving the problem at a finer scale. Scale focusing has a long tradition in linear scale-space theory (see e.g. Bergholm [6] for an early approach), and in spite of the fact that several theoretical problems exist, it has not lost its popularity due to its favourable practical behaviour. Detailed descriptions of linear scale-space theory can be found in [13, 15, 18, 19, 22, 29].

We proceed as follows. First, we introduce a linear scale factor in the parabolic PDE system in order to end up with

$$\frac{\partial u_\sigma}{\partial t} = C \operatorname{div} \left(D(\nabla G_\sigma * I_1) \nabla u_\sigma \right) +$$
$$+ \left(G_\sigma * I_1(\overline{x}) - G_\sigma * I_2(\overline{x} + h_\sigma(\overline{x})) \right) \frac{\partial (G_\sigma * I_2)}{\partial x} (\overline{x} + h_\sigma(\overline{x})), \qquad (11)$$

$$\frac{\partial v_\sigma}{\partial t} = C \operatorname{div} \left(D(\nabla G_\sigma * I_1) \nabla v_\sigma \right) +$$
$$+ \left(G_\sigma * I_1(\overline{x}) - G_\sigma * I_2(\overline{x} + h_\sigma(\overline{x})) \right) \frac{\partial (G_\sigma * I_2)}{\partial y} (\overline{x} + h_\sigma(\overline{x})), \qquad (12)$$

where $G_\sigma * I$ represents the convolution of I with a Gaussian of standard deviation σ.

The convolution with a Gaussian blends the information in the images and allows us to recover a connection between the objects in I_1 and I_2. We start with a large initial scale σ_0. Then we compute the optical flow $(u_{\sigma_0}, v_{\sigma_0})$ at scale σ_0 as the asymptotic state of the solution of the above PDE system using as initial data $u \equiv v \equiv 0$. Next, we choose a number of scales $\sigma_n < \sigma_{n-1} < \dots < \sigma_0$, and for each scale σ_i we compute the optical flow $(u_{\sigma_i}, v_{\sigma_i})$ as the asymptotic state of the above PDE system with initial data $(u_{\sigma_{i-1}}, v_{\sigma_{i-1}})$. The final computed flow corresponds to the smallest scale σ_n. In accordance with the logarithmic sampling strategy in linear scale-space theory [20], we choose $\sigma_i := \eta^i \sigma_0$ with some decay rate $\eta \in (0, 1)$.

4 Numerical Scheme

We discretize the parabolic system (11)–(12) by finite differences. All spatial derivatives are approximated by central differences, and for the discretization in t direction we use an explicit (Euler forward) scheme. Gaussian convolution was performed in the spatial domain with renormalized Gaussians, which where truncated at 5 times their standard deviation. Let $D(\nabla G_\sigma * I_1) = \begin{pmatrix} a & b \\ b & c \end{pmatrix}$. Then our explicit scheme has the structure

$$
\frac{u_{i,j}^{k+1} - u_{i,j}^k}{\tau} = C \left(\frac{a_{i+1,j} + a_{i,j}}{2} \frac{u_{i+1,j}^k - u_{i,j}^k}{h_1^2} + \frac{a_{i-1,j} + a_{i,j}}{2} \frac{u_{i-1,j}^k - u_{i,j}^k}{h_1^2} + \right.
$$

$$
+ \frac{c_{i,j+1} + c_{i,j}}{2} \frac{u_{i,j+1}^k - u_{i,j}^k}{h_2^2} + \frac{c_{i,j-1} + c_{i,j}}{2} \frac{u_{i,j-1}^k - u_{i,j}^k}{h_2^2} +
$$

$$
+ \frac{b_{i+1,j+1} + b_{i,j}}{2} \frac{u_{i+1,j+1}^k - u_{i,j}^k}{2h_1 h_2} + \frac{b_{i-1,j-1} + b_{i,j}}{2} \frac{u_{i-1,j-1}^k - u_{i,j}^k}{2h_1 h_2} -
$$

$$
\left. - \frac{b_{i+1,j-1} + b_{i,j}}{2} \frac{u_{i+1,j-1}^k - u_{i,j}^k}{2h_1 h_2} - \frac{b_{i-1,j+1} + b_{i,j}}{2} \frac{u_{i-1,j+1}^k - u_{i,j}^k}{2h_1 h_2} \right) +
$$

$$
+ \left(I_{1,\sigma}(\overline{x}_{i,j}^k) - I_{2,\sigma}(\overline{x}_{i,j} + \overline{h}_{\sigma,i,j}^k) \right) I_{2,x,\sigma}(\overline{x}_{i,j} + \overline{h}_{\sigma,i,j}^k), \qquad (13)
$$

$$
\frac{v_{i,j}^{k+1} - v_{i,j}^k}{\tau} = C \left(\frac{a_{i+1,j} + a_{i,j}}{2} \frac{v_{i+1,j}^k - v_{i,j}^k}{h_1^2} + \frac{a_{i-1,j} + a_{i,j}}{2} \frac{v_{i-1,j}^k - v_{i,j}^k}{h_1^2} + \right.
$$

$$
+ \frac{c_{i,j+1} + c_{i,j}}{2} \frac{v_{i,j+1}^k - v_{i,j}^k}{h_2^2} + \frac{c_{i,j-1} + c_{i,j}}{2} \frac{v_{i,j-1}^k - v_{i,j}^k}{h_2^2} +
$$

$$
+ \frac{b_{i+1,j+1} + b_{i,j}}{2} \frac{v_{i+1,j+1}^k - v_{i,j}^k}{2h_1 h_2} + \frac{b_{i-1,j-1} + b_{i,j}}{2} \frac{v_{i-1,j-1}^k - v_{i,j}^k}{2h_1 h_2} -
$$

$$
\left. - \frac{b_{i+1,j-1} + b_{i,j}}{2} \frac{v_{i+1,j-1}^k - v_{i,j}^k}{2h_1 h_2} - \frac{b_{i-1,j+1} + b_{i,j}}{2} \frac{v_{i-1,j+1}^k - v_{i,j}^k}{2h_1 h_2} \right) +
$$

$$
+ \left(I_{1,\sigma}(\overline{x}_{i,j}^k) - I_{2,\sigma}(\overline{x}_{i,j} + \overline{h}_{\sigma,i,j}^k) \right) I_{2,y,\sigma}(\overline{x}_{i,j} + \overline{h}_{\sigma,i,j}^k). \qquad (14)
$$

The notations are almost selfexplaining: for instance, τ is the time step size, h_1 and h_2 denote the pixel size in x and y direction, respectively, $u_{i,j}^k$ approximates u_σ in some grid point $\overline{x}_{i,j}$ at time $k\tau$, and $I_{1,x,\sigma}$ is an approximation to $G_\sigma * \frac{\partial I_1}{\partial x}$. We calculate values of type $I_{2,\sigma}(\overline{x}_{i,j} + \overline{h}_{\sigma,i,j}^k)$ by linear interpolation, and we use the time step size

$$
\tau = \frac{0.5}{4C + \max_{i,j}(|I_{1,x,\sigma}(\overline{x}_{i,j})|^2, |I_{1,y,\sigma}(\overline{x}_{i,j})|^2)}. \qquad (15)
$$

This step size can be motivated from a stability analysis in the maximum norm applied to a simplification of (13)–(14) where a scalar-valued diffusivity and a linearized optical flow constraint is used.

5   Experimental Results

The complete algorithm for computing the optical flow depends on a number of parameters which have an intuitive meaning:

- The regularization parameter C specifies the balance between the smoothing term and the optical flow constraint. Larger values lead to smoother flow fields by filling in information from image edges where flow measurements with higher reliability are available. Recent results show that there is also a close relationship between the parameter C of a regularization method and the scale parameter of a diffusion scale-space [26].
- The constant λ in the smoothing term serves as a contrast parameter: locations where the image gradient magnitude is larger than λ are regarded as edges. The diffusion process smoothes anisotropically along these edges. In our experiments we used $\lambda := 1$. The results were not very sensitive to underestimations of λ.
- The scale σ_0 denotes the standard deviation of the largest Gaussian. In general, σ_0 is chosen according to the maximum displacement expected. In our case we used $\sigma_0 := 10$.
- The decay rate $\eta \in (0,1)$ for the computation of the scales $\sigma_m := \eta^m \sigma_0$. We may expect a good focusing if η is close to 1. We have chosen $\eta := 0.95$.
- The smallest scale is given by σ_n. It should be close to the inner scale of the image in order to achieve optimal flow localization.
- The stopping time T for solving the system (11)–(12) at each scale σ_m. When good initializations from coarser scales are available, we observed that $T := 20$ gives results which are sufficiently close to the asymptotic state.

Figure 1 shows our first experiment. We use a synthetic image composed of four black squares on a white background. Each square moves in a different direction and with a different displacement magnitude: under the assumption that the x axis is oriented from left to right and the y axis from top to bottom, the left square on the top moves with $(u,v) = (10,5)$, the right square on the top is displaced with $(u,v) = (-10,0)$, the left square on the bottom is shifted by $(u,v) = (0,-5)$, and the right square on the bottom undergoes a translation by $(-10,-10)$. In order to visualize the flow field (u,v) we use two grey level images (u_{gl}, v_{gl}) defined by $u_{gl} := 128 + 8u$ and $v_{gl} := 128 + 8v$. We use the regularization parameter $C = 15000$. The depicted optical flow was obtained without scale-space focusing, i.e. with $\sigma_0 = 0$. As can be expected, the algorithm gets trapped in a physically irrelevant local minimum.

Figure 2 shows that the proposed scale-space focusing leads to significantly improved results. We start with initial scale $\sigma_0 = 10$ and show the results for focusing to the scales $\sigma_{10} = 5.99$, $\sigma_{20} = 3.58$, $\sigma_{30} = 2.15$, $\sigma_{40} = 1.29$, $\sigma_{50} = 0.77$, $\sigma_{60} = 0.46$, and $\sigma_{70} = 0.28$, respectively. The other parameters are identical with those in Figure 1. We notice that the computed flow is a good approximation of the expected flow. In fact, not only the orientation of the flow is correct, but also the flow magnitude is surprisingly accurate: the maximum of the computed optic flow magnitude is 14.13, which is a very good approximation of the ground truth maximum $10\sqrt{2} \approx 14.14$. It results from the square which moves in $(-10,-10)$ direction. This indicates that – under specific circumstances – our method may even lead to optical flow results with subpixel accuracy.

This observation is confirmed in the quantitative evaluations carried out in Figure 3. The left plot shows the average angular errors in the four squares of the

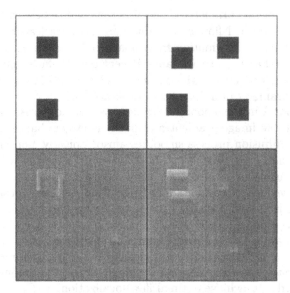

Fig. 1. Optic flow obtained without scale-space focusing ($T = 800$).

first frame. The angels between the correct flow (u_c, v_c) and the estimated flow (u_e, v_e) have been calculated in the same way as in [5]. The right plot depicts the Euclidean error $\sqrt{(u_e - u_c)^2 + (v_e - v_c)^2}$ averaged over all pixels within the four squares of the first frame. In both cases we observe that the error is reduced dramatically by focusing down in scale-space until it reaches a very small value when the Gaussian width σ approaches the inner scale of the image. Further reductions of σ leads to slightly higher errors. It appears that this is caused by discretization effects.

In the fourth experiment, we use the classical taxi sequence, but instead of taking two consecutive frames – as is usually done – we consider the frames 15 and 19. The dark car at the left creates a largest displacement magnitude of approximately 12 pixels. In Figure 4 we present the computed flow using the regularization parameter $C = 500$ and focusing from $\sigma_0 = 10$ to $\sigma_{70} = 0.28$. The computed maximal flow magnitude is 11.68, which is a good approximation of the actual displacement of the dark car. Figure 5 shows a vector plot of the computed flow field.

6 Conclusions

Usually, when computer vision researchers deal with variational methods for optical flow calculations, they linearize the optical flow constraint. Except for those cases where the images a sufficiently slowly varying in space, linearization, however, does only work for small displacements. In this paper we investigate

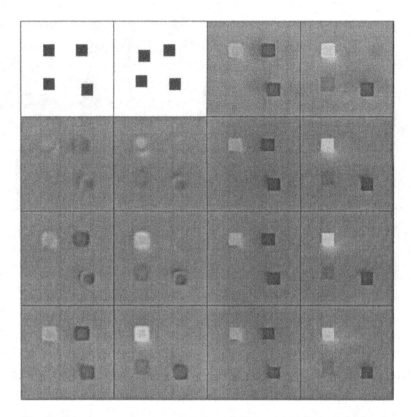

Fig. 2. From top to bottom and from left to right: the original pair of images I_1 and I_2, and the flow components (u_n, v_n) resulting from focusing to the scales $\sigma_{10} = 5.99$, $\sigma_{20} = 3.58$, $\sigma_{30} = 2.15$, $\sigma_{40} = 1.29$, $\sigma_{50} = 0.77$, $\sigma_{60} = 0.46$, and $\sigma_{70} = 0.28$, respectively.

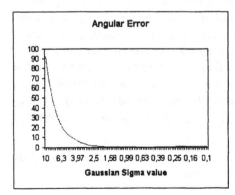
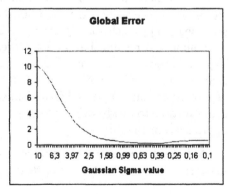

Fig. 3. Left: Average angular error of the optic flow calculations for the squares in the first frame of Figure 2. **Right:** Corresponding average Euclidean error.

Fig. 4. Optic flow computation of the taxi sequence using frames 15 and 19.

an improved formulation of a classical method by Nagel and Enkelmann where no linearization is used. We identify this method with two coupled anisotropic diffusion filters with a nonlinear reaction term. We showed that this parabolic system is well-posed from a mathematical viewpoint, and we presented a finite difference scheme for its numerical solution. In order to avoid that the algorithms converges to physically irrelevant local minima, we embedded it into a linear scale-space approach for focusing the solution from a coarse to a fine scale. The numerical results that we have presented for a synthetic and a real-world sequence are very encouraging: it was possible to recover displacements of more than 10 pixels with high accuracy. It is our hope that this successful blend of nonlinear anisotropic PDEs and linear scale-space techniques may serve as a motivation to study other combinations of linear and nonlinear scale-space approaches in the future.

Acknowledgements. This work has been supported by the European TMR network *Viscosity Solutions and their Applications*.

References

1. L. Alvarez, J. Esclarín, M. Lefébure and J. Sánchez, *A PDE model for computing the optical flow*, Proc. XVI Congreso de Ecuaciones Diferenciales y Aplicaciones (C.E.D.Y.A. XVI, Las Palmas de Gran Canaria, Sept. 21–24, 1999), in press.

245

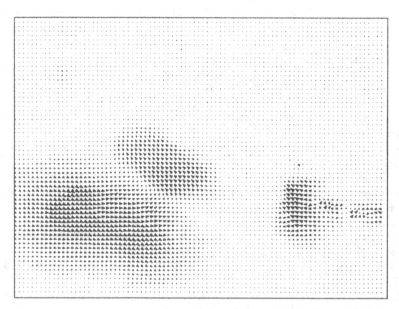

Fig. 5. Vector plot of the optic flow between the frames 15 and 19 of the taxi sequence.

2. L. Alvarez, F. Guichard, P.-L. Lions, J.-M. Morel, *Axioms and fundamental equations in image processing*, Arch. Rational Mech. Anal., Vol. 123, 199–257, 1993.

3. L. Alvarez, P.-L. Lions, J.-M. Morel, *Image selective smoothing and edge detection by nonlinear diffusion. II*, SIAM J. Numer. Anal., Vol. 29, 845–866, 1992.

4. P. Anandan, *A computational framework and an algorithm for the measurement of visual motion*, Int. J. Comput. Vision, Vol. 2, 283–310, 1989.

5. J.L. Barron, D.J. Fleet, S.S. Beauchemin, *Performance of optical flow techniques*, Int. J. Comput. Vision, Vol. 12, 43–77, 1994.

6. F. Bergholm, *Edge focusing*, IEEE Trans. Pattern Anal. Mach. Intell., Vol. 9, 726–741, 1987.

7. M. Bertero, T.A. Poggio, V. Torre, *Ill-posed problems in early vision*, Proc. IEEE, Vol. 76, 869–889, 1988.

8. M.J. Black, P. Anandan, *Robust dynamic motion estimation over time*, Proc. IEEE Comp. Soc. Conf. on Computer Vision and Pattern Recognition (CVPR '91, Maui, June 3–6, 1991), IEEE Computer Society Press, Los Alamitos, 292–302, 1991.

9. A. Blake, A. Zisserman, *Visual reconstruction*, MIT Press, Cambridge (Mass.), 1987.

10. I. Cohen, *Nonlinear variational method for optical flow computation*, Proc. Eighth Scandinavian Conf. on Image Analysis (SCIA '93, Tromsø, May 25–28, 1993), Vol. 1, 523–530, 1993.

11. R. Deriche, P. Kornprobst, G. Aubert, *Optical-flow estimation while preserving its discontinuities: A variational approach*, Proc. Second Asian Conf. Computer Vision (ACCV '95, Singapore, December 5–8, 1995), Vol. 2, 290–295, 1995.

12. W. Enkelmann, *Investigation of multigrid algorithms for the estimation of optical flow fields in image sequences*, Computer Vision, Graphics and Image Processing, Vol. 43, 150-177, 1988.

13. L. Florack, *Image structure*, Kluwer, Dordrecht, 1997.

14. L.M.J. Florack, W.J. Niessen, M. Nielsen, *The intrinsic structure of the optic flow incorporating measurement duality*, Int. J. Comput. Vision, Vol. 27, 263-286, 1998.

15. B. ter Haar Romeny, L. Florack, J. Koenderink, M. Viergever (Eds.), *Scale-space theory in computer vision*, Lecture Notes in Computer Science, Vol. 1252, Springer, Berlin, 1997.

16. B. Horn, B. Schunck, *Determining optical flow*, Artif. Intell., Vol. 17, 185-203, 1981.

17. T. Iijima, *Basic theory on normalization of pattern (in case of typical one-dimensional pattern)*, Bulletin of the Electrotechnical Laboratory, Vol. 26, 368-388, 1962 (in Japanese).

18. T. Iijima, *Pattern recognition*, Corona-sha, 1973 (in Japanese).

19. T. Iijima, *Theory of pattern recognition*, Series of Basic Information Technology, Vol. 6, Morishita Publishing, 1989 (in Japanese).

20. J.J. Koenderink, *The structure of images*, Biological Cybernetics, Vol. 50, 363-370, 1984.

21. A. Kumar, A.R. Tannenbaum, G.J. Balas, *Optic flow: a curve evolution approach*, IEEE Trans. Image Proc., Vol. 5, 598-610, 1996.

22. T. Lindeberg, *Scale-space theory in computer vision*, Kluwer, Boston, 1994.

23. A. Mitiche, P. Bouthemy, *Computation and analysis of image motion: a synopsis of current problems and methods*, Int. J. Comput. Vision, Vol. 19, 29-55, 1996.

24. H.H. Nagel, W. Enkelmann, *An investigation of smoothness constraints for the estimation of displacement vector fields from images sequences*, IEEE Trans. Pattern Anal. Mach. Intell., Vol. 8, 565-593, 1986.

25. M. Proesmans, L. Van Gool, E. Pauwels, A. Oosterlinck, *Determination of optical flow and its discontinuities using non-linear diffusion*, J.-O. Eklundh (Ed.), Computer vision – ECCV '94, Lecture Notes in Computer Science, Vol. 801, Springer, Berlin, 295-304, 1994.

26. E. Radmoser, O. Scherzer, J. Weickert, *Scale-space properties of regularization methods*, this volume.

27. C. Schnörr, *Segmentation of visual motion by minimizing convex non-quadratic functionals*, Proc. 12th Int. Conf. Pattern Recognition (ICPR 12, Jerusalem, Oct. 9-13, 1994), Vol. A, IEEE Computer Society Press, Los Alamitos, 661-663, 1994.

28. J. Shah, *A nonlinear diffusion model for discontinuous disparity and half-occlusions in stereo*, Proc. IEEE Comp. Soc. Conf. Computer Vision and Pattern Recognition (CVPR '93, New York, June 15-17, 1993), IEEE Computer Society Press, Los Alamitos, 34-40, 1993.

29. J. Sporring, M. Nielsen, L. Florack, P. Johansen (Eds.), *Gaussian scale-space theory*, Kluwer, Dordrecht, 1997.

30. J. Weickert, *Theoretical foundations of anisotropic diffusion in image processing*, Computing, Suppl. 11, 221-236, 1996.

31. J. Weickert, *Anisotropic diffusion in image processing*, Teubner, Stuttgart, 1998.

32. J. Weickert, *On discontinuity-preserving optic flow*, S. Orphanoudakis, P. Trahanias, J. Crowley, N. Katevas (Eds.), Proc. Computer Vision and Mobile Robotics Workshop (CVMR '98, Santorini, Sept. 17-18, 1998), 115-122, 1998.

33. J. Weickert, S. Ishikawa, A. Imiya, *Linear scale-space has first been proposed in Japan*, J. Math. Imag. Vision, Vol. 10, 237-252, 1999.

Scales in Natural Images and a Consequence on their Bounded Variation Norm

Luis Alvarez[1], Yann Gousseau[2], and Jean-Michel Morel[2]

[1] Departamento de Informatica y Sistemas, Universidad de Las Palmas, Campus de Tafira, 35017 Las Palmas, Spain. luis@amihp710.dis.ulpgc.es
[2] Centre de Mathématiques et leurs Applications, ENS Cachan, 61 av. du Président Wilson, 94235 Cachan Cedex, France. gousseau@cmla.ens-cachan.fr, morel@cmla.ens-cachan.fr

Abstract. This paper introduces a new method for analyzing scaling phenomena in natural images, and draws some consequences as to whether natural images belong to the space of functions with bounded variation.

1 Introduction

A digital, gray level image may be seen as the realization of a random vector of size $H \times L$ taking values in a discrete set $V = 1, ..., G$. For typical values like $H = L = G = 256$, the number of possible realizations, $G^{HL} = 2^{524288}$, is huge. Obviously, "natural images", i.e. digital photographs of natural scenes, only form a small subset of all possible realizations. Looking at random realizations of such vectors is enough to be convinced of this fact. Natural images are highly improbable events. It is therefore interesting to look for statistical characteristics of such images: what are the relationships between gray level values at distant pixels? Is it possible to define a probability law for natural images? Moreover, statistics of texture images may be useful for synthesis purposes (see [9], [24], [23]).

Most of the statistical studies of natural images are concerned with first or second order statistics (through the power spectrum, the covariances, the cooccurrences) or with additive decompositions of images. The power spectrum $P(\omega, \nu)$ is known to be well approximated by a power function $\frac{C}{(\omega^2 + \nu^2)^\gamma}$, where γ is an image dependant number usually close to 2 (see [5], [7]). The histogram of natural images has been found to have a peculiar, non-Gaussian shape (see [20], [10]). Nearest neighbors coocurences functions also exhibit non-Gaussian distributions (see [10]). Principal and independant component analysis on databases of such images yield localized and oriented images bases (see [17], [2]). We have a different approach, working in the image domain on items that can have a straightforward visual interpretation, and involve (relatively) long and high order interactions between pixels. We shall show that in natural images, there is a constant form for the size distribution of such items. The definitions of sizes we consider are of two types: area and boundary length. An experimental program which we performed on many photographs of very diverse natural scenes indicates that the size distribution of homogeneous parts in images obeys a law

$$\text{Card}\{\text{Homogeneous regions with size s}\} = \frac{K}{s^\alpha},$$

where K is an image dependent constant. When the size s denotes the area, in most photographs, α is close to 2. We will define in Section 2 what we mean by homogeneous parts, the connected components of image domains where contrast does not exceed a certain threshold. Let us mention that power laws have been previously observed, e.g. for points statistics (see [18], [19]) or density of extrema in scale space (see [11]).

As a consequence of the size power law, some information can be obtained about the "natural" function space for images, as will be shown in Section 3: we focus our attention on the space BV of functions with bounded variation. We are in a position to tell when a given image is not in this space, provided the observed size distribution model remains true at smaller (not observable) scales as well.

2   Sizes of sections in natural images

2.1   The distribution of areas

We'll now make clearer what we mean by homogeneous region of an image. We begin by equalizing the image histogram, and uniformly quantify it in the following way. We consider a digital image I of size $H \times L$, with G integer gray levels, and write $I(i,j)$ for the gray level at pixel (i,j). Let k be an integer less than G. Let N_1 be the first integer such that more than $\frac{HL}{k}$ pixels have a gray level less than N_1, then N_2 the first integer such that more than $2\frac{HL}{k}$ have a gray level less than N_2, then $N_3, ..., N_k = G$ defined the same way, this sequence being possibly constant at some point. For l varying from 1 to k, let I_l be the binary image with $I_l(i,j) = 1$ if $I(i,j) \in [N_{l-1}, N_l)$ and $I_l(i,j) = 0$ otherwise. We call those images k-bilevels of I. Each bilevel image represents a quantization level of the equalized image.

Next, we look at the area histogram of the connected components of the bilevels. For s an integer varying from 0 to HL, let $f(s)$ be the number of connected components with area s of the set of 1's pixels, in any of the k-bilevels of I. We will both consider 4-connectivity (each pixel has 4 neighbors: up, down, right, left) and 8-connectivity (we add the diagonal neighbors, so that each pixel has 8 neighbors).

We computed the function f on many digital photographs. We did not attempt to use a single source of images; the digitized images either are scanned photographs or from a digital camera, with diverse optical systems and exposures. Those functions are of the form $f(s) = \frac{C}{s^\alpha}$, with C a constant and α a real number close to two, for values of s in a certain range and reasonable values of k (basically between 4 and 30). The observed fit is excellent, as can be seen from

Figure 2, which actually corresponds to one of the worst cases we observed. For fixed k, we consider the set of points

$$S = \{(\log(s), \log(f(s)), 0 \le s \le T_{\max}\},$$

where $T_{max} + 1$ is the smallest value of s such that $f(s) = 0$. We perform a linear regression on this set S so as to find the straight line (in the log-log coordinates) $g(\log(i)) = A - \alpha \log(i)$ the closest to S in the least squares sense, and write E for the least squares error.

2.2 The distribution of areas in digital photographs

We present the results for two pictures having different scales and textures in Table 1. The value of α appears to be related to the amount of texture in the image; the more textured the image, the bigger the value of α. Typically, for photographs of natural scenes, the value of alpha is between 1.5 and 3 (the values close to 3 being reached for images as the baboon (Figure 1), which present textured areas), whereas for textures (e.g. from the Brodatz's album), it is typically between 2.5 and 3.5.

Fig. 1. baboon (512 × 512) and city (612 × 792) images

image	k	α	E	T_{max}	A
city	20	2.03	.32	184	11.7
city	16	1.94	.30	165	11.3
city	12	1.91	.42	202	11.1
city	8	1.80	.44	191	10.3

image	k	α	E	T_{max}	A
baboon	20	2.55	.30	70	11.7
baboon	16	2.38	.33	82	11.3
baboon	12	2.42	.47	78	11.4
baboon	8	2.35	.41	76	11.2

Table 1. different values of the quantization number k for the city and baboon images, 8-connectivity. Area distribution is $f(s) = As^{-\alpha}$, T_{max} is the maximal considered area

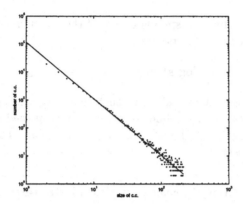

Fig. 2. function f (area distribution) for the city image (Figure 1), $k = 12$, 8-connectivity, $T_{max} = 202$

We also performed the linear regression on sets of points

$$S_{Tmin} = \{(\log(s), \log(f(s)), T_{min} \leq s \leq T_{max}\}$$

for various values of T_{min} to show that the fit of S to the power law was not forced by small areas only, and moreover that if the contribution of E mainly comes from the large areas, the value of α computed with those large areas was close to the initial value. The results for the image of the city are shown in Table 2. Those results about the stability of the slope of the regression across scales are of great importance in view of the hypothesis to be made in Section 3.

image	T_{min}	α	E	A
city	5	1.97	.30	11.6
city	10	1.98	.30	11.6
city	20	1.96	.31	11.5
city	40	1.91	.36	11.3

Table 2. different values of T_{min} for the city image, $k = 16$, 8-connectivity

2.3 The distribution of boundary lengths in digital photographs

We performed exactly the same analysis on the boundary lengths of connected components of bilevels as we did before on areas of those components. As a discrete definition of the length of a discrete connected set S (8-connectivity), we chose to count the pixels not belonging to S that are neighbors of some pixel of S in the 4-connectivity sense. There are many other ways to define discrete boundary length. We tried several other methods that gave basically the same results as the one we detail here. The notations k, E, A, T_{min} and T_{max} refer to the same quantities as before; β now stands for the exponent of the power law whose fit to the boundary length distribution is the best in the least square sense. We chose $T_{min} = 10$, because some small values for the boundary lengths are attained only for regions touching the border of the image. The fit to the power law is again very good, and the exponent β is usually between 2 and 3. We present the results for the images of the city and the baboon in Table 3 . We note that $\beta \simeq 2\alpha - 1$ accounts for connected components of bilevel sets satisfying on the average a decent isoperimetric ratio, $c \leq \frac{area^{\frac{1}{2}}}{boundary\ length} \leq C$. This is not the case in general, except for some images of textures.

image	k	β	E	T_{max}	A
city	20	2.42	.32	184	13.7
city	16	2.41	.35	184	13.7
city	12	2.28	.33	187	13.0
city	8	2.23	.48	192	12.4

image	k	β	E	T_{max}	A
baboon	20	3.02	.28	82	14.2
baboon	16	2.91	.35	81	13.9
baboon	12	2.93	.41	100	14.0
baboon	8	2.89	.33	96	13.8

Table 3. boundary lengths for the city and baboon images, with different values of the quantization number k

Let us mention that the length distribution of intersections of the homogeneous part of the image with lines (the so-called intercepts) also follows a power law. In a forecoming paper (see [1]), we use a morphological model, the dead-leaves model of G. Matheron (see [14]), as an object-based model for images. An image is defined as a sequential superposition of random objects. If we interpret the homogeneous parts as being the visible parts of objects after the occlusion process, it is possible to deduce the form of the length distribution of the intercepts from a power law distribution of the size of objects. This result is closely related to the ones of [19], where objects are defined in the image by visual segmentation, and where a power law is observed for the covariances.

2.4 Other types of images

In order to see whether the power law is in some sense characterizing digital photographs, we computed histograms of areas of bilevels for other types of images. We looked at noises images, white or correlated and text images.

White noise images, that is to say images in which the gray level values at distinct pixels are independent random variables, present an histogram of the form $f(s) = \exp(-Cs)$, with C a constant. We observed this fact on two different kinds of white noises: uniform and Gaussian. Text images produced by text editor do lead, as one would guess, to an histogram consisting of isolated peaks, whose height is not directly related to the value of s.

Then we looked at correlated noise. We performed convolutions between white noises and a Gaussian $\exp(-\frac{1}{2\sigma^2}(x^2+y^2))$, where σ is a variable parameter. This was done by multiplication in the frequency domain. Such a convolution can be seen as a crude approximation of the effect of an optical lens. The results we obtain for those images were similar to the ones for digital photographs of textures. We present the results obtained in the case of the uniform white noise in Table 4. We also tested the effect of the convolution with Bessel functions (Fourier transform of disks) and the results were very similar.

image convolved with a Gaussian	σ	α	E	T_{max}	A
noise convolved with a Gaussian	0.71	3.88	0.60	26	13.3
noise convolved with a Gaussian	0.85	3.57	0.50	30	13.1
noise convolved with a Gaussian	1.12	3.27	0.55	39	13.0

Table 4. Uniform white noise image, after convolution with a Gaussian of parameter σ, $k=12$, 8-connectivity

Those "non-natural images" lead to two remarks about the $\frac{1}{area^2}$ law. First, this law does not characterize natural images, even though a correlated noise looks similar to a natural texture. Secondly, the size law could be related to the way the optical photographic device captures the image, as suggested by the behavior of noises convolved with a Gaussian. More precisely, we observed that the convolution with a Gaussian increases the value of α for images where the initial α is small (such as text and synthetic images) whereas it tends to decrease its value when it is initially bigger than 2 (noises).

Another, and more satisfactory explanation of this power law is scale invariance. The assumption that natural images are scale invariant, so that all observed statistics should be scale (zoom) invariant, has been confirmed by the shape of the power spectrum mentioned in the introduction (see [7]), and also by the fact that some statistics are preserved when shrinking the image (see [20], [16]). Our experiments also confirm this assumption, since scale invariance yields the $\frac{1}{area^2}$ law. Indeed, if we suppose that the total area occupied by regions having an area between A and A' is the same as the total area occupied by regions with area between tA and tA', for all t, A, A', then the power law with exponent 2 is the only acceptable size distribution.

3 Size of sections and the BV norm of natural images

The aim of this section is to give a computational tool to decide whether an image can belong to the space BV of functions with bounded variations. The BV assumption for natural images is far ranging, from image restoration ([21], [22]) to image compression.

The space BV is the space of functions for which the sum of the perimeters of the level sets is finite. The space BV is of great importance in image modeling, since such a simple image as a white disk on a black background is not in any Sobolev space, but belongs to BV. However, if the disk is replaced by an object whose boundary has an infinite length, such as a bidimensional Cantor set, then the corresponding function is no longer in BV. There is also another way for a function not to be in BV. Each of its level sets may be of finite perimeter, while the sum of those perimeters tends towards infinity. According to our analysis, this is the case with natural images, for which, in a sense, small objects are too numerous for the function to be in BV.

3.1 A lower bound for the BV norm

We consider $I \in BV(\Omega)$ a bounded image belonging to the space of functions with bounded variation ([25], [6]) on a domain (e.g. rectangular) $\Omega \subset \mathbb{R}^2$. For $\lambda \in \mathbb{R}$, define the level set of I with level λ by

$$\chi_\lambda I = \{x, I(x) \geq \lambda\}.$$

Recall that a function is of bounded variation if, for almost every $\lambda \in \mathbb{R}$, $\chi_\lambda I$ is a set with finite perimeter and, denoting by $\text{per}(\chi_\lambda I)$ this perimeter (for a precise definition of the perimeter and the essential boundary we refer to [6]),

$$\|I\|_{BV} = \int_{\mathbb{R}} \text{per}(\chi_\lambda I) d\lambda. \tag{1}$$

(By the coarea formula, see [6], we also have $\|I\|_{BV} = \int_\Omega |DI|$)

In addition, by the classical isoperimetric inequality, we have for every set O with finite perimeter,

$$\text{per}(O) \geq 2\pi^{\frac{1}{2}} \nu(O)^{\frac{1}{2}}, \tag{2}$$

where $\nu(O)$ denotes the Lebesgue measure of O. In the following, we shall consider sections of the image. We always assume that the image I satisfies $0 \leq I(x) \leq C$. We first fix two parameters γ, λ, with $0 \leq \lambda \leq \gamma$. For any $n \in \mathbb{N}$, we consider the bilevel sets of I

$$\{x, \lambda + (n-1)\gamma \leq I(x) < \lambda + n\gamma\} = \chi_{\lambda+(n-1)\gamma} I \setminus \chi_{\lambda+n\gamma} I.$$

We call (γ, λ)-section of I any set which is a connected component of a bilevel set $\chi_{\lambda+(n-1)\gamma} I \setminus \chi_{\lambda+n\gamma} I$ for some n. We denote each one of them by $S_{\gamma,\lambda,i}$ for $i \in J(\gamma, \lambda)$, a set of indices. Notice that the (γ, λ)-sections are disjoint and their union is the image domain Ω,

$$\bigcup_{i \in J(\gamma,\lambda)} S_{\gamma,\lambda,i} = \Omega. \tag{3}$$

There are several ways to define the connected components of a set with finite perimeter, since such a set is defined up to a set with zero Lebesgue measure. We denote by H^1 the one-dimensional Hausdorff measure, that is to say the length. In the following, we call Jordan curve a simple closed curve of $I\!\!R^2$, i.e. the range of a continuous map $c : [0, 1] \to I\!\!R^2$, such that $c(s) \neq c(t)$ for all $0 < s < t < 1$, and $c(0) = c(1)$. A Jordan curve defines two and only two connected components (in the usual sense) of $I\!\!R^2 \setminus c([0, 1])$, one bounded and one unbounded. We shall say that a Jordan curve separates two points x and y if they do not belong to the same connected component of $I\!\!R^2 \setminus c([0, 1])$. One can prove ([8], [3]) that a definition of connected components for a set with finite perimeter permits the following statements :

Theorem 1 *(and definition)*
Let O be a set with finite perimeter.
(i) The essential boundary of O consists, up to a set of zero H^1-measure, of a countable set of noncrossing simple rectifiable closed curves c_j with finite length such that $per(O) = \sum_j H^1(c_j)$
(ii) Two points are in the same connected component of O if and only if for any representation of the essential boundary by a family of Jordan curves of the preceding kind, c_j, they are not separated by one of the c_j.
(iii) With this definition, the perimeter of a set with finite perimeter is the sum of the perimeters of its connected components.

We denote by $J(n) \subset J(\gamma, \lambda)$ the set of indices of sections which are connected components of $\chi_{\lambda+(n-1)\gamma} I \setminus \chi_{\lambda+n\gamma} I$. As an obvious consequence of Proposition 1, we have

Corollary 1

$$per(\chi_{\lambda+(n-1)\gamma} I \setminus \chi_{\lambda+n\gamma} I) = \sum_{i \in J(n)} per(S_{\lambda,\gamma,i}).$$

When A is a set with finite perimeter, we have ([6])

$$per(A) = ||1\!\!1_A||_{BV}.$$

Lemma 1 *If $B \subset A$ are two sets with finite perimeter, then*

$$per(A \setminus B) \leq per(A) + per(B).$$

Proof Indeed, by the subadditivity of the BV norm, we deduce from

$$1\!\!1_{A \setminus B} = 1\!\!1_A - 1\!\!1_B$$

that

$$per(A \setminus B) \leq per(A) + per(B).$$

$\square$

In the following theorem, we analyze the statistics of sizes of sections as follows. We fix γ, that is, the overall contrast of considered sections and for each

$0 \leq \lambda \leq \gamma$, we count all sections $S_{\gamma,\lambda,i}$ which have an area between s and $s + ds$. In other terms we consider the integer

$$\text{Card}\{i, s \leq |S_{\gamma,\lambda,i}| \leq s + ds\}.$$

We average this number over all λ's in $[0, \gamma]$, and assume that this average number has a density $f(\gamma, s)$ with respect to s. In other terms,

$$\frac{1}{\gamma} \int_0^\gamma \text{Card}\{i, s \leq |S_{\gamma,\lambda,i}| \leq s + ds\} d\lambda = f(\gamma, s) ds \tag{4}$$

Theorem 2 *Assume that there exists some $\gamma > 0$ such that (4) holds, i.e. the average number of sections with area s, for $0 \leq \lambda \leq \gamma$, has a density $f(\gamma, s)$. Then there is a constant c, not depending on I, such that*

$$\|I\|_{BV} \geq c \int_0^{\nu(\Omega)} s^{\frac{1}{2}} f(\gamma, s) ds. \tag{5}$$

Proof Applying Corollary 1 and Lemma 1

$$\|I\|_{BV} = \int_{\mathbf{R}} \text{per}\{x, I(x) \geq \lambda\} d\lambda$$

$$= \frac{1}{2}\Big(\int_{\mathbf{R}} \text{per}\{x, I(x) \geq \lambda\} d\lambda + \int_{\mathbf{R}} \text{per}\{x, I(x) \geq \lambda - \gamma\} d\lambda$$

$$\geq \frac{1}{2} \int_{\mathbf{R}} \text{per}(\chi_{\lambda-\gamma} I \setminus \chi_\lambda I) d\lambda$$

$$= \frac{1}{2} \sum_{n \in \mathbf{Z}} \int_{n\gamma}^{(n+1)\gamma} \text{per}(\chi_{\lambda-\gamma} I \setminus \chi_\lambda I) d\lambda$$

$$= \frac{1}{2} \int_0^\gamma \sum_{n \in \mathbf{Z}} \text{per}(\chi_{\lambda+(n-1)\gamma} I \setminus \chi_{\lambda+n\gamma} I) d\lambda$$

$$= \frac{1}{2} \int_0^\gamma \sum_{i \in J(\gamma,\lambda)} \text{per}(S_{\gamma,\lambda,i}) d\lambda.$$

By isoperimetric inequality (2), we therefore obtain

$$\|I\|_{BV} \geq \pi^{\frac{1}{2}} \int_0^\gamma \sum_{i \in J(\gamma,\lambda)} |S_{\gamma,\lambda,i}|^{\frac{1}{2}} d\lambda.$$

Applying Fubini-Tonelli Theorem, some slicing and the assumption (4), we get

$$\|I\|_{BV} \geq \pi^{\frac{1}{2}} \int_0^\gamma d\lambda \int_0^{\nu(\Omega)} \text{Card}\{i \in J(\gamma,\lambda), s \leq |S_{\gamma,\lambda,i}| \leq s + ds\} s^{\frac{1}{2}}$$

$$= \pi^{\frac{1}{2}} \int_0^{\nu(\Omega)} \int_0^\gamma d\lambda \text{Card}\{i \in J(\gamma,\lambda), s \leq |S_{\gamma,\lambda,i}| \leq s + ds\} s^{\frac{1}{2}}$$

$$= \gamma \pi^{\frac{1}{2}} \int_0^{\nu(\Omega)} s^{\frac{1}{2}} f(\gamma, s) ds.$$

□

We can repeat the preceding analysis by assuming now that

$$\frac{1}{\gamma} \int_0^\gamma \text{Card}\{i, p \leq \text{per}(S_{\gamma,\lambda,i}) \leq p + dp\}d\lambda = g(\gamma, p)dp. \tag{6}$$

Then we have the analog of Theorem 2 for the perimeters of sections:

Theorem 3 *Assume that there exists some $\gamma > 0$ such that (6) holds, i.e. the average number of sections with perimeter s, for $0 \leq \lambda \leq \gamma$, has a density $g(\gamma, p)$. Then*

$$\|I\|_{BV} \geq \frac{1}{2} \int_0^{+\infty} pg(\gamma, p)dp. \tag{7}$$

Proof The proof is essentially the same as for Theorem 2.

3.2 Application to natural images

In this section, we draw the consequences of Theorems 2 and 3 for the images analyzed in Section 2. According to the results of this section, we can assume that the considered images satisfy

$$f(\gamma, s) = \frac{C}{s^\alpha} \tag{8}$$

$$g(\gamma, p) = \frac{C}{p^\beta} \tag{9}$$

for some constants $\alpha > 0$, $\beta > 0$. This law has been experimentally checked for several values of $\gamma = \frac{256}{k}$, k ranging from 8 to 20. We also checked that the value of α was almost not modified when the bilevels were not defined from gray level 0, but from some gray level less that $\frac{256}{k}$ (that is to say, in the continuous model, for different values of λ). By Theorem 2 we have

$$\|I\|_{BV} \geq c \int_0^{\nu(\Omega)} \frac{Cs^{\frac{1}{2}}}{s^\alpha} ds = +\infty \text{ if } \alpha > \frac{3}{2}$$

and in the same way,

$$\|I\|_{BV} \geq c \int_0^{+\infty} \frac{Cp}{p^\beta} dp = +\infty \text{ if } \beta > 2.$$

thus if we admit that (8) and (9) indeed hold for natural images when $s \to 0$, as is indicated by the experiments of section 3.1, we obtain that the considered images are not in BV if $\alpha > \frac{3}{2}$, or $\beta > 2$. This strong assumption about the small scales behavior is motivated by the goodness of the fit at every scales and by the stability of the fit with respect to T_{min}, see Section 2, Table 2. Notice, however, that $\alpha > 2$, which happens for several of the considered images, is not compatible with a finite image area, since then $\int \frac{s\,ds}{s^\alpha} = +\infty$. As suggested to us by Vicent Caselles and Stéphane Mallat, this raises the question of whether the area is correctly measured by covering pixels. In fact, if a region is very ragged, the cardinality of covering pixels may be related to its perimeter as well, in which case the estimate of $g(\gamma, s)$ is more reliable. This cardinality could also be related to a fractional Hausdorff measure.

We point out here that wavelet coefficients (see [15], [13] for an introduction to wavelet decompositions) also give a way to decide whether or not an image belongs to the space BV. Let (c_k) be the wavelets coefficients of the image I, ordered in a nonincreasing sequence. Let us suppose that the wavelets have compact supports. We say that the c_k's are in l^1 if $\sum |c_k| < +\infty$, and that they are in weak-l^1 if there exists a constant C such that $c_k \leq \frac{C}{k}$. Obviously l^1 is included in weak-l^1. It is quite easy to prove that if the c_k are in l^1, then I is in BV. In the other direction, Cohen and al., [4], recently proved that if I is in BV, then the c_k's are in weak-l^1. Thus it is possible to decide whether an image belongs or not to BV by looking at its wavelet coefficients decay, except if they decrease like $\frac{C}{k}$, which happens to be often the case ([12]). Moreover, it is worth noticing that the wavelet coefficients produced by the characteristic function of a simple shape already decay like $\frac{1}{k}$. We do not present here a precise comparison between the two criteria. Let us just mention that in the case of the baboon image (Figure 1), both methods agree: this image is not in BV. For the well-known image of Lena, our approach gives an α of 1.9 (for $k = 16$), which suggests Lena being out of BV, whereas from the wavelet approach, the image is in BV. In fact, according to our analysis, natural images are not in the space BV. Of course, one may objects the presence of an inner scale cut off, but our results indicate that the BV norm of continuous representations of natural images blows up as we consider smaller and smaller scales.

4 Conclusions

We realized experimentally that the size distribution of homogeneous parts in digital natural images follows a power law. This power law confirms the scale invariance of natural images. Moreover, this enables us to show that, provided this power law is valid for small, non-observable scales, most natural images are not in the space BV of functions with bounded variations.

Acknowledgments

We would like to thank Vicent Caselles, Stuart Geman, Stéphane Mallat and David Mumford for several helpful comments and discussions. We also thank Les Treilles foundation which made some of these discussions possible.

258

References

1. L. Alvarez, Y. Gousseau, and J.-M. Morel. The size of objects in natural and artificial images. *Advances in Imaging and Electron Physics*, 111,1999.
2. A. J. Bell and T. J. Sejnowski. The "independent components" of natural scenes are edge filters. *Vision Research*, 37:3327–3338, 1997.
3. V. Caselles and J.-M. Morel. The connected components of sets of finite perimeters in the plane. Preprint, 1998.
4. A. Cohen, R. DeVore, P. Petrushev, and H. Xu. Non linear approximation and the space $BV(\mathbb{R}^2)$. Preprint, submitted to Amer. J. Math., 1998.
5. N. G. Deriugin. The power spectrum and the correlation function of the television signal. *Telecomunications*, 1:1–12, 1956.
6. L. C. Evans and R. F. Gariepy. *Measure Theory and Fine Properties of Functions*. Studies in Advanced Math. CRC Press, 1992.
7. D. J. Field. Relations between the statistics of natural images and the response properties of cortical cells. *Jour. Opt. Soc. Amer.*, A4:2379–2394, 1987.
8. E. De Giorgi. Su una teoria generale della misura $(r - 1)$-dimensionale in uno spazio ad r dimensioni. *Ann. Mat. Pura ed Appl.*, IV. Ser., 36:191–213, 1954.
9. D. J. Heeger and J. R. Bergen. Pyramid based texture analysis/synthesis. *Computer Graphics Proceedings*, pages 229–238, 1995.
10. J. Huang and D. Mumford. Statistics of natural images and models. *To be published*, 1998.
11. T. Lindenberg. Detecting salient blob-like image structure and their scales with a scale-space primal sketch: A method for focus-of-attention. *International Journal of Computer Vision*, 11(3):283–318, 1993.
12. S. Mallat. Personal communication.
13. S Mallat. *A Wavelet Tour of Signal Processing*. Academic Press, 1997.
14. G. Matheron. Modèle séquentiel de partition aléatoire. Technical report, CMM, 1968.
15. Y. Meyer. *Wavelets: Algorithms and Applications*. SIAM, 1993.
16. D. Mumford, S. C. Zhu, and B. Gidas. Stochastic models for generic images. Working draft, 1997.
17. B. A. Olshausen and D. J. Field. Natural images statistics and efficient image coding. *Network: Computation in Neural Systems*, 7:333–339, 1996.
18. A. P. Pentland. Fractal based description of natural scenes. *IEEE Trans. on Pattern Analysis and Machine Intelligence*, 6(6):661–674, November 1984.
19. D. L. Ruderman. Origins of scaling in natural images. *Vision Research*, 37(23):3385–3398, 1997.
20. D. L. Ruderman and W. Bialek. Statistics of natural images: Scaling in the woods. *Physical Review Letters*, pages 814–817, 1994.
21. L. Rudin. *Images, Numerical Analysis of Singularities and Shock Filters*. PhD thesis, California Institute of Technology, 1987.
22. L. Rudin, S. Osher, and E. Fatemi. Nonlinear total variation based noise removal algorithms. *Physica D*, 60:259–268, 1992.
23. E. P. Simoncelli and J. Portilla. Texture characterisation via joint statistics of wavelet coefficient magnitudes. In *5th International Conference on Image Processing*, 1998.
24. S. W. Zhu, Y. Wu, and D. Mumford. Filters, random fields and maximum entropy (FRAME). *Int'l Journal of Computer Vision*, 27:1–20, 1998.
25. W. P. Ziemer. *Weakly Differentiable Functions*. Springer Verlag, 1989.

Edges as Outliers: Anisotropic Smoothing Using Local Image Statistics

Michael J. Black[1] and Guillermo Sapiro[2]

[1] Xerox Palo Alto Research Center,
3333 Coyote Hill Road, Palo Alto, CA 94304 USA.
black@parc.xerox.com
[2] Dept. of Electrical and Computer Eng., University of Minnesota
200 Union Street SE, Minneapolis, MN 55455.
guille@ece.umn.edu

Abstract. Edges are viewed as statistical outliers with respect to local image gradient magnitudes. Within local image regions we compute a robust statistical measure of the gradient variation and use this in an anisotropic diffusion framework to determine a spatially varying "edge-stopping" parameter σ. We show how to determine this parameter for two edge-stopping functions described in the literature (Perona-Malik and the Tukey biweight). Smoothing of the image is related the local texture and in regions of low texture, small gradient values may be treated as edges whereas in regions of high texture, large gradient magnitudes are necessary before an edge is preserved. Intuitively these results have similarities with human perceptual phenomena such as masking and "popout". Results are shown on a variety of standard images.

1 Introduction

Anisotropic diffusion has been widely used for "edge-preserving" smoothing of images. Little attention, however, has been paid to defining exactly what is meant by an "edge." In the traditional formulation of Perona and Malik [8], edges are related to pixels with large gradient magnitudes and an anisotropic smoothing function is one that inhibits smoothing across such boundaries. The effect of this smoothing is determined by some parameter, σ, which implicitly defines what is meant by an edge. This paper addresses how the σ parameter can be determined automatically from the image data in such a way that edges correspond to statistical outliers with respect to local image gradients. With this method, σ varies across the image and hence, what is considered to be an edge is dependent on local statistical properties of the image.

Consider for example the image in Figure 1. Regions **A** and **B** illustrate areas where there is little gradient variation and the fairly small gradient magnitudes of the features are locally significant. Intuitively, we would say that the eyebrow and the shoulder crease are significant image structures. In contrast, region **C** is highly textured and there is a great deal of variation in the gradient magnitudes. Intuitively, in this region, the gradient magnitudes of features like those in regions

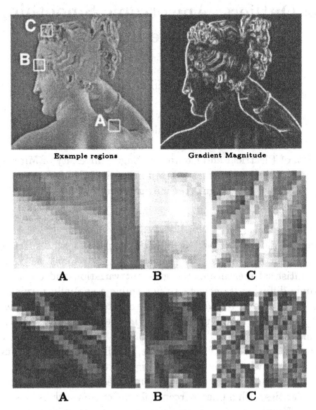

Fig. 1. Consider the image regions (**A, B, C**) in the upper left image. The middle row shows each image region in detail while the bottom row shows the gradient magnitude for each region. The faint image structures in regions **A** and **B** are statistically significant with respect the variation of intensity within the regions. The same variation in the highly textured region **C** would not be statistically significant due to the much larger image variation.

A and **B** might be considered insignificant. To be considered an edge in region **C** we would like the gradient magnitude to be much larger.

Here we adopt the robust statistical interpretation of anisotropic diffusion elaborated in [1]. Anisotropic diffusion is viewed as a robust statistical procedure that estimates a piecewise smooth image from noisy input data. This work formalized the relationship between the "edge-stopping" function in the anisotropic diffusion equation and the error norm and influence function in a robust estimation framework. This robust statistical interpretation provides a principled means for defining and detecting the boundaries (edges) between the piecewise smooth regions in an image that has been smoothed with anisotropic diffusion. Edges are considered statistical outliers in this framework.

The robust statistical approach also provides a framework to locally define edges and stopping functions, as demonstrated in this paper (see [11] for a different approach to spatially adaptive anisotropic diffusion). In particular, the

σ parameter in the edge stopping function has also a statistical interpretation. This statistical interpretation gives, among other properties, a completely automatic diffusion algorithm, since all the parameters are computed from the image. Our approach is to compute a statistically robust *local* measure of the brightness variation within image regions. From this we obtain a local definition of edges and a space-variant edge stopping function.

2 Review

We briefly review the traditional anisotropic diffusion formulation as presented by Perona and Malik [8].

2.1 Anisotropic diffusion: Perona-Malik formulation

Diffusion algorithms smooth images via a partial differential equation (PDE). For example, consider applying the isotropic diffusion equation (the heat equation) given by $\frac{\partial I(x,y,t)}{\partial t} = \text{div}(\nabla I)$, using the original (degraded/noisy) image $I(x, y, 0)$ as the initial condition, where $I(x, y, 0) : \mathbb{R}^2 \rightarrow \mathbb{R}^+$ is an image in the continuous domain, (x, y) specifies spatial position, t is an artificial time parameter, and where ∇I is the image gradient. Modifying the image according to this isotropic diffusion equation is equivalent to filtering the image with a Gaussian filter.

Perona and Malik [8] replace the classical isotropic diffusion equation with

$$\frac{\partial I(x, y, t)}{\partial t} = \text{div}(g(\| \nabla I \|, \sigma)\nabla I), \tag{1}$$

where $\| \nabla I \|$ is the gradient magnitude, and $g(\| \nabla I \|)$ is an "edge-stopping" function and σ is a scale parameter. This function is chosen to satisfy $g(x, \sigma) \rightarrow 0$ when $x \rightarrow \infty$ so that the diffusion is "stopped" across edges.

2.2 Perona-Malik discrete formulation

Perona and Malik discretized their anisotropic diffusion equation as follows:

$$I_s^{t+1} = I_s^t + \frac{\lambda}{|\eta_s|} \sum_{p \in \eta_s} g(\nabla I_{s,p}, \sigma)\nabla I_{s,p}, \tag{2}$$

where I_s^t is a discretely-sampled image, s denotes the pixel position in a discrete, two-dimensional grid, and t now denotes discrete time steps (iterations). The constant $\lambda \in \mathbb{R}^+$ is a scalar that determines the rate of diffusion, η_s represents the spatial neighborhood of pixel s, and $|\eta_s|$ is the number of neighbors (usually 4, except at the image boundaries). Perona and Malik linearly approximated the image gradient in a particular direction as

$$\nabla I_{s,p} = I_p - I_s^t, \quad p \in \eta_s. \tag{3}$$

Qualitatively, the effect of anisotropic diffusion is to smooth the original image while preserving brightness discontinuities. The choice of $g(x, \sigma)$ and the value of σ can greatly affect the extent to which discontinuities are preserved.

2.3 Related Work

In related work, a number of authors have explored the estimation of the scale at which to estimate edges in images [2, 5]. These methods find the optimal local scale for detecting edges with Gaussian filters; they do not explicitly use local image statistics. The approach described here might be augmented using these ideas to determine the size of the local area within which to compute image statistics.

Marimont and Rubner [6] computed local statistics of zero-crossings and used these to define the probability of a pixel belonging to an edge. Liang and Wang [4] also used the statistics of zero-crossings to set a local noise measure in an anisotropic diffusion formulation.

In contrast, the work here provides a robust statistical view which allows a principled choice of both the g-function and the scale parameter. Related to this is work on human perception that models feature saliency using a statistical test for outliers [9].

3 Robust Statistical View

For the majority of pixels in Figure 1 **A**, the image gradient values can be approximately modeled as being constant (zero) with random Gaussian noise. The large gradient values due to the image feature however are statistical "outliers" [3] with respect to the Gaussian distribution; the distribution of these outliers is unknown. We seek a function $g(x, \sigma)$ and a scale parameter σ that will appropriately smooth the image when the variation in the gradient is roughly Gaussian and will inhibit smoothing when the gradient can be viewed as an outlier.

First we need to relate the form of the g-functions used for anisotropic diffusion to the tools used in robust statistics (see [1] for details). From a robust statistical perspective the goal of anisotropic smoothing is to iteratively find an image I that satisfies the following optimization criterion:

$$\min_{I} \sum_{s \in I} \sum_{p \in \eta_s} \rho(I_p - I_s, \sigma) \tag{4}$$

where $\rho(\cdot)$ is a robust error function and σ is a "scale" parameter.

In this formulation large image differences $|I_p - I_s|$ are assumed to be outliers which should not have a large effect on the solution. To analyze the behavior of a given ρ-function with respect to outliers, we consider its derivative (denoted ψ), which is proportional to its *influence function* [3]. This function characterizes the bias that a particular measurement has on the solution and by analyzing the shape of this function we can infer the behavior of a particular robust ρ-function with respect to outliers.

In [1] (see also [12] for a related approach) it was shown that

$$g(x, \sigma)x = \psi(x, \sigma) = \rho'(x, \sigma). \tag{5}$$

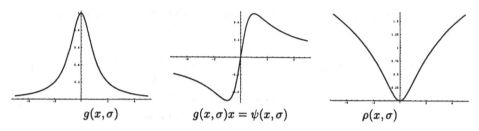

Fig. 2. Lorentzian error norm and the Perona-Malik g stopping function.

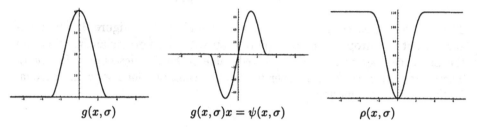

Fig. 3. Tukey's biweight.

This relationship means that we can analyze the behavior of a particular anisotropic edge-stopping function g in terms of its outlier rejection properties by examining the influence function ψ.

For example, consider the edge-stopping function proposed by Perona and Malik [8]

$$g(x,\sigma)x = \frac{2x}{2 + \frac{x^2}{\sigma^2}} = \psi(x,\sigma), \tag{6}$$

where $\psi(x,\sigma) = \rho'(x,\sigma)$. We can compute ρ by integrating $g(x,\sigma)x$ with respect to x to derive

$$\int g(x,\sigma)x \, dx = \sigma^2 \log\left(1 + \frac{1}{2}\left(\frac{x^2}{\sigma^2}\right)\right) = \rho(x,\sigma). \tag{7}$$

This function $\rho(x,\sigma)$ is proportional to the Lorentzian error norm use in robust statistics and $g(x)x = \rho'(x) = \psi(x)$ is proportional to the influence function (Figure 2).

The function $g(x,\sigma)$ acts as a "weight" and from the plot in Figure 2 we can see that small values of x (i.e. small gradient magnitudes) will receive high weight. As we move out to the tails of this function it flattens out and the weight assigned to some large x will be roughly the same as the weight assigned to some nearby $x+\epsilon$. This behavior is visible in the shape of the ψ-function which reaches a peak and then begins to descend. Outlying values of x beyond a point receive roughly equivalent weights and hence there is little preference for one outlying value over another. In this sense outliers have little "influence" on the solution. In the anisotropic diffusion context, $g(x,\sigma)x$ will be relatively small for outliers and, hence, each iteration in (2) will produce only a small change in the image.

In [1] a more robust edge stopping function was derived from Tukey's biweight ρ-error:

$$\rho(x,\sigma) = \begin{cases} \frac{x^2}{\sigma^2} - \frac{x^4}{\sigma^4} + \frac{x^6}{3\sigma^6} & |x| \leq \sigma, \\ \frac{1}{3} & \text{otherwise,} \end{cases} \tag{8}$$

$$\psi(x,\sigma) = \begin{cases} x(1-(x/\sigma)^2)^2 & |x| \leq \sigma, \\ 0 & \text{otherwise,} \end{cases} \tag{9}$$

$$g(x,\sigma) = \begin{cases} \frac{1}{2}(1-(x/\sigma)^2)^2 & |x| \leq \sigma, \\ 0 & \text{otherwise.} \end{cases} \tag{10}$$

The functions $g(x,\sigma)$, $\psi(x,\sigma)$ and $\rho(x,\sigma)$ are plotted in Figure 3: The influence of outliers drops off more rapidly than with the Lorentzian function and the influence goes to zero after a fixed value (a hard redescending function). These properties result in sharper boundaries than obtained with the Perona-Malik/Lorentzian function [1].

4 Local Measure of Edges

Both functions defined in the previous section reduce the influence of large gradient magnitudes on the smoothed image. The point at which gradient values begin to be treated as outliers is dependent on the parameter σ. In this section we consider how to globally and *locally* compute an estimate of σ directly from the image gradients. The main idea is that σ should characterize the variance of the majority of the data within a region. So, for example in Figure 1 A, σ should characterize the amount of variation in the gradients at all locations except where the feature is located. Outliers will then be determined relative to this background variation.

In deriving σ we appeal to tools from robust statistics to automatically estimate the "robust scale," σ_e, of the image as [10]

$$\sigma_e = 1.4826 \, \text{MAD}(\nabla I)$$
$$= 1.4826 \, \text{median}_I(\| \nabla I - \text{median}_I(\| \nabla I \|) \|) \tag{11}$$

where "MAD" denotes the median absolute deviation and the constant is derived from the fact that the MAD of a zero-mean normal distribution with unit variance is $0.6745 = 1/1.4826$. We consider σ_e to be the gradient magnitude at which outliers begin to be downweighted.

We choose values for the scale parameters σ to dilate each of the influence functions so that they begin rejecting outliers at the same value: σ_e. The point where the influence of outliers first begins to decrease occurs when the derivative of the ψ-function is zero. For the Lorentzian ρ-function this occurs at $\sigma_e = \sqrt{2}\sigma$ and for the Tukey function it occurs at $\sigma_e = \sigma/\sqrt{5}$. Defining σ with respect to σ_e in this way we plot the influence functions for a range of values of x in Figure 4a. Note how each function begins reducing the influence of measurements at the same point.

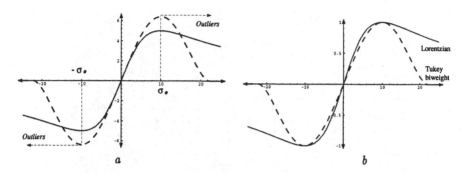

Fig. 4. Lorentzian and Tukey ψ-functions. *(a)* values of σ chosen as a function of σ_e so that outlier "rejection" begins at the same value for each function; *(b)* the functions aligned and scaled.

We also scale the influence functions so that they return values in the same range. To do this we take λ in (2) to be one over the value of $\psi(\sigma_e, \sigma)$. The scaled ψ-functions are plotted in Figure 4*b*.

Now we can directly compare the results of anisotropic smoothing with the different edge-stopping functions. The Tukey function gives *zero* weight to outliers whose magnitude is above a certain value while the Lorentzian (or Perona-Malik) downweights outliers but still gives them some weight.

4.1 Spatially Varying σ

In previous work we took the region for computing σ_e to be the entire image. This approach works well when edges are distributed homogeneously across the image but this is rarely the case. Here we explore the computation of this measure in image patches. In particular we consider computing a local scale $\sigma_l(x, y)$, which is a function of spatial position, in $n \times n$ pixel patches at every location in the image. We take this value to be the larger of the σ_e estimated for the entire image and the value in the local patch. Then $\sigma_l(x, y)$ is defined as

$$\sigma_l(x, y) = \max(\sigma_e, 1.4826 \, \mathrm{MAD}_{-\frac{n}{2} \leq i, j \leq \frac{n}{2}} (\nabla I_{x+i, y+j})). \tag{12}$$

In practice σ_e provides a reasonable lower bound on the overall spatial image variation and the setting of σ_l to be the maximum of the global and local variation prevents the amplification of noise in relatively homogeneous image regions.

Figure 5 shows the results of estimating σ_l in 15×15 pixel patches. Bright areas have higher values of σ_l and correspond to more textured image regions.

To see the effects of the spatially varying σ_l consider the results in Figure 6. The images show the results of applying diffusion using the $g(x, \sigma)$ corresponding to the Tukey biweight function. The top row uses a fixed value of σ_e estimated over the entire image while the bottom row shows the results with a spatially varying σ_l. We can detect edges in the smoothed images very simply by detecting those points that are treated as outliers by the given ρ-function. Figure 6 shows

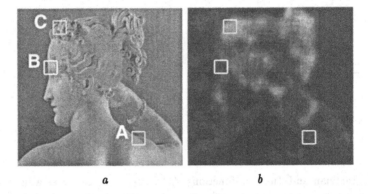

Fig. 5. Local estimate of scale, $\sigma_l(x,y)$. Bright areas in *(b)* correspond to larger values of σ_l.

the outliers (edge points) in each of the images, where outliers are given by those points having $|\nabla I_{x,y}| > \sigma_e$ (global, first row) or $|\nabla I_{x,y}| > \sigma_l(x,y)$ (local, second row).

In areas containing little texture the results are identical since in these areas the sigma estimated locally is likely to be less than σ_e and hence, σ_l is set to σ_e. The differences become apparent in the textured regions of the image. A detail is shown for a region of hair. With a fixed global σ_e, discontinuities are detected densely in the hair region as the large gradients are considered outliers with respect to the rest of the image which has relatively few large gradients. With the spatially varying σ_l, these regions are smoothed more heavily and only the statistically significant discontinuities remain.

5 Experimental Results

In this section we test the spatially varying smoothing method with both the Lorentzian and Tukey g-functions. Figure 7 compares the results for the Tukey function at 500 iterations and the Lorentzian at 50 iterations. The Lorentzian must be stopped sooner as, unlike the Tukey function, outliers have a finite influence and hence the image will eventually become oversmoothed; for a discussion of the edge-stopping properties of the Tukey biweight function see [1]. In both cases note that the edges detected in the highly textured regions have a spatial density similar to that of other regions of image structure.

Figure 8 shows a more textured image. Note that the highest scale values correspond to the steps in the lower middle portion of the image. The discontinuities here are smoothed while the boundaries of the people against a relatively uniform background are preserved. One can also see in this image the difference between the Lorentzian and Tukey functions in that the Tukey g-function results in sharper brightness discontinuities.

The Magnetic Resonance image in Figure 9 is challenging because there are areas of high contrast as well as detailed brain structures of very low contrast.

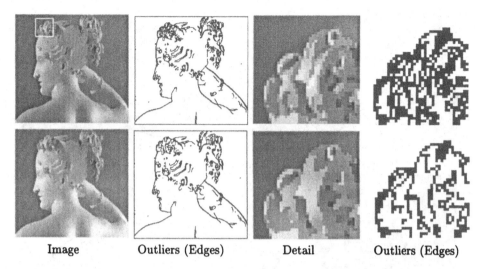

| Image | Outliers (Edges) | Detail | Outliers (Edges) |

Fig. 6. Anisotropic smoothing with the Tukey function (500 iterations). Top row shows smoothing with a fixed value of σ_e. Bottom row shows a spatially varying σ_l.

No single scale term will suffice for an image such as this. The results with the Tukey function preserve much of the fine detail and the detected edges reveal structure in both the high and low contrast regions.

6 Conclusions

One of the crucial steps in anisotropic diffusion is to define an edge, and from this definition, an edge stopping function. Several attempts have been reported in the literature, mainly dealing with global definitions. In this paper we have addressed the search for a local definition of edges. We have described a simple method for determining a spatially varying scale function based on robust statistical techniques. From this, we have provided a local definition of edges and a space-varying edge stopping function.

A number of topics remain open. First, the only parameter left in the proposed anisotropic diffusion algorithm is the size of the window within which σ_l is computed. This also should be space-variant, and needs to be automatically determined from the image itself. This is an area of ongoing research.

We are interested in comparing the output of our simple local edge detector with others as for example those proposed by Perona [7] or Elder and Zucker [2]. They use much more sophisticated techniques that might not be computationally efficient if the goal is to compute stopping functions for anisotropic diffusion. On the other hand, a more accurate computation of edges might be crucial for anisotropic diffusion applications such as the enhancement of medical images.

Finally, it would be interesting to explore the relationship to human perception of image features which can be effected by the local image statistics [9].

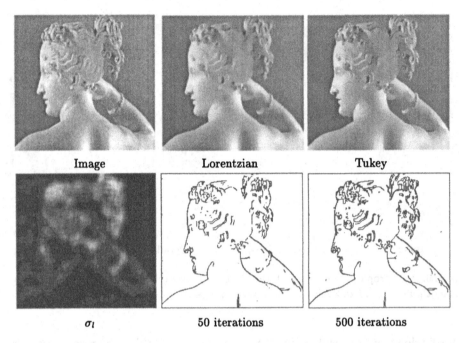

Fig. 7. Results for both the Perona-Malik (Lorentzian) function and the Tukey function.

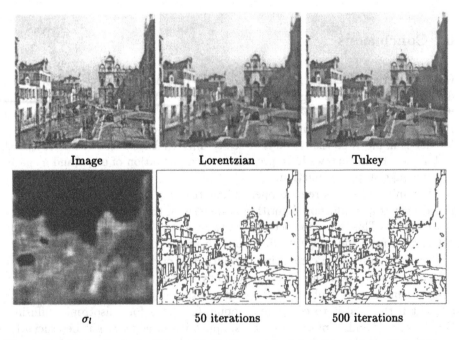

Fig. 8. Results for both the Perona-Malik (Lorentzian) function and the Tukey function.

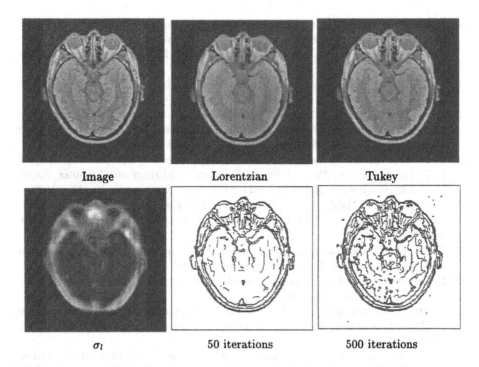

<table>
<tr><td>Image</td><td>Lorentzian</td><td>Tukey</td></tr>
<tr><td>σ_l</td><td>50 iterations</td><td>500 iterations</td></tr>
</table>

Fig. 9. Magnetic Resonance Image. Results for both the Perona-Malik (Lorentzian) function and the Tukey function.

Such an exploration may lead to a new statistical model more closely aligned with human perception of edges.

Acknowledgements. GS is partially supported by a grant from the Office of Naval Research ONR-N00014-97-1-0509, the Office of Naval Research Young Investigator Award, the Presidential Early Career Awards for Scientists and Engineers (PECASE), and by the National Science Foundation Learning and Intelligent Systems Program (LIS).

References

1. M. J. Black, G. Sapiro, D. Marimont, and D. Heeger. Robust anisotropic diffusion. *IEEE Trans. on Image Processing*, 7(3):421–432, 1998.
2. J. H. Elder and S. W. Zucker. Scale space localization, blur, and contour-based image coding. In *Proc. Computer Vision and Pattern Recognition, CVPR-96*, pages 27–34, San Francisco, June 1996.
3. F. R. Hampel, E. M. Ronchetti, P. J. Rousseeuw, and W. A. Stahel. *Robust Statistics: The Approach Based on Influence Functions*. John Wiley and Sons, New York, NY, 1986.

4. P. Liang and Y. F. Wang. Local scale controlled ansiotropic diffusion with local noise estimate for image smoothing and edge detection. In *Proceedings of the International Conference on Computer Vision*, pages 193–200, Mumbai, India, January 1998.

5. T. Lindeberg. Edge detection and ridge detection with automatic scale selection. *International Journal of Computer Vision*, 30(2):117–154, 1998.

6. D. H. Marimont and Y. Rubner. A probabilistic framework for edge detection and scale selection. In *Proceedings of the International Conference on Computer Vision*, pages 207–214, Mumbai, India, January 1998.

7. P. Perona. Steerable-scalable kernals for edge detection and junction analysis. In G. Sandini, editor, *Proc. of Second European Conference on Computer Vision, ECCV-92*, volume 588 of *LNCS-Series*, pages 3–23. Springer-Verlag, May 1992.

8. P. Perona and J. Malik. Scale-space and edge detection using anisotropic diffusion. *IEEE Transactions on Pattern Analysis and Machine Intelligence*, 12(7):629–639, July 1990.

9. R. Rosenholtz. General-purpose localization of textured image regions. In *Advances in Neural Information Processing Systems, 11*, 1999.

10. P. J. Rousseeuw and A. M. Leroy. *Robust Regression and Outlier Detection*. John Wiley & Sons, New York, 1987.

11. D. Strong, P. Blomgren, and T. F. Chan. Spatially adaptive local feature-driven total variation minimizing image restoration. Technical Report 97-32, UCLA-CAM Report, July 1997.

12. Y. L. You, W. Xu, A. Tannenbaum, and M. Kaveh. Behavioral analysis of anisotropic diffusion in image processing. *IEEE Trans. Image Processing*, 5:1539–1553, 1996.

The Hausdorff Dimension and Scale-Space Normalisation of Natural Images

Kim Steenstrup Pedersen and Mads Nielsen

DIKU, Universitetsparken 1
2100 Copenhagen, Denmark

Abstract. Fractal Brownian motions have been introduced as a statistical description of natural images. We analyze the Gaussian scale-space scaling of derivatives of fractal images. On the basis of this analysis we propose a method for estimation of the fractal dimension of images and scale-space normalisation used in conjunction with automatic scale selection assuming either constant energy over scale or self similar energy scaling.

Keywords: Fractal dimension, natural images, self-similarity, Gaussian scale-space, image derivatives, scale-selection, feature detection.

1   Introduction

In the literature [1–8] one finds several investigations into the fractal nature of natural images and in this article we will look at some scale-space properties of images of natural scenes. Here we use the term *natural image* to denote any image of a real world scene, which may be assumed to have a fractal intensity surface (or volume). A fractal function is self-similar, which means that if one looks at the function as a random function then its distribution is independent of the scale. To characterize a fractal function one uses the fractal dimension.

The fractal dimension of an image intuitively describes the roughness of the image intensity graph and the fractal dimension of the intensity surface of 2D images must a priori lie between 2 and 3. There has for some time been a general consent that 2D images of natural scenes have a fractal dimension (Hausdorff dimension[1]) $D_H = 2.5$, which is the same dimension as the classical 2D Brownian motion. But resent studies by Bialek et al. [6] has shown that 2D images of natural scenes[2] not necessarily have to come from a Gaussian process and that the fractal dimension can vary in the interval between 2 and 3.

Fractal Brownian motions (fBm) can be used as a model for images of natural scenes. By using this model we have the freedom to model images of any fractal dimension. The classical Brownian motion is a special case of the fBm. The fBms are in general continuous, but not differentiable. In the limit $D_H \to 2$, the 2D

---

[1] In this article we will use the Hausdorff dimension as the definition of the fractal dimension. See [9] for a mathematical definition of the Hausdorff dimension.

[2] The studies by Bialek et al. is based on a series of images in a forest.

fBms generically become smooth (C^∞). Whereas in the limit $D_H \to 3$, the 2D fBms become spatially uncorrelated.

The estimation of the fractal dimension of regions of interest in images has different interesting prospects. It has been proposed [7,8] that the fractal dimension of x-ray images of trabecular bone can give an indication of the micro structure of the bone and thereby also the biomechanical strength of the bone. This can be a helpful tool for the research of osteoporosis and other bone diseases. Other uses of the fractal dimension could be as a quality measure of surfaces produced in different kinds of industries, e.g. metal plates, wood etc.

Linear scale-space [10–12] is a mathematical formalization of the concept of scale (or aperture) in physical measurements. By Gaussian convolution, images at higher inner scales than the measurement scale can be simulated, enabling us to create an artificial scale-space of an image. By using this type of scale-space we bypass the problem of differentiability of digital images, because differentiation of the image in scale-space may be obtained by differentiation of the Gauss function prior to the convolution.

By the use of a non-linear combination of image derivatives, called measures of feature strength, it is possible to detect features in images [13]. In order to get dimensionless derivatives Florack et al. [14] has proposed normalisation of image derivatives where the derivatives are multiplied by the scale σ, $(\partial/\partial x)_{norm} = \sigma \partial/\partial x$. Lindeberg [15–17] operates with scale-normalized derivatives in order to detect the most significant scale for the features. He uses a normalisation which is defined through a scaling exponent γ. In application to feature detection, this normalisation exponent γ depend on the feature in question. Lindeberg determines this parameter on the basis of analysis of feature models. In this analysis the parameter varies in the interval $[\frac{1}{2}; 1]$. Our intuition[3] is that this parameter must reflect the local complexity of the image, and may be modelled through the fractal dimension of the local image. In this paper we reveal a simple relation between the topological dimension of a feature and the fractal dimension of the local image for determining the scale-normalisation.

We will in this paper assume, that the fBms constitute a model of images of natural scenes. Using this model we establish a method of scale-space normalisation of derivatives, changing the analytical expression of Lindeberg's γ-normalisation. This expression includes the fractal dimension of the image in a neighbourhood of the feature we want to detect. We can furthermore use this normalisation method for estimation of the fractal dimension of images.

2 Fractal Brownian Motions and Natural Images

The 1D fBm was first defined by Mandelbrot and van Ness [18] in an integral form, which later on was restated in terms of self similarity of a distribution function. In this form it is straightforward to state the fBm defined over an N-D space [5]. A function $f_H(x) : \mathbb{R}^N \mapsto \mathbb{R}$ is called a N-D fBm if for all positions

---

[3] Developed during discussions with Lindeberg.

$x \in \mathbb{R}^N$ and all displacements $\lambda \in \mathbb{R}^N$

$$P\left(\frac{f_H(x+\lambda) - f_H(x)}{||\lambda||^H} < y\right) = F(y),$$

where $F(y)$ is a cumulative distribution function and P the probability. The scaling exponent $H \in]0;1[$ determines the fractal dimension of the fBm. This definition implies that any 1D straight line through the image is a 1D fBm of same scaling exponent H.

One can find experimental data to support the assertion that images of natural scenes may satisfy the definition of the fBm [1,3,4,6], but $F(y)$ is not in general a cumulated Gaussian distribution [6] as commonly presumed [1,3].

The power spectrum of the N-D fBm $f_H(x)$ is given by

$$|\tilde{f}_H(\omega)|^2 \propto |\omega|^{-\alpha} \tag{1}$$

where $\tilde{f}_H(\omega)$ is the Fourier transform of the fBm and $\alpha = 2H + 1$, [5,18,19] which is independent of the dimensionality N. Voss and Pentland [5,19] note the relation, $D_H = N + (1 - H)$, between the Hausdorff dimension[4] D_H of a N-D fBm $f_H(x)$ and the scaling exponent H. The estimation of α in (1) is, together with the relation between D_H and H, a well known method for estimation of the fractal dimension of images, [8].

Lindeberg [15,20] argues that in the case of N-dimensional natural images the assumption of a uniform energy distribution at all scales leads to a power spectrum proportional to $|\omega|^{-N}$. With reference to Field [1], Lindeberg utilizes the assertion that the power spectrum has equal energy at all scale-invariant frequency intervals. We find that this only coincides with $H = 1/2$ for 2D images, which is the case where the images can be modelled by classical Brownian motions. For Lindeberg's proportionality to hold for other values of H the value of H must be $H = \frac{N-1}{2}$ which only makes sense for $N < 3$, because of the constraint $0 < H < 1$. So in general we cannot assume that $|\tilde{f}_H(\omega)|^2 \propto |\omega|^{-N}$ under the assumption that N-D natural images can be modelled as fBms.

3   Scale-Space Scaling of Derivatives of Fractal Images

In this section we will first give a short introduction to the Gaussian scale-space and its normalized derivatives. Then we will state our proposal for an extension of Lindeberg's normalisation method based on the fractal dimension.

3.1   Scale-Space and Normalisation

Linear scale-space of images was independently introduced by Iijima [10], Witkin [11] and Koenderink [12]. The linear Gaussian scale-space of an image $L(x)$:

---

[4] The Hausdorff dimension can intuitively be viewed as a scaling exponent of the space filling of the graph in question.

$\mathbb{R}^N \mapsto \mathbb{R}$ can be defined as a solution to the diffusion equation, which is given by

$$L(x;t) = G(x;t) *_x L(x)$$

where t is the scaling parameter and the notation $*_x$ denotes convolution over x. $G(x;t) : \mathbb{R}^N \times \mathbb{R} \mapsto \mathbb{R}$ is the Gauss function

$$G(x;t) = \frac{1}{(2\pi\sigma^2)^{N/2}} \exp\left(-\frac{\|x\|_2^2}{2\sigma^2}\right)$$

where $t = \sigma^2$. The nth order partial derivative of an image in scale-space can be found as

$$\frac{\partial^n}{\partial x_i^n}(G(x;t) *_x L(x)) = \frac{\partial^n G(x;t)}{\partial x_i^n} *_x L(x)$$

where x_i denotes the ith element of x. In this paper we will in general use tensor notation and Einstein's summation convention when using image derivatives.

Normalisation of image derivatives has been proposed by several authors [15, 21, 14]. The standard normalisation of the nth image derivative in scale-space, based on dimensional analysis [14], is

$$L_{i_1 \cdots i_n, norm} = t^{n/2} L_{i_1 \cdots i_n},$$

which for the 1st order of derivation is the same as $(\partial/\partial x)_{norm} = \sigma\partial/\partial x$. Lindeberg proposes [15–17] another method of normalisation of image derivatives. He proposes that the nth order derivatives could be normalised as

$$L_{i_1 \cdots i_n, \gamma_n - norm} = t^{\gamma_n} L_{i_1 \cdots i_n}$$

where $\gamma_n = n\gamma/2$ and γ is a free normalisation parameter. In conjunction with feature detection Lindeberg has determined γ by an analysis of model patterns reflecting the features under consideration.

3.2 Scale-Space Normalisation Using the Fractal Dimension

We propose that γ_n can be stated as a relation of α (i.e. H), the topological dimension N of the image, and the order n of derivation. This is based on an assumption that images of natural scenes may be modelled as fBms and that *normalised* derivatives must have equal energy at all scales.

We will investigate quadratic differential image invariants on the form

$$I^{(n)} = L_{i_1 \cdots i_n} L_{i_1 \cdots i_n}.$$

We say that this kind of invariants are of the nth order of derivation. In the following we examine the L_1-norm of such invariants. This corresponds to looking at the L_2-norm of image derivatives. That is, we examine scaling of energy of image derivatives. Note furthermore that $\|I^{(n)}\|_1$ also equals the L_1-norm of any other invariant quadratic in L of total order of derivation $2n$ (see [22]).

Theorem 1. *If $f_H(x) : \mathbb{R}^N \mapsto \mathbb{R}$ is a N-D fBm and $L(x;t) : \mathbb{R}^N \times \mathbb{R} \mapsto \mathbb{R}$ is the scale-space of $f_H(x)$, then the nth order invariants $I^{(n)}(x;t)$ in this scale-space can be normalised to equal energy on all scales by the following relation*

$$I^{(n)}_{norm}(x;t) = t^{\gamma_n} I^{(n)}(x;t)$$

where $\gamma_n = -\alpha/2 + n + N/2$.

Proof. The proof is inspired by a similar analysis of the power spectrum of images of natural scenes by Lindeberg [15, 20]. By usage of Parseval's identity we find

$$\|I^{(n)}\|_1 = \int_{\omega \in \mathbb{R}^N} |\tilde{G}^2_{i_1 \cdots i_n}(\omega;t) \tilde{f}^2_H(\omega)| d\omega$$

$$= \int_{\omega \in \mathbb{R}^N} \left| \imath^n |\omega|^{2n} e^{-|\omega|^2 t} \tilde{f}^2_H(\omega) \right| d\omega$$

$$= \int_{\omega \in \mathbb{R}^N} e^{-|\omega|^2 t} |\omega|^{-\alpha+2n} d\omega,$$

where $\imath^2 = -1$, and $\tilde{f}_\alpha(\omega)$ and $\tilde{G}_{i_1 \cdots i_n}(\omega;t)$ respectively are the Fourier transformed image and the nth order differentiated Gaussian. Using

$$\int_0^\infty x^m e^{-ax^2} dx = \frac{\Gamma((m+1)/2)}{2a^{(m+1)/2}},$$

and introducing N-D spherical coordinates, we find

$$\int_{\rho \in [0,\infty[;\varphi_1,\ldots,\varphi_{N-1} \in [0,2\pi]} \rho^{-\alpha+2n+N-1} e^{-\rho^2 t} \cdot d\rho d\varphi_1 \cdots d\varphi_{N-1} =$$

$$(2\pi)^{N-1} \frac{\Gamma(-\frac{\alpha}{2} + n + \frac{N}{2})}{2t^{-\frac{\alpha}{2}+n+\frac{N}{2}}} = K \cdot t^{\frac{\alpha}{2}-n-\frac{N}{2}} = K \cdot t^{-\gamma_n},$$

where K is an arbitrary constant, and hereby we arrive at $\gamma_n = -\alpha/2 + n + N/2$. $\square$

The normalisation relation of Theorem 1 gives us a special case when handling the 0th order of derivation, meaning the case of the undifferentiated scale-space. That is, we scale-normalise the scale-space by an exponent introduced by the fractal dimension of the original image. After doing so, the normalisation of the nth order derivation is just the normalisation based on dimensional analysis. This special case of the 0th order of derivation comes from the fact that the fBm is the fractional derivative or integral of the Brownian motion.

A benefit of the proposed normalisation method is that the normalisation relation can be used as a method for estimation of the fractal dimension of images. This can be done by calculating the L_1-norm of a collection of differentiated scale-space images and then fit the logarithmic norm values to a straight line. We use this method in Sec. 4 to estimate the fractal dimension of synthetic and

Table 1. This table shows the measure of feature strength used by Lindeberg for feature detection with automatic scale selection using his γ-normalisation. We have calculated the corresponding values of H and D_H using our definition of γ. This table is a reproduction of a table from [17] with an extension of the columns for H, D_H and topological dimension T of the features. Note that a simple relation exists between the fractal dimension D_H and the topological dimension T. The relation between γ and T is not as straight forward.

Feature type	Normalized strength measure	γ	H	D_H	T
Edge	$t^{\gamma/2}L_v$	1/2	1	2	1
Ridge	$t^{2\gamma}(L_{pp} - L_{qq})^2$	3/4	1	2	1
Corner	$t^{2\gamma}L_v^2 L_{uu}$	1	1/2	2.5	0
Blob	$t^{\gamma}\nabla^2 L$	1	1/2	2.5	0

real images. We will not conduct a comparative study of this method and other methods for estimation of the fractal dimension of images (see [8] for a study of other methods), but merely point out the existence of the method.

In conjunction with feature detection, we must use the fractal dimension of the image in a neighbourhood of the feature of interest. This suggests a simple relation between the topological dimension of the feature and a suitable choice of fractal dimension. In Table 1 we have listed Lindeberg's [17] suggested normalized measures of feature strength. For each feature we have calculated the H and D_H values that correspond to his suggested γ values. It is interesting to notice that corners and blobs have a fractal dimension of 2.5 and edges and ridges only have a fractal dimension of 2. The topological dimension of corners and blobs is 0, while edges and ridges have a topological dimension of 1. Round a corner or a blob, we would expect the void hypothesis of $H = \frac{1}{2}$. This is not expected to be true in a neighbourhood of 1D features owned to the spatial extend and we see that Lindeberg's choice of γ leads us to the hypothesis of $H = 1$ for both 1D features.

4 Experiments

We have conducted several experiments on synthetic and real 2D images in order to study the normalisation of digitized images. We can as stated earlier use the normalisation method to find the fractal dimension of images by calculating unnormalized derivatives of the scale-space of the considered image. From this unnormalized scale-space we can estimate the value of γ and calculate the Hausdorff dimension D_H. In the same manner one can get estimates of the local fractal dimension at a point in the original image. The fractal dimension of a point could be viewed as a contradiction in terms, but it is never the less possible to assign some meaning to this concept due to the intrinsic property of scale-space: A point in scale-space correspond to a neighbourhood in the underlying image.

Table 2. These tables show our estimated γ values for synthetic images. The synthetic images used, and the corresponding graphs of the L_1-norm of L_iL_i and $L_{ij}L_{ji}$, are depicted in Fig. 1. The top table show the values for a 2-D image differentiated $n = 1$ times (L_iL_i) and the bottom table show the values for a 2-D image differentiated $n = 2$ times $(L_{ij}L_{ji})$. In each of the tables there are 4 synthetic images with different α values. The γ values are estimated by first constructing the synthetic image with the specified α parameter and then calculating a series of 10 differentiated scale-space images of ascending scales. For each of these 10 images we have calculated the L_1-norm, which can be seen in the graphs of Fig. 1. These graphs reveal an inaccuracy of the estimated L_1-norms at high scales, which is why we chose to use only the L_1-norms of the first 5 images of the scale-space ($\sigma \in [2.0; 6.7[$) for our estimation of γ. The γ value is estimated by calculating the logarithmic slope of the L_1-norms of the scale-space images. The slope is the estimated γ value. The reason why the estimated values of the synthetic images are not exact is because the images we used where small. That is, the span from the inner scale to the outer scale of the images are not sufficient to establish γ as a single global average over all scales. Note that, $\alpha = 2$ corresponds to a classical Brownian motion.

α	Estimated γ values	Actual γ values	Relative error
1	-1.57	-1.5	-4.46 %
2	-1.15	-1	-15.0 %
2.5	-0.96	-0.75	-28.0 %
3	-0.78	-0.5	-56.0 %
α	Estimated γ values	Actual γ values	Relative error
1	-2.55	-2.5	-2.0 %
2	-2.11	-2	-5.5 %
2.5	-1.89	-1.75	-8.0 %
3	-1.68	-1.5	-12.0 %

It is the authors opinion that in principal all theory of fractal measures may be reformulated in the inherently well-posed framework of linear scale-space theory, thereby easing operationalisation of fractal measures.

In Table 2 we show some results for small synthetic images (see the images in Fig. 1). The synthetic images used for these experiments were constructed in the frequency domain and were given a power spectrum proportional to $|\omega|^2$ and a random phase. We have calculated the L_1-norm of different images from two scale spaces of L_iL_i and $L_{ij}L_{ji}$ images. On this basis we have estimated the γ values for the synthetic images and compared them to the theoretical values from the continuous domain theory.

The method of finding the fractal dimension that we propose is fairly accurate on synthetic images of known fractal dimensions. From Table 2 we see that our method delivers an inaccurate result for increasing α values. The reason for this inaccuracy is that when the α value is increased, the synthetic image will have structure on an increasing scale and when the α value of the image becomes

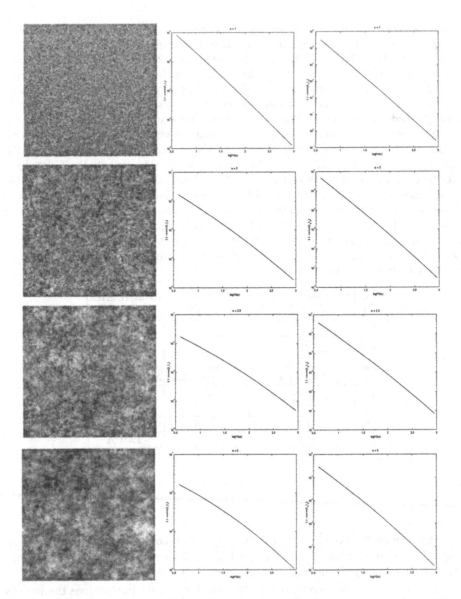

Fig. 1. In this figure we show the synthetic images with different α values and their corresponding graphs of the L_1-norm of $L_i L_i$ and $L_{ij} L_{ji}$ which we used for estimation of the γ values in Table 2. The synthetic images all have 256×256 pixels and $\alpha = 1, 2, 2.5, 3$ from the top down. The L_1-norm graphs were produced by calculating a scale space for the two set of derivatives. This scale space has 10 different scales between $\sigma = 2$ and $\sigma = 30$ with exponential growing increments. On the graphs it can be seen that high scales makes the estimate of the L_1-norm inaccurate, i.e. the estimate become too small. The reason for this inaccuracy is discretisation effects introduced by the outer scale of the image.

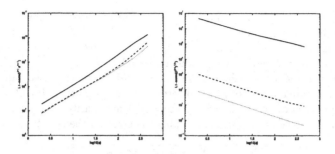

Fig. 2. We have calculated the invariants $L_i L_i$, $L_{ij} L_{ji}$ and $L_{ijk} L_{kji}$ scale-space images of the garden image from Fig. 3. These graphs show the L_1-norm of $I^{(n)} t^{n+1}$ and $(I^{(n)})^{1/n}$ of these 3 scale-space invariants. The solid lines corresponds to $L_i L_i$, the dashed lines to $L_{ij} L_{ji}$ and the dotted lines to $L_{ijk} L_{kji}$. The estimated slopes are for $I^{(n)} t^{n+1}$, $\gamma = 1.13, 1.10, 1.12$ ($n = 1, 2, 3$), and for $(I^{(n)})^{1/n}$, $\gamma = -0.87, -0.95, -0.96$ ($n = 1, 2, 3$).

large enough the outer scale of the large structures will exceed the outer scale of the image thereby misleading our method. Furthermore our results are biased by spectral leakage, because artificial periods is introduced into the images by the Fourier Transform. It can also be seen from Table 2 that when we increase the order of differentiation we also increases the accuracy of the method. The reason for this is that when we derive our image we enhance the fine structure of the image by effectively looking at a scale interval, which has been moved towards smaller scales. In real examples, image noise from the capture device will exhibit another structure than the random process of the scene. In general this is more uncorrelated noise, and a scale interval of smaller scales will exhibit structure merely from the capture device. That is, we must choose an appropriate scale if we wish to measure scale characteristics.

We expect a logarithmic relation between the scale and $\|I^{(n)}\|_1$. From Table 2 and Fig. 1 we can see that our proposed method for normalisation is quite reasonable for synthetic images. In order to examine our method on real images, we have calculated the L_1-norm of invariants of increasing order of differentiation of the garden image from Fig. 3. We have normalised the calculated invariants by $I^{(n)} t^{n+1}$, which corresponds to our normalisation method, and $(I^{(n)})^{1/n}$, which corresponds to the standard normalisation method, in order to examine the scaling property of the image independently of the order of derivation. The slope of the logarithmic plot corresponds to γ and we would expect that this slope should be approximately the same for all orders of derivation only for our normalisation method $I^{(n)} t^{n+1}$. The results can be viewed in Fig. 2. From this figure it can be concluded that our normalisation method seems as a reasonable choice, but we can also see that the γ of the standard normalisation method for this image is fairly independent of the order of derivation. This inconclusive experiment therefore calls for a thorough evaluation of the scaling properties of a large ensemble of images of natural scenes.

Table 3. This table show our estimated γ values and the corresponding H and Hausdorff dimension D_H. The values of H were calculated through $H = n + \frac{N}{2} - \gamma - \frac{1}{2}$ and the values of D_H were calculated through $D_H = N + (1 - H)$. The dimension of the images were $N = 2$ and they were differentiated by $L_{ij} L_{ji}$ ($n = 2$). The γ values were estimated in the same fashion as in table 2 and the images used can be seen in Fig. 3. The estimated values of D_H indicates the same results as Bialek [6] that the Hausdorff dimension of images of natural scenes not necessarily are close to $D_H = 2.5$. Unfortunately we have no way of determining the error on the results in this table.

Title	Estimated γ values	H	D_H
Garden	-1.90	0.60	2.40
X-rayed bone	-1.62	0.88	2.12
Water Lilly	-1.53	0.97	2.03
Sea weed	-1.98	0.52	2.48
Grains of sand	-2.09	0.41	2.59
Satellite clouds	-1.89	0.61	2.39
Landscape	-1.75	0.75	2.25
Trees	-1.82	0.68	2.32

We have also tried to estimate the Hausdorff dimension of some 2-D images of natural scenes. The results can be viewed in table 3.

5 Conclusion

We have related Lindeberg's [15–17] scale-space normalisation method to the notion of fractal dimension, assuming that images of natural scenes can be modelled by fractal Brownian motions and we propose that feature strength measures are normalized using the Hausdorff dimension of the local image.

We have found a normalisation expression that has the Hausdorff dimension as a parameter. Through this expression we have also found a relation between the topological dimension and the fractal dimension of the local image round a feature (see Table 1). We conjecture (for future experimental testing):

The topological dimension of the feature uniquely determines the scale-space normalisation parameter.

We propose a further investigation into the relation between different features and their Hausdorff dimension. It would be interesting to see whether it is possible to generalize the results described in table 1 and further establish a general relation between the topological dimension of features and the fractal dimension locally in the image. Furthermore we suggest a thorough investigation of the scaling properties of images of natural scenes using a large ensemble of images.

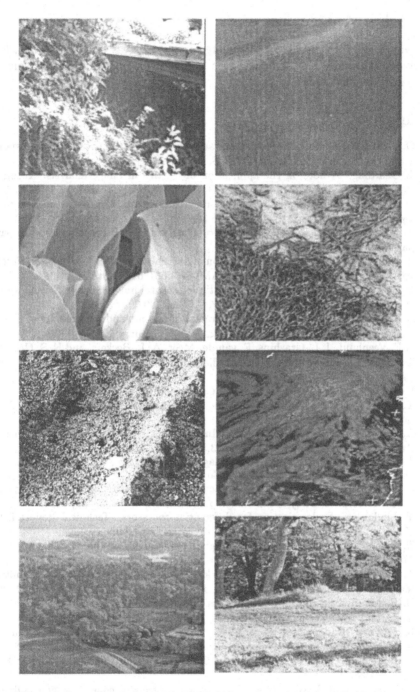

Fig. 3. Here we have shown the images for which we have estimated the fractal dimension (see table 3). All images are gray level images and the first six images all have 256×256 pixels and the last two have 512×512 pixels. We have called the images from the top left corner going in the reading direction; Garden, X-rayed bone, Water Lilly, Sea weed, Grains of sand, Satellite clouds, Landscape and Trees.

6 Acknowledgements

We would like to thank Tony Lindeberg for inspiring us to do this work. Furthermore we would like to thank Peter Johansen for his comments on some of the theory of this paper.

References

1. D. J. Field. Relations between the statistics of natural images and the response proporties of cortical cells. *J. Optic. Soc. Am.*, 4(12):2379–2394, Dec. 1987.
2. J. Gaarding. A note on the application of fractals in image analysis. Technical Report TRITA-NA-P8716 CVAP 49, Royal Institute of Technology, Dec. 1987.
3. D. C. Knill, D. Field, and D. Kersten. Human discrimination of fractal images. *J. Optic. Soc. Am.*, 7(6):1113–1123, June 1990.
4. B. B. Mandelbrot. *The fractal geometry of nature.* W. H. Freeman and company, San Francisco, 1982.
5. A. P. Pentland. Fractal-based desciption of natural scenes. *IEEE Trans. on Pattern Analysis and Machine Intelligence*, PAMI-6(6):661–674, November 1984.
6. D. L. Ruderman and W. Bialek. Statistics of natural images: Scaling in the woods. *Physical Review Letters*, 73(6):814–817, August 1994.
7. N. L. Fazzalari and I. H. Parkinson. Fractal dimension and architecture of trabecular bone. *Journal of Pathology*, 82(1):100–105, January 1996.
8. J. F. Veenland, J. L. Grashius, F. van der Meer, A. L. Beckers, and E. S. Gelsema. Estimation of fractal dimension in radiographs. *Med. Phys.*, 82(4):585–594, April 1996.
9. E. Ott. *Chaos in dynamical systems.* Cambridge University Press, 1993.
10. T. Iijima. Basic theory on normalization of a pattern. *Bulletin of Electrical Laboratory*, 26:368–388, 1962. In Japanese.
11. A. P. Witkin. Scale space filtering. In *Proc. International Joint Conference on Artificial Intelligence*, pages 1019–1023, Karlsruhe, Germany, 1983.
12. J. J. Koenderink. The structure of images. *Biol. Cybern.*, 50:363–370, 1984.
13. D. Marr. *Vision.* W. H. Freeman & Co., 1882.
14. L. M. J. Florack, B. M. ter Haar Romeny, J. J. Koenderink, and M. A. Viergever. Linear scalespace. *J. of Math. Imaging and Vision*, 4(4):325–351, 1994.
15. T. Lindeberg. Scale selection for differential operators. Technical Report ISRN KTH/NA/P–9403-SE, Royal Institute of Technology, January 1994.
16. T. Lindeberg. Edge detection and ridge detection with automatic scale selection. *IJCV*, 30(2):117–156, 1998.
17. T. Lindeberg. Scale-space: A framework for handling image structures at multiple scales. Technical Report CVAP-TN15, Royal Institute of Technology, Sep. 1996.
18. B. B. Mandelbrot and J. W. van Ness. Fractional brownian motions, fractional noises and applications. *SIAM Review*, 10(4):422–437, October 1968.
19. R. F. Voss. Random fractal forgeries. In R. A. Earnshaw, editor, *Fundamental Algorithms for Computer Graphics*, volume 17, pages 805–835. Springer, 1985.
20. T. Lindeberg. *Scale-Space Theory in Computer Vision.* Kluwer Academic Publishers, 1994.
21. J. H. Elder and S. W. Zucker. Local scale control for edge detection and blur estimation. In B. Baxton and R. Cipolla, editors, *ECCV'96*, pages 57–69. Springer, 1996.
22. M. Nielsen, L. Florack, and R. Deriche. Regularization, scale-space, and edge detection filters. *Journal of Mathematical Imaging and Vision*, (7):291–307, 1997.

Lattice Boltzmann Models for Nonlinear Diffusion Filtering*

Björn Jawerth[1], Peng Lin[1], and Eric Sinzinger[2]

[1] Dept. of Mathematics, Univ. of South Carolina, Columbia, SC 29208, USA
[2] Dept. of Computer Science, Univ. of South Carolina, Columbia, SC 29208, USA

Abstract. The lattice Boltzmann method has attracted more and more attention as an alternative numerical scheme to traditional numerical methods for solving partial differential equations and modeling physical systems. The idea of the lattice Boltzmann method is to construct a simplified discrete microscopic dynamics to simulate the macroscopic model described by the partial differential equations. In this paper, we present the lattice Boltzmann models for nonlinear diffusion filtering. We show that image feature selective smoothing can be achieved by making the relaxation parameter in the lattice Boltzmann equation be image feature and direction dependent. The models naturally lead to the numerical algorithms that are easy to implement. Experimental results on both synthetic and real images are described.

1   Introduction

Broadly speaking, there are two ways to use computers to make progress in understanding physical phenomenon. The first approach is to use computers as a tool to solve the partial differential equations (PDE's) that describe the macroscopic model. In this approach, the computers are used to treat the mathematical equations not directly the physical phenomenon. As the equstions become more and more complicate, the task for solving these equations becomes more and more diffficult. The second approach is to use computers as a kind of experimental laboratory, to simulate the phenomenon of interest. The idea is to design a synthetic model in which the physical laws are expressed in terms of simple local rules on a discrete space-time structure. Such models include so called lattice gas automata (LGA) and the more recent lattice Boltzmann (LB) models in fluid dynamics.

In lattice gas and lattice Boltzmann models, particles hop from site to site on a lattice at each tick of a clock. When particles meet they collide, but they always stay on the grid and appropriate physical quantities are always conserved. The long time evolution of this discrete microscopic dynamics is able to reproduce the complex physical phenomena investigated. The advantage of lattice gas and lattice Boltzmann methods is that they provide insight into the microscopic

* The research of the authors was supported by ARO Grant DAA HO 49610326, ONR Grant N00014-90-J1343, and DEPSCoR Grant N00014-97-10806.

process and easily implemented highly parallel algorithms and that they have the capability of handling complicated boundary and initial conditions.

The use of the lattice Boltzmann method has allowed the study of a broad class of systems that would have been difficult by other means. An example is flow through porous media [4]. In recent years, the adoption of the Bhatnagar-Gross-Krook (BGK) collision operator [10] in the lattice Boltzmann calculations has made the lattice Boltzmann model computationally more efficient.

In this work we apply the lattice Boltzmann method to image processing, especially to nonlinear anisotropic diffusion of images. Anisotropic diffusion has been extensively used as an efficient nonlinear filtering technique in image processing. A considerable amount of research has been done in this area during the last decade [1–3, 9, 5, 6, 12]. For a complete list of references and an overview of nonlinear diffusion filtering see [13].

In this paper, we report the lattice Boltzmann models presented in [7] for nonlinear diffusion filtering. We also present a lattice Boltzmann model for image smoothing by reaction-diffusion. We show that image feature selective smoothing can be achieved by making the relaxation parameter in the lattice Boltzmann equation be image feature (e.g., edge) and direction dependent.

The paper is organized as follows. In Section 2 we give a brief introduction to the general lattice Boltzmann model. Section 3 describes the lattice Boltzmann model for nonlinear isotropic diffusion filtering. In Section 4, we discuss the lattice Boltzmann model for anisotropic diffusion filtering. Next, in Section 5 we present the lattice Boltzmann model for reaction-diffusion filtering. Experimental results are shown in Section 6. We conclude with a summary in Section 7.

2 The General Lattice Boltzmann Model

In general, lattice Boltzmann model is built with a lattice together with the lattice vectors e_α ($\alpha = 0, 1, \cdots, b$). On each node there are a set of particle distribution functions $\{f_\alpha\}$ ($\alpha = 0, 1, \cdots, b$), with each f_α corresponding to the vector direction e_α. e_α can be considered as the particle velocity. Usually e_0 denotes the rest particles. The microscopic dynamics consists of two steps: translation from node to node along direction e_α and redistribution of the particle density at each node during the collision step. These two steps are described by the following lattice Boltzmann equation

$$f_\alpha(x + e_\alpha, t + 1) = f_\alpha(x, t) + \Omega_\alpha(x, t), \quad (\alpha = 0, 1, \cdots, b), \tag{1}$$

where $\Omega_\alpha(x, t)$ is the collision operator which depends on the distribution functions f_α.

Usually, the only restrictions on the collision operator $\Omega_\alpha(x, t)$ are that it conserves mass,

$$\sum_{\alpha=0}^{b} \Omega_\alpha(x, t) = 0, \tag{2}$$

and that it conserves momentum,

$$\sum_{\alpha=0}^{b} \mathbf{e}_\alpha \Omega_\alpha(\mathbf{x}, t) = 0. \tag{3}$$

The mass $m(\mathbf{x}, t)$ (or other quantity for different problem of interest) at position $\mathbf{x}$ and time t is given by

$$m(\mathbf{x}, t) = \sum_{\alpha=0}^{b} f_\alpha(\mathbf{x}, t). \tag{4}$$

By adopting the simple lattice-BGK model [10], the collision term Ω_α in (1) can be replaced by the single-time-relaxation approximation, $\Omega_\alpha = -(f_\alpha - f_\alpha^{eq})/\tau$, and (1) becomes

$$f_\alpha(\mathbf{x} + \mathbf{e}_\alpha, t+1) = f_\alpha(\mathbf{x}, t) - \frac{f_\alpha(\mathbf{x}, t) - f_\alpha^{eq}(\mathbf{x}, t)}{\tau}, \quad (\alpha = 0, 1, \cdots, b), \tag{5}$$

where $f_\alpha^{eq}(\mathbf{x}, t)$ denotes the appropriately chosen local equilibrium distribution functions, and τ is the relaxation time which controls the rate of approach to equilibrium. τ must be chosen greater than $1/2$ to ensure numerical stability [10].

On one hand, the lattice Boltzmann models can be used as PDE solvers. By chosing appropriate collision operator or equilibrium distribution, the lattice Boltzmann model is able to recover the PDE of interest. On the other hand, the lattice Boltzmann models can be used as simulators. By specifying the microscopic collision rules, the lattice Boltzmann model can directly simulate the under-investigated phenomena. The microscopic approach in the lattice Boltzmann model provides clear physical pictures, easy implementation of boundaries and fully parallel algorithms.

3   LB Model for Nonlinear Isotropic Diffusion Filtering

For two-dimensional discrete image of size $M \times M$, the image domain can be naturally considered to be a square lattice. In this paper, we use the 9-velocity model for square lattice with the velocity vectors,

$$\mathbf{e}_\alpha = \begin{cases} (0, 0) & \alpha = 0 \\ (\cos[2\pi(\alpha - 1)/8], \sin[2\pi(\alpha - 1)/8]) & \alpha = 1, 3, 5, 7 \\ \sqrt{2}(\cos[2\pi(\alpha - 1)/8], \sin[2\pi(\alpha - 1)/8]) & \alpha = 2, 4, 6, 8, \end{cases} \tag{6}$$

where $\mathbf{e}_0$ corresponds to the rest particles which have speed 0. Here the quantity that we are intersted in is the image intensity $I(\mathbf{x}, t)$ instead of the mass at position $\mathbf{x}$ and time t. Parallel to the general LB model described in Section 2, we have at some time t and position $\mathbf{x}$ the particle distribution functions $I_\alpha(\mathbf{x}, t)$ ($\alpha = 0, 1, \cdots, 8$), which can be imagined as the amount of the intensity moving into the direction $\mathbf{e}_\alpha$. Corresponding to (4), we have

$$I(\mathbf{x}, t) = \sum_{\alpha=0}^{8} I_\alpha(\mathbf{x}, t). \tag{7}$$

We will use the lattice-BGK model (5). In order to achieve the selective smoothing of image, we make the relaxation parameter τ to be space, time, and image feature (edge) dependent, i.e.,

$$\tau(\mathbf{x}, t) = \phi(|\nabla G_\sigma * I|), \tag{8}$$

where ϕ is some positive nonincreasing function, and

$$G_\sigma(\mathbf{x}) = \frac{1}{2\pi\sigma^2} \exp\left(-\frac{\mathbf{x}^2}{2\sigma^2}\right) \tag{9}$$

is the Gaussian kernel.

We choose the local equilibrium distribution functions $I_\alpha^{eq}(\mathbf{x}, t)$ as follows:

$$I_\alpha^{eq}(\mathbf{x}, t) = c_\alpha I(\mathbf{x}, t), \tag{10}$$

where the distribution factors c_α's are defined by

$$c_\alpha = \begin{cases} \frac{4}{9} & \alpha = 0 \\ \frac{1}{9} & \alpha = 1, 3, 5, 7 \\ \frac{1}{36} & \alpha = 2, 4, 6, 8. \end{cases} \tag{11}$$

Note that $\sum_{\alpha=0}^{8} c_\alpha = 1$.

The evolution of I_α ($\alpha = 0, 1, \cdots, 8$) is then governed by the following lattice Boltzmann equation

$$I_\alpha(\mathbf{x} + \mathbf{e}_\alpha, t+1) = I_\alpha(\mathbf{x}, t) - \frac{I_\alpha(\mathbf{x}, t) - I_\alpha^{eq}(\mathbf{x}, t)}{\phi(|\nabla G_\sigma * I|)}, \quad (\alpha = 0, 1, \cdots, 8). \tag{12}$$

From Section 2 we know that the relaxation parameter τ must be greater than $1/2$ to ensure numerical stability. Therefore the nonincreasing function ϕ must be chosen such that $\phi(|\nabla G_\sigma * I|) > 1/2$. One possible choice of $\phi(|\nabla G_\sigma * I|)$ is

$$\phi(|\nabla G_\sigma * I|) = \frac{1}{2} + \frac{C}{1 + |\nabla G_\sigma * I|^2} \quad \text{for some positive constant } C. \tag{13}$$

Using the so-called Chapman-Enskog expansion we showed in [7] that the long time behavior of the LB model described above recovers the following type of nonlinear isotropic diffusion equation

$$\partial_t I = \text{div}(g(|\nabla G_\sigma * I|)\nabla I). \tag{14}$$

Equation (14) was proposed in [2] as an improvement of the Perona-Malik model [9]. In [2] and [9] the function g is chosen as some positive nonincreasing function vanishing at infinite.

The relation between the diffusion coefficient g in the diffusion equation (14) and the relaxation parameter ϕ in the LB equation (12) is

$$g(|\nabla G_\sigma * I|) = \frac{4}{9}(\phi(|\nabla G_\sigma * I|) - \frac{1}{2}). \tag{15}$$

4   LB Model for Anisotropic Diffusion Filtering

In order to achieve anisotropic diffusion, we need to make the relaxation parameter τ also depend on the direction vectors $\mathbf{e}_\alpha$ ($\alpha = 0, 1, \cdots, 8$),

$$\tau(\mathbf{x}, t, \alpha) = \phi_\alpha(\nabla G_\sigma * I). \tag{16}$$

We can use the same equilibrium distribution functions as in Section 3,

$$I_\alpha^{eq}(\mathbf{x}, t) = c_\alpha I(\mathbf{x}, t), \tag{17}$$

where the c_α's are the same as in Section 3. But if we still use the same LB equation (12), the total mass (intensity in our case) will not be conserved. To fix this problem, the natural approach is to choose different equilibrium distribution functions; an alternative way is to simply add another term to the equation [8]. We will follow the approach in [8]. In this case the lattice Boltzmann equation becomes

$$I_\alpha(\mathbf{x} + \mathbf{e}_\alpha, t+1) = I_\alpha(\mathbf{x}, t) - \frac{I_\alpha(\mathbf{x}, t) - I_\alpha^{eq}(\mathbf{x}, t)}{\phi_\alpha(\nabla G_\sigma * I)} + \tilde{\Omega}_\alpha, \tag{18}$$

where

$$\tilde{\Omega}_\alpha = c_\alpha \sum_{\beta=0}^{8} \frac{I_\beta(\mathbf{x}, t) - I_\beta^{eq}(\mathbf{x}, t)}{\phi_\beta(\nabla G_\sigma * I)}, \tag{19}$$

which is added in equation (18) for mass (intensity) conservation.

As in Section 3, we also have

$$I(\mathbf{x}, t) = \sum_{\alpha=0}^{8} I_\alpha(\mathbf{x}, t). \tag{20}$$

The relaxation parameter functions $\phi_\alpha(\nabla G_\sigma * I)$ ($\alpha = 0, 1, \cdots, 8$) in (18) are some nonincreasing functions of some kind of quantities of $\nabla G_\sigma * I$. Again, $\phi_\alpha(\nabla G_\sigma * I)$ must be greater than $1/2$ to ensure numerical stability. In order to keep with the symmetry of the lattice ($\mathbf{e}_\alpha = \mathbf{e}_{\alpha+4}$), we will require $\phi_\alpha = \phi_{\alpha+4}$. One possible choice of $\phi_\alpha(\nabla G_\sigma * I)$ is

$$\phi_\alpha(\nabla G_\sigma * I) = \frac{1}{2} + \frac{C}{1 + |\langle \mathbf{e}_\alpha, \nabla G_\sigma * I \rangle|^2} \quad \text{for some positive constant } C. \tag{21}$$

In [7] we showed that the long time evolution of $I(\mathbf{x}, t) = \sum_{\alpha=0}^{8} I_\alpha(\mathbf{x}, t)$ according to the LB equation (18) recovers the following nonlinear anisotropic diffusion equation

$$\partial_t I = \text{div}(D\nabla I),\qquad(22)$$

where D is the diffusion tensor with

$$D_{ij} = \sum_{\alpha=0}^{8}(\phi_\alpha(\nabla G_\sigma * I) - \frac{1}{2})c_\alpha e_{\alpha i}e_{\alpha j}.\qquad(23)$$

Nonlinear anisotropic diffusion filtering by equation (22) with different diffusion tensors has been studied in [12] and [3]. Some applications have been presented in [11].

Equation (21) only gives one possible choice of the relaxation parameter $\phi_\alpha(\nabla G_\sigma * I)$. For different purpose of filtering, one can use different form of $\phi_\alpha(\nabla G_\sigma * I)$.

5   LB Model for Reaction-Diffusion Filtering

In this section we propose the lattice Boltzmann model for reaction-diffusion filtering.

For diffusion based filtering, one can also use reaction-diffusion equation instead of pure diffusion equation:

$$\partial_t I = \text{div}(g(|\nabla G_\sigma * I|)\nabla I) + \mu(I_0 - I)\qquad(24)$$

where I_0 is the original image. The advantage of adding a reaction term is that it provides a nontrivial steady state, therefore eliminates the problem of choosing a stopping time in using pure diffusion equation. But the trade off is that one has to determine μ.

In this section we use the same notations as those in Section 3. To get the LB model for the reaction-diffusion equation (24), we simply add another term to equation (12) resulting in the following LB equation:

$$I_\alpha(\mathbf{x}+\mathbf{e}_\alpha, t+1) = I_\alpha(\mathbf{x}, t) - \frac{I_\alpha(\mathbf{x}, t) - I_\alpha^{eq}(\mathbf{x}, t)}{\phi(|\nabla G_\sigma * I|)} + c_\alpha\gamma(I_0(\mathbf{x}, t) - I(\mathbf{x}, t))\quad(25)$$

where $\phi(|\nabla G_\sigma * I|)$ is the same as in Section 3 and γ is a parameter controlling the reaction speed. As in Section 3 and 4, we use the LB equation (25) to update I_α ($\alpha = 0, 1, \cdots, 8$), use

$$I(\mathbf{x}, t) = \sum_{\alpha=0}^{8} I_\alpha(\mathbf{x}, t)\qquad(26)$$

to update I, and use

$$I_\alpha^{eq}(\mathbf{x}, t) = c_\alpha I(\mathbf{x}, t)\qquad(27)$$

as the equilibrium distribution functions.

Using a similar procedure as in [7], one can derive the macroscopic equation (24) from the lattice Boltzmann equation (25) and equation (26).

6 Numerical Experiments

The implementations of our LB models are straightforward. Once an initial image $I(\mathbf{x}, 0)$ is given, we use $c_\alpha I(\mathbf{x}, 0)$ ($\alpha = 0, 1, \cdots, 8$) as the initial values for the LB equations, where c_α's are given by (11). The relaxation parameters $\phi(|\nabla G_\sigma * I|)$ and $\phi_\alpha(\nabla G_\sigma * I)$ are calculated using the corresponding equations given in Section 3 and 4 respectively. The equilibrium distribution functions $I_\alpha^{eq}(\mathbf{x}, t)$ are calculated using equation (10). I_α ($\alpha = 0, 1, \cdots, 8$) are updated by the LB equations (12), (18), and (25) for different models in Section 3, 4, and 5 respectively. After getting the updated I_α, I is updated by equation (7). Then start the next iteration.

Figure 1 shows a synthetic image (256 × 256) with 35% of the pixels are degraded and its "cleaned" version by the LB model in Sction 3 with $\phi(|\nabla G_\sigma * I|) = 0.5 + 50/(1 + |\nabla G_\sigma * I|^2)$ ($\sigma = 1$) and 60 iterations. Figure 2 shows the same synthetic image with 70% of the pixels are degraded and its "cleaned" version by the LB model in Section 4 with $\phi_\alpha(\nabla G_\sigma * I) = 0.5 + 25/(1 + |\langle e_\alpha, \nabla G_\sigma * I \rangle|^2)$ ($\sigma = 1$) and 90 iterations. Figure 3 shows an enlarged detail (256 × 256) of an original infrared airborne radar image and its processed version by the LB model in Section 3 with $\phi(|\nabla G_\sigma * I|) = 0.5 + 25/(1 + |\nabla G_\sigma * I|^2)$ ($\sigma = 1$) and 12 iterations. Figure 4 shows a part of an original airborne Doppler radar image (256 × 256) and its processed version by the LB model in Section 4 with $\phi_\alpha(\nabla G_\sigma * I) = 0.56 + 10/(1 + |\langle e_\alpha, \nabla G_\sigma * I \rangle|^2)$ ($\sigma = 1$) and 65 iterations.

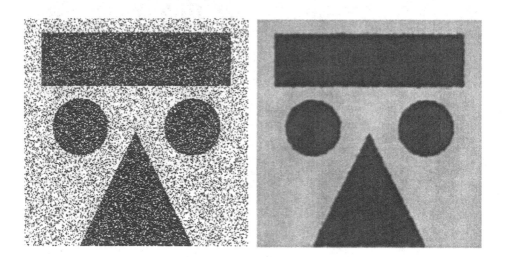

Fig. 1. A synthetic image (256 × 256) with 35% of the pixels are degraded (left) and its "cleaned" version by the LB model in Section 3 with 60 iterations (right).

Figure 5 shows an original image (256 × 256) with added Gaussian noise with

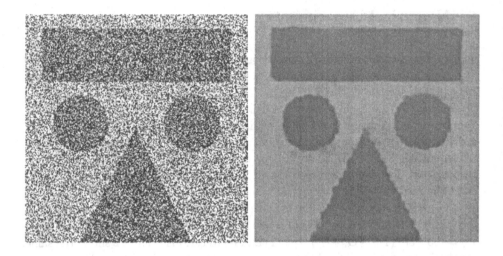

Fig. 2. A synthetic image (256 × 256) with 70% of the pixels are degraded (left) and its "cleaned" version by the LB model in Sction 4 with 90 iterations (right).

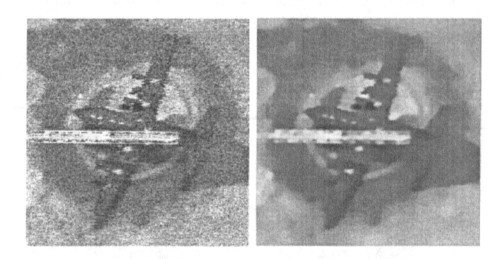

Fig. 3. An enlarged detail (256 × 256) of an original infrared airborne radar image (left) and its processed version by the LB model in Section 3 with 12 iterations (right).

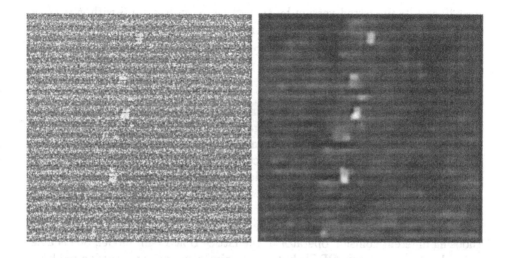

Fig. 4. A part of an original airborne Doppler radar image (256×256) (left) and its processed version by the LB model in Section 4 with 65 iterations (renormalized) (right).

Fig. 5. An original image (256×256) with added Gaussian noise with $\sigma = 30$ (left) and its processed version by the LB model in Section 5 (renormalized) (right).

$\sigma = 30$ and its processed version by the LB model in Section 5 with $\phi(|\nabla G_\sigma * I|) = 0.5 + 30/(1 + |\nabla G_\sigma * I|^2)$ ($\sigma = 1$) and $\gamma = 0.03$.

7 Concluding Remarks

In this paper, we have described the lattice Boltzmann models for nonlinear diffusion filtering. We have shown that image feature selective smoothing can be achieved by making the relaxation parameter in the lattice Boltzmann equation be image feature (e.g., edge) and direction dependent. The advantage of the lattice Boltzmann model is that it provides insight into the microscopic process and easily implemented highly parallel algorithms. We believe that the lattice Boltzmann method is also very helpful in exploring new models. By choosing different equilibrium distribution in the lattice BGK model or more generally choosing different collision operator in the lattice Boltzmann model, one is able not only to recover some PDE's but also to give new image processing models.

References

1. Alvarez, L., Guichard, F., Lions, P.-L., Morel, J.-M.: Axioms and fundamental equations in image processing. Arch. Rat. Mech. Anal. **123** (1993) 199–257
2. Catté, F., Lions, P.-L., Morel, J.-M., Coll, T.: Image selective smoothing and edge detection by nonlinear diffusion. SIAM J. Num. Anal. **29** (1992) 182–193
3. Cottet, G.-H., Ayyadi, M. EL: Nonlinear PDE operators with memory terms for image processing. Proc. IEEE Int. Conf. Image Processing (ICP-96, Lausanne, Sept. 16-19, 1996) **78** (1996) 481–483
4. Gunstensen, A. K., Rothman, D. H.: Lattice-Boltzmann studies of two-phase flow through porous media. J. Geophys. Res. **98** (1993) 6431–6441
5. Haar Romeny, B.M. ter (Ed.): Geometry-driven diffusion in Computer Vision. Kluwer, Dordrecht (1994)
6. Haar Romeny, B.M. ter, Florack, L., Koenderink, J., Viergever (Eds.), M.: Scale-Space Theory in Computer Vision. Springer (1997)
7. Jawerth, B., Lin, P., Sinzinger, E.: Lattice Boltzmann models for anisotropic diffusion of images. Journal of Mathematical Imaging and Vision (to appear)
8. Maillot, B., Main, I. G.: A Lattice BGK model for the diffusion of pore fluid pressure, including anisotropy, heterogeneity, and gravity effects. Geophys. Res. Lett. **23** (1996) 13–16
9. Perona, P. and Malik, J.: Scale-space and edge detection using anisotropic diffusion. IEEE Trans. Pattern Anal. Machine Intell. **12** (1990) 629–639
10. Qian, Y. H., d'Humières, D., Lallemand, P.: Lattice BGK models for Navier-Stokes equation. Europhys. Lett. **17** (1992) 479–484
11. Weickert, J.: Anisotropic diffusion filters for image processing based quality control. A. Fasano, M. Primicerio (Eds.), Proc. Seventh European Conf. on Mathematics in Industry. Teubner, Stuttgart (1994) 355–362
12. Weickert, J.: Multiscale texture enhancement. V. Hlaváč, R. Šára (Eds.), Computer analysis of images and patterns, Lecture Notes in Comp. Science **970** Springer, Berlin (1995) 230–237

13. Weickert, J.: A review of nonlinear diffusion filtering. B.M. ter Haar Romeny, L. Florack, J. Koenderink, and M. Viergever(Eds.), Scale-Space Theory in Computer Vision, Springer (1997) 3–28

Geometric-Variational Approach for Color Image Enhancement and Segmentation

Ron Kimmel[1] and Nir A. Sochen[2]

[1] CS Department, Technion - Israel Institute of Technology
Technion City, Haifa 32000, ISRAEL
ron@cs.technion.ac.il,
WWW home page: http://www.cs.technion.ac.il/~ron
[2] EE Department, Technion - Israel Institute of Technology
Technion City, Haifa 32000, ISRAEL
sochen@ee.technion.ac.il

Abstract. *We merge techniques developed in the Beltrami framework to deal with multi-channel, i.e. color images, and the Mumford-Shah functional for segmentation. The result is a color image enhancement and segmentation algorithm. The generalization of the Mumford-Shah idea includes a higher dimension and codimension and a novel smoothing measure for the color components and for the segmenting function which is introduced via the Γ-convergence approach. We use the Γ-convergence technique to derive, through the gradient descent method, a system of coupled PDEs for the color coordinates and for the segmenting function.*

1 Introduction

Segmentation is one of the important tasks of image analysis and much efforts have been consecrated to solve it. One can roughly classify the segmentation methods into two classes: 1) Global, i.e. histogram based techniques, and 2) Local, i.e. edge based techniques. In the second class it was shown that a large number of algorithms, including different region growing methods coupled with edge detection based techniques, are closely related to the Mumford-Shah functional minimization [11]. This functional involves an interplay between an image, which is a two dimensional object, and the contours that surround the objects in the image, which are one-dimensional curves. This functional was first suggested and analyzed by Mumford and Shah for gray-level images in [12]. It was later extensively studied, see e.g. [11] for an overview.

In particular, the Γ-convergence framework [1–3, 15] was invented to overcome the problem of dealing with objects with different dimensionalities in the same functional. In the Γ-convergence framework, one replaces the functional by a different, parameter dependent, functional. The parameter controls the degree of approximation, such that the approximating functional is equal to the Mumford-Shah functional in the limit, as the parameter goes to zero. In the approximating functional, the edge contours are replaced by a two-dimensional function which is close in shape to an edge indicator with certain smoothness around the edges. The degree of smoothness depends on the approximation parameter, and the function approaches a Dirac delta function for the edges, as the approximation parameter approaches zero.

In this study we address the question of the generalization of this approach to color images. Methods that disregard the coupling between the spectral channels give up important information given by the correlation between the color channels. Moreover, there is an underlying assumption in the Mumford-Shah model of the smoothness of the image in the non-boundary regions, which is formulated through an L_2 measure. It is known, though, that the L_1 performs better as an adaptive smoothing measure [17]. It is desirable, therefor, to incorporate the L_1 norm or another adaptive smoothing scheme in the Mumford-Shah formulation for the segmentation problem. Recently, it was shown [19] that the Beltrami framework provides a proper generalization of the L_1 norm from gray-level to color images.

In the Beltrami framework, an image is treated as a two-dimensional Riemannian surface, restricted as a graph, embedded in a higher dimensional spatial-feature space. A grey-level image is embedded in $\mathbb{R}^3$ whose coordinates are (x, y, I) and it is simply the graph of the intensity function $I(x, y)$. Similarly, a color image is embedded in a five-dimensional space whose coordinates are (x, y, R, G, B). The induced metric of these surfaces is easily extracted and a measure, known as the Polyakov action in high-energy physics, is used as a generalization of the L_2 norm to any dimension and codimension, and for any geometry of the surface and of the embedding space. We and others have shown that this "geometric L_2" norm interpolates via a scaling parameter between the conventional, i.e. flat L_1 and L_2 norms for gray level images. It interpolates, for color images, between the flat L_2 and a different norm, which is interpreted as the proper generalization of the Euclidean L_1 norm for color images [9, 6].

Our current study merges the Γ-convergence technique and the Beltrami framework for color images to yield a color and smoothing generalization for the Mumford-Shah segmentation functional.

The paper is organized as follows: In Section 2 we briefly review the Γ-convergence and its application for the gray-level image segmentation. Section 3 reviews the Beltrami framework. We present, in Section 4, our color segmentation functional and derive a non-linear coupled Partial Differential Equations (PDE) as gradient descent equations for this functional. Results are presented in Section 5, and we summaries and conclude in Section 6.

2 Γ-Convergence Formulation

The Mumford-Shah functional includes three terms: A fidelity term, a smoothing term, and a penalty on the total length of the discontinuities. Let

$$F[I, K] = \int_{\Omega \setminus K} \left(\alpha (I - I_0)^2 + \beta |\nabla I|^2 \right) dx dy + \mathcal{H}(K) \tag{1}$$

where I_0 is the observed image, I is the denoised image, Ω is the images domain, and K is the set of discontinuities. The Hausdorff measure $\mathcal{H}(K)$, measures the total length of the discontinuity set. The implicit assumption that underlies this functional is that an image is a piecewise smooth function. The first term penalizes a function that differs from the observed one, the second term penalizes large gradients, and the last term penalizes excessive use of segmentation curves. The minimizer places the segmenting curves along the most significant gradients and tries to smooth the function everywhere else without diverting too much from the original image. The parameters α and β control the relative weight of the three terms.

It is difficult to minimize this functional numerically because of the large number of possibilities of placing the set of boundaries K inside Ω. In order to have a better control of the problem, both mathematically and numerically, it is convenient to approximate the functional. In the Γ-convergence framework, a new functional is proposed [2] in the form

$$F_c[I, E] = \int_\Omega \left(\alpha(I - I_0)^2 + \beta E^2 |\nabla I|^2 + c|\nabla E|^2 + \psi_c(E) \right) dx dy, \qquad (2)$$

where, ideally the function $E(x, y)$ is an edge indicator, such that $E(x_0, y_0) = 0$ when an edge passes through (x_0, y_0) and $E(x, y) = 1$ otherwise. In this case, the second term in the approximating functional is identical to the second term in the Mumford-Shah functional. In fact, we demand that the segmenting function E is a smooth function and use the L_2 norm to penalize discontinuities in E. The last term is constructed in such a way that it forces E to behave as an edge indicator, i.e. it pushes E to 1 far from an edge. In the vicinity of an edge, the term $E^2 |\nabla I|^2$ pushes E to zero. Explicitly, Ambrosio and Tortorelly have chosen:

$$F_c[I, E] = \int_\Omega \left(\alpha(I - I_0)^2 + \beta E^2 |\nabla I|^2 + c|\nabla E|^2 + \frac{(E - 1)^2}{4c} \right) dx dy. \qquad (3)$$

One can show that in the limit as $c \to 0$, the functional $F_c[I, E]$ approaches $F[I, K]$ such that the minimizers of F_c converge to the minimizer of F.

One can naturally envisage using a different norm, i.e. L_1 norm for the gradients of the denoised image and the segmenting function. The question is how to extend this idea for a color image.

3   The Polyakov action

Let us introduce a geometric viewpoint that enables us to generalize an adaptive smoothing algorithm to a higher dimensional and codimensional images.

There is an extensive literature on functionals of the type

$$F[I] = \int dx dy \rho(|\nabla I|) = \int dx dy \rho \left(\sqrt{I_x^2 + I_y^2} \right), \qquad (4)$$

where $\rho(s)$ is a function which has a lower bound. We suggest to generalize it in the following way:

$$F[I, a, b, c] = \int dx dy f(a, b, c) \rho \left(\sqrt{a I_x^2 + 2b I_x I_y + c I_y^2} \right), \qquad (5)$$

where a, b, c and f are functions of x and y, and f is positive definite. The interpretation of this generalization is geometric. Images are viewed as embedding maps. Let us consider the important example $\mathbf{X} : \Sigma \to \mathbb{R}^3$. Denote the local coordinates on the two-dimensional manifold Σ by (σ^1, σ^2), these are analogous to arc-length for the one-dimensional manifold, i.e. a curve. The map $\mathbf{X}$ is explicitly given by

$$(X^1(\sigma^1, \sigma^2) = \sigma^1, X^2(\sigma^1, \sigma^2) = \sigma^2, X^3(\sigma^1, \sigma^2) = I(\sigma^1, \sigma^2)). \tag{6}$$

Since the local coordinates σ^i are curvilinear, the squared distance is given by a positive definite symmetric bilinear form called the metric whose components are denoted by $g_{\mu\nu}(\sigma^1, \sigma^2)$,

$$ds^2 = g_{\mu\nu}d\sigma^\mu d\sigma^\nu \equiv g_{11}(d\sigma^1)^2 + 2g_{12}d\sigma^1 d\sigma^2 + g_{22}(d\sigma^2)^2, \tag{7}$$

where we used Einstein summation convention in the second equality; identical indices that appear one up and one down are summed over, see [4, 18] for a short introduction to tensor calculus and covariance in the context of image analysis. We denote the inverse of the metric by $(g^{\mu\nu})$, and its determinant by g.

The Polyakov action is a generalization of L_2. It depends on *both* the image manifold and the embedding space. Denote by $(\Sigma, (g_{\mu\nu}))$ the image manifold and its metric and by $(M, (h_{ij}))$ the space-feature manifold and its metric. We choose $\rho(|s|) = s \cdot s \equiv s^i s^j h_{ij}$, then the map $\mathbf{X} : \Sigma \to M$ has the following weight [13]

$$F[X^i, g_{\mu\nu}, h_{ij}] = \int d^m \sigma \sqrt{g} g^{\mu\nu} (\partial_\mu X^i)(\partial_\nu X^j) h_{ij}(\mathbf{X}), \tag{8}$$

where m is the dimension of Σ and the range of indices is $\mu, \nu = 1, \ldots, \dim \Sigma$, and $i, j = 1, \ldots, \dim M$. In the above expression $d^m \sigma \sqrt{g}$ is a volume element of the image manifold. The rest, i.e. $g^{\mu\nu}(\partial_\mu X^i)(\partial_\nu X^j) h_{ij}(\mathbf{X})$, is a generalization of L_2. It is important to note that this expression, as well as the volume element, do not depend on the local coordinates one chooses.

For our example in Eq. (6), we assume a diagonal form for the embedding space, i.e. $h_{ij}(x, y, I) = f_i(x, y, I)\delta_{ij}$ (no summation over indices here). We get the following functional

$$F[I, g_{\mu\nu}] = \int dx dy \sqrt{g} \left(g^{11} f_1 + g^{22} f_2 + (g^{11} I_x^2 + 2g^{12} I_x I_y + g^{22} I_y^2) f_3\right) \tag{9}$$

which is reduced, up to terms independent of I, to the form of the functional in Eq. (5) when the f_i's are constants.

The minimization of F with respect to the metric can be solved analyticly, for two-dimensional manifolds. The minimizing metric is the induced metric of the isometric embedding. Explicitly, it is given in terms of the embedding map and the metric of the embedding space,

$$g_{\mu\nu}(\sigma^1, \sigma^2) = h_{ij}(\mathbf{X})(\partial_\mu X^i)(\partial_\nu X^j). \tag{10}$$

Using standard methods in variation calculus, the Euler-Lagrange (EL) equations with respect to the embedding are (see [18] for derivation)

$$-\frac{1}{2\sqrt{g}}h^{il}\frac{\delta F}{\delta X^l} = \Delta_g X^i + \Gamma^i_{jk}(\partial_\mu X^j)(\partial_\nu X^k)g^{\mu\nu}, \tag{11}$$

where the operator that is acting on X^i in the first term is the natural generalization of the Laplacian from flat spaces to manifolds and is called *the second order differential parameter of Beltrami* [10], or in short *Beltrami operator*. It is given in term of the metric as

$$\Delta_g X^i = \frac{1}{\sqrt{g}}\partial_\mu(\sqrt{g}g^{\mu\nu}\partial_\nu X^i). \tag{12}$$

In the second term of Eq. (11), the Γ^i_{jk} are the Levi-Civita connection's coefficients with respect to the metric h_{ij} that describes the geometry of the embedding space [23]

$$\Gamma^i_{jk} = \frac{1}{2}h^{il}(\partial_j h_{lk} + \partial_k h_{jl} - \partial_l h_{jk}). \tag{13}$$

This term is in particular important in color image analysis and processing since some of the models of color perception assume non-Euclidean color space.

We view scale-space as the gradient descent,

$$X^i_t \equiv \frac{\partial X^i}{\partial t} = -\frac{1}{2\sqrt{g}}h^{il}\frac{\delta F}{\delta X^l}. \tag{14}$$

Notice that we used our freedom to multiply the Euler-Lagrange equations by a strictly positive function and a positive definite matrix. This factor is the simplest one that does not change the minimization solution while giving a reparameterization invariant expression. This choice guarantees that the flow is geometric and does not depend on the parameterization.

Choosing the induced metric and minimizing the feature coordinates results in a system of coupled partial differential equations that describe the flow of the image surface inside the spatial-feature space. This flow has the effect of smoothing more rapidly areas between edges than the edges themselves. This effect is achieved by the projection of the mean curvature vector to the feature space. Since normals to the surface at an edge lie almost entirely in the spatial space, their projection to the feature space is small and does not change the value or location of an edge.

This technique was used to denoise and enhance a variety of gray-level, color, 3D images, like movies, and volumetric medical images, and texture [7, 19, 18]. Next, we show that it is a useful measure in color image segmentation.

4 Color Segmentation Functional

According to the Beltrami framework [19], a color image is represented as an embedding map of a two-dimensional Riemannian manifold in a five-dimensional spatial-color Riemannian manifold. The coordinates of the two-dimensional manifold are (σ^1, σ^2), and those of the five-dimensional one are $(X^1, X^2, X^3, X^3, X^4, X^5)$. The embedding map is

$$\{X^1 = \sigma^1, X^2 = \sigma^2, X^3 = R(\sigma^1, \sigma^2), X^4 = G(\sigma^1, \sigma^2), X^5 = B(\sigma^1, \sigma^2)\}. \quad (15)$$

We identify X^1 with x and X^2 with y and by abuse of notations we write $\{x, y, R(x, y), G(x, y), B(x, y)\}$. We also use below the notation I^i for $i =$r,g,b to denote the different color channels.

The metric of the embedding space is

$$ds^2 = dx^2 + dy^2 + ds^2_{color}, \quad (16)$$

where the metric in the color space is model dependent, see [23] for a general discussion and [20, 21] for the analysis of different color models in the Beltrami framework. We choose, for sake of simplicity, to adopt a Euclidean metric for the color space, see [24] for a related effort.

Two different approaches are possible in the treatment of the segmenting function. We can think of it as a function on the image manifold or as a function on the spatial part of the embedding space. The two approaches lead to somewhat different equations even though the spatial part and the image manifold coordinates are identified in the embedding map.

4.1 Segmenting function on the image manifold

The metric in the image manifold is given by the induced metric (see Eq. (10)). We assume further that the segmenting function is defined over the two-dimensional image manifold, see Figure 1. We use the Polyakov action as an adaptive smoothing metric for both the color coordinates and the segmenting function. The functional we propose reads

$$F_c[I^1, I^2, I^3, E] = \int_\Sigma d^2\sigma \sqrt{g} \left(\frac{\alpha}{2}(X^i - X^i_0)h_{ij}(\mathbf{X})(X^j - X^j_0) + \right.$$

$$\left. \frac{\beta}{2}E(\sigma^1, \sigma^2)^2 g^{\mu\nu}(\partial_\mu X^i)(\partial_\nu X^j)h_{ij}(\mathbf{X}) + \frac{c}{2}g^{\mu\nu}(\partial_\mu E)(\partial_\nu E) + \frac{(E-1)^2}{4c} \right) (17)$$

We take the color metric to be the unit matrix $h_{ij} = \delta_{ij}$ from now on. We minimize this functional by the gradient descent method. Formally, the equations are

$$I^i_t \equiv \frac{\partial I^i}{\partial t} = -\frac{1}{\sqrt{g}}\frac{\delta F}{\delta I^i}$$

$$E_t \equiv \frac{\partial E}{\partial t} = -\frac{\delta F}{\delta E}.$$

The functional variations yield the following explicit partial differential equations

$$I^i_t = \beta E^2 \Delta_g(I^i) + \beta g^{\mu\nu}(\partial_\mu E)(\partial_\nu I^i) - \alpha(I^i - I^i_0)$$

$$E_t = -\sqrt{g}\left(2\beta E - \frac{1-E}{2c} - c\Delta_g(E)\right)$$

where $i = [R, G, B]$, and

$$\Delta_g(X) = \frac{1}{\sqrt{g}} \partial_\mu(\sqrt{g} g^{\mu\nu} \partial_\nu X),$$

is the Laplace-Beltrami operator on the image manifold. The factor 2 in the first term of the equation for E comes from the choice of the metric as the induced one given in Eq. (10). We find that

$$g^{\mu\nu}(\partial_\mu I^i)(\partial_\nu I^j)h_{ij}(\mathbf{X}) = g^{\mu\nu} g_{\mu\nu} = \mathrm{Tr}(\mathrm{Id}_{2\times 2}) = 2. \tag{18}$$

The first term in the equation for I smoothes the function when $E = 1$ and is ineffective around an edge when E approaches zero. The second term sharpens gradients and create shocks. The last term pushes I towards I_0.

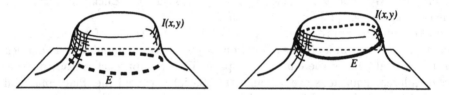

Fig. 1. Left is the edge indicator function E defined over the image plane $\{x, y\}$. Right: the edge indicator function E defined on the image surface manifold $\{x, y, I(x, y)\}$.

4.2 Segmenting function on the embedding space

The metric is, as before, the induced metric but this time the Polyakov action is used only for the feature coordinates. The segmenting function is defined over the Euclidean spatial part of the embedding space and therefor it is smoothed using the usual L_2 norm. The functional, in this case, is

$$F_c[I^1, I^2, I^3, E] = \int_\Sigma d^2\sigma \sqrt{g} \left(\frac{\alpha}{2}(X^i - X_0^i)h_{ij}(\mathbf{X})(X^j - X_0^j) + \right.$$
$$\left. \frac{\beta}{2}E(x, y)^2 g^{\mu\nu}(\partial_\mu X^i)(\partial_\nu X^j)h_{ij}(\mathbf{X}) \right) + \int dx dy \left(\frac{c}{2}|\nabla E|^2 + \frac{(E-1)^2}{4c} \right) \tag{19}$$

The gradient descent equations are

$$I_t^i = \beta E^2 \Delta_g(I^i) + \beta g^{\mu\nu}(\partial_\mu E)(\partial_\nu I^i) - \alpha(I^i - I_0^i)$$
$$E_t = -2\beta \sqrt{g} E + \frac{1-E}{2c} + c\Delta(E),$$

where i=[R,G,B], and $\Delta(E)$ is the usual Laplacian. The first term in the equation for E decreases the values of E for large g. The second term of the equation pushes the values of E toward 1, as c approaches zero. The last term is a smoothing term.

5 Experimental results

Fig. 2. Upper row, left to right: The original noisy image, followed by the final edge indicator function E, and the final image. At the bottom are zoom-in frames of a square section cropped from the initial and final images.

We tested both cases, where the segmentation function E is defined on the image manifold and then on the embedding space. The time derivatives are approximated by an explicit forward numerical approximation (Euler scheme). The spatial derivatives were taken first by forward followed by backwards approximation, see [17]. This is a simple way to keep the numerical support tight and centralized. The examples demonstrate color image enhancement for both noisy and clean images. In all examples we set $\alpha = 7 \cdot 10^{-2}, \beta = 2 \cdot 10^{-4}, c = 10^{-3}$. We also decreased the value of c along the iterations by setting $c^{n+1} = c^n/1.002$. as proposed in [15].

In Figure 2 we use the segmentation function E on the image flat manifold. The embedding space was taken Euclidean in color space. Figure 3 tests the segmentation function E on the embedding space. This example takes a clean benchmark image into a piecewise smooth one. Here the embedding space is based on Helmholtz's arclength in color $ds^2_{color} = (d\log R)^2 + (d\log G)^2 + (d\log B)^2$, see also [5, 22, 23, 20]. In some cases the edges appear as 'edge regions' rather than

Fig. 3. Upper row, left to right: The original image, followed by the final edge indicator function E, and the final image. At the bottom are zoom-in frames of a square section cropped from the initial and the final images.

one dimensional curves as expected. The reason is our numerical approximation for E. We use an edge image with the same resolution as that of the original image, adding central difference approximation yield the edge regions. One possible solution is to apply the refined numerical approximation to the edge map as in [15]. Finally, in Figure 4 we apply the segmentation function E in the embedding space, to a noisy image. The source of the noise comes from a digital camera compression distortions, followed by a scanned version of a printout picture.

Fig. 4. The original noisy image is on the left, followed by the edge indicator field E, and the final result. Bottom line shows a zoom in on the original noisy on the left and filtered image.

6 Summary and Conclusions

We presented a generalization of the Mumford-Shah enhancement and segmentation method. The generalization is in two aspects: Multi-channel images, i.e. color images are analyzed, and the L_2 measure is replaced by the Polyakov action. The generalization is a natural application of the Beltrami framework that represent images as an embedding map of the image manifold in a spatial-feature space.

References

1. L. Ambrosio and V. M. Tortorelli, "Approximation of functionals depending on jumps by elliptic functionals via Γ-convergence", *Comm. Pure Appl. Math.*, 43 (1990), 999-1036.
2. L. Ambrosio and V. M. Tortorelli, "On the approximation of free discontinuity problems", *Boll. Un. Mat. It.*, 7 (1992), 105-123.
3. E. Di Giorgi, M. Carriero, and A. Leaci, "Existence theorem for a minimum problem with free discontinuity set", *Arch. Rat. Mech. Anal.*, 108 (1989), 195-218.
4. L. M. J. Florac, A. H. Salden, B. M. ter Haar Romeny, J. J. Koenderink and M. A. Viergever, "Nonlinear Scale-Space",*Image and Vision Computing*, 13 (1995) 279-294.
5. H Helmholtz von, "Handbuch der Psychologischen Optik", Voss, Hamburg, 1896.
6. R Kimmel and R Malladi and N Sochen, "Images as Embedding Maps and Minimal Surfaces: Movies, Color, Texture, and Volumetric Medical Images", *Proc. of IEEE CVPR'97*, (1997) 350-355.
7. R. Kimmel and N Sochen and R Malladi, "On the geometry of texture", Report, Berkeley Labs. UC, LBNL-39640, UC-405, November,1996.
8. R Kimmel and N Sochen and R Malladi, "From High Energy Physics to Low Level Vision", *Lecture Notes In Computer Science:* 1252, First International Conference on Scale-Space Theory in Computer Vision, Springer-Verlag, 1997, 236-247.
9. R Kimmel, "A natural norm for color processing", *Proc. of 3-rd Asian Conf. on Computer Vision*, Hong Kong, Springer-Verlag, LNCS 1351, 1998, 88-95.
10. E Kreyszing, "Differential Geometry", Dover Publications, Inc., New York, 1991.
11. J. M. Morel and S. Solimini, Variational methods in image segmentation, Birkhauser, Boston, MA, 1995.
12. D. Mumford and J. Shah, "Optimal approximations by piecewise smooth functions and associated variational problems," *Comm. Pure Appl. Math.*, 42 (1989), 577-685.
13. A M Polyakov, "Quantum geometry of bosonic strings", *Physics Letters*, **103B** (1981) 207-210.
14. M Proesmans and E Pauwels and L van Gool, "Coupled geometry-driven diffusion equations for low level vision", In Geometric–Driven Diffusion in Computer Vision, Ed. B M ter Haar Romeny, Kluwer Academic Publishers, 1994.
15. T Richardson and S Mitter, "Approximation, computation, and distortion in the variational formulation", In Geometric–Driven Diffusion in Computer Vision, Ed. B M ter Haar Romeny, Kluwer Academic Publishers, 1994.
16. Geometric–Driven Diffusion in Computer Vision, Ed. B M ter Haar Romeny, Kluwer Academic Publishers, 1994.
17. L Rudin and S Osher and E Fatemi, "Nonlinear total variation based noise removal algorithms", *Physica D*, 60 (1991) 259-268.
18. N Sochen and R Kimmel and R Malladi, "From high energy physics to low level vision", Report, LBNL, UC Berkeley, LBNL 39243, August, Presented in ONR workshop, UCLA, Sept. 5 1996.
19. N Sochen and R Kimmel and R Malladi , "A general framework for low level vision", *IEEE Trans. on Image Processing*, 7, (1998) 310-318.
20. N Sochen and Y Y Zeevi, "Images as manifolds embedded in a spatial-feature non-Euclidean space", November 1998, EE-Technion report no. 1181.
21. N Sochen and Y Y Zeevi, "Representation of colored images by manifolds embedded in higher dimensional non-Euclidean space", IEEE ICIP'98, Chicago, 1998.

22. W S Stiles, "A modified Helmholtz line element in brightness-colour space, *Proc. Phys. Soc. (London)*, 58 (1946) 41.

23. G Wyszecki and W S Stiles, "Color Science: Concepts and Methods, Qualitative Data and Formulae", (2nd edition), Jhon Wiley & Sons, 1982 .

24. A Yezzi, "Modified curvature motion for image smoothing and enhancement", *IEEE Trans. on Image Processing*, 7 (1998) 345-352 .

A Level Set Model for Image Classification

Christophe Samson[1]*, Laure Blanc-Féraud[1], Gilles Aubert[2], and Josiane Zerubia[1]

[1] Ariana projet commun CNRS/INRIA/UNSA,
INRIA, 2004 route des lucioles, BP 93,
06902 Sophia Antipolis cedex, France.
{csamson,blancf,zerubia}@sophia.inria.fr
tel: +33 (0)4 92 38 75 67, Fax: +33 (0)4 92 38 76 43
[2] Laboratoire J.A. Dieudonné, UMR 6621 CNRS,
Université de Nice-Sophia Antipolis, 06108 Nice Cedex 2, France.

Abstract. We present a supervised classification model based on a variational approach. This model is devoted to find an optimal partition compound of homogeneous classes with regular interfaces. We represent the regions of the image defined by the classes and their interfaces by level set functions, and we define a functional whose minimum is an optimal partition. The coupled Partial Differential Equations (PDE) related to the minimization of the functional are considered through a dynamical scheme. Given an initial interface set (zero level set), the different terms of the PDE's are governing the motion of interfaces such that, at convergence, we get an optimal partition as defined above. Each interface is guided by internal forces (regularity of the interface), and external ones (data term, no vacuum, no regions overlapping). Several experiments were conducted on both synthetic an real images.

1 Introduction

Image classification, which consists of assigning a label to each pixel of an observed image, is one of the basic problems in image processing. This concerns many applications as, for instance, land use management in teledetection. The classification problem is closely related to the segmentation one, in the sense that we want to get a partition compound of homogeneous regions. Nevertheless, within the classification procedure, each partition represents a class, i.e. a set of pixels with the same label. In the following, the feature criterion we are interested in is the spatial distribution of intensity (or grey level). This work takes place in the general framework of supervised classification which means that the number and the parameters of the classes are known. The proposed method could be extended to other discriminant features than grey-level such as texture for instance. The unsupervised case, including a parameter estimation capability, will be studied in the future.

---

* author for correspondence

Many classification models have been developed with structural notions as region growing methods for example [9], or by stochastic approach as in [1], but rarely in the field of variational approach. In [11] we proposed a supervised variational classification model based on Cahn-Hilliard models, such that the solution we get is compound of homogeneous regions separated by regularized boundaries. The classes are considered as phases separated by interfaces boundaries. The model was developed through considerations of regularity on the phases by defining a set of functionals whose expected minimum at convergence is an image with expected properties of regularity.

Herein, the approach is different, mainly because the proposed model is based on active contours, and the functional of interest is defined over the regions with associated interfaces through a level set model. The resulting dynamical Partial Differential Equations (PDE's), governing the evolution of the set of interfaces, consist of a moving front converging to a regularized partition. This model is inspired by the work of Zhao et al. about multiphase evolution [13], and takes place in the general framework of active contours [2, 3, 7] for region segmentation [14]. We use a level set formulation [8] which is convenient to write functional depending on regions and contours, and allows a change of topology of the evolving fronts. Each active interface is coupled to the other ones through a term which penalizes overlapping regions (i.e. pixels with two labels) and the formation of vacuum (i.e. pixels without any label). The evolution of each interface is guided by forces which impose the following constraints : the interface exhibits a minimal perimeter (internal force) and it encloses one and only one homogeneous class (external force).

First, we state the problem of classification as a partitioning problem. We clearly set the framework and define the properties we expect on the classification. Second, we expose the classification statement through a level set formulation. The Euler-Lagrange derivative of the proposed functional leads to a dynamical scheme we propose to implement. We finally present some experimental results on both synthetic and real images (see also [10] for more experiments).

2 Image classification as a partitioning problem

This section is devoted to present the properties we want the classification model to satisfy. In the following, we consider a classification problem in which a partition of the observed data u_0, with respect to the predefined classes, is searched. This partition is compound of homogeneous regions, say the classes, separated by regularized interfaces. Herein, we suppose that the classes have a Gaussian distribution of intensity, therefore a class is characterized by its mean μ_i and its standard deviation σ_i. The number K of classes and the parameters $(\mu_i; \sigma_i)_{i=1...K}$ are supposed to be given from a previous estimation. We choose to assign the label value μ_i to each element of the ith class. All indexes i or j are going from 1 to K. The proposed method is not limited to images in which the intensity homogeneity is a good classifier. The same approach could be used to classify data according to a texture parameter for example, or other discriminant attributes.

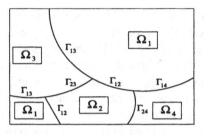

Fig. 1. A partition of Ω.

On can think of first computing the discriminant attributes on the observed data, then determine the classes using an algorithm giving the number of classes and their parameters. We can assume that the repartition inside each class is Gaussian and apply the proposed algorithm in order to determine a regularized classification.

Let Ω be an open domain subset of $\mathbb{R}^2$ with smooth boundary, and let $u_0 : \Omega \to \mathbb{R}$ represent the observed data function. Let Ω_i be the region defined as

$$\Omega_i = \{x \in \Omega / x \text{ belongs to the } i^{th} \text{ class}\}. \tag{1}$$

A partitioning of Ω consists of finding a set $\{\Omega_i\}_{i=1...K}$ such that (see Fig. 1)

$$\Omega = \bigcup_{i=1}^{K} \Omega_i \quad \text{and} \quad \Omega_i \bigcap_{i \neq j} \Omega_j = \varnothing. \tag{2}$$

We note $\Gamma_i = \partial \Omega_i \cap \Omega$ the intersection of the boundary of Ω_i with the open domain Ω, and let the interface between Ω_i and Ω_j be

$$\Gamma_{ij} = \Gamma_{ji} = \Gamma_i \cap \Gamma_j \cap \Omega, \quad \forall i \neq j. \tag{3}$$

We have

$$\Gamma_i = \bigcup_{j \neq i} \Gamma_{ij}. \tag{4}$$

Let remark that in (3) and (4) we eventually have $\Gamma_{ij} = \varnothing$. We note $|\Gamma_i|$ the one-dimensional Hausdorff measure of Γ_i verifying

$$|\Gamma_i| = \sum_{j \neq i} |\Gamma_{ij}| \text{ and } |\varnothing| = 0. \tag{5}$$

The classification model we consider for an image u_o defined over Ω, is a set $\{\Omega_i\}_i$ defined by (1) and satisfying :

Condition a : $\{\Omega_i\}_i$ is a partition of Ω :

$$\Omega = \bigcup_i \Omega_i \quad \text{and} \quad \Omega_i \bigcap_{i \neq j} \Omega_j = \varnothing.$$

Condition b : The partition $\{\Omega_i\}_i$ is a classification of the observed data u_0 and takes into account the Gaussian distribution property of the classes (data term) :

$$\text{minimize} \sum_i \int_{\Omega_i} \left(\frac{u_0 - \mu_i}{\sigma_i}\right)^2 \quad \text{with respect to } \Omega_i.$$

Condition c : The partition is regular in the sense that the sum of the length of interfaces Γ_{ij} is minimum :

$$\text{minimize} \sum_{i,j} \xi_{ij} |\Gamma_{ij}| \quad \text{with respect to } \Gamma_{ij} \quad (\xi_{ij} \in \mathbb{R} \text{ are fixed}).$$

The solution of the classification model proposed in the next section have to take into account the three conditions. This is done by associating a functional to the set of interfaces such that minimizers will respect CONDITIONS A, B and C.

3 Multiphase model : image classification in terms of level set

The classification model developed further is based on coupled active interfaces, and the approach we adopt is inspired from Zhao *et al.* [13]. The evolution of each interface is guided by forces constraining the solution to respect CONDITIONS A, B and C exposed in the previous section. We use a level set formulation to represent each interface and also each region Ω_i element of the partition $\{\Omega_i\}_i$.

3.1 Preliminaries

Let $\Phi_i : \Omega \times \mathbb{R}^+ \to \mathbb{R}$ be a Lipschitz function associated to region Ω_i (we assume the existence of such a Φ_i) such that

$$\begin{cases} \Phi_i(x;t) > 0 & \text{if } x \in \Omega_i \\ \Phi_i(x;t) = 0 & \text{if } x \in \Gamma_i \\ \Phi_i(x;t) < 0 & \text{otherwise .} \end{cases} \tag{6}$$

Thus, the region Ω_i is entirely described by the function Φ_i. In the following, for a sake of clarity, we will sometimes omit spatial parameter x and time parameter t in $\Phi_i(x;t)$.

Let define the approximations δ_α and H_α of Dirac and Heaviside distributions with $\alpha \in \mathbb{R}^+$

$$\delta_\alpha(s) = \begin{cases} \frac{1}{2\alpha}\left(1 + \cos(\frac{\pi s}{\alpha})\right) & \text{if } |s| \leq \alpha \\ 0 & \text{if } |s| > \alpha \end{cases} \tag{7}$$

$$H_\alpha(s) = \begin{cases} \frac{1}{2}\left(1 + \frac{s}{\alpha} + \frac{1}{\pi}\sin(\frac{\pi s}{\alpha})\right) & \text{if } |s| \le \alpha \\ 1 & \text{if } s > \alpha \\ 0 & \text{if } s < -\alpha \end{cases} \qquad (8)$$

and we have

$$\begin{cases} \delta_\alpha \xrightarrow{\mathcal{D}'(\Omega)} \delta & \text{as } \alpha \to 0^+ \\ H_\alpha \xrightarrow{\mathcal{D}'(\Omega)} H & \text{as } \alpha \to 0^+ \end{cases}$$

where $\mathcal{D}'(\Omega)$ is the space of distributions defined over Ω. From (6),(7) and (8) we can write

$$\{x \in \Omega / \lim_{\alpha \to 0^+} H_\alpha(\Phi_i(x;t)) = 1\} = \Omega_i \qquad (9)$$

$$\{x \in \Omega / \lim_{\alpha \to 0^+} \delta_\alpha(\Phi_i(x;t)) \ne 0\} = \Gamma_i. \qquad (10)$$

3.2 Multiphase functional

Let $u_0 : \Omega \to \mathbb{R}$ be the observed data (grey level for instance).

Thanks to the level set Φ_i's defined in (6) and by the use of (9) and (10), a partition $\{\Omega_i\}_i$ respecting CONDITIONS A, B and C stated in section 2 can be found through the minimization of a global functional depending on the Φ_i's. This functional contains three terms, each one being related to one of the three conditions. In the following, we express each condition in term of functional minimization. Minimizers of the following functionals are supposed to exist.

• FUNCTIONAL RELATED TO CONDITION A (PARTITION CONDITION) :
Let define the following functional :

$$F_\alpha^A(\Phi_1, ..., \Phi_K) = \frac{\lambda}{2} \int_\Omega \left(\sum_{i=1}^{K} H_\alpha(\Phi_i) - 1\right)^2 dx \quad \text{with } \lambda \in \mathbb{R}^+ . \qquad (11)$$

The minimization of F_α^A, as $\alpha \to 0^+$, penalizes the formation of vacuum (pixels with no label) and regions overlapping (pixels with more than one label).

• FUNCTIONAL RELATED TO CONDITION B (DATA TERM) :
Taking into account the observed data and the Gaussian distribution property of the classes, we consider :

$$F_\alpha^B(\Phi_1, ..., \Phi_K) = \sum_{i=1}^{K} e_i \int_\Omega H_\alpha(\Phi_i) \frac{(u_o - \mu_i)^2}{\sigma_i^2} dx \quad \text{with } e_i \in \mathbb{R}, \forall i. \qquad (12)$$

The family $\{\Phi\}_i$ minimizing F_α^B as $\alpha \to 0^+$ leads to a partition $\{\Omega_i\}_i$ satisfying CONDITION B.

- FUNCTIONAL RELATED TO CONDITION C (LENGTH SHORTENING OF INTER-FACE SET) :

The last functional we want to introduce is related to CONDITION C about the minimization of the interfaces length. We would like to minimize

$$\frac{1}{2} \sum_{i,j} \xi_{ij} |\Gamma_{ij}| \quad \text{with } \xi_{ij} \text{ being real constants.} \tag{13}$$

The factor $\frac{1}{2}$ expresses the symmetry $\Gamma_{ij} = \Gamma_{ji}$ and will be introduced in the weighting parameters ξ_{ij}. We turn the minimization of interfaces length into the minimization of boundaries length :

$$\sum_{i=1}^{K} \gamma_i |\Gamma_i| \quad \text{with } \gamma_i \text{ being real constants.} \tag{14}$$

From (13) and (14) we obtain the constraint $\xi_{ij} = \gamma_i + \gamma_j$ which permits to select the weighting parameters γ_i in the problem of boundaries length minimization to retrieve the interfaces length minimization one. According to the Lemma exposed below, the minimization of (14) is operated by minimizing the functional (as $\alpha \to 0^+$) :

$$F_\alpha^C(\Phi_1, ..., \Phi_K) = \sum_{i=1}^{K} \gamma_i \int_\Omega \delta_\alpha(\Phi_i) |\nabla \Phi_i| dx. \tag{15}$$

Lemma : *According to the previous definitions, let define*

$$L_\alpha(\Phi_i) = \int_\Omega \delta_\alpha(\Phi_i(x;t)) |\nabla \Phi_i(x;t)| dx,$$

then we have

$$\lim_{\alpha \to 0} L_\alpha(\Phi_i) = \int_{\Phi_i = 0} ds = |\Gamma_i|.$$

Proof : using the Coarea formula [4], we have

$$L_\alpha(\Phi_i) = \int_{\mathbb{R}} \left[\int_{\Phi_i = \rho} \delta_\alpha(\Phi_i(x;t)) ds \right] d\rho = \int_{\mathbb{R}} \left[\delta_\alpha(\rho) \int_{\Phi_i = \rho} ds \right] d\rho$$

By setting $h(\rho) = \int_{\Phi_i = \rho} ds$ we obtain

$$L_\alpha(\Phi_i) = \int_{\mathbb{R}} \delta_\alpha(\rho) h(\rho) d\rho = \frac{1}{2\alpha} \int_{-\alpha}^{\alpha} \left(1 + \cos(\frac{\pi \rho}{\alpha})\right) h(\rho) d\rho$$

If we take $\theta = \frac{\rho}{\alpha}$ we have

$$L_\alpha(\Phi_i) = \frac{1}{2} \int_{-1}^{1} \left(1 + \cos(\pi \theta)\right) h(\alpha \theta) d\theta$$

Thus, when $\alpha \to 0$ we obtain

$$\lim_{\alpha \to 0} L_\alpha(\Phi_i) = \frac{1}{2}h(0) \int_{-1}^{1} \left(1 + \cos(\pi\theta)\right) d\theta = h(0) = \int_{\Phi_i=0} ds = |\Gamma_i|$$

• GLOBAL FUNCTIONAL :
The sum $F_\alpha^{\text{A}} + F_\alpha^{\text{B}} + F_\alpha^{\text{C}}$ leads to the global functional :

$$F_\alpha(\Phi_1, ..., \Phi_K) = \sum_{i=1}^{K} e_i \int_\Omega H_\alpha(\Phi_i) \frac{(u_o - \mu_i)^2}{\sigma_i^2} dx + \sum_{i=1}^{K} \gamma_i \int_\Omega \delta_\alpha(\Phi_i)|\nabla\Phi_i|dx$$

$$+ \frac{\lambda}{2} \int_\Omega \left(\sum_{i=1}^{K} H_\alpha(\Phi_i) - 1\right)^2 dx$$

$$(16)$$

As $\alpha \to 0^+$, the solution set $\{\Phi_i\}_i$ minimizing $F_\alpha(\Phi_1, ..., \Phi_K)$, if it exists[1] and according to (6), defines a classification compound of homogeneous classes (the so-called Ω_i *phases*) separated by regularized interfaces.

3.3 Remark about length minimization

Consider the length functional :

$$L(t) = \int_0^1 |\frac{\partial C(p; t)}{\partial t}| dt \qquad (17)$$

where $\{C(p; t)\}_t$ is a set of closed parametrized ($p \in [0; 1]$) curves over Ω such that $C(0; t) = C(1; t)$ and $\frac{\partial C(0;t)}{\partial t} = \frac{\partial C(1;t)}{\partial t}$. Then, $L(t)$ is decreasing most rapidly if

$$\frac{\partial C(p; t)}{\partial t} = \kappa N \qquad (18)$$

κ being the local curvature of $C(p; t)$ and N the inward normal. Curve evolution through PDE (18) is known as *mean curvature motion* (see [6] for instance). Active contours guided by (18) tends to regular curves in the sense that the length is minimized. PDE (18) can be written through a level set formulation [8] which is more convenient to manage curves breaking and merging. Assume that $d : \Omega \times \mathbb{R}^+ \to \mathbb{R}$ is a smooth continuous function such that, from the value of $d(x; t)$, we can determine if x is interior, exterior or belongs to $C(p; t)$. Let suppose that : $C(p; t) = \{x \in \Omega/d(x; t) = a\}$ (i.e. the contour is represented by level set a of function d). PDE (18) formulated by the use of level set becomes

$$\frac{\partial d(x; t)}{\partial t} = div(\frac{\nabla d}{|\nabla d|})|\nabla d|, \qquad (19)$$

----

[1] If they exist, minimizers $\{\Phi_i\}_i$ should be found in the space $\{\Phi_i : \Omega \times \mathbb{R}^+ \to \mathbb{R}/|\nabla\Phi_i| \in L^1(\Omega)\}$

with $div(\frac{\nabla d}{|\nabla d|})$ being the local curvature of level set a. Equation (19) was studied for instance in [5]. Evolution of level sets of function d (and so evolution of contour $C(p;t)$ through level set a) from (19) is the level set formulation of mean curvature motion. The level set formulation allows breaking and merging fronts which is not possible from formulation (18). Since contour $C(p;t)$ is represented by level set a, we only need to update PDE (19) in a narrow band around a. In this case, the level set formulation (19) comes from a reformulation of (18) to track the motion of contours $C(p;t)$. In our case, we directly define a length functional F_α^C over contours Γ_i's by the use of level set Φ_i's. The associated Euler-Lagrange equations lead to K PDE's of the form

$$\frac{\partial \Phi_i(x;t)}{\partial t} = div(\frac{\nabla \Phi_i}{|\nabla \Phi_i|})\delta_\alpha(\Phi_i). \tag{20}$$

Compared to PDE (19), we get from (20) a "natural" narrow band from the Dirac operator δ_α whose width depends on the value of α (for Φ_i's defined as signed distance in (6)).

4 Multiphase evolution scheme

Using Neumann conditions $(\frac{\partial \Phi_i}{\partial n}(x;t) = 0, \forall x \in \partial \Omega)$, the Euler Lagrange equations associated to F_α give the K following coupled PDE's $(i = 1...K)$

$$\frac{\partial F_\alpha}{\partial \Phi_i} = \delta_\alpha(\Phi_i)\left[e_i \frac{(u_0 - \mu_i)^2}{\sigma_i^2} - \gamma_i div\left(\frac{\nabla \Phi_i}{|\nabla \Phi_i|}\right) + \lambda\left(\sum_{i=1}^{K} H_\alpha(\Phi_i) - 1\right)\right] = 0, \tag{21}$$

with div denoting the divergence operator, and $div(\frac{\nabla \Phi_i}{|\nabla \Phi_i|})$ being the (mean) curvature of level set Φ_i at point x. We note that the term $\delta_\alpha(\Phi_i)$ in (21) delimits a "natural" band in which the ith PDE is non zero valued (for Φ_i's being signed distance functions) : $B_\alpha^i = \{x \in \Omega/|\Phi_i(x;t)| \leq \alpha\}$.

We embed (21) into a dynamical scheme, and we get a system of K coupled equations $(i = 1...K)$, where dt is the step in time :

$$\Phi_i^{t+1} = \Phi_i^t - dt\left(\delta_\alpha(\Phi_i)\left[e_i \frac{(u_0 - \mu_i)^2}{\sigma_i^2} - \gamma_i div\left(\frac{\nabla \Phi_i}{|\nabla \Phi_i|}\right) + \lambda\left(\sum_{i=1}^{K} H_\alpha(\Phi_i) - 1\right)\right]\right), \tag{22}$$

Let remark that we initially set the Φ_i's to signed distance functions which is commonly used for level set schemes. But as for (19), PDE's (20) and (22) do not maintain the the constraint $|\nabla \Phi_i| = 1$, and we regularly need to regularize the level sets Φ_i to be sure they remain signed distance functions. This can be done for instance by the use of PDE defined in [12].

5 Experimental results

We present some results for synthetic and real images. More experiments were conducted in [10], including noisy data.

Synthetic data presented on Fig. 2 are provided by the Research Group GDR ISIS. This image contains three classes of predefined parameters μ_i and σ_i. We initialized three Φ_i's whose zero level sets (ZLS's) are circular. We show the evolution of the ZLS's, and the resulting classification is given with false colors. We choose a small value for the γ_i's in order to retrieve the non smooth boundary of the class 3 object on the right handside of the data. Black pixels of false color image are pixels of vacuum (unclassified pixels).

The image treated on Fig. 3 is a SPOT satellite image provided by the French Space Agency CNES. This image contains four classes whose parameters μ_i and σ_i were estimated in [1]. We show the evolution of the ZLS's and the final classification (false color image). For these data, we use an automatic method for the initialization of the Φ_i's that we call "seed initialization". This method consists of cutting the data image of u_0 into N windows $W_{l, l=1..N}$ of predefined size. We compute the average m_l of u_0 on each window W_l. We then select the index k such that $k = arg \min_j (m_l - \mu_j)^2$. And we initialize the corresponding circular signed distance function Φ_k on each W_l. Windows are not overlapping and each of them is supporting one and only one function Φ_k, therefore we avoid overlapping of initial Φ_k's. The size of the windows is related to the smallest details we expect to detect. The major advantages of this simple initialization method are : it is automatic (only the size of the windows has to be fixed), it accelerates the speed of convergence (the smaller the windows, the faster the convergence), and it is less sensitive to noise (in the sense that we compute the average m_l of u_0 over each window before selecting the function Φ_k whose mean μ_k is the closest one to m_l).

6 Conclusion

We have presented a variational model based on level set formulation for image classification. The level set formulation is a way to represent regions and set of interfaces with a continuous function defined over the whole support of the image. The minimization of the functional leads to a set of coupled PDE's which are considered through a dynamical scheme. Each PDE is guiding a level set function according to internal forces (length minimization), and external ones (data term, no vacuum and no region overlapping). Results on both synthetic and satellite images are given. In [10] we proposed a way of introducing an additional restoration term in the model through the minimization of the functional :

$$G_\alpha(u, \Phi_1, ..., \Phi_K) = \sum_{i=1}^K \gamma_i \int_\Omega \delta_\alpha(\Phi_i)|\nabla\Phi_i|dx + \frac{\lambda_1}{2}\int_\Omega \Big(\sum_{i=1}^K H_\alpha(\Phi_i) - 1\Big)^2 dx$$

$$+ \sum_{i=1}^K e_i \int_\Omega H_\alpha(\Phi_i)\frac{(u-\mu_i)^2}{\sigma_i^2}dx$$

$$+ \Lambda\Big[\int_\Omega (Ru - u_o)^2 + \lambda_2 \int_\Omega \varphi(|\nabla u|)\Big]$$

$$(23)$$

with φ being a regularizing function and R being the impulse response of the physical system. We alternatively minimize G_α with respect to u (restoration) and with respect to the Φ_i's (classification). First results are promising, and we will study more precisely this model in future work. Further work will also be conducted to deal with the estimation of the class parameters (unsupervised classification). We also envisage to extend this model to multispectral data (with applications to multiband satellite data and applications to color imaging).

References

1. M. Berthod, Z. Kato, S. Yu, and J. Zerubia. "Bayesian image classification using Markov random fields". *Image and Vision Computing*, 14(4):285–293, 1996.
2. V. Caselles, F. Catte, T. Coll, and F. Dibos. "A geometric model for active contours". *Numerische Mathematik*, 66:1–31, 1993.
3. V. Caselles, R. Kimmel, and G. Sapiro. "Geodesic active contours". *International J. of Computer Vision*, 22(1):61–79, 1997.
4. L. C. Evans and R. F. Gariepy. *"Measure theory and fine properties of functions"*. CRC Press, 1992.
5. L.C. Evans and J. Spruck. "Motion of level sets by mean curvature. II". *Trans. of the American Mathematical Society*, 330(1):321–332, 1992.
6. S. Kichenassamy, A. Kumar, P. Olver, A. Tannenbaum, and A. Yezzi Jr. "Conformal curvature flows : from phase transitions to active vision". *Arch. Rational Mech. Anal.*, 134:275–301, 1996.
7. R. Malladi, J.A. Sethian, and B.C. Vemuri. "Evolutionary fronts for topology independent shape modeling and recovery". In *Proc. of the 3rd ECCV*, pages 3–13, Stockholm, Sweden, 1994.
8. S. Osher and J.A. Sethian. "Fronts propagating with curvature dependent speed : algorithms based on the Hamilton-Jacobi formulation". *J. of Computational Physics*, 79:12–49, 1988.
9. T. Pavlidis and Y.-T. Liow. "Integrating region growing and edge detection". In *Proc. of IEEE CVPR*, 1988.
10. C. Samson, L. Blanc-Fraud, G. Aubert, and J. Zerubia. "Multiphase evolution and variational image classification". INRIA Research Report RR-3662 (http://www.inria.fr/RRRT/RR-3662.html), April 1999.
11. C. Samson, L. Blanc-Fraud, G. Aubert, and J. Zerubia. "Simultaneous image classification and restoration using a variational approach". In *Proc. of IEEE CVPR, Fort-Collins, USA*, June 1999.
12. M. Sussman, P. Smereka, and S. Osher. "A level set approach for computing solutions to incompressible two-phase flow". *J. of Computational Physics*, 114:146–159, 1994.
13. H-K. Zhao, T. Chan, B. Merriman, and S. Osher. "A variational level set approach to multiphase motion". *J. of Computational Physics*, 127:179–195, 1996.
14. S. C. Zhu and A. Yuille. "Integrating region growing and edge detection". *IEEE Trans. on Pattern Analysis and Machine Intelligence*, 18(9):884–900, 1996.

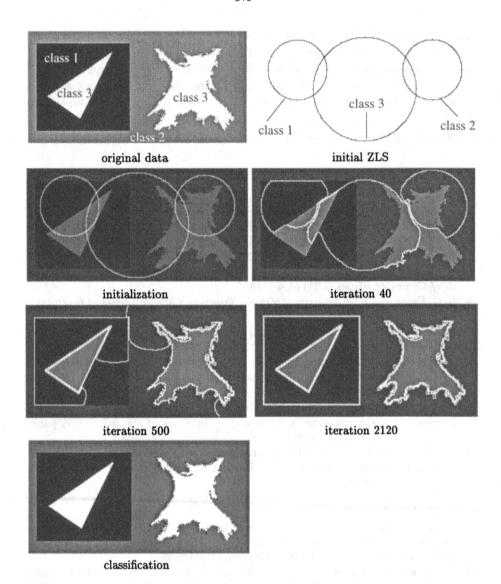

Fig. 2. ZLS evolution and classification for synthetic data containing three classes ($\mu_1 = 100.0$, $\mu_2 = 128.0$ and $\mu_3 = 160.0$). Parameters are : $\lambda = 5.0$, $dt = 0.2$, and for all i we have $\gamma_i = 0.1$ and $e_i = 0.01$. Final figure is the classification result with false colors.

SPOT data

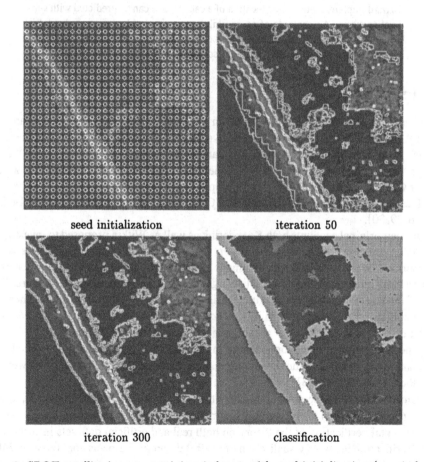

seed initialization   iteration 50

iteration 300   classification

Fig. 3. SPOT satellite image containing 4 classes with seed initialization (on windows of size 9×9) : We show three steps of the ZLS evolution. Final figure is the classification result with false colors.

Calculations on Critical Points under Gaussian Blurring

Arjan Kuijper and Luc Florack

Utrecht University, Department of Computer Science
Padualaan 14
NL-3584 CH Utrecht, The Netherlands
arjan@cs.uu.nl, florack@cs.uu.nl

Abstract. The behaviour of critical points of Gaussian scale-space images is mainly described by their creation and annihilation. In existing literature these events are determined in so-called canonical coordinates. A description in a user-defined Cartesian coordinate system is stated, as well as the results of a straight-forward implementation. The location of a catastrophe can be predicted with sub-pixel accuracy. An example of an annihilation is given. Also an upper bound is derived for the area where critical points can be created. Experimental data of an MR, a CT, and an artificial noise image satisfy this result.

1 Introduction

One way to understand the structure of an image is to embed it in a one-parameter family. In this way the image can be endowed with a topology. If a scale-parametrised Gaussian filter is applied, the parameter can be regarded as the "scale" or the "resolution" at which the image is observed. The resulting structure has become known as linear Gaussian scale-space. In view of ample literature on the subject we will henceforth assume familiarity with the basics of Gaussian scale-space theory [4, 8, 9, 14, 23, 24, 26, 29, 30].

In their original accounts both Koenderink as well as Witkin proposed to investigate the "deep structure" of an image, *i.e. structure at all levels of resolution simultaneously*. Encouraged by the results in specific image analysis applications an increasing interest has recently emerged trying to establish a generic underpinning of deep structure. Results from this could serve as a common basis for a diversity of multiresolution schemes. Such bottom-up approaches often rely on *catastrophe theory* [1, 6, 25, 27, 28], which is in the context of the scale-space paradigm now fairly well-established.

The application of catastrophe theory in Gaussian scale space has been studied *e.g.* by Damon [3]—probably the most comprehensive account on the subject—as well as by others [7, 10–13, 15–23]

Closely related to the present article is the work by Florack and Kuijper [5], introducing new theoretical tools. We will summarise some results in section 2 and give an experimental verification of the theory on both real and artificial data sets in section 3. This verification includes visualisation of several theoretical aspects applied on an MR, a CT, and an artificial noise image. Furthermore we show that the location in scale space of a catastrophe point can be predicted with subpixel accuracy. Of special interest are creations. We will show experimentally and theoretically that the regions in the image in which they can occur is typically small.

2 Theory

The behaviour of critical points as the (scale) parameter changes is described by catastrophe theory. As the parameter changes continuously, the critical points move along critical curves. If the determinant of the Hessian does not become zero, these critical points are called *Morse critical points*. In a typical image these points are extrema (minima and maxima) and saddles. *The Morse lemma* states that the neighbourhood of a Morse critical point can essentially be described by a second order polynomial. At isolated points on a critical curve the determinant of the Hessian may become zero. These points are called *non-Morse points*. Neighbourhoods of such points need a third or higher order polynomial, as described by *Thom's theorem*. If an image is slightly perturbed, the Morse critical points may undergo a small displacement, but nothing happens to them qualitatively. A non-Morse point however will change. In general it will split into a number of Morse critical points. This event is called *morsification*. Thom's theorem provides a list of elementary catastrophes with canonical formulas[1] for the catastrophe germs and the perturbations. The Thom splitting lemma states that there exist *canonical coordinates* in which these events can be described. These coordinates however do in general not coincide with the user-defined coordinates, but are used for notational convenience. In Gaussian scale space the only generic events are *annihilations* and *creations* of a pair of Morse points: an extremum and a saddle in the 2D case. All other events can be split into a combination of one of these events and one 'in which nothing happens'. See Damon [3] for a proof. Canonical descriptions of these events are given by the following formulae:

$$f^{A}(x, y; t) \overset{\text{def}}{=} x^3 + 6xt \pm (y^2 + 2t) \tag{1}$$

$$f^{c}(x, y; t) \overset{\text{def}}{=} x^3 - 6x(y^2 + t) \pm (y^2 + 2t). \tag{2}$$

Note that Eq. (1) and Eq. (2), describing annihilation and creation respectively, satisfy the diffusion equation

$$\frac{\partial u}{\partial t} = \Delta u. \tag{3}$$

Here Δ denotes the Laplacean operator. The reader can easily verify that the the form $f^{A}(x, y; t)$ corresponds to an annihilation via the critical path $(\sqrt{-2t}, 0, t)$, $t \leq 0$ at the origin, whereas $f^{c}(x, y; t)$ corresponds to a creation at the origin via the critical path $(\sqrt{+2t}, 0, t)$ $t \geq 0$.

In general the user-defined coordinates will not equal the canonical coordinates. Therefore it would be helpful to have a so-called covariant formalism, in which results are stated in an arbitrary coordinate system. Then the first order approximation of a non-Morse point is given by the linear system

$$\begin{bmatrix} \mathbf{H} & \mathbf{w} \\ \mathbf{z}^T & c \end{bmatrix} \begin{bmatrix} \mathbf{x} \\ t \end{bmatrix} = - \begin{bmatrix} \mathbf{g} \\ \det \mathbf{H} \end{bmatrix}, \tag{4}$$

---

[1] Notation due to Gilmore [6]. Also the terminology *normal forms* is used in literature, *e.g.* by Poston and Steward [25].

in which the coefficients are determined by the first order derivatives of the image's gradient g and Hessian determinant $\det H$, evaluated at the point of expansion near the critical point of interest (x_0, t_0), as follows:

$$H = \nabla g, w = \partial_t g, z = \nabla \det H, c = \partial_t \det H. \tag{5}$$

See Florack and Kuijper [5] for more details. In 2D images, where $x = (x, y)$, this becomes

$$H = \begin{bmatrix} L_{xx} & L_{xy} \\ L_{xy} & L_{yy} \end{bmatrix}, \tag{6}$$

$$w = \begin{bmatrix} \Delta L_x \\ \Delta L_y \end{bmatrix}, \tag{7}$$

$$z = \begin{bmatrix} L_{xxx}L_{yy} + L_{xx}L_{xyy} - 2L_{xy}L_{xxy} \\ L_{yyy}L_{xx} + L_{yy}L_{xxy} - 2L_{xy}L_{xyy} \end{bmatrix}, \tag{8}$$

and

$$c = L_{xx}\Delta L_{yy} - 2L_{xy}\Delta L_{xy} + L_{yy}\Delta L_{xx}, \tag{9}$$

where Eq. (3) has been used. Apparently the first order scheme requires spatial derivatives up to *fourth* order. These derivatives are obtained at any scale by linear filtering:

$$\frac{\partial^{m+n}u(x,y;\sigma)}{\partial x^m \, \partial y^n} \stackrel{\text{def}}{=} (-1)^{m+n} \int u(x',y') \frac{\partial^{m+n}\phi(x'-x,y'-y;\sigma)}{\partial x'^m \, \partial y'^n} dx' dy',$$

where $u(x,y)$ is the input image and $\phi(x,y;\sigma)$ a normalised Gaussian of scale σ. It has been shown by Blom [2] that we can take derivatives up to fourth order without problems with respect to the results, provided scale is somewhat larger than pixelscale. It is important to note that Eqs. (4–9) hold *in any Cartesian coordinate system*. This property of form invariance is known as *covariance*.

At Morse critical points we must restrict ourselves to $Hx + wt = -g$, *i.e.* the first row of Eq. 4. The solution is easily found to be

$$x = -H^{\text{inv}}g - H^{\text{inv}}wt. \tag{10}$$

If we define $t \stackrel{\text{def}}{=} \det H\tau$, Eq. (10) becomes $x = -H^{\text{inv}}g - \tilde{H}w\tau$, where the matrix $\tilde{H}$ is the transposed cofactor matrix, defined by $H\tilde{H} = \det H\, I$. In 2D $\tilde{H}$ reads

$$\tilde{H} \stackrel{\text{def}}{=} \begin{bmatrix} L_{yy} & -L_{xy} \\ -L_{xy} & L_{xx} \end{bmatrix}. \tag{11}$$

Note that $\tilde{H}$ exists even if H is singular. At critical points the *scale-space velocity* is defined by

$$\overline{w} \stackrel{\text{def}}{=} -\tilde{H}w. \tag{12}$$

Thus instead of tracing the two branches of the critical curve with Lindeberg's *drift velocity of critical points* [22, 23], $v = -H^{\text{inv}}w$ (if defined), it is now parametrised by a continuous function that is non-degenerate at the catastrophe point. Note that the *scale-space velocity* $\overline{\mathbf{w}}$ has the direction of $\mathbf{v}$ at extrema, is opposite at saddles, and remains well-defined even if $\mathbf{v}$ does not exist.

At non-Morse critical points the determinant of $\mathbf{H}$ becomes zero and we need to invert the complete linear system, Eq. (4). If we define

$$\mathbf{M} \stackrel{\text{def}}{=} \begin{bmatrix} \mathbf{H} & \mathbf{w} \\ \mathbf{z}^{\mathrm{T}} & c \end{bmatrix}, \tag{13}$$

the solution of Eq. (4) becomes

$$\begin{bmatrix} \mathbf{x} \\ t \end{bmatrix} = -\mathbf{M}^{\text{inv}} \begin{bmatrix} \mathbf{g} \\ \det \mathbf{H} \end{bmatrix}, \tag{14}$$

In general this inverse matrix exists even if the Hessian is singular. Florack and Kuijper [5] have proven that at annihilations $\det \mathbf{M} < 0$ and at creations $\det \mathbf{M} > 0$, where

$$\det \mathbf{M} = c \det \mathbf{H} + \mathbf{z}^{\mathrm{T}}\overline{\mathbf{w}}. \tag{15}$$

In a full $(2+1)$D scale-space neighbourhood of a catastrophe the differential invariant $\det \mathbf{M}$ reads

$\det \mathbf{M} =$

$([L_{xxyy} + L_{yyyy}]L_{xx} + [L_{xxxx} + L_{xxyy}]L_{yy} - 2[L_{xxxy} + L_{xyyy}]L_{xy})(L_{xx}L_{yy} - L_{xy}^2) +$
$-\{L_{xx}[L_{xxy} + L_{yyy}][L_{yyy}L_{xx} + L_{yy}L_{xxy} - 2L_{xy}L_{xyy}] +$
$+L_{yy}[L_{xxx} + L_{xyy}][L_{xxx}L_{yy} + L_{xx}L_{xyy} - 2L_{xy}L_{xxy}] +$
$-L_{xy}([L_{xxx} + L_{xyy}][L_{yyy}L_{xx} + L_{yy}L_{xxy} - 2L_{xy}L_{xyy}] +$
$[L_{xxy} + L_{yyy}][L_{xxx}L_{yy} + L_{xx}L_{xyy} - 2L_{xy}L_{xxy}])\}.$

At catastrophes $\det \mathbf{H} = 0$, so Eq. (15) reduces to

$$\det \mathbf{M} = \mathbf{z}^{\mathrm{T}}\overline{\mathbf{w}}, \tag{16}$$

which is the innerproduct between the spatial derivative of $\det \mathbf{H}$, Eq. (5), and the scale-space velocity $\overline{\mathbf{w}}$, Eq. (12). It can be seen that only spatial derivatives up to third order are required at the catastrophe points. In the next section we will apply these results on several images.

3 Experimental results

In our experiments we used a 64 x 64 subimage of a 256 x 256 MR scan (Fig. 1a and b), CT scan (Fig. 1c and d), and a 64 x 64 artificial image with Gaussian noise of mean zero and standard deviation $\sigma = 10$, also denoted as N(0,10) (Fig. 1e).

3.1 Visualisation of $\mathbf{z}^{\mathrm{T}}$ and $\overline{\mathbf{w}}$

As an example of the vectors $\overline{\mathbf{w}}$ (see Eq. (12)) and $\mathbf{z}^{\mathrm{T}}$ (see Eq. (5)) we selected two critical points of the MR image (Fig. 1b) at scale $\sigma = 2.46$. This image with its critical

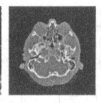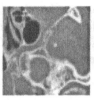

Fig. 1. a) Original 256 x 256 pixel MR image. b) 64 x 64 pixel subimage of a). c) original 256 x 256 pixel CT image. d) 64 x 64 pixel subimage of c). e) 64 x 64 artificial Gaussian N(0,10) noise image.

points is shown in Fig. 2a. Extrema (saddle points) are visualised by the white (black) dots. At the upper middle part of this image a critical isophote generated by a saddle and enclosing two extrema is shown (see also Fig. 2b). At a larger scale the saddle point will annihilate with the upper one of these extrema. At these two points we have calculated the direction and magnitude of the vectors $\overline{\mathbf{w}}$ and $\mathbf{z}^T$. The vectors are shown on these points at two successive scales $\sigma = 2.46$ (Fig. 2c) and $\sigma = 2.83$ (Fig. 2d). Indeed the velocity (given by $\overline{\mathbf{w}}$) of the extremum (dark arrow at the white dot) is in the direction of the saddle, and thus in the direction of the point of annihilation. The velocity vector at the saddle has the same direction, as the result of the parametrisation by Eq. (12))

Furthermore since the point where the annihilation takes place (at $\det \mathbf{H} = 0$) is between the two critical points, the vector $\mathbf{z}^T$, which is the normalvector (recall Eq.(5)) to the zero-crossing of $\det \mathbf{H}$, directs from the saddle towards the extremum both at the saddle and the extremum.

Finally it can be seen that the vectors of $\mathbf{z}^T$ and $\overline{\mathbf{w}}$ at the critical points have an angle of more than $\frac{\pi}{2}$. Since $\det \mathbf{M}$ is the innerproduct of these vectors at a catastrophe (see Eq. (16)), this leads to a negative sign of $\det \mathbf{M}$, indicating that the two critical points approach each other and disappear eventually.

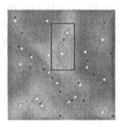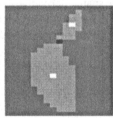

Fig. 2. a) Critical points (extrema white, saddles black) of Fig. 1b at scale $\sigma = 2.46$. At the field of interest the critical isophote through a saddle is shown; b) subimage of a, showing the field of interest more clearly. The saddle is about to annihilate with the upper extremum; c) Subimage of the two annihilating critical points and the vectors of $\overline{\mathbf{w}}$ (dark) and $\mathbf{z}^T$ (bright) at scale $\sigma = 2.46$; d) Same, at scale $\sigma = 2.83$.

3.2 Location of the catastrophe

Although the location of the critical points at the image can easily be calculated by using the zerocrossings of the derivatives, the subpixel position of the catastrophe point in scale space requires invertsion of the complete linear system, Eq. (4), yielding Eq. (14). As an example we took the same two critical points as in the previous section. The resulting vectors of 4 successive scales for the MR subimage (Fig. 2c) are shown in Fig. 3. At each pixel the projection of the vector on the spatial plane is shown. A bright (dark) arrow denotes a positive (negative) scale-coordinate. The approximate location of the catastrophe can be found with subpixel precision by averaging the arrows as shown in Table 1. The black dot in Fig. 3 is located at the estimated position of the catastrophe, the ellipse shows the standard deviation of the estimation.

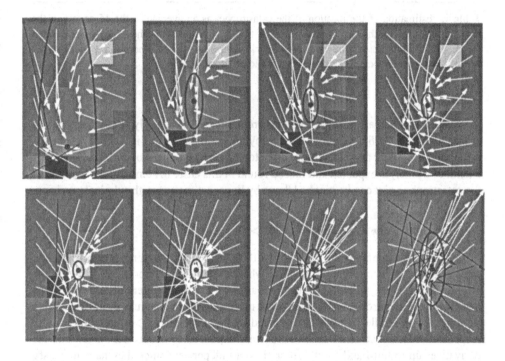

Fig. 3. Visualisation of Eq. (14) of the vector (x, y); a bright (dark) arrow signifies a positive (negative) value of the t-component. The black dot is located at the mean value of the inner 15 arrows, the ellipse shows the standard deviation (see Table 1). First row: a: scale $\sigma = 2.34$; b: scale $\sigma = 2.46$; c: scale $\sigma = 2.59$; d: scale $\sigma = 2.72$. Second row: e: scale $\sigma = 2.86$; f: scale $\sigma = 3.00$; g: scale $\sigma = 3.16$, a catastrophe has occurred; h: scale $\sigma = 3.32$.

Below the catastrophe-scale the location is accurate whereas at a scale above it (at $\sigma = 3.32$, see Fig. 3h) the estimated location turns out to be more uncertain. The estimation of the t-coordinate is positive below catastrophe-scale and negative above, as expected. The standard deviation is largely influenced by the cells that are distant from the critical curve, which also can be seen in Fig 3h. Since the relation between scale σ and coordinate t is given by $t = \frac{1}{2}\sigma^2$, we can easily calculate the estimated scale $\sigma_{est} = \sqrt{\sigma^2 + 2t_{calc}}$ with error $\delta\sigma_{est} = \partial_t\sigma_{est} \cdot \delta t_{calc} = \delta t_{calc}/\sigma_{est}$.

scale	x-coordinate	y-coordinate	t-coordinate	estimated scale
2.34	0.481197 ± 1.27275	−0.111758 ± 6.54458	0.630053 ± 3.7568	2.59501 ± 1.4477
2.46	0.869898 ± 0.401954	1.83346 ± 1.26546	1.58998 ± 0.663776	3.03808 ± 0.218489
2.59	0.893727 ± 0.340422	1.72886 ± 0.79602	1.3391 ± 0.447622	3.06008 ± 0.146278
2.72	0.92611 ± 0.286782	1.73222 ± 0.580028	1.10524 ± 0.434127	3.09831 ± 0.140117
2.86	0.95843 ± 0.250132	1.75858 ± 0.429409	0.824525 ± 0.483923	3.13293 ± 0.154464
3.00	0.991123 ± 0.26873	1.79548 ± 0.504445	0.466264 ± 0.597825	3.15556 ± 0.189451
3.16	1.02368 ± 0.380863	1.83618 ± 0.921176	−0.00573945 ± 0.792309	3.15638 ± 0.251019
3.32	1.05174 ± 0.603366	1.86346 ± 1.67306	−0.642702 ± 1.1066	3.12054 ± 0.354618

Table 1. Estimation of the location of the catastrophe, as an average of the 15 arrows in the rectangle spanned by the two critical points of Fig. 3a. The origin in the (x, y)-plane is fixed for all figures at the middle of the saddle (black square) of Fig. 3a. The average value of the t-direction is positive below catastrophe scale and negative above it.

By slightly increasing scales the catastrophe is experimentally found between the scales 3.050 and 3.053, which is covered by all estimated scales in Table 1. Since the estimation is a linear approximation of the top of a curve a small overestimation (*here:* a tenth of a pixel) is expected and indeed found in this case. In summary the location of the catastrophe point can be pinched down by linear estimation with subpixel precision.

3.3 Fraction of the area where det M > 0

Since creations can only occur at det $M > 0$, we calculated the number of pixels at the three different images (Figs. 1a, c and e) where this invariant is positive. If we for the moment assume that all elements of the matrix M are independent of each other, the distribution of catastrophes is in some sense random in the image, just as the distribution of extrema and saddle points, discriminated by the areas det $H > 0$ and det $H < 0$, respectively. However, since annihilations are supposed to occur more often and the derivatives up to third and fourth order are not independent since they have to satisfy the heat equation, we expect the area where det $M > 0$ to be small. In the following figures we show this fraction as a percentage of the total area of the image.

For the MR image we see a relative area of maximal 0.12 (Fig. 4, top-left). Furthermore the number of critical points decreases logarithmically with scale (Fig. 4, top-right). The slope is $-1.76 \pm .01$. An a priori estimation value is -2, see *e.g.* Florack's monograph [4].

In Fig. 5 the image of the sign of det M of the MR-subimage (Fig. 1b) is shown at four successive scales. It appears that the locations of the image where det M is positive are relatively small isolated areas.

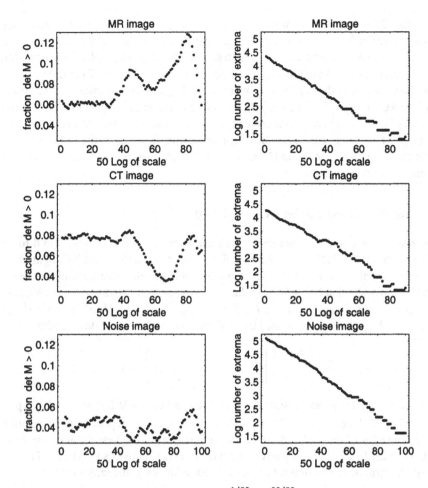

Fig. 4. Results of calculations; scales vary from $e^{1/50}$ to $e^{90/50}$; First row: MR image; Second row: CT image; Third row: artificial noise image. First column: Fraction of det **M** > 0, ranging from 0.04 to 0.12 for the MR and CT image, and less for the artificial noise image; Second column: Logarithm of the number of critical points, with slopes $-1.76 \pm .01$, $-1.74 \pm .02$, and $-1.84 \pm .01$, respectively;

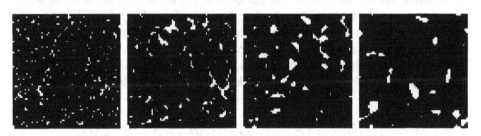

Fig. 5. In white the area where $det\mathbf{M} > 0$ a: at scale $\sigma = 1.57$, corresponding to the value 22.5 on the horizontal axis of Fig. 4 b: at scale $\sigma = 2.46$, (value 45) c: at scale $\sigma = 3.866$, (value 67.5) d: at scale $\sigma = 6.05$, (value 90)

For the CT image we see more or less the same results (Fig. 4, second row): the fraction where det M is positive is a bit higher at small scales ($\sigma < 2.22$, the value 40 at the horizontal axis) and a bit smaller at high scales. The slope of graph of the logarithm of the number of critical points at increasing scale is found to be -1.74 ± 0.02.

At the noise image the relative area where det M > 0 is significantly smaller than at the MR and CT images. This might indicate that creations require some global structure (like a ridge), that is absent in a noise image. The logarithm of the number of extrema has a slope of $-1.84 \pm .01$ (Fig. 4, bottom-right), which is closer to the expected value -2 than the slope at the MR and CT image. This might also be caused by the lack of structure in the noise image.

3.4 Estimation of the area where det M > 0

In the previous section the fraction of the area where det M > 0 was found to be ranging from 0.04 to 0.12. A mathematical survey on the sign of det M might show the expectation of creations. At non-Morse points this invariant can be simplified considerably. If the Hessian becomes singular, the rows (or, equivalently the columns) are dependent of each other, i.e. $(L_{xx}, L_{xy}) = \lambda(L_{xy}, L_{yy})$. Therefore[2] $L_{xx} = \lambda^2 L_{yy}$ and $L_{xy} = \lambda L_{yy}$. So in general, the Hessian at a catastrophe can be described by

$$\mathbf{H} = \begin{bmatrix} \lambda^2 & \lambda \\ \lambda & 1 \end{bmatrix} L_{yy} \, , \, \tilde{\mathbf{H}} = \begin{bmatrix} 1 & -\lambda \\ -\lambda & \lambda^2 \end{bmatrix} L_{yy} \tag{17}$$

The second order Taylor expansion of the image now reads $\frac{1}{2}\lambda^2 L_{yy} x^2 + \lambda L_{yy} xy + L_{yy} y^2$ which reduces to $\frac{1}{2}L_{yy}(\lambda x + y)^2$. The parameter λ depends on the rotation between the axes of the real and the canonical coordinates. If these coincide we have $\lambda = 0$, i.e. both L_{xx} and L_{xy} are zero, see Eqs.(1) and (2). With Eqs.(7-8), (12), (16-17) the explicit form of det M at a catastrophe in 2D reduces significantly to

$$\det \mathbf{M} = L_{yy}^2 (L_{xxx} - 3\lambda L_{xxy} + 3\lambda^2 L_{xyy} - \lambda^3 L_{yyy})(-L_{xxx} + \lambda L_{xxy} - L_{xyy} + \lambda L_{yyy}) \tag{18}$$

Equation (18) shows that the sign of det M only depends on third order derivatives and the orientation of the critical curve, as determined by λ. If we assume that all third order derivatives are independent, the zerocrossings of equation (18) can be regarded as the union of two linear planes in the 4-dimensional ($L_{xxx}, L_{xxy}, L_{xyy}, L_{yyy}$) space. The planes divide this space into 4 subspaces where the determinant is either positive or negative, whereas any point on the planes leads to det M $= 0$. The normal vectors to these planes are given by $n_1 = (1, -3\lambda, 3\lambda^2, -\lambda^3)$ and $n_2 = (-1, \lambda, -1, \lambda)$. The factor L_{yy}^2 does not change the sign of the determinant. By definition we then have

$$\cos\phi = \frac{n_1 \cdot n_2}{\|n_1\| \cdot \|n_2\|} = -\frac{1 + 6\lambda^2 + \lambda^4}{\sqrt{(2 + 2\lambda^2)(1 + 9\lambda^2 + 9\lambda^4 + \lambda^6)}} \tag{19}$$

---

[2] The choice of L_{yy} as leading term is of minor importance, we could just as well have chosen $\mu(L_{xx}, L_{xy}) = (L_{xy}, L_{yy})$, leading to $L_{yy} = \mu^2 L_{xx}$ and $L_{xy} = \mu L_{xx}$, which would be particularly prudent if L_{yy} is close to zero.

This angle is invariant with respect to the transformations $\lambda \to -\lambda$ and $\lambda \to \frac{1}{\lambda}$. Fig. 6a shows the cosine of the angle for different values of λ.

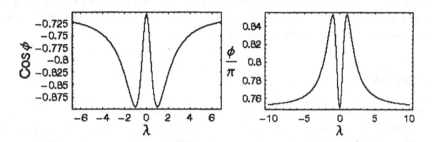

Fig. 6. Left: Cosine of the angle of planes given by Eq. (19). Right: Fraction of the 4D $(L_{xxx}, L_{xxy}, L_{xyy}, L_{yyy})$-space where det M is smaller than zero.

Lemma 1. *The fraction of the space (of third order derivatives) μ where creations can occur is bounded by $\frac{1}{\pi} \arccos(\frac{2}{5}\sqrt{5}) \leq \mu \leq \frac{1}{4}$.*

Proof. The fraction of the space where annihilations can occur is given by the fraction of the image where det $M < 0$ and det $H = 0$. Since Eq. (19) is negative definite and $\phi \in [0, \pi]$, the fraction $\frac{\phi}{\pi}$ gives the fraction of the space where annihilations can occur. This fraction varies from $\frac{3}{4}$ at both $\lambda = 0$ and $\lambda \to \infty$, to $\frac{1}{\pi} \arccos(-\frac{2}{5}\sqrt{5}) \approx 0.852\ldots$ at $\lambda = 1$, which follow directly from differentiation, see also Fig. 6b. Equivalently, creations can occur in at most $\frac{1}{4}$ of all possible tuples $(L_{xxx}, L_{xxy}, L_{xyy}, L_{yyy})$.

The usual generic events, *e.g.* discussed by Damon [3] and others [10] correspond to the case $\lambda = 0$. In the canonical coordinates the equations (1) and (2) are found. Then Eq. (18) reduces to det $M = -L_{yy}^2 L_{xxx} (L_{xxx} + L_{xyy})$ and it can easily be seen that the fraction of the space is $\frac{3}{4}$, *i.e.* in only $\frac{1}{4}$ of the possible values of L_{xxx} and L_{xyy} a creation can occur.

4 Conclusion and Discussion

We have used an operational scheme to characterise critical points in scale-space. The characteristic local property of a critical point is determined by its Hessian signature (saddle or extremum). Pairs of critical points with opposite signature can be annihilated or created. Close to such catastrophes, empirically observed properties of the critical points are consistent with the presented theory. The location of catastrophes in scale space can be found with subpixel accuracy. The approximate location of an annihilation and the idea of scale space velocity have been visualised. In general, more annihilations than creations are observed, probably because creations need a special structure of the neighbourhood. This is also indicated by the results of the noise image. We have shown that the area where creations can occur, determined by the third order derivatives, is at most $\frac{1}{4}$. In our experiments this fraction is even smaller than approximately 0.125 .... It remains to be investigated whether the relative volumes of det $\mathbf{M} > 0$ and det $\mathbf{M} < 0$ is indicative of a similar ratio between creations and annihilations. In future work we will therefore examine the correlation between the distributions of the various derivatives in the definition of det $\mathbf{M}$. Blom [2] has given a general framework, which might give a more precise explanation of the small number of creations.

References

1. V. I. Arnold. *Catastrophe Theory*. Springer-Verlag, Berlin, 1984.
2. J. Blom, B. M. ter Haar Romeny, A. Bel, and J. J. Koenderink. Spatial derivatives and the propagation of noise in Gaussian scale-space. *Journal of Visual Communication and Image Representation*, 4(1):1–13, March 1993.
3. J. Damon. Local Morse theory for solutions to the heat equation and Gaussian blurring. *Journal of Differential Equations*, 115(2):368–401, January 1995.
4. L. M. J. Florack. *Image Structure*, volume 10 of *Computational Imaging and Vision Series*. Kluwer Academic Publishers, Dordrecht, The Netherlands, 1997.
5. L. M. J. Florack and A. Kuijper. The Topological Structure of Scale-Space Images *To appear in Journal of Mathematical Imaging and Vision*.
6. R. Gilmore. *Catastrophe Theory for Scientists and Engineers*. Dover Publications, Inc., New York, 1993. Originally published by John Wiley & Sons, New York, 1981.
7. L. D. Griffin and A. C. F. Colchester. Superficial and deep structure in linear diffusion scale space: Isophotes, critical points and separatrices. *Image and Vision Computing*, 13(7):543–557, September 1995.
8. B. M. ter Haar Romeny, L. M. J. Florack, J. J. Koenderink, and M. A. Viergever, editors. *Scale-Space Theory in Computer Vision: Proceedings of the First International Conference, Scale-Space'97, Utrecht, The Netherlands*, volume 1252 of *Lecture Notes in Computer Science*. Springer-Verlag, Berlin, July 1997.
9. T. Iijima. Basic theory on normalization of a pattern (in case of typical one-dimensional pattern). *Bulletin of Electrical Laboratory*, 26:368–388, 1962. (In Japanese).
10. P. Johansen. On the classification of toppoints in scale space. *Journal of Mathematical Imaging and Vision*, 4(1):57–67, 1994.
11. P. Johansen. Local analysis of image scale space. In Sporring et al. [26], chapter 10, pages 139–146.
12. P. Johansen, S. Skelboe, K. Grue, and J. D. Andersen. Representing signals by their top points in scale-space. In *Proceedings of the 8th International Conference on Pattern Recognition (Paris, France, October 1986)*, pages 215–217. IEEE Computer Society Press, 1986.
13. S. N. Kalitzin, B. M. ter Haar Romeny, A. H. Salden, P. F. M. Nacken, and M. A. Viergever. Topological numbers and singularities in scalar images: Scale-space evolution properties. *Journal of Mathematical Imaging and Vision*, 9:253–269, 1998.
14. J. J. Koenderink. The structure of images. *Biological Cybernetics*, 50:363–370, 1984.
15. J. J. Koenderink. The structure of the visual field. In W. Güttinger and G. Dangelmayr, editors, *The Physics of Structure Formation: Theory and Simulation. Proceedings of an International Symposium*, Tübingen, Germany, October 27–November 2 1986. Springer-Verlag.
16. J. J. Koenderink. A hitherto unnoticed singularity of scale-space. *IEEE Transactions on Pattern Analysis and Machine Intelligence*, 11(11):1222–1224, November 1989.
17. J. J. Koenderink. *Solid Shape*. MIT Press, Cambridge, 1990.

18. J. J. Koenderink and A. J. van Doorn. Dynamic shape. *Biological Cybernetics*, 53:383–396, 1986.
19. J. J. Koenderink and A. J. van Doorn. The structure of two-dimensional scalar fields with applications to vision. *Biological Cybernetics*, 33:151–158, 1979.
20. L. M. Lifshitz and S. M. Pizer. A multiresolution hierarchical appraoch to image segmentation based on intensity extrema. *IEEE Transactions on Pattern Analysis and Machine Intelligence*, 12(6):529–540, June 1990.
21. T. Lindeberg. On the behaviour in scale-space of local extrema and blobs. In P. Johansen and S. Olsen, editors, *Theory & Applications of Image Analysis*, volume 2 of *Series in Machine Perception and Artificial Intelligence*, pages 38–47. World Scientific, Singapore, 1992. Selected papers from the 7th Scandinavian Conference on Image Analysis.
22. T. Lindeberg. Scale-space behaviour of local extrema and blobs. *Journal of Mathematical Imaging and Vision*, 1(1):65–99, March 1992.
23. T. Lindeberg. *Scale-Space Theory in Computer Vision*. The Kluwer International Series in Engineering and Computer Science. Kluwer Academic Publishers, 1994.
24. N. Otsu. *Mathematical Studies on Feature Extraction in Pattern Recognition*. PhD thesis, Electrotechnical Laboratory, Ibaraki, Japan, 1981. (In Japanese).
25. T. Poston and I. N. Stewart. *Catastrophe Theory and its Applications*. Pitman, London, 1978.
26. J. Sporring, M. Nielsen, L. M. J. Florack, and P. Johansen, editors. *Gaussian Scale-Space Theory*, volume 8 of *Computational Imaging and Vision Series*. Kluwer Academic Publishers, Dordrecht, 1997.
27. R. Thom. *Stabilité Structurelle et Morphogénèse*. Benjamin, Paris, 1972.
28. R. Thom. *Structural Stability and Morphogenesis (translated by D. H. Fowler)*. Benjamin-Addison Wesley, New York, 1975.
29. J. A. Weickert, S. Ishikawa, and A. Imiya. On the history of Gaussian scale-space axiomatics. In Sporring et al. [26], chapter 4, pages 45–59.
30. A. P. Witkin. Scale-space filtering. In *Proceedings of the International Joint Conference on Artificial Intelligence*, pages 1019–1022, Karlsruhe, Germany, 1983.

Region Tracking on Surfaces Deforming via Level-Sets Methods*

Marcelo Bertalmio[1], Guillermo Sapiro[1], and Gregory Randall[2]

[1] Electrical and Computer Engineering
University of Minnesota
Minneapolis, MN 55455
guille@ece.umn.edu
[2] I.I.E. Facultad de Ingenieria
Universidad de la Republica
Montevideo, Uruguay

Abstract. Since the work by Osher and Sethian on level-sets algorithms for numerical shape evolutions, this technique has been used for a large number of applications in numerous fields. In medical imaging, this numerical technique has been successfully used for example in segmentation and cortex unfolding algorithms. The migration from a Lagrangian implementation to an Eulerian one via implicit representations or level-sets brought some of the main advantages of the technique, mainly, topology independence and stability. This migration means also that the evolution is parametrization free, and therefore we do not know exactly how each part of the shape is deforming, and the point-wise correspondence is lost. In this note we present a technique to numerically track regions on surfaces that are being deformed using the level-sets method. The basic idea is to represent the region of interest as the intersection of two implicit surfaces, and then track its deformation from the deformation of these surfaces. This technique then solves one of the main shortcomings of the very useful level-sets approach. Applications include lesion localization in medical images, region tracking in functional MRI visualization, and geometric surface mapping.

Key words: Level-sets, region tracking and correspondence, medical imaging, segmentation, visualization, shape deformation.

1 Introduction

The use of level-sets for the numerical implementations of n-dimensional[1] shape deformations became extremely popular following the seminal work of Osher and Sethian [17] (see for example [14, 18] for some of the applications of this technique and a long list of references). In medical imaging, the technique has been successfully used for example for 2D and 3D segmentation [5, 10, 12, 15, 20,

---

* A journal version of this paper appears in the May 1999 issue of IEEE Trans. Medical Imaging.
[1] In this note we consider $n \geq 3$.

21]. The basic idea is to represent the deformation of an n-dimensional closed surface $\mathcal{S}$ as the deformation of an $n+1$-dimensional function Φ. The surface is represented in an implicit form in Φ, for example, via its zero level-set. Formally, let's represent the initial surface $\mathcal{S}(0)$ as the zero level-set of Φ, i.e., $\mathcal{S}(0) \equiv \{\mathbf{X} \in \mathbb{R}^n : \Phi(\mathbf{X}, 0) = 0\}$. If the surface is deforming according to

$$\frac{\partial \mathcal{S}(t)}{\partial t} = \beta \mathcal{N}_\mathcal{S}, \tag{1}$$

where $\mathcal{N}_\mathcal{S}$ is the unit normal to the surface, then this deformation is represented as the zero level-set of $\Phi(\mathbf{X}, t) : \mathbb{R}^n \times [0, \tau) \to \mathbb{R}$ deforming according to

$$\frac{\partial \Phi(\mathbf{X}, t)}{\partial t} = \beta(\mathbf{X}, t) \parallel \nabla \Phi(\mathbf{X}, t) \parallel, \tag{2}$$

where $\beta(\mathbf{X}, t)$ is computed on the level-sets of $\Phi(\mathbf{X}, t)$. The formal analysis of this algorithm can be found for example in [6, 7].

The basic idea behind this technique is that we migrate from a Lagrangian implementation (particles on the surface) to an Eulerian one, i.e., a fix Cartesian coordinate system. This allows for example to automatically follow changes in the topology of the deforming surface $\mathcal{S}$, since the topology of the function Φ is fixed. See the mentioned references for more details on the level-sets technique.

In a number of applications, it is important not just to know how the whole surface deforms, but also how some of its regions do. Since the parametrization is missing, this is not possible in a straightforward level-sets approach. This problem is related to the aperture problem in optical flow computation, and it is also the reason why the level-sets approach can only deal with parametrization independent flows that do not contain tangential velocities. Although tangential velocities do not affect the geometry of the deforming shape, they do affect the 'point correspondence' in the deformation. For example, with a straight level-sets approach, it is not possible to determine where a given point $\mathbf{X}_0 \in \mathcal{S}(0)$ is at certain time t. One way to solve this problem is to track isolated points with a set of ODE's, and this was done for example in grid generation and surface flattening; see [9, 18]. This is a possible solution if we are just interested in tracking a number of isolated points. If we want to track regions for example, then using 'particles' brings us back to a 'Lagrangian formulation' and some of the problems that actually motivated the level-sets approach. For example, what happens if the region splits during the deformation? What happens if the region of interest is represented by particles that start to come too close together in some parts of the region and too far from each other in others?

In this note we propose an alternative solution to the problem of region tracking on surface deformations implemented via level-sets.[2] The basic idea is to represent the boundary of the region of interest $\mathcal{R} \in \mathcal{S}$ as the intersection

---

[2] A different level-set approach for intrinsic motions of generic 3D curves, together with very deep and elegant theoretical results, is introduced in [1]. This approach is difficult to implement numerically, and in some cases not fully appropriate for numerical 3D curve evolution [16]. A variation of this technique, with very good

of the given surface S and an auxiliary surface $\hat{S}$, both of them given as zero level-sets of $n+1$-dimensional functions $\varPhi$ and $\hat{\varPhi}$ respectively.[3] The tracking of the region $\mathcal{R}$ is given by tracking the intersection of these two surfaces, that is, by the intersection of the level-sets of $\varPhi$ and $\hat{\varPhi}$. In the rest of this note we give details on the technique and present examples.

Note that although we use the proposed technique to track regions of interest on deforming surfaces, with the region deformation dictated by the surface deformation, the same general approach here presented of simultaneously deforming n hypersurfaces ($n \geq 2$) and looking at the intersection of their level-sets can be used for the numerical implementation of generic geometric deformations of curves and surfaces of high co-dimension.[4]

2 The algorithm

Assume the deformation of the surface S, given by (1), is implemented using the level-sets algorithm, i.e., Equation (2). Let $\mathcal{R} \in S$ be a region we want to track during this deformation, and $\partial\mathcal{R}$ its boundary. Define a new function $\hat{\varPhi}(\mathbf{X}, 0) : \mathbb{R}^n \to \mathbb{R}$ (a distance function for example), such that the intersection of its zero level-set $\hat{S}$ with S defines $\partial\mathcal{R}$ and then $\mathcal{R}$. In other words,

$$\partial\mathcal{R}(0) := S(0) \cap \hat{S}(0) = \{\mathbf{X} \in \mathbb{R}^n : \varPhi(\mathbf{X}, 0) = \hat{\varPhi}(\mathbf{X}, 0) = 0\}.$$

The tracking of $\mathcal{R}$ is done by simultaneously deforming $\varPhi$ and $\hat{\varPhi}$. The auxiliary function $\hat{\varPhi}$ deforms according to

$$\frac{\partial\hat{\varPhi}(\mathbf{X}, t)}{\partial t} = \hat{\beta}(\mathbf{X}, t) \parallel \nabla\hat{\varPhi}(\mathbf{X}, t) \parallel, \tag{3}$$

and then $\hat{S}$ deforms according to

$$\frac{\partial\hat{S}}{\partial t} = \hat{\beta}\mathcal{N}_{\hat{S}}. \tag{4}$$

We have then to find the velocity $\hat{\beta}$ as a function of β. In order to track the region of interest, $\partial\mathcal{R}$ must have exactly the same geometric velocity both in (2) and (3). The velocity in (2) (or (1)) is given by the problem in hand, and is

---

experimental results, is introduced in [11]. The Ambrosio-Soner approach and its variations deal with intrinsic curve-velocities and do not address the surface-velocity projection needed for the tracking in this paper.

[3] The use of multiple level-set functions was used in the past for problems like motion of junctions [13]. Both the problem and its solution are different from the ones in this paper.

[4] After this paper was accepted for publication, we became aware of recent work by Osher and colleagues using this general approach mainly to deform curves in 3D and curves on surfaces [4]. This work also does not deal with the projection of velocities as needed for our application.

$\beta\mathcal{N}_{\hat{S}}$. Therefore, the velocity in (4) will be the projection of this velocity into the normal direction $\mathcal{N}_{\hat{S}}$ (recall that the tangential component of the velocity does not affect the geometry of the flow). That is, for (at least) $\partial\mathcal{R}$,

$$\hat{\beta} = \beta\mathcal{N}_S \cdot \mathcal{N}_{\hat{S}}.$$

Outside of the region corresponding to $\mathcal{R}$, the velocity $\hat{\beta}$ can be any function that connects smoothly with the values in $\partial\mathcal{R}$.[5]

This technique, for the moment, requires to find the intersection of the zero-level sets of Φ and $\hat{\Phi}$ at every time step, in order to compute $\hat{\beta}$. To avoid this, we choose a particular extension of $\hat{\beta}$ outside of $\partial\mathcal{R}$, and simple define $\hat{\beta}$ as the projection of $\beta\mathcal{N}_S$ for *all* the values of $\mathbf{X}$ in the domain of Φ and $\hat{\Phi}$.[6] Therefore, the auxiliary level-sets flow is given by

$$\frac{\partial\hat{\Phi}}{\partial t}(\mathbf{X}, t) = \left(\beta(\mathbf{X}, t)\frac{\nabla\Phi(\mathbf{X}, t)}{\|\nabla\Phi(\mathbf{X}, t)\|} \cdot \frac{\nabla\hat{\Phi}(\mathbf{X}, t)}{\|\nabla\hat{\Phi}(\mathbf{X}, t)\|}\right)$$
$$\|\nabla\hat{\Phi}(\mathbf{X}, t)\|,$$

and the region of interest $\mathcal{R}(t)$ is given by the portion of the zero level-sets that belongs to $\Phi(\mathbf{X}, t) \cap \hat{\Phi}(\mathbf{X}, t)$:

$$\partial\mathcal{R}(t) = \{\mathbf{X} \in I\!R^n : \Phi(\mathbf{X}, t) = \hat{\Phi}(\mathbf{X}, t) = 0\}. \tag{5}$$

For a number of velocities β, short term existence of the solutions to the level-sets flow for $\hat{\Phi}$ (in the viscosity framework) can be obtained from the results of Evans and Spruck [8].

This formulation gives the basic region tracking algorithm. In the next section, we present some examples.

3 Examples and comments

We now present examples of the proposed technique. We should note that: (a) The numerical implementation of both the flows for Φ and $\hat{\Phi}$ follow the ordinary level-sets implementations developed by Osher and Sethian [17]; (b) Recently introduced fast techniques like narrow bands, fast-marching [18], or local methods [14], can also be used with the technique here proposed to evolve each one of the surfaces; (c) In the examples below, we compute a zero-order type of intersection between the implicit surfaces, meaning that we consider part of the intersection the full vortex where both surfaces go through (giving a jagged boundary). More

---

[5] To avoid the creation of spurious intersections during the deformation of Φ and $\hat{\Phi}$, these functions can be re-initialized every few steps, as frequently done in the level-sets approach.

[6] Note that although S and $\hat{S}$ do not occupy the same regions in the n dimensional space, their corresponding embedding functions Φ and $\hat{\Phi}$ do have the same domain, making this velocity extension straightforward.

accurate intersections can be easily computed using sub-divisions as in marching cubes. Recapping, the same numerical implementations used for the classical level-sets approaches are used to implement the deformation of $\hat{\Phi}$, and finding the intersection is straightforward from algorithms like marching cubes.

Four examples are given in Figure 1 and Figure 2, one per column. In each example, the first figure on the top shows the original surface with the marked regions to be tracked (brighter regions), followed by three different time steps of the geometric deformation and region tracking.

Figure 1 shows two toy examples. We track the painted regions on the surfaces while they are deforming with a morphing type velocity [2, 3]. ($\beta(\mathbf{X}, t)$ is simply the difference between the current surface $\Phi(\mathbf{X}, t)$ and a desired goal surface $\Phi(\mathbf{X}, \infty)$, two separate surfaces and two merged balls respectively, thereby morphing the initial surface toward the desired one [3].) Note how the region of interest changes topology (splits on the left example and merges on the next one).

Next, Figure 2 presents one of the main applications of this technique. Both these examples first show, on the top, a portion of the human cortex (white-matter/gray-matter boundary), obtained from MRI and segmented with the technique described in [19]. In order to visualize brain activities recorder via functional MRI in one of the non-visible folds (sulci), it is necessary to 'unfold' the surface, while tracking the color-coded regions (surface unfolding or flattening has a number of applications in 3D medical imaging beyond fMRI visualization; see also [9]). In the first of these two examples (left column), the different gray values simply indicate sign of Gaussian curvature on the original surface (roughly indicating the sulci), while two arbitrary regions are marked in the last example (one of them with a big portion hidden inside the fold). We track each one of the colored regions with the technique described in this note. In the first column, $\beta(\mathbf{X}, t) = \frac{\text{sign}(\kappa_1) + \text{sign}(\kappa_2)}{2} \min(|\kappa_1|, |\kappa_2|)$, where κ_1 and κ_2 are the principal curvatures. In the second column, we use a morphing type velocity like before [2, 3] (in this case, the desired destination shape is a convex surface). See [9] for additional possible unfolding velocities, including volume and area preserving ones. The colors on the deforming surfaces then indicate, respectively, the sign of the Gaussian curvature and the two marked regions in the *original* surfaces. Note how the surface is unfolded, hidden regions are made visible, and the tracking of the colored coded regions allow to find the matching places in the original 3D surface representing the cortex. This also allows for example to quantify, per each single tracked region, possible area/length distortions introduced by the flattening process. In order to track all the marked regions simultaneously in these two examples, we select the zero level-set of $\hat{\Phi}$ to intersect the zero level-set of Φ at all these regions. If we have regions with more than two color codes to track, as will frequently happen in fMRI, we just use one auxiliary function $\hat{\Phi}$ per color (region).

The same technique can be applied to visualize lesions that occur on the 'hidden' parts of the cortex. After unfolding, the regions become visible, and the region tracking allows to find their position in the original surface. When using level-sets techniques to deform two given shapes, one toward the other (a 3D cortex to a canonical cortex for example), this technique can be used to find the region-to-region correspondence. This technique then solves one of the basic shortcomings of the very useful level-sets approach.

Acknowledgments
GS wants to thank Prof. Brian Wandell from Stanford University for introducing him to the fMRI world and its unfolding issues. This was the motivation behind the algorithm described in this note. MB wants to thank the I.I.E. and the Facultad de Ingenieria, Montevideo, Uruguay for their continuous support through the M.Sc. Program and M.Sc. Scholarships. We thank Prof. Stanley Osher from UCLA and Prof. Olivier Faugeras from INRIA and MIT for making us aware of their related work. Comments from the anonymous reviewers are truly appreciated. This work was partially supported by NSF-LIS, by the Math, Computer, and Information Sciences Division at ONR, by an ONR Young Investigator Award, by the Presidential Early Career Awards for Scientists and Engineers (PECASE), by a National Science Foundation CAREER Award, by CSIC, and by CONICYT.

References

1. L. Ambrosio and M. Soner, "Level set approach to mean curvature flow in arbitrary codimension," *Journal of Differential Geometry* **43**, pp. 693-737, 1996.
2. M. Bertalmio, *Morphing Active Contours*, M.Sc. Thesis, I.I.E., Universidad de la Republica, Uruguay, June 1998.
3. M. Bertalmio, G. Sapiro, and G. Randall, "Morphing active contours," *Proc. IEEE-ICIP*, Chicago, October 1998.
4. P. Burchard, L. T. Cheng, B. Merriman, and S. Osher, "Level set based motion of curves in $\mathbb{R}^3$," *UCLA CAM Report*, May 1999.
5. V. Caselles, R. Kimmel, and G. Sapiro, "Geodesic active contours," *International Journal of Computer Vision* **22:1**, pp. 61-79, 19
6. Y. G. Chen, Y. Giga, and S. Goto, "Uniqueness and existence of viscosity solutions of generalized mean curvature flow equations," *Journal of Differential Geometry* **33**, 1991.
7. L. C. Evans and J. Spruck, "Motion of level sets by mean curvature, I," *Journal of Differential Geometry* **33**, 1991.
8. L. C. Evans and J. Spruck, "Motion of level sets by mean curvature, II," *Trans. Amer. Math. Soc.* **330**, pp. 321-332, 1992.
9. G. Hermosillo, O. Faugeras, and J. Gomes, "Cortex unfolding using level set methods," *INRIA Sophia Antipolis Technical Report* **3663**, April 1999.
10. L. M. Lorigo, O. Faugeras, W. E. L. Grimson, R. Keriven, and R. Kikinis, "Segmentation of bone in clinical knee MRI using texture-based geodesic active contours," *Proceedings Medical Image Computing and Computer-Assisted Intervention, MICCAI '98*, pp. 1195-1204, Cambridge, MA, Springer, 1998.
11. L. Lorigo, O. Faugeras, W.E.L. Grimson, R. Keriven, R. Kikinis, and C-F. Westin, "Co-dimension 2 geodesic active contours for MRA segmentation," *International Conference on Information Processing in Medical Imaging*, June 1999, forthcoming.

12. R. Malladi, J. A. Sethian and B. C. Vemuri, "Shape modeling with front propagation: A level set approach," *IEEE Trans. on PAMI* **17**, pp. 158-175, 1995.

13. B. Merriman, J. Bence, and S. Osher, "Motion of multiple junctions: A level-set approach,' *Journal of Computational Physics* **112**, pp. 334-363, 1994.

14. B. Merriman, R. Caflisch, and S. Osher, "Level set methods, with an application to modeling the growth of thin films, *UCLA CAM Report* **98-10**, February 1998.

15. W. J. Niessen, B. M. Romeny, and M. A. Viergever, "Geodesic deformable models for medical image analysis," *IEEE Trans. Medical Imaging* **17**, pp. 634-641, 1998.

16. S. Osher, Personal communication, March 1999.

17. S. Osher and J. Sethian, "Fronts propagating with curvature-dependent speed: Algorithms based on Hamilton-Jacobi formulations," *Journal of Computational Physics* **79**, pp. 12-49, 1988.

18. J. Sethian, *Level Set Methods: Evolving Interfaces in Geometry, Fluid Mechanics, Computer Vision and Material Sciences*, Cambridge University Press, Cambridge, UK, 1996.

19. P. Teo, G. Sapiro, and B. Wandell, "Creating connected representations of cortical gray matter for functional MRI visualization," *IEEE Trans. Medical Imaging* **16:06**, pp. 852-863, 1997.

20. A. Yezzi, S. Kichenassamy, P. Olver, and A. Tannenbaum, "Geometric active contours for segmentation of medical imagery," *IEEE Trans. Medical Imaging* **16**, pp. 199-210, 1997.

21. X. Zeng, L. H. Staib, R. T. Schultz, and J. S. Duncan, "Segmentation and measurement of the cortex from 3D MR Images," *Proceedings Medical Image Computing and Computer-Assisted Intervention, MICCAI '98*, pp. 519-530, Cambridge, MA, Springer, 1998.

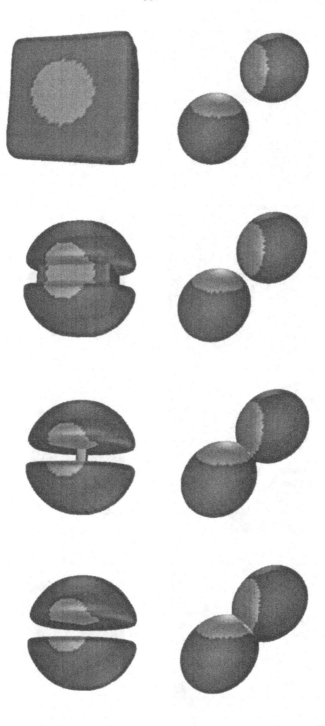

Fig. 1. *Two simple examples, one per column, of the algorithm introduced in this note (brighter regions are the ones being tracked), demonstrating possible topological changes on the tracked region.*

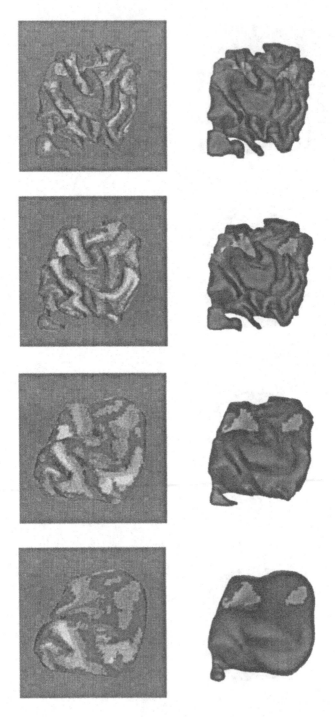

Fig. 2. *Unfolding the cortex, and tracking the marked regions, with a curvature based flow and a 3D morphing one, left and right columns respectively.*

Geometric Multiscale Representation of Numerical Images

Georges Koepfler[1,2] and Lionel Moisan[1]

[1] Centre de Mathématiques et de Leurs Applications (CNRS UMR 8536),
Ecole Normale Supérieure de Cachan,
61 avenue du président Wilson, 94235 Cachan cedex, France

[2] Université René Descartes
UFR de Mathématiques et Informatique, équipe PRISME,
Centre Universitaire des Saints-Pères,
45 rue des Saints-Pères, 75270 PARIS cedex 06, France

koepfler@cmla.ens-cachan.fr   moisan@cmla.ens-cachan.fr

Abstract. We explain how a discrete grey level image can be numerically translated into a completely pixel independent geometric structure made of oriented curves with grey levels attached to them. For that purpose, we prove that the Affine Morphological Scale Space of an image can be geometrically computed using a level set decomposition/reconstruction and a well adapted curve evolution scheme. Such an algorithm appears to be much more accurate than classical pixel-based ones, and allows continuous deformations of the original image.

1 Introduction

If a mathematician had to examine recent evolutions of image analysis, he would certainly notice a growing interest for geometric techniques, relying on the computation of differential operators like orientation, curvature, ... or on the analysis of more global objects like level curves. Of course Fourier or wavelet analysis are still very efficient for image compression for example, but in order to analyze larger scales geometric approaches seem to be more relevant. At large scales a real-world image can hardly be considered –like a sound signal– as a superimposition of waves (or wavelets), since the main formation process relies on occlusion, which is highly nonlinear. This is not without some mathematical consequences : in this context, images are more likely to be represented in a geometrical space like $BV(\mathbb{R}^2)$, the space of functions on $\mathbb{R}^2$ with bounded variation, than in the more classical $L^2(\mathbb{R}^2)$ space. From a practical point of view, the question of the numerical geometric representation of an image certainly deserves to be investigated, since images have been described so far by arrays of numbers (or wavelet/DCT coefficients for compressed images). It is likely that in the future alternative geometric descriptions will be commonly used, relying on some level-set/texture decomposition like the one proposed in [8].

In this paper, we show how it is possible to compute numerically a completely geometric and multiscale representation of an image, for which the notion of pixel disappears (though it can be recovered). Our algorithm is a fully geometrical implementation of the so-called Affine Morphological Scale Space (AMSS, see [1]), described in Sect. 2. Due to its contrast invariance, this scale space is equivalent to the affine curve shortening process described in [15], for which a fully geometrical algorithm has been recently proposed in [11]. A simplified version of this scheme, described in Sect. 3, allows to process all level curves of an image with a high precision in a couple of minutes. In association with level set decomposition and reconstruction algorithms, described in Sect. 4, we thus compute the AMSS of an image with much more accuracy than classical scalar schemes, as is shown in Sect. 5. Another interest of this method is that it yields a contrast-invariant multiscale geometric representation of the image that provides a framework for geometry based analyses and processing. We illustrate this in Sect. 6 by applying our algorithm to image deformation.

2 The Affine Morphological Scale Space

A natural way of extracting the geometry of an image consists in the level set decomposition inherited from Mathematical Morphology. Given an image u viewed as an intensity map from $\mathbb{R}^2$ to $\mathbb{R}$, one can define the (upper) level sets of u by

$$\chi_\lambda(u) = \{\mathbf{x} \in \mathbb{R}^2;\ u(\mathbf{x}) \geqslant \lambda\}.$$

This collection of planar sets is equivalent to the function u itself since one has the reconstruction formula

$$u(\mathbf{x}) = \sup\{\lambda;\ \mathbf{x} \in \chi_\lambda\}.$$

The main interest of this representation is its invariance under contrast changes : if g is an increasing map from $\mathbb{R}$ to $\mathbb{R}$ (i.e. a contrast change), then one has

$$\chi_{g(\lambda)}(g(u)) = \chi_\lambda(u).$$

Hence, the collection of all level sets of an image does not depend a priori on the global illumination conditions of this image, and is thus an interesting geometrical representation.

Now, because an image generally contains details of different sizes, the notion of scale-space has been introduced. It consists in representing an original image $u_0(\cdot)$ by a collection of images $(u(\cdot, t))_{t \geqslant 0}$ which are simplified versions of u_0 such that $u(\cdot, 0) = u_0(\cdot)$ and, with increasing scale t, the $u(., t)$'s represent more and more coarser versions of u_0. There are plenty of possibilities for such representations, but it is possible to reduce them by demanding strong invariance properties from the operator T_t which transforms $u_0(\cdot)$ into $u(\cdot, t)$. In particular, it is possible to enforce the level set decomposition evoked above to be compatible with the scale-space representation, in the sense that the λ-level set of $u(\cdot, t)$ only depends on the λ-level set of u_0. If one asks, in addition, for other properties like regularity, semi-group structure, and Euclidean Invariance (i.e. translation and rotation invariance), then according to [1] one reduces the possibilities to the choice of a nondecreasing continuous function F governing the scale space given by

$$\frac{\partial u}{\partial t} = |Du|\, F\left(\operatorname{div}\frac{Du}{|Du|}\right),\tag{1}$$

where Du represents the spatial gradient of u. In this paper we have chosen the particular case of the Affine Morphological Scale Space, given by $F(s) = s^{1/3}$, for mainly two reasons :

First it yields an interesting additional invariance property called Affine Invariance :

$$T_t(u_0 \circ \phi) = (T_t u_0) \circ \phi \quad \text{for any} \quad \phi(\mathbf{x}) = A\mathbf{x} + b,\ A \in SL(\mathbb{R}^2),\ b \in \mathbb{R}^2.\tag{2}$$

This property allows to perform affine-invariant shape recognition under occlusions (see [6]) and to compute local affine-invariant features like affine curvature for example.

Second, there exists a fully consistent geometric scheme (see [11]) for solving the level curve evolution induced by the AMSS,

$$\frac{\partial \mathbf{C}}{\partial t} = \kappa^{1/3}\, \mathbf{N}.\tag{3}$$

Here $\mathbf{C}$ is any point of a level curve, κ the local curvature and $\mathbf{N}$ the normal vector at this point. In particular, this scheme guarantees that the inclusion of any two sets is preserved by the evolution (inclusion principle). In the simplified version described in Sect. 3, it is fast (linear complexity) and robust, as only areas and middle points are computed.

3   A Fast Geometric Scheme

The numerical implementation of the affine scale space of a curve given by (3) can be realized in several ways. For our purpose, an ideal algorithm should satisfy, up to a given computer precision, the following properties :

P1: preserve inclusion, which is necessary for level set reconstruction;
P2: be affine invariant, since the scale-space is;
P3: have linear complexity, so that all level curves of an image can be processed with a high precision in a reasonable time.

Of course, algorithms based on scalar formulations (see [16]) are not relevant here, since our goal is precisely to get rid of pixel based representations. In any case, such algorithms satisfy neither P1 nor P2, and are not computationally efficient (in terms of time and memory) if an accurate precision is needed (e.g. 100 points per original pixel). The purpose of this paper is to present a scheme

Fig. 1. σ-affine erosion (- - -) of a convex non closed curve (—).

opposite to Sethian's formulation[1], since we want to solve a scalar (contrast-invariant) evolution equation with a geometric algorithm. We cannot either use local point evolution schemes (naive ones or more refined ones like in [10]) since they do not guarantee P1 (because they rely on a local estimation of the curvature that is not directly connected with a global property like inclusion), and for the same reason P2 would be uncertain (and might depend on the discretization). This is the reason why we started from the geometric scheme described in [11], for it satisfies P1 and P2. This scheme is based on a simple operator called *affine erosion*, which we define now.

Consider a (non necessarily closed) convex parameterized curve $C : [a, b] \to \mathbb{R}^2$ and an area parameter σ. Define a σ-chord set of C as the region with area σ that is enclosed by a segment $[C(s_1)C(s_2)]$ and the corresponding piece of curve $C([s_1, s_2])$. Then, the σ-affine erosion of C, written $E_\sigma(C)$, can be defined as the segment-side boundary of the union of these σ-chord sets (see Fig. 1). Without going into details (which might be found in [11] and [12]), we briefly recall two main results about the affine erosion :

First, the evoked boundary is essentially obtained by the middle points of the segments $[C(s_1)C(s_2)]$ defining the σ-chord sets (minus some "ghosts parts" that do not appear in general, and plus two end-segments if the curve is not closed)

Second, the infinitesimal iteration of such an operator asymptotically yields the affine scale space of the initial curve C_0 (with fixed endpoints if C_0 is not closed), one has

$$(E_\sigma)^n (C_0) \to C(\cdot, t)) \quad \text{as} \quad n \to +\infty, \ \sigma \to 0 \quad \text{and} \quad \frac{1}{2} \left(\frac{3}{2} \right)^{\frac{2}{3}} n\sigma^{2/3} \to t,$$

where $C(\cdot, t)$ is defined from C_0 by (3).

The scheme presented in [11] relies on a more general definition of the affine erosion that also applies to non-convex curves. Compared to the convex case, the computations are more complex since the computation of curve intersections may be needed, which requires careful programming and causes the complexity

---

[1] The main interest of scalar formulations is that they naturally handle topological changes of the level sets : it has however been proved in [2] that no such changes occur for the affine scale space.

of the algorithm to become quadratic in the number of vertices of the polygonal curve to be processed. This is the reason why, as suggested in [11], we have chosen an alternative scheme based on the separate treatment of each convex part. Given a possibly non-convex and non-necessarily closed polygonal curve, we iterate the following three-step process :

1. Break the curve into convex components (by "cutting" inflection segments at their middle point), and compute the minimum value σ_{min} of the area of any non-closed component.
2. Define $\sigma_{real} = \min(\sigma_{min}, \sigma)$ and apply a discrete affine erosion of area σ_{real} to each convex component.
3. Concatenate the obtained pieces of curves in order to obtain a new (possibly non-convex) curve.

This approach yields a good approximation of the exact affine-erosion of C. The main reason is that near an inflection point of C the curve is locally flat, thus, for reasonable values of σ, the tangents at the inflection point do not evolve much during step 2. This ensures that the convex pieces nicely fit together at step 3 and that the whole three-step process described above is not very sensitive to the precise location at which the curve is cut. These are unformal observations rather than theoretical statements, indeed for reasonable values of σ both evolutions give the same result (see [12]). The main advantage of this simplified algorithm is that it is fast (it has linear complexity) and it is robust, since each evolution is obtained by middle points of segments whose endpoints lie on the original curve and whose selection only relies on an area computation.

4 The Complete Algorithm

Our geometric multiscale representation algorithm for numerical images is made out of the following 5 steps.

Step 1: decomposition.
The level set extraction is done currently in a straightforward way. Using 4-connectedness, we extract, for each grey value which appears in the image, the corresponding level sets (upper or lower) and keep the oriented border such that the level set lies on the left of the curve. We thus obtain a set of curves which are either closed or start and end on the image border. For each curve we keep the associated grey level, so that we have a representation that is completely equivalent to the initial image. It is important to notice that no interpolation is made to extract these level curves : the pixels are simply considered as adjacent squares.

Step 2: symmetrization.
Then, in order to get Neumann boundary conditions for the affine scale space, we have the possibility to symmetrize the level lines which start and end on the border, which guarantees that the curve will remain orthogonal to the image border during the evolution. Curves with end points on the same side are reflected once, curves with end points on adjacent sides are reflected twice, thus yielding

closed curves. Finally curves with end points on opposite sides are reflected once at each side (they should, theoretically, be reflected infinitely many times, but in practice once is enough). Without this symmetrization the endpoints of the non-closed level curves would remain fixed.

Step 3 : AMSS.

At this stage, we process all level curves with the geometric implementation of the affine scale space described in Sect. 3. This involves two parameters : the scale of evolution t and the precision ε at which curves are computed. We normalize ε such that $1/\varepsilon$ corresponds to the number of points that will be used to describe a one-pixel-length curve.

Step 4: geometric transformation and/or computation.

Once achieved steps 1 to 3, we have a smooth geometric description of the image that allows to perform any geometric transformation and/or computation. We shall give an example of image deformation in section 6, but there are many other possibilities of geometric processing. For example, one can simply remove level sets that are too small, or too oscillatory (see [13]), or satisfying any geometric criterion that can be estimated on a smooth curve.

Step 5: rasterization and reconstruction.

After transforming the level lines of the initial image, we need to reconstruct the corresponding image. This is done by filling in the level sets and using the grey level information associated with each level line. This step is more complex than the extraction of level lines, since now the level curves are made of points with non-integer coordinates, and thus we have to decide whether a pixel is inside the set or not. We first rasterize the curves using an adaptation of Bresenham's algorithm[2] that satisfies the inclusion principle. In this algorithm a pixel belongs to the side of the curve where more than half of its area is (see Fig. 2) and a special treatment for very near points (sub-pixel) is added.

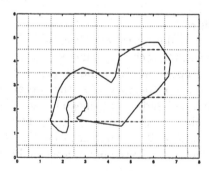

Fig. 2. Example of rasterization of a floating-point curve (—) into a pixel separating integer curve (- - -).

---

[2] Bresenham's algorithm is a well known algorithm from computer graphics which allows to join two points which have floating-point coordinates and are distant by more than a couple of pixels (see [3]).

Our implementation allows a good approximation of the real curves : only some very small, sub-pixel, details of the eroded curve might be lost during the rasterization, such as curves enclosing an area smaller than one pixel.

Complexity of the Algorithm

The complexity of the different steps of the algorithm depends on the following parameters : N, the number of pixels contained in the original image (typically 10^6) ; G, the number of grey-levels contained in the original image (typically 256) ; ε, the precision (number of points per pixel) at which the level curves need to be computed (typically from $1/100$ to $1/2$) ; t, the scale at which the level curves are smoothed, and N', the number of pixels contained in the reconstructed image. Table 1 gives upper bounds of time and memory complexity for the steps described above.

	computation time	memory
decomposition	$N \times G$	$N \times G$
affine scale space	$N \times G \times t/\varepsilon$	$N \times G/\varepsilon$
rasterization	$N \times G/\varepsilon$	$N \times G/\varepsilon$
reconstruction	$N' \times G$	$N' \times G$

Table 1. Complexity of the proposed algorithm

Notice that the upper bound of $N \times G$ points to describe all level lines of G is very rough. For the classical Lena image (see Fig 5, one has $N = 256^2$, $G = 238$, and the decomposition yields in 10 seconds about 48000 curves and 1.1 million points. Then the affine scale space computation for $\varepsilon = 1/2$ takes 2.5 minutes and yields 13000 curves and 0.78 million points. The final rasterization and reconstruction takes 10 seconds.

5 Comparison with Scalar Schemes

The purpose of this section is to compare the geometric algorithm we proposed with explicit scalar schemes based on the iteration of a process like

$$u^{n+1} = u^n + |Du^n| \left(\operatorname{div} \frac{Du^n}{|Du^n|} \right)^{1/3},$$

where Du^n and $\operatorname{div} \frac{Du^n}{|Du^n|}$ are computed either by using finite differences on a 3x3 neighborhood of the current pixel (see [7]) or by using a non local estimation of the image derivatives, as obtained by a Gaussian convolution (see [14]). Such a scheme is strongly limited by the grid : the localization of the level curves is known up to a precision of the order of the pixel size (even when interpolation is used), and affine-invariance could only be achieved at large scales (but even rotation-invariance is difficult to ensure at all scales, as noticed in [14]). Another striking side effect of such scalar schemes is that they need to produce artificial diffusion in the gradient direction. In other terms, a scalar scheme cannot be contrast invariant, and in practice new grey levels (and consequently new level curves) are created. The reason is the following : for a purely contrast-invariant algorithm defined on a fixed grid, a point of a level curve either does not move or moves by at least one pixel. This constraint causes small (i.e. large scale) curvatures to be treated as zero, and is for that reason incompatible with a curvature-driven evolution like AMSS.

These effects are illustrated on Fig. 3. We have chosen an image of size 100×70 which has been magnified 10 times and subsampled to only 10 20-spaced grey levels (see the first row). The left column presents the image, the right column the level lines. In the second row we show the result of our algorithm : no level sets (i.e. grey levels) are created and the level lines are smoothed. The last row presents the result of a classical scalar algorithm. As expected, this scheme produces artificial scalar diffusion and creates new grey levels, thus causes a multiplication of the level lines. This can be seen in the left half of the level lines image where 5-spaced level lines are represented; in the right part, 20-spaced level lines are represented which should be the only present. One can also remark some anisotropy in that side effect diffusion : it is more attenuated along the directions aligned with the grid (i.e. horizontal or vertical directions), which enforces the visual perception of this grid.

6 Applications

6.1 Visualization of Level Curves

The level sets of an image are generally so irregular that only a few of them can be visualized at the same time. Extracting and processing independently each level curve of an image produces an interesting tool to visualize clearly the level lines of a given image, as illustrated in Fig. 5. In that image we can see all 4-spaced level lines of the Lena image thanks to the smooth geometric representation provided by the geometric Affine Morphological Scale Space. Such a superimposition shows interesting shape information about the geometric structure of the image.

6.2 Image Deformation

In this part, we show how our algorithm can be used to apply a geometric transform to an image. In the experiments that follow, projective or affine transforms are used, but more complex geometric transform will work as well. Let $u(i,j)$ be a given, discrete image, how can one define an approximation (or interpolation) $\tilde{u}$ of u that allows to build the transformed image

$$v(i,j) = \tilde{u}\left(\frac{ai+bj+c}{di+ej+1}, \frac{fi+gj+h}{di+ej+1}\right),$$

where a, b, c, d, e, f, g, h are given coefficients (that may vary) ? One can distinguish between two kinds of methods. The first are continuous (and explicit) methods, for which a continuous model for $\tilde{u}$ is explicitly given and computed from u once and for all. The second are discrete (and implicit) methods, for which $\tilde{u}$ is implicitly defined and must be estimated for each discrete grid.

For example, zero order interpolation defined by $\tilde{u}(i, j) = u([i + 1/2], [j + 1/2])$, where $[x]$ represent the integer part of x, or bilinear interpolation and higher order generalizations are explicit methods. On the opposite, image interpolation/approximation algorithms based on the minimization of a certain error between discrete images (like the Total Variation used in [9]) are implicit methods. In fact, this distinction is rather formal if the practical criterion is not "how is $\tilde{u}$ defined ?", but "how much time does it take to compute $\tilde{u}$?". For example, Fourier representation is an explicit method, but for non-Euclidean transformations it is computationally expensive. Indeed if N is the number of pixels of the original image u, it requires N operations to compute the value of $\tilde{u}$ at a given point. From that point of view, our representation is a compromise between computation time (once the level lines have been extracted and smoothed, the deformation and the reconstruction processes are fast) and accuracy (the geometry of the level sets is precisely known). We do not affirm that the Affine Morphological Scale Space yields the best image approximation : it is geometrically better than bilinear interpolation (for which pixelization effects remain), but less accurate than sophisticated image interpolation algorithms like [9]. However, we proved that it can be precisely computed in a reasonable time and then allowing any kind of geometric deformation.

We compared deformations yielded by our method, zero and bilinear interpolation on two images :

On a simple binary image (left in Fig. 4), we applied an affine deformation using three different methods : 1. a bilinear interpolation (left part of middle image); 2. a zero-order interpolation (right part of middle image); 3. the geometric representation described in this paper (right hand image). In order to gain space we have put zero-order and bilinear interpolation in the same picture. Contrary to classical methods, a geometric curve shortening quickly provides a good compromise between pixelization effects, accuracy and diffusion effects.

In Fig. 6 we present a satellite image from which we have simulated a projective view (from right to left as indicated by the black trapezoid). Fig. 7 left shows the results with zero-order interpolation (left part) and bilinear interpolation (right part). Our algorithm, using the geometric implementation of the affine morphological scale space gives the result shown in Fig. 7, right hand image.

7   Conclusion

In this paper, we described how the Affine Morphological Scale Space of an image can be implemented in a geometric manner. Compared to classical scalar schemes, the main advantages are a much higher accuracy both in terms of image definition and in terms of fidelity to the scale space properties (contrast-invariance and affine-invariance). The algorithm needs a large amount of memory but is still rather fast, and the representation it induces also allows very fast geometric image deformations and contrast changes.

Our method relies on a level set decomposition/reconstruction and on a particular geometric algorithm for affine curve shortening, but it could be generalized to other curve evolutions, as similar geometric algorithms for general curvature driven curve evolutions begin to appear (see [4]). Another generalization could be made by using some image interpolation for the extraction of the level sets : however, in this case the representation will generally no be contrast-invariant any more. A more geometric extension of the algorithm relying on the interpolation of new level lines using the Absolute Minimizing Lipschitz Extension (see [5]) could also be investigated for visualization tasks.

References

1. L. Alvarez, F. Guichard, P.L. Lions, J.M. Morel, "Axioms and fundamental equations of image processing", *Archives for Rational Mechanics* 123, pp. 199-257, 1993.
2. S. Angenent, G. , A. Tannenbaum, "On the affine heat equation for nonconvex curves", preprint.
3. J. E. Bresenham, "Algorithm for computer control of a digital plotter", *IBM Syst. J.* 4:1, pp. 25-30, 1965.
4. F. Cao, L. Moisan, "Geometric Computation of Curvature Driven Plane Curve Evolutions", in preparation.
5. V. Caselles, J.-M. Morel "An Axiomatic Approach to Image Interpolation", *IEEE Transactions On Image Processing*, vol. 7:3, pp. 376-386, march 1998.
6. T. Cohignac, "Reconnaissance de formes planes", PhD dissertation, Ceremade, 1994.
7. T. Cohignac, F. Eve, F. Guichard, J.-M. Morel, "Numerical analysis of the fundamental equation of image processing", preprint Ceremade, 1992.
8. J. Froment, "A Functional Analysis Model for Natural Images Permitting Structured Compression", preprint CMLA, 1998.
9. F. Guichard, F. Malgouyres, "Total Variation Based Interpolation", *Proceedings of Eusipco'98*, vol. 3, pp.1741-1744.
10. K. Mikula, "Solution of nonlinear curvature driven evolution of plane convex curves", *Applied Numerical Mathematics*, vol. 23, pp. 347-360, 1997.
11. L. Moisan, "Affine Plane Curve Evolution : a Fully Consistent Scheme", *IEEE Transactions On Image Processing*, vol. 7:3, pp. 411-420, march 1998.
12. L. Moisan, "Traitement numérique d'images et de films : équations aux dérivées partielles préservant forme et relief", PhD dissertation, Ceremade, 1997.
13. P. Monasse, F. Guichard, "Fast computation of a contrast-invariant image representation", preprint CMLA, 1998.
14. W.J. Niessen, B. M. ter Haar Romeny, M. A. Viergever, "Numerical Analysis of Geometry-Driven Diffusion Equations", in *Geometry-Driven Diffusion in Computer Vision*, Bart M. ter Haar Romeny Ed., Kluwer Acad. Pub., 1994.
15. G. Sapiro, A. Tannenbaum, "Affine invariant scale-space", *Int. J. Comp. Vision*, vol. 11, pp. 25-44, 1993.
16. J.A. Sethian, *Level Set Methods*, Cambridge University Press, 1996.

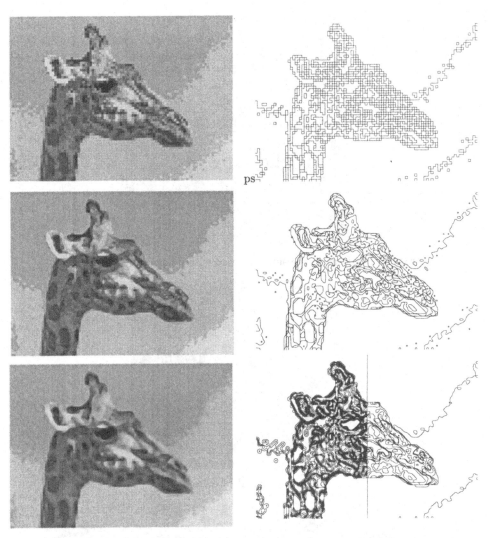

Fig. 3. AMSS of giraffe, original top left, level lines on the right.

Fig. 4. Affine transform of an ellipse image.

Fig. 5. The Lena image superimposed with its smoothed level lines.

Fig. 6. Original satellite image.

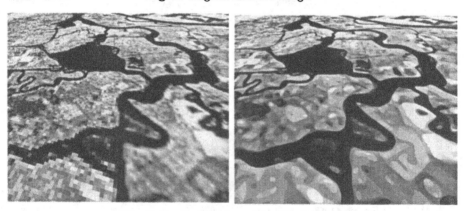

Fig. 7. Projective view of satellite image.

Multiscale Morphological Segmentations Based on Watershed, Flooding, and Eikonal PDE

Fernand Meyer[1] and Petros Maragos[2]

[1] Centre de Morphologie Mathématique, Ecole des Mines de Paris,
35, Rue Saint Honoré, 77305 Fontainebleau, France. Email: meyer@cmm.ensmp.fr
[2] National Technical University of Athens, Dept. of Electrical & Computer
Engineering, Zografou 15773, Athens, Greece. Email: maragos@cs.ntua.gr

Abstract. The classical morphological segmentation paradigm is based on the watershed transform, constructed by flooding the gradient image seen as a topographic surface. For flooding a topographic surface, a topographic distance is defined from which a minimum distance algorithm is derived for the watershed. In a continuous formulation, this is modeled via the eikonal PDE, which can be solved using curve evolution algorithms. Various ultrametric distances between the catchment basins may then be associated to the flooding itself. To each ultrametric distance is associated a multiscale segmentation; each scale being the closed balls of the ultrametric distance.

1 Introduction

Segmentation is one of the most challenging tasks in image processing, as it requires to some extent a semantic understanding of the image. The morphological segmentation paradigm, based on the watershed transform and markers, has been extremely successful, both for interactive as for automatic segmentation. Its principle is simple: a) a gradient image of the scene is constructed; b) for each object of interest, an inside particle is detected, either in an automatic manner or in an interactive manner; c) construction of the watershed associated to the markers. Its avantage is the robustness: the result is independent of the shape or the placement of the markers in the zones of interest. The result is obtained by a global minimization implying both the topography of the surface and the complete set of markers.

This paradigm has met its limits with the emergence of new segmentation tasks in the area of communications and multimedia industry. The development of games, teleworking, teleshopping, television on demand, videoconferences etc. has multiplied situations where images and sequences have not only to be transmitted but also manipulated, selected, assembled in new ways. This evolution is most challenging for segmentation techniques: one has to segment complex sequences of color images in real time, be automatic but also able to deal with user interaction.

Object oriented coding represents an even greater challenge for segmentation techniques. Such encoders segment the scene into homogeneous zones for which contours, motion and texture have to be transmitted. Depending upon the targeted bitstream and the complexity of the scene, a variable number of regions has to be transmitted. Hence an automatic segmentation with a variable number of regions is required for sequences for which the content or even content type is not known a priori. Hence, there is no possibility to devise a strategy for finding markers, and as a consequence the traditional morphological segmentation based on watershed and markers fails.

This situation has triggered the development of new techniques of multiscale segmentation, where no markers are required. In such cases it is of interest to construct a sequence of nested partitions going from coarse to fine; each boundary of a coarse segmentation also being a boundary of all finer segmentations. We will call such a series of nested partitions a multiscale cube (we do not call it pyramid, as the resolution of the images is not reduced when going from fine to coarse). Such a multiscale cube may be used in various ways:

- chose in the cube a slice with the appropriate number of regions
- compose a segmentation by extracting regions from different slices of the cube. This may be done in an interactive way. It may also result by minimizing some global criterion (for instance, if a texture model is adopted for each region, it is possible to measure the distance between the model and the original image in each region. It is then possible to minimize a weighted sum of the length of the contours and of the global distortion of the image).
- use the pyramid for defining new dissimilarity measures between the adjacent catchment basins, which may be used for segmenting with markers and yield better results as the traditional segmentation with markers, using the altitude of the gradient.

In absence of any knowledge of the image content, it is important to find good psychovisual criteria for constructing the cube.

In this paper, we first discuss the monoscale watershed segmentation by flooding both from a discrete formulation of the shortest topographic distance as well as from a continuous viewpoint of the eikonal PDE and curve evolution. Further, for multiscale segmentation, we use ultrametric distances to generalize the flooding and improve the segmentation.

2 The classical morphological segmentation paradigm

2.1 Flooding a topographic surface

The classical morphological tool for segmentation is the watershed transform. For segmenting an image f, first its edges are enhanced by computing its gradient magnitude $\|\nabla f\|$. This is approximated by the discrete morphological gradient $\delta(f) - \varepsilon(f)$, where $\delta(f) = f \oplus B$ is the flat dilation of f by a small disk B and $\varepsilon(f) = f \ominus B$ is the flat erosion of f by B. After the edge enhancement, the segmentation process starts with creating flooding waves that emanate from a set of markers (feature points inside desired regions) and flood the topographic surface $\|\nabla f\|$. The points where these flooding waves meet each other form the segmentation boundaries. The simplest markers are the regional minima of the gradient image. Very often, the minima are extremely numerous, leading to an oversegmentation. For this reason, in many practical cases, the watershed will take as sources of the flooding a smaller set of markers, which have been identified by a preliminary analysis step as inside germs of the desired segmentation.

2.2 Modifying a topographic surface: Swamping

In the case where the sources for the flooding are not all minima of the topographic surface, two solutions are possible. Either use the markers as sources. In this case, catchment basins without sources are flooded from already flooded neighbouring region. Such a flooding algorithm, using hierarchical queues has been described in [1].

The second solution consists in modifying the topographic surface as slightly as possible, in such a way that the markers become its only regional minima. This operation is called swamping. If $m_1, m_2, ... m_k$ are the binary markers we construct a marker function g defined as follows : $g = White$ outside the markers and $g = Black$ inside the markers. On the other hand, the topographic surface f is modified by assigning the value $Black$ to all regional minima. We then perform a closing by reconstruction of f from the marker function g. This can be accomplished by an iterative algorithm which at each iteration forms a conditional erosion, i.e., a supremum $(\vee)$ of the erosion of the previous iterate and the original function:

$$\begin{aligned} g_0 &= g \vee f \\ g_k &= \varepsilon(g_{k-1}) \vee f \quad , \quad k = 1, 2, 3, ... \end{aligned} \tag{1}$$

In the limit as $k \to \infty$ we obtain the function g_∞ which is the result of the closing by reconstruction. This new function is as similar as possible to the function f, except that its only regional minima are the family $\{m_i\}$. Hence, its catchment basins will give the desired segmentation.

3 Watershed Segmentation: Discrete and Continuous

3.1 Discrete Watershed and Topographic Distance

We consider first images in a digital framework. Images are represented on regular graphs where the nodes represent the pixels and the edges the neighborhood relations. A connected component of uniform grey tone is called plateau. A plateau without lower (resp. higher) neighbors is a regional minimum (resp. maximum).

Let us now consider a drop of water falling on a topographic surface f for which the regional minima are the only plateaus. If it falls outside a plateau, it will glide along a path of steepest descent. If the altitude of a pixel x is $f(x)$, the altitude of its lowest neighbor defines the erosion $\varepsilon(f)(x)$ of size 1

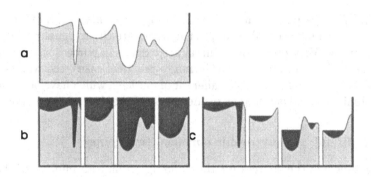

Fig. 1. (a) Initial topographic surface. (b) Creation of the marker. (c) Result of the swamping.

at pixel x. Hence the altitude of the steepest descending slope at pixel x is $\text{slope}(x) = f(x) - \varepsilon(f)(x)$. If x and y are two neighboring pixels, we will define the topographic variation $\text{topvar}(x, y)$ between x and y as $\text{slope}(x)$ if $f(x) > f(y)$ and as $\frac{\text{slope}(x) + \text{slope}(y)}{2}$ if $f(x) = f(y)$.

If π is a path $(x = p_1, p_2, ..., y = p_n)$ between two pixels x and y, we define the topographical variation along the path π as the sum $\sum_{i=1, n-1} \text{topvar}(p_i, p_{i+1})$ of the elementary topographical variations along the path π. The topographical distance between two pixels x and y is defined as the minimal topographical variation along all paths between x and y. By construction, the trajectory of a drop of water falling on the surface is a geodesic line of the topographic distance. A pixel p belongs to the upstream of a pixel q if and only if the topographic distance between both pixels is equal to $\mid f(p) - f(q) \mid$. Let us now transform the topographic surface by putting all regional minima at altitude 0.

Definition 1. *We call catchment basin* $\text{CB}(m_i)$ *of a regional minimum* m_i *the set of pixels which are closer to* m_i *than to any other regional minimum for the topographical distance*

A more general description of the topographic distance, also valid for images with plateaus may be found in [7]. Within each catchment basin, the set of pixels closer to the minimum than a given topographic distance h are all pixels of this basin with an altitude below h. In this framework the construction of the catchment basins becomes a shortest path problem, i.e., finding the path between a marker and an image point that corresponds to the minimum weighted distance. Computing this minimum weighted distance at all image points from any marker is also equivalent to finding the *gray-weighted distance transform (GWDT)* of the image. There are several types of discrete algorithms to compute the GWDT which include iterated (sequential or parallel) min-sum differences [13] and hierarchical queues [7]. Instead of elaborating more on discrete GWDT algorithms, we prefer now to proceed to our next formulation of watershed that will be based on a continuous (PDE-based) model. Afterwards, the discrete GWDT will be re-interpreted as one possible discrete approximation to the solution of the continuous problem.

3.2 Continuous Watershed and Eikonal PDE

The watershed transforms an image $f(x,y)$ to the crest lines separating adjacent catchment basins that surround regional minima or other 'marker' sets of feature points. In a continuous formulation, the topographic distance of f along a path becomes the line integral of $\|\nabla f\|$ along this path. Viewing the domain of f as a 2D optical medium with a refractive index field $\eta(x,y) = \|\nabla f\|$, makes the continuous topographic distance function equivalent to the optical path length which is proportional to the time required for light to travel this path. This leads to the *eikonal PDE*

$$\|\nabla U(x,y)\| = \eta(x,y), \quad \eta(x,y) = \|\nabla f(x,y)\| \tag{2}$$

whose solution for any field $\eta(x,y)$ is a weighted distance function [11, 2]. In the continuous domain and assuming that the image is smooth and has isolated critical points, the continuous watershed is equivalent to finding a skeleton by influence zones with respect to a weighted distance function that uses points in the regional minima of the image as sources and $\eta = \|\nabla f\|$ as the field of indices [9, 7]. If other markers different than the minima are to be used as sources, then the homotopy of the function must be modified via morphological reconstruction to impose these markers as the only minima.

Modeling the watershed via the eikonal has the advantage of a more isotropic flooding but also poses some challenges for its implementation. This problem can be approached by viewing the solution of the eikonal PDE as a *gray-weighted distance transform (GWDT)* whose values at each pixel give the minimum distance from the light sources weighted by the gray values of the refractive index field. Next we outline two ways of solving the eikonal PDE as applied to segmentation.

3.3 GWDT based on Chamfer Metrics

Let $\eta[i,j]$ be a sampled nonnegative gray-level image and let us view it as a discrete refractive index field. Also let S be a set of reference points or the 'sources' of some wave or the location of the wavefront at time $t = 0$. As discussed earlier, the GWDT finds at each pixel $p = [i,j]$ the smallest sum of values of η over all possible paths connecting p to the sources S.

This discrete GWDT can be computed by running a 2D min-sum difference equation like the one implementing the chamfer distance transform of binary images but with spatially-varying coefficients proportional to the gray image values [13]:

$$U_k[i,j] = \min\{U_k[i-1,j] + a\eta[i,j], U_k[i,j-1] + a\eta[i,j],$$
$$U_k[i-1,j-1] + b\eta[i,j], U_k[i-1,j+1] + b\eta[i,j], U_{k-1}[i,j]\} \tag{3}$$

where U_0 is the $0/\infty$ indicator function of the source set S. Starting from U_0, a sequence of functions U_k is iteratively computed by running (3) over the image domain in a forward scan for even k, whereas for odd k an equation as in (3) but with a reflected coefficient mask is run in a backward scan. In the limit $k \to \infty$ the final GWDT U_∞ is obtained. In practice, this limit is reached after a finite number of passes. The above implementation can also be viewed as a procedure of finding paths of minimal 'cost' among nodes of a weighted graph or as discrete dynamic programming. As such it is actually known as Dijkstra's algorithm. There are also other faster implementations using queues [13, 6]. The above GWDT based on discrete chamfer metrics is shown in [13] and [4] to be a discrete approximate solution of the eikonal PDE $||\nabla U|| = \eta$.

The constants a and b are the distance steps by which the planar chamfer distances are propagated within a 3×3 neighborhood. To improve the GWDT approximation to the eikonal's solution, one can optimize (a, b) to minimize the error between the chamfer and Euclidean distances and/or use larger neighborhoods (at the cost of a slower implementation). However, using a neighborhood larger than 5×5 may give erroneous results since the large masks can bridge over a thin line that separates two segmentation regions. Overall, this chamfer metric approach to GWDT is fast and easy to implement, but due to the required small neighborhoods is not isotropic and cannot achieve high accuracy.

3.4   GWDT based on Curve Evolution

In the standard digital watershed algorithm [8, 14], the flooding at each level is achieved by a planar distance propagation that uses the chess-board metric. This kind of distance propagation is non-isotropic and could give wrong results, particularly for images with large plateaus, as we found experimentally. Eikonal segmentation using GWDTs based on chamfer metrics improves this situation a little but not entirely. In contrast, for images with large plateaus/regions, segmentation via the eikonal PDE and curve evolution GWDT gives results close to ideal.

In the PDE-based watershed approach [5], at time $t = 0$ the boundary of each source is modeled as a curve $\gamma(0)$ which is then propagated with normal speed $c(x, y) = c_0/\eta(x, y) = c_0/||\nabla f(x, y)||$, where c_0 is the largest constant speed (e.g., the speed of light in vacuum). The propagating curve $\gamma(t)$ is embedded as the zero-level curve of a function $F(x, y, t)$, where $F(x, y, 0) = F_0(x, y)$ is the signed (positive in the curve interior) distance from $\gamma(0)$. The function F evolves according to the PDE

$$\frac{\partial F}{\partial t} = c(x, y)||\nabla F|| \tag{4}$$

As analyzed in [10, 12], this PDE implies that all the level curves of F propagate with a position-dependent normal speed $c(x, y) > 0$. This is a time-dependent formulation of the eikonal PDE and can be solved via the entropy condition satisfying numerical algorithm of [10]. The value of the resulting GWDT at any pixel (x, y) of the image is the time it takes for the evolving curve to reach this pixel, i.e. the smallest t such that $F(x, y, t) \geq 0$. The wateshed is then found along the lines where wavefronts emanating from different markers collide and extinguish themselves.

To reduce the computational complexity of solving general eikonal PDE problems via curve evolution a 'fast marching' algorithm was developed in [12, 3] that tracks only a narrow band of pixels at the boundary of the propagating wavefront. For the eikonal PDE segmentation problem, a queue-based algorithm has been developed in [5] that combines features from the fast marching method to computing GWDTs and can deal with the case of multiple sources where triple points develop at the collision of several wavefronts.

As Fig. 2 shows, compared on a test image that is difficult (because expanding wavefronts meet watershed lines at many angles ranging from being perpendicular to almost parallel), the continuous segmentation approach based on the eikonal PDE and curve evolution outperforms the discrete segmentation results (using either the digital watershed flooding algorithm or chamfer metric GWDTs). However, some real images may not contain many plateaus or only large regions, in which cases the digital watershed flooding algorithm may give comparable results than the eikonal PDE approach.

4 Ultrametric distances associated to flooding

4.1 Ultrametric distance and multiscale partitions

The first part of the paper has described the tools for producing the finest partition, from which a multiscale representation may be derived. Let $P_0 = (P_{01}, P_{02}, ...P_{0n})$ be the list of regions forming the finest partition. We are interested in constructing a series of nested partitions $P_k = (P_{k1}, P_{k2}, ...P_{kn})$, where each region P_{kj} is the union of a number of regions of finer partitions P_l, for $l < k$.

It is classical to associate to the series of nested partitions (P_k) an ultrametric distance :
$d(P_{0i}, P_{0j}) = \min(l \mid \exists P_{lh} \in P_l$ for which $P_{0i} \subset P_{lh}$ and $P_{0j} \subset P_{lh})$. In other words, the ultrametric distance is the smallest index of a partition P_h, of which one of the sets P_{lh} contains both regions P_{0i} and P_{0j}.

It is an ultrametric distance as it verifies the following axioms :
* reflexivity : $d(P_{0i}, P_{0i}) = 0$
* symmetry: $d(P_{0i}, P_{0j}) = d(P_{0j}, P_{0i})$
* ultrametric inequality : for all i, j, k:
$d(P_{0i}, P_{0j}) \leq \max\{d(P_{0i}, P_{0k}), d(P_{0k}, P_{0j})\}$
The first two axioms are obviously verified. The last one may be interpreted as follows : the smallest index l of a region P_{lh} containing both regions P_{0i} and P_{0j} is necessarily smaller or equal than the smallest index u of a region P_{uv} containing all three regions P_{0i}, P_{0j} and P_{0k}

An ultrametric distance is a distance, as the ultrametric inequality is stronger than the triangular inequality. A closed ball for the ultrametric distance with

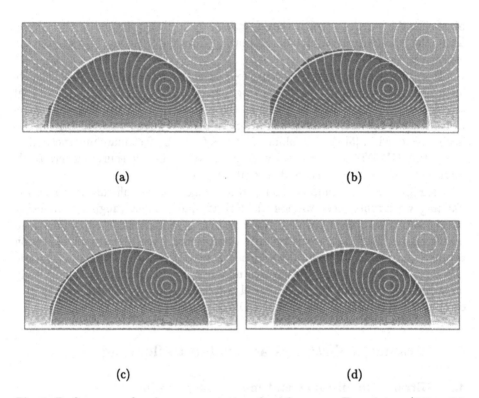

(a) (b)

(c) (d)

Fig. 2. Performance of various segmentation algorithms on a TEST image (250 × 400 pixels). This image is the minimum of two potential functions. Its contour plot (thin bright curves) is superimposed on all segmentation results. Markers are the two source points of the potential functions. Segmentation results based on: (a) Digital watershed flooding algorithm. (b) GDWT based on optimal 3 × 3 chamfer metric. (c) GDWT based on optimal 5 × 5 chamfer metric. (d) GDWT based on curve evolution. (The thick bright curve shows the correct segmentation.)

centre P_{0k} and radius n is the set of all regions P_{0i} for which $d(P_{0i}, P_{0j}) \leq n$. The balls associated to an ultrametric distance have two unique features, which will be useful in segmentation. The radius of a ball is equal to its diameter, i.e. to the largest distance between two elements in the ball. Each element of a ball is the centre of this ball. It is easy to check that the union of all closed balls of radius n precisely constitute the partition P_n.

Inversely we will associate a series of nested partitions to each ultrametric distance, by taking for partition of rank n, the set of closed balls of radius n. We will now define several ultrametric distances, naturally associated to the flooding of a topographic surface. Each of them will yield a different partition cube.

4.2 Flooding Tree

A finer analysis of the flooding will show the apparition of a tree in which the nodes are the catchment basins and the edges represent relations between neighboring nodes. Let us observe the creation and successive fusions of lakes during the flooding. The level of the flood is uniform over the topographic surface and increases with constant speed : new lakes appear as the flood reaches the various regional minima. At the time of apparition, each lake is isolated. As the level increases and reaches the lowest passpoint separating the corresponding CB from a neighboring CB, two lakes will merge. Two types of passpoints are to be distinguished. When the level of the flood reaches the first type, two lakes previously completely disconnected merge ; we will call these passpoints first meeting passes. When the flood reaches the second type, two branches of a unique lake meet and form a closed loop around an island. Representing each first meeting pass as an edge of a graph and the adjacent catchment basins as the nodes linked by this edge will create a graph. It is easy to see that this graph is a tree, spanning all nodes. It is in fact the minimum spanning tree (MST) of the neighborhood graph obtained by linking all neighboring catchment basins by an edge weighted by the altitude of the passpoint between them.

4.3 Flooding via Ultrametric Distances

Each edge of the spanning tree represents a passpoint where two disconnected lakes meet. We will assign to this edge a weight derived by measuring some geometric features on each of the adjacent lakes. We consider four different measures. The simplest is the altitude of the passpoint itself. The others are measured on each lake separately : they are respectively the depth, the area and the volume of the lakes For each of these four types a weight is derived as follows. Let us consider for instance the volume : the volumes of both lakes are compared and the smallest value is chosen as volumic weight of the edge. Depth and area measures are treated similarly leading respectively to weight distributions called dynamics for the depth and surfacic weight distributions. If the height is chosen, we get the usual weight distribution of the watershed.

We will now define an ultrametric distance associated to each weight distribution on the MST : the distance $d(x,y)$ is defined as the highest weight encountered on the unique path going from x to y along the spanning tree. This relation obviously is reflexive and symmetrical. The ultrametric inequality also is verified : for all $x, y, z, d(x,y) \leq \max\{d(x,z), d(z,y)\}$; since the highest weight on the unique path going from x to y along the spanning tree is smaller or equal to the highest way on the unique path which goes first from x to z and then from z to y along the spanning tree.

The closed balls of the ultrametric distance precisely correspond to the segmentation tree induced by the minimum spanning tree. The balls of radius 0 are the individual nodes, corresponding to the catchment basins. Each ball of radius n is the union of all nodes belonging to one of the subtrees of the MST obtained by cutting all edges with a valuation higher than n. A closed ball of radius R and centre C is the set of nodes which belong to the same subtree of the MST, obtained by cutting the edges at altitude higher than or equal to R and containing C. Obviously replacing the centre C by any other node of the subtree yields the same subtree.

Cutting the $(k-1)$ highest edges of the minimum spanning tree creates a forest of k trees. This is the forest of k trees of minimal weight contained in the neighborhood graph. Depending on the criterion on which the ultrametric distance is based, the nested segmentations will be more or less useful. The ultrametric distance based on altitude is the less useful. The segmentation based on depth are useful for ranking the particles according to their contrast. The area ultrametric distance will focus on the size of the particles. The volumic ultrametric distance has particularly good psychovisual properties [15]: the resulting segmentation trees offer a good balance between size and contrast. as illustrated in the following figures. The topographical surface to be flooded is a color gradient of the initial image (maximum of the morphological gradients computed in each of the R, G and B color channels). The volumic ultrametric distance has been used, and 3 levels of fusions have been represented, corresponding respectively to 15, 35 and 60 regions.

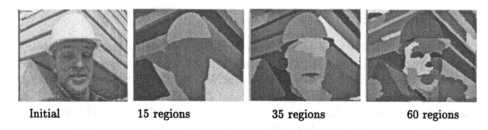

| Initial | 15 regions | 35 regions | 60 regions |

Fig. 3. Multiscale segmentation example.

5 Applications

5.1 Interactive segmentation with nested segmentations

A toolbox for interactive editing is currently constructed at the CMM [16], based on nested segmentations. A mouse position is defined by its x-y coordinates and its depth in the segmentation tree. If the mouse is active, the whole tile containing the cursor is activated. Moving the mouse in the x-y plane permits to select or deselect regions at the current level of segmentation. Going up will produce a coarser region, going down a smaller region. This technique permits to "paint" the segmentation with a kind of brush, whose shape adapts itself to the contours and whose size may be interactively changed by the user.

6 The watershed from markers

In many situations one has a seed for the objects to segment. It may be the segmentation produced in the preceding frame when one has to track an object in a sequence. It may also be some markers produced by hand, in interactive segmentation scenarios. As a result, some nodes of the minimum spanning tree may be identified as markers. The resulting segmentation associated to these markers will then still be a minimum spanning forest, but constrained in that each tree is rooted in a marker. The algorithm for constructing the minimum spanning forest is closely related to the classical algorithms for constructing the MST itself (see ref[17]. for more details). Each marker gets a different label and constitutes the initial part of a tree. The edges are ranked and processed in increasing order. The smallest unprocessed edge linking one of the tree T to an outside node is considered ; if this node does not already belong to another tree, it is assigned to the tree T. If it belongs to another tree, the edge is discarded and the next edge is processed.

Segmenting with markers constitutes the classical morphological method for segmentation. For optimal results, it is important to correctly chose the underlying ultrametric distance. We have presented 3 new distances giving often better results than the classically used flooding distance (where the weights are the altitude of the passpoints) This is illustrated by the following figures, where the same set of markers has been used alternatively with the flooding distance and with the volumic distance. The superiority of the volumic distance clearly appears here : it correctly detects the face, whereas the flooding distance follows the boundary of a shadow and cuts the face in two.

markers   flooding dist.   volumic dist.

Fig. 4. Segmentations with different ultrametric floodings.

7 Conclusion

A multiscale segmentation scheme has been presented, embedded in the flooding mechanism of the watershed itself. It opens many new possibilities for segmentation, either in supervised or unsupervised mode.

Acknowledgements: P. Maragos' work in this paper was partially supported by the European TMR/Networks Project ERBFMRXCT970160.

References

1. S. Beucher and F. Meyer. The morphological approach to segmentation: the watershed transformation. In E. Dougherty, editor, *Mathematical morphology in image processing*, chapter 12, pages 433–481. Marcel Dekker, 1993.
2. R. Kimmel, N. Kiryati, and A. M. Bruckstein, "Sub-Pixel Distance Maps and Weighted Distance Transforms", *J. Math. Imaging & Vision*, 6:223–233, 1996.
3. R. Malladi, J. A. Sethian, and B. C. Vemuri, "A Fast Level Set Based Algorithm for Topology-Independent Shape Modeling", *J. Math. Imaging and Vision*, 6, pp. 269–289, 1996.
4. P. Maragos, "Differential Morphology and Image Processing" *IEEE Trans. Image Processing*, vol. 78, pp. 922–937, June 1996.
5. P. Maragos and M. A. Butt, "Advances in Differential Morphology: Image Segmentation via Eikonal PDE & Curve Evolution and Reconstruction via Constrained Dilation Flow", in *Mathematical Morphology and Its Applications to Image and Signal Processing*, H. Heijmans and J. Roerdink, Eds., Kluwer Acad. Publ., 1998, pp. 167–174.
6. F. Meyer, "Integrals and Gradients of Images", *Proc. SPIE vol. 1769: Image Algebra and Morphological Image Processing III*, pp.200-211, 1992.
7. F. Meyer, "Topographic Distance and Watershed Lines", *Signal Processing*, 38, pp. 113–125, 1994.
8. F. Meyer and S. Beucher, "Morphological Segmentation", *J. Visual Commun. Image Representation*, 1(1):21–45, 1990.
9. L. Najman and M. Schmitt, "Watershed of a Continuous Function", *Signal Processing*, vol. 38, pp. 99-112, July 1994.
10. S. Osher and J. Sethian, "Fronts Propagating with Curvature-Dependent Speed: Algorithms Based on Hamilton-Jacobi Formulations", *J. Comput. Physics*, 79, pp. 12–49, 1988.
11. E. Rouy and A. Tourin, "A Viscocity Solutions Approach to Shape from Shading", *SIAM J. Numer. Anal.*, vol. 29 (3), pp. 867-884, June 1992.
12. J. A. Sethian, *Level Set Methods*, Cambridge Univ. Press, 1996.
13. P. Verbeek and B. Verwer, "Shading from shape, the eikonal equation solved by grey-weighted distance transform", *Pattern Recogn. Lett.*, 11:618–690, 1990.
14. L. Vincent and P. Soille, "Watershed In Digital Spaces: An Efficient Algorithm Based On Immersion Simulations", *IEEE Trans. Pattern Anal. Mach. Intellig.*, vol. 13, pp. 583–598, June 1991.
15. C. Vachier. *Extraction de Caractéristiques, Segmentation d'Image et Morphologie Mathématique.* PhD thesis, E.N.S. des Mines de Paris, 1995.
16. F. Zanoguera, B. Marcotegui and F. Meyer, "An interactive colour image segmentation system", *Wiamis'99: Workshop on Image Analysis for Multimedia Interactive Services*, pp.137–141. Heinrich-Hertz Institut Berlin, 1999.
17. F. Meyer. Minimal spanning forests for morphological segmentation. *ISMM94 : Mathematical Morphology and its applications to Signal Processing*, pages 77–84, 1994.

Nonlinear PDEs and Numerical Algorithms for Modeling Levelings and Reconstruction Filters

Petros Maragos[1] and Fernand Meyer[2]

[1] National Technical University of Athens, Dept. of Electrical & Computer Engineering, Zografou 15773, Athens, Greece. Email: maragos@cs.ntua.gr
[2] Centre de Morphologie Mathématique, Ecole des Mines de Paris, 35, Rue Saint Honoré, 77305 Fontainebleau, France. Email: meyer@cmm.ensmp.fr

Abstract. In this paper we develop partial differential equations (PDEs) that model the generation of a large class of morphological filters, the levelings and the openings/closings by reconstruction. These types of filters are very useful in numerous image analysis and vision tasks ranging from enhancement, to geometric feature detection, to segmentation. The developed PDEs are nonlinear functions of the first spatial derivatives and model these nonlinear filters as the limit of a controlled growth starting from an initial seed signal. This growth is of the multiscale dilation or erosion type and the controlling mechanism is a switch that reverses the growth when the difference between the current evolution and a reference signal switches signs. We discuss theoretical aspects of these PDEs, propose discrete algorithms for their numerical solution and corresponding filter implementation, and provide insights via several experiments. Finally, we outline the use of these PDEs for improving the Gaussian scale-space by using the latter as initial seed to generate multiscale levelings that have a superior preservation of image edges and boundaries.

1 Introduction

For several tasks in computer vision, especially the ones related to scale-space image analysis, there have been proposed continuous models based on partial differential equations (PDEs). Motivations for using PDEs include better and more intuitive mathematical modeling, connections with physics, and better approximation to the Euclidean geometry of the problem. While many such continuous approaches have been linear (the most notable example being the isotropic heat diffusion PDE for modeling the Gaussian scale-space), many among the most useful ones are nonlinear. This is partly due to a general understanding about the limitations or inability of linear systems to successfully model several important vision problems.

Areas where there is a need to develop nonlinear approaches include the class of problems related to scale-space analysis and multiscale image smoothing. In contrast to the shifting and blurring of image edges caused by linear smoothers, there is a large variety of nonlinear smoothers that either suffer less from or completely avoid these shortcomings. Simple examples are the classic morphological openings and closings (cascades of erosions and dilations) as well as the median filters. The openings suppress signals peaks, the closings eliminate valleys, whereas the medians have a more symmetric behavior. All three filter types preserve well vertical image edges but may shift and blur horizontal edges/boundaries. A much more powerful class of filters are the *reconstruction openings and closings* which, starting from a *reference* signal f consisting of several parts and a *marker* (initial seed) g inside some of these parts, can reconstruct whole objects with exact preservation of their boundaries and edges. In this reconstruction process they simplify the original image by completely eliminating smaller objects inside which the marker cannot fit. The reconstruction filters enlarge the flat zones of the image [15]. One of their disadvantages is that they treat asymmetrically the image foreground and background. A recent solution to this asymmetry problem came from the development of a more general powerful class of morphological filters, the levelings [10, 11], which include as special cases the reconstruction openings and closings. They are transformations $\Psi(f, g)$ that depend on two signals, the reference f and the marker g. Reconstruction filters and levelings have found numerous applications in a large variety of problems involving image enhancement and simplification, geometric feature detection, and segmentation. They also possess many useful algebraic and scale-space properties, discussed in a companion paper [12].

In this paper we develop PDEs that can model and generate levelings. These PDEs work by growing a marker (initial seed) signal g in a way that the growth extent is controlled by a reference signal f and its type (expansion or shrinking growth) is switched by the sign of the difference between f and the current evolution. This growth is modeled by PDEs that can generate multiscale dilations or erosions. Therefore, we start first with a background section on dilation PDEs. Afterwards, we introduce a PDE for levelings of 1D signals and a PDE for levelings of 2D images, propose discrete numerical algorithms for their implementation, and provide insights via experiments. We also discuss how to obtain reconstruction openings and closings from the general leveling PDE. Further, we develop alternative PDEs for modeling generalized levelings that create quasi-flat zones. Finally, we outline the use of these PDEs for improving the Gaussian scale-space by using the latter as initial seed to generate multiscale levelings that have a superior preservation of image edges and boundaries.

2 Dilation/Erosion PDEs

All multiscale morphological operations, at their most basic level, are generated by multiscale dilations and erosions, which are obtained by replacing in the standard dilations/erosions the unit-scale kernel (structuring element) $K(x, y)$ with a multiscale version $K^{(t)}(x, y) \equiv tK(x/t, y/t), t > 0$. The *multiscale dilation* of a 2D signal $f(x, y)$ by $K^{(t)}$ is the space-scale function

$$\delta(x, y, t) \equiv (f \oplus K^{(t)})(x, y) = \sup_{(a,b)} \{f(x - a, y - b) + tK(a/t, b/t)\}, \quad t > 0$$

where $\delta(x, y, 0) = f(x, y)$. Similarly, the multiscale erosion of f is defined as

$$\varepsilon(x, y, t) \equiv (f \ominus K^{(t)})(x, y) = \inf_{(a,b)} \{f(x + a, y + b) - tK(a/t, b/t)\}$$

Until recently the vast majority of implementations of multiscale morphological filtering had been discrete. In 1992, three teams of researchers independently published nonlinear PDEs that model the continuous multiscale morphological scale-space. In [1] PDEs were obtained for multiscale flat dilation and erosion by compact convex sets as part of a general work on developing PDE-based models for multiscale image processing that satisfy certain axiomatic principles. In [4] PDEs were developed that model multiscale dilation, erosion, opening and closing by compact-support convex sets or concave functions which may have non-smooth boundaries or graphs, respectively. This work was based on the semigroup structure of the multiscale dilation and erosion operators and the use of sup/inf derivatives to deal with the development of shocks. In [18] PDEs were obtained by studying the propagation of boundaries of 2D sets or signal graphs under multiscale dilation and erosion, provided that these boundaries contain no linear segments, are smooth and possess a unique normal at each point. Refinements of the above three works for PDEs modeling multiscale morphology followed in [2, 5, 6, 8, 9, 19]. The basic dilation PDE was applied in [3, 16] for modeling continuous-scale morphology, where its superior performance over discrete morphology was noted in terms of isotropy and subpixel accuracy. Next we provide a few examples.[1]

For 1D signals $f(x)$, and if $K(x)$ is the $0/-\infty$ indicator function of the interval $[-1, 1]$, then the PDEs generating the multiscale flat dilation $\delta(x, t)$ and erosion $\varepsilon(x, t)$ of f are:

$$\delta_t = |\delta_x| \quad , \quad \varepsilon_t = -|\varepsilon_x| \tag{1}$$

with initial values $\delta(x, 0) = \varepsilon(x, 0) = f(x)$.

For 2D signals $f(x, y)$, and if $K(x, y)$ is the $0/-\infty$ indicator function of the unit disk, then the PDEs generating the multiscale flat dilation $\delta(x, y, t)$ and erosion $\varepsilon(x, y, t)$ of f are:

$$\delta_t = \|\nabla\delta\| = \sqrt{(\delta_x)^2 + (\delta_y)^2}; \quad , \quad \varepsilon_t = -\|\nabla\varepsilon\| \tag{2}$$

with initial values $\delta(x, y, 0) = \varepsilon(x, y, 0) = f(x, y)$.

These simple but nonlinear PDEs are satisfied at points where the data are smooth, i.e., the partial derivatives exist. However, even if the initial image/signal f is smooth, at finite scales $t > 0$ the above multiscale dilation evolution may create discontinuities in the derivatives of δ, called *shocks*, which then continue propagating in scale-space. Thus, the multiscale dilations are *weak solutions* of the corresponding PDEs.

The above PDEs for dilations of graylevel images by flat structuring elements directly apply to binary images, because flat dilations commute with thresholding and hence, when the graylevel image is dilated, each one of its thresholded

---

[1] Notation: For $u = u(x, y, t)$, $u_t = \partial u/\partial t$, $u_x = \partial u/\partial x$, $u_y = \partial u/\partial y$, $\nabla u = (u_x, u_y)$.

versions representing a binary image is simultaneously dilated by the same element and at the same scale. However, this is not the case with graylevel structuring functions. For example, if $K(x, y) = -a(x^2+y^2)$, $a > 0$, is an infinite-support parabolic function, the dilation PDE becomes

$$\delta_t = ||\nabla \delta||^2 / 4a = [(\delta_x)^2 + (\delta_y)^2]/4a \qquad (3)$$

3 PDE for 1D Leveling

Consider a 1D signal $f(x)$ and a marker signal $g(x)$ from which a leveling $\Psi(f, g)$ will be produced.

If $g \leq f$ everywhere and we start iteratively growing g via incremental flat dilations with an infinitesimally small element $[-\Delta t, \Delta t]$ but without ever growing the result above the graph of f, then in the limit we shall have produced the *opening by reconstruction* of f (with respect to the marker g), which is a special leveling. The infinitesimal generator of this signal evolution can be modeled via a dilation PDE that has a mechanism to stop the growth whenever the intermediate result attempts to create a function larger than f. Specifically, let $u(x, t)$ represent the evolutions of f with initial value $u_0(x) = u(x, 0) = g(x)$. Then, u is a weak solution of the following initial-value PDE system

$$u_t = \text{sign}(f - u)|u_x| = \begin{cases} |u_x|, & u < f \\ 0, & u = f \text{ or } u_x = 0 \end{cases} \qquad (4)$$

$$u(x, 0) = g(x) \leq f(x) \qquad (5)$$

where $\text{sign}(r)$ is equal to $+1$ if $r > 0$, -1 if $r < 0$ and 0 if $r = 0$. This PDE models a *conditional dilation* that grows the intermediate result as long as it does not exceed f. In the limit we obtain the final result $u_\infty(x) = \lim_{t \to \infty} u(x, t)$. The mapping $u_0 \mapsto u_\infty$ is the *opening by reconstruction filter*.

If in the above paradigm we reverse the order between f and g, i.e., assume that $g(x) \geq f(x) \, \forall x$, and replace the positive growth (dilation) of g with negative growth via erosion that stops when the intermediate result attempts to become smaller than f, then we obtain the *closing by reconstruction* of f with respect to the marker g. This is another special case of a leveling, whose generation can be modeled by the following PDE:

$$u_t = -\text{sign}(u - f)|u_x| = \begin{cases} -|u_x|, & u > f \\ 0, & u = f \text{ or } u_x = 0 \end{cases} \qquad (6)$$

$$u(x, 0) = g(x) \geq f(x) \qquad (7)$$

What happens if we use any of the above two PDEs when there is no specific order between f and g? The signal evolutions are stored in a function $u(x, t)$ that is a weak solution of the initial-value PDE system

$$u_t(x, t) = |u_x(x, t)| \text{sign}[f(x) - u(x, t)]$$
$$u(x, 0) = g(x) \qquad (8)$$

This PDE has a varying coefficient sign$(f - u)$ with spatio-temporal dependence which controls the instantaneous growth and stops it whenever $f = u$. (Of course, there is no growth also at extrema where $u_x = 0$.) The control mechanism is of a switching type: For each t, at points x where $u(x, t) < f(x)$ it acts as a dilation PDE and hence shifts parts of the graph of $u(x, t)$ with positive (negative) slope to the left (right) but does not move the extrema points. Wherever $u(x, t) > f(x)$ the PDE acts as an erosion PDE and reverses the direction of propagation. The final result $u_\infty(x) = \lim_{t \to \infty} u(x, t)$ is a general *leveling* of f with respect to g. We call (8) a *switched dilation* PDE. The switching action of this PDE model occurs at zero crossings of $f - u$ where shocks are developed. Obviously, the PDEs generating the opening and closing by reconstruction are special cases where $g \leq f$ and $g \geq f$, respectively. However, the PDEs generating the reconstruction filters do not involve switching of growth.

The switching between a dilation- or erosion-type PDE also occurs in a class of nonlinear time-dependent PDEs which was proposed in [13] to deblur images and/or enhance their contrast by generating shocks and hence sharpening edges. For 1D images a special case of such a PDE is

$$u_t = -|u_x|\text{sign}(u_{xx}) \tag{9}$$

A major conceptual difference between the above edge-sharpening PDE and our PDE generating levelings is that in the former the switching is determined by the edges, i.e., the inflection points of u itself whereas in the latter the switching is controlled by comparing u against the reference signal f. Note also that, if at some point there is an edge in the leveling output, then there must exist an edge of equal or bigger size in the initial (reference) image.

3.1 Discretization, Algorithm, Experiments

To produce a shock-capturing and entropy-satisfying numerical method for solving the general leveling PDE (8), we use ideas from the technology of solving PDEs corresponding to hyperbolic conservation laws [7] and Hamilton-Jacobi formulations [14]. Thus, we propose the following discretization sheme, which is an adaptation of a scheme proposed in [13] for solving (9).

Let U_i^n be the approximation of $u(x, t)$ on a grid $(i\Delta x, n\Delta t)$. Consider the forward and backward difference operators:

$$D_+^x u \equiv \frac{u(x + \Delta x, t) - u(x, t)}{\Delta x}, \quad D_-^x u \equiv \frac{u(x, t) - u(x - \Delta x, t)}{\Delta x} \tag{10}$$

(Similarly we define the difference operators D_+^y and D_-^y along the y direction.) Then we approximate the leveling PDE (8) by the following nonlinear difference equation:

$$U_i^{n+1} = U_i^n - \Delta t[\, (S_i^n)^+ \sqrt{((D_-^x U_i^n)^+)^2 + ((D_+^x U_i^n)^-)^2} \\ + (S_i^n)^- \sqrt{((D_+^x U_i^n)^+)^2 + ((D_-^x U_i^n)^-)^2} \,] \tag{11}$$

where $S_i^n = \text{sign}(f(i\Delta x) - U_i^n)$, $r^+ = \max(0, r)$, and $r^- = \min(0, r)$. For stability, $(\Delta t / \Delta x) \leq 0.5$ is required. Further, at each iteration we enforce the sign consistency

$$\text{sign}(U^n - f) = \text{sign}(g - f) \tag{12}$$

We have not proved theoretically that the above iterated scheme converges when $n \to \infty$, but through many experiments we have observed that it converges in a finite number of steps. Examples are shown in Fig. 1.

4 PDE for 2D Leveling

A straighforward extension of the leveling PDE from 1D to 2D signals is to replace the 1D dilation PDE with the PDE generating multiscale dilations by a disk. Then the 2D leveling PDE becomes:

$$\begin{aligned} u_t(x, y, t) &= \|\nabla u(x, y, t)\| \text{sign}[f(x, y) - u(x, y, t)] \\ u(x, y, 0) &= g(x, y) \end{aligned} \tag{13}$$

Of course, we could select any other PDE modeling dilations by shapes other than the disk, but the disk has the advantage of creating an isotropic growth.

For discretization, let $U_{i,j}^n$ be the approximation of $u(x, y, t)$ on a computational grid $(i\Delta x, j\Delta y, n\Delta t)$. Then we approximate the leveling PDE (13) by the following 2D nonlinear difference equation:

$$\begin{aligned} U_{i,j}^{n+1} = U_{i,j}^n - \Delta t[\cdots \\ (S_{i,j}^n)^+ \sqrt{((D_-^x U_{i,j}^n)^+)^2 + ((D_+^x U_{i,j}^n)^-)^2 + ((D_-^y U_{i,j}^n)^+)^2 + ((D_+^y U_{i,j}^n)^-)^2} \\ + (S_{i,j}^n)^- \sqrt{((D_+^x U_{i,j}^n)^+)^2 + ((D_-^x U_{i,j}^n)^-)^2 + ((D_+^y U_{i,j}^n)^+)^2 + ((D_-^y U_{i,j}^n)^-)^2}\,] \end{aligned} \tag{14}$$

where $S_{i,j}^n = \text{sign}(f(i\Delta x, j\Delta y) - U_{i,j}^n)$. For stability, $(\Delta t / \Delta x + \Delta t / \Delta y) \leq 0.5$ is required. Also, the sign consistency (12) is enforced at each iteration.

Three examples of the action of the above 2D algorithm are shown in Fig. 2.

5 Discussion and Extensions

5.1 PDEs for Levelings with Quasi-Flat Zones

So far all the previous leveling PDEs produce filtering outputs that consist of portions of the original (reference) signal and of flat zones (plateaus). Actually they enlarge the flat zones of the reference signal. Is it possible to generate via PDEs generalized levelings that have quasi-flat zones? For example, zones with constant linear slope or zones with parabolic surface? The answer is yes. We illustrate it via the parabolic example. If we replace the flat dilation PDE generator in (8) with the PDE generator for multiscale dilations by a 1D unit-scale parabola $K(x) = -ax^2$ we obtain the PDE for 1D parabolic levelings:

$$\begin{aligned} u_t(x, t) &= \tfrac{1}{4a} |u_x(x, t)|^2 \text{sign}[f(x) - u(x, t)] \\ u(x, 0) &= g(x) \end{aligned} \tag{15}$$

To obtain the PDE for 2D parabolic levelings we replace $|u_x|$ with $\|\nabla u\|$.

5.2   Why Use PDEs For Levelings?

In addition to the well-known advantages of the PDE approach (such as more insightful mathematical modeling, more connections with physics, better isotropy, better approximation of Euclidean geometry, and subpixel accuracy), during construction of levelings or reconstruction filters it is possible in some applications to need to stop the marker growth before convergence. In such cases, the isotropy of the partially grown marker offered by the PDE is an advantage. Further, there are no simple digital algorithms for constructing levelings with quasi-flat zones, whereas for the PDE approach only a simple change of the generator is needed.

5.3   From Gaussian Scale-Space to Multiscale Levelings

Consider a reference signal f and a leveling Ψ. If we can produce various markers g_i, $i = 1, 2, 3, ...$, that are related to some increasing scale parameter i and produce the levelings of f with respect to these markers, then we can generate multiscale levelings in some approximate sense. This scenario will be endowed with an important property if we slightly change it to the following hierarchy:

$$h_1 = \Psi(f, g_1), \ h_2 = \Psi(h_1, g_2), \ h_3 = \Psi(h_2, g_3), ... \tag{16}$$

The above sequence of steps insures that h_j is a leveling of h_i for $j > i$.

The sequence of markers g_i may be obtained from f in any meaningful way. In this paper we consider the case where the g_i are multiscale convolutions of f with Gaussians of increasing standard deviations σ_i. Examples of constructing multiscale levelings from Gaussian convolution markers according to (16) are shown in Fig. 3 for a 1D signal and in Fig. 4 for an image f. The sequence of the multiscale markers can be viewed as a scale-sampled Gaussian scale-space. As shown in the experiments, the image edges and boundaries which have been blurred and shifted by the Gaussian scale-space are better preserved across scales by the multiscale levelings that use the Gaussian convolutions as markers.

Acknowledgements

We wish to thank Profs. J. Barrera and R. Lotufo for inviting us to talk at SIBGRAPI'98 in Brazil. The ideas in this paper were formed from our collaboration during this research visit.

P. Maragos' work in this paper was partially supported by the European TMR/Networks Project ERBFMRXCT970160.

References

1. L. Alvarez, F. Guichard, P.L. Lions, and J.M. Morel, "Axiomatization et nouveaux operateurs de la morphologie mathematique", *C. R. Acad. Sci. Paris*, pp. 265-268, t.315, Serie I, 1992.

2. L. Alvarez, F. Guichard, P.L. Lions, and J.M. Morel, "Axioms and Fundamental Equations of Image Processing", *Archiv. Rat. Mech.*, vol. 123 (3), pp. 199–257, 1993.

3. A. Arehart, L. Vincent and B. Kimia, "Mathematical Morphology: The Hamilton-Jacobi Connection", in *Proc. Int'l Conf. Comp. Vision*, pp. 215–219, 1993.

4. R. W. Brockett and P. Maragos, "Evolution Equations for Continuous-Scale Morphology", *Proc. IEEE Int'l Conf. Acoust., Speech, Signal Processing*, San Francisco, CA, March 1992.

5. R. Brockett and P. Maragos, "Evolution Equations for Continuous-Scale Morphological Filtering", *IEEE Trans. Signal Processing*, vol. 42, pp. 3377-3386, Dec. 1994.

6. H.J.A.M. Heijmans and P. Maragos, "Lattice Calculus and the Morphological Slope Transform", *Signal Processing*, vol. 59, pp. 17–42, 1997.

7. P. D. Lax, *Hyperbolic Systems of Conservation Laws and the Mathematical Theory of Schock Waves*, SIAM, Philadelphia, PA, 1973.

8. P. Maragos, "Differential Morphology and Image Processing" *IEEE Trans. Image Processing*, vol. 78, pp. 922–937, June 1996.

9. P. Maragos and M. A. Butt, "Curve Evolution, Differential Morphology, and Distance Transforms Applied to Multiscale and Eikonal Problems", *Fundamentae Informatica*, to appear.

10. F. Meyer, "From Connected Operators to Levelings", in *Mathematical Morphology and Its Applications to Image and Signal Processing*, H. Heijmans and J. Roerdink, editors, Kluwer Acad. Publ., 1998.

11. F. Meyer, "The Levelings", in *Mathematical Morphology and Its Applications to Image and Signal Processing*, H. Heijmans and J. Roerdink, editors, Kluwer Acad. Publ., 1998.

12. F. Meyer and P. Maragos, "Morphological Scale-Space Representation with Levelings", *Proc. 2nd Int'l. Conf. on Scale-Space Theories in Computer Vision*, Corfu, Greece, Sep. 1999.

13. S. Osher and L. I. Rudin, "Feature-Oriented Image Enhancement Using Schock Filters", *SIAM J. Numer. Anal.*, vol. 27, no. 4, pp. 919–940, Aug. 1990.

14. S. Osher and J. Sethian, "Fronts Propagating with Curvature-Dependent Speed: Algorithms Based on Hamilton-Jacobi Formulations", *J. Comput. Physics*, 79, pp. 12–49, 1988.

15. P. Salembier and J. Serra, "Flat Zones Filtering, Conencted Operators, and Filters by Reconstruction", *IEEE Trans. Image Process.*, vol. 4, pp.1153-1160, Aug. 1995.

16. G. Sapiro, R. Kimmel, D. Shaked, B. Kimia, and A. Bruckstein, "Implementing Continuous-scale Morphology via Curve Evolution", *Pattern Recognition*, 26(9), pp. 1363–1372, 1993.

17. J. A. Sethian, *Level Set Methods*, Cambridge Univ. Press, 1996.

18. R. Van den Boomgaard, *Mathematical Morphology: Extensions towards Computer Vision*, Ph.D. Thesis, Univ. of Amsterdam, The Netherlands, 1992.

19. R. Van den Boomgaard and A. Smeulders, "The Morphological Structure of Images: The Differential Equations of Morphological Scale-Space", *IEEE Trans. Pattern Anal. Mach. Intellig.*, vol. 16, pp.1101-1113, Nov. 1994.

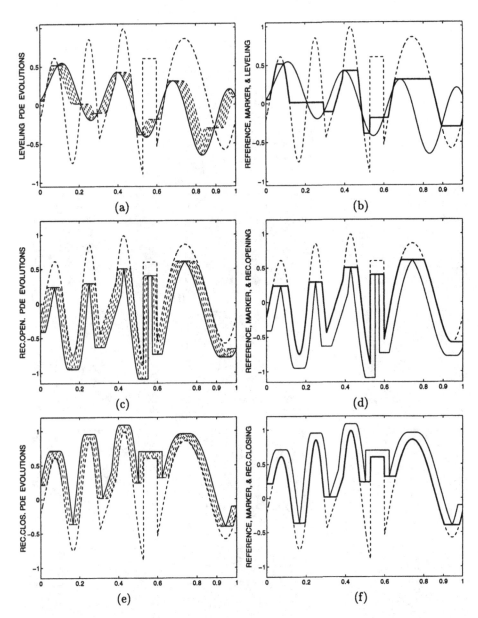

Fig. 1. Evolutions of 1D leveling PDE for 3 different markers. For each row, the right column shows the reference signal f (dash line), the marker (thin solid line), and the leveling (thick solid line). The left column shows the marker and 5 of its evolutions at times $t = n20\Delta t$, $n = 1, 2, 3, 4, 5$. In row (a,b) we see the general leveling evolutions for an arbitrary marker. In row (c,d) the marker was an erosion of f minus a constant, and hence the leveling is a reconstruction opening. In row (e,f) the marker was a dilation of f plus a constant, and hence the leveling is a reconstruction closing. ($\Delta x = 0.001$, $\Delta t = 0.0005$.)

Fig. 2. Evolutions of the 2D leveling PDE on the reference top image (a) using 3 markers. Each column shows evolutions from the same marker. On second row the markers ($t = 0$) are shown, on third and fourth rows two evolutions at $t = 10\Delta t$ and $t = 20\Delta t$, and on fifth row the final levelings (after convergence). For left column (b-e), the marker (b) was obtained from a 2D convolution of f with a Gaussian of $\sigma = 4$. For middle column (f-i), the marker (f) was a simple opening by a square of 9×9 pixels and hence the corresponding leveling (i) is a reconstruction opening. For right column (j-m), the marker (j) was a simple closing by a square of 9×9 pixels and hence the corresponding leveling (m) is a reconstruction closing. ($\Delta x = \Delta y = 1$, $\Delta t = 0.25$.)

373

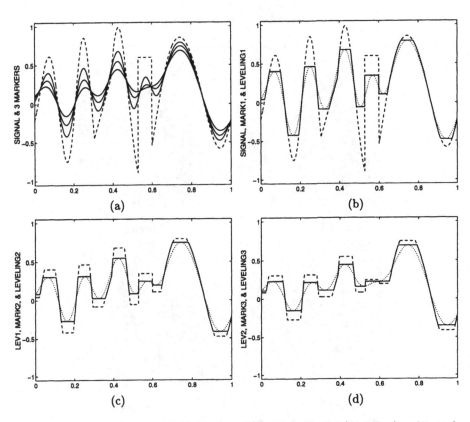

Fig. 3. 1D Multiscale levelings. (a) Original (reference) signal f (dash line) and 3 markers g_i obtained by convolving f with Gaussians of standard deviations $\sigma_i = 30, 40, 50$. (b)-(d) show reference signals g_i (dash line), markers g_{i+1} (dotted line), and levelings $\Psi(g_i, g_{i+1})$ (solid line) for $i = 0, 1, 2$, where $g_0 = f$. ($\Delta x = 0.001$, $\Delta t = 0.0005$.)

Original Reference

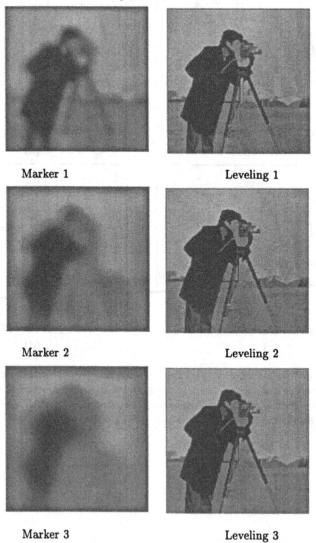

Marker 1

Leveling 1

Marker 2

Leveling 2

Marker 3

Leveling 3

Fig. 4. Multiscale image levelings. The markers were obtained by convolving reference image with 2D Gaussians of standard deviations $\sigma = 3, 5, 7$. ($\Delta x = \Delta y = 1$, $\Delta t = 0.25$.)

Proper Scales of Shapes
A Curved Scale Space

Ph. G. Batchelor[1,*], A. D. Castellano Smith[1], D.L.G. Hill[1]

Div. of Radiological Sciences and Medical Engineering,
The Guy's King's and St Thomas' Medical and Dental School,
King's College London
London SE1 9RT, UK
p.batchelor@umds.ac.uk

Abstract. We present an extension of the scale space idea to surfaces, with the aim of extending ideas like Gaussian derivatives to function on curved spaces. This is done by using the fact, also valid for normal images, that among the continuous range of scales at which one can look at an image, or surface, there is a infinite discrete subset which has a natural geometric interpretation. We call them "proper scales", as they are defined by eigenvalues of an elliptic partial differential operator associated with the image, or shape. The computations are performed using the Finite Element technique.

1   Introduction

Scale space theory studies the dependence of image structure on the level of resolution [8]. Most of the time, an observer is interested in the object imaged and not purely the complete image. Such an object generically has features at very different scales.

On the other hand, not all possible values of scale show interesting features, for example scale lengths smaller than the resolution, and at the other extreme, lengths greater than the "window" of the image. This also depends on the shape of the window, if it is square or cubic, circular, etc...

The imaging process has an influence on the extracted object, which is only an approximation of the imaged one, and thus measurements on the object are also approximations. The degree of approximation is dependent on the scale, in a broad sense, at which the measurement is made.

These reasons show a need for the definition of the "right scales" [8] associated with an object. Such a scale space theory for objects should show properties similar to the ones of the image scale space. The luminance function defining an image is a measurement of a given part of the physical world, and it is embedded in a family of derived images. In the same way, a measurement on a shape should have a corresponding family of derived measurements at a specified resolution.

---

* We would like to thank the referees for the useful suggestions

Our claim is that there is a list of "proper" scales, where by proper we mean that they are *specific* to the shape.

We present the necessary theory for calculating a scale space on curved manifolds, analogous to the use of Gaussians on standard images. We then describe how to implement this theory on discrete data using Finite Element methods. Finally, we give example results from simple geometrical shapes.

2 Theory

We start by stating some notations and definitions. An image I is a mapping $I : \Omega \to \mathbb{R}^n$, where $\Omega \subset \mathbb{R}^m$. In concrete cases, m is 2 or 3, $n = 1$, Ω is an open bounded set with piecewise smooth (C^∞) boundary, e.g. a square or a cube. For discrete images, one should take the intersection of such a domain with a lattice. To be very precise, we should also specify to which class of functions I belongs, for the moment we will just call $H(\Omega)$ the set of possible images on Ω.

The image I is extended to a family of images parametrised by S, i.e. $I_S : \Omega \times S \to \mathbb{R}^n$. $I_S(\cdot, t) =: I_t(\cdot)$, and the central point is that I_t is defined by convolution with a parameter dependent kernel

$$\mathcal{K}^\Omega : \Omega \times \Omega \times S \to \mathbb{R}$$

$$(x, y, t) \mapsto \mathcal{K}_t^\Omega(x, y) \ .$$

We write $I_t = I * \mathcal{K}_t^\Omega$.

The choice of the kernel is central to this theory. Normally, $S = \mathbb{R}^+$ and the Gaussian kernel is chosen:

$$\mathcal{K}_t^\Omega(x, y) = G_t(x - y) = \frac{1}{(2\pi t^2)^{m/2}} e^{\frac{-\|(x-y)\|^2}{2t^2}} \ . \tag{1}$$

There are many approaches which lead to this choice, for an historical account, see e.g. [10]. The mathematical foundations for the following can be found in [6] or for a more introductory text [9].

We are interested in shapes, usually extracted from an image by segmentation. We will denote a shape with the letter X, and define it as being a 2D-surface, or if one wants other dimensions, an m dimensional manifold.

Examples would be a sphere, or more interestingly, the cortical surface of a brain extracted by segmentation.

Scale Space on Shapes. The main difference with the case described above is that X has usually no linear structure: one can't add $x \in X$ to $y \in X$. The Gaussian kernel is meaningless in this case, as well as the axioms based on linearity. Nevertheless, there is one approach which can be used straightforwardly here: Iijima's axiomatic of 1971 ([10]). Given an image $I : X \to \mathbb{R}$, let I_t be the scale space of X which we want to define. F is the corresponding image flow, i.e. it is a vector field on the manifold X which gives the strength and direction of the "intensity" change at time t. The first principle is the *Conservation principle*, i.e.

$$\frac{\partial}{\partial t}I_t + \operatorname{div}^X F = 0. \tag{2}$$

The second condition is what is called *Principle of maximum loss of figure impression*, which is translated by saying that the flux direction should be the direction of maximal image gradient, i.e. $F = -\nabla^X I_t$. Using this in equation 2, we have:

$$\frac{\partial}{\partial t}I_t = \Delta^X I_t \quad \text{on } X \tag{3}$$

$$I_0 = I \tag{4}$$

The corresponding kernel is the special solution such that:

$$\frac{\partial}{\partial t}\mathcal{K}_t^X(x,y,t) = \Delta^X \mathcal{K}_t^X(x,y,t) \quad \text{on } X$$

$$\lim_{t\to 0}\int_X \mathcal{K}^X(x,y,t)I(y) = I(x)$$

For a standard image, the kernel $\mathcal{K}^X$ is a Gaussian, and the Laplacian takes its usual form.

Deriving the Form of the Scale Space Kernel and the Laplacian for a Manifold. First, the degree of differentiability of the manifolds X have not been specified. The most general assumptions do not require it to be differentiable, and indeed fractal domains are a current area of research in mathematics for the existence of solution to such heat equations. Here, it is simply assumed that X is at least a C^2 manifold. They can have a boundary, with finitely many corners out of which the boundary is also smooth. At none of these points should there be a zero angle. Another very important concrete assumption is that X is compact, i.e. in particular bounded. The space $H(X)$ of possible "images" should be such that the partial differential equation above can be defined within that space, so one is first tempted to take $C^2(X)$ or even $C^\infty(X)$, but this choice often turns out to be too restrictive, and not well adapted to the numerical computations. The idea is to complete C^2 by limits of sequences of C^2 functions, where the limit is taken in the sense of the function norm: $\|I\|_{H^{1,2}}^2 = \int_X I^2 + \int_X |\nabla^X I|^2$, and to use partial integration to interpret the diffusion equation above in the weak form. The space is called the Sobolev space $H^1(X)$, where the index refers to the fact that we only use one degree of differentiability, as the differential equations are taken in the weak sense. $H^1(X)$ contains non differentiable functions, for example Lipschitz continuous functions belong to it.

We are interested in X which is a curved space, or *Riemannian manifold* and this allows us to define the differential operators div^X, ∇^X to be defined on differentiable vector fields and functions over X^1. From these, one can define the *Laplace Beltrami* operator $\Delta^X := \operatorname{div}^X \nabla^X$ over C^2.

---

[1] See [9] for expression in local coordinates

We can use these operators to construct a nonlinear scale space on a manifold X. Interestingly a special example of shape can be the graph surface defined by the points $(x, y, I(x, y))$ for $x, y \in \Omega$. This approach appears in [7], see also [4], which contains an introduction to Riemannian geometry adapted to this field. Note that it is different to considering Ω as a flat surface with boundary, e.g. a rectangular window which corresponds to the classical scale space. There is still a need to construct the kernel explicitly. We will describe such a construction by introducing the main object of this work: the spectrum of the Laplace Beltrami operator, which will define the set of "natural scales" of the shape.

It can be shown that the Laplace Beltrami operator can be extended to the complete space $H(X)$ as defined above. It is a linear operator, and thus one can study the eigenvalues of such an operator. Note that a discrete spectrum is by no means guaranteed for a partial differential operator, but here we can state that there is a sequence of infinitely many eigenvalues, all of the same sign (which by convention is positive). Every eigenvalue has finite multiplicity, i.e. there exist only finitely many linearly independent eigenfunctions. These eigenfunctions are differentiable, and generate the L^2 functions. The two messages of this work are thus:

1. There is an infinite but discrete set of *natural* scales $(s_n)_{n \in \mathbb{N}}$ associated with a shape. These scales are defined by the eigenvalues $(\lambda_n)_{n \in \mathbb{N}}$. Explicitly: $s_n = \frac{1}{\sqrt{\lambda_n}}$.

2. The heat kernel associated to this shape can be constructed from the eigenfunctions. Explicitly, if u_n is a normalised eigenfunction associated to λ_n,

$$\mathcal{K}^X(x, y, t) = \sum_{n=0}^{\infty} u_n(x) u_n(y) e^{-\lambda_n t} \tag{5}$$

Example 1. On a flat square with either free boundary condition (Neumann problem), or fixed boundary condition (Dirichlet problem), the eigenfunctions are the usual trigonometric functions, and the expansion of a function according to the eigenfunctions is just the Fourier series of the function.

Example 2. On a sphere (radius 1), the metric tensor in polar coordinates is

$$\begin{pmatrix} 1 & 0 \\ 0 & \sin^2 \theta \end{pmatrix}$$

thus the Laplace Beltrami operator is

$$\Delta_{\text{Sphere}} = \frac{1}{\sin \theta} \left(\partial_\theta (\sin \theta \partial_\theta) + \frac{1}{\sin \theta} \partial_\phi^2 \right)$$

the eigenvalue equation is separable, the equation in θ transforms into a Legendre equation with the change variable $t := \cos^2 \theta$. The equation in ϕ becomes a simple harmonic equation. the eigenfunctions are the spherical harmonics $Y_{m,n}(\theta, \phi)$ with associated eigenvalues $\lambda_n = n(n+1)$. This means in particular that λ_n has high multiplicity $2n+1$, a sign of the high symmetry of the sphere, cf. [1, 2, 3].

Interpretation. The eigenvalues of the Laplace Beltrami operator have units $1/m^2$, and can be interpreted as wavelengths for small variation of the shape. Intuitively, a large scale corresponds to information on global aspect of the shape, whereas on a small scale, the assumption of the shapes being locally like Euclidean space means that the behaviour should be the same as the one expected on flat surface patches. This is indeed the case, as stated by *Weyl's asymptotic formula* ([1, 2, 3, 6, 9]):

$$\lambda_n \sim \left(\frac{n}{Area(X)}\right)^{\frac{2}{dim(X)}} \quad \text{up to a multiplicative constant}$$

The theory of spectral geometry is exposed among others in [1, 2, 3, 6, 9]. One has the following development for *any* scale space:

$$I_t(x) = \sum_{n=0}^{\infty} e^{-t/s_n^2}(I, u_n)u_n(x)$$

Now, the first eigenvalue (written λ_0) is zero, so the scale space "image" can be interpreted as a sum of weighted "proper" scale images, where the weights are exponential in the corresponding scale. This explains the asymptotic behaviour: as t becomes large, only the "proper" mode u_0, corresponding to infinite scale $s_0 \to \infty$ remains: this gives a *constant* eigenfunction: $I_t \to \bar{I}$ the mean value of I. All the "grey values" are spread over the complete domain. At the other limit, $(t \to 0)$, one gets the initial condition.

Use of the Finite Element Method to Compute Eigenvalues, Eigenfunctions and the Scale Space Kernel. Up to now, we have supposed that everything was continuous. Now, our typical application is a surface extracted from an image by segmentation. The image itself, instead of being a differentiable function on a domain becomes a function on a lattice. After segmentation-reconstruction, one typically gets a discrete version of the surface. As standard reconstruction techniques usually give triangular facets, we will use triangulated surfaces in the examples. The Laplace Beltrami operator is an elliptic partial differential operator, and thus the Finite Element method is perfectly adapted to the computation of eigenvalues and eigenfunctions. For this, the eigenvalue equation is written in weak form:

$$(\nabla u, \nabla v) = \lambda(u, v)$$

theoretically for *all* v in the solution space. Here, we choose a Finite Element space $S_X(T)$ generated by piecewise linear functions N_i, where i runs over the vertices of a triangulation T of X, $N_i \in C^0(X)$, the global condition, $N_i(\text{vertex}_j) = \delta_{ij}$. We seek approximate solutions in $S_X(T)$: $u_T = \sum_i U^i N_i$. The equation has thus to be valid for all $v = N_j$, i.e.:

$$\sum_i U^i(\nabla u_i, \nabla u_j) = \lambda \sum_i U^i(u_i, u_j).$$

Writing $K_{ij} := (\nabla N_i, \nabla N_j)_S$, we get the global *stiffness matrix* and $M_{ij} := (u_i, u_j)_S$ gives the *global mass matrix*, so the problem becomes the one of finding the *generalised* eigenvalues of the matrices K and M:

$$KU = \lambda MU.$$

These are assembled from their values on individual facets,

$$K_{ij} = \sum_k \int_{T_k} (\nabla N_i|_{T_k}, \nabla N_j|_{T_k}) \, dA$$

and

$$M_{ij} = \sum_k \int_{T_k} (N_i|_{T_k}, N_j|_{T_k}) \, dA$$

Each triangle T_k is the affine image of a standard fixed triangle T_0 (isoparametric FE). Let us call this affine map $F_k : \boldsymbol{\xi} \mapsto \boldsymbol{x}$. Dropping the index k, and using $\frac{\partial}{\partial \boldsymbol{x}} = \frac{\partial \boldsymbol{\xi}}{\partial \boldsymbol{x}} \frac{\partial}{\partial \boldsymbol{\xi}}$, $dA(\boldsymbol{x}) = \left| \frac{\partial \boldsymbol{x}}{\partial \boldsymbol{\xi}} \right| dA(\boldsymbol{\xi})$, we need to compute for every facet the integrals:

$$\int_{F(T_0)} (\nabla N_i(\boldsymbol{x}), \nabla N_j(\boldsymbol{x})) \, dA(\boldsymbol{x}) =$$
$$\int_{T_0} \left(J^{-1}(F(\boldsymbol{\xi})) \, \nabla N_i(F(\boldsymbol{\xi})), J^{-1}(F(\boldsymbol{\xi})) \, \nabla N_j(F(\boldsymbol{\xi})) \right) |J(\boldsymbol{\xi})| \, dA(\boldsymbol{\xi})$$

where we have written $J(\boldsymbol{\xi}) := \frac{\partial \boldsymbol{x}}{\partial \boldsymbol{\xi}}(\boldsymbol{\xi})$. For the simple choice of linear elements that we have made here, there is a big simplification: the derivative of an affine map is just the linear part of this map, and thus is constant, and the Jacobian determinant is the ratio of areas of the triangles. This allows high speed computations for the matrix assembly.

3 Example

Figure 3 shows the computation of the 50 first eigenvalues on a sphere (*), plotted alongside the 50 first for a discrete sphere (+) and a "voxelised" reconstructed sphere (o)(shown below). This sphere was constructed by filling voxels at a given distance from a centre, which allows to artificially specify the resolution, then using standard reconstruction algorithm (here *Nuages*, [5]) to get a triangulated shape, the other one has been directly constructed in a more classical manner by using a triangulation of the parameter domain. Values have been scaled by area to make them comparable.

This example was designed to illustrate a typical problem from surface reconstruction: if the surfaces look similar from far, the reconstructed sphere has a very different small scale structure.

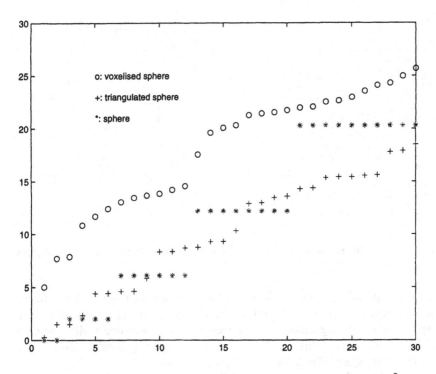

Fig. 1. *x-axis*: index n of the eigenvalue, *y-axis*: value of λ_n, in $1/m^2$. The area is normalised to approximately 4π. dark *: real sphere

Fig. 2. *Left*, the shape on the left looks like a sphere on a "large" scale (radius 1), but at a scale of the size of a voxel, it is very different, see also 3

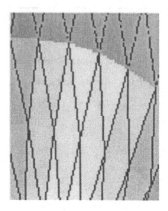

Fig. 3. At an other scale: zooming on a detail shows the difference between the objects

Their corresponding spectra reflect this fact: the one for the voxelised sphere is shifted upwards, which we interpret as showing that the small scale structure of the sphere has a strong influence. The reconstruction was done with the help of the *Nuages* software. This can be shown by computing local measures, for example curvatures, see Fig. 5 for a simulated example.

The next figure (Fig. 3) shows the "diffusion" on such a sphere: on the left the initial situation. A random function I has been defined on the set of vertices, with value 0 or 1. If the value at vertex i is larger than 0.5, the facets which contain vertex i are coloured red, it it is between 0.1 and 0.5, they are coloured light red. We compute the eigenvalues and eigenfunctions for this sphere, and then $I_t := \sum_{n=0}^{N} e^{-\lambda_n t}(I, u_n)u_n$, and apply the same colouring rule. Even for this rough example, one can see how most of the gaps were filled.

A more concrete example is given in Fig. 5. The first torus on the left has 450 facets, and its Gauss curvature is displayed. The settings are such that the curvature range is approximately -0.13 to 0.15. The second torus shows this curvature which has been perturbed by addition of a random value (generated by Matlab) within the range 0 to 0.1. The last one shows this perturbed curvature after diffusion, at time $t = 0.1$. The aim is to illustrate the blurring property of this technique, similarly to the usual Gauss kernel: the dark blue and dark red have already disappeared [2].

---

[2] The figures and some supplementary material will be made available at http://carmen.umds.ac.uk/p.batchelor

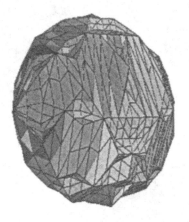

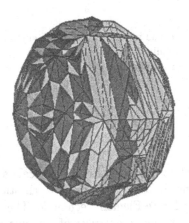

Fig. 4. top: the dark red facets simulate some initial data, bottom: this initial data has been diffused, resulting in a blurred, more homogeneous pattern

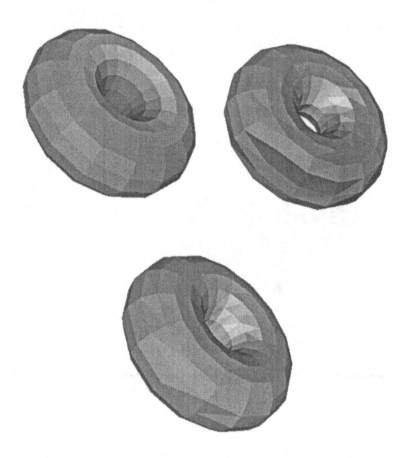

Fig. 5. *Left* : the Gauss curvature, *right:* the initial scalar on the surface is the Gauss curvature randomly perturbed, *below* finally the diffused value ($t = 0.1$ cf text), flat shading was chosen in order to avoid any confusion

4 Discusssion

The main contribution of this work is the extension of the scale space idea to curved spaces. It is concretely done by using techniques of elliptic partial differential equations, solved with the Finite Element technique. These techniques are well understood and commonly applied in a variety of domains ranging from fluid mechanics to elasticity theory. This extension of the concept of scale space will allow a wider variety of real world problems to be addressed within a mathematically rigorous, yet computationally viable, framework.

Applications may include the smoothing of surface shape measures made on discretised surfaces, for example in the brain mapping problem. They also permit a natural, observer independent, definition of the scale of objects of interest in such problems, for example sulci and gyri.

Future work Work in progress include the application of these techniques to a variety of other geometrical shapes. Future work will include the characterisation of brain surface features from both normal and abnormal human brains within a multi scale paradigm.

References

[1] P.H. Bérard. *Spectral geometry: Direct and Inverse Problems*, volume 1207 of *Lect. Notes Math.* Springer Verlag, Berlin, 1986.

[2] M. Berger, P. Gauduchon, and E. Mazet. *Le Spectre d'une Variété Riemannienne.* Number 194 in Lect. Notes Math. Springer Verlag, Berlin, 1974.

[3] I. Chavel. *Eigenvalues in Riemannian Geometry.* Academic Press, 1984.

[4] L.M.J. Florack, A.H. Salden, B.M. ter Haar Romeny, J.J. Koenderink, and M.A. Viergever. Nonlinear scale-space. *Image and Vision Computing*, 13(4):279–294, 1995.

[5] B. Geiger. Contruction et utilisation des modèles d'organes en vue de l'assitance au diagnostic et aux interventions chirurgicales. Technical report, INRIA, 6902 Sophia Antipolis, France, April 1993.

[6] P.B. Gilkey. *Invariance Theory, the Heat Equation, and the Atiyah-Singer Index Theorem.* Publish or Perish, 1984.

[7] R. Kimmel, R. Malladi, and N. Sochen. Image processing via the beltrami operator. In *Proceedings of Asian Conference on Computer Vision*, volume 1351 of *LNCS*, pages 574–581, 1998.

[8] J.J Koenderink. The structure of images. *Biol. Cybern.*, (50):363–370, 1984.

[9] S. Rosenberg. *The Laplacian on a Riemannian Manifold.* Number 31 in Student Texts. London Mathematical Society, 1997.

[10] J. Weickert, S. Ishikawa, and A. Imiya. Scale-space has been discovered in Japan. Technical report, Department of Computer Science, University of Copenhagen, 1997.

Nonlinear Anisotropic Diffusion in Three-Dimensional Electron Microscopy

Achilleas S. Frangakis and Reiner Hegerl

Max Planck Institute for Biochemistry
Am Klopferspitz 18a, D-82152 Martinsried, Germany
frangak@biochem.mpg.de
hegerl@biochem.mpg.de

Abstract. Electron tomography is a powerful tool for investigating the three-dimensional (3D) structure of biological objects at a resolution in the nanometer range. However, visualization and interpretation of the resulting volumetric data is a very difficult task due to the extremely low signal to noise ratio (<0dB). In this paper, an approach for noise reduction in volumetric data is presented, based on nonlinear anisotropic diffusion, using a hybrid of the edge enhancing and the coherence enhancing techniques. When applied to both, artificial or real data sets, the method turns out to be superior to conventional filters. In order to assess noise reduction and structure preservation experimentally, resolution tests commonly used in structure analysis are applied to the data in the frequency domain.

1   Introduction

Transmission electron microscopy is used to investigate the structural organization of biological objects (e.g. macromolecular assemblies or cellular organelles) at a resolution in the nanometer range. In good approximation, the obtained two-dimensional (2D) images are parallel projections of the three-dimensional (3D) density distribution of the object. By means of techniques similar to medical computer tomography, it is possible to reconstruct the 3D density of the specimen and to reveal the 3D structure of the biological object [4]. Although electron microscopes are able to image biological objects with a resolution down to 0.3nm, the structural information is not directly accessible since most of the signal is buried in noise (SNR<0dB). The standard method in the field is correlation averaging, where many thousand identical particles are averaged in order to reveal structural information with a resolution down to 0.8nm. In the case of unique objects (e.g. cells) averaging is not possible and denoising exigently necessary. Particularly with regard to the three-dimensionality of the observed objects, denoising plays an essential role, since the human eye is not able to extract the same amount of information (by interpolation, lowpass filtering, classification, etc.) as in the 2D case. An interpretation of the volumes using surface and volume rendering techniques is difficult due to the noise sensitivity of rendering algorithms. A denoising algorithm suitable for such applications must be able to preserve as much signal as possible while reducing the noise to a sufficiently low level. Nonlinear anisotropic diffusion appears to be a good basis for such an algorithm, as demonstrated by test calculations and applications presented below.

2 3D electron tomographic reconstruction

The 3D electron tomographic reconstruction is a method similar to the well known tomographic reconstruction in medical imaging (X-ray tomography, etc.). All these methods are based theoretically on the "central section theorem", stating: The Fourier transform of the 2D-projection image corresponds to the central section through the 3D Fourier transform of the object, which is perpendicular to the projection direction [8]. This theorem can be used to perform a 3D reconstruction: The 2D Fourier transforms of the projections are derived and placed in the 3D Fourier domain, according to the corresponding angle. After interpolation and 3D inverse Fourier transformation, the reconstructed object appears in real space. In practice, a different algorithm, namely filtered backprojection is mainly used for reconstruction in electron tomography due to its simple and general applicability [3]

The typical experimental approach in electron tomography is to tilt the specimen in the microscope about an axis perpendicular to the electron beam and to record an image for each tilt view. Unfortunately, the specimen cannot be tilted over the full angular range from −90 to +90 degrees, because the specimen holder masks the object at high tilt angles. Additionally, the total electron dose has to be kept below a critical limit in order to avoid excessive radiation damage. Therefore the number of projection views has to be limited and the images suffer from an extremely low signal-to-noise ratio. Image shifts resulting from mechanical inaccuracies of the tilt stage and from specimen drift require an alignment of the projection images with respect to a common origin, a process also prone to errors. As a consequence of all these effects, the interpretation of volumetric data obtained by electron tomography is severely aggravated by artifacts and a noisy appearance. Of all the artifacts, those arising from the limited tilt range are easy to understand in the Fourier domain ("missing wedge") [4] and, in real space, may be described by a point spread function expressing an anisotropic resolution. Any approach for noise reduction must not amplify artifacts.

3 Anisotropic diffusion

The idea introduced in the pioneering work of Perona and Malik [7] is to prefer intraregional smoothing and, consequently, to preserve semantically important features as edges. Many methods have been proposed how to control diffusion in order to achieve the best signal preservation. In the implementation described below different nonlinear anisotropic diffusion methods have been combined, realized in 3D, and accommodated to the filtering of electron tomographic reconstructions [2].

The nonlinear anisotropic diffusion procedure applied to a 2D image or 3D volume I can be described in a general form by the following equation:

$$\frac{\partial I}{\partial t} = \mathrm{div}(g(\nabla I) \cdot \nabla I), \tag{1}$$

where t denotes the evolution time and ∇I the local gradient. In the following we concentrate on the 3D case. The diffusivity g is either a scalar or a matrix function. The crucial question is how the diffusivity has to be designed in order to achieve maximum noise reduction and optimum signal preservation. Following the setup proposed by Weickert [15], the diffusivity is advantageously derived from the structure tensor $\mathbf{J}_0$ averaged by convolution with the Gaussian K_ρ :

$$\mathbf{J}_\rho(\nabla I) = K_\rho * \mathbf{J}_0 \text{ with } \mathbf{J}_0 = \nabla I \cdot \nabla I^\mathrm{T}, \tag{2}$$

Local structural features of I within a neighborhood of size $O(\rho)$ are characterized by the local eigenvectors and eigenvalues of the matrix $\mathbf{J}_\rho$. Generally, the eigenvalues describe the variance of the volume data in the direction of the corresponding eigenvectors. In the presence of noise and for $\rho > 0$, all eigenvalues μ_i are positive since the matrix is positive semidefinite.

$$\mu_1 \geq \mu_2 \geq \mu_3 > 0 \tag{3}$$

The first eigenvector is parallel to the average gradient orientation and the corresponding eigenvalue μ_1 reflects the strength of the local gradient. μ_2 provides further information about structural features, e.g. the existence of a surface or a line and μ_3 can be used as a measure for the noise level.

For 2D applications, Weickert has proposed to use two different realizations of the diffusion tensor depending on what structural features should be emphasized [13, 14, 15]. The first one - called edge enhancing diffusion (EED) - is basically a correctly discretized Perona-Malik model and shows a good performance at a low signal-to-noise ratio. Edges are evenly enhanced and piecewise constant subvolumes are produced in between. The second method is called coherence enhancing diffusion (CED). It averages the gradient over a rather large field of the volume and calculates the mean orientation. It is capable of connecting lines interrupted by noise.

In order to cover the larger variety of structural features in 3D as well as the high noise level, one can take advantage of both methods by combining them according to the following strategy. The difference-value between the first and third eigenvalue reflects the local relation of structure and noise, therefore it can be used as a switch: EED is applied when this value is smaller than a suitably chosen threshold parameter and CED otherwise. A useful threshold parameter can be derived ad hoc from the variance, calculated over a subvolume of I that only contains noise. It is possible to verify the appropriate choice of the subvolume by lowpass filtering or even by visual control of the backprojected images.

It is obvious that during the first iterations EED highlights the edges while, subsequently, CED connects the lines and enhances flow-like structures. Both processes take place simultaneously within one iteration step, depending on the local threshold parameter. If the build-up of a specific edge takes more iterations, the other edges are going to be preserved and enhanced, so that no signal degradation takes place.

For the discretization of the model central differences are utilized. The additive operator splitting (AOS) [12] schemes definitely showed a superior performance to the standard iterative methods, but in order to switch between the different diffusion types, the simulations were performed with the simple explicit Euler method. In order to preserve small structures, with a size of only a few pixels, the gradient approximation, proposed by Sethian [10] is used. It shows a better performance than the standard central-difference gradient approximation.

4   Applications

In this chapter two impressive examples for the applicability of the hybrid model for 3D visualization in the field of electron microscopy are given. In the first example the object under scruting is a vesicle with actin filaments [1]. The size of the object is 100nm in diameter and the resolution is ca. 7nm. The position, connectivity and strength of the filaments, pictured as dark lines in Fig. 1, or as thin white fibers running parallel to the direction of the cylinder in Fig. 2, are the features of interest. The quality of representation of these features can also be used as a criterion for the judgement of the performance of the respective method. For this volume a comparison with standard techniques in image processing is presented. The second example is one of the first 3D reconstructions of a mitochondrion in vitrified ice [5]. Strength and connectivity of the white fibers are here again the criterion for the judgement.

The vesicle is filtered with a simple lowpass and a median filter. In the case of low pass filtering the noise and the signal are simultaneously degraded. Though producing a satisfactory smooth background, the filaments are thickened and interrupted. The isosurface representation appears corrupted due to a lack of most of the information. Median filtering results in a good edge preservation, but the noise reduction is not satisfactory. Fig.1 and Fig. 2 show the results of different types of filtering for the vesicle with actin filaments in tomographic and isosurface representation. The results after application of either EED or CED confirm the properties described in the previous section. EED produces the typical staircase effects and imposes an artificial appearance in the volumes. The connectivity of the filaments is not improved or even preserved. It shows basically a behavior opposite to CED. At last the result of the hybrid model is presented. It combines an excellent noise reduction of the background with a clear representation of the filaments

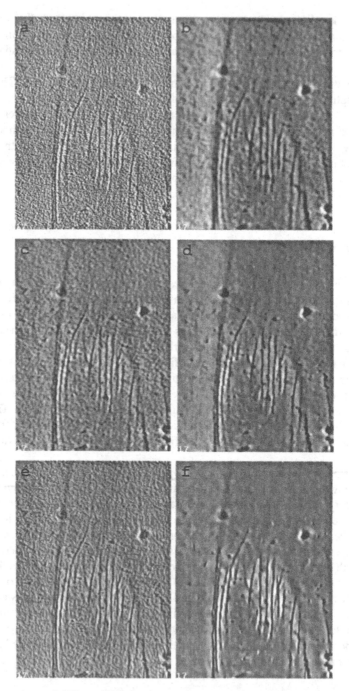

Fig. 1. Comparison of different filtration types of a x-y slice from an electron tomographic reconstructed volume of a vesicle with actin filaments. (a) slice from the original reconstruction, (b) Gaussian f., (c) median f., (d) EED f., (e) CED f. and (f) hybrid EED/CED

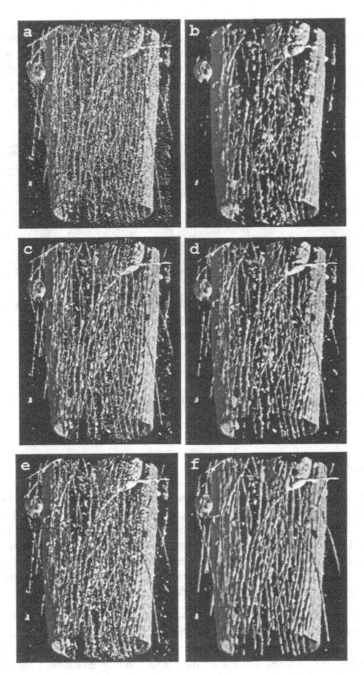

Fig. 2. Isosurface representation of a vesicle with actin filaments (Volume 256*256*128 Voxels). The diameter of the cylinder is about 100nm and the thickness of the white fibers 7nm. The order of the representation is the same as in Fig.1.

The 3D reconstruction of a mitochondrion also gives an impressive example of the applicability of the method (Fig. 3). The goal of this reconstruction was to investigate the 3D structure of the mitochondrion. The structures as obtained by electron tomography, cannot be visualized satisfactorily without filtering. The 3D diffusion filtering using the hybrid EED/CED approach drastically improves the connectivity and thus provides a clear picture of the complicated internal network of the object.

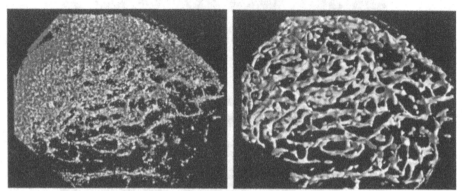

Fig. 3. Isosurface representation of a mitochondrion (800*600*200nm). At the left side the original data. At the right side the result of denoising with the hybrid model.

5 Assessment of signal preservation

5.1 Correlation averaging

In electron microscopy, efficient noise reduction of macromolecules is normally achieved by correlation averaging. Before averaging, the signals are brought into register using cross-correlation functions. The method combines the information contained in the images of many individual, however structurally identical molecules. Each volume is considered to be a single realization of a statistical process. It provides a signal corresponding to the structure of the object, e.g. a projection view or a density map, degraded by noise. Adding up equivalent signals of n volumes increases the signal-to-noise ratio by a factor $\sqrt{n}$, thereby assuming additive, signal-independent noise. In the context of this approach it is possible to estimate the resolution of the averaged volume by comparing the averages of two statistically independent, equal-sized subsets of the corresponding ensemble. The comparison occurs by subdividing the Fourier domain into shells and calculating cross-correlation coefficients between the subsets for each of these shells. The resulting radial correlation function (RCF) is a frequency-dependent measure of similarity between the two subsets, and therefore can be used to estimate the resolution [9].

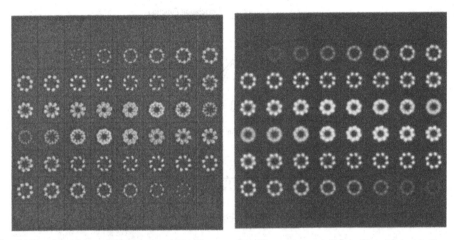

Fig. 4. Results of correlation averaging of two ensembles represented by slices through the volumetric data. On the left side the average of the original particles (noisy ensemble). On the right side the average of the particles denoised by EED (denoised ensemble).

Averaging is conceptually free from signal degradation, while all other denoising methods smooth the noise and more or less also the signal. In order to study how the signal is affected by nonlinear anisotropic diffusion, a set of real volumes of a biological macromolecule was subjected to denoising and averaging. The results were assessed in the frequency domain by means of the RCF. For this purpose, 500 copies were produced from the known 3D density map of the *Thermosome* molecule [6] and degraded by additive colored noise. Using EED, a denoised version was created from each individual copy. Finally, averaged volumes were calculated from both, the original "noisy" volumes (noisy ensemble) and the denoised versions (denoised ensemble). The results are presented in Fig. 4. The average of the denoised ensemble appears smoother and significant details are suppressed. Obviously, the signal is degraded by the diffusion process.

In contrast to the apparent signal degradation, the cross-correlation coefficients of the denoised ensemble are higher than those of the noisy ensemble, indicating a higher resolution. This surprising result does not reflect a contradiction, because nonlinear anisotropic diffusion enhances the SNR and simultaneously reduces the magnitude of the Fourier coefficients. The statement may become clearer when linear diffusion is considered. In this case, the average volume is also blurred but the RCF is not changed at all. Since linear diffusion is equivalent to a linear filtration using a gaussian kernel, the data in the Fourier domain are damped by a factor which is constant within shells, and the cross-correlation coefficients used for the RCF remain unchanged. Obviously, the RCF-curves in Fig. 5 reflect the gain in the SNR when linear diffusion is replaced by the edge-enhancing approach.

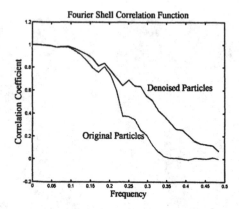

Fig. 5. Fourier shell correlation function of the denoised and original particles.

5.2 Frequency equalization

Edge enhancing diffusion is a nonlinear process and cannot be described by a linear time invariant theory. Nevertheless, the improvement of the SNR described above gives some justification to improve the visual appearance of the average volume by a linear frequency enhancement. The global energy in the volume decreases with increasing evolution time when diffusion is applied (Lyapunov functional [13]). Due to Parseval's theorem, the energy in the Fourier domain decreases correspondingly. The amount of this decrease can be determined as a function of frequency by investigating volume ensembles. As above, original and denoised volume data representing the *Thermosome* molecule are used to calculate the root mean square amplitudes on each shell in the Fourier domain. The curve in Fig. 6 shows the ratio of mean amplitudes of the original and the denoised data and reveals a "bandstop" characteristic of edge-enhancing diffusion.

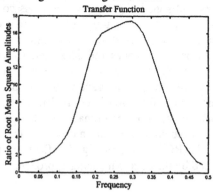

Fig. 6. Ratio of the root mean square amplitudes in the Fourier domain.

This function can be used for equalization in conventional manner. The result when equalizing the average of the denoised particle is shown in Fig.7. The edges are more distinct and the output looks similar to the average of the original particles. Furthermore, the noise enhancement is minimal.

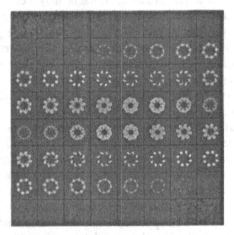

Fig. 7. Equalization of the nonlinear diffusion process

The idea arising from this observation is to determine a global "transfer function" and to equalize the data in the Fourier domain after the diffusion process. It is an open question whether or not such a function can be applied to all objects. We expect that the answer will be no, considering the non-linearity of the diffusion procedure and the diversity of objects studied by electron tomography. It is perhaps possible to define transfer functions for distinct classes of objects. In any case, further investigations are needed to clarify this point.

6 Discussion

An EED/CED hybrid model of nonlinear anisotropic diffusion techniques has been realized in 3D and adapted to the field of electron tomography. The examples presented in Figs 1-3 demonstrate a satisfactory performance especially in the case of very "noisy" data (SNR<-1dB). The smooth background indicates that an efficient noise reduction is achieved while the signal is well preserved. The diffusion approach turns out to be clearly superior to conventional methods of noise filtration, e.g. low-pass filtering or median filtering. Most important for electron tomography, the visualization of very complex volume data by isosurface representations or volume rendering is considerably improved, and the interpretation of the results from the biological point of view is facilitated. It is worth to note that the approach takes advantage from both, EED and CED, by avoiding artifacts arising from each of these methods. Connectivity and flow-like structures are preserved, while noise reduction and edge enhancement produce a significant SNR improvement.

The design of the diffusion flux is more complicated in 3D than in 2D. An optimum setup should use the full structural information specified locally by all three eigenvalues of the averaged structure tensor. For instance, the second eigenvalue μ_2

can be used to switch between 2D and 1D flux. However, tests based on this approach gave unsatisfactory results because μ_2 is very sensitive to noise. When a 2D flux is applied erroneously to a 1D structure, artifacts may occur; e.g., a line may be degraded to a sword-like structure due to the Gaussian elongation in the additional direction. Further investigations are necessary to optimize the procedure. This is also true for another drawback of the method, namely the discretization stencil. In the present implementation, central differences are used for the model discretization and consequently, signals belonging to frequencies near the Nyquist frequency are totally eliminated. This may be improved in a straightforward way by better gradient approximating methods.

One might also ask, whether a 2D denoising of the projection images could replace the more complicated and time-consuming 3D denoising of the final tomographic reconstruction. However, the tomographic reconstruction process relies on a linear relationship between the projection images and the density values. Nonlinear diffusion would destroy this relationship, possibly causing severe artifacts. According to previous experiences with another nonlinear denoising technique, the so-called wavelet denoising [11], such an approach cannot be recommended.

A fascinating idea is to use the wavelet transformation in conjunction with nonlinear anisotropic diffusion. Obviously, the transformation could be applied in order to obtain more reliable information on local structures. Recently we have used the wavelet coefficients for estimating the diffusivity parameter. Preliminary results are very encouraging, apart from a slowing down of the process. An extended use of the wavelet transformation requires more detailed investigation. Unfortunately there is a lack of motivation to develop such an approach because higher dimensional applications of the wavelet transformation suffer from artifacts while more sophisticated translation- and rotation-invariant realizations require an intolerable effort in computer power. For electron tomography, the present setup of nonlinear anisotropic diffusion appears to be the most favorable approach regarding the efficiency of noise reduction, signal preservation and computing effort.

Acknowledgments

We are grateful to Dr. Michael Nitsch, Dr. Rudo Grimm and Dr. Daniela Nicastro for providing the *Thermosome*, vesicle and mitochondrion data respectively. Special thanks to Jochen Böhm and Dr. Dieter Typke for critically reading the manuscript. The work has been supported by the Deutsche Forschungsgemeinschaft Projekt He. 1404/9-1

References

1. Grimm, R., Bärmann, M., Häckl, W., Typke, D., Sackmann, E., Baumeister, W.: Energy filtered electron tomography of ice-embedded actin and vesicles, Biophysical Journal, vol. 72 (1996), pp.482-489
2. Hegerl, R., Stoschek, A.: Noise reduction in electron tomographic reconstructions, International Congress of Electron Microscopy 1998, vol.4, pp.451-452

3. Hegerl, R.: The EM program package: A platform for image processing in biological electron microscopy, Journal of Structural Biology, vol.116 (1996), pp. 30-34

4. Koster, A.J., Grimm, R., Typke, D., Hegerl, R., Stoschek, A., Walz, J., Baumeister, W.: Perspectives of molecular and cellular electron tomography, Journal of Structural Biology, vol. 120 (1998), pp. 276-308

5. Nicastro, D., Frangakis, A. S., Nickell, S., Baumeister, W.: Three-dimensional structure of *Neurospora* mitochondria: New insights provided by electron tomography of the frozen-hydrated organelles, Microscopy and Microanalysis 1999, in press

6. Nitsch, M., Walz, J., Typke, D., Klumpp, M., Essen, L.O., Baumeister, W., Group II chaperonin in an open conformation examined by electron tomography, Nature Structure Biology, vol. 5 n. 10 (1998), pp.855-857.

7. Perona, P., Malik, J.: Scale-space and edge detection using anisotropic diffusion, IEEE trans. on Pattern Analysis and Machine Intelligence, vol.12 (1990), no. 7

8. Radon, J.: Über die Bestimmung von Funktionen durch ihre Integralwerte längs gewisser Mannigfaltigkeiten, Berlin Sächsische Akad. Wissen, vol. 29 (1917), pp. 262-279

9. Saxton, W.O. and Baumeister, W.: The correlation averaging of a regularly arranged bacterial cell envelope protein. Journal of Microscopy, Vol. 127 (1982) 127-138

10. Sethian, J.A.: Level set methods evolving interfaces in geometry, Fluid Mechanics, Computer Vision and Materials Science, Cambridge University Press, 1996

11. Stoschek, A. and Hegerl, R.: Denoising of electron tomographic reconstructions using multiscale transformations, Journal of Structural Biology, vol. 120 (1998), pp. 257-265

12. Weickert, J. Zuiderveld, K.L.,ter Harr Romeny, B.M., Niessen, W.J.: Parallel implementations of AOS schemes: A fast way of nonlinear diffusion filtering, IEEE Int. Conf. on Image Processing, vol. 3 (1997), pp. 396-399

13. Weickert, J.: Anisotropic diffusion in image processing, B.G.Teubner Stuttgart, 1998

14. Weickert, J.: Coherence-enhancing diffusion filtering, Journal of Computer Vision, (1999), 1-18

15. Weickert, J.: Scale-space properties of nonlinear diffusion filtering with a diffusion Tensor, Report No. 110, Laboratory of Technomathematics, University of Kaiserslautern

Polygon Evolution by Vertex Deletion

Longin Jan Latecki and Rolf Lakämper

Institut für Angewandte Mathematik, Universität Hamburg
Bundesstr. 55, 20146 Hamburg
{latecki, lakaemper}@math.uni-hamburg.de

Abstract. We propose a simple approach to evolution of polygonal curves that is specially designed to fit discrete nature of curves in digital images. It leads to simplification of shape complexity with no blurring (i.e., shape rounding) effects and no dislocation of relevant features. Moreover, in our approach the problem to determine the size of discrete steps for numerical implementations does not occur, since our evolution method leads in a natural way to a finite number of discrete evolution steps which are just the iterations of a basic procedure of vertex deletion.

Keywords: discrete curve evolution, shape simplification, shape recognition

1 Introduction

We assume that a closed polygon P is given (that does not need to be simple). In particular, any boundary curve in a digital image can be regarded as a polygon without loss of information, with possibly a large number of vertices.

The main motivation for the presented discrete curve evolution is the fact that *the boundary of a segmented object in a digital image contains misinformation but misses no information.* Clearly, there is digitization and segmentation noise on the boundary of a segmented object, that results in displacement of the boundary points. However, as long as it is possible to recognize the overall shape of the object, the shape information is contained in the given contour.

Most of the standard approaches in computer vision try to compute the original position of the displaced boundary points. This is only possible if the class of shapes to which the analyzed shape belongs is explicitly known and is sufficiently restrictive, e.g., fitting ellipses.

On the other hand, it is not necessary to recover the original position of the boundary points in order to recognize the shape. A pointwise interpretation of this fact is that there exists a subset A of the set of the boundary points B that is sufficient to represent the shape of the object. The other points in $B \setminus A$ either are redundant for the shape or had been influenced by noise. Clearly, the points in the set A may also be displaced due to noise, but nevertheless they are sufficient to recognize the shape, if the amount of displacement is such that people can still recognize the shape. For example, this is the case for the contour of the building obtained from an aerial image in Figure 1 (cf. Brunn et al. [3], Fig. 4), where it is still possible to recognize the overall shape, although the amount of displacement of boundary points is relatively large.

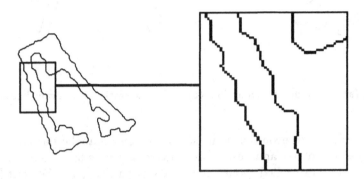

Fig. 1. It is possible to recognize the overall shape of the building, although the amount of displacement of boundary points is relatively large.

The presented discrete curve evolution allows us for a given object boundary to find a subset A of the set of the boundary points B that is sufficient to represent the shape of the object, i.e., points important for the object shape remain after the application of the discrete curve evolution. For example, compare the contour (a) with (c) in Figure 2, where the contours (b) and (c) are obtained from (a) by our discrete curve evolution. Observe also an enormous data reduction: contour (c) in Figure 2 contains only 3% of points of contour (a).

The fact that the discrete curve evolution allows us to find a subset A of the set of the boundary points B that is sufficient to represent the shape of the object is not only justified by experimental results, some of which we present in this paper, but also by the continuity theorem in [7]. This theorem states that if polygon B is sufficiently close to a polygon A, then the evolved version of polygon B will remain close to polygon A.

In *scale-space theory* a curve (or surface) Γ is embedded into a continuous family $\{\Gamma_t : t \geq 0\}$ of gradually simplified versions. The main idea of *scale-spaces* is that the original curve (or surface) $\Gamma = \Gamma_0$ should get more and more simplified and noise and small structures should vanish as parameter t increases. Thus, due to different scales (values of t), it is possible to separate small details from relevant shape properties. The ordered sequence $\{\Gamma_t : t \geq 0\}$ is referred to as *evolution* of Γ. Scale-spaces find wide application in computer vision, in particular, due to smoothing ($\Rightarrow$ noise influence is reduced) and elimination of small details ($\Rightarrow$ relevant shape features remain). Some of the main applications are quality enhancement of images, noise removal, and shape description and recognition (e.g., see Sethian [12]).

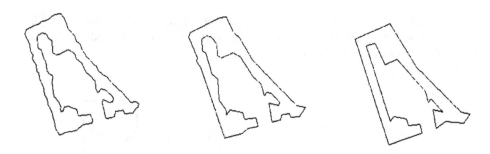

Fig. 2. (a) → (b): noise elimination. (b) → (c): extraction of relevant line segments.

The scale-space evolution is mostly based on parabolic partial differential equations. The oldest and best-studied are scale-spaces based on a linear diffusion equation (also called geometric heat equation), e.g., see Weickert [15]. The solutions of diffusion equations can be obtained by convolution of the original curve (or surface) with a Gaussian function with parameter t (Kimia and Siddiqi [5]). Hence the solutions correspond to Gaussian smoothing of the original curve (or surfaces) with support size t. This leads to a multiscale, curvature-based shape representation.

Along with the advantages of evolution based on the linear diffusion equation, there are also some serious problems (Weickert [15], p. 6):

(a) *"Gaussian smoothing does not only reduce noise, but also blurs important features such as edges and, thus, makes them harder to identify. Since Gaussian scale-space is designed to be completely uncommitted, it cannot take into account any a-priori information on structures which are worth being preserved (or even enhanced).*

(b) *Diffusion dislocates features when moving from finer to coarser scales. So features identified at a coarse scale do not give the right location and have to be traced back to the original image [16]. In practice, relating dislocated information obtained at different scales is difficult and bifurcations may give rise to instabilities. These coarse-to-fine tracking difficulties are generally denoted as the correspondence problem."*

To reduce these problems, many anisotropic and nonlinear diffusion processes have been proposed for scale-spaces (for an overview see, Weickert [15]). Also reaction-diffusion equations, which lead to reaction-diffusion scale spaces, have been considered (Kimia, et al [6]).

We propose a different approach to scale-space evolution in which both problems simply do not occur. Our departing point is a discrete nature of curves and surfaces in digital images. In opposite to standard approaches in scale-spaces, our evolution is guided neither by differential equations nor Gaussian smoothing, and it is not a discrete version of an evolution by differential equations, as it is the case in Bruckstein, et al. [2]. The main properties of the proposed evolution are (see Figure 3):

- Although it leads to noise elimination, it does not introduce any blurring effects.
- Although irrelevant features vanish during our evolution, there is no dislocation of relevant features.

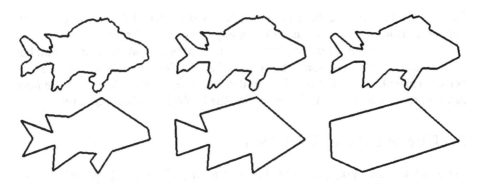

Fig. 3. A few stages of our curve evolution. The first contour is a distorted version of the contour on www-site [17].

In comparison to scale-space methods, the main differences are

1. By numerical implementations of diffusion equations, every vertex of the polygon is translated at a single evolution step, whereas in our approach the remaining vertices do not change their positions.
2. The translation vector of each point in a diffusion process is locally determined, whereas our polygonal evolution is guided by a relevance measure that is not a local property with respect to the original polygon.
3. The process of the polygonal evolution is parameter-free.

Although there exist diffusion process that are parameter-free in the sense that constant values for parameters are known that apply to large classes of curves, for most numerical implementations of parabolic differential equations several parameters are necessary and it is theoretically unknown how to relate and determine the parameters. This is due to

(c) problems with stability and computation time of discrete, numeric realizations of diffusion processes.

An example problem is to specify the discrete time steps t necessary for a stable numeric computation. Since the scale-space theories are continuous theories, i.e., scale (or time) parameter t varies over positive real numbers, the determination of discrete steps is a non-trivial problem; if the steps are too large, it can happen that too many relevant features vanish, and on the other hand, too small discrete steps lead to an inefficient computation. Additionally, a given digital curve (or surface) has some fixed grid resolution that cannot be made infinitely small, and this resolution not always satisfies the requirements for stabile numerical solutions of partial differential equations. A different but related problem is the following:

(d) *"Diffusion filters with a constant steady-state require to specify a stopping time if one wants to get nontrivial results."* (Weickert [15], p.19)

Clearly, if the stopping time (i.e., stopping parameter t) is too large, it can happen that all relevant features do not any more exist at scale t.

The proposed evolution method leads in a natural way to a finite number of discrete evolution steps which are just the iterations of a basic procedure of vertex removal. Thus, the problem to determine the size of discrete steps does not occur. This also drastically simplifies the problem of stopping time.

2 Discrete Curve Evolution

Let P be a closed polygon (that does not need to be simple). We will denote the vertices of P with $Vertices(P)$. A *discrete curve evolution* produces a sequence of polygons $P = P^0, ..., P^m$ such that $|Vertices(P^m)| \leq 3$, where $|\ .\ |$ is the cardinality function. Each vertex v in P^i is assigned a relevance measure $K(v, P^i) \in \mathbb{R}_{\geq 0}$. The relevance measure $K(v, P^i)$ that we used for our experiments is defined below. The process of the *discrete curve evolution* is very simple:

For every evolution step $i = 0, ..., m - 1$, a polygon P^{i+1} is obtained after the vertices whose relevance measure is minimal have been deleted from P^i.

In order to give a precise definition of the discrete curve evolution, we first define

Definition: $K_{min}(P^i)$ to be the smallest value of the relevance measures for vertices of P^i:

$$K_{min}(P^i) = \min\{K(u, P^i) : u \in Vertices(P^i)\}$$

and the set $V_{min}(P^i)$ to contain the vertices whose relevance measure is minimal in P^i:

$$V_{min}(P^i) = \{u \in Vertices(P^i) : K(u, P^i) = K_{min}(P^i)\}$$

for $i = 0, ..., m - 1$.

Definition: For a given polygon P and a relevance measure K, we call a **discrete curve evolution** a process that produces a sequence of polygons $P = P^0, ..., P^m$ such that

$$Vertices(P^{i+1}) = Vertices(P^i) \setminus V_{min}(P^i),$$

where $|Vertices(P^m)| \leq 3$.

The process of the discrete curve evolution is guaranteed to terminate, since in every evolution step, the number of vertices decreases by at least one. It is also obvious that this evolution converges to a convex polygon, since the evolution will reach a state where there are exactly three, two, one, or no vertices in P^m. Clearly, the only polygon with three vertices is a triangle. Of course, for many curves, a convex polygon with more then three vertices can be obtained in an earlier stage of the evolution. The only polygon with two vertices is a line segment. A polygon with one vertex is also trivially convex. Only when the set $Vertices(P^m)$ is empty, we obtain a degenerated polygon equal to the empty set, which is trivially convex. Thus, we obtain for every relevance measure

Proposition 1. *The discrete curve evolution converges to a convex polygon, i.e., there exists $0 \leq i \leq m$ such that P^i is convex, and if $0 \leq i < m$, all polygons $P^{i+1}, ..., P^m$ are convex.* ∎

This proposition demonstrates mathematical simplicity of the relation between our evolution approach and the geometric properties of the evolved polygons. Observe that this proposition also holds for polygons that are not simple (i.e., have self-intersections). An analog theorem for evolution of continuous planar curves by diffusion equations is a deep and highly non-trivial result of differential geometry. It holds only for simple closed smooth curves evolved by the heat equation:

Theorem (Grayson [4]) *An embedded planar curve converges to a simple convex curve when evolving according to:*

$$\begin{cases} \frac{\partial C(s,t)}{\partial t} = \frac{\partial^2 C(s,t)}{\partial s^2} = \kappa(s,t)N(s,t) \\ C(s,0) = C_0(s), \end{cases} \tag{1}$$

where $C : S^1 \times [0,T) \to \mathbb{R}^2$ is a family of smooth simple curves, s is the Euclidean arc-length, κ the Euclidean curvature, and N the inward unit normal. The diffusion equation (1) is called a *geometric heat equation* for a curve. The flow given by (1) is called the *Euclidean shortening flow*.

Polygonal analogs of the evolution by diffusion equations are presented in Bruckstein, et al. [2]. The experiments in [2] indicate that an arbitrary initial polygon converges to a convex polygon (polygonal circle). However, the proof of this fact in the Euclidean case is an open question. In [2] as well as in evolutions by numerical solutions of differential equations, each vertex of the polygon with nonzero curvature is displaced at a single evolution step, whereas in our approach some vertices are removed and the remaining vertices do not change their positions. This is an important difference which leads to several properties of our approach (described in the next section) that are favorable for many applications.

The convexity result (and some other properties of the discrete curve evolution) holds for any relevance measure. However, there are some important properties like continuity that depend on the choice of the relevance measure (see Section 3).

The key property of the evolution we used for our experiments is the order of the deletion determined by the relevance measure. Our relevance measure

$K(v, P^i)$ depends on vertex v and its two neighbor vertices u, w in P^i, i.e., $K(v, P^i) = K(v, u, w)$. It is given by the formula

$$K(v, u, w) = K(\beta, l_1, l_2) = \frac{\beta l_1 l_2}{l_1 + l_2}, \tag{2}$$

where β is the turn angle at vertex v in P^i, l_1 is the length of $\overline{vu}$, and l_2 is the length of $\overline{vw}$. (Both lengths are normalized with respect to the total length of polygon P^i.) Intuitively it reflects the shape contribution of vertex v in P^i. The main property is the following

- The higher the value of $K(v, u, w)$, the larger is the contribution of arc $\overline{vu} \cup \overline{vw}$ to the shape of polygon P^i.

Observe that this relevance measure is not a local property with respect to the polygon P, although its computation is local in P^i for every vertex v. A motivation for this measure and its properties are discussed in [8].

An algorithmic definition of the discrete curve evolution is given in [8] and live examples can be found our www-site [9]. The curve evolution in [8] differs from the one defined here if two or more vertices in P^i have the same relevance measure. The evolution in [8] removes in a single step only one vertex. If in the course of the evolution no two vertices in P^i have the same relevance measure, then the algorithmic definition in [8] and the above definitions are equivalent.

3 Properties of the Discrete Curve Evolution

We will show in this section that our discrete curve evolution has the following properties that do not depend on the choice of the relevance measure:

(P_1) It leads to a simplification of shape complexity.
(P_2) It does not introduce any blurring (i.e., shape rounding) effects and
(P_3) there is no dislocation of relevant features,

due to the fact that the remaining vertices do not change their positions. Two more important properties of our curve evolution are based on the relevance measure defined in Section 2:

(P_4) It is stable with respect to noisy deformations and noise elimination takes place in early stages of the evolution.
(P_5) It allows to find line segments in noisy images, due to the relevance order of the repeated process of linearization (e.g., Figure 2).

We begin with some examples to illustrate these properties. A few stages of the proposed curve evolution in Figure 3 illustrate the shape complexity reduction. Observe that our curve evolution does not introduce any blurring effects, which result in shape rounding for curves. (for a comparison see the curve evolution on www-site [17], based on [10]). There is no dislocation of the remaining relevant shape features, since the planar position of the remaining points of the

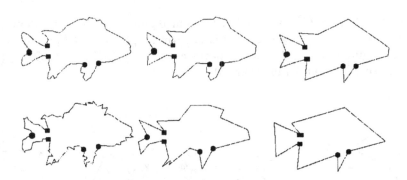

Fig. 4. Discrete curve evolution is stable with respect to distortions. The same planar position of the points marked with the same symbols demonstrates that there is no displacement of the remaining feature points.

digital polygon is unchanged. This is demonstrated by marking the corresponding points with the same symbols in Figure 4. Observe also the stability of feature points with respect to noise deformations shown in the second row in Figure 4.

By comparison of the curves (a) and (b) in Figure 2, it can be seen that our evolution method allows us first to eliminate noise influence without changing the shape of objects (P_4). If we continue to evolve the curve (b), the deletion of vertices guided by our relevance measure results in a process of repeated linearization. This way the original line segments can be recovered in noisy images, see Figure 2(c) (cf. Brunn et al. [3], Fig. 4).

Now we give a more formal justification of the above properties. The reduction of shape complexity of a polygonal curve during the evolution process (P_1) is justified by Proposition 1. Additionally, the shape complexity of a polygonal curve can be measured by the sum of the absolute values of the turn angles. Let C be a closed polygonal curve with vertices $v_0, ..., v_{n-1}$. Then the **shape complexity** of C is given by

$$SC(C) = \sum_{i=0}^{n-1} |turn(v_i)|,$$

where $turn(v_i)$ is the turn angle at vertex v_i in C. Clearly, the shape complexity of any closed convex curve is 2π and the shape complexity of a closed non-convex curve is greater than 2π.

Proposition 2. *The shape complexity $SC(C)$ of a closed polygonal curve C is monotonically decreasing in the course of the discrete evolution, i.e., if $C = C^0, ..., C^m$ with $|C^m| \leq 3$ is a sequence of simplified curves obtained by the evolution of C, then $SC(C^k) \geq SC(C^{k+1})$ for $0 \leq k \leq m-1$.*

Proof: The curves C^k and C^{k+1} differ by at least one vertex, say $v_d \in C^k \setminus C^{k+1}$. Let v_{d-1} and v_{d+1} denote the neighbor vertices of v_d in C^k, and let A be the polygonal subarc of C^k composed of the four digital line segments whose end-points are vertices v_{d-1}, v_d, v_{d-1}. If A is a convex arc, then $SC(C^k) = SC(C^{k+1})$ (e.g, see Figure 5(a)). If A is not a convex arc, then $SC(C^k) > SC(C^{k+1})$ (e.g, see cases (b), (c), and (d) in Figure 5).   ■

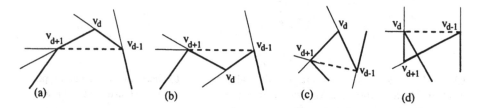

Fig. 5. The shape complexity remains the same (a) or decreases (b), (c), and (d) after a single vertex has been deleted.

The following proposition is a direct consequence of the definition of the evolution procedure:

Proposition 3. *Let $C = C^0, ..., C^m$ with $|C^m| \leq 3$ be a sequence of simplified curves obtained by the discrete evolution. For every vertex v of digital polygonal curve C that also belongs to C^k, the position of v on the plane as vertex of C is the same as the position of v as a vertex of C^k.*   □

From Proposition 3, it clearly follows that there is no dislocation of the remaining features during the curve evolution. Thus, in our approach the corre-spondence problem of coarse-to-fine tracking difficulties does not occur. In con-trary, in the course of curve evolution guided by diffusion equations, all points with non-zero curvature change their positions during the evolution. Proposition 3 also explains why our curve evolution does not introduce any blurring (i.e., rounding) effects: In a single evolution step, all vertices remain at their Euclidean positions with exception of the removed vertices. The two neighbor vertices of a removed vertex are joined by a new line segment, which does not lead to any rounding effects.

We proved that the discrete curve evolution with the relevance measure $K(v, u, w)$ is continuous (Theorem 1 in [7]): if polygon Q is close to polygon P, then the polygons obtained by their evolution are close. Continuity guaran-tees us the stability of the discrete curve evolution with respect to noise (P_4), which we observed in numerous experimental results.

The fact that noise elimination takes place in early stages of the evolution is justified by the relative small values of the relevance measure for vertices resulting by noise:

Mostly, if two adjacent line segments result from noise distortions, then when-ever their turn angle is relatively large, their length is very small, and whenever their length is relatively large, their turn angle is very small. This implies that if arc $\overline{vu} \cup \overline{vw}$ results from noise distortions, the value $K(v, u, w)$ of the relevance measure at vertex v will be relatively low with high probability. Hence noise elimination will take place in early stages of the evolution. This fact also contributes to the stability of our curve evolution with respect to distortions introduced by noise.

The justification of property (P_5) is based on the fact that the evolution of polygon Q corresponds to the evolution of polygon P if Q approximates P (Theorem 2 in [7]): If polygon Q is close to polygon P, then first all vertices of Q are deleted that are not close to any vertex of P, and then, whenever a vertex of P is deleted, then a vertex of Q that is close to it is deleted in the corresponding evolution step of Q. Therefore, the linear parts of the original polygon will be recovered during the discrete curve evolution.

4 Topology-Preserving Discrete Evolutions

Our discrete curve evolution yields results consistent with our visual perception even if the original polygonal curve P have self-intersections. However, it may introduce self-intersections even if the original curve were simple (e.g., see Figure 6). Now we present a simple modification that does not introduce any self-intersections for a simple polygon P.

We say that a vertex $v_i \in Vertices(P^i)$ is **blocked** in P^i if triangle $v_{i-1}v_iv_{i+1}$ contains a vertex of P^i different from v_{i-1}, v_i, v_{i+1}. We will denote the set of all blocked vertices in P^i by $Blocked(P^i)$.

Definition: For a given polygon P and a relevance measure K, the process of the discrete curve evolution in which

$$K_{min}(P^i) = \min\{K(u, P^i) : u \in Vertices(P^i) \setminus Blocked(P^i)\}$$

and

$$V_{min}(P^i) = \{u \in Vertices(P^i) \setminus Blocked(P^i) : K(u, P^i) = K_{min}(P^i)\}$$

will be called a **topology-preserving discrete curve evolution** (e.g., see Figure 6).

The question is whether this modified curve evolution will not prematurely terminate. This would be the case if $Vertices(P^i) = Blocked(P^i)$. It can be shown that this is not the case, i.e., it holds for $i = 0, ..., m - 1$

$$Vertices(P^i) \setminus Blocked(P^i) \neq \emptyset.$$

5 Conclusions and Future Work

We presented a discrete approach to curve evolution that is based on the observation that in digital image processing and analysis, we deal only with digital curves that can be interpreted as polygonal curves without loss of information.

The main properties of the proposed discrete evolution approach are the following:

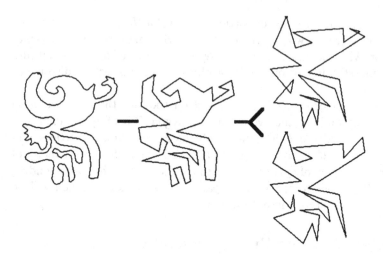

Fig. 6. The discrete curve evolution may introduce self-intersections, but after a small modification it is guaranteed to be topology-preserving.

(P_1) Analog to evolutions guided by diffusion equations, it leads to shape simplification but

(P_2) no blurring (i.e., shape rounding) effects occur and

(P_3) there is no dislocation of feature points.

(P_4) It is stable with respect to noisy deformations.

(P_5) It allows to find line segments in noisy images.

These properties are not only justified by theoretical considerations but also by numerous experimental results. Additionally, the mathematical simplicity of the proposed evolution process makes various modifications very simple, e.g., by a simple modification, a set of chosen points can be kept fixed during the evolution.

Our evolution method can be also interpreted as hierarchical approximation of the original curve by a polygonal curve whose vertices lie on the original curve. Our approximation is fine-to-coarse and it does not require any error parameters, in opposite to many standard approximations, where starting with some initial coarse approximation to a curve, whereupon line segments that do not satisfy an error criterion are split (e.g., Ramer [11]). A newer and more sophisticated split-and-merge method for polygon approximation is presented in Bengtsson and Eklundh [1], where multiscale contour approximation is obtained by varying an error parameter t, which defines a scale in a similar manner as it is the case for diffusion scale-spaces. This implies similar problems as for scale-spaces, e.g., How to determine the step size for the parameter t? Additionally, the scale-space property of shape complexity simplification does not result automatically from the approach in [1], but is enforced ([1], p. 87): *"New breakpoints, not appearing at finer scales, can occur but are then inserted also at finer levels."*

There are numerous application possibilities of our method for curve evolution in which scale-space representations play an important role, e.g., noise elimination and quality enhancement, shape decomposition into visual parts, salience measure of visual parts, and detection of critical or dominant points (Teh and Chin [13], Ueda and Suzuki [14]). The specific properties of our curve evolution yield additional application possibilities like detection of straight line segments in noisy images, which can be used for model-based shape recovery (Brunn, et al. [3]), and polygonal approximation (cf. [1]).

A paper on a discrete surface evolution that is analog to the presented polygonal evolution is in preparation.

References

1. A. Bengtsson and J.-O. Eklundh. Shape representation by mutliscale contour approximation. *IEEE Trans. Pattern Analysis and Machine Intelligence*, 13:85–93, 1991.

2. A.M. Bruckstein, G. Shapiro, and C. Shaked. Evolutions of planer polygons. *Int. J. of of Pattern Recognition and AI*, 9:991–1014, 1995.

3. A. Brunn, U. Weidner, and W. Förstner. Model-based 2d-shape recovery. In *Proc. of 17. DAGM Conf. on Pattern Recognition (Mustererkennung)*, pages 260–268, Bielefeld, Springer-Verlag, Berlin, 1995.

4. M.A. Grayson. The heat equation shrinks embedded plane curves to round points. *Pattern Recognition*, 26:285–314, 1987.

5. B. B. Kimia and K. Siddiqi. Geometric heat eequation and nonlinear diffusion of shapes and images. *Computer Vision and Image Understanding*, 64:305–322, 1996.

6. B. B. Kimia, A. R. Tannenbaum, and S. W. Zucker. Shapes, shocks, and deformations. i: The components of shape and the reaction-diffusion space. *Int. J. Computer Vision*, 15:189–224, 1995.

7. L. J. Latecki, R.-R. Ghadially, R. Lakämper, and U. Eckhardt. Continuity of the discrete curve evolution. In *SPIE and SIAM Conf. on Vision Geometry VIII*, July 1999, to appear.

8. L. J. Latecki and R. Lakämper. Convexity rule for shape decomposition based on discrete contour evolution. *Computer Vision and Image Understanding*, 73:441–454, 1999.

9. L. J. Latecki, R. Lakämper, and U. Eckhardt. http://www.math.uni-hamburg.de/ home/lakaemper/shape.

10. F. Mokhtarian and A. K. Mackworth. A theory of multiscale, curvature-based shape representation for planar curves. *IEEE Trans. PAMI*, 14:789–805, 1992.

11. U. Ramer. An iterative procedure for the polygonal approximation of plane curves. *Computer Graphics and Image Processing*, 1:244–256, 1972.

12. J.A. Sethian. *Level Set Methods*. Cambridge University Press, Cambridge, 1996.

13. C.-H. Teh and R. T. Chin. On the detection of dominant points on digital curves. *IEEE Trans. PAMI*, 11:859–872, 1989.

14. N. Ueda and S. Suzuki. Learning visual models from shape contours using multiscale convex/concave structure matching. *IEEE Trans. PAMI*, 15:337–352, 1993.

15. J. Weickert. A review of nonlinear diffusion filtering. In B. M. ter Haar Romeny, L. Florack, J. Koenderink, and M. Viergever, editors, *Scale-Space Theory in Computer Vision*, pages 3–28. Springer, Berlin, 1997.

16. A.P. Witkin. Scale-space filtering. In *Proc. IJCAI*, volume 2, pages 1019–1022, 1983.

17. www site. http://www.ee.surrey.ac.uk/research/vssp/imagedb/demo.html.

A Scale-Space Based Approach for Deformable Contour Optimization *

Yusuf Sinan Akgul and Chandra Kambhamettu

Video/Image Modeling and Synthesis (VIMS) Lab
Department of Computer and Information Sciences
University of Delaware
Newark, Delaware, 19716
USA
{akgul,chandra}@cis.udel.edu

Abstract. Multiresolution techniques are often used to shorten the execution times of dynamic programming based deformable contour optimization methods by decreasing the image resolution. However, the speedup comes at the expense of contour optimality due to the loss of details and insufficient usage of the external energy in decreased resolutions. In this paper, we present a new scale-space based technique for deformable contour optimization, which achieves faster optimization times and performs better than the current multiresolution methods. The technique employs a multiscale representation of the underlying images to analyze the behavior of the external energy of the deformable contour with respect to the change in the scale dimension. The result of this analysis, which involves information theoretic comparisons between scales, is used in segmentation of the original images. Later, an exhaustive search on these segments is carried out by dynamic programming to optimize the contour energy. A novel gradient descent algorithm is employed to find optimal internal energy for large image segments, where the external energy remains constant due to segmentation.

We present the results of our contour tracking experiments performed on medical images. We also demonstrate the efficiency and the performance of our system by quantitatively comparing the results with the multiresolution methods, which confirm the effectiveness and the accuracy of our method.

1 Introduction

A deformable contour[8] is an energy minimizing model which is popularly used for automatic extraction and tracking of image contours. One of the main reasons of the popularity of deformable contours is their ability to integrate image level bottom up information, task dependent top down knowledge information

---

* This work is supported by Grant No. R01 DC01758 from NIH and Grant No. IRI 961924 from NSF.

and the desirable contour properties into a single optimization process. A deformable contour model has two types of energies associated with it: an internal energy, which characterizes the desirable attributes of the contour, and an external energy, which ties the contour with the underlying image. The framework is based on minimizing the sum of these energies. Formally, a discretized version of a deformable contour is an ordered set of points $V = [v_1, v_2, ..., v_n]$. Given an image I, the energy associated with a deformable contour, V, can be generally written as

$$E_{Snake}(V) = \sum_{i=1}^{n} \alpha E_{int}(v_i) + \beta E_{ext}(v_i, I) \tag{1}$$

where E_{int} is the internal and E_{ext} is the external energy of the contour element v_i, and α and β are the weighting parameters.

Although for the majority of the applications, the main framework for the formulation stayed more or less the same, there have been numerous proposals for minimization techniques. Original proposal[8] and many others used variations of gradient descent algorithms for the minimization of Equation(1). While the internal energy definitions are suitable for optimizations based on gradient descent, external energies usually include large amounts of noise, which makes gradient descent methods sensitive to convergence to local minima instead of global minima, numerical instability and inaccuracy problems.

Application of dynamic programming (DP) to deformable contour minimization[3][5] addresses these problems. As we will explain in section 2.1, DP solves the optimality, numerical stability and incorporating hard constraints problems. However, although the time complexity is polynomial, DP suffers from long execution times. In order to shorten execution times for practical applications, researchers commonly suggested[5] using a multiresolution framework. The main idea of using multiresolution techniques for DP is to decrease the number of degrees of freedom for each contour element. Since the underlying images are smaller at the lower resolutions, there are less number of image positions that a contour element can take, resulting in faster exhaustive enumeration times. The details of current multiresolution techniques are explained in section 2.2.

There are some problems with the above multiresolution techniques. First, during the construction of lower resolution levels, these techniques utilize the external energy of the deformable contour minimally. This is a serious problem because only the external energy ties the deformable contour to the new resolution image. Another problem with the current multiresolution methods is that, while the image size is decreased, the fact that the new resolution image will be used in an exhaustive enumeration, which is a very costly process, is completely neglected. Neighboring image locations that will produce the same energies should be unified to one location. We describe the details of these problems and a few others in Section 2.2.

This paper addresses the above problems by employing a multiscale representation instead of a multiresolution representation. The method segments the underlying images by analyzing their structures with respect to the external energy in the scale-space. The segments are formed in a way that, in the final segmentation the external energy related information is kept closer to the maximum by measuring the change of this information with respect to the scale change through an information theoretic approach. A special dynamic programming technique[1] is then applied to optimize the energy of Equation(1) by using the centroids of these segments as the degrees of freedom. This paper extends our previous work[1] by employing a different segmentation technique that uses information and scale-space theory.

2 Snakes, DP, and Problems with Multiresolution Methods

In this section we define the deformable contour energies, the details of DP methods and multiresolution methods. We will also describe the problems that we address in detail.

2.1 Snakes and DP

Equation(1) describes the general form of the snake energy. The internal energy of the snake serve to impose smoothness and continuity of the contour. As mentioned earlier, the external energy, on the other hand, ties the contour to the underlying image by pushing the snake toward application dependent image features like edges. One of the biggest advantages of using snakes is that specific applications can change the internal and external energy definitions without affecting the general framework.

We define the internal energy as follows:

$$E_{int}(v_i) = \left(1 - \frac{\overrightarrow{v_{i-1}v_i} \cdot \overrightarrow{v_i v_{i+1}}}{|\overrightarrow{v_{i-1}v_i}| \, |\overrightarrow{v_i v_{i+1}}|}\right) + \gamma||v_i - v_{i+1}| - d| \qquad (2)$$

where γ is the weighting parameter and d is the distance needed between the contour elements. The first part of this energy formulation, which is the dot product of two vectors(Figure 1), is for imposing smoothness of the contour.

Given an image I, one possible definition for the external energy is

$$E_{ext}(v_i, I) = -|\nabla I(v_i)| \qquad (3)$$

which is the negative of the image gradient ∇I at v_i. Given the above formulations and an image I, we can extract and track object boundaries by defining a search window around each contour element and selecting the candidates from these search windows that minimizes the snake energy (Figure 1). The desired contour, $V = [v_1, v_2, ..., v_n]$, can be obtained by

$$V = \arg\min_v \sum_{i=1}^{n} \alpha E_{int}(v_i) + \beta E_{ext}(v_i, I) \qquad (4)$$

Assuming there are m different positions that the contour element v_i can take in a search window W_i, the cost of iteratively testing each possible element configuration is $O(m^n)$, which grows exponentially. Fortunately, the optimization

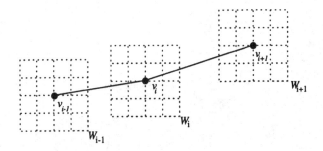

Fig. 1. Each contour element v_i has a search window W_i defined around it.

of the snake energy can be done in polynomial time using dynamic programming. Amini *et. al.*[3] and Geiger *et. al.*[5] proposed DP methods for deformable contour optimization. In this paper, we will use Amini *et. al.* formulation. Our system can easily be ported to the system of Geiger *et. al.*

The main idea under the DP method is that each contour element, v_i, can take only one possible position from the search window W_i. We also observe that the energy formula of Equation(1) can be written in terms of separate energy terms of $E_1, E_2, .., E_{n-2}$, such that each energy term E_{i-1} depends only on v_{i-1}, v_i, v_{i+1}.

$$E_{Snake}(v_1, v_2, ..., v_n) = E_1(v_1, v_2, v_3) + E_2(v_2, v_3, v_4) + ... + E_{n-2}(v_{n-2}, v_{n-1}, v_n)$$

where

$$E_{i-1}(v_{i-1}, v_i, v_{i+1}) = E_{int}(v_i) + E_{ext}(v_i). \tag{5}$$

Next we write a set of optimal value functions that hold the best energy configurations up to the current contour element.

$$s_1(v_2, v_3) = \min_{v_1} E_1(v_1, v_2, v_3)$$

$$s_2(v_3, v_4) = \min_{v_2} E_2(v_2, v_3, v_4) + s_1(v_2, v_3)$$

$$\cdots$$

$$s_{n-2}(v_{n-1}, v_n) = \min_{v_{n-2}} E_{n-2}(v_{n-2}, v_{n-1}, v_n) + s_{n-3}(v_{n-2}, v_{n-1})$$

Finally, we can write

$$\min E_{Snake} = \min_{v_{n-1}, v_n} s_{n-2}(v_{n-1}, v_n).$$

Since each optimal value function is calculated by iterating on three contour elements and there are $n - 2$ of them, the time complexity of DP algorithm is polynomial and it is $O(nm^3)$. The resulting contour produced by the DP algorithm is optimal since it checks every possible alternative.

Although the time complexity of DP algorithm is polynomial, it is still too slow for some practical applications. Application of DP in combination with multiresolution methods addresses this problem, which is explained in the next section.

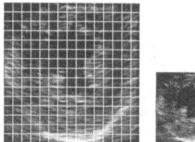

Fig. 2. A multiresolution representation of an echocardiographic image: The leftmost image is the original 240x240 image. The rightmost image is the 15x15 top level image. Each pixel in this 15x15 image represents a square shaped 16x16 segment marked on the original image.

2.2 DP with Multiresolution Methods and Problem Details

We will use the Gaussian pyramid as the basic multiresolution method[4] in explaining the general structure and describing the problems. Geiger *et. al.*[5] uses a different multiresolution scheme[6], which preserves discontinuity between the image resolutions. However, most of the problems with the existing techniques are also present in their method.

A Gaussian pyramid for an image I is a sequence of copies of I, where each successive copy has half the resolution and sample rate. The levels of a Gaussian pyramid for given image I is calculated as

$$G_I(ij0) = I(ij)$$
$$G_I(ijk) = \sum_{m,n} w(mn)G_I(2i - m, 2j - n, k - 1) \qquad (6)$$

where k is the pyramid level. The motivation in using a multiresolution method for the snake optimization is that lower the image resolution, smaller the search windows, which means lower number of candidate positions in each search window. Decreasing the resolution in a multiresolution representation may be viewed as segmenting the original image into equal sized square segments and representing each segment with a single pixel whose gray-level value is usually given by the average of the area around the segment(Figure 2). Deformable contour optimization algorithms are applied to the highest level of the pyramid. The obtained contour is an approximation of the final contour and it is used as the initial snake position for the next lower level. Using a smaller window size, the optimization is performed at the current level, and the process continues until the contour is optimized at the lowest level, which is the original image level. As expected, a multiresolution based DP does not necessarily produce optimal contours.

We mentioned before that only the external energy ties the deformable contour to the underlying image. However, during resolution decreasing steps, Equation (6) utilizes external energy minimally, which increases the loss of external energy related information. We argue that, unlike in Figure 2, the pixels in the lowest-resolution image should represent different sized segments in the original image. This will give us a possibility of choosing a smaller segment size on areas where external energy shows greater variations, resulting in better representation of external energy and less loss of external energy related information.

Another problem with the above multiresolution method is efficiency related. We know that the purpose of using a multiresolution method is to reduce the number of candidates in a search window so that the enumeration process gets faster. Therefore, during the construction of the newer resolutions, neighboring elements of search windows that will produce about the same energy should be unified into a single element. This modification can also be done by employing different sized segments – We choose a larger segment for areas where external energy remains relatively constant on the original image. This will increase the system efficiency without decreasing the performance because at the upper levels of the pyramid, we are not looking for the final version of the contour but only an approximation.

3 A New Scale-Space Based Approach for Deformable Contour Optimization

In the previous section, discussions on the problems of DP multiresolution methods suggested that in order to utilize external energy properly, each pixel in the lowest resolution pyramid image should represent a variable sized segment in the original image. However, achieving this is very difficult with the multiresolution techniques because of their inherent nature – A pixel in a multiresolution pyramid level can only represent a fixed sized segment in the lower pyramid level. Therefore our new method does not use the multiresolution approach.

Our solution is based on scale-space techniques, which have received a considerable amount of attention in the computer vision field[10]. The main idea of producing a multiscale representation is to simplify the underlying image by removing the fine scale details while continuously increasing the scale. This kind of approach gives us the possibility of analyzing the image structure with respect to scale. In other words, we can analyze the change of the image structure while the image undergoes a simplification transformation. There are major differences between a multiresolution representation and a multiscale representation. Lindeberg has a thorough discussion about the differences in [10] and we use the terminology used by him. As its name implies, a multiresolution representation decreases the image resolution while forming the pyramid levels. On the other hand, a multiscale representation keeps the spatial sampling constant while the scale changes.

Our new method for deformable contour optimization forms a separate scale-space for the search window of each contour element v_i of a snake V. Using an information theoretic approach, we then analyze the behavior of the external energy under the scale change to come up with a set of different sized square shaped segments of the search windows. We apply a special dynamic programming optimization[1] using the centroids of these segments as the possible positions for optimized contour elements v_i. The resulting contour is used as the initial contour position for the same kind of optimization with a smaller scale-space representation and smaller search window sizes. The process continues until the segments of the search windows correspond to an original image pixel, after which no segmentation is meaningful.

3.1 Analyzing the Underlying Images and the Segmentation

The scale-space for a search window is constructed by a repeated convolution of the search window with a Gaussian kernel of increasing standard deviation σ sampled at discrete intervals. Given a search window W_i, we construct the scale space $L_i(x, y; \sigma)$ by

$$L_i(x,y;\sigma) = g(x,y;\sigma) * W_i(x,y) = \int_\alpha \int_\beta \frac{1}{2\pi\sigma^2} e^{-\frac{\alpha^2+\beta^2}{2\sigma^2}} W_i(x-\alpha, y-\beta) d\alpha d\beta \quad (7)$$

where $L_i(x, y; 0) = W_i(x, y)$ and $g(x, y; \sigma)$ is the Gaussian kernel with standard deviation σ. Each sample of σ is called a level of the scale-space. Levels are numbered starting from 0, which is the original image level. The scale of the level l is represented by σ_l.

We first form all scale-spaces L_i, $i = 1..n$, where n is the number of contour elements. Then, we segment each search window W_i by analyzing the behavior of the external energy with respect to change in σ. In other words, we like to know how the external energy changes in various areas of the search window if the underlying image is simplified by increasing σ in the scale-space. If the external energy starts to behave differently, we conclude that the corresponding segment of that area should be chosen smaller in order to be able to reflect the behavioral change better in the final segmentation. On the other hand, if the external energy behaves the same between the scale changes, we conclude that a larger segment for the corresponding area should not decrease the external energy related information in the final segmentation. We prefer larger segments in terms of efficiency because larger segments means less number of segments in a search window. This segmentation process addresses all the problems of the segmentation that we mentioned before.

In order to measure the behavioral change of the external energy with respect to scale σ, we use an information theoretic approach. Let $s_{i,j}^k$ be the jth segment of the search window W_i defined on image $L_i(x, y; \sigma_k)$, which is the kth level of the scale-space L_i. We can measure the amount of external energy related information, $H(s_{i,j}^k)$, by the Shannon entropy.

$$H(s_{i,j}^k) = \sum_x \sum_y -p(s_{i,j}^k(x,y)) ln(p(s_{i,j}^k(x,y))) \quad (8)$$

where

$$p(s_{i,j}^k(x,y)) = \frac{E_{Ext}(s_{i,j}^k(x,y))}{\sum_u \sum_v E_{Ext}(s_{i,j}^k(u,v))}.$$

Similar types of information theoretic approaches were used in many scale-space studies by a number of researchers including Niessen *et. al.*[11] and Jagersand[7].

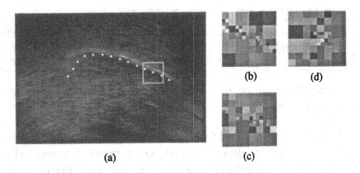

Fig. 3. Segmentation of the search window using different external energies. Please see the text for details.

We can measure the Shannon entropy of the same segment on the immediate upper level $k + 1$ by $H(s_{i,j}^{k+1})$. Finally, we get the normalized measure of the behavioral change of the external energy with respect to change in σ by

$$D(s_{i,j}^k) = \frac{H(s_{i,j}^{k+1}) - H(s_{i,j}^k)}{H(s_{i,j}^\infty)}. \tag{9}$$

Larger the value of $D(s_{i,j}^k)$, smaller the size of the segment should be.

The details of our segmentation is as follows. For a given m by m search window W_i, we form the scale-space L_i up to level l. The elements of the image at level k of this scale-space can be reached directly by $L_i(x, y; \sigma_k)$. We then form a set of segments S_i with four initial segments at the scale-space level $l - 1$.

$$S_i = \{s_{i,1}^{l-1}, s_{i,2}^{l-1}, s_{i,3}^{l-1}, s_{i,4}^{l-1}\}. \tag{10}$$

Each of these segments are $m/2$ by $m/2$ and they are not allowed to overlap. In other words, we segment the scale-space level $l - 1$ into four equal sized squares. We then choose the rth segment $s_{i,r}^{l-1}$ in S_i that gives the largest value for Equation (9). This means we are choosing the segment that has the highest behavioral change with respect to change in scale. $s_{i,r}^{l-1}$ is removed from the set S_i and we add four new segments to S_i that are all $m/4$ by $m/4$ and are defined on scale-space level $l - 2$ at the position of $s_{i,r}^{l-1}$ without any overlapping. The process continues by removing the segment producing the largest behavioral change value and adding four new square segments defined on the immediate lower scale level. This process continues until the number of segments in S_i reaches a user determined value.

Figure 3-a shows a midsagital ultrasound image of the tongue with the initial contour points superimposed. Figure 3-b shows the search window of the marked contour element segmented using an image intensity based external energy. Figure 3-c shows the same window segmented using the external energy defined by Equation (3). Figure 3-d shows the same search window segmented using an external energy that is sensitive to image gradient magnitude and the tangent angle of the contour at the marked contour element. Each segment is

$\sqrt{Number\ of\ Segments}$	64	32	16	8	4	2
Multiscale	8.1924	6.7940	5.3886	4.0486	2.6926	1.3669
Multiresolution	8.1924	6.8194	5.4500	4.0863	2.7301	1.3669
Constant Image	8.3178	6.9315	5.5452	4.1589	2.7726	1.3863

Table 1. Average Shannon entropy values for the segmentations by multiscale and multiresolution methods.

shaded with a random gray-level for visualization purposes. As the figures show, the final segmentations are different for different types of energy, which should be reflected in the DP optimization process by producing better contours.

Using the information theory, we can measure the information carried by a set of segments S_i by

$$H(S_i) = \sum_j -r(s_{i,j})ln(r(s_{i,j})) \qquad (11)$$

where $r(s_{i,j}) = E_{Ext}(\overline{s_{i,j}})/\sum_v E_{Ext}(\overline{s_{i,v}})$, $s_{i,j}$ is the jth element of the segment set S_i and $\overline{s_{i,j}}$ is the average gray-level value of the segment $s_{i,j}$. In order to demonstrate that our scheme produces sets of segments that have more external energy related information, we performed experiments on medical images by measuring the information of the produced segment sets using Equation (11). We then measured the information produced by the equal sized square shaped segmentation(Figure 2) of the usual multiresolution methods using the same formulation. We also measured the information produced by segmenting a constant gray level image, which has the least possible information. Notice that, the type of segmentation does not matter for the constant image because the resulting information produced by Equation (11) would be the same. Experiments were performed on the ultrasound image shown in Figure 3-a, by taking 64 by 64 search windows of each contour element and by segmenting each search window using our multiscale method and using the multiresolution method. Finally, for each segment set, we measured the information produced and took the average. Table 1 shows these average information values for our multiscale method and for the multiresolution method. As the table shows our method carries more information than the multiresolution methods because the difference between multiscale values and the constant image values are greater than the difference between multiresolution values and the constant image values. Figure 4 shows this visually where we normalized the average information values by dividing it with the constant image information value. As expected, both methods produce the same information amount where the number of segments is 64^2. This is because each segment corresponds to an original image pixel and both methods produce the same segmentation. Similarly, both methods produce the same information value where the number of segments is 2^2. It is because our multiscale method initializes the segment set S_i with equal sized segments as in Equation (10). Figure 4 also shows that our method carries much more external energy related information where the number of segments is around 16^2, which is the most widely used case.

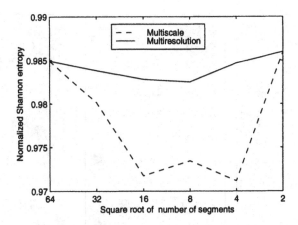

Fig. 4. Normalized average Shannon entropy values for Table 1.

Although there are major differences, our segmentation method shows resemblance to quad-tree type segmentation methods[9]. Our method uses scale-space techniques to analyze the behavior of the external energy with respect to change in the scale to decide which segment to divide. Quad-trees on the other hand do not pay attention to scale changes. They simply use the variance in the image to decide which segment to divide.

4 Experiments

We tested our system by performing experiments on medical images, which are known to be very problematic for contour analysis. In order to show the performance of our system we compared the contours of the multiresolution methods with our multiscale method at the highest level of the pyramid. This is because we know that final results are corrected by the contour optimizations at the lowest levels, which are the same for our method and for the multiresolution methods. This paper presents two of the test sets that we used.

The first test set is a sequence of midsagital ultrasound images of the tongue during speech. In addition to the usual ultrasound imaging problems, open contours and application specific problems makes contour analysis of these sequences very difficult[2]. Figure 5-(a) shows the tracked contours for four frames by our system. Figure 5-(b) shows the tracked contours produced by the multiresolution method. Our method spends about 28 seconds of CPU time for each contour. The multiresolution method spends about 43 seconds. We compared these contours against the ground truth obtained by a non-multiresolution dynamic programming system, which guarantees to give optimal results. The comparison is done by measuring the distances between the corresponding contour element positions of the two contours. Our system produced an average of 6.12 pixel difference. The other method produced an average of 12.91 pixel difference.

The experiments on ultrasound images confirmed the accuracy of our system. Next, we like to see if we can achieve the same performance using a smaller

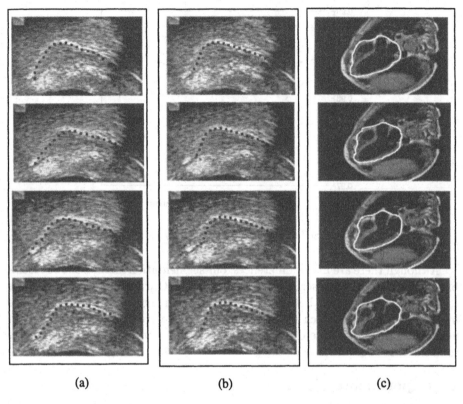

(a)   (b)   (c)

Fig. 5. Tracking results from (a) Multiscale method (b) Multiresolution method. (c) Results of our system applied to an MRI heart image sequence.

number of segments, which would result in faster execution times. For this experiment we used a sequence of four frames of a right anterior oblique (RAO) view contrast ventriculogram (CV) images from a normal human subject. Since they are less noisy and the contours are closed, MRI images are easier to analyze. Manually detected contours were used for verification of our results. First we run the multiresolution method on the sequence using the first frame's manually detected contour as the initial contour positions for all the frames in the sequence. We used 64 points for each 32 by 32 search window. Each contour extraction took an average of 26.78 CPU seconds. The average contour element difference with the manually detected contours was 2.88 pixels. We then did the same experiment using our multiscale method. We used only 25 points(segments) for each search window to speedup the optimization process. The average contour element difference with the manually detected contours was 2.87, which is almost the same with the multiresolution method. However, we saw a big difference in the time taken for each contour optimization: it took only an average of 7.42 CPU seconds for each contour extraction process with our method. Figure 5-(c) shows the tracking results from our system.

5 Conclusions

We presented a new multiscale approach for dynamic programming based deformable contour minimization. The system introduces a number of novel ideas that would be valuable for discovering new uses of scale-spaces in model based analysis of 2D and 3D images and image sequences. We confirmed through the experiments that the new method can achieve faster optimization times and performs better than the current dynamic programming optimization methods that are based on multiresolution techniques.

Our method reduces the number of possible locations that a contour element can take, dramatically shortening the execution time of the optimization. Although multiresolution methods use the same idea, our multiscale approach uses a scale-space approach to come up with a better set of candidate positions that makes the optimization process faster and increases the performance. Using information theory, the system analyzes the behavior of the external energy with respect to the scale change. This analysis gives us information on how to segment the underlying images so that reduced number of candidate positions carries more external energy related information. A previously developed dynamic programming method[1] is used to optimize the contour energy on these points to produce the final contours. The system can be generalized to different deformable contour and deformable model applications by changing the internal and external energies and the segmentation algorithm to fit the specific needs of the application.

References

1. Yusuf Sinan Akgul and Chandra Kambhamettu. A new multi-level framework for deformable contour optimization. In *CVPR99*, volume II, pages 465–470, 1999.
2. Yusuf Sinan Akgul, Chandra Kambhamettu, and Maureen Stone. Extraction and tracking of the tongue surface from ultrasound image sequences. In *CVPR*, pages 298–303, 1998.
3. A. A. Amini, T.E. Weymouth, and R.C. Jain. Using dynamic programming for solving variational problems in vision. *PAMI*, 12(9):855–867, 1990.
4. P.J. Burt and E.H. Adelson. The laplacian pyramid as a compact image code. *IEEE Trans. on Commun.*, 31(4):532–540, April 1983.
5. D. Geiger, A. Gupta, L. A. Costa, and J. Vlontzos. Dynamic programming for detecting, tracking, and matching deformable contours. *PAMI*, 17:294–302, 1995.
6. D. Geiger and J.E. Kogler, Jr. Scaling images and image features via the renormalization group. In *CVPR*, pages 47–53, 1993.
7. M. Jagersand. Saliency maps and attention selection in scale and spatial coordinates: An information theoretic approach. In *ICCV95*, pages 195–202, 1995.
8. M. Kass, A. Witkin, and D. Terzopoulos. Snakes: Active contour models. In *ICCV*, pages 259–269, 1987.
9. A. Klinger. Pattern and search statistics. In J.S. Rustagi, editor, *Optimizing Methods in Statistics*. Academic Press, 1971.
10. T. Lindeberg. *Scale-Space Theory in Computer Vision*. Kluwer Academic Publishers, 1994.
11. W.J. Niessen, K.L. Vincken, J.A. Weickert, and M.A. Viergever. Nonlinear multiscale representations for image segmentation. *CVIU*, 66(2):233–245, May 1997.

Self-Similarity of Noise in Scale-Space

Peter Majer

Institute for Statistics and Econometrics, University of Göttingen, Platz der Göttinger Sieben 5, Göttingen, Germany. E-mail: majer@wiso.uni-goettingen.de

Abstract. A simple derivation of properties of a normal white noise random field in linear scale-space is presented. The central observation is that the random field has a scaling invariance property. From this invariance it is easy to derive the scaling behaviour of measurements made on normal white noise random fields.

1 Introduction

Properties of normal white noise in scale-space have been studied previously for a number of reasons. Images may be corrupted by noise and scale-space smoothing may improve the signal to noise ratio. Noise has served as a model to study the behaviour across scales of properties such as the number of local extrema or the volume of grey-level blobs [4]. Deviations from the scaling behaviour of properties of white noise or ensembles of natural images [5] may provide useful information to a visual system. Apart from the covariance of normal white noise in scale-space [1] results have been achieved mostly by simulation. The purpose of this paper is to illustrate that some useful results are available analytically.

2 An invariance of noise in scale-space

It is well known [3] that the only *functions* that are form invariant under linear scale-space filtering are the derivative of Gaussian functions

$$G^{\mathbf{n}}(\mathbf{x};t) = \partial_1^{n_1}...\partial_N^{n_N} \frac{e^{-\frac{\mathbf{x}^T\mathbf{x}}{2t}}}{(2\pi t)^{N/2}}$$

Filtering these functions with a Gaussian kernel G^0 is equivalent to a rescaling as expressed by the invariance $\mathbf{x} \to s\mathbf{x}$, $t \to s^2t$, $G^{\mathbf{n}} \to s^{-n-N}G^{\mathbf{n}}$ or $G^{\mathbf{n}}(\mathbf{x};t) = s^{-n-N}G^{\mathbf{n}}(s\mathbf{x};s^2t)$. N denotes the dimension of space, $x \in R^N$, $\mathbf{n} = (n_1,...,n_N)$ specifies the derivative operator , and $n = \sum_i n_i$ its order. The squareroot of the second argument $0 < t \in R$ is the "scale" of $G^{\mathbf{n}}$.

There is also a family of *random fileds* that is invariant under scale-space filtering with a kernel G^0 in the sense that *a filtering of the random field is equivalent to a rescaling of the joint distribution function.*

Members $\xi^n(\mathbf{x};t)$ of this family are generated (and defined) by filtering a normal white noise $\xi^0(\mathbf{x};0)$ of zero mean and standard deviation σ with a derivative of Gaussian filter kernel G^n:

$$\xi^n(\mathbf{x};t) = (G^n(\cdot;t) * \xi^0(\cdot;0))(\mathbf{x})$$

These normal random fields are completely determined by their autocovariance function

$$\gamma^n(\mathbf{x}-\mathbf{x}',t+t') = \sigma^2(-1)^n\, G^{2n}(\mathbf{x}-\mathbf{x}';t+t')$$

that describes the covariance of $\xi^n(\mathbf{x};t)$ and $\xi^n(\mathbf{x}';t')$. It follows immediately that the form invariance of G^n is inherited by the random fields:

$$\gamma^n(\mathbf{x}-\mathbf{x}',t+t') = s^{-2n}s^{-N}\gamma^n(s(\mathbf{x}-\mathbf{x}'),s^2(t+t')) \qquad (1')$$

The (joint distribution function of the) random field ξ^n is invariant under the rescaling

$$\mathbf{x} \to s\mathbf{x}$$
$$t \to s^2 t \qquad (1)$$
$$\sigma \to s^{-n}s^{-N/2}\sigma$$

Figure (1) displays a one-dimensional realization of $\xi^0(x,8^2)$, the same realization filtered to $\xi^0(x,32^2)$, and lastly a rescaled *display* of the first graph.

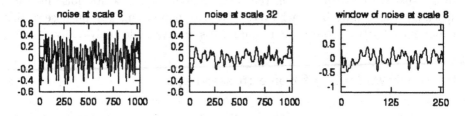

Fig. 1. Normal noise at scale $\sqrt{t} = 8$, filtered to scale 32, and a rescaled *display* of the noise at scale 8 showing only $0 < x < 256$.

Obviously the particular *function* that we have realized is not scaling invariant. Filtering the function in the first graph results in the second which is apparently different from the third graph that shows the appropriately rescaled version of the first. However, the similarity of these graphs serves to illustrate the fact that they are generated by identical random mechanisms, i.e. that *the random field is scaling invariant*.

The invariance of normal noise under the scaling transformation (1) allows to derive the *scaling behaviour* of any observations made on a random field $\xi^n(\mathbf{x};t)$.

Some examples follow.

3 Density of local extrema

The number of local extrema of normal white noise in scale-space has been studied as a model for the scale dependence of the number of features in a signal [4]. Computation of the expected value of the number of local extrema *at a fixed scale* is extremely difficult [4]. However, the scale invariance property (1) of normal white noise directly gives a relationship between the distributions of the numbers of local extrema at different scales.

From (1) we find that the distribution of the number N^{ext} of local extrema in a volume V of space at t is identical to the distribution of the number of local extrema in a volume $s^N V$ at $s^2 t$. More specifically:

- the probability $P_t(N^{ext})$ of observing less than N^{ext} local extrema in a unit volume ($\int_\Omega d\mathbf{x} = 1$) of filtered white noise $\xi^{\mathbf{n}}(\mathbf{x}; t)$ at scale $\sqrt{t}$ is related to $P_{s^2 t}(N^{ext})$ at scale $s\sqrt{t}$ by

$$P_t(N^{ext}) = s^N P_{s^2 t}(N^{ext}) \qquad (2)$$

- the expected number $E(N^{ext})$ of local extrema over space per unit volume of space behaves as

$$E(N^{ext}) \propto t^{-N/2} \qquad (3)$$

Note that (2) and (3) hold for any derivative $\mathbf{n}$ in $\xi^{\mathbf{n}}(\mathbf{x}; t)$.

Similar relations hold for the distribution and expectation of the number N^{ScSp} of local extrema over scale and space per unit volume of scale and space:

$$E(N^{ScSp}) \propto t^{-N/2-1} \qquad (4)$$

The scale-dependence (4) of the number of local extrema over scale and space is validated by simulation experiments. Figure (2) shows a plot of $\log N^{ScSp}$ against $\log t$ for one-dimensional and two-dimensional white noise.

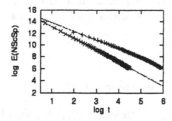

Fig. 2. Log-Log plot of the number of local extrema against scale for a one-dimensional (top curve) and a two-dimensional normal white noise. The theoretical curves are depicted as lines.

4 Edge lengths

The distribution of edge lengths l in normal noise $\xi^n(\mathbf{x}; t)$ at scale $\sqrt{t}$ is identical to the distribution of scaled edge lengths sl at scale $s\sqrt{t}$. Again this scaling invariance results directly from the invariance of the distribution of normal white noise under the scaling transformation (1) without the need to actually compute the distribution of edge lengths. It should be noted that for this scaling behaviour to hold it is essential that edges are computed by an algorithm that commutes with the scaling transformation, e.g. zero crossings of differential invariants.

Let us denote by $P_t(l)$ the relative frequency of edges of lengths less than l occurring in the set of all edges at scale $\sqrt{t}$ in a normal noise image $\xi^n(\mathbf{x}; t)$. $P_t(l)$ is identical to the probability $P_{s^2t}(sl)$ of edges of lengths less than sl occuring in a filtered image $\xi^n(\mathbf{x}; s^2t)$

$$P_t(l) = P_{s^2t}(sl)$$

so that the expected edge lengths grow linearly in scale $\sqrt{t}$

$$E(l) \propto \sqrt{t} \tag{5}$$

as shown on the left of figure (3).

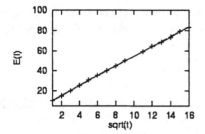 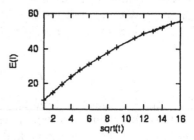

Fig. 3. Mean length of edges $E(l)$ as a function of scale $\sqrt{t}$. left: without boarder effects. right: with boarder effects. Theoretical relations are shown as lines.

4.1 Edge lengths with boarder effects

In contrast to dimensionless features the distribution of edge lengths is certainly affected by the image boarder cutting some edges short. We therefore attempt to describe the effect of this on the distribution of edge lengths.

Consider a two-step procedure to arrive at the measured edge lengths. First edges are computed from a hypothetical boarderless image. Then this is cropped to the observed image size. Thereby some edges are cut into two. One piece of each of these cut edges is kept. With probability one half it will be the long and with equal probability the short piece, so that the expected length after cutting is one half that before. If we denote by $p_t^c(l)$ the probability density of lengths of edges cut by the image boarder, we have

$$p_t^c(l) = 2p_t(2l)$$

where $p_t(l)$ is the density of lengths l, i.e. $P_t(l) = \int_0^l du \; p_t(u)$. Each edge has a certain probability p^b to be on the boarder of the image. This probability p^b depends on the length l of the edge. If we assume that p^b is linear in l — which should be a good assumption as long as the edge length is smaller than the length of the image — it will scale like

$$p^b(l) = s^{-1}p^b(sl)$$

The density of observed lengths at scale $\sqrt{t}$

$$(1 - p^b(l))p_t(l) + p^b(l)p_t^c(l)$$

then scales to

$$(1 - s^{-1}p^b(sl))sp_{s^2t}(sl) + 2p^b(sl)p_{s^2t}(2sl)$$

Thus the mean length depends on t as

$$E(l) \propto \sqrt{t} - at$$

with a constant a that depends inversely on the length of the image boarder and on the edge detection and linking algorithm used. Figure (3) shows a fit of the scale dependence of edge lengths in 512 by 512 pixel white noise images in scale-space. As edge-detection and linking algorithm we used Canny's non-maximum suppression and hysteresis thresholding [2] (for thresholding see below).

5 Blob volumes

Volumes of so called grey-level blobs have been used to construct a systematic approach for the extraction of important structures in images [4]. Their significance was assessed from a comparison to the expected blob volume in normal noise.

For the analysis of their scale dependence in normal noise it suffices to know that grey-level blob volumes are integrals of the (smoothed) intensity function over regions of the image domain, and that the regions are defined by geometric properties of the intensity [4]. Irrespective of whether each region grows or shrinks with increasing scale, the number of regions decreases like $t^{-N/2}$ and thus there average area A increases like

$$E(A) = t^{N/2} .$$

More generally, the distribution of areas of the regions of integration shows the invariance $P_t(A) = P_{s^2 t}(s^N A)$.

The values of the intensity function depend on scale as $t^{-N/4}$ so that the integrals over the above areas depend on scale like $t^{N/2-N/4}$

$$E(\text{blob volume}) \propto t^{N/4} \tag{6}$$

as reported in simulation studies by Lindeberg [4].

6 Scale dependent thresholds

The described scale dependencies hold only when the measurements commute with the scaling transformation. The introduction, for example, of a threshold in Canny's edge detection and hysteresis algorithm would destroy the scale dependence shown in figure (3).

Thresholds may however be modified to depend on scale such that their relative position within the distribution of values they are applied to is independent of scale. Or, conversely, the distribution of values to be thresholded may be rescaled. In the edge detection a threshold on the absolute value of the gradient should be be proportional to t^{-1} (for a two-dimensional image). Alternatively, as in figure (3) a fixed threshold was used and 'standardized' gradients

$$t^{1/2} t^{N/4} \, \partial_i \frac{e^{-\frac{x^T x}{2t}}}{(2\pi t)^{N/2}}$$

were computed. The use of standardized derivatives is superior to a scale-dependent threshold in that it may be numerically checked by setting the power of the filter kernel equal to 1.

7 Summary

Scale dependencies of distributions of properties of white noise in scale-space were derived from a scaling invariance of normal random fields. The method is usually much simpler than a direct computation of the distribution at fixed scales and subsequent derivation of the scale dependence.

References

1. J. Blom, B.M. ter Haar Romeny, A. Bel, J.J. Koenderink, *Spatial derivatives and the propagation of noise in Gaussian scale space* J. of Vis. Comm. and Im. Repr., **4**, 1, 1-13, 1993
2. J. F. Canny, *Finding Edges and Lines in Images*, AI-TR-720, M.I.T.
3. J.J. Koenderink, A.J.van Doorn, *Generic Neighborhood Operators*, IEEE Trans. Pattern Analysis and Machine Intell. **14**, 6, 597-605, 1992
4. T. Lindeberg, *Scale-space Theory*, Kluwer Academic, 1994
5. D. L. Ruderman, W. Bialek, *Statistics of Natural Images: Scaling in the Woods* Phys. Rev. Lett., bf 73, 6, 814-817, 1994

A New Time Dependent Model Based on Level Set Motion for Nonlinear Deblurring and Noise Removal

Antonio Marquina[1] and Stanley Osher[2]

[1] Departament de Matemàtica Aplicada,
Universitat de València,
Calle Dr. Moliner, 50, E-46100-Burjassot, Spain.
Supported by NSF Grant INT9602089 and DGICYT Grant PB97-1402.
marquina@uv.es
[2] Department of Mathematics,
University of California, Los Angeles,
405 Hilgard Avenue, Los Angeles, CA 90095-1555
Supported by NSF Grant DMS 9706827.
sjo@math.ucla.edu

Dedicated to the memory of Emad Fatemi

Abstract. In this paper we summarize the main features of a new time dependent model to approximate the solution to the nonlinear total variation optimization problem for deblurring and noise removal introduced by Rudin, Osher and Fatemi. Our model is based on level set motion whose steady state is quickly reached by means of an explicit procedure based on an ENO Hamilton-Jacobi version of Roe's scheme. We show numerical evidence of the speed, resolution and stability of this simple explicit procedure in two representative 1D and 2D numerical examples.

1 Introduction

The Total Variation (TV) deblurring and denoising models are based on a variational problem with constraints using the total variation norm as a nonlinear nondifferentiable functional. The formulation of these models was first given by Rudin, Osher and Fatemi in ([10]) for the denoising model and Rudin and Osher in ([9]) for the denoising and deblurring case. The main advantage is that their solutions preserve edges very well, avoiding *ringing*, but there are computational difficulties. Indeed, in spite of the fact that the variational problem is convex, the Euler-Lagrange equations are nonlinear and ill-conditioned. Linear semi-implicit fixed-point procedures devised by Vogel and Oman, (see [11]), and interior-point primal-dual implicit quadratic methods by Chan, Golub and Mulet, (see [3]), were introduced to solve the models. Those methods give good results when treating pure denoising problems, but the methods become highly ill-conditioned for the deblurring and denoising case where the computational cost is very high and parameter dependent. Furthermore, those methods also suffer from the undesirable *staircase effect*, namely the transformation of smooth regions (*ramps*) into piecewise constant regions (*stairs*).

In ([5]), a very simple time dependent model was constructed by evolving the Euler-Lagrange equation of the Rudin-Osher optimization problem, multiplied by the magnitude of the gradient of the solution. The two main analytic features of this formulation were the following: 1) the level contours of the image move quickly to the steady solution and 2) the presence of the gradient numerically regularizes the mean curvature term in a way that preserves and enhances edges and kills noise through the nonlinear diffusion acting on small scales. To approximate the solution we used a higher order accurate ENO version of Roe's scheme, for the convective term, and central differencing for the regularized mean curvature diffusion term. This explicit procedure is very simple, stable and computationally fast compared with other semi-implicit or implicit procedures. We show numerical evidence of the power of resolution and stability of this explicit procedure in two representative 1D and 2D numerical examples, consisting of a noisy and blurred signal and a noisy image, (we have used Gaussian white noise and Gausssian blur). We have observed in our experiments that our algorithm shows a substantially reduced staircase effect; we give an explanation for this in next section.

2 Deblurring and Denoising

Let us denote by u_0 the observed image and u the real image. A model of blurring comes from the degradation of u through some kind of averaging. The model of degradation we assume is

$$j * u + n = u_0, \tag{1}$$

where n is Gaussian white noise, i.e., the values n_i of n at the pixels i are independent random variables, each with a Gaussian distribution of zero mean and variance σ^2 and $j(x, y)$, is a kernel, where the blurring is defined through the convolution:

$$(j * u)(x, y) = \int_\Omega u(s, r) \, j(x - s, y - r) \, ds \, dr \tag{2}$$

For the sake of simplicity, we suppose that the blurring is coming from a convolution, through a kernel function j such that $j * u$ is a selfadjoint compact integral operator. For any $\alpha > 0$ the so-called *heat kernel*, defined as

$$j(x, y) = \frac{1}{4\pi\alpha} e^{-(x^2+y^2)/4\alpha} \tag{3}$$

is an important example that we will use in our numerical experiments.

Our objective is to estimate u from statistics of the noise, blur and some *a priori* knowledge of the image (smoothness, existence of edges). This knowledge is incorporated into the formulation by using a regularization functional R that measures the quality of the image u, in the sense that smaller values of $R(u)$ correspond to better images. The process, in other words, consists in the choice of the best quality image among those matching the constraints imposed by the statistics of the noise together with the blur induced by j.

In [10], the *Total Variation norm* or *TV-norm* is proposed as a regularization functional for the image restoration problem:

$$TV(u) = \int_\Omega |\nabla u|\, dx = \int_\Omega \sqrt{u_x^2 + u_y^2}\, dx. \tag{4}$$

The TV norm does not penalize discontinuities in u, and thus allows us to recover the edges of the original image. There are other functionals with similar properties introduced in the literature for different purposes, (see for instance, [4, 2]). The restoration problem can be thus written as the following constrained optimization problem:

$$\min_u \int_\Omega |\nabla u|\, dx \tag{5}$$

subject to

$$\frac{1}{2}\left(\int_\Omega (j*u - u_0)^2\, dx - |\Omega|\sigma^2\right) = 0. \tag{6}$$

and its Euler-Lagrange equation, with homogeneous Neumann boundary conditions for u is:

$$0 = -\nabla \cdot \left(\frac{\nabla u}{|\nabla u|}\right) + \lambda\left(j*(j*u - u_0)\right) \tag{7}$$

There are known techniques for solving the constrained optimization problem (5) by exploiting solvers for the corresponding unconstrained problem, whose Euler-Lagrange equation is (7) for λ fixed.

3 The time dependent model

Vogel and Oman and Chan, Golub and Mulet devised direct methods to approximate the solution to the Euler-Lagrange equation (7) with an *a priori* estimate of the Lagrange multiplier and homogeneous Neumann boundary conditions. Those methods work well for denoising problems but the removal of blur becomes very ill-conditioned with user-dependent choice of parameters. However, stable explicit schemes are preferable when the steady state is quickly reached because the choice of parameters is almost user-independent.Moreover, the programming for our algorithm is quite simple compared to the implicit inversions needed in the above mentioned methods.

Usually, time dependent approximations to the ill-conditioned Euler-Lagrange equation (7) are inefficient because the steady state is reached with a very small time step, when an explicit scheme is used. This is the case with the following formulation due to Rudin, Osher and Fatemi (see [10]) and Rudin and Osher (see [9]):

$$u_t = -\lambda j*(j*u - u_0) + \nabla \cdot \left(\frac{\nabla u}{|\nabla u|}\right). \tag{8}$$

with $u(x, y, 0)$ given as initial data, (we have used as initial guess the original blurry and noisy image u_0) and homogeneous Neumann boundary conditions, i.e., $\frac{\partial u}{\partial n} = 0$ on the boundary of the domain.

This solution procedure is a parabolic equation with time as an evolution parameter and resembles the gradient-projection method as used in [9] and [10]. In this formulation we assume an *a priori* estimate of the Lagrange multiplier, in contrast with the dynamically changing λ used in [9] and [10].

However, this evolution procedure is slow to reach steady state and is also stiff since the parabolic term is quite singular for small gradients. In fact, an *ad hoc* rule of thumb would indicate that the timestep Δt and the space stepsize Δx need to be related by

$$\frac{\Delta t}{\Delta x^2} \leq c |\Delta u|, \tag{9}$$

for fixed $c > 0$, for stability. This CFL restriction is what we shall relax to

$$\frac{\Delta t}{\Delta x^2} \leq c, \tag{10}$$

for c around 0.5. In order to avoid these difficulties, we propose a new time dependent model that accelerates the movement of level curves of u and regularizes the parabolic term in a nonlinear way. In order to regularize the parabolic term we multiply the whole Euler-Lagrange equation (7) by the magnitude of the gradient and our time evolution model reads as follows:

$$u_t = -|\nabla u| \lambda j * (j * u - u_0) + |\nabla u| \nabla \cdot \left(\frac{\nabla u}{|\nabla u|} \right). \tag{11}$$

We use as initial guess the original blurry and noisy image u_0 and homogeneous Neumann boundary conditions as above, with an *a priori* estimate of the Lagrange multiplier.

From the analytical point of view this solution procedure approaches the same steady state as the solution of (7) whenever u has nonzero gradient. The effect of this reformulation, (i.e. preconditioning) is positive in various aspects. The numerical scheme is simple to program, satisfies a maximum principle, it is at least an order of magnitude faster than standard TV implicit procedures. The resulting time evolution problem involves the motion of level sets and has a morphological flavor.

A very simple way to extend the Roe scheme to get high order accuracy is described in [8]. For more detail involving the numerical method see [5]. We note that the staircasing is minimized because our unconventional numerical method gives numerical steady states, based on nonoscillatory ideas. These numerical steady states will generally be different from those obtained by from those obtained by [10], [9], [11], [2] and [3] which used standard central differencing.

4 Numerical Experiments

We have used 1D signals with values in the range $[0, 255]$. The signal of (1, left) represents the original signal versus the blurred and noisy signal with $\sigma = 5$,

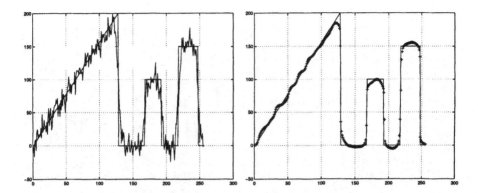

Fig. 1. Left,original vs. noisy and blurred 1D signal ; right, original vs. recovered 1D signal

and $SNR \approx 5$. The signal of (1, right) represents the original signal versus the recovered signal after 80 iterations with first order scheme with CFL 0.25. The estimated $\lambda = 0.25$ was computed as the maximum value allowed for stability, using explicit Euler time stepping.

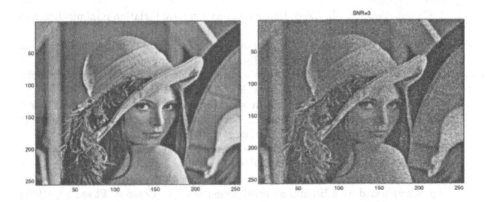

Fig. 2. Left: original image, right: noisy image, SNR$\approx$ 3.

Our 2D numerical experiments were performed on the original image (Fig 2, left) with 256×256 pixels and dynamic range in $[0, 255]$. The third order scheme we used in our 2D experiments was based on a third order accurate ENO Hamilton-Jacobi version of Roe's scheme described in [8], (see details in [5]). Our 2D experiment was made on the noisy image, (2, right), with a SNR which is approximately 3. Details of the approximate solutions using the Chan-Golub-Mulet primal-dual method and our time dependent model using the third order Roe's scheme, (described above), are shown in Fig. 3. We used $\lambda \approx 0.0713$ and we perform 50 iterations with CFL number 0.1.

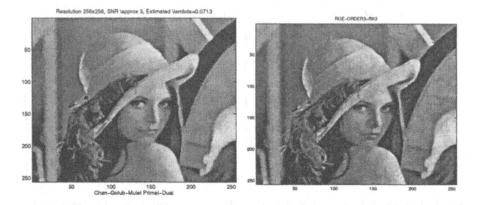

Fig. 3. Left: image obtained by the Chan-Golub-Mulet primal-dual method, right: image obtained by our time evolution model,with 50 timesteps and CFL-0.1

References

1. L. Álvarez, F. Guichard, P.L. Lions and J. M. Morel: Axioms and fundamental equations of image processing. Arch. Rational Mechanics and Anal., v. 16, IX, (1993) 199–257.
2. A. Chambolle and P.-L. Lions: Image recovery via total variation minimization and related problems. Numerische Mathematik, 76 (1997) 167–188.
3. T. Chan, G. Golub, and P. Mulet: A nonlinear primal-dual method for total variation-based image restoration. SISC, (1999) (To appear).
4. D. Geman and G. Reynolds: Constrained restoration and the recovery of disconti-nuities. IEEE Trans. on Pat. An. and Mach. Intel., 14 (1992) 367–383.
5. A. Marquina and S.J. Osher: Explicit algorithms for a new time dependent model based on level set motion for nonlinear deblurring and noise removal. CAM report 99-5, Math. Department, UCLA, January, (1999), (submitted).
6. S. J. Osher and L. I. Rudin. Feature-oriented image enhancement using shock filters. SIAM J. Numer. Anal., 27, (1990) 919–940.
7. S. J. Osher and J. A. Sethian: Fronts propagating with curvature dependent speed: algorithms based on a Hamilton-Jacobi formulation. J. Comput. Phys., 79, (1988) 12–49.
8. S. Osher and C.W. Shu: High-order essentially nonoscillatory schemes for Hamilton-Jacobi equations. SIAM J. Numer. Anal., 28, (1991) 907–922.
9. L. Rudin and S. Osher: Total variation based image restoration with free local constraints. Proc. IEEE Internat. Conf. Imag. Proc., (1994), 31–35.
10. L. Rudin, S. Osher, and E. Fatemi: Nonlinear total variation based noise removal algorithms. Physica D, 60 (1992) 259–268.
11. C. R. Vogel and M. E. Oman: Iterative methods for total variation denoising. SIAM J. Sci. Statist. Comput., 17 (1996) 227–238.

Curvature Scale Space with Affine Length Parametrisation

Sadegh Abbasi and Farzin Mokhtarian

Centre for Vision Speech and Signal Processing
University of Surrey
Guildford, Surrey GU2 5XH, UK
Tel: +44-1483-879842   Fax: +44-1483-876031
S.Abbasi,F.Mokhtarian@ee.surrey.ac.uk
http://www.ee.surrey.ac.uk/Research/VSSP/imagedb/demo.html

Abstract. The maxima of Curvature Scale Space (CSS) image have already been used to represent 2-D shapes under affine transforms. Since the CSS image employs the arc length parametrisation which is not affine invariant, we expect some deviation in the maxima of the CSS image under general affine transforms.

In this paper we examine the advantage of using affine length rather than arc length to parametrise the curve prior to computing its CSS image. The parametrisation has been proven to be invariant under affine transformation and has been used in many affine invariant shape recognition methods.

The CSS representation with affine length parametrisation has been used to find similar shapes from a large prototype database.

Keywords: Curvature scale space, Affine transformation, Image databases, Shape similarity retrieval, Affine length

1 Introduction

The CSS representation finds its roots in curvature deformation and heat equation. In fact, the *resampled* curvature scale space [6] implements curvature deformation [4]. This is carried out by convolving each coordinate of a closed planar curve, with a Gaussian function at different levels of scale. At each stage and before being convolved by a larger width Gaussian, the curve is represented in terms of arc length parameter. In *regular* curvature scale space [6] the resampling is not applied. As a result, the evolution is not a curvature deformation anymore. However, the implementation is carried out much faster and the representation has shown a good performance in shape similarity retrieval [1][5] under similarity transforms.

Both regular and resampled CSS image employ the arc length parametrisation which is not affine invariant. As a result, we expect some deviation in the maxima of the CSS image under general affine transformation. It has been shown

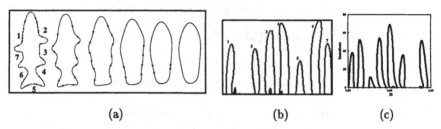

(a)   (b)   (c)

Fig. 1. a)Curve evolution, from left: $\sigma = 1, 4, 7, 10, 12, 14$. (b)The regular CSS image of the shape. (c) The resampled CSS image.

that affine invariance can only be achieved by an affine invariant parametrisation and affine length has been used by a number of authors [2][3]. In this paper we examine the utility of using affine length rather than arc length to parametrise the curve prior to computing its CSS image.

We have a database of 1100 images of marine creatures. The contours in this database demonstrate a great range of shape variation. A database of 5000 contours has been constructed using 500 real object boundaries and 4500 contours which are the affine transformed versions of real objects. Both regular and resampled CSS representations are constructed with affine length parametrisation and then used to find similar shapes from this prototype database.

2 The CSS image

This section describes the process of CSS construction for both regular and resampled CSS image. The use of affine length instead of arc length and finally the CSS matching are also briefly explained.

Construction of the regular CSS image; In order to use arc length, the curve is resampled and represented by 200 equally distant points. Considering the resampled curve as $\Gamma_0(s) = (x_0(s), y_0(s))$, we smooth the curve by Gaussian function:

$$X(s,t) = x_0(s) \star g(s,t) \qquad Y(s,t) = y_0(s) \star g(s,t).$$

The smoothed curve is called Γ_σ, where σ denotes the width of the Gaussian kernel. It is then possible to find the locations of curvature zero crossings on Γ_σ [5]. The process starts with $\sigma = 1$, and at each level, σ is increased by $\Delta\sigma$, chosen as 0.1 in our experiments. As σ increases, Γ_σ shrinks and becomes smoother, and the number of curvature zero crossing points on it decreases. Finally, when σ is sufficiently high, Γ_σ will be a convex curve with no curvature zero crossings (see Figure 1(a)). The process of creating ordered sequences of curves is referred to as the *evolution* of Γ.

If we determine the locations of curvature zero crossings of every Γ_σ during evolution, we can display the resulting points in (u, σ) plane, where u is an approximation of the normalised arc length and σ is the width of the Gaussian kernel. The result of this process can be represented as a binary image called *the regular CSS image* of the curve (see Figure 1(b)).

Construction of the resampled CSS image; The process of constructing the resampled CSS image is slightly different. It starts with convolving each coordinate of the initial curve $\Gamma_0(s)$ with a small width Gaussian filter. The resulting curve is re-parametrised by the normalised arc length and convolved again with the same filter. This process is repeated until the curve becomes convex and no longer has a curvature zero crossing. The curvature zero crossings of each curve are marked in the resampled CSS image.

Affine length; In order to achieve an affine invariant parametrisation, arc length, s, is usually replaced by affine length, τ, with the following definitions.

$$s = \frac{\int_0^u (\dot{x}^2 + \dot{y}^2)^{\frac{1}{2}}}{\int_0^1 (\dot{x}^2 + \dot{y}^2)^{\frac{1}{2}}} \qquad \tau = \frac{\int_0^u (\dot{x}\ddot{y} - \ddot{x}\dot{y})^{\frac{1}{3}}}{\int_0^1 (\dot{x}\ddot{y} - \ddot{x}\dot{y})^{\frac{1}{3}}}$$

The main disadvantage of the affine length is that its computation requires higher order derivatives. However, by using the method described in [5] , we can parametrise the curve using this formula.

Both regular and resampled CSS images can be reconstructed using affine length instead of arc length. In regular CSS image, only the initial representation is affine length and re-parametrisation is not applied. In resampled CSS image, however, after each iteration the resulting curve is re-parametrised using affine length parametrisation.

Curvature Scale Space Matching; We assume that the user enters his query by pointing to an image. The same preprocessing is done to find the maxima of the CSS contours of the input shape and compare them with the same descriptors of the database objects. The algorithm used for comparing two sets of maxima, one from the input and the other from one of the models, has been described in [5]. The algorithm first finds any possible changes in orientation which may have been occurred in one of the two shapes. A circular shift then is applied to one of the two sets to compensate the effects of change in orientation. The summation of the Euclidean distances between the relevant pairs of maxima is then defined to be the matching value between the two CSS images.

3 Experiments and results

In this paper, we examine the performance of the CSS representation under a combination of rotation and shear transform represented by the following matrices.

$$A_{rotation} = \begin{pmatrix} cos\theta & -sin\theta \\ sin\theta & cos\theta \end{pmatrix} \qquad A_{shear} = \begin{pmatrix} 1 & k \\ 0 & 1 \end{pmatrix}$$

The measure of shape deformation depends on the parameter k, *shear ratio*, in the matrix A_{shear}. In the present form of the matrix A_{shear}, x axis is called *shear axis*, as the shape is pulled toward this direction.

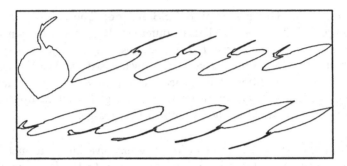

Fig. 2. The deformation of shapes is considerable even with $k = 1$ in shear transform. The original shape is presented in top left. Others represent transformation with $k = 1$ and $\theta = 20°, 40°, ..., 160°, 180°$.

Figure 2 shows the effects of affine transformation on shape deformation. In this Figure, shear ratio is selected as $k = 1$. In order to achieve different shear axes, we have changed the orientation of the original shape prior to applying the pure shear transformation. The values of θ range from 20° to 180°, with 20° intervals. As this Figure shows, the deformation is severe for $k = 1$. For larger values of k, e.g. 1.5 and 2, the deformation is much more severe.

In order to create three different databases, we chose three different values for shear ratio, 1.0, 2.0 and 3.0. We then applied the transformation on a database of 500 original object contours. From every original objects, we obtained 9 transformed shapes with different values of θ. Therefore, each database consisted of 500 original and 4500 transformed shapes.

In order to evaluate the performance of the method, every original shape was selected as the input query and the first n outputs of the system were observed to see if the transformed versions of the query are retrieved by the system. The results indicated that the performance of regular CSS is much better than the resampled CSS and using affine length parametrisation instead of arc length improves the performance of both representations.

Considering each original, ie not affine transformed, shape as an input query, we observed the first n outputs of the system and determined m, the number of outputs which are the affine transformed versions of the input. The success rate for a particular input is calculated as $\frac{m}{m_{max}}$; where m_{max} is the maximum possible value of m. Note that m_{max} is equal to n if $n \leq 10$; if not, m_{max} is equal to 10. The success rate of the system for the whole database will be the average of the success rates for each input query.

We chose different values for n, ranging from 2 to 40, and in each case found the average success rate of the system for *all* 500 original shapes. The same experiment was carried out on four different CSS representations, including regular and resampled CSS image with arc or affine length parametrisation. The results are presented in Figure 3(a) to 3(d). Each Figure includes three curves associated with three values of k, the shear ratio. Each curve shows the average success rate for the particular type of the CSS representation and for different values of n, the number of observed outputs.

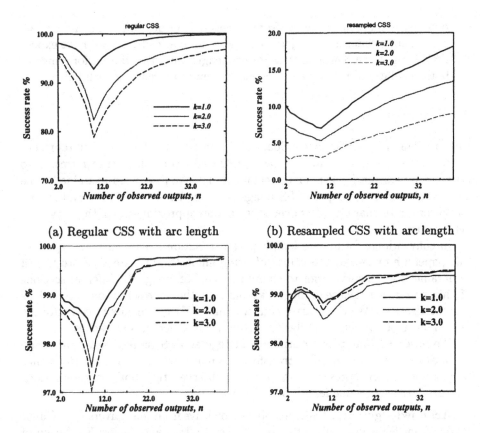

(a) Regular CSS with arc length (b) Resampled CSS with arc length

(c) Regular CSS, affine length (d) Resampled CSS, affine length

Fig. 3. Identifying transformed versions of the input query. k is the shear ratio and represents the measure of deformation. (see section 3)

Starting from 3(a), we observe that the conventional regular CSS image shows good results. For example, with $k = 1$ and in spite of severe deformation, more than 93% of outputs are always the affine transformed versions of the input query. This figure drops to 80% as k increases but it is still reasonably large.

The resampled CSS image with arc length parametrisation is quite vulnerable against affine transforms. In most cases, none of the transformed versions of the input query appear as the first few outputs of the system.

With affine length parameterisation, both regular and resampled CSS image show much better results. Almost all affine transformed versions of an input query appear among the first outputs of the system (see Figure 3(c) and (d)). The results are also robust with respect to k, the shear ratio.

In conclusion we observe the followings.

- Regular CSS image is almost robust with respect to affine transforms.
- Resampled CSS image with arc length parameterisation is not and with affine length parameterisation is robust with respect to affine transforms.
- Since the transformation is applied mathematically, the effects of pre-processing noise has not been considered. In real world applications, when the object

boundaries must be extracted from images taken from different camera viewpoints, noise changes the object boundaries dramatically. However, we expect that using affine length instead of arc length improves the performance of both regular and resampled CSS image even in presence of such noise.

4 Conclusion

The maxima of Curvature Scale Space (CSS) image have been used to represent closed planar curve in shape similarity retrieval under affine transforms. Two types of representations, namely regular and resampled were examined. The curve evolution in resampled CSS image is an implementation of curvature deformation. In regular CSS, however, it is only an approximation of the curvature deformation.

In conventional forms, arc length parametrisation is used in both types. In this paper we examined the utility of using affine length instead of arc length to parametrise the curve prior to computing its CSS image. In different sections of this paper, we reviewed the background of the representations as well as parametrisations. We then carried out a number of experiments to compare the performance of our shape similarity system using different approaches.

We observed that the performance of regular CSS representation in shape similarity retrieval under affine transforms is much better than the performance of resampled CSS representation. We also observed that both representations improved by using affine length parametrisation.

Acknowledgements Sadegh Abbasi is on leave from the University of Guilan, Rasht, Iran. He is grateful to the Ministry of Culture and Higher Education of Iran for its financial support during his research studies.

References

1. S. Abbasi, F. Mokhtarian, and J. Kittler. Reliable classification of chrysanthemum leaves through curvature scale space. In *Proceedings of the Scale-Space'97 Conference*, pages 284–295, Utrecht, Netherlands, July 1997.
2. K. Arbter et al. Applications of affine-invariant fourier descriptors to recognition of 3-d objects. *IEEE Trans. Pattern Analysis and Machine Intelligence*, 12(7):640–646, July 1990.
3. J. Flusser and T. Suk. Pattern recognition by affine moment invariants. *Pattern Recognition*, 26(1):167–174, Janaury 1993.
4. B. B. Kimia and K. Siddiqi. Geometric heat equation and nonlinear diffusion of shapes and images. *Computer Vision and Image Understanding*, 64(3):305–332, 1996.
5. F. Mokhtarian, S. Abbasi, and J. Kittler. Robust and efficient shape indexing through curvature scale space. In *Proceedings of the sixth British Machine Vision Conference, BMVC'96*, volume 1, pages 53–62, Edinburgh, September 1996.
6. F. Mokhtarian and A. K. Mackworth. A theory of multi-scale, curvature-based shape representation for planar curves. *IEEE Trans. on Pattern Anal. Mach. Intell.*, PAMI-14:789–805, August 1992.

A Stochastic Scale Space for Multiscale Image Representation

Uma S. Ranjan[1] and K. R. Ramakrishnan[1]

Department of Electrical Engineering
Indian Institute of Science
Bangalore 560 012, India
{kumaa,krr}@ee.iisc.ernet.in

Abstract. The notion of a stochastic scale space has been introduced through a stochastic approximation to the Perona-Malik equation. The approximate solution has been shown to preserve scale-space causality and is well-posed in an expected sense. The algorithm also converges to a (unique) constant image.

Keywords : stochastic scale space, discrete scale space, stochastic approximation

1 Introduction

Images can be represented at a variety of scales through a multiscale characterization [4]. Among the several methods used to obtain a multiscale characterization, it has been shown [1, 7] that the PDE approach is the most generic and most other approaches can be re-cast in the framework of PDEs. Interest in scale-space theories has increased after Perona and Malik [5] proposed a nonlinear scale-space based on a nonlinear diffusion PDE which smooths different regions of the image at different rates, thereby accentuating edges.

Although the Perona-Malik equation had impressive results, several modifications have been suggested to avoid its theoretical and numerical difficulties. This paper proposes a stochastic approximation to the discretized Perona-Malik equation using a system of particles distributed on the pixel array and evolving according to probabilistic rules. For a fixed pixel array, the stochastic algorithm is theoretically well-posed (has a unique stationary distribution and the expectation of the one-step evolution matrix is Lipschitz continuous). As the pixel distance goes to zero, the solution of the stochastic algorithm converges weakly [2] to a unique solution. If the Perona-Malik equation has a solution, at least in a weak sense, the stochastic algorithm converges to this solution. If however, the Perona-Malik equation has no solution[3], the algorithm is merely a stochastic aproximation which converges to a unique solution.

The motivation in using a particle system is that the state of the system (characterized by the number of particles at each site) directly corresponds to a set of gray-level values. Since digital images are invariably quantized, any non-integral solution, as obtained by classical numerical methods for example, has to be scaled and quantized, resulting in some loss of information and small inaccuracies. Further, the image at any particular scale is a quantization of the solution at a particular instant of time rather than the solution itself. The semigroup property (that an image at scale $t_1 + t_2$ may be obtained by observing at scale t_2 an image already approximated at scale t_1) then does not strictly hold for the quantized image since the intermediate image is different from the intermediate (real-valued) solution and hence, corresponds to a different initial value for further approximation. The particle system described in this paper has the advantage of maintaining a valid image as the solution at every instant.

2 A stochastic scale space

In this section, we first consider a discretization of the Perona-Malik equation. A stochastic algorithm is then formulated in such a manner that it is "locally consistent" with the discretized equation. By this we mean that the stochastic algorithm evolves for each iteration, in an expected sense, in the same way as the deterministic equation.

The Perona-Malik equation is given by

$$\frac{\partial f}{\partial t} = \operatorname{div}(D(\cdot)\nabla f) \tag{1}$$

where $f : S \times R^+ \to R$ represents the evolution with time of the image defined on a compact set S. $D(\cdot)$ is a decreasing function of the gradient computed from the solution $f(\cdot, t)$ at every instant of time.

$$D(x) = \exp\left\{-\left(\frac{\|\nabla f\|(x)}{2K}\right)^2\right\} \tag{2}$$

Using a standard second-order discretization, a discretized version of (1) can be obtained as

$$f^{(n+1)}(i) = f^{(n)}(i) + \lambda \sum_{j \in \mathcal{N}(i)} \left[D^{(n)}\left(\frac{i+j}{2}\right)(f^{(n)}(j) - f^{(n)}(i))\right] \tag{3}$$

where n denotes the discrete time instants and i the pixel coordinate. $\mathcal{N}(i)$ is the 4-neighbourhood of i.

We now formulate a stochastic algorithm with the same kind of behaviour as (3) in an expected sense.

2.1 Stochastic algorithm

To formulate a stochastic algorithm which represents (3) in an expected sense, we treat the image as a system of particles with the gray level at any pixel corresponding to the number of particles.

Let S denote the pixel array on which the image is defined and $\mathcal{N}(\cdot)$ the symmetric 4-neighbourhood. $X_i(n)$ denotes the number of particles at pixel i at time instant n.

At each instant of time 'n', each $X_i(\cdot)$ evolves according to the following probabilistic rule:

1. Each pixel i chooses one of its neighbours $j \in \mathcal{N}(i)$ according to a uniform selection probability.

2. The neighbour j is "accepted" with probability $D^{(n)}\left(\frac{i+j}{2}\right)$, $i \neq j$ where $i + j$ denotes the coordinate-wise addition of i and j. The total probability of a transition from i to j is then given by

$$\Pr(i, j) = \frac{1}{|\mathcal{N}(\cdot)|} D^{(n)}\left(\frac{i+j}{2}\right) \quad i \neq j \tag{4}$$

$$\Pr(i, i) = 1 - \sum_{i \neq j} \Pr(i, j) \tag{5}$$

3. If the neighbour is "accepted", $X_i(n)$ and $X_j(n)$ are both updated according to the rule

$$X_i(n + 1) = X_i(n) + int\left[\lambda\left(X_j(n) - X_i(n)\right)\right]$$
$$X_j(n + 1) = X_j(n) - int\left[\lambda\left(X_j(n) - X_i(n)\right)\right] \tag{6}$$

An additional particle is transferred (to the neighbour with lesser number of particles) with probability $\lambda\left|X_j(n) - X_i(n)\right| - int\left[\lambda\left|X_j(n) - X_i(n)\right|\right]$

Each $X_i(n+1)$ is thus a convex combination of its neighboring values and this effects a smoothing at i. Of course, this smoothing takes place with a probability inversely proportional to the strength of the edge, so that stronger edges are less likely to be smoothed while weaker edges are more likely to be smoothed.

The stochastic system evolves, in the expected sense, for one time step in the same way as (3).

Since the evolution algorithm is stochastic, the variance of the algorithm plays an important part. The variance should be small, if the same 'features' are to be preserved in every run of the algorithm. We show that the variance, particularly at the edges, is bounded by a "small" quantity.

For the specific form of $D(\cdot)$ that we choose, the variance of the increment $X^{(n+1)}(i) - X^{(n)}(i)$ at edge points (where $|X_j(n) - X_i(n)| > K$) is given by

$$\text{Var}\left(X_i(n + 1) - X_i(n)\right) \leq K \sum_{j \in \mathcal{N}(i)} \left(\frac{X_j(n) - X_i(n)}{K}\right)^{2-n} \tag{7}$$

where n is any positive integer.

Thus the algorithm preserves the same features in different runs although each run produces a slightly different result.

3 Properties of the stochastic algorithm

In this section, we state some properties of the stochastic algorithm which justify its application for a multiscale representation. Proofs are omitted here and may be found in [6].

- **Property 1:** *(Maximum principle) No local maximum is increased and no local minimum is decreased.*
- **Property 2** *The algorithm is well-posed in an expected sense.*
  Weickert[7] has shown that Lipschitz-continuity of the evolution matrix is sufficient for well-posedness. This can be proven in the L_1 norm

$$\|A\| = \sum_{i,j} \left| a_{ij} \right|$$

Note 1. Well-posedness fails for the nonlinear diffusion equation proposed by Perona and Malik because if the gradient value exceeds the threshold K, the equation behaves as an inverse diffusion equation. However, in the semi-discrete case, we use a finite difference rather than the gradient value and preserve Lipschitz continuity in the discrete norm. This is also the reason why some authors [7] note that a discretization on a finite lattice provides sufficient regularization for the Perona-Malik equation.

- **Property 3** *The Markov chain $X(\cdot)$ has a unique stationary distribution*
  It can be shown [6] that every state for which $\max_i X_i(\cdot) - \min_i X_i(\cdot) > 1$ is a transient state. The unique absorbing state of the system is the constant image which has the same number of particles at all pixels. The constant image is obtained if and only if the sum of gray values in the image is an exact multiple of the number of pixels. If such a state is not possible, the algorithm converges to an "almost constant" image where the maximum difference between the gray level at any two pixels is 1.

4 Results and Discussion

The stochastic algorithm has been tested on several real images. It has been found that the algorithm is able to preserve the sharpness of boundaries while smoothing region interiors effectively. Results on the cheetah image (Figure 1) show that the algorithm correctly identifies the spots of the cheetah as part of the region interiors and smooths them in preference to inter-region smoothing. This is in spite of the fact that no textural features have been used. The stochastic solution also gives almost segmented regions.

The images at multiple resolutions are obtained, as in other PDE formalisms, by stopping the evolution at various times. The difference is that the scale space generated by this algorithm is *stochastic* in nature, meaning thereby that the image approximated at any scale is obtained through a stochastic evolution. Hence, different runs of the algorithm could presumably result in slightly different images. However, experimentally, there was no perceivable difference in different runs.

Original image

After 50 iterations

After 100 iterations

After 200 iterations

Fig. 1. Results on cheetah image

References

1. L. Alvarez, F. Guichard, P.-L. Lions, and J.-M. Morel. Axioms and fundamental equations of image processing. *Arch. Rational Mech. Anal.*, 16:199–257, 1993.
2. P. Billingsley. *Convergence of Probability Measures.* John Wiley and Sons, 1968.
3. S. Kichenassamy. The Perona-Malik Paradox. *SIAM Journal of Applied Mathematics*, 57:1343 – 1372, 1997.
4. D. Marr and E. Hildreth. Theory of Edge-Detection. *Proc. R. Soc. Lond.*, 13(207):187–217, 1980.
5. P. Perona and J. Malik. Scale Space and Edge Detection Using Anisotropic Diffusion. *IEEE Transactions on Image Processing*, 12(7):629–639, July 1990.
6. Uma S. Ranjan. *Dynamical Systems in Image Processing.* PhD thesis, Indian Institute of Science, Bangalore 560 012, India, 1998.
7. Joachim Weickert. *Anisotropic Diffusion in Image Processing.* B. G. Teubner Stuttgart, 1998.

Original Image

After 20 iterations

After 100 iterations

After 500 iterations

After 1000 iterations

Fig. 2. Results on telephone booth image

Fast Marching to Moving Object Location

E. Sifakis and G. Tziritas

Institute of Computer Science - FORTH,
P.O. Box 1385, Heraklion, Greece
and,
Department of Computer Science, University of Crete
P.O. Box 1470, Heraklion, Greece
E-mails: tziritas@csi.forth.gr sifakis@csd.uch.gr

Abstract. In this paper we address two important problems in motion analysis: the detection of moving objects and their localization. Statistical and level set approaches are adopted in order to formulate these problems. For the change detection problem, the inter-frame difference is modeled by a mixture of two zero-mean Laplacian distributions. At first, statistical tests using criteria with negligible error probability are used for labeling as many as possible sites as changed or unchanged. All the connected components of the labeled sites are seed regions, which give the initial level sets, for which velocity fields for label propagation are provided. We introduce a new multi-label fast marching algorithm for expanding competitive regions. The solution of the localization problem is based on the map of changed pixels previously extracted. The boundary of the moving object is determined by a level set algorithm, which is initialized by two curves evolving in converging opposite directions. The sites of curve contact determine the position of the object boundary. For illustrating the efficiency of the proposed approach, experimental results are presented using real video sequences.

1 Introduction

Detection and localization of moving objects in an image sequence is a crucial issue of moving video [11], as well as for a variety of applications of Computer Vision, including object tracking, fixation and 2-D/3-D motion estimation. This paper deals with these two problems for the case of a static scene.

Spatial Markov Random Fields (MRFs), through Gibbs distribution have been widely used for modeling the change detection problem [1], [7] and [9]. On the other hand approaches based on contour evolution [5] [2], or on partial differential equations are also proposed in the literature. In [3] a three step algorithm is proposed including a contour detection, an estimation of the velocity field along the detected contours and finally the moving contours are determined. In [8], the contours to be detected and tracked are modeled as geodesic active contours.

In this paper we propose a new method based on level set approaches. An innovative idea here is that the propagation speed is label dependent. Thus for the problem of change detection, where two labels are characterizing image sites, an initial statistical test gives seeds for performing the contour propagation. The propagation of the labels is implemented using an extension of the fast marching algorithm, named multi-label fast marching algorithm. The change detection maps are used for initializing another level set algorithm, based on the spatial gradient, for tracking the moving object boundary. For more accurate results and for having an automatic stopping criterion, two fronts are propagated in converging opposite directions, and they are designed for contact on the object boundary, where the spatial gradient is maximum.

The remainder of this paper is organized as follows. In Section 2 we consider the motion detection problem and we propose a method for initially labeling sites with high confidence. In Section 3 a new algorithm based on level set approach is introduced for propagating the initial labels. In Section 4, we present the moving object localization problem, as well as a fast marching algorithm for locating the object's boundary. In order to check the efficiency and the robustness of the proposed method, experimental results are presented on real image sequences.

2 Detection of moving objects

Let $D = \{d(x,y) = I(x,y,t+1) - I(x,y,t), (x,y) \in S\}$ denote the gray level difference image. The change detection problem consists of a "binary" label $\Theta(x,y)$ for each pixel on the image grid. We associate the random field $\Theta(x,y)$ with two possible events, $\Theta(x,y) = static$ (or unchanged pixel), and $\Theta(x,y) = mobile$ (or changed pixel). Let $p_{D|static}(d|static)$ and $p_{D|mobile}(d|mobile)$ be the probability density functions of the observed inter-frame difference under the two hypotheses. These probability density functions are assumed to be homogeneous, i.e. independent of the pixel location, and usually they are under Laplacian or Gaussian law. We use here a zero-mean Laplacian distribution function to describe the statistical behavior of the pixels for both hypotheses. Thus the probability density function is a mixture of Laplacians, for which the principle of Maximum Likelihood is used to obtain an estimate of its parameters ([4], [6]).

An initial map of labeled sites is obtained using statistical tests. The first test detects changed sites with high confidence, that is with small probability of false alarm. Then a series of tests are used for finding unchanged sites with high confidence, that is with small probability of non-detection.

A multi-label fast marching level set algorithm, which is presented in the next section, is then applied for all sets of points initially labeled. This algorithm is an extension of the well-known fast marching algorithm [10]. The contour of each region propagates according to a motion field which depends on the label and on the absolute inter-frame difference. The exact propagation velocity for the "unchanged" label is $v_0(x,y) = 1/(1 + e^{\beta_0(|d(x,y)|-n\zeta-\theta_0)})$ and for the "changed" label $v_1(x,y) = 1/(1 + e^{\beta_1(\theta_1-|d(x,y)|-(n+\alpha)\zeta)})$, where n is the number of the neighbouring pixels already labeled with the same candidate label, and α takes a positive value, if the pixel at the same site of the previous label map is an interior point of a "changed" region, else it takes a zero value. The parameters $\beta_0, \beta_1, \theta_0, \theta_1$ and ζ are adapted to the data.

3 Multi-label fast marching algorithm

The fast marching level-set algorithm introduced by Sethian [10] computes a constructive solution to the stationary level set equation $|\nabla T(x, y)| = 1/v(x, y)$, where $v(x, y)$ corresponds to the velocity of the moving front, while $T(x, y)$ is a map of crossing times. The curves are advanced monotonically according to the propagation speed field.

The proposed multi-label version of the fast marching algorithm solves the same problem for the case of any number of independent contours propagating with possibly different velocities, which are supposed to "freeze", when they cross over each other. In this approach two properties of each pixel are calculated: the arrival time and the region or contour that first reached the specific pixel.

Our algorithm takes advantage of the fact that the fast marching algorithm sweep the pixels in a time-advancing fashion in order to limit redundant recalculations only to the pixels of contact between contours. For each pixel a list of label candidacies is maintained. A candidacy can only be introduced by a neighboring pixel being fixated to a certain label. It follows that no more than four candidacies may coexist per pixel. Additionally, multiple candidacies can occur in pixels belonging to the border between two labels only, which illustrates the fact that multiple recalculations of arrival times are rather scarce. Finally, the label carrying the smallest arrival time is selected for every pixel.

We now present the new multi-label fast marching level set algorithm.

Initialize
    For each pixel p in decision map
        If decision exists for p
            Set arrival time to zero for p
            For each neighboring pixel q lacking a decision
                - add label of pixel p to list of label candidacies for q,
                - mark it as trial,
                - give an initial estimate of the arrival time
        Else
            Set arrival time to infinity for p
Propagate
    While trial non alive label candidacies exist
        Select trial candidate c with smallest arrival time
        Mark c as an alive label candidacy
        If no decision exists for pixel p owning c
            Decide for p the label and arrival time of c
            For each undecided neighboring pixel q lacking a candidacy
            for the label of p
                - add label of pixel p to list of label candidacies for q,
                - mark it as trial

For each neighboring pixel q containing a trial candidacy d
for the label of c

      Recalculate arrival time of d

For the efficient location of the candidacy with the smallest arrival time a priority queue is utilized. Pixel candidacies themselves, being up to four, are keeped in a linked list for ease of implementation. The above facts indicate an execution cost of order $N \log N$ over the uninitialized pixels. Moreover, in practice it is expected to run in no more than twice the time of the traditional fast marching algorithms regardless of the actual number of labels used.

4 Moving Object Localization

The change detection stage could be used for initialization of the moving object tracker. The objective now is to localize the boundary of the moving object. The ideal change area is the union of sites which are occupied by the object in two successive time instants. It can easily be shown that

$$C(t, t+1) \cap C(t, t-1) = \{O(i, j, t)\} \cup (\{O(i, j, t+1)\} \cap \{O(i, j, t-1)\})$$

This means that the intersection of two successive change maps is a better initialization for moving object localization, than each of them. In addition sometimes it is $\{O(i, j, t)\} = C(t, t+1) \cap C(t, t-1)$. In Fig. 1 we give the initial position of the moving contours for the *Trevor White* sequence.

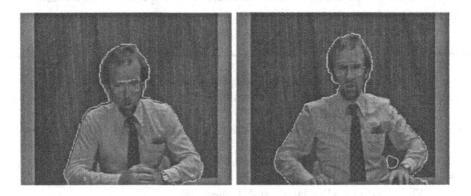

Fig. 1. Detection of Moving Objects: *Trevor White*

Knowing that there exist some errors in change detection and that sometimes under some assumptions the intersection of the two change maps gives the object location, we propose to initialize a level set contour search algorithm by this map. This search will be performed in two stages: first, an area containing the object's boundary is extracted, and second, the boundary is detected.

The first objective is to determine the area which contains the object's boundary with extremely high confidence. Because of errors resulting from the change detection stage, and also because of the fact that the initial boundary is, in principle, placed outside the object, it is needed to find an area large enough to contain the object's boundary. The task is simplified, if some knowledge about the background is acquired. In absence of knowledge concerning the background, the initial boundary could be relaxed in both directions, inside and outside, with a constant speed, which may be different for the two directions. In this area will then the photometric boundary be searched.

For cases where the background could be easily described, a level set approach extracts the zone of object's boundary. Let us suppose that the image intensity on the backround could be described by a Gaussian random variable with mean value, μ, and variance, σ^2. This model could be locally adapted. For the *White Trevor* sequence used here for illustrating results, a global backgound distribution is assumed.

The speed of uncertain area propagation is dependent on the label given by the initialization, and defined for the inner border as $v_o = c_o + d_o f(\bar{I})$, where $f(\bar{I}) = 1/(1 + e^{\frac{(I-\mu)^2}{\sigma^2} - 1})$, $\bar{I}$ being the mean value of the intensity in a 3×3 window centered at the examined point. For the outer border the speed is defined as $v_b = d_b(1 - f(\bar{I}))$. Thus for a point on the inner border, if its intensity is very different from that of the background, it is advancing with only the constant speed c_o. In contrast, the propagation of a point on the outer border is decelerated, if its intensity is similar to that of the background. The width of the uncertain zone depends on the size of the detected objects.

The last stage involves determining the boundary of the object based on the image gradient. The two extracted boundaries are propagated in opposite directions, the inner outside and the outer inside. The boundary is determined as the place of contact of the two borders. The propagation speed for both is $v = 1/(1 + e^{\gamma(\|\nabla I\| - \theta)})$. The parameters γ and θ are adapted to the data. Thus the two borders are propagating rapidly in the "smooth" area, and they are stopped on the boundaries of the object. In Fig. 2 are given the same frames as in Fig. 1 with the final result of localization.

5   Conclusions

In this article we propose at first a very interesting extension of the fast marching algorithm, in order to be able to consider multiple labels for the propagating contours. This allows to have purely automatic boundary search methods, and to obtain more robust results, as multiple labels are in competition. We have tested the new algorithm into the two stage problem of change detection and moving object localization. Of course, it is possible, and sometimes sufficient, to limit the algorithm into only one of these stages. This is the case for telesurveillance applications, where change detection with a reference frame gives the location of the moving object. In the case of a motion tracking application, the stage of localization could be used for refining the tracking result. In any case, in this

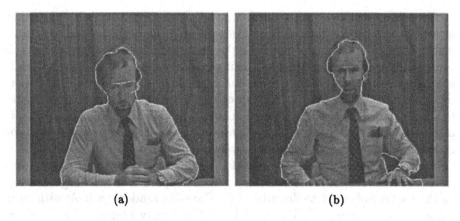

(a)   (b)

Fig. 2. Location of Moving Objects: *Trevor White*

article we show that it is possible to locate a moving object without motion estimation, which, if it is added, it could improve further the already sufficiently accurate results.

References

1. T. Aach and A. Kaup. Bayesian algorithms for adaptive change detection in image sequences using markov random fields. *Signal Processing: Image Communication*, 7:147–160, 1995.
2. A. Blake and M. Isard. *Active contours*. Springer, 1998.
3. V. Caselles and B. Coll. Snakes in movement. *SIAM Jour. on Numerical Analysis*, 33:2445–2456, Dec. 1996.
4. R. Duda and P. Hart. *Pattern Classification and Scene Analysis*. New York: Willey-Interscience, 1973.
5. M. Kass, A. Witkin, and D. Terzopoulos. Snakes: active contour models. *Intern. Jour. of Computer Vision*, 1:321–332, Jan. 1988.
6. G. McLachlan, D. Peel, and W. Whiten. Maximum likelihood clustering via normal mixture model. *Signal Processing: Image Communication*, 8:105–111, 1996.
7. J-M. Odobez and P. Bouthemy. Robust multiresolution estimation of parametric motion models.
   Visual Communication and Image Representation, pages 348–365, Dec. 1995.
8. N. Paragios and R. Deriche. Detecting multiple moving targets using deformable contours. *Intern. Conf. on Image Processing*, 1997.
9. N. Paragios and G. Tziritas. Adaptive detection and localization of moving objects in image
   sequences. *Signal Processing: Image Communication*, 14:277–296, Feb. 1999.
10. J. Sethian. Theory, algorithms, and applications of level set methods for propagating interfaces. *Acta Numerica*, pages 309–395, 1996.
11. G. Tziritas and C. Labit. *Motion analysis for image sequence coding*. Elsevier, 1994.

A Windows-based User Friendly System for Image Analysis with Partial Differential Equations *

Do Hyun Chung and Guillermo Sapiro

Electrical and Computer Engineering
University of Minnesota
Minneapolis, MN 55455
guille@ece.umn.edu

Abstract. In this paper we present and briefly describe a Windows user-friendly system designed to assist with the analysis of images in general, and biomedical images in particular. The system, which is being made publicly available to the research community, implements basic 2D image analysis operations based on partial differential equations (PDE's). The system is under continuous development, and already includes a large number of image enhancement and segmentation routines that have been tested for several applications.

1 Introduction

Partial differential equations (PDE's) are being used for image processing in general, and biomedical image processing in particular, with great success. The goal of this paper is to present a user friendly system developed under Windows NT/95/98 that implements and extends some of the most popular and useful algorithms based on this technique. The software package is in the process of being made publicly available to the research community.

Some of the algorithms included in the system are: (a) Anisotropic diffusion [3, 13]; (b) Curvature-based diffusion [1]; (c) Coherence enhancement [20]; (d) Vector-valued PDE's [6, 20]; (e) Geodesic active contours [5, 10, 14]; (f) Edge tracing [7, 19]; (g) Fast numerics [15]. Both the original algorithms and new improvements have been implemented.

As a form of example, we will describe two groups of operations implemented in the system, image enhancement and image segmentation, and during the conference we will demonstrate the system with a number of examples from different imaging modalities.

---

* This work was supported by a grant from the Office of Naval Research ONR-N00014-97-1-0509, the Office of Naval Research Young Investigator Award, the Presidential Early Career Awards for Scientists and Engineers (PECASE), the National Science Foundation CAREER Award, and the National Science Foundation Learning and Intelligent Systems Program (LIS).

The whole system is designed with two goals in mind: First, to assist researchers in the analysis of their data, and second, to allow its constant expansion and the introduction of new algorithms. Only a subgroup of the basic algorithms implemented in the system are here described, while it is understood that the package includes a large number of user friendly options that will be demonstrated at the conference. Details on the algorithms can be found in the mentioned references.

2 Image enhancement

Both for analysis and visualization, it is imperative to enhance images. This is of particular importance in biomedical images. Our software package includes a large number of PDE's based image enhancement procedures, both for scalar and vectorial (e.g., color) data. We have included directional diffusion, anisotropic diffusion, color anisotropic diffusion, coherence enhancement, and vectorial diffusion. We proceed to describe two of the algorithms implemented in the package.

2.1 Directional (curvature-based) diffusion

The algorithm in this section follows [1].

Let $I(x, y, 0) : I\!R^2 \to I\!R$ be the original image that we want to enhance. The basic idea behind image enhancement via directional diffusion is to define a family of images $I(x, y, t) : I\!R^2 \times [0, \tau) \to I\!R$ satisfying

$$\frac{\partial I}{\partial t} = g(\| \nabla I \|) \frac{\partial^2 I}{\partial \xi^2},$$

where $g(r) \to_{r \to \infty} 0$ is an edge stopping function, and ξ is a unit vector perpendicular to ∇I. This flow is equivalent to

$$\frac{\partial I}{\partial t} = g(\| \nabla I \|) \kappa \| \nabla I \|,$$

where κ is the curvature of the level-sets of I. The flow is processing the image in the direction of its edges, hereby preserving the basic edge information.

2.2 Robust anisotropic diffusion

The algorithm in this section follows [3, 13].

One of the most popular PDE's based algorithms for image enhancement is the anisotropic diffusion scheme pioneered by Perona and Malik. Our system includes these equations and the later improvements developed by Black *et al.* Letting $I(x, y, t) : I\!R^2 \times [0, \tau) \to I\!R$ be the deforming image, with the original image as initial condition, the image enhancement flow is obtained from the gradient descent of

$$\int_\Omega \rho(\| \nabla I \|) d\Omega,$$

which is given by

$$\frac{\partial I}{\partial t} = \text{div} \left(\rho'(\| \nabla I \|) \frac{\nabla I}{\| \nabla I \|} \right),$$

where ρ is, for example, the Lorentzian or Tukey's biweight robust function.

3 Segmentation

One of the most commonly used approaches to segment objects, particularly in medical images, are *active contours* or *snakes* [8, 17]. This technique is based on deforming a curve toward the minimization of a given energy. This energy is mainly composed by two terms, one attracting the curve to the objects boundaries, and the other one addressing regularization properties of the deforming curve. In [4, 5], it was shown that a re-interpretation of the classical snakes model leads to the formulation of the segmentation problem as the minimization of a weighted length given by

$$\int_{\mathcal{C}} (g(\| \nabla(I) \|))ds, \tag{1}$$

where $\mathcal{C} : \mathbb{R} \to \mathbb{R}^2$ is the deforming curve, $I : \mathbb{R}^2 \to \mathbb{R}$ the image, ds stands for the curve arc-length ($\| \partial \mathcal{C}/\partial s \| = 1$), $\nabla(\cdot)$ stands for the gradient, and $g(\cdot)$ is such that $g(r) \to 0$ while $r \to \infty$ (the "edge detector"). This model means that finding the object boundaries is equivalent to computing a path of minimal weighted distance, a *geodesic curve*, with weight given by $g(\cdot)$ (see also [10, 16, 21]). This model not only improves classical snakes, but also provides a formal mathematical framework that connects between previous models (e.g., between [8] and [11]); see [5] for details.

There are two main techniques to find the geodesic curve, that is, the minimizer of (1). Both are part of the system we have developed, and are briefly described now.

3.1 Curve evolution approach

The algorithm in this section follows [5, 10, 14].

This technique is based on computing the gradient descent of (1), and starting from a closed curve either inside or outside the object, deform it toward the (possibly local) minima, finding a geodesic curve. This approach gives a curve evolution flow of the form

$$\frac{\partial \mathcal{C}}{\partial t} = g\kappa \mathcal{N} - (\nabla g \cdot \mathcal{N})\mathcal{N}, \tag{2}$$

where κ and $\mathcal{N}$ are the Euclidean curvature and Euclidean unit norm respectively (additional velocities can be added as well and they are part of our implementation). This was the approach followed in [5, 10], inspired by [11], where the model was first introduced. The implementation is based on the numerical technique developed by Osher and Sethian [12]. This model gives a completely automatic segmentation procedure (modulo initialization). This approach works very well for images that are not extremely noisy. For extremely noisy images, like the neuron data presented in the examples section, spurious objects are detected, and is left to the user to manually eliminate them. In addition, since the boundary might be very weak, this is not always detected. An initialization very close to the goal might then be required. This motivates the next approach.

3.2 Geodesic edge tracing

The algorithm in this section follows [7, 19].

This technique of solving (1) is based on connecting between a few points marked by the user on the neuron's boundary, while keeping the weighted length (1) to a minimum. This was developed in [7]. In contrast with the technique described above, this approach always needs user intervention to mark the initial points. On the other hand, for very noisy images, it permits a better handling of the noise.

We now describe the algorithm used to compute the minimal weighted path between points on the objects boundary. That is, given a set of boundary points $\{\mathcal{P}\}_{i=1}^{N+1}$, and following (1), we have to find the N curves that minimize ($\mathcal{P}_{N+1} \equiv \mathcal{P}_1$)

$$d(I(\mathcal{P}_i), I(\mathcal{P}_{i+1})) := \int_{\mathcal{P}_i}^{\mathcal{P}_{i+1}} (g(\| \nabla I \|) ds. \tag{3}$$

The algorithm is composed of three main steps: 1- Image regularization, 2- Computation of equal distance contours, 3- Back propagation. We briefly describe each one of these steps now.

Image regularization As in the curve evolution approach, the image is first enhanced (noise removal and edge enhancement), using the PDE's based algorithms described before. The result of this step is the image $\hat{I}$ (working on the subsampled data, following [19], is part of the software package as well).

Equal distance contours computation After the image $\hat{I}$ is computed, we have to compute, for every point $\mathcal{P}_i$, the weighted distance map, according to the weighted distance d. That is, we have to compute the function

$$\mathcal{D}_i(x, y) := d(\hat{I}(\mathcal{P}_i), \hat{I}(x, y)),$$

or in words, the weighted distance between the pair of image points $\mathcal{P}_i$ and (x, y).

There are basically two ways of making this computation, computing equal distance contours, or directly computing $\mathcal{D}_i$. We briefly describe each one of these now.

Equal distance contours $\mathcal{C}_i$ are curves such that all the points on the contour have the same distance d to $\mathcal{P}_i$. That is, the curves $\mathcal{C}_i$ are the level-sets or isophotes of $\mathcal{D}_i$. It is easy to see, [7], that following the definition of d, these contours are obtained as the solution of the curve evolution flow

$$\frac{\partial \mathcal{C}_i(x,y,t)}{\partial t} = \frac{1}{g(\|\nabla \hat{I}\|)}\mathcal{N},$$

where $\mathcal{N}$ is in this case the outer unit normal to $\mathcal{C}_i(x,y,t)$. This type of flow should be implemented using the standard level-sets method [12].

A different approach is based on the fact that the distance function $\mathcal{D}_i$ holds the following Hamilton-Jacobi equation [9, 15, 18]:

$$\frac{1}{g(\|\nabla \hat{I}\|)}\|\nabla \mathcal{D}_i\| = 1.$$

Optimal numerical techniques have been proposed to solve this static Hamilton-Jacobi equation [9, 15, 18]. Due to this optimality, this is the approach we follow in our software package. At the end of this step, we have $\mathcal{D}_i$ for each point $\mathcal{P}_i$. We should note that we do not need to compute $\mathcal{D}_i$ for all the image plane. It is actually enough to stop the computations when the value at $\mathcal{P}_{i+1}$ is obtained.

Back propagation After the distance functions $\mathcal{D}_i$ are computed, we have to trace the actual minimal path between $\mathcal{P}_i$ and $\mathcal{P}_{i+1}$ that minimizes d. Once again it is easy to show (see for example [9, 15]), that this path should be perpendicular to the level-curves $\mathcal{C}_i$ of $\mathcal{D}_i$, and therefore tangent to $\nabla \mathcal{D}_i$. The path is then computed backing from $\mathcal{P}_{i+1}$, in the gradient direction, until we return to the point $\mathcal{P}_i$. This back propagation is of course guaranteed to converge to the point $\mathcal{P}_i$, and then gives the path of minimal weighted distance. We have implemented both a full back propagation scheme and a discrete one that just looks at the neighboring pixels.

4 Concluding remarks

In this paper we introduced a system for image analysis via PDE's. Some of the algorithms implemented in our package have been shown to outperform commercially available packages that perform similar operations. For example, we have shown, [19], that the edge tracing algorithm normally outperforms the one in *PictureIT*, Microsoft's image processing package. As mentioned in the introduction, the system will be available to the research community. The system is under constant development, and additional features, like an improvement of the tracking scheme introduced in [2], are expected to be available soon.

References

1. L. Alvarez, P. L. Lions, and J. M. Morel, "Image selective smoothing and edge detection by nonlinear diffusion," *SIAM J. Numer. Anal.* **29**, pp. 845-866, 1992.

2. M. Bertalmio, G. Sapiro, and G. Randall, "Morphing active contours: A geometric, topology-free, technique for image segmentation and tracking," *Proc. IEEE ICIP*, Chicago, October 1998.

3. M. Black, G. Sapiro, D. Marimont, and D. Heeger, "Robust anisotropic diffusion," *IEEE Trans. Image Processing*, March 1998.

4. V. Caselles, R. Kimmel, and G. Sapiro, "Geodesic active contours," *Proc. Int. Conf. Comp. Vision '95*, Cambridge, June 1995.

5. V. Caselles, R. Kimmel, and G. Sapiro, "Geodesic active contours," *International Journal of Computer Vision* **22:1**, pp. 61-79, 1997.

6. V. Caselles, G. Sapiro, and D. H. Chung, "Vector median filters, inf-sup operations, and coupled PDE's: Theoretical connections," *ECE-University of Minnesota Technical Report*, September 1998.

7. L. Cohen and R. Kimmel, "Global minimum for active contours models: A minimal path approach," *Int. J. of Computer Vision* **24**, pp. 57-78, 1997.

8. M. Kass, A. Witkin, and D. Terzopoulos, "Snakes: Active contour models," *International Journal of Computer Vision* **1**, pp. 321-331, 1988.

9. R. Kimmel and J. A. Sethian, "Fast marching method for computation of distance maps," *LBNL Report* **38451**, UC Berkeley, February, 1996

10. S. Kichenassamy, A. Kumar, P. Olver, A. Tannenbaum, and A. Yezzi, "Conformal curvature flows: from phase transitions to active vision," *Archive for Rational Mechanics and Analysis* **134**, pp. 275-301, 1996.

11. R. Malladi, J. A. Sethian and B. C. Vemuri, "Shape modeling with front propagation: A level set approach," *IEEE-PAMI* **17**, pp. 158-175, 1995.

12. S. J. Osher and J. A. Sethian, "Fronts propagation with curvature dependent speed: Algorithms based on Hamilton-Jacobi formulations," *Journal of Computational Physics* **79**, pp. 12-49, 1988.

13. P. Perona and J. Malik, "Scale-space and edge detection using anisotropic diffusion," *IEEE-PAMI* **12**, pp. 629-639, 1990.

14. G. Sapiro, "Color snakes," *Computer Vision and Image Understanding* **68:2**, pp. 247-253, 1997.

15. J. Sethian, *Level Set Methods: Evolving Interfaces in Geometry, Fluid Mechanics, Computer Vision and Materials Sciences*, Cambridge University Press, Cambridge-UK, 1996.

16. J. Shah, "Recovery of shapes by evolution of zero-crossings," Technical Report, Math. Dept. Northeastern Univ. Boston MA, 1995.

17. D. Terzopoulos, A. Witkin, and M. Kass, "Constraints on deformable models: Recovering 3D shape and nonrigid motions," *AI* **36**, 1988.

18. J. N. Tsitsiklis, "Efficient algorithms for globally optimal trajectories," *IEEE Transactions on Automatic Control* **40** pp. 1528-1538, 1995.

19. L. Vazquez, G. Sapiro, and G. Randall, "Segmenting neurons in electronic microscopy via geometric tracing," *Proc. IEEE ICIP*, Chicago, October 1998.

20. J. Weickert, "Coherence-enhancing diffusion of color images," *Proc. VII National Symp. on Pattern Recognition and Image Analysis*, pp. 239-244, Barcelona, Spain, 1997.

21. R. T. Whitaker, "Algorithms for implicit deformable models," *Proc. ICCV'95*, pp. 822-827, Cambridge, June 1995.

Color Invariant Edge Detection

Jan-Mark Geusebroek[1,2], Anuj Dev[1], Rein van den Boomgaard[1], Arnold W.M. Smeulders[1], Frans Cornelissen[2], and Hugo Geerts[2]

[1] Department of Computer Science, Faculty of Science, University of Amsterdam, Kruislaan 403, 1098 SJ Amsterdam, The Netherlands
[2] Biological Imaging Laboratory, Life Sciences, Janssen Research Foundation, Turnhoutseweg 30, B2340 Beerse, Belgium.
mark@wins.uva.nl

Abstract. Segmentation based on color, instead of intensity only, provides an easier distinction between materials, on the condition that robustness against irrelevant parameters is achieved, such as illumination source, shadows, geometry and camera sensitivities. Modeling the physical process of the image formation provides insight into the effect of different parameters on object color.
In this paper, a color differential geometry approach is used to detect material edges, invariant with respect to illumination color and imaging conditions. The performance of the color invariants is demonstrated by some real-world examples, showing the invariants to be successful in discounting shadow edges and illumination color.

1 Introduction

Color is a powerful clue in the distinction between objects. Segmentation based on color, instead of intensity only, provides an easier discrimination between colored regions. It is well known that values obtained by a color camera are affected by the specific imaging conditions, such as illumination color, shadow and geometry, and sensor sensitivity. Therefore, object properties independent of the imaging conditions should be derived from the measured color values. Modeling the physical process of the image formation provides insight into the effect of different parameters on object color [4, 5, 10, 12]. We consider the determination of material changes, independent of the illumination color and intensity, camera sensitivities, and geometric parameters as shadow, orientation and scale.

When considering the estimation of material properties on the basis of local measurements, differential equations constitute a natural framework to describe the physical process of image formation. A well known technique from scale-space theory is the convolution of a signal with a derivative of the Gaussian kernel to obtain the derivative of the signal [8]. The introduction of wavelength in the scale-space paradigm leads to a spatio-spectral family of Gaussian aperture functions, introduced in [2] as the Gaussian color model. As a result, measurements from color images of analytically derived differential expressions may be obtained by applying the Gaussian color model. Thus, the model defines how to measure material properties as derived from the photometric model.

In this paper, the problem of determining material changes independent of the illumination color and intensity is addressed. Additionally, robustness against changes in the imaging conditions is considered, such as camera viewpoint, illumination direction and sensor sensitivities and gains. The problem is approached by considering a Lambertian reflectance model, leading to differential expressions which are robust to a change in imaging conditions. The performance of these color invariants is demonstrated on a real-world scene of colored objects, and on transmission microscopic preparations.

2 Determination of Object Borders

Any method for finding invariant color properties relies on a photometric model *and* on assumptions about the physical variables involved. For example, hue and saturation are well known object properties for matte, dull surfaces, illuminated by white light [5]. Normalized rgb is known to be insensitive to surface orientation, illumination direction and intensity, under a white illumination. When the illumination color varies or is not white, other object properties which are related to constant physical parameters should be measured. In this section, expressions for determining material changes in images will be derived, under the assumption that the scene is uniformly illuminated by a colored source, and taking into account the Lambertian photometric model.

Consider a homogeneously colored material patch illuminated by incident light with spectral distribution $e(\lambda)$. When assuming Lambertian reflectance, the reflected spectrum by the material in the viewing direction v, ignoring secondary scattering after internal boundary reflection, is given by [7,13]

$$E(\lambda) = e(\lambda) \left(1 - \rho_f(n, s, v)\right)^2 R_\infty(\lambda) \tag{1}$$

where n is the surface patch normal and s the direction of the illumination source, and ρ_f the Fresnel front surface reflectance coefficient in the viewing direction, and R_∞ denotes the body reflectance.

Because of projection of the energy distribution on the image plane vectors n, s and v will depend on the position at the imaging plane. The energy of the incoming spectrum at a point x on the image plane is then related to

$$E(\lambda, x) = e(\lambda, x) \left(1 - \rho_f(x)\right)^2 R_\infty(\lambda, x) \tag{2}$$

where the spectral distribution at each point x is generated off a specific material patch.

Consider the photometric reflection model (2) and an illumination with locally constant color. Hence, the illumination may be decomposed into a spectral component $e(\lambda)$ representing the illumination color, and a spatial component $i(x)$ denoting the illumination intensity, resulting in

$$E(\lambda, x) = e(\lambda)i(x) \left(1 - \rho_f(x)\right)^2 R_\infty(\lambda, x) . \tag{3}$$

The aim is to derive expressions describing material changes independent of the illumination. Without loss of generality, we restrict ourselves to the one dimensional case; two dimensional expressions will be derived later. The procedure of deriving material properties can be formulated as finding expressions depending on the material parameters in the given physical model only.

Differentiation of (3) with respect to λ results in

$$\frac{\partial E}{\partial \lambda} = i(x)(1 - \rho_f(x))^2 R_\infty(\lambda, x) \frac{\partial e}{\partial \lambda} + e(\lambda)i(x)(1 - \rho_f(x))^2 \frac{\partial R_\infty}{\partial \lambda} . \qquad (4)$$

Dividing (4) by (3) gives the relative differential,

$$\frac{1}{E} \frac{\partial E}{\partial \lambda} = \frac{1}{e(\lambda)} \frac{\partial e}{\partial \lambda} + \frac{1}{R_\infty(\lambda, x)} \frac{\partial R_\infty}{\partial \lambda} . \qquad (5)$$

The result consists of two terms, the former depending on the illumination color only and the latter depending on the body reflectance. Since the illumination depends on λ only, differentiation to x yields a reflectance property.

Lemma 1. *Assuming matte, dull surfaces and an illumination with locally constant color,*

$$\frac{\partial}{\partial x} \left\{ \frac{1}{E} \frac{\partial E}{\partial \lambda} \right\} \qquad (6)$$

determines material changes independent of the viewpoint, surface orientation, illumination direction, illumination intensity and illumination color.

Proof. See (4)—(5). Further, the reflectivity R_∞ and its derivative with respect to λ depend on the material characteristics only, that is on the material absorption- and scattering coefficient. Hence, the spatial derivative of their product is determined by material transitions. $\qquad \square$

Note that Lemma 1 holds whenever Fresnel (mirror) reflectance is neglectable, thus in the absence of interreflections and specularities. The expression given by (6) is the fundamental lowest order illumination invariant. Any spatio-spectral derivative of (6) inherently depends on the body reflectance only. According to [11], a complete and irreducible set of differential invariants is obtained by taking all higher order derivatives of the fundamental invariant.

Proposition 2. *Assuming matte, dull surfaces and an illumination with locally constant color, N is a complete set of irreducible invariants, independent of the viewpoint, surface orientation, illumination direction, illumination intensity and illumination color,*

$$N = \frac{\partial^{n+m}}{\partial \lambda^n \partial x^m} \left\{ \frac{1}{E} \frac{\partial E}{\partial \lambda} \right\} \qquad (7)$$

for $m \geq 1$, $n \geq 0$.

These invariants may be interpreted as the spatial derivatives of the normalized slope (N_λ) and curvature ($N_{\lambda\lambda}$) of the reflectance function R_∞.

3   Measurement of Spatio-Spectral Energy

So far, we have established invariant expressions describing material changes under different illuminations. These are formal expressions, assumed to be measurable at an infinitesimal small spatial resolution and spectral bandwidth. The physical measurement of electro-magnetic energy inherently implies integration over a certain spatial extent and spectral bandwidth. In this section, physically realizable measurement of spatio-spectral energy distributions is described. We emphasize that no essentially new color model is proposed here, but rather a theory of color *measurement*. The specific choice of color representation, often referred to as color coordinates or color model, is irrelevant for our purpose.

Let $E(\lambda)$ be the energy distribution of the incident light, and let $G(\lambda_0; \sigma_\lambda)$ be the Gaussian at spectral scale σ_λ positioned at λ_0. Measurement of the spectral energy distribution with a Gaussian aperture yields a weighted integration over the spectrum. The observed energy in the Gaussian color model, at infinitely small spatial resolution, approaches in second order to [2, 9]

$$\hat{E}^{\sigma_\lambda}(\lambda) = \hat{E}^{\lambda_0,\sigma_\lambda} + \lambda \hat{E}_\lambda^{\lambda_0,\sigma_\lambda} + \frac{1}{2}\lambda^2 \hat{E}_{\lambda\lambda}^{\lambda_0,\sigma_\lambda} + \dots \tag{8}$$

$$\hat{E}^{\lambda_0,\sigma_\lambda} = \int E(\lambda)G(\lambda; \lambda_0, \sigma_\lambda)d\lambda \tag{9}$$

$$\hat{E}_\lambda^{\lambda_0,\sigma_\lambda} = \int E(\lambda)G_\lambda(\lambda; \lambda_0, \sigma_\lambda)d\lambda \tag{10}$$

$$\hat{E}_{\lambda\lambda}^{\lambda_0,\sigma_\lambda} = \int E(\lambda)G_{\lambda\lambda}(\lambda; \lambda_0, \sigma_\lambda)d\lambda \tag{11}$$

were $G_\lambda(.)$ and $G_{\lambda\lambda}(.)$ denote derivatives of the Gaussian with respect to λ.

Definition 3. *The Gaussian color model measures, up to the 2nd order, the coefficients $\hat{E}^{\lambda_0,\sigma_\lambda}$, $\hat{E}_\lambda^{\lambda_0,\sigma_\lambda}$ and $\hat{E}_{\lambda\lambda}^{\lambda_0,\sigma_\lambda}$ of the Taylor expansion of the Gaussian weighted spectral energy distribution at λ_0 [9].*

Introduction of spatial extent in the Gaussian color model yields a local Taylor expansion at wavelength λ_0 and position x_0 [2]. Each measurement of a spatio-spectral energy distribution has a spatial as well as spectral resolution. The measurement is obtained by probing an energy density volume in a three-dimensional spatio-spectral space, where the size of the probe is determined by the observation scale σ_λ and σ_x,

$$\hat{E}(\lambda, x) = \hat{E} + \begin{pmatrix} x \\ \lambda \end{pmatrix}^T \begin{bmatrix} \hat{E}_x \\ \hat{E}_\lambda \end{bmatrix} + \frac{1}{2}\begin{pmatrix} x \\ \lambda \end{pmatrix}^T \begin{bmatrix} \hat{E}_{xx} & \hat{E}_{x\lambda} \\ \hat{E}_{\lambda x} & \hat{E}_{\lambda\lambda} \end{bmatrix} \begin{pmatrix} x \\ \lambda \end{pmatrix} + \dots \tag{12}$$

where

$$\hat{E}_{x^i\lambda^j}(\lambda, x) = E(\lambda, x) * G_{x^i\lambda^j}(\lambda, x; \sigma_x) \ . \tag{13}$$

Here, $G_{\boldsymbol{x}^i\lambda^j}(\lambda, \boldsymbol{x}; \sigma_{\boldsymbol{x}})$ are the spatio-spectral probes, or color receptive fields. The coefficients of the Taylor expansion of $\hat{E}(\lambda, \boldsymbol{x})$ represents the local image structure completely. Truncation of the Taylor expansions results in an approximate representation, which is best possible in the least squares sense [8].

For human vision, the Taylor expansion is spectrally truncated at second order [6]. Hence, higher order derivatives do not affect color as observed by the human visual system. The Gaussian color model approximates the Hering basis for human color vision when taking the parameters $\lambda_0 \simeq 515$ nm and $\sigma_\lambda \simeq 55$ nm [2]. Again, this approximation is optimal in least square sense.

For an RGB camera, principle component analysis of all triplets results in a decomposition of the image independent of camera gains and dark-current. The principle components may be interpreted as the intensity of the underlying spectral distribution, and the first- and second-order derivative, describing the largest and one but largest variation in the distribution. Hence, the principal components of the RGB values denote the spectral derivatives as approximated by the camera sensor sensitivities.

Concluding, measurement of spatio-spectral energy implies probing the energy distribution with Gaussian apertures at a given observation scale. The human visual system measures the intensity, slope and curvature of the spectral energy distribution, at fixed λ_0 and fixed σ_λ. Hence, the spectral intensity and its first and second order derivatives, combined in the spatial derivatives up to a given order, describe the local structure of a color image.

4 Results

Geometrical invariants are obtained by combining the color invariants N_λ and $N_{\lambda\lambda}$ in the polynomial expressions proposed by Florack et al. [3]. For example, the first order spatial derivatives yields the edge detectors

$$N_{\lambda x}^2 + N_{\lambda y}^2 \quad \text{and} \quad N_{\lambda\lambda x}^2 + N_{\lambda\lambda y}^2 . \tag{14}$$

Figure 1a–c shows the result of applying the edge detector $\sqrt{N_{\lambda x}^2 + N_{\lambda y}^2}$ under different illuminants.

Color edges can be detected by examination of the directional derivatives in the color gradient direction [1], by solving for

$$N_{\lambda ww} = \frac{N_{\lambda y}^2 N_{\lambda yy} + 2N_{\lambda y}N_{\lambda x}N_{\lambda xy} + N_{\lambda x}^2 N_{\lambda xx}}{N_{\lambda x}^2 + N_{\lambda y}^2} = 0$$

$$N_{\lambda w} = \sqrt{N_{\lambda x}^2 + N_{\lambda y}^2} \geq \alpha$$

and similar for $N_{\lambda\lambda}$. Salient edges are determined by the value of α. An example is shown in Fig. 1d.

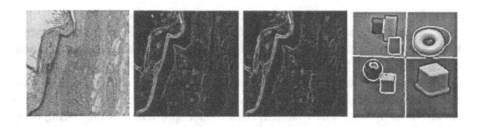

Fig. 1. Illumination invariant edges for epithelial tissue (a) visualized by transmission light microscopy. Edges $N_{\lambda w} = \sqrt{N_{\lambda x}{}^2 + N_{\lambda y}{}^2}$ are shown for (b) a white illumination (halogen 3400K), and (c) a reddish illumination (halogen 2450K). Despite the different illuminants, edge strength is comparable. Figure d shows zero crossing detection in an image of colored objects. In white the $N_{\lambda ww}$ crossings (bluish-yellow edges), in black the $N_{\lambda\lambda ww}$ crossings (reddish-green edges).

References

1. Cumani, A.: Edge detection in multispectral images. CVGIP: Graphical Models and Image Processing **53** (1991) 40–51
2. Dev, A., van den Boomgaard, R.: Color and scale: The spatial structure of color images, Technical report, ISIS institute, Department of Computer Science, University of Amsterdam, Amsterdam, The Netherlands (1999)
3. Florack, L.M.J., Romeny, B.M.tH., Koenderink, J.J., Viergever, M.A.: Cartesian differential invariants in scale-space. Journal of Mathematical Imaging and Vision **3** (1993) 327–348
4. Gershon, R., Jepson, D., Tsotsos, J.K.: Ambient illumination and the determination of material changes. J. Opt. Soc. Am. A **3** (1986) 1700–1707
5. Gevers, T., Smeulders, A.W.M.: Color based object recognition. Pat. Rec. **32** (1999) 453–464
6. Hering, E.: Outlines of a Theory of the Light Sense. Harvard University Press, Cambridge, MS (1964)
7. Judd, D.B., Wyszecki, G.: Color in Business, Science, and Industry. Wiley, New York, NY (1975)
8. Koenderink, J.J., van Doorn, A.J.: Receptive field families. Biol. Cybern. **63** (1990) 291–297
9. Koenderink, J.J., Kappers, A.: Color Space. Utrecht University, The Netherlands (1998)
10. Mielenz, K.D., Eckerle, K.L., Madden, R.P., Reader, J.: New reference spectrophotometer. Appl. Optics **12** (1973) 1630–1641
11. Olver, P., Sapiro, G., Tannenbaum, A.: Differential invariant signatures and flows in computer vision: A symmetry group approach. In: Geometry-Driven Diffusion in Computer Vision, ter Haar Romeny BM (ed). Kluwer Academic Publishers, Boston (1994) 255–306
12. Shafer, S.A.: Using color to separate reflection components. Color Res. Appl. **10** (1985) 210–218
13. Wyszecki, G., Stiles, W.S.: Color Science: Concepts and Methods, Quantitative Data and Formulae. Wiley, New York, NY (1982)

Scale Space Range Image Aspect Graph

Satoru MORITA

Utrecht University, Heidelberglaan 100, 3584 CX, Utrecht, NL
Yamaguchi University, Tokiwadai Ube 755 Japan

Abstract. This paper introduces a new approach for computing a hierarchical aspect graph of curved objects using multiple range images. Characteristic deformations occur in the neighborhood of a cusp point as viewpoint moves. We analyze the division types of viewpoint space in scale space in order to generate aspect graphs from a limited number of viewpoints. Moreover, the aspect graph can be automatically generated using an algorithm of the minimization criteria.

1 Introduction

Koenderink and van Doorn introduced the notion of aspect graphs for representing an object shape [KD]. An aspect is defined as a qualitatively distinct view of an object as seen from a set of connected viewpoints in the viewpoint space. Every viewpoint in each set gives a qualitatively similar projection of the object. In an aspect graph, nodes represent aspects and arcs denote visual events connecting two aspects. It is possible to compute the aspect graph by deriving the exact partition of viewpoint space from its geometric model for that of polyhedral objects[GC].Many researchers have shown an interest in visual events and boundary viewpoints for piecewise-curved objects [RI][PK].

A panel discussed the theme "Why Aspect Graphs Are Not (Yet) Practical for Computer Vision"[FA]. One issue raised by the panel is that aspect graph research has not included any notion of scale. As an object's complexity increases, the aspect number also increases. Therefore, this method can only be applied to simple objects, such as solids of revolution. If an object is complex, the size of its aspect graph is too big to match an object. By introducing the concept of scale, it is hoped that this large set of theoretical aspects can be reduced to a smaller set. From this viewpoint, Eggert has proposed the scale space aspect graph for polyhedra [EB]. These approaches address the case of a camera having finite resolution [SP][EB]. From the same viewpoint, we proposed a method to generate a hierarchical aspect graph using silhouettes of curved objects [MK]. The strict direction of the objects cannot be matched using only silhouettes, though objects can be matched quickly. Thus we proposed a method for generating a hierarchical aspect graph using multiple range data for curved objects.

2 Primitive techniques and overview of aspect analysis

The curvatures used here are defined as follows.

Suppose a parametric form of a surface $X(u,v) = (x(u,v), y(u,v), z(u,v))$. A tangential line at $X(u,v)$ is denoted by $t(u,v) = du X_u(u,v) + dv X_v(u,v)$.

The curvature at X along (du, dv) is defined as $\lambda(du, dv) = \frac{\delta_2(du,dv)}{\delta_1(du,dv)}$,

where $\delta_1(du, dv) = \begin{pmatrix} du & dv \end{pmatrix} \begin{pmatrix} X_u X_u & X_v X_u \\ X_v X_u & X_v X_v \end{pmatrix} \begin{pmatrix} du \\ dv \end{pmatrix}$ and

$$\delta_2(du, dv) = \begin{pmatrix} du & dv \end{pmatrix} \begin{pmatrix} X_{uu} n & X_{uv} n \\ X_{uv} n & X_{vv} n \end{pmatrix} \begin{pmatrix} du \\ dv \end{pmatrix}$$

$$X_u = \frac{\partial X}{\partial u}, X_v = \frac{\partial X}{\partial v}, X_{uu} = \frac{\partial^2 X}{\partial u^2}, X_{uv} = \frac{\partial^2 X}{\partial v \partial u}, X_{vv} = \frac{\partial^2 X}{\partial v^2}$$

With the directional vectors which maximize and minimize the curvature at the point p as $(u,v)=(\zeta_1,\eta_1)$ and (ζ_2,η_1), the maximum curvature κ_1, the minimum curvature κ_2, the mean curvature H, and the Gaussian curvature H are defined as:
$\kappa_1 = \lambda(\zeta_1,\eta_1), \kappa_2 = \lambda(\zeta_2,\eta_2), H = \frac{\kappa_1+\kappa_2}{2}$, and $K = \kappa_1\kappa_2$, respectively.

Characteristic contours which satisfy $H = \frac{\kappa_1+\kappa_2}{2} = 0$, and $K = \kappa_1\kappa_2 = 0$ are called H0 contours and K0 contours, respectively.

Scale-space filtering is a useful method for analyzing a signal qualitatively by managing the ambiguity of scale in an organized and natural way. In this section, we extend the scale-space filtering for 2-D contour to 3-D surface analysis. The Gaussian convolution to the surface ϕ is formulated by a diffusion equation:

$$\frac{\partial^2 \phi}{\partial u^2} + \frac{\partial^2 \phi}{\partial v^2} = \frac{1}{t}\frac{\partial \phi}{\partial t} \cdots (1)$$

where $\phi(u, v) = (x(u, v), y(u, v), z(u, v))$ is a parametric representation of a surface. This equation is approximated by the difference equation:

$$\phi(u, v, t + \Delta t) = \phi(u, v, t) + \Delta t \frac{\phi(u - \Delta u, v, t) - 2\phi(u, v, t) + \phi(u + \Delta u, v, t)}{\Delta u^2}$$

$$+ \Delta t \frac{\phi(u, v - \Delta v, t) - 2\phi(u, v, t) + \phi(u, v + \Delta v, t)}{\Delta v^2} \cdots (2)$$

Iterating (2), the curvature at each sample point converges to a constant.

Figure 1 shows the primitive causing the unique changes in the topologies of the zero-crossing surface, when the shape is smooth. Diagrams 1a and 2a in Figure 1 show the vertical section of the zero-crossing surface in which u coordinate has the constant values u1 and u2. and figure 1b and 2b of Figure 1 show the horizontal section of the zero-crossing surfaces in which scale t has the constant values t1 and t2. Diagrams 1a and 1b in Figure 1 show the changes occurring when a zero-crossing surface comes into contact with another surface. Diagrams 2a and 2b show the changes occurring when a zero-crossing surface comes into existence. Diagrams 1a and 1b in Figure 1 show the non-monotonous causes of scale-space[YP]. As the scale t decreases, the surface first opens in the top level, then closes in the next step, and later appears again.

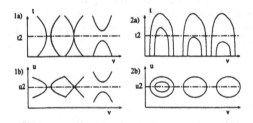

Fig. 1. The primitive causes topology changes of zero-crossing surfaces.

We generate a hierarchical aspect graph from orthographic projections obtained from a limited number of viewpoints. If the viewpoint space $(\alpha[0, 360], \theta[0, 360])$ is divided into pieces of size $(\frac{360}{n}, \frac{360}{n})$, then the number of sample viewpoints is $n/2 * n(n = 2, 4, 6, 8, 10...)$. The number of sample viewpoints is 36*18 (n=10) in this paper.

3 The Hierarchical Partition Method of a Viewpoint Space

3.1 Aspect Analysis of Occluding Contour

If the observed image is the same, the classification of the orthographic image does not change, as the differential geometric characters, which are the mean curvature and Gaussian curvature, do not change.

The orthographic image deforms in the following two cases. In the first case, a surface occluded by other surfaces appears. In the second case, a surface is occluded by the other surfaces. In these two cases the differential geometrical continuity isn't satisfied and occluding contours come into existence.

We analyze aspect changes in the neighborhood of cusp points where occluding contours occur. This is important in the case of describing an aspect, such as the contour topology which includes occluding contours. By convolving the depth image of the orthographic projection Gaussian, a unique deformation process occurs at this discontinuity point. The appearance of occluding contours has three prototypes [TH]:lips, beaks and swallows. We partition the viewpoint space using the unique events from the observation of limited viewpoints. The partitioning of the viewpoint is reliable because it is restricted by the unique events, where occluding contours occur.

3.2 Hierarchical events

Every viewpoint in a viewpoint space can be classified into two different types: a stable viewpoint or an accidental viewpoint. For stable viewpoints, there exists an open neighborhood of viewpoints that gives the same aspect of the object.

In partitioning viewpoint space into aspects, the boundary between two aspects is called an event. Each visual event type can be characterized by alterations in the feature configurations . As the number of processes increase, an aspect is partitioned into finer aspects. The deformation processes in a deformation number differ in the boundary between two scales. The boundary between two aspects and between two scales is called a hierarchical event. In order to generate a hierarchical aspect graph automatically from depth maps of limited observed viewpoints and scales, we must analyze the hierarchical and visual events. The number of deformation processes is the applied number of event.

The number of different hierarchical events is finite, and they depend on the difference in zero-crossing contour topology of scale-space images A hierarchical event occurs when the following occurs in scale-space images.

Type 1. A zero-crossing surface comes into contact with another surface.

Type 2. The singularity of two zero-crossing surfaces is at the same height.

Type 3. A zero-crossing surface disappears.

Figure 2(a)(b) shows three types of hierarchical events. a0 represents a zero-crossing surface. Lines of a0 illustrate the intersection of a zero-crossing surface, where the u coordinate is constant and the dotted lines of a0 represent the intersection of a zero-crossing surface, where the t coordinate is zero. a1, a2 and a3 are zero-crossing contours in the u, and v coordinates. The label a1 changes a3, as scale t decreases.

Type 1-a and 1-b show the difference of singularity heights. A and C are two stable views, and B is an accidental view. One zero-crossing surface is higher than the other in

A, but lower than the other zero-crossing surface in C, which means A and C differ in the order of deformation. B deforms in two places at once. A zero-crossing surface does not exist between the two surfaces in 1-a, but does in 1-b.

Type 2-a and 2-b show a zero-crossing surface which comes into contact with another contour in a scale-space image. Type 2-a shows two zero-crossing surfaces which are inscribed, and type 2-b shows two zero-crossing surfaces which are circumscribed. Since the topology of the zero-crossing surfaces are the same in the first frame a0 of type 2-a, the viewpoint space belongs to an aspect. However, in the next deformation process, a zero-crossing surface comes into contact with another surface, and a difference occurs. A and C are two stable views, and B is an accidental view. A zero-crossing surface contacts with another zero-crossing surface accidentally. B is the boundary of the two aspects A and C and the event.

Type 3-a and 3-b show a zero-crossing surface which disappears in a scale-space image. If the outline is a circle, it will never deform. As the surface is smooth, it does not deform without reaching the comparable process number. C1 and C2 are two stable views and B is the accidental view. The zero-crossing surface disappears in the viewpoint B.

Hierarchical events can be classified into these three events, depending on the properties of scale-space. If the projection depth image changes smoothly, then the zero-crossing surface also changes smoothly. These events are all considered in this paper. This discussion is based on the Morse theory[TH] studying the theoretical behavior of extrema and saddle points.

3.3 The Partition Types of a Viewpoint Space

The partition type and the changes of the partition type are limited by three hierarchical events. It is important to analyze the points in which the boundary lines of the viewpoint space intersect. Two hierarchical events occur in the intersection point at the same time. If Type 1-b and Type 2-a events in Figure 2(a)(b) occurs at the same time, then the two boundary lines dividing the viewing space intersect as in Figure 2(c) and Figure 3(a). If Type 1-a and Type 2-b events occur at the same time, then the two boundary lines dividing the viewing space intersect as in Figure 2(c) and Figure 3(a). a0 shows the zero-crossing surfaces of the nine viewpoints, such as (B1, B2) and (C1, C2). The lines inside of nine square frames of a0 are the intersections of zero-crossing surfaces, where the u coordinate is constant. The dotted lines inside of nine square frames of a0 are the intersections of zero-crossing surfaces, where the t coordinate is zero. The label a1 is the coarse level and a3 is the fine level and they represent the value of the scale t. The square frame of a0, a1, a2, and a3 represents the viewpoint space, which have nine viewpoints. The circle frame means that zero-crossing contours occurred in u and v coordinates. In this case, Type2-a and Type 1-b occurred, and the aspect of the viewpoint space is the same. In the scale a1, there is one viewpoint space. In the scale a2, the viewpoint space is divided into three, and the events (B2, C1), (B1, C2) and (A1, B2) occur. In the scale a3, the viewpoint space is divided into four, and the event (B2, B1) happens. The number of the partitions primitive is limited to 15 because the combinations of two events ,which we select from 6 hierarchical events. Each event is classified in more detail depending on whether the combinations of the zero-crossing surfaces are K0 or H0 surfaces. The viewpoint space is partitioned using the stable viewpoint and the neighboring viewpoints from the limited viewpoints.

Three hierarchical events happen in the intersection point at the same time. However, we don't use events where three types exist at one viewpoint and scale, because they seldom actually occur. A combination of more than three events is regarded as a sequential change of two hierarchical events. Thus, all visual events are considered.

4 Generating an Algorithm of Hierarchical Aspect Graphs

Our algorithm to generate an aspect graph can be outlined in the following steps, as figure 4 shows the flow chart of the algorithm

1. We observe an object in 36*18 viewpoints and detect the depth map of the orthographic projection using a laser range finder.

2. We filter in the limited resolutions for each depth map.

3. The depth map, after the filtering is divided into regions using the signs of the mean curvature and Gaussian curvature.

4. By detecting the topology changes of the K0 and H0 contours on the KH-image from the top level, the zero-crossing surfaces are inferred using KH-images of the limited resolution. Actually the changes of KH-images over scale are registered as sets of the primitive operator.

5. The topology changes of the K0 and H0 contours is recorded over scale. If the topology changes cannot be determined because of a limited number of resolutions examined, all deformation processes capable of being obtained from observed images are recorded.

6. The minimum process in the possible deformation processes without inconsisentcy in the neighboring viewpoints is selected. The inconsistency is found using the partition types of a viewpoint space.

The dividing map of viewpoint space observed using range sensor are showed in Figure 4. y axis is latitude, which is $\eta = 0° \sim 180°$, and x axis is longitude, which is $\zeta = 0° \sim 360°$ ((A)t=20, (B)t=90, (C)t=270).

We analyzed the division types of viewpoint space in the neighborhood of a cusp point in order to generate aspect graphs from a limited number of viewpoints. The aspect graph can be automatically generated using an algorithm of the minimization criteria.

References

[YP] A. L. Yuille and T. Poggio.: Scaling theorem for zero crossing .IEEE Trans. PAMI-8.1.pp. 15-25.(1986)

[FA] O. Faugeras, J. Mundy , N. Ahuja , C. Dyer .: Panel theme: Why aspect graphs are not (yet) practical for computer vision .CVGIP: Image Understanding .55.pp. 212-218.(1992)

[SP] I. Shimshoni and J. Ponce.: Finite resolution aspect graph of Polyhedral Objects .Proc. of the IEEE Workshop on Qualitative Vision..pp. 140-150.(1993)

[MK] S. Morita, T. Kawashima and Y. Aoki.: Generating Hierarchical Aspect Graph Based on Shilouette Contours .MVA'92-IAPR..pp. 149-152.(1992)

[GC] Z. Gigus, J. Canny and R. Seidel.: Efficiently Computing and Representing Aspect Graphs of Polyhedra Objects .IEEE Trans. PAMI-13..pp. 542-551.(1991)

[KD] J. J. Koenderink, A. J. van Doorn.: The Internal Representation of Solid Shapes with Respect to Vision .Biblogical Cybernetics.32.pp. 211-216.(1984)

[EB] D. W. Eggert, K. W. Bowyer, C. R. Dyer, H. I. Christensen and D. B. Goldgof.: The Scale Space Aspect Graph .IEEE trans. PAMI-14.2.pp. 1114-1130.(1993)

[PK] J. Ponce and D. J. Kriegman, "Computing exact aspect graphs of curved objects : parametric patches," UIUCDCS-R-90-1579, University of Illinois (1990)

[RI] J. H. Rieger.: The geometry of view space of opaque objects bounded by smooth surfaces .Artificial Intelligence.44.pp. 1-40.(1990)

[TH] R. Thom, "Structural Stability and Morphogenesis," W. A. Benjamin, Inc. (1975)

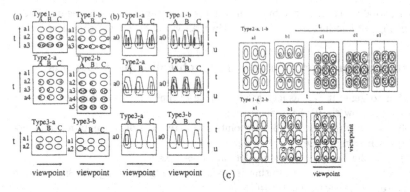

Fig. 2. Hierarchical events.(a) KH-image changes as viewpoint moves. (b)Zero-crossing surface changes as viewpoint moves. (c) KH-image changes as viewpoint moves.

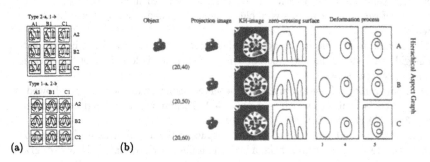

Fig. 3. (a)Zero-crossing surface changes as viewpoint moves. (b)Algorithm for generating hierarchical aspect graph.

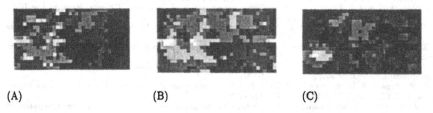

Fig. 4. The dividing maps of viewpoint space observed using range sensor are showed. y axis is latitude, which is $\eta = 0° \sim 180°$, and x axis is longitude, which is $\zeta = 0° \sim 360°$. ((A)t=20, (B)t=90, (C)t=270)

Hierarchical Non-rigid Density Object Analysis

Satoru MORITA

Utrecht University, Heidelberglaan 100, 3584 CX, Utrecht, NL
Faculty of engineering,Yamaguchi University Tokiwadai Ube 755 Japan

Abstract. This paper introduces a new approach for generating the hierarchical description of a non-rigid density object. Scale-space is useful for the hierarchical analysis. Process-grammar which describes the deformation process between a circle and the shape is proposed. We use these two approaches to track the deformation of a non-rigid density object. We extend 2D process-grammar to 3D density process-grammar. We analyze the event that the topology of zero-crossing surface of scale-space changes, as a density object changes smoothly. The analysis is useful to generate 3D density process-grammar from a limited number of observations. This method can be used for tracking a non-rigid object using MRI data.

1 Introduction

Scale-space[Wi1] is used to analyze signal sets and contours with several resolutions. 3D medical data is analyzed using scale-space to obtain the surface of the internal organs [VK]. On the other hand, many studies have been devoted to the analysis of motion in magnetic resonance images. The most frequently used method consists of reconstructing the motion by using a deformable model [TW][CC][MT]. The purpose is mainly to find the surface of a non-rigid shape.

We propose the hierarchical description of the internal structure for a medical non-rigid density object. We define a non-rigid density object as an object which includes the density and changes in the internal structure of density over time. In comparison with surface analysis using the deformable object and the statistical segmentation using scale-space, our purpose is not to analyze a surface, but to analyze the internal structure of a medical density object.

Koenderink and van Doorn introduced the notion of aspect graphs for representing a shape [KV]. An aspect is defined as a qualitatively distinct view of an object as seen from a set of connected viewpoints in the viewpoint space. We extend the concept of aspect graph to the concept of a non-rigid density object. In this paper, we define an aspect as a qualitatively distinct internal structure as a non-rigid density object changes in density. We extend the 2D process-grammar[LE] to 3D density process-grammar, in order to generate the description of a non-rigid density object. 2D process-grammar describes the deformation process of 2D contour between a circle and the shape. We define 3D density process-grammar as the deformation process between a flat density and the density. We use the scale-space filtering to generate 3D density process-grammar automatically. We analyze the events that the topology of zero-crossing surface changes as a density object changes smoothly. The analysis is useful to generate 3D density process-grammar from a limited number of observations.

2 3D Density Scale-space Filtering

3D density scale-space filtering can be used to analyze a density non-rigid object hierarchically.

Assuming that a mesh has a parametric form, then $f(u, v, w) = h(x(u, v, w), y(u, v, w), z(u, v, w))$ for the density value for the image coordinate $x(u, v, w), y(u, v, w), z(u, v, w)$ on the mesh coordinate (u, v, w). A point on the derived mesh is the result of the convolution $\phi(u, v, w, \sigma) = f(u, v, w) * g(u, v, w, \sigma)$. The mesh convolved Gaussian satisfies the following diffusion equation.

$$\frac{\partial^2 \phi}{\partial u^2} + \frac{\partial^2 \phi}{\partial v^2} + \frac{\partial^2 \phi}{\partial w^2} = \frac{1}{t} \frac{\partial \phi}{\partial t} \tag{1}$$

This equation can be approximated by the diffusion equation.

2.1 Hierarchical density analysis based on 3D density scale-space filtering

A mesh $\phi(u, v, w)$ is divided into elements using the positive and negative values of the Gaussian curvature K and mean curvature H.

The curvature used here is defined as follows. Assuming that a mesh has a parametric form, $X(u, v, w) = \phi(u, v, w)$.

The curvature at X along (du, dv, dw) is defined as $\lambda(du, dv, dw) = \frac{\delta_2(du, dv, dw)}{\delta_1(du, dv, dw)}$, where

$$\delta_1(du, dv, dw) = (\,du\ dv\ dw\,) \begin{pmatrix} X_u X_u & X_u X_v & X_u X_w \\ X_v X_u & X_v X_v & X_v X_w \\ X_w X_u & X_w X_v & X_w X_w \end{pmatrix} \begin{pmatrix} du \\ dv \\ dw \end{pmatrix}$$

$$\delta_2(du, dv, dw) = (\,du\ dv\ dw\,) \begin{pmatrix} X_{uu} & X_{uv} & X_{uw} \\ X_{vu} & X_{vv} & X_{vw} \\ X_{wu} & X_{wv} & X_{ww} \end{pmatrix} \begin{pmatrix} du \\ dv \\ dw \end{pmatrix}$$

$X_u = \frac{\partial X}{\partial u}, X_v = \frac{\partial X}{\partial u}$ $X_{uu} = \frac{\partial^2 X}{\partial u^2}, X_{vv} = \frac{\partial^2 X}{\partial v^2}, X_{uv} = \frac{\partial^2 X}{\partial u \partial v}$

With the directional vectors which maximize and minimize the curvature at the points p being defined as $(u, v, w) = (\eta_1, \zeta_1, \gamma_1)$ and $(\eta_2, \zeta_2, \gamma_2)$, then the maximum curvature κ_1, the minimum curvature κ_2, the mean curvature H, and the Gaussian curvature H are defined as:

$\kappa_1 = \lambda(\eta_1, \zeta_1, \gamma_1)$, $\kappa_2 = \lambda(\eta_2, \zeta_2, \gamma_2)$, $H = \frac{\kappa_1 + \kappa_2}{2}$, and $K = \kappa_1 \kappa_2$, respectively.

Characteristic surfaces which satisfy $H = \frac{\kappa_1 + \kappa_2}{2} = 0$ and $K = \kappa_1 \kappa_2 = 0$ are called H0

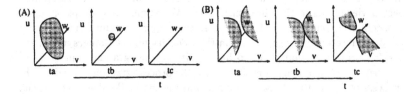

Fig. 1. The primitive causes topology changes of zero-crossing surfaces.

surfaces and K0 surfaces respectively. We divided the density into elements using positive and negative values of the Gaussian curvature K and the mean curvature H. This image is termed to a KH-image. Figure 1 shows the primitive causing the unique changes in the topologies of the zero-crossing surface, when a non-rigid density object changes smoothly. Figure 1(a) shows the changes occurring when a zero-crossing surface disappear. Figure 1(b) shows the changes occurring when a zero-crossing surface comes into contact with another surface.

3 Hierarchical Event of 3D Density Object Space

3.1 Hierarchical events

We describe the changes of aspects on the density object space. In partitioning the density object space into aspects, the boundary between two aspects is called an event. As the scale increase, an aspect is partitioned into finer aspects. The boundary between two aspects and between two scales is called a hierarchical event.

The number of different hierarchical events is finite, and they depend on the difference in zero-crossing surface topology of 3-D density scale-space. A hierarchical event occurs when the following three types occurs in 3-D density scale-space. In type 1, a zero-crossing surface comes into contact with another surface. In type 2, the singularity of two zero-crossing surfaces is at the same height. In type 3, a zero-crossing surface disappears. Figure 2 (a) (b) shows three types of hierarchical events. a0 represents a zero-crossing surface. Lines of a0 illustrate the intersection of a zero-crossing surface, where the u coordinate is constant and the dotted lines of a0 represent the intersection of a zero-crossing surface, where the t coordinate is zero. a1, a2 and a3 are zero-crossing contours in the u, and v coordinates. The label a1 changes a3, as scale t decreases.

Type 1-a and 1-b show the difference of singularity heights. A and C are two stable density objects, and B is an accidental density object. One zero-crossing surface is higher than the other in A, but lower than the other zero-crossing surface in C, which means A and C differ in the order of deformation.

Type 2-a and 2-b show a zero-crossing surface which comes into contact with another contour in a scale-space image. Type 2-a shows two zero-crossing surfaces which are inscribed, and type 2-b shows two zero-crossing surfaces which are circumscribed.

Type 3-a and 3-b show a zero-crossing surface which disappears in a scale-space image. If the outline is a circle, it will never deform. As the surface is smooth, it does not deform without reaching the comparable process number. The zero-crossing surface disappears in the density object B.

By studying the theoretical behavior of extrema and saddle points [TH], it is possible to repropriate blob events in four basic types: annihiration, merge, split, and creation[CB][LI]. These events are all considered in this paper.

3.2 The Partition Types of Density Object Space

Two hierarchical events occur in the intersection point at the same time. If Type 1-b and Type 2-a events in Figure 2(a)(b) occur at the same time, the two boundary lines dividing the viewing space intersect as in Figure 2(c). If Type 1-a and Type 2-b events occur at the same time, then the two boundary lines dividing the viewing space intersect as in Figure 4.

The number of partitions primitive is limited to 15 because of the combinations of two events ,which we select from 6 hierarchical events. Each event is classified in more detail depending on whether the combinations of the zero-crossing surfaces are K0 or H0 surfaces. The density object space is partitioned using the stable density object and the neighboring density objects from the limited observations.

We don't use events where three types exist at a voxel of one density object and scale, because they seldom actually occur. A combination of more than three events is regarded as a sequential change of two hierarchical events. Thus, all events are considered.

3.3 3D Density Process-grammar based on Scale-space Topological Analysis

We extend the process-grammar to analyze a 3D density object. All densities are transformed from the a flat density in the same way as 2D contours are transformed from the circle in 2D process-grammar. The four elements $M+, M-, m-, m+$ of 2D process-grammar are defined as the primitive elements. The primitive elements of 3D density process-grammar are defined using the four elements $G > 0 H > 0, G > 0 H < 0, G < 0 H > 0, G < 0 H < 0$. All smoothed densities are described using these primitive elements. Just as the relation between adjacent primitive elements is described by 2D process-grammar, so is the relation between adjacent primitive elements described by 3D density process-grammar. The process is described on 3D density process-grammar such as the process that the density is transformed from a flat density.

We generate the deformation process based on the analysis of sections 3.1 and 3.2 We described the density in terms of the K0 blobs only because the appearance and disappearance of the H0 surface depends on the appearance and disappearance of the K0 blob. We used 3D density scale-space filtering because the density becomes a flat density as scale t increases. When two H0 surfaces come into contact, the number of surfaces does not decrease monotonously as the scale t increases. The K0 and H0 surfaces contact without affecting the multi-resolution when K0 and H0 blob are very close. For this reason we did not use the contact of the K0 blob as the deformation process in this paper. This discussion is based on the morse theory[TH]. The K0 surface of 3D scale-space can be generated by linking the K0 blobs as scale t increases. After that, the 3D density process-grammar is generated by using 3D scale-space.

We then transformed the set of K0 blob to $\{Mm_1, Mm_2, \cdots, Mm_{a+b}\}$. If the order satisfies $t_i > t_j$, the order reflects the deformation process of 3D density process-grammar. Mm_i is represented as $(g(i), t_{Ai}, d_i)$. $g(i)$ is the value (x_i, y_i, z_i) on xyz coordinate. The positive and negative values of H are indicated by $+1$ and -1 using the last element d_i. The deformation of Mm_1 occurs first, followed by that of Mm_2, and subsequently that of Mm_{a+b}.

4 Matching using Geometric Invariance Features

An object can be matched to another object by using 3D density process-grammar hierachically. To relate one feature to a second feature, we use geometric invariance features. We consider the polyhedron that 3 surfaces contact at a vertex. If we assume the co-ordinate value of the polyhedron n_i, the invariance [RF] of this polyhedron is defined as:

$$I_1 = \frac{detN_{3561} \cdot detN_{3542}}{detN_{3564} \cdot detN_{3512}}, I_2 = \frac{detN_{3561} \cdot detN_{3142}}{detN_{3512} \cdot detN_{3642}}, I_3 = \frac{detN_{3564} \cdot detN_{5612}}{detN_{3561} \cdot detN_{3642}}$$

where $N_{ijkl} = [n_i, n_j, n_k, n_l]$ and which is a 4×4 matrix. We use 6 K0 blobs generated when the scale is high at first. We generate the polyhedron which 3 surfaces contact at a vertex using 6 blobs. After that, we calculate the geometric invariance obtained from the polyhedron. Thus, the K0 blobs for one scale-space corresponds to the K0 blobs of the another scale-space in turn. Subsequently, we evaluate the similarity of the objects by comparing two deformation process using the geometric invariance.

5 Medical Data Analysis

We show the algorithm for the moving heart analysis using the following steps:

- 1. A 3D density scale-space is generated from a density object (2.).
- 2. We transform the 3D scale-space to the 3D density process-grammar using topological analysis (3.).
- 3. We track the change in these points over time.
- 4. We repeat processes 1 through process 3.
- 5. We evaluate the similarity of the density objects hierachically using geometric invariance features of 3D density process-grammar (4.).

We used the sequential images of a moving heart obtained via MRI. The size of the image was 100*100*100. Figure 3(A)(B)(C) show KH-image (z=50), (y=50) and (x=50). Figure 3(D)(E)(F) show the zero-crossing surfaces (z=50), (y=50) and (x=50) that K0 blob which is $K > 0, H > 0$ are stacked. Figure 3(G) shows KH-image which is $K > 0H > 0$, when the iteration number is 8, 32, 128, and 496. KH-images on 4 sequential images of a heart are shown when the iteration number t is 270. We obtain the deformation process $\{Mm_1, Mm_2, Mm_3, Mm_4, Mm_5, Mm_6, Mm_7, Mm_8, Mm_9\}$ from the 4 hearts $s1, s2, s3, s4$. First, we calculate a geometric invariance using 6 kO blobs represended by $Mm1 - Mm6$. After that, we calculate the geometric invariances using the sets composed of 6 blobs in turn. The results are shown in Table 1. Figure 3(H) show K0 blobs, which is $K > 0H > 0$, obtained from 4 sequential images. The value of the geometric invariance of 4 sequential objects nearly equal, though the value changes slightly over time.

We analyzed the hierachical event that the topology of zero-crossing surface of scale-space changes, as a density object changes smoothly. The analysis is useful to generate 3D density process-grammar from limited number of observations. The tool is useful for analyzing a non-rigid density object hierachically.

	I1	I2	I3		I1	I2	I3
s1 Mm1-Mm6	1.060174	0.860518	2.143412	s1 Mm2-Mm7	1.103340	0.927175	3.230862
s1 Mm3-Mm8	1.116745	0.948955	3.939625	s1 Mm4-Mm9	1.114275	0.985219	4.950984
s2 Mm1-Mm6	1.060174	0.860518	2.143412	s2 Mm2-Mm7	1.103340	0.927175	3.230862
s2 Mm3-Mm8	1.116745	0.948955	3.939625	s2 Mm4-Mm9	1.114275	0.985219	4.950984
s3 Mm1-Mm6	1.062561	0.856981	2.143711	s3 Mm2-Mm7	1.113535	0.915727	3.256538
s3 Mm3-Mm8	1.127873	0.934663	3.927846	s3 Mm4-Mm9	1.114944	0.985621	4.999187
s4 Mm1-Mm6	1.062669	0.855323	2.136194	s4 Mm2-Mm7	1.111324	0.903093	3.049251
s4 Mm3-Mm8	1.129468	0.933878	3.954875	s4 Mm4-Mm9	1.114350	0.993526	5.314854

Table 1. Table 1. The geometric invariance obtained from 3D density scale-space is calculated for 4 sequential images of a moving heart.

References

[Wi1] A.P.Witkin, "Scale-space filtering," Proc. of IJCAI, pp.1019-1022, (1983)
[KV] J. J. Koenderink, A. J. van Doorn, "The Internal Representation of Solid Shapes with Respect to Vision," Bio. Cybernetics, 32, pp. 211-216, (1984)
[LE] M. Leyton, "A process-grammar for shape," Artiftial intelligence, 34, pp. 213-247, (1988)
[TH] R. Thom, "Structural Stability and Morphogenesis," W. A. Benjamin., Inc., (1975)
[RF] C. A. Rothewell etal. "Extracting projective structure from single perspective views of 3D point sets", Proc. of the 4th ICCV, pp. 573-582 (1993)

476

[VK] K. L. Vinken etal. "Probabilistic segmentation of partial volume voxels, Pattern Recognition Letters, pp. 477-484, (1994)

[LI] T. Lindeberg, "Scale-space theory in computer vision", Kluwer Academic, (1994)

[CB] O. Coulon etal., proc. of Scale-space 97 (1997)

[TW] D. Terzopoulos etal., "Constraints on deformable models: recovering 3D shapes and nonrigid motion," Artificial Intelligence, 36(1), pp. 91-123, (1988)

[CC] L. D. Cohen and I. Cohen, "Finite element methods for active contour models and balloons for 2-D and 3-D images," IEEE Trans. on Pattern Anal. and Machine Intelligence, Vol. 15 (11), (1993)

[MT] T. McInerney and D. Terzopoulos, Computerized Medical Imaging and Graphics, 19(10), pp. 69-83 (1995)

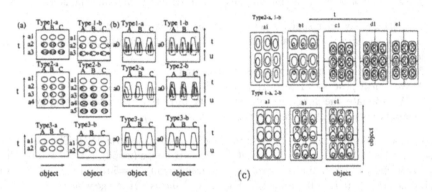

Fig. 2. Hierarchical events.(a)KH-image changes as a density object changes. (b) Zero-crossing surface changes as scale increases. (c)Partition changes of a density object space.

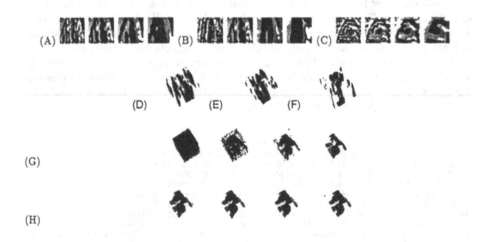

Fig. 3. (A)KH-images(z=50)(B)KH-image(y=50)(C)KH-image(x=50), The zero-crossing surfaces of $K > 0, H > 0$ (D)z = 50, (E)y = 50, (F)x = 50. (G)KH-images($K > 0 H > 0$)t= 8, 32, 128, 496. (H)The sequence KH-images of a heart($K > 0 H > 0$)t=270

Discrete Mean Curvature Flow

Atsushi Imiya[1] and Ulrich Eckhardt[2]

[1]Dept. of Information and Image Sciences, Chiba University
1-33 Yayoi-cho, Inage-ku, Chiba 263-8522, Japan
[2]Dept. of Applied Mathematics, University of Hamburg
Bundesstrasse 55, 20146 Hamburg, Germany

Abstract. In this paper, we introduce the linear scale-space theory for functions on finite graphs. This theory permits us to derive a discrete version of the mean curvature flow. This discrete version yields a deformation procedure for polyhedrons. The adjacent matrix and the degree matrix of a polyhedral graph describe the system equation of this polyhedral deformation. The spectral thepry of graphs derive the stability condition of the polyhedral deformation.

1   Introduction

Mean curvature flow has advantages for shape deformation and signal smoothing [1] [2]. The two-dimensional version of mean curvature flow is applied for shape analysis by means of the boundary curve and iso-level counter evolutions [2]. Bruckstein *et al.* in [3] proposed a discrete version of mean curvature flow for planar closed polygonal curves. Lindeberg [4] proposed a theory of discrete linear scale-space for the infinite lattice space. We derive the linear scale-space theory for finite graphs. This theory permits us to define the discrete linear scale-space theory for grids in finite regions with appropriate boundary conditions.

In this paper, we derive a theory of discrete mean curvature flow for the higher dimensional discrete objects that is applicable for open curves and open surfaces with appropriate boundary conditions. We define the diffusion procedure on graphs. This theory permits us to derive the scale-space theory for functions on graphs and a discrete version of the mean curvature flow. The discrete version of this equation extends the treatments in reference [3] for closed polygonal curves to the case of polyhedrons and closed and open spatial curves, and we also show that our extension contains results in reference [3].

2   Discrete Curvature Flow

A polyhedron consists from a triplet of graphs with indices on vertices which topologically have the same structure. These indices express the x, y, and z coordinates of vector of a polyhedron, respectively. Setting a finite set of three-dimensional vectors $\mathbf{V} = \{\boldsymbol{p}_i\}_{i=0}^{N-1}$ to be the vertices of a polyhedron, we define the neighbor of each vertex $\boldsymbol{p}_i$ as

$$\mathbf{V}(i) = \{\boldsymbol{p}_{i(1)}, \boldsymbol{p}_{i(2)}, \cdots, \boldsymbol{p}_{i(k)} \,|\, i(k+1) = i(1)\}, \tag{1}$$

such that $p_{i(j)}$ and $p_{i(j+1)}$ are connected with an edge.

Using vector p_i, we define the edge vector v_{ij} and the face vector f_{ij} as

$$v_{ij} = p_i - p_j, \; f_{ij} = (p_{i(j)} - p_i) \times (p_{i(j+1)} - p_i). \qquad (2)$$

The edge vector is the vector which connects a vertex and a vertex in its neighborhood. The face vector is the normal vector of a triangle defined by a vertex and a pair of vertices in its neighborhood which are connected by an edge. Furthermore, we define the following vectors,

$$v_i = \sum_{j=i(1)}^{i(k)} v_{ij}, \; f_i = \sum_{j=i(1)}^{i(k)} f_{ij}, \; t_{mn}(i) = (p_i - p_m) + (p_i - p_n), \qquad (3)$$

where p_m and p_n do not lie on the same face. We call v_i, f_i, and $t_{mn}(i)$ the vertex normal, the face normal, and a path normal of vertex p_i. The vertex normal is the sum of all edge vectors which are connected to a vertex. the face normal is the sum of all normal vectors of the triangles formed by a points and two points in the neighborhood which are connected by an edge. The path normal is the sum of a pair of edge vectors. From these notations, the following definitions are deived.

Definition 1 *The path normal and face normal vectors classify the geometric properties of a vertex in each neighborhood as follows.*

1. *For all m and n in $\mathbf{V}(i)$, if $t_{mn}(i)^\top f_i > 0$, then p_i is quasi-convex.*
2. *For all m and n in $\mathbf{V}(i)$, if $t_{mn}(i)^\top f_i = 0$, then p_i is flat.*
3. *For all m and n in $\mathbf{V}(i)$, if $t_{mn}(i)^\top f_i < 0$, then p_i is quasi-concave.*
4. *For all m and n in $\mathbf{V}(i)$, if $sgn t_{mn}(i)^\top f_i$ depends on m and n, then p_i is a saddle point.*

Since, in the nonlinear diffusion operation, the localization conditions are described as a function of the magnitude of the gradient of each point, we define the vector operations for the polyhedral vertices. We define the gradient on the polyhedral surfaces by

$$\nabla p_i = (p_{i(1)i}, \cdots, p_{i(k)i})^\top, \; p_{ji} = p_j - p_i. \qquad (4)$$

The total sum of the lengths of the gradients on a surface can be used as a total roughness measure of this surface [5]. Therefore, we define the mean curvature of vertex p_i using the lengths of the gradients on a polyhedron.

Definition 2 *Setting r_i to be the average of the elements of the gradient at vertex p_i, we define a discrete version of the mean curvature on each vertex as*

$$k_i = sgn(v_i^\top f_i) \cdot r_i, \; r_i = \frac{1}{i(k)} \sum_{j=1}^{i(k)} |p_{i(j)i}|. \qquad (5)$$

This definition is used to derive a discrete version of mean curvature flow

$$p_i(t+1) - p_i(t) = k_i(t) \times \text{sgn}(v_i^\top f_i) \frac{v_i(t)}{|v_i(t)|}, \tag{6}$$

where t is the step of the iterations, since $k_i(t)$ and $v_i(t)/|v_i(t)|$ are the discrete mean curvature of vertex v_i and the outer normal of vertex v_i, respectively. v_i is the outward vector if p_i is qusi-convex, otherwise v_i is the inward vector. Therefore, $\text{sgn}(v_i(t)^\top f_i(t))v_i(t)/|v_i(t)|$ determines the outward normal at vertex $p_i(t)$.

A linearization of eq. (6) is

$$p_i(t+1) - p_i(t) = \alpha v_i \tag{7}$$

for a nonzero constant α. Here, we deal with eq.(7), and show some topological and geometrical properties of this equation. Setting

$$X(t) = \big(p_0(t), p_1(t), \cdots, p_{N-1}(t)\big)^\top, \ X(0) = \big(p_0(0), p_1(0), \cdots, p_{N-1}(0)\big)^\top \tag{8}$$

for $p_i = (x_i^t, y_i^t, z_i^t)^\top$ and $p_i(0) = (x_i, y_i, z_i)^\top$, we have the matrix notation of eq. (7) as

$$X(t+1) - X(t) = \alpha(A - D)X(t), \tag{9}$$

where A and D are the adjacent matrix and the degree matrix of the graph derived by polyhedron V, respectively. Here, $X(t)$ and $(A - D)$ are a $N \times 3$ matrix function and a $N \times N$ matrix operator, respectively. Therefore, eq. (9) can be understood as the curvature flow on a geometric graph in three-dimensional Euclidean space. The method deforms polyhedrons, changing the positions of vertices of a polyhedron using a linear sum of the edge vectors.

Setting λ_i and w_i to be the eigenvalue of unit length and the corresponding eigenvector of L, since $L^* = L$, the unitary matrix $W = (w_0, w_1, \cdots, w_{N-1})$ diagonalizes L as $LW = WD$ for diagonal matrix $D = \text{diag}(\lambda_0, \lambda_1, \cdots, \lambda_{N-1})$. The singular decomposition of L such that $L = WDW^*$ yields equation

$$X(t+1) = W(I + \alpha D)^t W^* X(0), \tag{10}$$

for the computation of $X(\infty)$. We assume that the Laplacian matrix is normalized such that $|1 + \alpha\lambda_i| \leq 1$ for $i = 0, 1, \cdots, n-1$, since we deal with a shape in a finite region of $\mathbf{R}^3$. The geometric version of theorem 1 is as follows.

Theorem 1 Setting $\{w_0, w_1, \cdots, w_\gamma\}$ such that $1 \leq \gamma \leq n$ to be the eigenvectors of Laplaceian matrix of a polyhedron which hold the properties $|1 + \alpha\lambda_i| = 1$, for $i = 0, 1, \cdots, \gamma$, we have

$$\lim_{t \to \infty} X(t) = WW^* X(0), \tag{11}$$

for $W = (w_0, w_1, \cdots, w_\gamma)$.

Similar to the case of graphs, the process orthogonally projects each $e_i^\top X(0)$ to the space spanned by $\{w_i\}_{i=0}^\gamma$. Furthermore, this result shows that the analysis employed above is not restricted to a graph which represents polyhedrons in $\mathbf{R}^3$. Theorem 1 holds for any polytope in $\mathbf{R}^n$. In this case, $X(t)$ is a $N \times n$ matrix, each column vector of which indicates the position of a vertex vector.

3 Deformation as Signal Processing

3.1 Matrix and Topology

If a graph is regular, then the relation $D = cI$ is obvious, where c is a positive integer and I is the identity matrix, and matrices A and L have the same eigenvectors. Furthermore, if γ is an eigenvalue of A, then $(\gamma - c)$ is an eigenvalue of L. Therefore, in this section, our concern is regular graphs since the degree matrix of regular graphs is cI. We write down adjacent matrices which define topological properties of geometric objects such as a torus and a sphere. Setting $m \times m$ matrices F_m and C_m to be

$$F_m = \begin{pmatrix} 0 & 1 & 0 & 0 & \cdots & 1 \\ 1 & 0 & 1 & 0 & \cdots & 0 \\ \vdots & & 1 & 0 & 1 & \cdots & 0 \\ & & & & & \\ 0 & \cdots & 0 & 1 & 0 & 1 \\ 1 & \cdots & 0 & 0 & 1 & 0 \end{pmatrix}, \quad C_m = \begin{pmatrix} 1 & 1 & 0 & 0 & \cdots & 0 \\ 1 & 0 & 1 & 0 & \cdots & 0 \\ \vdots & & 1 & 0 & 1 & \cdots & 0 \\ & & & & & \\ 0 & \cdots & 0 & 1 & 0 & 1 \\ 0 & \cdots & 0 & 0 & 1 & 1 \end{pmatrix}, \tag{12}$$

where F_m is the circulant matrix of the order 2, matrices T and S,

$$T = F_m \otimes I + I \otimes F_n, \quad S = F_m \otimes I + I \otimes C_n, \tag{13}$$

define the systems of grids which are topologically equivalent to the torus and a sphere. These matrices are the adjacent matrices of the systems of grids, the degree of which are four. Therefore, setting

$$D_4 = \text{diag}(4, 4, \cdots, 4), \tag{14}$$

the matrices $L_T = T - D_4$ and $L_S = S - D_4$ are the discrete Laplacian operators with the circliar boundary condition $f(x, y) = f(x + 1, y)$ and $f(x, y) = f(x, y + 1)$, and the boundary condition $f'(0, 0, 1) = f'(0, 0, -1) = 0$, respectively [6,7]. A line graph, the adjacent matrix of which is expressed by C_m has a self-loop at each endpoint. It means this graph is not regular. However, this graph has similar properties as regular graphs. Therefore, it is possible to deal with a graph which is described by S as a regular graph with the degree four.

3.2 Eigenvectors of Deformations

The eigenvalues and eigenvectors of matrix F_m are

$$\lambda_k^m = 2 \cos 2\alpha_k^n, \quad u_k^m = (1, \omega^k, \cdots, \omega^{(m-1)k})^\top, \tag{15}$$

for $\alpha_k^m = k\pi/m$ and $\omega^m = 1$ such that $\omega \neq 1$. This means that the eigenvectors of matrix F_m define the discrete Fourier transform [7,8]. Furthermore, the eigenvalues and eigenvectors of C_n are

$$\sigma_k^n = 2 \cos 2\beta_k, \quad v_k^n = (\cos \beta_k^n, \cos 3\beta_k^n, \cdots, \cos(2n - 1)\beta_k^n)^\top, \tag{16}$$

for $\beta_k^n = k\pi/2n$. This means that the eigenvectors of C_n define the discrete cosine transform [7,8]. Moreover, for $i = 0, 1, \cdots, m-1$ and $j = 0, 1, \cdots, n-1$, we can adopt

$$x_{ij} = u_i^m \otimes u_j^n, \quad y_{ij} = u_i^m \otimes v_j^n \qquad (17)$$

as the discrete spherical harmonics on the torus and sphere, respectively, since T and S describe topological properties of systems of grids on the toruses and spheres, respectively, and vectors x_{ij} and y_{ij} are the eigenvectors of matrices T and S, respectively.

The DFT matrix U and the DCT (Discrete Cosine Transform) matrix V such that

$$U = \frac{1}{\sqrt{m}}(u_0, u_1, \cdots, u_{m-1}), \quad V = \frac{1}{\sqrt{n}}(v_0, v_1, \cdots, v_{n-1}) \qquad (18)$$

diagonalize F_m and C_n, respectively. Therefore, these structures of the transformation imply that properties of the discrete curvature flow are described using DFT and DCT if shapes are approximated using appropriate graphs, that is, if the grids for the computation of curvature flow are appropriately small, the linear approximation of the equations on polyhedrons are sufficient such that FFT (Fast Fourier Transform) and FCT (Fast Cosine Transform) achieve rapid numerical computation of the flow on polyhedrons.

3.3 Stability and Convergence

Using the properties of eigenvalues and eigenvectors of transformations, we obtain the following theorems for the stabilities and final shapes of polyhedrons, the connection of vertices of which are expressed by matrices T and S.

Theorem 2 *Two discrete systems*

$$X(t+1) = \{I + \alpha_T(T - D_4)\} X(t), \quad X(t+1) = \{I + \alpha_S(S - D_4)\} X(t), \quad (19)$$

are stable if α_T and α_S hold the inequalities such that,

$$0 \le \alpha_T \le \frac{1}{4}, \ 0 \le \alpha_S \le \frac{1}{3}, \qquad (20)$$

respectively.

Theorem 3 *The final shapes of polyhedrons whose topological connections of vertices are expressed using T and S are the centroids.*

Theorem 4 *The asymptotic shapes of polyhedrons whose topological connections of vertices are expressed using T and S are general ellipsoids [1] if t, the times of iterations, approaches to infinity.*

---

[1] Setting $\{\partial E_i\}_{i=1}^k$ to be a collection of the boundaies of ellipses, we call $\partial E = \partial E_1 \oplus \partial E_2 \oplus \cdots \oplus \partial E_k$ a general discrete ellipse, where $A \oplus B$ expresses the Minkowski addition of two point-sets A and B. Let A be a set of points in three-dimensional Euclidean space. If all slices of A which are perpendicular to $(1,0,0)^\top$, $(0,1,0)^\top$, and $(0,0,1)^\top$ are general ellipses, we call the set a general ellipse.

Since our definitions of the adjacent matrices are valid for nonsimple polyhedrons, these theorems imply that discrete mean curvature flow does not preserve the topologies of objects in the final and asymptotic forms. Similar properties were proven for planar polygons by Bruckstein et al. [3]. Our results agree with their results, if our objects are planar polygons. Furthermore, our results agree with that the results of Bruckstein et al. if planar polygons are valid also for both simple and nonsimple spatial polygons. For the proofs of these theorems see reference [9].

4 Conclusions

We derived a discrete approximation of curvature flow and showed that it has relations with graph theory. The graph theory description of the problem shows the mechanical aspects of the discrete curvature flow, that is, the graph theory treatment combines a theory of linear approximation of the curvature flow and numerical analysis. We also showed that a polyhedral approximation of a surface is described by a system of grids with the degree four, if we approximate a surface using two parameters. This approximation implies that properties of the discrete curvature flow are described using DFT (Discrete Fourier Transform) and DCT (Discrete Cosine Transform) since the eigenvectors of adjacent matrices of these grids define DFT and DCT matrices.

References

1. Huisken, G.: Flow by mean curvature of convex surface into sphere, Journal of Differential Geometry, Vol.20, pp.237-266, 1984.
2. Sethian, J.A.:*Level Set Methods: Evolving Interfaces in Geometry Fluid Mechanics, Computer Vision, and Material Science.* Cambridge University Press, Cambridge, 1996.
3. Bruckstein, A.M., Shapiro, G., Shaked, D.: Evolution of planar polygons, Journal of Pattern Recognition and Artificial Intelligence, Vol.9, pp.991-1014, 1995.
4. Lindeberg, T.:*Scale-Space Theory,* Kluwer Academic Publishers, Dordercht, 1994.
5. Rippa, S.:Minimal roughness property of the Delaunay triangulation, Computer Aided Geometric Design, Vol. 7, pp.489-497, 1990.
6. Collatz, L., Sinogowitz, U.: Spektren sndicher Grafen, Abhandlungen aus dem Mathematischen Seminar der Universtaet Hamburg, Band 21, pp.63-77, 1957.
7. Cvetković, M.D., Doob, M, Sachs, H.: *Spectra of Graphs*, Academic Press: New York, 1980.
8. Huppert, B.: *Angewandte Lineare Algebra*, Walter de Gruyter, Berlin, 1990.
9. Imiya, A., Eckhardt, U.: Discrete mean curvature flows:Analysis and computation, Technical Report of IEICE, PRMU98-1, 1998.

An Adaptive Local Smoothing
for Contour Figure Approximation

Hidekata Hontani[1] and Koichiro Deguchi[2]

[1] University of Tokyo, Hongo, Bunkyo, Tokyo, 113-8656 JAPAN
honn@meip7.t.u-tokyo.ac.jp
[2] Tohoku University, Sendai, Miyagi, 980-8579 JAPAN
kodeg@fractal.is.tohoku.ac.jp

Abstract. We propose a method for contour figure approximation which does not assume the shape of primitives for contours. By smoothing out only local details by curvature flow process, a given contour figure is approximated. The amount of smoothing is determined adaptively based on the sizes of the local details. To detect local details and to determine the amount of the local smoothing, the method uses the technique of the scale space analysis. Experimental results show that this approximation method has preferable properties for contour figure recognition, e.g. only finite number of approximations are obtained from a given contour figure.

1 Introduction

Describing global shapes of a contour figure is essential for contour figure recognition. To describe global shape of a given contour is to approximate a contour figure. A contour can be approximated by replacing local details with simple shape primitives. For example, a line segment approximation replaces small shape details with line segments. Many approximation methods of a contour figure have been proposed, and almost of which assume the shape of the replacing primitives. As the result, those methods often fail to describe global shape of a given contour. For example, a line segment approximation fails to approximate a round circular contour.

We propose an approximation method which do not assume primitive shapes. The method approximates a given contour by smoothing out only local details. To detect local details and to determine the amount of the local smoothing adaptively, we use a smoothing process which is known as curvature flow. The curvature flow is one of the smoothing processes of a contour which has a *scale* parameter. As the scale increases, the contour is more smoothed, and the curvature of the contour becomes constant. We define a *shape component* on a given contour with inflection points of the curvature. As the scale increases, shape components on the given contour disappear next by next. The *size* of each shape component is defined as the scale at which the shape component disappears. Shape components of small sizes correspond to local details and large ones correspond to global shapes[1].

Our method, first, smoothes a given contour figure, and obtains a finger print pattern of curvature inflection points in the scale space. Then, referring to the finger print pattern, shape components smaller than a given scale are detected. This scale is called the *base scale* in this paper. Finally, the given contour figure is approximated by smoothing only smaller shape components. The amount of the smoothing is determined adaptively based on the size of each shape component. As shown in later, even if the base scale is changed continuously, this method produces only a finite number of approximations from a given contour. It is also shown that the approximations obtained from an approximated contour figure are included in the approximations obtained from the original contour figure.

2 Smoothing of Contour Figure

In order to detect shape components on a given contour, we use a smoothing process which is known as the curvature flow. Let us consider a contour represented as $C(u) = (x(u), y(u))$ where u is a position parameter along the contour. From this contour $C(u)$, smoothed contours $F(u, t)$ are obtained by solving next equations.

$$\begin{cases} F(u, 0) = C(u), \\ \partial F(u, t)/\partial t = -\kappa N, \end{cases} \tag{1}$$

where κ is the curvature, and N is the unit outward normal vector of $F(u, t)$. The parameter $t(\geq 0)$ is called the *scale parameter*. We assume that $C(u)$ is a simple, closed, and piecewise C^1 plane curve. As t increases, the contour becomes more smoothed. This smoothing process has preferable properties for our purpose as followings[2].

- Increasing t generates no new curvature inflection point.
- An inflection point disappears only when it meets with another inflection point.
- Any contour converges to a round circle, then to a point, and disappears when t becomes $A/2\pi$ where A is the area of the given original contour.

An example of a set of $F(u, t)$ is shown in Fig.1(left). As t increases, the shape of the contour becomes close to a round circle.

To obtain smoothed contours $F(u, t)$, the level set method[3] or the Gaussian filtering[4] is available. We employ the latter method because, in the proposed method, every point on a given contour is traced through the smoothing process.

3 Adaptive Local Smoothing for Approximation

As described, any contour figure converges to a round circle in the smoothing process. This means that as the scale t increases, the curvature of the smoothed contour becomes more even and constant. When we plot u-κ graph at every scale, the graph becomes even and flat as the scale increases.

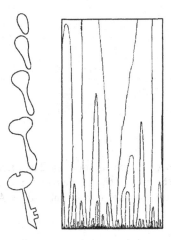

Fig. 1. Left: An example of smoothed contours. The total length of the given contour is 540, and $t = 0$, 100, 500, 900, and 1300 respectively from bottom to top. Right: An example of a finger print pattern of inflection points.

We define a shape component of a contour figure with inflection points of the curvature. An inflection point of the curvature is defined as a point between the concave part and the convex part of the u-κ graph of the contour figure. As the scale t increases, the number of the inflection points decreases, and the u-κ graph becomes flat. Increasing t, no new inflection point is generated, and inflection points disappear only when two or more inflection points meet together. We define a shape component as a part of a given contour between two inflection points which meet together when they disappear. We also define the size of the shape component as the scale at which the two inflection points meet and disappear.

In general, an original contour figure has many shape components of various sizes. In the smoothing process, as the scale t increases, shape components disappear next by next, and finally, all shape components disappear to become a round circle.

Our method approximates a given contour figure by smoothing out only small shape components. The amount of smoothing for each shape component is determined adaptively based on the size of the components. In order to detect shape components and their sizes of a given contour, we use the technique of a scale space analysis.

When we plot the inflection points in the scale space, we obtain so-called finger print pattern. Figure 1 shows an example of the finger print pattern of inflection points. Here, the scale space is a space of the original position u and the scale t. Every curve of the finger print pattern closes upward as shown in Fig.1. In the scale space, each area closed by each curve of the finger print pattern corresponds to a shape component. Referring to the height of each area, we detect the size of each shape component.

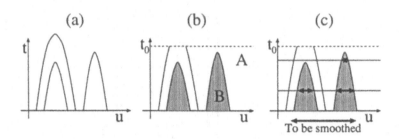

Fig. 2. The proposed approximation method. (a)The finger print pattern of inflection points. (b) Area B shows the area of the shape components whose scale is smaller than t_0. (c) At each scale, the area on the contour showed by Area B is smoothed.

We approximate a given contour figure by smoothing out shape components whose sizes are smaller than a given scale t_0. We call this scale t_0 as base scale. The amount of local smoothing is determined adaptively based on the size of each shape component. Because the shape components larger than t_0 remain as it is on the original figure, the results may still contain small notches belong to larger shape components. The algorithm is as followings.

1. Obtain the finger print pattern of a given contour on a scale space with an axis of original arc length u and the scale value t. See Fig.2(a).
2. Set the base scale t_0, and draw a line $t = t_0$ on the scale space.
3. Divide the scale space into areas A and B with the boundary of the inflection points pattern, where the area A includes the line $t = t_0$, and the area B does not. See Fig.2(b).
4. Smooth only shape components of the given contour which are smaller than t_0, that is, obtain a contour $H(s, t_0)$ which satisfies (2). See Fig.2(c).

$$\begin{cases} H(s,0) = C(s), \\ \partial H(s,t)/\partial t = 0 \quad (\text{ if } (s,t) \in \text{area A}), \\ \partial H(s,t)/\partial t = \kappa N \text{ (if } (s,t) \in \text{area B}). \end{cases} \quad (2)$$

It should be noted that, by changing the base scale t_0 continuously, we have only a finite number of approximations by this process. This is because the shape of $H(s, t_0)$ will change only when t_0 crosses over some closing point of inflection pattern. We will show some preferable properties of this approximation method with experimental results in the next section.

4   Experimental Results of Approximations

Figure 3(A) and (B) show approximations obtained from two contours of key silhouettes, respectively. As just described in previous section, by changing the base scale t_0, we obtain only finite number of approximated contours from a given contour. Fig.3 shows all approximated contours obtained from the original

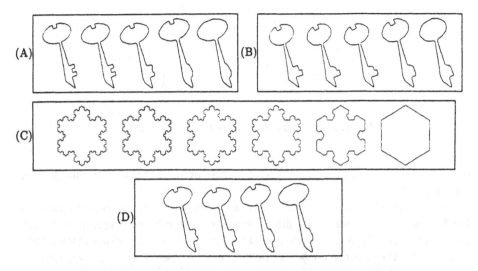

Fig. 3. Results of proposed approximation method for key silhouette contours. In each box, the left one is the original contour. All approximated results obtained from the originals are shown in this figure. Contours in box(D) shows approximations obtained from the approximated contour shown in box(A).

ones. Two keys shown in Fig.3 are different only at local shapes of their head parts. The approximations of the two keys with large base scales t_0 have similar shapes because only head parts of them are smoothed adaptively.

Figure 3(C) shows another experimental result. From a given snow-flake type contour, 6 approximations were obtained. Every approximation characterizes the global shape of a given contour at their respective level. A series of approximations obtained from a given contour is a kind of hierarchical shape description of the contour.

Figure 3(D) shows approximations of an approximated contour. The series of approximations of an approximated contour in (A) is entirely included in the series of approximations of the original contour figure. This property of inclusion is important for discriminating the similarities of the shape of contour figures.

As shown in Fig.3, in the series of approximations of a given contour, some parts change their shapes several times, but some parts do not. In order to construct a hierarchical description for each part of a given contour, we split the approximated contours at corner points.

A corner point on a contour figure is a point at which the absolute value of the curvature is locally maximal. In the smoothing process, as the scale t increases, the number of corner points decreases, and no new corner point is generated. In order to split the approximated contours appropriately, we split the approximated contours at corner points which do not disappear in the smoothing process until the largest shape component disappears. We call such corner points as dominant corner points[5]. By splitting the approximated contours at

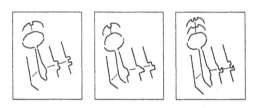

Fig. 4. Hierarchical descriptions of key silhouettes

dominant corner points, we construct a hierarchical description for each part of a given contour.

The obtained hierarchical descriptions of three key contours are shown in Fig.4. Each contour was split into five parts at dominant corner points, and hierarchical description of each part was constructed. This description shows clearly that these three contours have similar shapes from a global point of view, and that the shapes of hollow parts and the head parts are different.

5 Conclusion

In this paper, we propose a method of contour figure approximation, which smoothes out only small shape components and remains large shape clearly. The amount of smoothing for detail shape components are determined adaptively based on the scale space analysis.

This method has following properties: First, only a finite number of approximated contours which characterize the hierarchical structure of the original contour are obtained. Next, a series of approximations of an approximated contour is entirely included in the series of approximations of the original contour. This property of inclusion is important for discriminating the similarities of the shape of contour figures. These properties promise a step of preferable recognition method for contour figures.

References

1. Koichiro Deguchi and Hidekata Hontani. Multiscale Contour Approximation Based on Scale Space Analysis with A Stable Gaussian Smoothing. In *2nd International Workshop on Visual Form, Capri, Italy*, pages 139–148, 1994.
2. Matthew A.Grayson. The Heat Equation Shrinks Embedded Plane Curves To Round Points. *J.Differential Geometry*, 26:285–314, 1987.
3. James A. Sethian. *Level Set Methods : Evolving interfaces in geometry, Fluid Mechanics, Computer Vision, and Material Science*. Cambridge University Press, 1996.
4. Farzin Mokhtarian and Alan K.Mackworth. A Theory of Multiscale, Curvature-Based Shape Representation for Planar Curves. *IEEE Transactions on Pattern Analysis and Machine Intelligence*, 14(8):789–805, 8 1992.
5. Anothai Rattarangsi and Roland T. Chin. Scale-Based Detection of Corners of Planar Curves. *IEEE Transactions on Pattern Analysis and Machine Intelligence*, 14(4):430–449, Apr. 1992.

Negative Results for Multilevel Preconditioners in Image Deblurring

C. R. Vogel

Department of Mathematical Sciences
Montana State University
Bozeman, MT 59717-0240 USA

Abstract. A one-dimensional deconvolution problem is discretized and certain multilevel preconditioned iterative methods are applied to solve the resulting linear system. The numerical results suggest that multilevel multiplicative preconditioners may have no advantage over two-level multiplicative preconditioners. In fact, in the numerical experiments they perform *worse* than comparable two-level preconditioners.

1   Introduction

In image deblurring, the goal is to estimate the true image u_{true} from noisy, blurred data
$$z(x) = \int k(x - y)\, u_{true}(y)\, dy + \eta(x). \tag{1}$$

Here η represents noise in the recorded data, and the convolution kernel function k, which is called the point spread function in this application, is known. Since deconvolution is unstable with respect to perturbations in the data, regularization (i.e., stabilization which retains certain desired features of the true solution) must be applied. To a discretized version of the model equation (1), $\mathbf{z} = K\mathbf{u}_{true} + \eta$, we apply standard (zero order) Tikhonov regularization, i.e., we minimize
$$T_\alpha(\mathbf{u}) = ||K\mathbf{u} - \mathbf{z}||^2 + \alpha ||\mathbf{u}||^2, \qquad \alpha > 0. \tag{2}$$

The α is the regularization parameter. The resulting minimizer $\mathbf{u}_\alpha$ solves the symmetric, positive definite (SPD) linear system
$$A\mathbf{u} = \mathbf{b}, \qquad A = K^*K + \alpha I, \tag{3}$$

with $\mathbf{b} = K^*\mathbf{z}$. The superscript "$*$" denotes matrix conjugate transpose.

The system (3) is often quite large. For example, $n = 256^2 = 65{,}536$ unknowns arise from two-dimensional image data recorded on a 256×256 pixel array. For real-time imaging applications, it is necessary to solve these systems very quickly. Due to these size and time constraints, iterative methods are required. Since the coefficient matrix A in (3) is SPD, the conjugate gradient (CG) method is appropriate. A tends to be highly ill-conditioned, so preconditioning is needed to increase the convergence rate. (It should be noted that CG can be applied to the unregularized system, and the iteration count becomes the regularization parameter. See for example [4] for details. We will not take this approach here.) Convolution integral operators typically lead to matrices K with Toeplitz structure (see [2]). Circulant preconditioners [7, 2, 3] have proven to be highly effective for large Toeplitz systems. Standard multigrid methods have also been implemented (see for example [1]), but their utility seems limited by the inability to find a good "smoother", i.e., an iterative scheme which quickly damps high frequency components of solutions on fine grids.

It is well-known that wavelet multilevel decompositions tend to "sparsify" the matrices which arise in the discretization of integral operators. The task which remains is to efficiently solve the transformed system. Rieder [6] showed that fairly standard block iterative schemes (e.g., Jacobi and Gauss-Seidel iterations) are effective. (The correspondence between block index and grid level makes these methods "multilevel".) Hanke and Vogel [5, 8] extended Rieder's results to two-level preconditioners. Their analysis showed that multiplicative (i.e., Gauss-Seidel-like) preconditioners are generally far superior to additive (Jacobi-like) preconditioners in terms of convergence properties. In particular, they obtained the bounds on the condition numbers,

$$\text{cond}(C_{add}^{-1}A) \le b_1\,\alpha^{-2} \quad \text{as} \quad \alpha \to 0, \tag{4}$$

$$\text{cond}(C_{mult}^{-1}A) \le b_2\,\alpha^{-1} \quad \text{as} \quad \alpha \to 0, \tag{5}$$

where C_{add} and C_{mult} denote the additive and multiplicative preconditioning matrices, respectively. They also presented numerical results indicating that these bounds were sharp.

In addition to rapid convergence, these two-level schemes offer other advantages. Toeplitz structure is not required for efficient implementation. Essentially all that is needed is a means of computing matrix-vector products Av and a means of computing coarse-grid projections of vectors. See [8] for details. A disadvantage in certain situations is the need to invert the "coarse-grid representation" of the matrix A, which is the A_{11} in equation (8) below. The constants b_i in (4)-(5) depend on how well the integral operator is represented on the coarse grid. If α is relatively small, then the b_i's also must be relatively small to maintain rapid convergence. This typically means that A_{11} must be relatively large, and hence, expensive to invert.

The cost of inverting relatively large coarse-grid representation matrices A_{11} in the two-level case motivated our interest in multilevel schemes. We conducted a preliminary numerical study which suggested that, at least with obvious implementations, multilevel schemes offer *no* advantage over two-level schemes. In the final section, we present the test problem used in this study. This is preceded by a brief sketch of multilevel iterative methods.

2 Multilevel Decomposition and Iterative Schemes

Let the columns of V comprise the discrete Haar wavelet basis for $\mathbf{R}^n$, $n = 2^p$, normalized so that $V^*V = I$. Note that the discrete Haar wavelet vectors are orthogonal with respect to the usual Euclidean inner product, so orthonormality can be achieved simply by rescaling these vectors. The system (3) can be transformed to

$$\bar{A}\mathbf{x} = \bar{b}, \tag{6}$$

where

$$\bar{A} = V^*AV, \quad \mathbf{u} = V\mathbf{x}, \quad \bar{b} = V^*\mathbf{b}. \tag{7}$$

Partition the wavelet transformed matrix $\bar{A}$ into blocks A_{ij}, $1 \le i, j \le m$,

$$\bar{A} = \begin{bmatrix} A_{11} & A_{12} & \dots & A_{1m} \\ A_{21} & A_{22} & \dots & A_{2m} \\ \vdots & & \ddots & \vdots \\ A_{m1} & A_{m2} & \dots & A_{mm} \end{bmatrix}. \tag{8}$$

Multilevel iterative methods can be derived from a natural splitting of these blocks, i.e.,

$$\bar{A} = L + D + U, \tag{9}$$

where U consists of the upper triangular blocks $A_{ij}, j > i$, D consists of the diagonal blocks A_{ii}, and $L = U^*$. For instance, to derive a multilevel additive Jacobi iteration to solve (3), take an initial guess $\mathbf{u}^0$, set $\mathbf{x}^0 = V^*\mathbf{u}^0$, iterate

$$\mathbf{x}^{\nu+1} = D^{-1}(\bar{b} - (L+U)\mathbf{x}^\nu), \quad \nu = 0, 1, \dots,$$

and then back-transform via (7) to obtain an approximate solution to the original system (3). To derive the additive Schwarz iteration presented by Rieder in [6], replace the A_{mm} block in the block diagonal matrix D by αI, where I is the identity matrix of the appropriate size.

Similarly, one can derive multilevel Jacobi and additive Schwarz preconditioners. To apply such a Jacobi preconditioner to a vector $\mathbf{r} \in R^n$, one first applies the Haar wavelet transform to this vector, obtaining $\bar{\mathbf{r}} = V^*\mathbf{r}$. One then computes $\mathbf{x} = D^{-1}\bar{\mathbf{r}}$, and then back-transforms via (7) to get

$$\mathbf{u} = VD^{-1}V^*\mathbf{r} = C_J^{-1}\mathbf{r}.$$

The matrix $C_J = VDV^*$ is the multilevel Jacobi preconditioning matrix. To derive a multilevel additive Schwarz preconditioner, one again replaces the A_{mm} block in D by αI.

These Jacobi/additive Schwarz iterative methods neglect off-diagonal terms in the block decomposition (8). Incorporating these off-diagonal terms leads to multiplicative iterative methods. Perhaps the simplest example is multilevel Gauss-Seidel iteration, which can be expressed as $\mathbf{u}^\nu = V\mathbf{x}^\nu$, where $\mathbf{x}^\nu$ is obtained from

$$\mathbf{x}^{\nu+1} = (L+D)^{-1}(\bar{b} - U\mathbf{x}^\nu). \tag{10}$$

A multilevel multiplicative Schwarz iteration is obtained by again replacing the A_{mm} block of D by αI.

To obtain *symmetric* Gauss-Seidel/multiplicative Schwarz iterations, follow (10) by

$$\mathbf{x}^{\nu+2} = (D + U)^{-1}(\bar{b} - L\mathbf{x}^{\nu+1}). \tag{11}$$

To obtain the action of a multilevel symmetric Gauss-Seidel preconditioner on a vector $\mathbf{r}$, replace $\bar{b}$ in (10)-(11) by $\bar{r} = V^*\mathbf{r}$, set $\mathbf{x}^\nu = 0$, and then back-transform via (7) to obtain

$$\begin{aligned} C_{SGS}^{-1}\mathbf{r} &= V(D + U)^{-1}(V^*\mathbf{r} - L(L + D)^{-1}V^*\mathbf{r}) \\ &= V(D + U)^{-1}D(L + D)^{-1}V^*\mathbf{r}. \end{aligned} \tag{12}$$

Consequently, the symmetric Gauss-Seidel preconditioning matrix is

$$C_{SGS} = V(L + D)D^{-1}(D + U)V^*. \tag{13}$$

Once again replacing the A_{mm} block in D by αI yields a corresponding multilevel symmetric multiplicative Schwarz preconditioner (SMS) denoted C_{SMS}.

3 Numerical Results

A symmetric Toeplitz matrix $K = h \times \texttt{toeplitz}(\mathbf{k})$ was generated from a discretization $\mathbf{k} = (k(x_1), \ldots, k(x_n))$ of the Gaussian kernel function

$$k(x) = \frac{\exp(-x^2/\sigma^2)}{\sqrt{2\pi\sigma^2}}, \quad 0 \le x \le 1, \tag{14}$$

Here $h = 1/n$ and $x_i = (i - 1)h$, $i = 1, \ldots, n$. We selected the kernel width parameter $\sigma = 0.05$ and the number of grid points $n = 2^7 = 128$. The $n \times n$ matrix K is extremely ill-conditioned, having eigenvalues which decay to zero like $\exp(-\sigma^2 j^2)$ for large j. The matrix $A = K^*K + \alpha I$ was computed with regularization parameter $\alpha = 10^{-3}$. The distribution of the eigenvalues of A is shown in the upper left subplot of Fig. 1. From this distribution, it can be seen that the eigencomponents corresponding to roughly the smallest 110 eigenvalues of K have been filtered out by the regularization. The value of the regularization parameter is nearly optimal for error-contaminated data whose signal-to-noise ratio is 100.

We computed several two- and three-level SMS preconditioners for the system (3). The notation $C_{SMS}(r)$ denotes the two-level ($m = 2$ in equation (8)) SMS preconditioner with the "coarse grid" block A_{11} of size $r \times r$. To obtain $C_{SMS}(r)$ the matrix A is transformed and partitioned into 2×2 blocks, cf. (8). The $(n - r) \times (n - r)$ submatrix A_{22} is replaced by αI_{n-r}, the splitting (9) is applied, and the right-hand-side of (13) is computed. The eigenvalues of the matrix products $C_{SMS}(r)^{-1} A$ were computed for coarse grid block sizes $r = 16$ and $r = 32$. The distributions of these eigenvalues are displayed in the upper right and lower left subplots of Fig. 1. The reduced relative spread and clustering of these eigenvalues ensures rapid CG convergence. Recall the eigenvalue relative spread can be quantified by the condition number, which is the ratio of the largest to the smallest eigenvalue. With course grid block size $r = 16$, the condition number of $C_{SMS}(r)^{-1}A$ is 48.419, while for block size $r = 32$, the corresponding condition number is 1.4244. As one might expect, doubling the size of the coarse grid block A_{11} substantially decreased the condition number. In contrast, the condition number of the matrix A (without preconditioning) is nearly 1000.

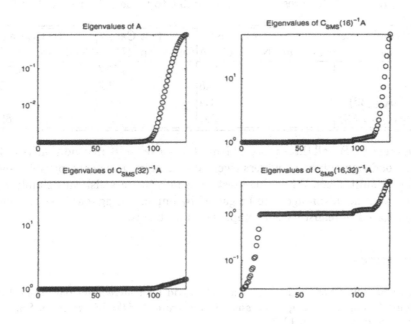

Fig. 1. *Eigenvalue distributions for various multilevel symmetric multiplicative Schwarz preconditioned systems.*

Let $C_{SMS}(r, s)$ denote the three-level multiplicative Schwarz preconditioner whose coarse grid block A_{11} in (8) has size $r \times r$ and whose second diagonal block A_{22} has size $(s - r) \times (s - r)$. The third diagonal block A_{33} is replaced by αI_{n-s}. With $r = 16$ and $s = 32$, the distribution of the eigenvalues of $C_{SMS}(r, s)^{-1}A$ is shown in the lower right subplot of Fig. 1. The corresponding condition number is 200.85. This is substantially worse than the result for the two-level preconditioner with coarse grid block size 32×32. What is surprising is that this is worse than the result for the two-level preconditioner with coarse grid block size 16×16. This comes in spite of the fact that much more work is required to apply $C_{SMS}(16, 32)^{-1}$ than to apply $C_{SMS}(16)^{-1}$.

The condition numbers for the various matrix products $C^{-1}A$ in the example presented above are summarized in column 2 (Test Case 1) of the table below. The I in column 1 indicates that no preconditioning is applied, i.e., the condition number of A appears across the corresponding row. In column 3 (Test Case 2), results are presented for the same kernel function, cf., equation

(14), but the kernel width $\sigma = .1$ is increased, and the regularization parameter $\alpha = 10^{-4}$ is decreased. As in Case 1, the two-level preconditioners outperform comparable three-level preconditioners. The difference in performance is even more pronounced with the broader kernel than with the narrower kernel. In column 4 (Test Case 3), we present results for the sinc squared kernel, $k(x) = (\sin(\pi x/\sigma)/(\pi x/\sigma))^2$, with kernel width $\sigma = .2$, and regularization parameter $\alpha = 10^{-5}$. The results are comparable to those obtained in Case 2.

Preconditioner C	Test Case 1 Condition No. of $C^{-1}A$	Test Case 2 Cond. No. $C^{-1}A$	Test Case 3 Cond. No. $C^{-1}A$
I	824	8777	3175
$C_{SMS}(16)$	48	2.2	1.5
$C_{SMS}(32)$	1.4	1.1	1.1
$C_{SMS}(16, 32)$	201	254	86

Conclusions. For all three test problems, the 3-level SMS preconditioners yielded larger condition numbers and less eigenvalue clustering than comparable 2-level SMS preconditioners. While these test cases may be unrealistically simple, they suggest that no advantage is to be gained by implementing multilevel preconditioners for more realistic (and complicated) problems.

References

1. R. Chan, T. Chan, and W. L. Wan, Multigrid for Differential-Convolution Problems Arising from Image Processing, in *Proceedings of the Workshop on Sci. Comput.*, Springer Verlag, 1997.
2. R. H. Chan and M. K. Ng, Conjugate Gradient Method for Toeplitz Systems, SIAM Review, **38** (1996), pp. 427-482.
3. R. H. Chan, M. K. Ng and R. J. Plemmons, Generalization of Strang's preconditioner with applications to Toeplitz least squares problems, Numerical Lin. Alg. and Applications, **3** (1996), pp. 45–64.
4. H. Engl, M. Hanke, and A. Neubauer, *Regularization of Inverse Problems*, Kluwer Academic Publishers, Dordrecht, 1996.
5. M. Hanke and C. R. Vogel, Two-Level Preconditioners for Regularized Inverse Problems I: Theory, Numer. Math., to appear.
6. A. Rieder, A wavelet multilevel method for ill-posed problems stablized by Tikhonov regularization, Numer. Math., **75** (1997), 501-522.
7. G. Strang, A Proposal for Toeplitz Matrix Calculations, Stud. Appl. Math, **74** (1986), 171-176.
8. C. R. Vogel and M. Hanke, Two-level preconditioners for regularized inverse problems II: Implementation and numerical results, SIAM J. Sci. Comput., to appear.

Decomposition and Hierarchy: Efficient Structural Matching of Large Multi-scale Representations

Simon Massey and Graeme A. Jones

Kingston University,
Penrhyn Road, Kingston upon Thames, Surrey KT1 2EE, United Kingdom
G.Jones@kingston.ac.uk

Abstract. Using the registration of remote imagery as an example domain, this work describes an efficient approach to the structural matching of multi-resolution representations where the scale difference, rotation and translation are unknown. The matching process is posed within an optimisation framework in which the parameter space is the probability hyperspace of all possible matches. In this application, searching for corresponding features at all scales generates a parameter space of enormous dimensions - typically 1-10 million. In this work we use feature's hierarchical relationships to decompose the parameter space into a series of smaller subspaces over which optimisation is computationally feasible.

Key Words: Multi-Scale Matching, Structural Matching, Optimisation

1 Introduction

Extracting extended image features and their relationships from images will enable the application of structural matching techniques to *image-to-image* remote sensing registration problems[7]. A multi-resolution contour representation of the coastline is constructed in the next section for two reasons. First in different modalities, coastlines may be captured at different scales[5, 6]. Second, match results at higher levels within the hierarchy can be propagated down to lower levels[3]. While we restrict ourselves to coastlines, the problem generalises to any non-iconic multi-scale structural representation where both the number of candidate matches is enormous and the proportion of correct matches is very small. Ensuring the global convexity of our match functional or recovering an initial probability estimate close to the global optimum is practically impossible. In section 3 we formulate the registration as an optimisation problem, and introduce the decomposition principle which underpins our approach. The existance of hierarchical relationships between features at different scales enable the optimisation functional defined over an enormous parameter space to be decomposed into a recursive series of functionals defined over smaller subspaces over which optimisation is computationally feasible. A *Genetic Algorithm*[1, 4, 2] is employed to both facilitate escape from local optima, and to generate multiple *good* hypotheses for the the recursive optimisation procedure.

2 Multi-Resolution Segmentation of Coastline Contours

As images of a coastline may be captured by different types of sensor at arbitrary heights, matching may have to be performed between a pair of images taken at different resolutions. A pyramidal multi-resolution representation of each image may be generated by repeated subsampling. By choosing a small level of subsampling between levels in our image pyramid, we may ensure that the two images are similar at some scale difference (see figure 1). Moreover, additional levels of match constraint are available by demanding that the correct solution generates a consistent set of corresepondences at all levels of the hierarchy.

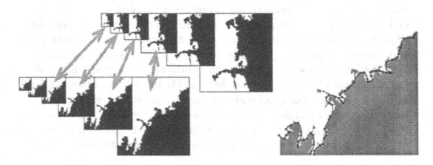

Fig. 1. (a) Matching Multi-Resolution Representations (b) Segmented Codons

Extraction of the coastline contours in each image is achieved by first binarising satellite images into land and sea regions, and then extracting edge chains using a region boundary extraction algorithm. These contour chains are then segmented into *codons* - significant contour segments[5]. Natural points at which to segment the contours are curvature extrema and curvature zero-crossings. Examples of extracted codons are shown in figure 1(b).

The multi-resolution segmentation technique outlined above produces a series of hierarchically related image features. At the lowest level in this hierarchy (highest resolution), are the original set of codons Λ_0 and Ω_0 generated from each image respectively. At the next level, the feature sets Λ_1 and Ω_1 are generated by subsampling the image of the previous layer. This is repeated until the feature sets Λ_{L-1} and Ω_{L-1} of the topmost layer are recovered. Where the scale rises by a factor of $\sqrt{2}$ through the hierarchy, the number of features in each layer reduces approximately by a factor of $\sqrt{2}$.

The hierarchical relationships between features from adjoining layers in the multi-resolution pyramid may be captured by the sets $\mathcal{H}_\lambda^l$; $\lambda \in \Lambda_l, 1 \leq l < L$ and $\mathcal{H}_\omega^l$; $\omega \in \Omega_l, 1 \leq l < L$. Each set $\mathcal{H}_\lambda^l$ contains the set of features from the higher resolution $l-1$ layer which are contained in the lower resolution feature λ. (Since features in sets Λ_0 and Ω_0 are at the bottom-most level of the hierarchy, hierarchical sets cannot be computed.)

3 Posing Registration as an Optimisation Problem

A match γ is constructed using one feature from each image such that $\gamma = \{\lambda, \omega\}$ where features λ and ω are drawn from feature sets Λ and Ω respectively. Let $p(\gamma)$ be the probability of the match γ. The matching process may now be defined as a procedure for computing the set of match probabilities. The requirement to enable matching between two contours of potentially different scales necessitates allowing matches between any feature in one image with features in all scales in the second image. The set of candidate matches Γ from which γ is drawn is therefore defined as

$$\Gamma = \Lambda \times \Omega \qquad (1)$$

Thus the size of the candidate match set is given by the outer product of the full hierarchy of features. For typical satellite imagery enjoying image sizes of 2000×2000, at least 1000 codons may be generated at the highest resolution of the feature hierarchy, resulting in potentially $10M$ matches.

Irrespective of whether it plays an inhibiting or supportive role, each match can be considered as a source of contextual information about other matches and may therefore aid their interpretation. Structural match constraint may be defined as the degree to which pairs of matches are mutually compatible. Sources of such constraint are usually derived from world knowledge such as *uniqueness*, *continuity*, *topology* and *hierarchy*[3]. The degree of compatibility between any pair of matches γ and γ' is captured by the expression

$$-1 \leq C(\gamma, \gamma') \leq 1 \qquad (2)$$

Pairs of correct matches should ideally enjoy a strong level of mutual compatibility while pairs containing a false match should generate low levels of compatibility. This suggests the following suitable optimisation functional. If $\mathbf{p} = (p(\gamma_1), \dots, p(\gamma_M))$ is the vector containing the probabilities of all M matches in Γ, then a suitable functional $F(\mathbf{p})$ which measures the degree of mutual compatibility for a mapping $\mathbf{p}$ may be defined as

$$F_{\mathcal{P}}(\mathbf{p}) = \sum_{\gamma \in \Gamma} \sum_{\substack{\gamma' \in \Gamma \\ \gamma' \neq \gamma}} C(\gamma, \gamma') p(\gamma) p(\gamma') \qquad (3)$$

which may be maximised by eliminating matches (*i.e.* $p(\gamma) \to 0$) which increase the degree of incompatibility. $F_{\mathcal{P}}(\mathbf{p})$ describes a functional defined over a M-dimensional space $\mathcal{P} = p(\gamma_1) \times p(\gamma_2) \times \cdots \times p(\gamma_M)$ where the correct mapping is represented by that probability vector $\hat{\mathbf{p}}$ which maximises equation 3 *i.e.*

$$\hat{\mathbf{p}} = \underset{\mathbf{p} \in \mathcal{P}}{\text{argmax}} \, F_{\mathcal{P}}(\mathbf{p}) \qquad (4)$$

This optimisation functional may be rewritten in vector matrix form

$$F_{\mathcal{P}}(\mathbf{p}) = \frac{1}{2} \mathbf{p} Q \mathbf{p}^T \qquad (5)$$

where the matrix Q stores the symmetric compatibility terms.

4 Hierarchical Subspace Decomposition

Where $|\Lambda \times \Omega|$ is very large, direct optimisation of equation 5 is impractical. However, for the hierarchically organised features of this application, it is possible to partition the probability space $\mathcal{P}$ into a series of smaller subspaces over which the optimisation process may be performed independently.

Let $\mathcal{P}'$ represent a subspace of the full probability space $\mathcal{P}$. Let us assume that the position of the global maximum $\hat{p}$ of a functional $F_{\mathcal{P}}$ defined over $\mathcal{P}$ contains the position of the global maximum $\hat{p}'$ of a functional $F_{\mathcal{P}'}$ defined over the smaller subspace $\mathcal{P}'$. This is true if the matches whose probabilities are contained in $\mathcal{P}'$ are hierarchical *parents* of the matches whose probabilities are contained in $\mathcal{P}$. In this case, the maximisation may be decomposed into two independent problems each over a smaller probability space *i.e.* first maximise $F_{\mathcal{P}'}$ before maximising the full functional $F_{\mathcal{P}}$.

In fact we can partition $\mathcal{P}$ into an ordered series of N smaller subspaces $\mathcal{P}_0, \mathcal{P}_1, \cdots \mathcal{P}_{N-1}$ such that the position of the maximum $\hat{p}_n$ of each functional $F_{\mathcal{P}_n}$ defined over $\mathcal{P}_n$ is contained within the position of maximum $\hat{p}$ of the functional $F_{\mathcal{P}}$ defined over the full probability space $\mathcal{P}$. Thus the global maximum of the functional $F_{\mathcal{P}}$ is defined as the concatenation of each of the *local* maxima

$$\hat{p} = \underset{p \in \mathcal{P}}{\text{argmax}} \; F_{\mathcal{P}}(p) \quad = \quad (\hat{p}_0, \hat{p}_1, \cdots, \hat{p}_{N-1}) \qquad (6)$$

Each of these *local* maxima (global maxima in their respective subspaces) is defined as before *i.e.* that vector $\hat{p}_n \in \mathcal{P}_n$ which maximises the functional $F_{\mathcal{P}_n}$

$$\hat{p}_n = \underset{p_n \in \mathcal{P}_n}{\text{argmax}} \, F_{\mathcal{P}_n}(p_n) \qquad (7)$$

where $F_{\mathcal{P}_n}$ is defined in recursive form as

$$F_{\mathcal{P}_n}(p_n) = \frac{1}{2} p_n Q_n p_n^T + p_n.h_n + F_{\mathcal{P}_{n-1}}(\hat{p}_{n-1})$$
$$h_n = H_n(\hat{p}_0, \ldots, \hat{p}_{n-1})^T \qquad (8)$$
$$F_{\mathcal{P}_0}(p_0) = \frac{1}{2} p_0 Q_0 p_0^T$$

The minimisation of $F_{\mathcal{P}_n}$ depends on the position of earlier minima $\hat{p}_0, \cdots \hat{p}_{n-1}$ implying that the functionals must be maximised in a particular order. Consequently, equation 7 specifies an estimator which converges on the global maximum $\hat{p}$ over progressively larger proportions of the full parameter space $\mathcal{P}$.

Features from higher up the feature hierarchy tend to capture the larger scale structure in the image. Feature matches are ordered hierarchically allowing solutions at higher levels to guide the match process further down the hierarchy. Our *hierarchical propagation* strategy partitions this full ordered match probability space into a series of smaller *subspaces*. A *genetic algorithm* is used to recover a number of good yet disparate solutions in each partition. The union of these solution is used in conjunction with the hierarchical relations $\mathcal{H}_\gamma; \gamma \in \Gamma$ generated in section 2 to generate the next partition. Note also that as the process progresses, the descendants of all matches not selected are pruned from the search space. This has the effect of dramatically reducing the dimensionality of the problem!

Generating the Initial Subspace Partition Depending on the scale difference between the two images, the correct mapping will map EITHER the highest most feature set Λ_{L-1} onto one of the feature sets $\Omega_0, \dots \Omega_{L-1}$ OR the highest most set Ω_{L-1} onto one of the feature sets $\Lambda_0, \dots \Lambda_{L-1}$. Thus the first partition Γ_0 should be restricted to locating the first correct mapping among this most salient feature match set *i.e.*

$$\Gamma_0 = \bigcup_{l=L-1,\cdots,0} \{\{\Lambda_{L-1} \times \Omega_l\} \cup \{\Lambda_l \times \Omega_{L-1}\}\} \qquad (9)$$

Any limits on the expected scale difference between the pair of images will significantly reduce the size of Γ_0. There are typically 20-30 codon features at the highest level of our hierarchy while the expected scale difference is no greater two or three octave generating an initial partition $|\Gamma_0| < 6000$. While still a very large space, this is considerably smaller than Γ whose size can be several million.

Since we are not employing the full match hierarchical match constraint available, there is an increased likelihood that the best solution will not coincide with the global solution. Consequently, we recover the best N_0 solutions from which the set $\mathcal{M}_0$ of matches for this most salient partition are recovered.

Propagating Match Information Having found the match solution $\mathcal{M}_{n-1}$ from a previous partition Γ_{n-1}, the hierarchical relations $\mathcal{H}$ may be used to dramatically prune the set of as yet unprocessed matches $\Gamma - \{\Gamma_{n-1} \cup \cdots \cup \Gamma_0\}$. The next partition Γ_n need only contain matches whose parent features belong to a match in the previous match pool $\mathcal{M}_{n-1}$. Thus if γ represents a match between two features λ and ω, then

$$\Gamma_n = \bigcup_{\gamma \in \mathcal{M}_{n-1}} \mathcal{H}_\lambda \times \mathcal{H}_\omega \qquad (10)$$

On average each hierarchical set $\mathcal{H}$ has $\sqrt{2}$ features. Consequently the size of the next partition is given by $|\Gamma_n| \approx 2|\mathcal{M}_{n-1}|$. Unlike the first partition, this is typically a few hundred matches which enables rapid optimisation.

The sets of multiple solutions from these repeated optimisations are ordered to recover the best N_n solutions which in turn are propagated to the next partition. The above procedure is merely repeated until all of the matches within Γ have been included within a partition and optimised. The solution of the first partition effectively recovers the scale difference ΔS of the mapping between the image pair. Thus the number of subsequent partitions is $L - \Delta S - 1$ where L is the multi-resolution number of levels in the codon pyramid.

5 Conclusions

A graph matching framework for registering images has been proposed which enjoys a number of advantages over traditional techniques relying on similarity of tokens. First there is no requirement for both images to be captured at the same scale or resolution. Second, as only local topological constraint is used, no global transformation between the images is assumed. This is particularly useful where the images may contain severe local geometric distortions. The graph matching problem has been formulated within an optimisation framework. This not only provides a principled manner of combining complex match constraint, but enables us to explore a number of different optimisation techniques already reported in the optimisation and computer vision literature.

The primary difficulties of the problem is the extremely high dimensionality of the optimisation space, the very low levels of correct match density, and the non-convexity of the match functional. Two strategies have been employed to ameliorate this problem. First, exploiting the multi-scale representation already built for each image, a multi-scale matching (or *hierarchical propagation*) strategy delivers a considerable increase in speed by partitioning the match problem into a number of decomposed steps. Matching is first performed at higher levels in the hierarchy and the recovered mappings are then propagated down to lower levels. To exploit this hierarchical decomposition, the optimisation functional itself required decomposing to enable match probabilities computed for matches higher up the hierarchy to contribute to the optimsation process. Second, as direct descent optimisation tecchniques will not perform well where the match density is low or the functional is highly non-convex, a search strategy based on the genetic algorithm ensures a global optimum is recovered.

References

1. D.E. Goldberg. *"Genetic Algorithms in Search, Optimisation and Machine Learning"*. Addison–Wesley Publishing Company Inc., Reading, Mass., 1989.
2. J. Eshelman J.D. Schaffer, R.A. Caruana and R. Das. "A Study of Control Parameters Affecting Online Performance of Genetic Alogrithms". In *Proceedings of the Third International Conference of Genetic Algorithms and Machine Learning*, pages 51–60, San Mateo, Cal., June 1989. Morgan Kaufmann Publishers Inc.
3. G.A. Jones. "Constraint,Optimisation and Hierarchy: Reviewing Stereoscopic Correspondence of Complex Features". *Computer Vision and Image Understanding*, 65(1):57–78, January 1997.
4. M. Mitchell. *"An Introduction to Genetic Algorithms"*. MIT Press, 1996.
5. W. Richards and D. Hoffman. *"Readings in Computer Vision: Issues, Problems, Principles and Paradigms"*, chapter "Codon Constraints on Closed 2D Shapes", pages 700–708. Morgan Kauffman, 1987. Edited by M.A. Fischler and O. Firschein.
6. P.L. Rosin. "Determining Local Scales of Curves". *Pattern Recognition Letters*, 19(1):63–75, 1998.
7. D.P. Roy, B. Deveraux, B. Grainger, and S.J. White. "Parametric Geometric Correction of Airborne Thematic Mapper Imagery". *International Journal of Remote Sensing*, 18(9):1865–1887, June 1997.

Tracing of Curvilinear Structures in 3D Images with Single Scale Diameter Measurement

G.J. Streekstra, A.W.M.Smeulders, R. van den Boomgaard

Dept. Intelligent Sensory Information Systems, WINS,
University of Amsterdam, Kruislaan 403, 1098 SJ Amsterdam, the Netherlands
geert@wins.uva.nl

Abstract. We introduce a 3D tracing method based on differential geometry in Gaussian blurred images. The line point detection part of the tracing method starts with calculation of the line direction from the eigenvectors of the Hessian matrix. The sub-voxel center line position is estimated from a second order Taylor approximation of the 2D intensity profile perpendicular to the line. The line diameter is obtained at a single scale using the theoretical scale dependencies of the 0-th and 2nd order Gaussian derivatives at the line center. Experiments on synthetic images reveal that the localization of the centerline is mainly affected by line curvature. The diameter measurement is accurate for diameters as low as 4 voxels.

1 Introduction

Quantitative analysis of curvilinear structures in images is of interest in various research fields. In medicine and biology researchers need estimates of length and diameter of line-like structures like chromosomes [11] blood vessels or neuron dendrites [1] for diagnostic or scientific purposes. In the technical sciences there is an interest in center line positions of line structures in engineering drawings [2] or automatic detection of roads in aerial images [3].

Any method for detection of the centerline of curvilinear structures needs a criterion for a certain position in the image to be part of a center line. Methods differ in the definition of such a criterion and in the way the criterion is evaluated.

In a first class of methods a line point is defined as a local grey value maximum relative to neighboring pixels or voxels [4] [5]. Since no reference is made to properties of line structures in an image this class will generate many false hypotheses of line points if noise is present.

A better criterion for a line point is to consider it to be part of a structure which length is larger than its diameter [6]. This criterion can be materialized within the framework of differential geometry [3], [6], [7], [8].

There are several computational approaches to computing the differential structure in an image. In the facet model of Haralick [8] image derivatives in a 2D image are calculated from a third order polynomial fit to the image data in a 5x5 neighborhood. Along the line perpendicular to the direction of the line structure the sub pixel position where the first derivative vanishes is estimated from the polynomial. A pixel is declared a line point if this position is within the pixel boundaries. The main drawback of this method is that the differential structure of the image is calculated at the fixed inner scale of the image which may lead to erroneous line center positions in case of noise or bar shaped intensity profiles.

An essentially different computational approach is to calculate image derivatives at a scale adapted to the line diameter by convolution of the image with Gaussian derivative kernels [9]. The properties of the Gaussian kernel reduce the influence of noise and ensures meaningful first and second order derivatives even in the case of plateau-like intensity profiles across the line [3] [10].

Few line detection or tracing methods provide an estimate of the line width [6] [11]. In [11] the diameter is estimated from a fit of a function describing the line profile. This method suffers from the same noise sensitivity as the facet model [8]. This problem can be avoided by using the scale dependency of normalized second derivatives to estimate line diameter [6]. However, in [6] no evaluation of the method is presented and the diameter is found by iteration over scale which is computational expensive.

In this paper we present a 3D line tracer which uses the line point detection method as presented in [10] [3] and measures diameter at a single scale based on the theorectical scale dependency of Gaussian derivatives in the image.

2 Tracing of 3D curvilinear structures

Our tracing procedure starts by selecting a discrete point P_d at position (x, y, z) in the image close to a center line position. At this position we calculate the Gaussian derivatives up to order two. The second order derivatives are used to build up the Hessian matrix $\mathbf{H}$ from which we calculate the 3 eigenvalues $\lambda_t, \lambda_n, \lambda_m$ and the corresponding eigenvectors t, n and m. The eigenvectors form an orthonormal base for a local Cartesian coordinate system through the center of the voxel. The vector t which is aligned to the line direction is the eigenvector with the smallest eigenvalue in magnitude λ_t [6].

Locally around point P_d the grey value distribution in the plane perpendicular to the line direction is approximated by the second order Taylor polynomial

$$I(\xi, \eta) \approx I + p \cdot \nabla I + \frac{1}{2} p^T \cdot \mathbf{H} \cdot p \tag{1}$$

where I and ∇I are the Gaussian blurred grey value and gradient vector at the current discrete voxel position P_d . In (1) p is a vector in the plane perpendicular to the line direction defined by n and m i.e. $p = \xi n + \eta m$.

The center line position p_c relative to the voxel center is found by setting the first derivatives of the local Taylor polynomial along ξ and η to zero [10] and solving η and ξ from the resulting linear equation. The sub voxel center line position P_s is calculated by $P_s = P_d + p_c$. If P_s is not within the boundaries of the current voxel the line point estimation procedure is carried out again at the discrete voxel position closest to P_s . This procedure is repeated until P_s

is within the boundaries of the current voxel. The tracing proceeds by taking a step from the estimated position P_s in the t-direction.

3   Diameter estimation

For diameter estimation it is necessary to take the shape of the 2D grey value profile perpendicular to the line into account [6]. This grey value profile $I(r)$ is assumed to obey the following conditions:

$$I(r) = \begin{cases} I_0 f(r), & (r \leq R) \\ 0, & (r > R). \end{cases} \quad (2)$$

In (2), I_0 is the grey value at the center line, $r = \sqrt{\xi^2 + \eta^2}$ is the distance from the center line position and R the radius of the line structure. The first derivative of $f(r)$ is assumed to vanish at the centerline.

We use the scale dependencies of $I(r)$ convolved with a Gaussian and the second Gaussian derivatives of $I(r)$ at $r = 0$ to estimate the line diameter. For this purpose expressions are derived for the Gaussian blurred intensity $I(R, \sigma)$ and the Laplacean $\Delta^\perp I(R, \sigma)$ restricted to the span of n and m :

$$I(R, \sigma) = I_0 \int_0^{2\pi} \int_0^R f(r) g(r, \sigma) r \, dr \, d\theta \quad (3)$$

$$\Delta^\perp I(R, \sigma) = I_0 \int_0^{2\pi} \int_0^R f(r) g_{rr}(r, \sigma) r \, dr \, d\theta \quad . \quad (4)$$

In (3) and (4) $g(r, \sigma)$ and $g_{rr}(r, \sigma)$ are the 2D Gaussian and its second derivative in r-direction. The expressions for $I(R, \sigma)$ and the normalized Laplacean $\sigma^2 \frac{1}{2} \Delta^\perp I(R, \sigma)$ are used to construct a non-linear filter which is rotation invariant with respect to the line direction and independent of I_0 :

$$h(R, \sigma) = \frac{I(R, \sigma)}{-\sigma^2 \frac{1}{2} \Delta^\perp I(R, \sigma)} \quad . \quad (5)$$

The filter output $h(R, \sigma)$ is dependent on the choice of $f(r)$. For a parabolic and a pillbox profile the integrals appearing in eqs. (3) and (4) can be evaluated analytically and $h(R, \sigma)$ turns out to be only dependent on the dimensionless parameter $q = \frac{1}{2} (R/\sigma)^2$. Figure 1 hows that $h(R, \sigma)$ is a monotonically increasing function of q which makes it easy to estimate q from a measured filter output h_m. Provided that h_m is measured and a priory knowledge concerning the shape of the profile is available q_0 can be estimated by solving $h(q_0) - h_m = 0$. The corresponding R is found by applying $R = \sigma \sqrt{2q_0}$.

4   Experiments

The localization accuracy and robustness of the tracing and the diameter estimation methods was evaluated using a set of synthetic test images which reflects

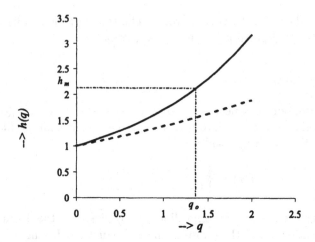

Fig. 1. Line diameter filter output $h(q)$ for a pillbox profile (solid line) and a parabolic profile (dashed line). ($q = \frac{1}{2}(R/\sigma)^2$).

possible properties of curvilinear structures. Properties which are considered are the shape of the grey value profile perpendicular to the line, the curvature of the center line of the structure and the noise level.

4.1 Bias in center line position

Images of straight rods with pillbox profiles and parabolic profiles were created with R ranging between 2 and 15. In case the line center was set to the central position in the voxel the estimated center line position turned out to be bias free. A sub voxel shift d_s in the plane perpendicular to the line leads to an experimentally observed bias ΔP_s which increases with d_s but never exceeds 0.08 ($R = 2$, $\sigma = 2$). Experiments with larger R and larger kernel size σ show a smaller bias.

To investigate bias introduced in center line position due to line curvature we estimated center line positions in a torus with a parabolic line profile. An analysis of the mathematical expressions used to calculate the line center revealed that the relative bias $\Delta P_s/R$ in the center line position depends only on R_t/R and R/σ. The experiments show that $\Delta P_s/R$ decreases with R_t/R and R/σ (Fig.2.).

4.2 Bias in diameter estimate

To test the performance of the line diameter estimation method images containing straight line segments with circular cross section were used. The diameter estimate turned out to be independent of the setting of σ in the range where $0.2 < R/\sigma < 2$. In images without noise the bias in the estimated diameter is always below 5% (Fig.3.). In an additional experiment Gaussian noise in the

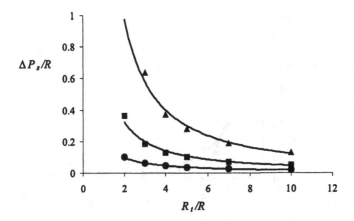

Fig. 2. Relative bias in center line position ($\Delta P_s/R$) as function of R_t/R for settings of R/σ of 0.62 (triangles) 1.0 (squares) and 1.67 (dots).

range between 0 and 30% was added to the image with a pillbox shaped intensity profile and $R = 20$. The measurements show a bias of 5% in the diameter estimation at a noise level of 10%. This bias increases to a level of 30% at a noise level of 30%.

5 Discussion

In our tracing method the Gaussian derivatives are calculated only at a limited amount of points at one single scale in the neighborhood of the center line position. Consequently, the method provides for sufficiently small response times to allow interactive measurement of both center line location and diamerter.

One of the criteria for a point to be on the centerline of the curvilinear structure ($\nabla I \cdot \boldsymbol{p} = 0$) implies that the localization of the line center is only bias free for a straight line with the centerline positioned in the center of the voxel. A sub voxel shift of the center line introduces a small bias in the center line position.

High curvature is a serious source of bias in the center line location. This can be understood by realizing that at high curvature the position where $\nabla I \cdot \boldsymbol{p} = 0$ will be significantly shifted due to the spatial extend of the derivative kernels.

The diameter measurement based on the scale dependency of the 0-th and the second Gaussian derivatives performs well in the noiseless situation even for R as small as 2 times the voxel size. In the diameter estimation procedure noise added to the image introduces a bias in the line diameter estimate.

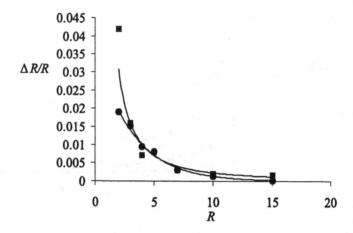

Fig. 3. Relative bias in estimation of radius R of the line structure as a function of R for a parabolic profile (squares) and a pillbox profile (dots)

References

1. Capowsky, J.J.: Computer Techniques in Neuroanatomy. Plenum Press, New York (1989)
2. Jonk, A.: A Line Tracker. ISIS Techn. report, University of Amsterdam (1998)
3. Steger, C.: An Unbiased Detector of Curvilinear Structures. IEEE trans. PAMI. **20(2)** (1998) 113-125
4. Bevaqua, G., Floris, R.: A Surface Specific-Line and Slope Recognition Algorithm. Computer Vision, Graphics, and Image Processing **40** (1987) 219-227
5. Collerec, R., Coatrieux, J.L.: Vectorial Tracking and directed contour finder for vascular network in digital subtraction angiography. Pattern Recognition Letters **8** (1988) 353-358
6. Lorenz, C., Carlsen, I.C., Buzug, T.M., Fassnacht, C., Weese, J.: Multi-scale Line Segmentation with Automatic Estimation of Width, Contrast and Tangential Direction in 2D and 3D Medical Images. Proceedings of the First Joint Conference on Computer Vision, Virtual Reality and Robotics in Medicine and Medical Robotics and Computer-Assited Surgery (1997) 233-242
7. Eberly, D.: Ridges in Image and Data Analysis. Computational Imaging and Vision, Vol. 7. Kluwer Academic Publishers, Dordrecht, The Netherlands (1996)
8. Haralick, R.M.: Ridges and Valleys on Digital Images. Computer Vision, Graphics, and Image Processing **22** (1983) 28-38
9. Lindeberg, T.: Edge Detection and Ridge Detection with Automatic Scale Selection. Computer Vision and Pattern Recognition. IEEE Computer Society Press, Los Alamitos (1996) 465-470
10. Steger, C.: Unbiased Extraction of Cuvilinear Structures from 2D and 3D Images. PhD thesis, Muenchen (1998)
11. Noordmans, H.J.: Interactive Analysis of 3D Microscope Images. PhD thesis, Amsterdam (1997)

A Geometric Functional for Derivatives Approximation

Nir A. Sochen[1], Robert M. Haralick[2], and Yehoshua Y. Zeevi[1]

[1] EE Department, Technion - Israel Institute of Technology
Technion City, Haifa 32000, ISRAEL
sochen,zeevi@ee.technion.ac.il
[2] EE Department, University of Washington
Seattle, WA 98195, USA
haralick@ee.washington.edu

Abstract. *We develop on estimation method, for the derivative field of an image based on Bayesian approach which is formulated in a geometric way. The Maximum probability configuration of the derivative field is found by a gradient descent method which leads to a non-linear diffusion type equation with added constraints. The derivatives are assumed to be piecewise smoothe and the Beltrami framework is used in the development of an adaptive smoothing process.*

1   Introduction

It is widely accepted that gradients are of utmost importance in early vision analysis such as image enhancement and edge detection. Several numerical recipes are known for derivatives estimation. All based on fixed square or rectangular neighborhoods of different sizes. This type of estimation does not account for the structure of images and bound to produce errors especially near edges where the estimate on one side of the edge may wrongly influence the estimate on the other side of it. In places where the image is relatively smooth, least square estimates of derivatives computed over large area neighborhoods will give best results (e.g the facet approach [2], see also [1]). But, in places where the underlying image intensity surface is not smooth, and therefore can not be fitted by a small degree bivariate polynomial, the neighborhood should be smaller and rectangular, with the long axis of the rectangle aligned along the orientation of the directional derivative.

From this viewpoint, it is natural to suggest a varying size and shape neighborhood in order to increase both the robustness of the estimate to noise, and its correctness. Calculating directly for each point of the image its optimal neighborhood for gradient estimation is possible but cumbersome. We Therefore propose an alternative approach, which uses a geometry driven diffusion [8] that produces implicitly, and in a sub-pixel accuracy, the desirable effect. We are not concerned, in this approach, with finding an optimal derivative filter but formulate directly a Bayesian reasoning for the derivative functions themselves.

The paper is organized as follows: In Section 2 we review the Beltrami framework. A Bayesian formulation of the problem, in its linear form, is presented in

Section 3. We incorporate, in Section 4, The Beltrami framework in the Bayesian paradigm, and derive partial differential equations (PDEs) by means of the gradient descent method. Preliminary results are presented in Section 5.

2 A Geometric Measure on Embedded Maps

We represent an image as a two-dimensional Riemannian surface embedded in a higher dimensional spatial-feature Riemannian manifold [11, 10, 3–5, 13, 12]. Let σ^μ, $\mu = 1, 2$, be the local coordinates on the image surface and let X^i, $i = 1, 2, \ldots, m$, be the coordinates on the embedding space than the embedding map is given by

$$(X^1(\sigma^1, \sigma^2), X^2(\sigma^1, \sigma^2), \ldots, X^m(\sigma^1, \sigma^2)). \tag{1}$$

Riemannian manifolds are manifolds endowed with a bi-linear positive-definite symmetric tensor which is called a *metric*. Denote by $(\Sigma, (g_{\mu\nu}))$ the image manifold and its metric and by $(M, (h_{ij}))$ the space-feature manifold and its corresponding metric. Then the map $\mathbf{X} : \Sigma \to M$ has the following weight [7]

$$E[X^i, g_{\mu\nu}, h_{ij}] = \int d^2\sigma \sqrt{g} g^{\mu\nu} (\partial_\mu X^i)(\partial_\nu X^j) h_{ij}(\mathbf{X}), \tag{2}$$

where the range of indices is $\mu, \nu = 1, 2$, and $i, j = 1, \ldots, m = \dim M$, and we use the Einstein summation convention: identical indices that appear one up and one down are summed over. We denote by g the determinant of $(g_{\mu\nu})$ and by $(g^{\mu\nu})$ its inverse. In the above expression $d^2\sigma \sqrt{g}$ is an area element of the image manifold. The rest, i.e. $g^{\mu\nu}(\partial_\mu X^i)(\partial_\nu X^j)h_{ij}(\mathbf{X})$, is a generalization of L_2. It is important to note that this expression (as well as the area element) does not depend on the local coordinates one chooses.

The feature evolves in a geometric way via the gradient descent equations

$$X_t^i \equiv \frac{\partial X^i}{\partial t} = -\frac{1}{2\sqrt{g}} h^{il} \frac{\delta E}{\delta X^l}. \tag{3}$$

Note that we used our freedom to multiply the Euler-Lagrange equations by a strictly positive function and a positive definite matrix. This factor is the simplest one that does not change the minimization solution while giving a reparameterization invariant expression. This choice guarantees that the flow is geometric and does not depend on the parameterization.

Given that the embedding space is Euclidean, The variational derivative of E with respect to the coordinate functions is given by

$$-\frac{1}{2\sqrt{g}} h^{il} \frac{\delta F}{\delta X^l} = \Delta_g X^i = \frac{1}{\sqrt{g}} \partial_\mu(\sqrt{g} g^{\mu\nu} \partial_\nu X^i), \tag{4}$$

where the operator that is acting on X^i in the first term is the natural generalization of the Laplacian from flat spaces to manifolds and is called *the second order differential parameter of Beltrami* [6], or in short *Beltrami operator*.

3 Bayesian formulation for derivatives estimate

Denote by (x_r, y_s) the sampling points and by $I^0_{rs} \equiv I^0(x_r, y_s)$ the grey-levels at the sampling points.

From the data i.e. (x_r, y_s), I^0_{rs} we want to infer the underlying function $I(x, y)$ and its gradient vector field $\mathbf{V}(x, y)$. The analysis is easier in the continuum and we refer from now on to I^0 as to a continuous function. In practice we can skip a stage and find the derivatives without referring to the underlying function. The inference is described by the posterior probability distribution

$$P(\mathbf{I}(x, y), \mathbf{V}(x, y) | I^0(x, y)) = \frac{P(I^0(x, y) | \mathbf{I}(x, y), \mathbf{V}(x, y)) P(\mathbf{I}(x, y), \mathbf{V}(x, y))}{P(I^0(x, y))}$$

In the numerator the first term $P(I^0(x, y)) | \mathbf{V}(x, y))$ is the probability of the sampled grey-level values given the vector field $\mathbf{V}(x, y)$ and the second term is the prior distribution on vector fields assumed by our model. The denominator is independent of $\mathbf{V}$ and will be ignored from now on.

Assuming that $P(A|B)$ is given by a Gibbsian form :

$$P(A|B) = Ce^{-\alpha E(A,B)},$$

we get

$$-\log P(\mathbf{V}(x, y) | I^0(x, y)) = \alpha E_1(I^0(x, y), \mathbf{V}(x, y)) + \beta E_2(\mathbf{V}(x, y)).$$

If we use the Euclidean L_2 norm we get

$$E_1(I^0(x, y), \mathbf{V}(x, y)) = \frac{1}{2} C_1 \int dx dy \left(|\mathbf{V} - \nabla I|^2 \right)$$
$$E_2(\mathbf{V}(x, y)) = \frac{1}{2} C_2 \int dx dy \left(|\nabla \mathbf{V}|^2 \right) + E_3, \tag{5}$$

where the first term is a fidelity term that forces the vector field $\mathbf{V}$ to be close enough to the gradient vector field of $I(x, y)$. The second term intoduces regularization that guarantees certain smoothness properties of the solution. The second term in E_2 constraints the vector field to be a gradient of a function. Its form is:

$$E_3(I(x, y), \mathbf{V}(x, y) = \frac{1}{2} C_3 \int dx dy (\epsilon^{\mu\nu} \partial_\mu V_\nu)^2 = \frac{1}{2} C_3 \int dx dy (V1_y - V2_x)^2,$$

where $\epsilon^{\mu\nu}$ is the antisymmetric tensor.

Alternatively we may adopt a more sophisticated regularization based on geometric ideas. These are treated in the next section.

Maximization of the posterior probability amounts to the minimization of the energy. We do that by means of the gradient descent method which leads eventually to non-linear diffusion type equations.

4   Derivatives Estimation: Geometric Method

In this section we incorporate the Beltrami framework into the Byesian paradigm. We consider the intensity to be part of the feature space, and the fifth-dimensional embedding map is

$$(X^1 = x, X^2 = y, X^3 = I(x,y), X^4 = V_1(x,y), X^5 = V_2(x,y)). \qquad (6)$$

Again we assume that these are Cartesian coordinates of $\mathbb{R}^5$ and therefore $h_{ij} = \delta_{ij}$. That implies the following induced metric:

$$(g_{\mu\nu}(x,y)) = \begin{pmatrix} 1 + I_x^2 + V1_x^2 + V2_x^2 & I_xI_y + V1_xV1_y + V2_xV2_y \\ I_xI_y + V1_xV1_y + V2_xV2_y & 1 + I_y^2 + V1_y^2 + V2_y^2 \end{pmatrix}. \qquad (7)$$

The energy functionals have two more terms: The first is a fidelity term of the denoised image with respect to the observed one, and the last is an adaptive smoothing term. The functionals are

$$E_0(I(x,y), I^0(x,y)) = \frac{1}{2}C_0 \int dx dy \sqrt{g}(I - I^0)^2$$

$$E_1(I^0(x,y), \mathbf{V}(x,y)) = \frac{1}{2}C_1 \int dx dy \sqrt{g}\left(|\mathbf{V} - \nabla I^0|^2\right)$$

$$E_2(\mathbf{V}(x,y)) = \frac{1}{2}C_2 \int dx dy \sqrt{g}g^{\mu\nu}(\partial_\mu X^i)(\partial_\nu X^i)$$

$$E_3(\mathbf{V}(x,y)) = \frac{1}{2}C_3 \int dx dy \sqrt{g}(\epsilon^{\mu\nu}\partial_\nu V_\mu)^2, \qquad (8)$$

and since the Levi-Civita connection's coefficients are zero, we get the following gradient descent system of equations:

$$I_t = C_2 \Delta_g I - C_0(I - I^0)$$

$$V_{\rho t} = C_2 \Delta_g V_\rho - C_1(V_\rho - \partial_\rho I^0) + \frac{C_3}{\sqrt{g}}\partial_\rho(\sqrt{g}\epsilon^{\mu\nu}\partial_\nu V_\mu), \qquad (9)$$

with the initial conditions

$$I(x,y,t=0) = I^0(x,y)$$

$$V_\rho(x,y,t=0) = \partial_\rho I^0(x,y), \qquad (10)$$

where $I^0(x,y)$ is the given image.

It is important to understand that V_1 and V_2 are estimates of I_{0x} and I_{0y} and not of the denoised I_x and I_y.

5   Results and discusssion

The solution of the PDE's was obtained by using the explicit Euler scheme, where the time derivative is forward and the spatial derivatives are central. The stencil was taken as 3×3.

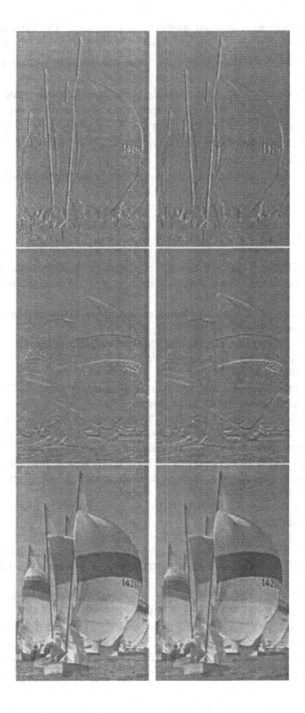

Fig. 1. Upper row, left: The original noisy x derivative. Upper row, right: The x derivative estimation. Middle row, left: The original noisy y derivative. Middle row, right: The y derivative estimation. Lower row, left: The original noisy image. Lower row, right: The denoised image.

We did not optimize any parameter, nor the size of the time steps. For the Euclidean embedding algorithm we chose $C_1 = 0.5$, $C_2 = 1$, $C_3 = 8.5$ and the time step was $\Delta t = 0.005$. The results after 150 iterations are depicted in Fig. (1).

This demonstrates that it is possible to merge Bayesian reasoning and the geometric Beltrami framework in computation of derivative estimations. The requirement that the obtained functions are the x and y derivatives of some underlying function is formulated through a Lagrange multiplier. Close inspection reveals that this requirement is fulfilled only approximately.

An analysis and comparison with statistical based method will appear elsewhere[9].

References

1. M Azaria, I Vitsnudel and Y Y Zeevi "The Design of Tow-Dimensional Gradient estimators Based on One-Dimensional Operators", *IEEE Trans. on Image Processing*, 5, (1996) 155-159.
2. R M Haralick and L G Shapiro *Computer and Robot Vision*, Addison-Wesley Publishing Company, New York, 1992, Chapter 8.
3. R Kimmel, R Malladi and N Sochen, "Images as Embedding Maps and Minimal Surfaces: Movies, Color, Texture, and Volumetric Medical Images", *Proc. of IEEE CVPR'97*, (1997) 350-355.
4. R Kimmel, N Sochen and R Malladi, "On the geometry of texture", Report, Berkeley Labs. UC, LBNL-39640, UC-405, November,1996.
5. R Kimmel, N Sochen and R Malladi, "From High Energy Physics to Low Level Vision", *Lecture Notes In Computer Science:* 1252, First International Conference on Scale-Space Theory in Computer Vision, Springer-Verlag, 1997, 236-247.
6. E Kreyszing, "Differential Geometry", Dover Publications, Inc., New York, 1991.
7. A M Polyakov, "Quantum geometry of bosonic strings", *Physics Letters*, **103B** (1981) 207-210.
8. B M ter Haar Romeny Ed., Geometry Driven Diffusion in Computer Vision, Kluwer Academic Publishers, 1994.
9. N A Sochen, R M Haralick and Y Y Zeevi *in preparation*
10. N Sochen, R Kimmel and R Malladi, "From high energy physics to low level vision", Report, LBNL, UC Berkeley, LBNL 39243, August, Presented in ONR workshop, UCLA, Sept. 5 1996.
11. N Sochen, R Kimmel and R Malladi , "A general framework for low level vision", *IEEE Trans. on Image Processing*, 7, (1998) 310-318.
12. N Sochen and Y Y Zeevi, "Images as manifolds embedded in a spatial-feature non-Euclidean space", November 1998, EE-Technion report no. 1181.
13. N Sochen and Y Y Zeevi, "Representation of colored images by manifolds embedded in higher dimensional non-Euclidean space", IEEE ICIP'98, Chicago, 1998.

Segmenting by Compression Using Linear Scale-Space and Watersheds

Jon Sporring[1] and Ole Fogh Olsen[2]

[1] Institute of Computer Science, Foundation for Research and Technology – Hellas,
Vassilika Vouton, P.O. Box 1385, GR 71110 Heraklion, Crete, GREECE
sporring@ics.forth.gr
[2] Department of Computer Science, University of Copenhagen,
Universitetsparken 1, DK 2100 Copenhagen, DENMARK
fogh@diku.dk

Abstract. Automatic segmentation is performed using watersheds of the gradient magnitude and compression techniques. Linear Scale-Space is used to discover the neighbourhood structure and catchment basins are locally merged with Minimum Description Length. The algorithm can form a basis for a large range of automatic segmentation algorithms based on watersheds, scale-spaces, and compression.

1 Introduction

A semantically meaningful segmentation of an indoor scene would be piecewise smooth regions corresponding to walls, floor, etc.. Such segmentation tasks are often solved indirectly using some similarity measure, and this article will focus on the gradient magnitude, since discontinuities are most likely where the gradient magnitude is high.

Generally, segmentation is an NP-complete problem [2] for two dimensional images, however reasonable solutions may be found in polynomial time. Segmentation algorithms may be divided into three broad categories: Intensity thresholding [9], regional split and merge [9], variational and partial differential equation (PDE) based approaches [6, 14], and mixes of the previous three [8, 4, 5].

The algorithm presented in this article uses a PDE based technique [8] for hierarchical splitting regions based on a *well-founded*, *thoroughly studied*, and *least committed* scale analysis [3, 8]. The regions are merged with *consistent* modelling by Minimum Description Length (MDL) [10] to yield *parametric descriptions* of segments.

2 Least Committed Splitting

Watersheds on the gradient magnitude partition an image into homogeneous areas in a fast manner, and in contrast to the Mumford-Shah functional, the

* Supported in part by EC Contract No. ERBFMRY-CT96-0049
(VIRGO http://www.ics.forth.gr/virgo) under the TMR Programme.

watersheds are not restricted to intersect in T-junctions at 120 degree angles. To regularise the gradient operator several authors have investigated the properties of the watersheds of the gradient magnitude in various scale-spaces [3, 8, 4, 14]. In the linear scale-space [15], this has lead to the development of a semi-automatic segmentation tool [7], henceforth called Olsen's segmentation tool.

Olsen's segmentation tool organises segments in a hierarchical data structure, making it convenient to use as a splitting operation. At each scale the image is partitioned by the watersheds of the gradient magnitude, and the catchment basins are linked across scale exploiting the deep structure [8]. The linking graph can be approximated with a tree, called the Scale-Space Tree. The tool can pragmatically be extended to other similarity measures disregarding deep structure merely with the use of area overlap between scales.

In Figure 1 are given examples of partitions for two similar images. The

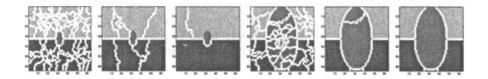

Fig. 1. The Scale-Space Tree captures ellipses of varying size. The white lines are the watersheds. Two ellipses are shown using three different integration scales.

original images consists of 3 intensity values (64, 128, 192) plus i.i.d. normal noise with zero mean and standard deviation 5. The ellipses are one pixel further into the light than the dark area. The segments at measurement scale zero are shown for three different integration scales. We observe that the ellipses are captured at low and high integration scale respectively, indicating that structure of varying size is captured by the Scale-Space Tree at corresponding levels. Hence, the task of the merge algorithm is to perform local scale-selection.

3 Specifying Semantics by Compression

For models where increasing the number of degrees of freedom monotonically decreases the distance to the data, we need some criterion to balance model complexity and model deviation. There are at present three competing model selection methods: Akaike's Information Criterion (AIC), Schwarz's Bayes Information Criterion (BIC), and Rissanen's Minimum Description Length (MDL) [1]. The original formulation by Akaike AIC is known to be inconsistent in the sense that it will not always converge to the correct model with increasing samples. In contrast, both BIC and MDL have been shown to be consistent and converge to each other, but MDL is the only method that is derived from a principle outside the problem of model selection. Thus in contrast to AIC and BIC, MDL gives a clear interpretation of the resulting model selection, as that which achieves optimal compression. Therefore will MDL be used to merge segments created by Olsen's segmentation tool.

For the model selection criterion to be consistent, every investigated model, must include everything that is needed to completely reproduce the data set. Mixing models from deterministic and stochastic domains is quite natural, since every physical signal contains a portion of randomness. A typical MDL functional is the sum of the number of bits used to describe the model $L(\theta)$ and the deviation from the model $L(x|\theta)$, where x and θ denotes vectors of data and model parameters [10]. Model selection performed by minimizing this sum,

$$\bar{\theta} = \arg\min_{\theta} L(x|\theta) + L(\theta) \tag{1}$$

For compression it is quite natural to study a quantisation of the parameter space with respect to the total code length. In broad terms, the needed precision is in practice inversely proportional to the second order structure of the sum in (1), which in turn is inversely proportional to the variance of the estimator. For almost all estimators this variance is inversely proportional to the number of data points. Except for the square root we are intuitively led to the classical result of [10]:

$$\lim_{|x|\to\infty} L(x|\bar{\theta}) + L(\bar{\theta}) = L(x|\hat{\theta}) + L(\hat{\theta}) + \frac{|\theta|}{2}\log n + \mathcal{O}(|\theta|) \tag{2}$$

where $\bar{\theta}$ denotes the truncated parameters, $\hat{\theta}$ are the maximum likelihood estimates, and $|\theta|$ is the number of parameters. This limit has recently been sharpened to be an $o(1)$ estimate [1]. However, since the per data point improvement is ignorable when $|x| \gg |\theta|$, (2) suffices for large segments.

A coding scheme for segmentation naturally divides into a code for the border and the interior [5]. For many large segments there will be a natural tendency for code length of the border to be diminished by the code length of the interior. It is noted that there is a large group of shapes, where this is not the case, however we do not expect these shapes to be typical. A simple chain code for the border will therefore suffice. A better and model driven code for borders may be found in [12]. For the interior, the choice of model class is much more interesting. In the piecewise smooth case, low order polynomials are obviously suitable and can be interpreted as the extension of the local structure. Harmonic representations are definitely also possible, and cosine waves may be versatile enough to handle both smooth regions and texture like regions. For simplicity however, we will use the class of lower order polynomials plus i.i.d. normal noise with zero mean. We will use the centroid of a segment as origin, and the parameters will be coded as the universal prior of integers [10].

The least squares fitting procedure is well suited for the normal distributed noise. However, it is ill suited in the case of outliers since just a single deviating point can make the fit arbitrarily bad. Such outliers do occur for simple image structure such as corners and T-junctions. In the spirit of Least Median of Squares [11], we have implemented a method that uses 1% of a segment's pixels as test-inliers (an elemental subset), refits the model on this subset, and calculates the median of squared deviation of the inliers as a quality measure. This process is iterated till sufficient confidence, and the parameters for the subset that minimises the quality measure are used to dissect the segment into inliers and outliers. In contrast to statistical models of outliers [11], we order the outliers by their distance to the robust fit, and by coding the outliers by the universal distribution of integers for outliers we may iteratively find the optimal division between inliers and outliers. This has proven to be a very effective outlier detector.

We finally derive the total MDL functional for a segment as,

$$L_k = \frac{|x|}{2} \left(\log 2\pi e + \log \sum_i (x_i - f(x_i, \theta))^2 \right)$$
$$+ \sum_j \log^*(\theta_j) + \frac{|\theta| + 1}{2} \log |x| + |\partial x| + \log^*(\text{outlier}) \tag{3}$$

where the maximum likelihood estimate, $\sigma^2 = \sum_i (x_i - f(x_i, \theta))^2 / |x|$, has been used, f is a function from the class, $\log^*$ is minus the logarithm to the universal distribution [10], and a 4-connected chain code of the boundary, ∂x, has been used. We have divided the code length estimate for the chain code by two, since almost all border points are used for exactly two segments. To code the outliers the coordinate and value as integers must be supplied. The total code length for the image is given by independence as, $L = \sum_k L_k$. The task of the merge algorithm is thus to find a minimum for L over the number and placement of segments. This is in general an intractable problem [2]. In the following section will a reasonable, fast, but suboptimal algorithm be given.

3.1 A General Merge Algorithm

The goal of our merge algorithm is only to consider local neighbourhoods in a fine to coarse manner. A single iteration of the algorithm is illustrated in Figure 2. Leaves A, B, C, and D are all segments tracked to measurement scale. At bottom

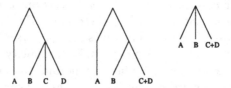

Fig. 2. A single step of the merge algorithm. LEFT: the original tree, MIDDLE: Subtree B,C, and D is merged into B and C+D. RIGHT: Children replace parents.

level, we find the best local merge. In this case, segment A has no siblings to merge with, while all possible merges of B, C, and D are examined. For the example we assume that merging C and D is the optimal local solution. When all sibling tuples have been optimally locally merged, the remaining siblings take the place of their parent, and the algorithm is reiterated on the smaller tree.

Since there is no direct cross-talk between neighbouring sibling tuples, the tree *defines* a hierarchical neighbourhood structure, and the final segmentation result cannot be better than defined by the neighbourhood structure of the tree. As all merge algorithms, this algorithm does not guarantee global optimum, but the advantage of this algorithm is that the search space is restricted by the geometrical structure of the image defined by the Scale-Space Tree.

4 Shapes in Data

Interpreting data has two basic steps: Firstly, a proper syntax must be found, which can contain all data sets to be considered. Secondly a sentence must be composed that describes a particular data set. This article has described an algorithm that uses the Scale-Space Tree to define the neighbourhood structure of regions and seeks the particular combination of neighbourhoods that reduces the description length according to a prespecified preference. In Figure 3 are shown several examples of segmentations produced by the algorithm. On the simple im-

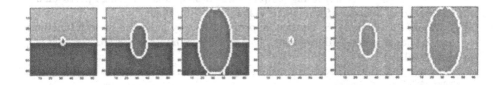

Fig. 3. Segmentation of simple structures. Left images are as Figure 1, and right images show light ellipses on a lighter background (values 112, 128 and standard deviation 5).

ages we observe that the algorithm correctly joins segments from various levels of the Scale-Space Tree for a remarkable range of sizes and intensity differences. On more complex images such as shown in Figure 4 the algorithm displays a range of behaviours. It is difficult if not impossible to obtain the 'correct' segmentation of such images, but we conclude that the algorithm does distinguish a number of significant regions, and that the concept of lossless coding allows for a consistent discussion of different segmentation algorithms.

References

1. Andrew Barron, Jorma Rissanen, and Bin Yu. The minimum description length principle in coding and modeling. *IEEE Transactions on Information Theory*, 44(6):2743–2760, 1998.

518

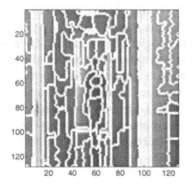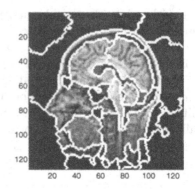

Fig. 4. Segmentation of an indoor scene and an MR slice.

2. Martin C. Cooper. The tractability of segmentation and scene analysis. *International Journal of Computer Vision*, 30(1):27–42, 1998.
3. Lewis D. Griffin, Alan C. F. Colchester, and G. P. Robinson. Scale and segmentation of grey-level images using maximum gradient paths. *Image and Vision Computing*, 10(6):389–402, July/August 1992.
4. Paul T. Jackway. Gradient watersheds in morphological scale-space. *IEEE Transactions on Image Processing*, 5(6):913–921, 1996.
5. Yvan C. Leclerc. Constructing simple stable descriptions for image partitioning. *International Journal of Computer Vision*, 3:73–102, 1989.
6. D. Mumford and J. Shah. Optimal approximations by piecewise smooth functions and asociated variational problems. *Comm. on Pure and Applied Mathematics*, 42, July 1989.
7. Ole Fogh Olsen. Multi-scale watershed segmentation. In Sporring et al. [13], pages 191–200.
8. Ole Fogh Olsen and Mads Nielsen. Generic events for the gradient squared with application to multi-scale segmentation. In *Scale-Space Theory in Computer Vision, Proc. 1st International Conference*, volume 1252 of *Lecture Notes in Computer Science*, pages 101–112, Utrecht, The Netherlands, July 1997.
9. N. R. Pal and S. K Pal. A review on image segmentation techniques. *Pattern Recognition*, 26:1277–1294, 1993.
10. J. Rissanen. *Stochastic Complexity in Statistical Inquiry*. World Scientific, Singapore, 1989.
11. P. J. Rousseeuw and A. M. Leroy. *Robust Regression and Outlier Detection*. John Wiley & Sons, 1987.
12. Jon Sporring. *Measuring and Modelling Image Structure*. PhD thesis, DIKU, Datalogisk Institut ved Københavns Universitet, Copenhagen, Denmark, 1999.
13. Jon Sporring, Mads Nielsen, Luc Florack, and Peter Johansen, editors. *Gaussian Scale-Space Theory*. Kluwer Academic Publishers, Dordrecht, The Netherlands, 1997.
14. J. Weickert. Efficient image segmentation using partial differential equations and morphology. Technical Report DIKU-98/10, Dept. of Computer Science, University of Copenhagen, Universitetsparken 1, DK-2100 Copenhagen, Denmark, 1998.
15. J. Weickert, S. Ishikawa, and A. Imiya. On the history of Gaussian scale-space axiomatics. In Sporring et al. [13], chapter 4, pages 45–59.

A Multiscale Taylor Series Approach to Optic Flow and Stereo: A Generalization of Optic Flow under the Aperture

Robert Maas *, Bart M. ter Haar Romeny and Max A. Viergever

Image Sciences Institute, University Medical Center Utrecht, Heidelberglaan 100 E01.334, NL-3584 CX Utrecht, The Netherlands

Abstract. In this paper binocular stereo in a linear scale-space setting is studied. A theoretical extension of previous work involving the optic flow constraint equation is obtained, which is embedded in a robust top-down algorithm. The method is illustrated by some examples.

1 Introduction

Stereo and optic flow are closely related. One method to study motion and short baseline stereo is by the optic flow equation [3]. Recently, it has been realized that, because we are dealing with observed data, the equation consequently has to be embedded in scale-space ("brought under the aperture") [1]. This has been successfully applied to optic flow and binocular stereo extraction, which is not necessary short baseline stereo anymore because of the scale involved [8, 7].

This paper extends the theory of [1] (and [7] for binocular stereo) by taking time discrete, i.e., no filtering is performed in that direction. This is of course the case in binocular stereo, where only two frames are present. We show that in that case higher order polynomials in the disparity are obtained. Then the disparity has to be expanded in a spatial series to obtain a solution, like in [1].

We incorporate this method in a top-down patch-based stereo algorithm. During the descending over scale, consistency is enforced based on the scale and the residual (i.e. the value of the function minimized using a least squares process), like in [5].

2 Review of optic flow under the aperture

In this section a brief review of the optic flow equation under the aperture [1, 7, 8] is given. The classical optic flow constraint equation for a spatio-temporal image I in 2D+time is given by:

$$I_t + u^x I_x + u^y I_y = 0 \tag{1}$$

where the subscript denotes partial differentiation and the superscript denotes the component of the flow. In discrete images we can not take derivatives directly, so we have

---

* This work was supported by the NWO-Council Earth and Life Sciences (ALW), which is subsidized by the Netherlands Organization for Scientific Research (NWO).

to obtain an equation with regularized derivatives, i.e. Gaussian derivatives at a certain scale.

In order now to get an optic flow equation involving regularized derivatives we (formally) convolve both sides of eq. (1) with γ, the Gaussian kernel at a certain scale (see also [1, 7, 8]):

$$(I_t + u^x I_x + u^y I_y) * \gamma = 0 \qquad (2)$$

(Since the values u^x and u^y depend on the position, the left-hand side of the equation is generally not equal to $L_t + u^x L_x + u^y L_y$.) To move the differentiation operator from the image to the aperture we have to use partial integration. For this reason we have to *model* the unknown velocity (or disparity) field u^x and u^y with a polynomial function to some order. For u^x we get a local, spatial series:

$$u^x(x, y) = \sum_{m=0}^{M} \sum_{n=0}^{m} U_{n(m-n)}^x (x_0, y_0)(x - x_0)^n (y - y_0)^{m-n} \qquad (3)$$

A similar equation is derived for u^y. Using the fact that derivatives of γ are Hermite polynomials times the kernel γ itself, partial integration gives an equation in $(M+2)*(M+1)$ unknowns (the U_{ij}^x-s and U_{ij}^y-s), with the derivatives moved from the image to the aperture. We clarify this by an example: take $M = 1$ in the series expansions, then eq. (1) is replaced by:

$$L_t + U^x L_x + \sigma^2 U_x^x L_{xx} + \sigma^2 U_y^x L_{xy} + U^y L_y + \sigma^2 U_x^y L_{xy} + \sigma^2 U_y^y L_{yy} = 0 \quad (4)$$

where σ is the scale of the Gaussian operator γ. We can not solve for six unknowns from one equation. Therefore we have to use additional equations. In [1] extra equations are obtained by taking partial derivatives of the equation up till the order of the truncation. Due to the aperture problem additional knowledge has to be included, e.g., that the flow is only horizontally. One gets a linear system, which can easily be solved. In binocular stereo the temporal derivative is replaced by the difference between the right and the left images. The additional scale parameter can be used to select a proper scale for the computations [7–9].

3 Higher order Taylor expansion

The mathematical idea behind the approach discussed in the previous section is to compute the infinitesimal velocity. However, although a theoretically sound continuous interpretation can be given for the discretely sampled space-time, we actually want the displacement between two adjacent slices in temporal direction and not the infinitesimal displacement. In binocular stereo, the main focus of our approach, it is not at all possible to perform a temporal smoothing.

Let $I(x, y, t)$ be a spatio-temporal image. To obtain the displacements between two frames, one taken at $t = t_0$ and one taken at $t = t_1$, we have to solve:

$$I\left(x - \frac{a_c^x(x, y)}{2}, y - \frac{a_c^y(x, y)}{2}, t_0\right) = I\left(x + \frac{a_c^x(x, y)}{2}, y + \frac{a_c^y(x, y)}{2}, t_1\right) \qquad (5)$$

a_c^x and a_c^y are the presumed model for the flow (disparity). We use $a^x \equiv a_c^x(x,y)$ and $a^y \equiv a_c^y(x,y)$ for clarity in the formulas below. Both $I(x - \frac{a^x(x,y)}{2}, y - \frac{a^y(x,y)}{2}, t_0)$ and $I(x + \frac{a^x(x,y)}{2}, y + \frac{a^y(x,y)}{2}, t_1)$ are expanded in a Taylor Series. Then we truncate the series at some order K to obtain the displacement.

$$0 = I(x + \frac{a^x}{2}, y + \frac{a^y}{2}, t_1) - I(x - \frac{a^x}{2}, y - \frac{a^y}{2}, t_0) \approx$$

$$\sum_{k=0}^{K} \sum_{l=0}^{k} \frac{(a^x)^l (a^y)^{k-l}}{2^k l!(k-l)!} \left(\frac{\partial^k}{\partial x^l \partial y^{k-l}} I(x,y,t_1) - (-1)^k \frac{\partial^k}{\partial x^l \partial y^{k-l}} I(x,y,t_0) \right) \quad (6)$$

for certain K. So far we formally differentiated $I(x,y,t)$, but now we put the equation under the aperture. Following the lines of section 2 we obtain:

$$\sum_{k=0}^{K} \sum_{l=0}^{k} (a^x)^l (a^y)^{k-l} \frac{1}{2^k l!(k-l)!} \left(\frac{\partial^k}{\partial x^l \partial y^{k-l}} I(x,y,t_1) - (-1)^k \frac{\partial^k}{\partial x^l \partial y^{k-l}} I(x,y,t_0) \right) * \gamma = 0 \quad (7)$$

We have to move the derivative operator from the images to the aperture. Before we are able to do so we have to expand a^x and a^y in a truncated series. Note that it is not a truncated Taylor Series, and actually depending on σ, since eq. (7) has to be satisfied for the approximation.

$$a^x(x,y) = \sum_{m=0}^{M} \sum_{n=0}^{m} a_{n(m-n)}^x \frac{1}{n!(m-n)!} x^n y^{m-n} \quad (8)$$

and similar for a^y. Using this expansion the derivatives can be moved from the images to the aperture in eq. (7). This yields one equation involving regularized derivatives.

We could obtain more equations by using in addition to γ in eq. (7) certain derivatives of γ, just as is done in the method discussed in the previous section. Adding physical constraints, necessary due to the aperture problem, leads to a finite number of possible solutions, from which the proper one should be chosen.

In this paper we use a different approach to obtain a solution from eq. (7), in combination with eq. (8) (and the similar one for a^y). The motion in a point is given by the least squares solution to the equations in a neighborhood of that point. We explain the developed algorithm in the next section. We finish with an example of the above derived equation:

Example 1. $K = 2$, $M = 1$, horizontal flow:

$$(L^1 - L^0) + a_{00}^x \frac{L_x^1 + L_x^0}{2} + a_{10}^x \sigma^2 \frac{L_{xx}^1 + L_{xx}^0}{2} + a_{01}^x \sigma^2 \frac{L_{xy}^1 + L_{xy}^0}{2} +$$

$$(a_{00}^x)^2 \frac{L_{xx}^1 - L_{xx}^0}{8} + (a_{10}^x)^2 \sigma^2 \frac{\sigma^2 L_{xxxx}^1 + L_{xx}^1 - \sigma^2 L_{xxxx}^0 - L_{xx}^0}{8} +$$

$$(a_{01}^x)^2 \sigma^2 \frac{\sigma^2 L_{xxyy}^1 + L_{xx}^1 - \sigma^2 L_{xxyy}^0 - L_{xx}^0}{8} + a_{00}^x a_{10}^x \sigma^2 \frac{L_{xxx}^1 - L_{xxx}^0}{4} +$$

$$a_{00}^x a_{01}^x \sigma^2 \frac{L_{xxy}^1 - L_{xxy}^0}{4} + a_{10}^x a_{01}^x \sigma^4 \frac{L_{xxxy}^1 - L_{xxxy}^0}{4} = 0 \quad (9)$$

4 Over-constrained systems

Using the derivatives from one point, although computed using a filter of finite width, can give rise to noisy results. Another severe problem which occurs in practice is the difference in illumination between the left and right images.

Possible solutions for these problems are preprocessing the images with a small Laplacian filter, or to use higher order derivatives of γ instead of γ as initial aperture filter. These approaches will be studied in further work on this subject, but in this paper we propose a least squares solution to eq. (7) over a patch, where we add a new variable to account for the local greyvalue difference between the images. It is a generalization of [6] (which is our case with $K = 1$ and $M = 0$).

For this generalization we write eq. (7) with the additional greyvalue offset g and with the expansion for a^x and a^y (eq. (8)) as follows:

$$f(\mathbf{a_M}, x, y, t_0, t_1, K) + g = 0 \tag{10}$$

where $\mathbf{a_M}$ is the vector containing all coefficients of eq. (8) and the expansion of a^y, and g is the greyvalue offset, that needs to be computed. Of course the least squares solution is given by

$$(\mathbf{a_M}^{\text{opt}}, g^{\text{opt}})^T = \underset{(\mathbf{a_M}, g) \in \mathbf{R}^{(M+1)(M+2)+1}}{\operatorname{argmin}} \sum_{(x,y) \in \Omega} (f(\mathbf{a_M}, x, y, t_0, t_1, K) + g)^2 \tag{11}$$

The neighborhood Ω has to contain at least $(M + 1)(M + 2) + 2$ points to make the system over-constrained.

In the case of $M = 0$ and only horizontal displacement ($a_{00}^y = 0$) we find the optimal parameter as follows:
In the minimum of $\tilde{f}(a_{00}^x, x, y, t_0, t_1, K, g) := \sum_{(x,y) \in \Omega} (f(\mathbf{a_M}, x, y, t_0, t_1, K) + g)^2$ both $\frac{\partial \tilde{f}}{\partial a_{00}^x} = 0$ and $\frac{\partial \tilde{f}}{\partial g} = 0$. From $\frac{\partial \tilde{f}}{\partial g} = 0$ it follows that in a singular point g can be written as a polynomial in a_{00}^x. Inserting this polynomial in $\frac{\partial \tilde{f}}{\partial a_{00}^x} = 0$ yields that we have to solve a polynomial equation of degree $(2K - 1)$ in a_{00}^x to find the global minimum. In case we have to deal with both horizontal and vertical displacement and $K > 1$, or if we have only horizontal displacements and $M > 0$ and $K > 1$, we have to use a minimization algorithm [10], which might yield only a local minimum.

5 Top-down algorithm

The above described approach is implemented in a top-down algorithm, where the solution on every scale level has to fulfill certain conditions, similar to some ones used in [5], to be labeled as reliable.

The filter size used and the size of the correlation region, which we take equal to the filter size (similar to [4, Ch. 14]), restrict the size of solution. If the solution is much larger than the filter size it becomes more unreliable. Therefore we should only allow solutions which are in order of magnitude equal to σ. So we compute the disparity for a stack of scales and allow for every scale only those u and v, which are both smaller than σ.

We put in another restriction, that is the size of the found minimum of the function that has been minimized. If the value of that so-called residual ([5]) is larger than a certain threshold, the found displacement is regarded as wrong (e.g., a local minimum instead of a global minimum, or an occluded point), and therefore removed.

Using the points which fulfill both restrictions, a displacement field for the whole image is obtained by interpolation. Going down in scale now we first compensate for the obtained flow field and repeat the procedure. For $M = 1$, $|u_x| < 2$ and $|u_y| < 1$ are taken (note that the restriction on u_x is imposed by the ordering constraint).

6 Results

We show some results of the methods on a synthetic random dot pair, of which the 3-D scene is a paraboloid on a flat background, and Bill Hoff's fruit pair [2]. On every level in the algorithm we first checked the size of results, after which 10 % of the remaining points were removed using the size of the residual.

In Fig 1 the input random dot pair is shown, together with the results for $K = 1$ and $M = 0$, $K = 3$ and $M = 0$, and $K = 2$ and $M = 1$. The results for all methods are quite similar. The method with $K = 1$ and $M = 0$ retains a little more points than the method with $K = 2$ and $M = 1$, but the standard deviation of the error (compared with the ground truth) is a little smaller for the method with $K = 2$ and $M = 1$.

On the fruit image we see some more differences. In the first row the results of the same expansions as used in the random dot example are shown. The method with $K = 2$ and $M = 1$, throws away more points than the other methods, but also yields less points with the wrong disparity . In order to compare the methods better we have varied the number of points that was thrown away based on the residual, such that in every method 60 % of all points was retained by the algorithm. The result using $K = 2$ and $M = 1$ still contains less outliers.

7 Discussion

Binocular stereo in scale-space has been studied. A theoretical, extension to the optic flow work in [1], especially suited for stereo, has been described. This theory has been embedded in a robust top-down algorithm. Some examples have been given to illustrate the derived results, but more study has to be done. For instance: what are the results if we replace the patch approach with a preprocessing step on the images to overcome illumination differences? For the same purpose, could we use different filters instead of γ, especially higher order derivatives of γ?
*

References

1. L Florack, W. Niessen, and M. Nielsen. The intrinsic structure of optic flow incorporating measurement duality. *International Journal of Computer Vision*, 27:263–286, 1998.

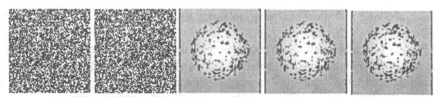

Fig. 1. From left to right: the left input image, the right input image, results for $K = 1$ and $M = 0$, $K = 3$ and $M = 0$, and $K = 2$ and $M = 1$.

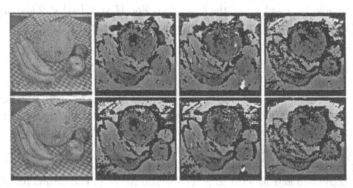

Fig. 2. In the left column the input images are displayed. In the remaining part of the top row the results for $K = 1$ and $M = 0$, $K = 3$ and $M = 0$, and $K = 2$ and $M = 1$ are displayed. In the second row the same expansions are used, but now 60 % of all points are retained.

2. W. Hoff and N. Ahuja. Surfaces from stereo: Integrating feature matching, disparity estimation, and contour detection. *IEEE Transactions on Pattern Analysis and Machine Intelligence*, 11:121–136, 1989.

3. B. K. P. Horn and B. G. Schunck. Determining optical flow. *Artificial Intelligence*, 23:185–203, 1981.

4. T. Lindeberg. *Scale-Space Theory in Computer Vision*. The Kluwer International Series in Engineering and Computer Science. Kluwer Academic Publishers, Dordrecht, the Netherlands, 1994.

5. T. Lindeberg. A scale selection principle for estimating image deformations. *Image and Vision Computing*, 16:961–977, 1998.

6. B. D. Lucas and T. Kanade. An iterative image registration technique with an application to stereo vision. In *Proceeding of the 7th International Joint Conference on Artificial Intelligence*, pages 674–679, 1981.

7. M. Nielsen, R. Maas, W. J. Niessen, L. M. J. Florack, and B. M. ter Haar Romeny. Binocular stereo from grey-scale images. *Journal of Mathematical Imaging and Vision*, 10:103–122, 1999.

8. W. J. Niessen, J. S. Duncan, M. Nielsen, L. M. J. Florack, B. M. ter Haar Romeny, and M. A. Viergever. A multi-scale approach to image sequence analysis. *Computer Vision and Image Understanding*, 65(2):259–268, 1997.

9. W. J. Niessen and R. Maas. Multiscale optic flow and stereo. In J. Sporring, M. Nielsen, L. Florack, and P. Johansen, editors, *Gaussian Scale-Space Theory*, Computational Imaging and Vision, pages 31–42. Dordrecht: Kluwer Academic Publishers, 1997.

10. W. H. Press, S. A. Teukolsky, W. T. Vetterling, and B. P. Flannery. *Numerical Recipes in C, the Art of Scientific Computing - Second Edition*. Cambridge University Press, Cambridge, UK, 1995.

Global Convergence Rates of Nonlinear Diffusion for Time-Varying Images

Winfried Lohmiller and Jean-Jacques E. Slotine

Nonlinear Systems Laboratory, Massachusetts Institute of Technology
Cambridge, Massachusetts, 02139, USA
wslohmil@mit.edu, jjs@mit.edu

Abstract. In this paper, classical nonlinear diffusion methods of machine vision are revisited in the light of recent results in nonlinear stability analysis. Global exponential convergence rates are quantified, and suggest specific choices of nonlinearities and image coupling terms. In particular, global stability and exponential convergence can be guaranteed for nonlinear filtering of time-varying images.

1 Introduction

Nonlinear reaction-diffusion processes are pervasive in physics [7]. In [11, 12], we extended recent results on stability theory, referred to as contraction analysis [10], to partial differential equations describing time-varying nonlinear reaction-diffusion processes, and showed that analyzing global stability and determining convergence rates is very simple indeed for such processes. In this paper, classical nonlinear diffusion methods of machine vision [1–3, 5, 6, 8, 9, 13, 16–20] are revisited in the light of these recent results.

Section 2 summarizes the contraction properties of nonlinear reaction-diffusion-convection equations of the form

$$\frac{\partial \phi}{\partial t} = \mathrm{div}\ \mathbf{h}(\nabla\phi, t) + \mathbf{v}^T(t)\ \nabla\phi + f(\phi, \mathbf{x}, t) \tag{1}$$

and explicitly quantifies stability and convergence rates. In section 3, rhese results are then applied to classical nonlinear diffusion methods of machine vision, and suggest specific choices of nonlinearities and image coupling terms. In particular, global stability and exponential convergence can be guaranteed for nonlinear filtering of time-varying (video) images. Brief concluding remarks are offered in section 4.

2 Contraction Analysis of Nonlinear Diffusion Processes

Differential approximation is the basis of all linearized stability analysis. What is new in contraction analysis is that differential stability analysis can be made *exact*, and in turn yield *global* exponential stability results [10].

The theory can be applied simply to important classes of physical ditributed processes. In particular, consider the system (1) on an bounded m-dimensional continuum V, let $l_{k,max}$ be the diameter (maximum length) of V along the kth axis, and $\lambda_{\frac{\partial h}{\partial \nabla \phi}}$ be a lower bound on the smallest eigenvalue of the symmetric part of $\frac{\partial h}{\partial \nabla \phi} \geq 0$ on V. It can then be shown [11,12] that

Theorem 1. *Consider the nonlinear reaction-diffusion-convection equation (1), where*
$\partial h / \partial \nabla (\phi, t) \geq 0$, *and assume that*

$$\lambda_{diff} + max\left(\frac{\partial f}{\partial \phi}\right)$$

is uniformly negative, where

$$\lambda_{diff} = -\lambda_{\frac{\partial h}{\partial \nabla \phi}} \sum_{k=1}^{m} \frac{2\pi^2}{l_{k,max}^2} \qquad (2)$$

for a (perhaps time-varying) Dirichlet condition (i.e., $\phi(t)$ specified on the boundary), and

$$\lambda_{diff} = 0 \qquad (3)$$

for a (perhaps time-varying) Neumann condition. Then, all system trajectories converge exponentially to a single field $\Phi_d(\mathbf{x}, t)$, with minimal convergence rate $|\lambda_{diff} + max(\frac{\partial f}{\partial \phi})|$.
In the autonomous case ($f = f(\phi, \mathbf{x}), \mathbf{v}$ constant, and with constant boundary conditions) the system converges exponentially to a steady-state $\Phi_d(\mathbf{x})$, which is the unique solution of the generalized Poisson equation

$$0 = \text{div } \mathbf{h}(\nabla \phi_d) + \mathbf{v}^T \nabla \phi_d + f(\phi_d, \mathbf{x})$$

The method of proof implies that all the results on contracting systems in [10] can be extended to contracting reaction-diffusion processes, with boundary conditions acting as additional inputs to the system. For instance, any autonomous contracting reaction-diffusion process, when subjected to boundary conditions periodic in time, will tend exponentially to a periodic solution of the same period. Also, any autonomous contracting reaction-diffusion process will tend exponentially to a unique steady-state. The convergence is robust to bounded or linearly increasing disturbances. The stability guarantees also hold for any orthonormal Cartesian discretization of the continuum. Finally, chains or hierarchies of contracting processes are themselves contracting, and thus converge exponentially, allowing multiple levels of stable preprocessing if desired.

3 Machine Vision

The above results can be used in particular in problems of function approximation and nonlinear filtering. One such application is machine vision, where they suggest a different perspective and systematic extensions (notably to time-varying images) for the now classical results of scale-space analysis and anisotropic diffusion (see [1–3, 5, 6, 9, 13, 16–20]). Similar questions occur in models of physiological vision and eye movement [4].

Consider the problem of computing a smooth estimate $\hat{\phi}(\mathbf{x}, t)$ of a noisy time-varying image $\phi(\mathbf{x}, t)$, while preserving meaningful discontinuities such as edges at given scales [20, 14]. Define the filter

$$\frac{\partial \bar{\phi}}{\partial t} = \operatorname{div} \mathbf{h}(\nabla \hat{\phi}, t) + \mathbf{v}^T \nabla \hat{\phi} + f(\hat{\phi} - \phi) \tag{4}$$

$$\hat{\phi} = \bar{\phi} + \phi$$

where $\mathbf{v}(t)$ accounts for camera motion. The system thus verifies the nonlinear reaction-diffusion-convection equation

$$\frac{\partial \hat{\phi}}{\partial t} - \frac{\partial \phi}{\partial t}(t) = \operatorname{div} \mathbf{h}(\nabla \hat{\phi}, t) + \mathbf{v}^T \nabla \hat{\phi} + f(\hat{\phi} - \phi(t))$$

Thus the dynamics of $\hat{\phi}$ contains $\frac{\partial \phi}{\partial t}$, although the actual computation is done using equation (4) and hence $\frac{\partial \phi}{\partial t}$ is not explicitly used.

According to Theorem 1, global exponential convergence to a unique time-varying image can be guaranteed by choosing the nonlinear function f to be strictly decreasing, and the field $\mathbf{h}$ to have a positive semi-definite Jacobian. These can be used to shape the performance of the filter design. For instance,

– Choosing $\mathbf{h}$ in the usual form

$$\mathbf{h} = g(\|\nabla \hat{\phi}\|) \, \nabla \hat{\phi}$$

and letting $r = \|\nabla \hat{\phi}\|$, the corresponding Jacobian is symmetric and can be written

$$g\mathbf{I} + r \, \frac{\partial g(r)}{\partial r} \, \frac{\nabla \hat{\phi}}{\|\nabla \hat{\phi}\|} \, \frac{\nabla \hat{\phi}}{\|\nabla \hat{\phi}\|}^T$$

Since the largest eigenvalue of the last dyadic product is 1, the system is globally contracting for $g \geq 0$ and $\frac{\partial (rg(r))}{\partial r} \geq 0$. One might e.g. choose $g = \tanh(\alpha r)/(\alpha r)$ or $g = \sin\left(\frac{\pi}{2} \operatorname{sat}(\alpha \operatorname{grad} \hat{\phi})\right)/(\alpha r)$ (with α a constant) to filter small r and leave large r unfiltered. More generally one may choose $g = 0$ for specific r ranges, leaving the corresponding part of the image unfiltered.

– Outliers ϕ can be cut off e.g. with a sigmoidal f.

Furthermore, chains or hierarchies of contracting processes are themselves contracting, as mentioned earlier. This implies, for instance, that the velocity $\mathbf{v}$ above, the input coupling f, or the time-dependence of $\mathbf{h}$ (e.g. the choice of threshold) could themselves result from "higher" contracting processes. Similarly, prefiltering in time or space of the signal can be straightforwardly incorporated.

Finally, note that in the case that **v** is actually unknown, but constant or slowly varying, it is straightforward to design versions of the above which are adaptive in **v**.

4 Concluding Remarks

This paper exploits the contraction properties of nonlinear reaction-diffusion-convection equations to suggest a different perspective on classical results on nonlinear diffusion for machine vision. In particular, it explicitly quantifies global exponential convergence rates, and extends systematically to stable nonlinear diffusion of time-varying images. Relationships between noise models and specific choices of f and **h** or of higher contracting processes need to be studied further. Additional flexibility may be also be obtained by shaping the system metric while still preserving global exponential stability [10], and could parallel recent developments [8]. Numerical implementation on actual video images will be presented at the conference.

Acknowledgements: We would like to thank Martin Grepl for the numerical simulations.

References

1. Alvarez, L., Lions, P-L., Morel, J-M., *SIAM J. Num. An.*, **29**:845-866, (1992).
2. Alvarez, L and Mazorra, L., *SIAM J. Num. Analysis*, **31(2)**:590-605, (1994).
3. Aubert, G., Barlaud, M., Blanc-Feraud, L., and Charbonnier, P., *IEEE Trans. Imag. Process.*, **5(12)**, (1996).
4. Berthoz, A., ed., Multisensory Control of Movement, *Oxford U.P.*, (1993).
5. Catte, F., Lions P.L., Morel, J.M., Coll, T., *SIAM J. Num. An.*, **29(1)**, (1992).
6. Deriche, R and Faugeras, O., *Traitement du Signal*, **13(6)**, (1996).
7. Evans, L.C., Partial Differential Equations, *Amer. Math. Soc.*, (1998).
8. Florack, L., *International Journal of Computer Vision*, **31(2/3)**, (1999).
9. Kornprobst, P., Deriche, R., and Aubert, G. Image coupling, restoration, and enhancement via PDE's., preprint, (1997).
10. Lohmiller, W., and Slotine, J.J.E., *Automatica*, **34(6)**, (1998).
11. Lohmiller, W., and Slotine, J.J.E., in *New Trends in Nonlinear Observer Design*, Nijmeijer H. and Fossen, T., eds., Springer Verlag, (1999).
12. Lohmiller, W., and Slotine, J.J.E., *European Control Conference*, Karlsruhe, (1999).
13. Malladi, R. and Sethian, J.A., *Graph. Mod. Im. Proc.*, **58(2)**:127-141, (1996).
14. Mallat, S., A Wavelet Tour of Signal Processing, *Univeristy Press*, (1998).
15. Mumford, D., and Shah, J., *Comm. Pure Appl. Math.*, **42** (1989).
16. Nordstsrom, N., *Image and Vision Computing*, **8(11)**:318-327, (1990).
17. Osher, S. and Rudin, L.I., *SIAM J. Num. An.*, **27(4)**:919-940, (1990).
18. Perona, P. and Malik, J., *IEEE Trans. P.A.M.I.*, **12(7)**:629-639, (1990).
19. Rudin, L., Osher, S., and Fatemi, E., *Physica D*, **60**:259-268, (1992).
20. ter Haar Romeny, B.M., ed., Geometry-Driven Diffusion in Computer Vision, *Kluwer*, (1994).

529

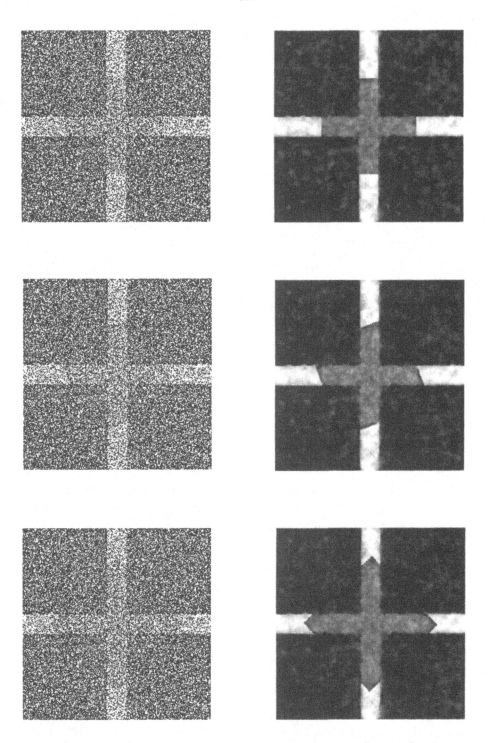

Fig. 1. Applying the basic algorithm to the "pulsating square" illusion. Original and filtered images at time $t = 1, 2, 3$, using a sampling rate of $1/20$. Note that in such an observer design, each new image is processed in only one iteration step.

Author Index

Lecture Notes in Computer Science

For information about Vols. 1–1606
please contact your bookseller or Springer-Verlag